Carolyn McCarthy

Trekking
IN THE PATAGONIAN ANDES

THE ARAUCANÍA

5

3

1 LAGUNA TERMAL

Ascending the steep and sandy Volcán Copahue (p41), gusts might blow you sideways and fumes might tear your eyes but it is this boiling turquoise crater lake that will take your breath away.

2 HOT SPRINGS SOAKS

Is there anything better after a long, dusty adventure? Choose from the Araucanía's hundreds of hot springs (p55) – ranging from posh to primitive – to melt away a hard walk's afterburn.

3 AROUND VOLCÁN VILLARICA

Definitely the wilder side of Pucón (p57), this long traverse follows a scenic puzzlescape of calderas, alpine lakes, forest and lava flows. Watch for rare maras streaking through the brush.

4 MAPUCHE HERITAGE

The Araucanía is the cradle of Mapuche nation. Chile's largest indigenous population, the Mapuche (p60) have been known for their rebellion, as well as their amazing handicrafts and strong traditions. Visitors shouldn't shy away from a closer look at this culture and its modern-day challenges.

5 ARAUCARIA TREES

Spindly and strange, this once-prevalent conifer is also called a monkey-puzzle tree (p40). Take a sunset walk and you might find flocks of lime-green parakeets merging on these prickly silhouettes to feast on their piñon nuts.

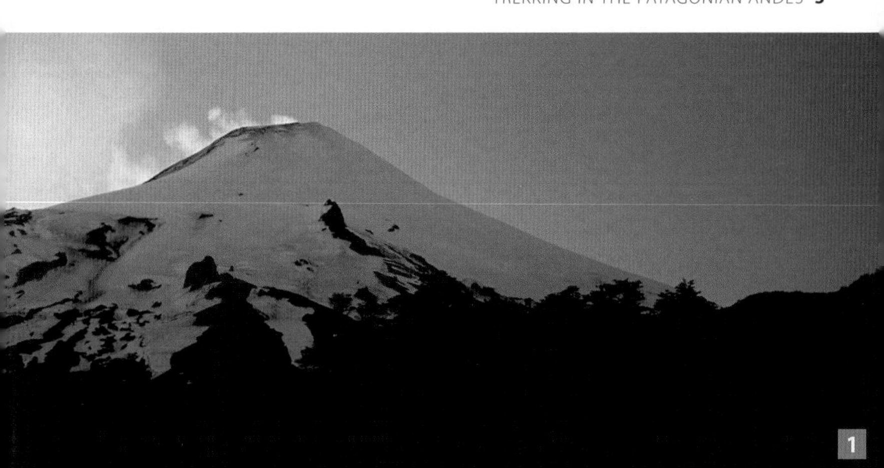
1

4

LAKES DISTRICT

1 VOLCANOES

Climb one for the spine-tingling sensation of feeling a mountain alive beneath you. The masses choose Volcán Villarica (p61) and the masochists, Volcán Lanín (p81).

2 NAHUEL HUAPI TRAVERSE

A rugged terrain of snow-patched meadows, scree and windy passes, this is Switzerland disguised as Latin America. Traversing the heart of Lakes District wilderness (p103), this challenging classic offers gaping views to match.

3 LAKES

With hundreds of ponds, lagoons and lakes, this region is celebrated in summer with cool dips and kayak trips. The biggest – Lago Llanquihue (p123) and Nahuel Huapi (p103) – put perspective on the landscape, but for a private getaway, make for their backwoods.

4 PARQUE NACIONAL VICENTE PÉREZ ROSALES

Chile's first national park is its wettest and greenest, with its centerpiece Lago Todo Los Santos (p96) ringed by volcanoes and a cool Valdivian rainforest. Whether you stumble upon a black sand beach or camp gazing on galaxies thick with stars, this is what getting away is all about.

5 SEAFOOD

Satisfy oceanic appetites in the portside market kitchens *(cocinas costumbristas)* of Puerto Montt (p127), Ancud and other seaside towns. Do like locals and opt for pottery bowls of steamed mussels (*choritos al vapor*), crab casserole (*chupe de jaiva*) or shellfish stew (*paila marina*).

1

2

CENTRAL PATAGONIA

4

3

1 CERRO CASTILLO

Under Castillo's (p145) pinnacle ramparts, a winding route takes in wild glaciated landscapes of snow-covered saddles that dip into fragrant *lenga* forest. You won't be alone though – condors and *huemul* deer are often sighted.

2 BIG RIVERS

Ranging from turquoise to crystalline, the great waterways of Central Patagonia (p130) are wonders of wilderness, which have flown undisturbed for millennia, though proposals to place dams throughout the region would certainly change all that.

3 ALERCES

Today's oldest alerces sprouted before the Chinese invented writing. There is no mistaking the grandeur of this hardwood (p134) native to chilly southern forests. Nearly indestructible, its popularity as a building material led alerce to the verge of extinction. Now, even finding one is an adventure.

4 ASADO A PALO

Barbecuing (p231) is a slow Sunday ritual that defines the Patagonian summer. Lamb is slow-seared on an open fire pit for hours and served with potatoes and salad tossed from the garden plot.

5 COMARCA ANDINA

Verdant valleys with rushing rivers, wooden huts and mountain meadows bursting with wildflowers. This nature haven hugs the shadow of El Bolsón (p136), but you will have to brave some rickety bridges to get there!

1
2

SOUTHERN PATAGONIA

1 TORRES DEL PAINE

We know no parallel – whether it's the full Paine Circuit or the W (the shorter version), these treks (p182,186) follow a mesmerising landscape of turquoise lakes, pinnacle peaks and glaciers.

2 RUTA 40

Epic in scope – around 3000km from San Martín de los Andes (p128) to El Calafate (p195) – this is the king of road trips. Sure, it takes in Patagonia's hot spots, but in its loneliest stretches, you're more likely to see the flightless, ostrich-like bird *ñandú* racing tumbleweeds than passing cars.

3 MONTE FITZ ROY & CERRO TORRE

If views could be heartbreakers, we would nominate this legendary duo – granite towers (p171) almost arrogant in their beauty and impervious to the hubbub all around them. But, ah, what a view.

4 MATÉ

Energizing and invigorating, this bitter brew is always shared, served in gourds and sipped through metal straws (p232). Maté in Patagonia is a rite of passage; just remember *gracias* means you're done.

5 GUANACO

Maybe the world's coolest camelid. Overhunting and cattle grazing reduced their vast numbers, but safe havens like Valle Chacabuco (p193) and Torres del Paine (p177) are helping this leggy native make a comeback.

5

3

1
4

TIERRA DEL FUEGO

1 DIENTES DE NAVARINO

The sense of no man's land is palpable – in fact, you'll feel the last soul on earth, treading the narrow path through moors and misty passes of the southernmost trek (p217) in the world.

2 SOUTHERN SUNSETS

Don't miss that godly moment when the sun sets in these austral extremes, painting mountains and seascapes in broad luminous strokes (p203).

3 PASO DE LA OVEJA

Above you condors float, beneath you alpine meadows are choked with wildflowers. This pleasant trek (p212) ascends *lenga* forest to an old herder's pass that dips down to Ushuaia.

4 SAILING THE BEAGLE

You don't have to be Darwin to discover the magic of the Beagle Channel (p212), island-hopping the many rocky islets that sea lions, penguins and cormorants call home.

4
2

TREKKING IN THE PATAGONIAN ANDES

Vast and varied, Patagonia is muddy rainforest, wild rivers, glaciated peaks and the windblown steppe skating to some lost horizon. You can't deny its grandeur. It whispers possibility. Shared by Chile and Argentina, this remote region sits at the tip of the continent. It has been the opiate of great adventurers, those who attempt to climb its sheer towers, traverse the continental ice cap or, like writer Bruce Chatwin, simply lose themselves wandering its great expanse. Today, a number of outstanding parks and private reserves frame this two-thousand-kilometer stretch of Andean wilderness. The maps stoke our imagination. Patagonia still has hundreds of unnamed mountains, contours inaccessible and unexplored, stories frozen in their layers.

The truth is that in Patagonia much remains to be discovered. That mere notion should put the thud in your pulse. You can start with the world-renowned treks around Torres del Paine and the Fitz Roy range, but on dozens of others you are more likely to spot a condor than another human being. Patagonian trails can take you through pristine forests to the rim of glaciers, under granite monoliths and over rickety suspension bridges, well beyond the crowds. Its remoteness doesn't make it hard to travel. Though characteristically slow-paced, Patagonia is one of the safest destinations in South America.

Yet, since the Patagonian ethos is built on deep solitude and bullying weather, the going isn't always easy. But that's probably what hooked you in the first place.

Contents

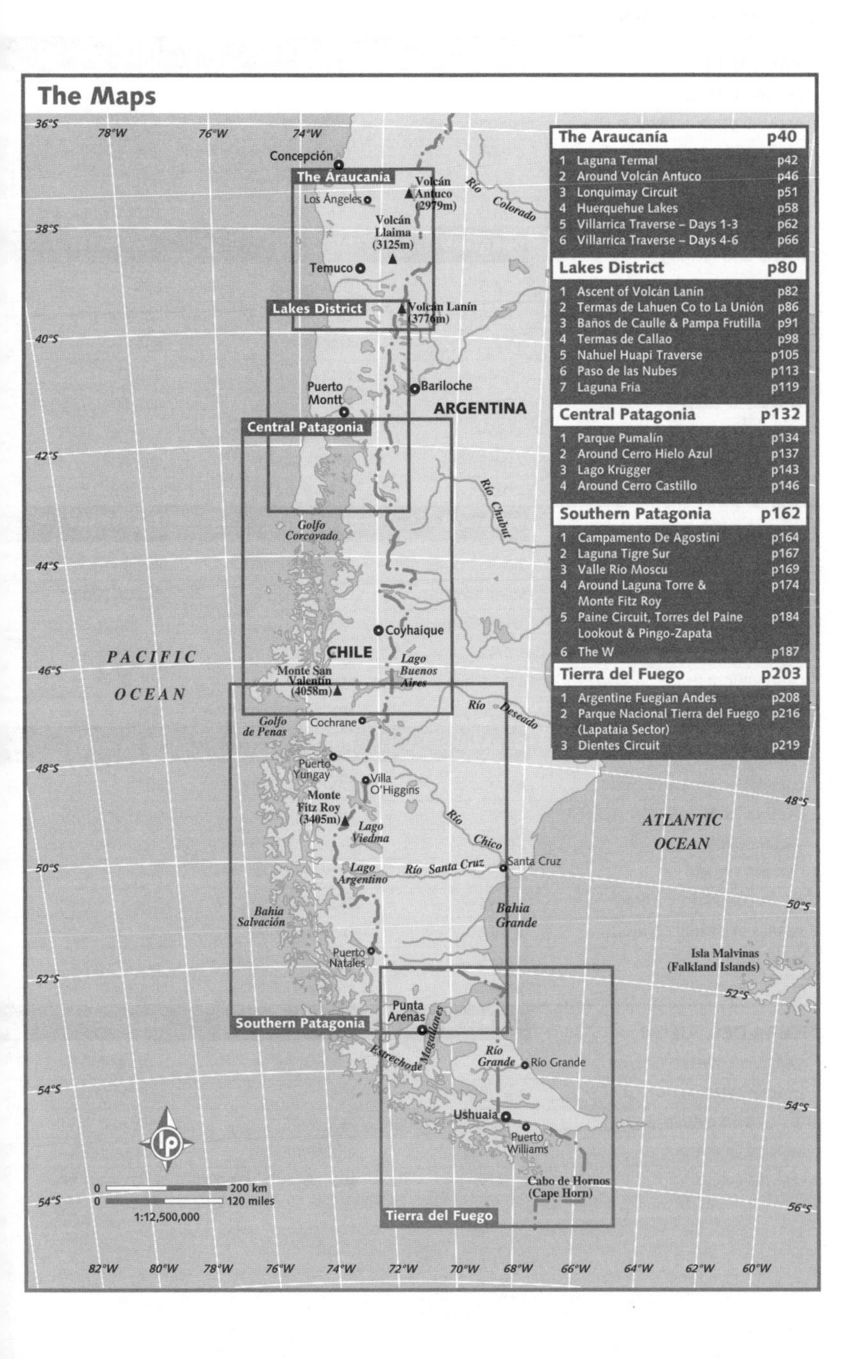

The Maps
The Araucanía p40
1 Laguna Termal p42
2 Around Volcán Antuco p46
3 Lonquimay Circuit p51
4 Huerquehue Lakes p58
5 Villarrica Traverse – Days 1-3 p62
6 Villarrica Traverse – Days 4-6 p66
Lakes District p80
1 Ascent of Volcán Lanín p82
2 Termas de Lahuen Co to La Unión p86
3 Baños de Caulle & Pampa Frutilla p91
4 Termas de Callao p98
5 Nahuel Huapi Traverse p105
6 Paso de las Nubes p113
7 Laguna Fría p119
Central Patagonia p132
1 Parque Pumalín p134
2 Around Cerro Hielo Azul p137
3 Lago Krügger p143
4 Around Cerro Castillo p146
Southern Patagonia p162
1 Campamento De Agostini p164
2 Laguna Tigre Sur p167
3 Valle Río Moscu p169
4 Around Laguna Torre & Monte Fitz Roy p174
5 Paine Circuit, Torres del Paine Lookout & Pingo-Zapata p184
6 The W p187
Tierra del Fuego p203
1 Argentine Fuegian Andes p208
2 Parque Nacional Tierra del Fuego (Lapataia Sector) p216
3 Dientes Circuit p219
Concepción
Los Ángeles
Volcán Antuco (2979m)
Volcán Llaima (3125m)
Temuco
Volcán Lanín (3776m)
Puerto Montt
Bariloche
ARGENTINA
CHILE
Coyhaique
Monte San Valentín (4058m)
Cochrane
Puerto Yungay
Villa O'Higgins
Monte Fitz Roy (3405m)
Santa Cruz
Puerto Natales
Punta Arenas
Río Grande
Ushuaia
Puerto Williams
Cabo de Hornos (Cape Horn)
Isla Malvinas (Falkland Islands)
PACIFIC OCEAN
ATLANTIC OCEAN
Golfo Corcovado
Golfo de Penas
Bahía Salvación
Bahía Grande
Lago Buenos Aires
Lago Viedma
Lago Argentino
Río Colorado
Río Chubut
Río Deseado
Río Chico
Río Santa Cruz
Río Grande
Estrecho de Magallanes
0 200 km
0 120 miles
1:12,500,000

Table of Treks

ARAUCANÍA	DURATION	DIFFICULTY	TRANSPORT
LAGUNA TERMAL	6½–8¼ HOURS	MODERATE	BUS
AROUND VOLCÁN ANTUCO	3 DAYS	MODERATE	BUS, WALK
LONQUIMAY CIRCUIT	6 DAYS	MODERATE–DEMANDING	BUS
HUERQUEHUE LAKES	4 DAYS	EASY–MODERATE	BUS
VILLARRICA TRAVERSE	6 DAYS	DEMANDING	TOUR OR TAXI; BUS

LAKES DISTRICT	DURATION	DIFFICULTY	TRANSPORT
ASCENT OF VOLCÁN LANÍN	3 DAYS	DEMANDING	BUS
TERMAS DE LAHUEN CO TO LA UNIÓN	2 DAYS	EASY	TOUR OR TAXI
BAÑOS DE CAULLE	4 DAYS	MODERATE	BUS
PAMPA FRUTILLA	2 DAYS	EASY–MODERATE	BUS
TERMAS DE CALLAO	3 DAYS	EASY	BUS, BOAT
NAHUEL HUAPI TRAVERSE	5 DAYS	MODERATE–DEMANDING	BUS
PASO DE LAS NUBES	2 DAYS	MODERATE	BUS, BOAT
LAGUNA FRÍA	2 DAYS	EASY–MODERATE	BUS & WALK

CENTRAL PATAGONIA	DURATION	DIFFICULTY	TRANSPORT
LAGUNA TRONADOR	2½–3½ HOURS	EASY–MODERATE	BUS OR TOUR
SENDERO ALERCES	30–40 MINUTES	EASY	BUS OR TOUR
CASCADAS ESCONDIDAS	1½–2 HOURS	EASY	BUS OR TOUR
AROUND CERRO HIELO AZUL	3 DAYS	MODERATE	BUS OR TAXI
LAGO KRÜGGER	3 DAYS	MODERATE	BUS
AROUND CERRO CASTILLO	4–6 DAYS	MODERATE–DEMANDING	BUS

SOUTHERN PATAGONIA	DURATION	DIFFICULTY	TRANSPORT
CAMPAMENTO DE AGOSTINI	4 DAYS	EASY–MODERATE	BUS
LAGUNA TIGRE SUR	2 DAYS	MODERATE	TAXI
VALLE RÍO MOSCU	2 DAYS	EASY	BUS, PLANE
LAGUNA TORRE	2 DAYS	EASY	BUS
AROUND MONTE FITZ ROY	3 DAYS	EASY–MODERATE	BUS
TORRES DEL PAINE LOOKOUT	4½–6 HOURS	EASY–MODERATE	BUS
PAINE CIRCUIT	8 DAYS	MODERATE–DEMANDING	BUS
PINGO-ZAPATA	2 DAYS	EASY	PRIVATE

TIERRA DEL FUEGO	DURATION	DIFFICULTY	TRANSPORT
SIERRA VALDIVIESO CIRCUIT	4 DAYS	DEMANDING	VAN OR TAXI
LAGUNA ESMERALDA	3–4 HOURS	EASY	VAN OR TAXI
GLACIAR VINCIGUERRA	5–6½ HOURS RETURN	MODERATE	VAN OR TAXI
PASO DE LA OVEJA	2–3 DAYS	MODERATE	VAN, TAXI, BUS
DIENTES CIRCUIT	5 DAYS	MODERATE–DEMANDING	BOAT OR PLANE

BEST TIME	SUMMARY	PAGE
DEC–APR	**Trek to a remarkable steaming volcanic lake**	41
DEC–APR	**Circuit over a scenic col past a large lake dammed by lava**	45
DEC–APR	**Circumnavigation of a dormant volcano through a fascinating post-eruption landscape**	50
NOV–APR	**Exploration of a subalpine lake basin to some remote hot springs**	57
DEC–MAR	**Scenic high-level route along the rugged complex volcanic range**	61

BEST TIME	SUMMARY	PAGE
NOV-FEB	**Climb to the top of an awesomely panoramic volcano cone**	81
NOV–MAY	**An uncomplicated trek to the scenic shores of Lago Paimún**	85
DEC–APR	**Popular trek to a thermal field with fumeroles, geysers and hot springs**	89
NOV–APR	**Gentle rise to tarns among rolling grassy alpine meadows**	94
OCT–MAY	**Laid back amble via hot springs with volcano views**	97
DEC–APR	**Classic pass-hopping route amid finest Lakes District scenery**	103
DEC–APR	**Link between rainforested valleys below hanging glaciers on Monte Tronador massif**	111
NOV–APR	**Trek to giant alerce trees among subalpine lakes**	118

BEST TIME	SUMMARY	PAGE
NOV–MAY	**Energetic trek to a jewel of a lake among luxuriant rainforest**	133
NOV–MAY	**Brief return trek to stands of glorious old alerces**	134
NOV–MAY	**Short rainforest trek to several 'hidden cascades'**	135
NOV–APR	**Route linking two lovely alpine valleys fringing the Argentine steppes**	136
DEC–APR	**Trek past lakeside beaches lined by graceful arrayán trees**	141
NOV–MAR	**Route through a raw alpine landscape with hanging glaciers, craggy peaks and tumbling waterfalls**	145

BEST TIME	SUMMARY	PAGE
NOV–APRIL	**Little-traveled route into a wild remote valley under Monte San Lorenzo**	163
DEC–APRIL	**Exploration of a wild upper valley frequented by huemul**	166
NOV–APR	**Simple trek to a glaciated valley drained by a spectacular roaring torrent**	168
NOV–APR	**Short walk to a viewpoint opposite the legendary Cerro Torre**	171
NOV–APR	**Exploration of valleys surrounding the one of the world's great summits**	172
NOV–APR	**Day trek to a lookout at the base of incredible granite towers**	181
DEC–MAR	**Classic rounding of the stunning Paine massif through steppes, forest and moors**	182
NOV–APR	**Ramble to glaciers at the head of a tranquil valley beside the southern icecap**	191

BEST TIME	SUMMARY	PAGE
DEC–MAR	**Pass-hopping route through rugged Fuegian-Andean wilderness**	205
NOV–APR	**Short overnight trek to a lovely subalpine lake below a tiny icecap**	210
NOV–APR	**A short jaunt to stunning glacial lakes**	211
NOV–APR	**Pass route linking two idyllic forested Fuegian valleys behind Ushuaia**	212
DEC–MAR	**World's most southerly loop across tiny passes in windswept subantarctic ranges**	217

The Author

CAROLYN MCCARTHY

Writer Carolyn McCarthy first traveled to Torres del Paine on vacation. She returned to Chile seasonally as a trekking guide, and moved there in 2003 on a Fulbright grant to document pioneer Patagonia. In spite of her deep resistance to powdered coffee, she proudly calls Chile's magnificent south home. She writes on travel, culture and the environment. Her work has appeared in *National Geographic,* the *Boston Globe, Salt Lake Tribune,* and other publications. For Lonely Planet, she has authored guides to Argentina, Chile, Central America and Yellowstone & Grand Teton National Parks. You can check out her blog at www.carolynswildblueyonder.blogspot.com.

MY FAVORITE WALK

Patagonia is full of potent landscapes, but my favorite trek is the Dientes Circuit (p217). The southernmost hike in the world, this 53.5km loop winds through Austral beech forest, rusty moors, and teacup lagoons, but most of the time it travels a strange theater of rock above the tree line. Trail…what trail? True, the weather can be less than welcoming – at this latitude the landscape whinges gray for days, with sharp winds, hail and disappearing trail lines. But finding the track – and keeping it – is surely part of the fun. The rest is matching Isla Navarino with its storied past of sailors and nearby shipwrecks, Yaghan canoe communities and roaming guanaco.

PATAGONIAN PIONEER CLEM LINDENMAYER

Clem Lindenmayer, the creator and original author of this book, passed away in 2007 while hiking in China's remote Gongga Shan. Though we never met, walking in his footsteps has been an education. For starters, he knew wilderness. His directions were precise, his pace was tireless (those hiking times!) and his humor dry. I got used to subtle 'Clemisms' – when a steep scree traverse was described as 'mildly uncomfortable,' I got ready to suffer.

In addition to documenting popular routes, Lindenmayer pioneered some of Patagonia's most remote and wild treks. On Isla Navarino, locals credit him with creating the Dientes de Navarino circuit. The southernmost trek in the world, the wild high alpine traverse takes trekkers through mesmerizing landscapes of rock and spire. In 2001, Chile's Ministerio de Bienes Nacionales (Ministry of National Resources) took names Lindenmayer had christened for the Dientes Circuit and made them official, adding in tribute Cerro Clem and Montes Lindenmayer. In the Lonely Planet guide, Lindenmayer deferred credit for the route to the native guanaco.

Yet even an innovation as seemingly light and recreational as a trekking route has repercussions. In the sluggish economy of Isla Navarino, locals who provide transport, groceries and lodgings to trekkers in their own homes literally live off the route. Few of them have been able to do it themselves.

Not every trekker is a pioneer, but may we all journey with that same spirit of wonder and perseverance.

Route Descriptions

This book contains 32 route descriptions ranging from day trips to multiday treks, plus suggestions for more treks, side trips and alternative routes. Each trek description has a brief introduction outlining the natural features you may encounter, plus information to help you plan your walk – transport options, level of difficulty, time frame and any permits required.

Day treks highlight areas of uncommon beauty. Multiday treks include information on campsites, *refugios* (mountain huts), hostels or other accommodation, and places to get water and supplies.

TIMES & DISTANCES

These are provided only as a guide. Times are based on actual walking time and do not include breaks for snacks, taking photographs, rest or side trips. Be sure to factor these in when planning. Distances are provided but should be read in conjunction with altitude gain. Significant elevation changes can make a greater difference to your walking time than lateral distance.

In most cases, the daily stages are flexible and can be varied. It is important to recognize that short stages are sometimes recommended in order to acclimatize in mountain areas or because there are interesting features to explore en route.

LEVEL OF DIFFICULTY

Grading systems are always arbitrary. However, having an indication of the grade may help you choose between walks. Our authors use the following grading guidelines:

Easy – a walk on flat terrain or with minor elevation changes usually over short distances on well-travelled routes with no navigational difficulties.
Moderate – a walk with challenging terrain, often involving longer distances and steep climbs.
Demanding – a walk with long daily distances and difficult terrain with significant elevation changes; may involve challenging route-finding and high-altitude or glacier travel.

TRUE LEFT & TRUE RIGHT

The terms 'true left' and 'true right', used to describe the bank of a stream or river, sometimes throw readers. The 'true left bank' simply means the left bank as you look downstream.

Planning

It's the stuff of legend: a million square kilometers of iconic peaks fast rivers and hurling winds. Let's face it, even clothing catalogues wax poetic about this place. And rightly so. A trip to Patagonia is a dream for most trekkers. It is strangely marvelous, low key, and even easy to organize, but hard to do without a hitch, particularly the first time around. Given Patagonia's remoteness and seasonality, it is important to plan your trip here carefully.

While the luxury travel market has transformed Patagonia into a gold card destination, with careful planning budget travelers can still do well. For small budgets, think camping, family lodgings and self-catering, with the luxury of the occasional bottle of red. Those seeking guided trips will find package tours priced to international standards, though local services may not meet the same lofty rates. Food quality and price particularly suffers; remember that hard pink tomato traveled nearly as far as you did to get here.

There are challenges: weather can be unstable, Patagonian transport is unreliable and the distances are tedious and large. If you're doing it all on your own, remember your happiness will increase in direct proportion to your patience and flexibility. Logistics are most challenging in Central Patagonia, where transport connections are infrequent and subject to change. With the great exception of Parque Nacional Torres del Paine, trekking infrastructure is more developed in Argentina, where trails tend to be well-marked and accessible by public transport.

For general travel information, consult Lonely Planet's *Chile & Easter Island* and *Argentina* guides.

WHEN TO TREK

Trekking in the Patagonian Andes is possible from early November until late April. In colder years, snowfalls may close trails a month earlier or later. Although each month has its own charms and drawbacks, for peak season services and better weather, February and March are the best months to trek.

The Patagonian summer lasts from early December to late February. Trekkers should be prepared for variable conditions, though hot

DON'T LEAVE HOME WITHOUT...

- Warm waterproof gear
- Sunblock, lip block and sun hat
- Polarized dark sunglasses for glaciers
- A cozy sleeping bag
- Camping gear – it's available but expensive, so best bring it from home
- A pocket knife with corkscrew
- Extra memory cards for digital snaps – they're hard to find outside cities
- An adapter to plug in battery chargers
- Zoom lens or binoculars to capture Chile's more bashful wildlife
- Medical items – see p254

BEST IN SHOW

- A purebred consoles an out-of-work mechanic in *Bombón, El Perro* (*The Dog*; 2004), directed by Carlos Sorin, set on the Argentine steppe
- Chaos descends on a remote fishing village in Chilean Patagonia in *La Fiebre de Locos* (*Abalone Fever*; 2001), directed by Andres Wood, set during the lucrative abalone harvest
- A visually delicious homage to travel, *The Motorcycle Diaries* (2004), directed by Walter Salles, recreates Che Guevara's cross-continental journey
- Chilean and Argentine troops share a war and a soccer match in *Mi Mejor Enemigo* (*My Best Enemy*; 2004), an original take on the 1978 Beagle conflict

weather sometimes prevails, particularly in the Araucanía and Lakes District. During the busy local holiday season (January to mid-February), lodging and transport are often heavily booked. On the other hand, services start to wind down after the end of February. Another seasonal problem are *tábanos*, these horseflies proliferate on low-level routes in the Araucanía and Lakes District for a couple weeks during January.

Early fall (autumn), from March to mid-April, typically brings cooler but more stable weather. The red-gold colors of deciduous trees make this an especially pleasant time to trek. Toward mid-May, the days become short and temperatures fall steadily, yet conditions are often still suitable for trekking in the Araucanía and Lakes District. Parties undertaking treks at this time should be equipped for possible heavy snowfalls.

COSTS & MONEY

Prices in this book are given in Argentine Pesos (AR$) or Chilean Pesos (CH$), unless quoted in US Dollars (US$). Though not cheap by South American standards, Chile and Argentina remain more economical than Europe or North America. Prices can double during the late-December to mid-March high season, but bargain accommodations or airfares appear in low season.

Shoestring travelers should budget a minimum of CH$20,000 in Chile or AR$80 in Argentina per day for food and lodging, though costs are considerably lower while trekking (factoring transport, park entry fees and provisions).

HOW MUCH?

Camping (per person) US$8

Dorm bed US$18

B&B (per person sharing) US$30

Box of wine US$3.50

BACKGROUND READING

Reading anything on Patagonia is sure to enrich your experience of it, though apart from ship logs, this part of the world is underrepresented. The literary first stop should be Bruce Chatwin's classic *In Patagonia*. This fun, enigmatic book is dubbed Cubist synthesis of Patagonian characters and landscape. For more about the modern challenges of rural life, read Nick Reding's *The Last Cowboys at the End of the World: The Story of the Gauchos of Patagonia*.

To understand this region's short but phenomenal history, first check out E Lucas Bridges' classic memoir *Uttermost Part of the Earth*. Bridges grew up the son of a missionary in the Wild West days of Tierra del Fuego. He played with seafaring Yahgan and later sought out the nomadic Selk'nam. The book tells of his adventures with these fascinating now-extinct cultures – its perspective on these 'savages' stands in stark contrast to Charles Darwin's. Those who can't resist comparison can read Darwin's *Voyage of the Beagle.*

Che Guevara's iconic *Motorcycle Diaries* gets readers behind the scenes in the making of a revolutionary. Che counted his continental journey as formative. The 'school of hard knocks' includes a hypothermic crossing of the Lakes District in winter. To bring the story up to date, try Patrick Symmes' *Chasing Che.*

Armchair andinistas should read *Against the Wall* by Simon Yates (of *Touching the Void* fame). This ripping yarn describes Yates' punishing climb of the world's largest vertical rock face, Paine's 4000-ft (1220m) central tower in Chile.

Visitors to Patagonia inevitably wonder what it would be like to see Torres del Paine through Victorian eyes. So satisfies Lady Florence Dixie's *Across Patagonia,* which takes her from British high society in 1880 to the ends of the earth to 'taste a more vigorous emotion.'

INTERNET RESOURCES

Argentina Turistica (www.argentinaturistica.com) A great source of general information.

Buenos Aires Herald (www.buenosairesherald.com) An English-language newspaper based in BA.

Setur (www.turismo.gov.ar) The official Argentine state tourism board site.

Chile Information Project (www.chip.cl) Umbrella for English-language *Santiago Times.*

Chiloé (www.chiloeweb.com, in Spanish) Terrific information on the island of Chiloé.

Go Chile (www.gochile.cl) General tourist information.

Interpatagonia (www.interpatagonia.com) All things touristy in Patagonia.

Sernatur (www.visitchile.org or www.sernatur.cl) Chile's national tourism organization.

Latin American Network Information Center (www.lanic.utexas.edu/la/chile or www.lanic.utexas.edu/la/argentina) Links to Chilean and Argentine government, politics, culture, environment and more.

Lonely Planet (www.lonelyplanet.com) Has travel news and tips. Consult fellow travelers on the Thorn Tree bulletin board, see trekking and mountaineering discussions.

SUSTAINABLE PATAGONIA: RURAL TOURISM

Rural Patagonia offers a rare and privileged glimpse of a fading way of life. To help the rural economy, government and nonprofit initiatives have created local guide and homestay associations in Chile.

These family enterprises range from comfortable roadside hospedajes and farmstays to wild multiday treks and horse trips through wonderland terrain. Prices are reasonable, starting from CH$10,000 per day for lodging and CH$25,000 for guided day trips, although extras include horses, and only Spanish is spoken.

Casa del Turismo Rural (☎ 214-031; www.casaturismorural.cl; Dussen 357b, Coyhaique) operates from Palena to Cerro Castillo, south of Coyhaique. Further north, the tourist office in the **Municipalidad de Cochamo** (www.cochamo.cl) arranges similar trips in the Puelo Valley. It's best to book a week or more in advance, as intermediaries will have to make radio contact with the most remote hosts. That's right – no phones, no electricity, no worries.

TOP FIVES

PATAGONIA'S GREATEST HITS

Bucket listers and soloists seeking company will hit pay dirt with these popular favorites:

- The W, Parque Nacional Torres del Paine (p186)
- Around Monte Fitz Roy, Parque Nacional Los Glaciares (p169)
- Volcán Villarrica, Parque Nacional Villarrica (p61)
- Circuito Chico, Parque Nacional Nahuel Huapi (p103)
- Huerquehue Lakes, Parque Nacional Huerquehue (p57)

FEELING HOT HOT HOT

Thermal features, geysers, bubbling mud pits…there's something about a rugged climate that makes you long for a little steam. Satisfy the urge at:

- Baños de Caulle (p89)
- Huerquehue Lakes (p57)
- Termas de Lahuen Co (p85)
- Termas de Callao (p97)
- Laguna Termal (p41)

BEST WILDLIFE WALKS

Bring binoculars and tread lightly to spy the shy Patagonian fauna. With luck, abundant birds, endangered *huemul* deer, guanaco and puma may cross your viewfinder at these locations:

- Parque Nacional Torres del Paine (p194)
- Valle Chacabuco (p193)
- Reserva Nacional Tamango (p192)
- Chepú, Parque Nacional Chiloé (p124)
- Parque Nacional Conguillío (p69)

REMOTE & RUGGED TREKS

If life's a stroll since retiring from the Special Forces, we have the solution. These treks lack shelter, trail markings, hand railings, etc. Five great excuses to test your top gear:

- Dientes Circuit, Isla Navarino (p217)
- Lonquimay Circuit (p50)
- Parque Nacional Perito Moreno (p194)
- Sierra Valdivieso Circuit (p205)
- Reserva Nacional Jeinimeini (p192)

IN THE PRIMEVAL FOREST

One of Patagonia's main attractions is its fresh, cool forests. Those seeking a lush green scene will find bliss under canopy at these parks:

- Parque Nacional Alerce Andino (p117)
- Parque Nacional Puyehue (p88)
- Parque Pumalín (p131)
- El Cañi (p70)
- PN Tierra del Fuego (p202)

BACKYARD WILDERNESS

If it's the icy beer, hot stone massage or hot tub at the finish line that motivates you, on these treks, civilization never lies too far behind:

- Villarrica Traverse to Pucón (p61)
- Campamento De Agostini to El Chaltén (p163)
- Paso de la Oveja to Ushuaia (p212)
- Around Cerro Hielo Azul to El Bolsón (p136)
- Valle Francés to Cabañas Los Cuernos in Parque Nacional Torres del Paine (p177)

GUIDED & GROUP TREKS

With this guidebook, trekkers have the necessary tools and information to trek independently, but those less confident in mountain terrain may opt to join an organized trekking tour. A wide range of foreign operators organize guided treks in the Patagonian Andes. Some of the best are listed below. Readers can also find local operators in their respective chapters.

International Operators

Andean Trails (☎ 0131-4677086; www.andeantrails.co.uk; The Clockhouse, Bonnington Mill Business Center, 72 Newhaven Rd, Edinburgh EH6 5QG, Scotland) Torres del Paine, Los Glaciares, with some winter trips.

Andes (☎ 01556-503929; www.andes.org.uk; 37a St Andrew St, Castle Douglas, Kirkcudbrightshire, DG7 1EN, Scotland) Southern Patagonia treks as well as climbing and ski trips to volcanoes in the Chilean Araucanía.

Aventuras Patagónicas (☎ 888-2039354; www.patagonicas.com; 1303 Sumac Ave, Boulder, CO 80304) This adventure group does 18-day trekking tours to Torres del Paine and Los Glaciares as well as climbing and skiing trips in Patagonia.

Backroads (☎ 800-4622848, 510-5271555; www.backroads.com; 801 Cedar St, Berkeley, CA 94710-1800) Biking the Lakes District and hiking Southern Patagonia.

Hauser Exkursionen (☎ 89-2350060; www.hauser-exkursionen.de; Spiegelstrasse 9, D-81241 München, Germany) Chilean Araucanía and Lakes District and Southern Patagonia, Tierra del Fuego.

Mountain Travel Sobek (☎ 888-8317526; 510-5946000; www.mtsobek.com; 1266 66th St, Suite 4, Emeryville, CA 94608) The usual suspects plus Central Patagonia's Aysen Glacier Trail and Southern Ice Cap.

Off the Beaten Path (☎ 800-4452995; www.offthebeatenpath.com; 7 East Beall St, Bozeman, MT 59715) Highly-regarded tours to the Argentine Lakes District and Los Glaciares.

Wilderness Travel (☎ 800-3682794; www.wildernesstravel.com; 1102 Ninth St, Berkeley, CA 94710) From Chile's Lake District to Tierra del Fuego, with interesting remote options.

Willis's Walkabouts (☎ 08-89852134; www.bushwalkingholidays.com.au; 12 Carrington St, Millner, NT 0810, Australia) Original, off the beaten path itineraries including Cerro Castillo, Cochamo Valley.

World Expeditions (☎ 613-2412700; www.worldexpeditions.com) 78 George St, Ottawa, Ontario, K1N 5W1, Canada. Lakes District, Southern Patagonia and Southern Ice Field.

Regional Operators

Andes Mountain Expediciones (☎ 02-2074699; www.andesmountain.cl; Nuestra Señora del Rosario 1411, Vitacura, Santiago, Chile) Torres del Paine and Los Glaciares.

Azimut (☎ 02-2351519; www.azimut360.com; Gral. Salvo 159, Providencia, Santiago) Central and Southern Patagonia, with trips to Cerro Castillo and Glaciar La Leona with base in Terra Luna (p194).

Compañia de Guias (☎ 02901-437-753; www.companiadeguias.com.ar; San Martín 654, Ushuaia) Glacier trekking, Paso de la Oveja and Ushuaia-based trips.

Escuela de Guias (www.escueladeguias.cl; Casilla 73, Coyhaique) Not an operator, this community NGO trains guides but also incorporates client trips. Treks in central Patagonia, including San Lorenzo trek and Cerro Castillo (see p145).

Patagonia-Argentina (☎ 011-4342-0931; www.patagonia-argentina.com; Venezuela 574 loft C, Buenos Aires 1012, Argentina) Argentine Patagonia.

Patagonia Adventure Trip (☎/fax 011-43432048; www.patagoniaadventuretrip.com; Room 162, 6th Floor, Maipu 42, C1084ABB, Buenos Aires, Argentina) Torres del Paine, Los Glaciares and Tierra del Fuego.

Patagonia Guide Service/Salvaje Corazón (☎/fax 067-211488; www.patagoniaguideservice.com; Casilla 311, Coyhaique, Chile) For Central Patagonia.

Environment

Active volcanoes, temperate rainforest, tumbling glaciers and sprawling steppe that make up the diverse landscapes of Patagonia inspire human passion. As a region it has been explored, colonized and very much popularized, but the sense of its potential never seems to diminish. Perhaps it's all that space – over a million square kilometers – and its sparse population (about two people per square kilometer) that remind us what a unique environment this is. While most of the world is depleted of forests, water and glaciers, here these precious features persist in obscene abundance. At least for now. In recent years, mining, salmon farming and hydroelectric proposals have put many parts of this once-pristine environment under imminent threat.

For information about trekking responsibly, see p36.

Glaciologists calculate that each snowflake that falls on the continental icecaps is trapped for 300 years or more before being finally released at the termination of a glacier.

THE LAND

Young, as mountain chains go, the Andes were created over the last 70 million years as the oceanic Nazca plate was slowly wedged under the continental South American plate. So mountain ranges gradually rose, blocking the passage of moisture from the Pacific, which in effect dried out the Andes' eastern side. This division is still noticable when traveling in northern Patagonia from the dryer Argentine side to the wetter, green landscape of Chilean Patagonia.

Volcanic activity centers on the Andes' western edge in Chile, where most of the dormant and active volcanoes are located, their cones scattered along the divide between 36°S and 43°S, with one volcano roughly every 30km. Though the region is stable, there are eruptions; the most recent being Volcán Llalma and Volcán Chaitén (see p133). The volcanic past is written into the landscape, in features like lava flows that have dammed rivers to create large new lakes, and the hundreds of thermal springs which dot the countryside, most still undeveloped.

The Carretera Austral runs 1240 mostly unpaved kilometers through Chilean Patagonia. Completed in 1996, it took US$300 million and 20 years to build, and cost 11 workers their lives.

DEFINITIONS OF PATAGONIA

In its widest definition, Patagonia comprises around one million square kilometers. The region represents just under one-third of the land area of both Chile and Argentina, but less than 5% of either nation's population actually lives there.

Chilean Patagonia is geographically very different from Argentine Patagonia. While the coast of southern Chile is a wild and wet strip of densely forested mountainous country, the greater part of Argentine Patagonia is a broad semiarid plateau out of which rise eroded tablelands (called *mesetas*).

In Argentina, Patagonia officially includes all the land south of the Río Colorado (at 36°S), from the Argentine Lakes District in the provinces of Neuquén and Río Negro, to the provinces of Chubut and Santa Cruz and the territories of Tierra del Fuego and the Falkland (Malvinas) Islands. In Chile, the situation is less definite. Only the strip of land extending south from Puerto Montt (which Chilean geographers call the Sur Grande) is normally considered Patagonia, a definition that excludes the Chilean side of the Araucanía and Lakes District and the island of Chiloé.

Even this narrow definition would come as a surprise to some Chileans, many of whom use the term Patagonia exclusively for the southern steppes of the Argentine known as *la pampa*. However, since the Araucanía and Lakes District on either side of the Andes show a high degree of geographical homogeneity, this book uses 'Patagonia' to include all the Chilean territory south of the Río Bíobío (at roughly 37°S), in addition to the 'true' Patagonia of the Argentine steppes.

PATAGONIA'S UNESCO WORLD HERITAGE SITES

- Parque Nacional Conguíllo (p69)
- Torres del Paine Biosphere Reserve (p177)
- Cabo de Hornos Biosphere Reserve (p203)
- Parque Nacional Los Glaciares (p169)

In the Lakes District, dozens of great lakes were gouged into the precordilleran landscape during the last ice age, complemented by the hundreds of alpine lagoons set among snowcapped peaks. Lush native rainforest still covers the higher ranges and large parts of the coast, but the Chilean valley has been largely cleared for farming and grazing. Flanked by smaller islands, Chile's largest island, Isla Grande de Chiloé, hangs off the continent here, battered by Pacific winds and storms. This region is drenched by high rainfall, most of which dumps between May and September, but no month is excluded.

Argentine Patagonia begins south of the Río Colorado, which flows southeast from the Andes and passes just north of the city of Neuquén. Blocking wet Pacific storm systems, the eastern Andes are notably drier, with snowfalls suitable for winter skiing around San Martín and Bariloche. Here too, volcanoes have left their mark in fascinating formations, including the petrified forests further south where thick layers of volcanic ash smothered forests of protoaraucaria and other coniferous trees.

Descending the backbone of the Andes, Chile's Aisén region is an intoxicating mix of fjords, raging rivers, impenetrable forests and high peaks. To the east, mountainous rainforest gives way to barren Patagonia steppe. Here South America's deepest lake, the enormous Lago General Carrera (or Lago Buenos Aires), is shared with Argentina.

Visiting a national park may be child's play, but creating one certainly isn't. Converting **Valle Chacabuco** from an *estancia* to park required dismantling 644km of fencing so native guanaco and huemul could return.

For such a southerly location, temperatures on the eastern slope are relatively mild, even in winter, when more uniform atmospheric pressure moderates the strong gales that blow most of the year. The cool, arid Patagonian steppes of Argentina support huge flocks of sheep, whose wool is almost entirely exported to Europe.

Heading south, the landscape hits a frozen curtain of glacial ice – the most extensive outside the world's polar regions. With 19 major glaciers, Campo de Hielo Norte (Northern Ice Field) stretches 100km. Its 4500 sq km include Monte San Valentín (4058m), generally considered to be the highest peak in Patagonia. Almost triple in size, the Campo de Hielo Sur (Southern Ice Field) stretches 320km from north to south and is shared with Argentina.

Overgrazing has serious consequences: Argentina's Ministerio de Agricultura estimates around 30% of Patagonia to be in some stage of desertification.

Fed by extremely heavy snowfalls, these icecaps are kept from melting by almost continuous cloud cover. The great icebound ranges are southern Patagonia's highest peaks (over 3000m) – coveted classics like Cerro Torre, Monte Fitz Roy and Cerro Paine Grande.

South of the Hielo Sur, the Patagonian Andes rapidly diminish. At Puerto Natales the dry zone of Patagonian steppes extends westward right to the Pacific coast. The barren eastern pampas stretch through northern Tierra del Fuego, abruptly halting by the Cordillera Darwin.

The world's southernmost permanently inhabited territory, Tierra del Fuego, consists of one large island (Isla Grande), unequally divided between Chile and Argentina, and many smaller ones, some of which have been a long-running point of contention between the two countries. When Europeans first passed through the Strait of Magellan, the fires stemmed from the activities of the now endangered Yahgan people; nowadays, the fires result from the flaring of natural gas in the region's oil fields.

The northern half of Isla Grande, resembling the Patagonian steppes, is devoted to sheep grazing, while its southern half is mountainous and

READING THE GLACIAL LANDSCAPE

Patagonia was sculpted by several periods of intense glaciation over the last two million years. During these ice ages, an ice sheet hundreds of meters thick blanketed entire ranges and part of the lowlands. Retreating glaciers released enormous quantities of debris known as 'moraine' over the steppes of southern Argentina.

Many of the world's finest treks lead through landscapes substantially shaped by glaciers. The most obvious is the U-shaped valley (1), gouged out by a glacier moving downhill, often with one or more bowl-shaped cirques (2) at its head. Cirques are found along high mountain ridges or at mountain passes or cols (3). Where an alpine glacier – which flows off the upper slopes and ridges of a mountain range – has joined a deeper, more substantial valley glacier, a dramatic hanging valley (4) is often the result. Hanging valleys and cirques commonly shelter hidden alpine lakes or tarns (5). The thin ridge, which separates adjacent glacial valleys, is known as an arête (6).

As a glacier grinds its way forward it usually leaves long, lateral moraine (7) ridges along its course – debris mounds deposit along the flanks of the glacier or remain from sub-ice streams within its heart (an esker). At the snout of a glacier is the terminal moraine (8), the point where the giant conveyor belt of ice drops its load of rocks and grit. Both high up in the hanging valleys and in the surrounding valleys and plains, moraine lakes (9) may form behind a dam of glacial rubble.

The plains surrounding a glaciated range may feature a confusing variety of moraine ridges, mounds and outwash fans – material left by rivers flowing from the glaciers. Perched randomly, erratics (10) are rocks carried far from their origin by the moving ice, and are left stranded when it melts.

partly covered by forests and glaciers. As in Patagonia, winter conditions are rarely extreme, although trekking and outdoor camping are not advisable except for experienced mountaineers. For most visitors, though, the brief daylight hours during this season may be a greater deterrent than the weather.

FLORA & FAUNA

Compared to temperate South America, Patagonia is not a wildlife-driven destination. The destruction of forest and loss of native habitat through livestock grazing have had a strong impact on the populations of native species. Yet, visitors can still enjoy and engage with the unique flora and fauna found here.

For the scoop on Chile's foundering salmon industry, check out **Fundación Terram** (www.terram.cl), which closely monitors the industry.

Animals

Many of Patagonia's native animals are shy, nocturnal and increasingly scarce, and are thus seldom seen. It's not uncommon to spot dropping or hoof print but sightings are fleeting, so don't expect shots of that puma or *huemul*. Guanacos, foxes and many bird species are easily sighted, however, and there's a fair chance of spotting a *coipo*, *huillín* or *pudu*. The following animals may be seen in a range of parks.

Among the world's 25 biodiversity hot spots, Chiloe's **Parque Tantauco** (www.parquetantauco.cl) is home to whales, otters and foxes. Just created in 2005, you won't even find it on most maps.

SMALL MAMMALS

The **coipo,** an aquatic rodent, has prominent, sharp front teeth useful for chomping herbs and roots. To deter predators it burrows under the banks of lakes and slow-flowing streams and rarely comes out before dusk. Once trapped almost to extinction for its pelt, the coipo is now protected by law.

The tawny grey mouse **oopossum** (*monito del monte*) is one of the southern Andes' few marsupials. The female nurtures young in a belly-pouch. This tree-dwelling 'little monkey of the mountains' has highly adapted, monkeylike hands with four fingers and an opposable thumb to facilitate climbing. You can see it in Parque Nacional Vicente Peréz Rosales (see p96).

LEAVE IT TO BEAVERS

Forget guns, germs and steel, Canadian beavers (*Castor canadensis*) have colonized Tierra del Fuego using only buckteeth and broad tails.

It all goes back to the 1940s, when Argentina's military government imported 25 pairs of beavers from Canada, hoping they would generate a lucrative fur industry in this largely undeveloped area. Without natural predators, the beavers did multiply but, in turn, felted beaver hats skidded out of fashion.

These days there are some 250,000 beavers on Tierra del Fuego and the surrounding islands, where they are officially considered a plague. Beavers' damaging effects are many. A sole beaver couple has the chewing power to create their own lake, felling hundreds of trees. Flooding from beaver dams destroys roads and meadows, ruining infrastructure and creating havoc for livestock. Beavers also pass giardia into the lakes, which can get into water supplies and work its black magic on human intestines.

Yet, since beavers must live in water, they can only spread so far across the land and they don't reproduce as wildly as rabbits or other rodents. However, there is great concern that they have already crossed the Strait of Magellan, spreading the beaver plague to the rest of the South American continent.

If you're eager to do your part, look for beaver meat on Fuegian menus.

The omnivorous **Patagonian skunk** (known locally as *chingue*) has typical skunk features and, like its cousins, protects itself by ejecting an acidic liquid with a powerfully unpleasant odor from under its tail.

Standing just 45cm and weighing only 9kg, the **pudu** is the world's smallest deer. Males have pointed, branched horns. This shy animal is spotted in the dense rainforest of the Araucanía and Lakes District.

Half a dozen species of **tucotuco**, relatives of the hamster, are found throughout the Patagonian Andes and Tierra del Fuego. The tucotuco has powerful incisor teeth, which it uses to burrow through the earth. The endangered **mara**, also called the Patagonian hare, is actually another larger relative of the hamster that inhabits the Patagonian steppes.

The **vizcacha** (also called *chinchillón*, related to domesticated chinchillas) build extensive burrows in steep, rocky terrain. Resembling a bearded squirrel, it has thick greyish fur and a darker brushlike tail. Older members of the colony scan for predators, letting out a shrill warning at the slightest sign of danger. It can be spotted in Valle Chacabuco (see p193).

The docile *huemul* is the world's fifth-most endangered species of deer and could disappear from mainland Chile in the next few years if radical steps are not taken to protect it.

LARGER HERBIVORES

The **guanaco** is found mainly on the Patagonian steppes, but also inhabits mountainous areas of Tierra del Fuego. Closely related to the alpaca and llama, this camelid is sleek but powerful, with a tawny body and long neck. Guanaco herds have been drastically reduced on the steppes, but the animal manages to hold its own due to continuing human persecution of its main predator, the puma.

Chile's national symbol, the endangered **huemul** is an agile deer, once abundant in the southern Andes. Deforestation, hunting and habitat destruction for pasture have been the main causes of the decreasing numbers in southern Aisén, where only a few hundred remain. After several reintroductions into Parque Nacional Torres del Paine, the population there is still considered low. Your best bet to see a wild *huemul* is in Reserva Nacional Tamango (see p192), though chances even there are slim.

Before you hit the trail, you can check out the weather coming your way at www.meteochile.cl (in Spanish); click on Prognóstico General.

PREDATORS

The **huillín**, or southern river otter, inhabits inland waterways and coastal areas of Patagonia. Growing to over 1m in length and weighing 10kg at maturity, its long tail and broad, short paws make the *huillín* an excellent swimmer and diver, while its thick, oily fur insulates it from cold water. It ventures out at dusk in search of crabs and mussels.

The small grey Azara's fox or **pampas fox** (*zorro gris*) prefers open country and has few natural enemies, apparently due to its unpalatable flesh. Once prized by trappers, the larger Patagonian **red fox** (*zorro culpeo* or *zorro colorado*) lives primarily in lightly forested country. A subspecies, known as the Fuegian fox (*zorro fueguino*) is found on Tierra del Fuego.

The adaptable **puma** (North American cougar or mountain lion) can be found anywhere on the Patagonian mainland, with its only enemy being people. Sandy-brown with a white muzzle, it reaches over 2m from head to tail. Its prints are about the size of a man's fist. Pumas traditionally prey on guanaco or pudu. In spite of their taste for livestock, pumas are an illegal target for ranchers. Trekkers will be lucky to glimpse this mainly nocturnal animal.

Plants

The Patagonian Andes are divided into four vegetation zones – temperate, highland, alpine and continental – determined by altitude and distance from the coast. Temperate rainforest and highland forest zones appear at lower altitudes with the further south you travel.

The temperate zone is covered in **Valdivian rainforest** (*bosque valdiviano*), with mixed evergreen tree species. The most diverse of the four zones, it occupies all lower areas west of the Cordillera with strong coastal influence (and heavy rainfall). In the Araucanía and Lakes District, temperate rainforest is species-rich and grows from sea level up to about 1400m.

Above the temperate zone is the highland zone, which is covered by subalpine **Magellanic forest** (*bosque magellánico*), dominated by deciduous southern beech species (chiefly *lenga*). In southern Patagonia, where there is little undergrowth, mosses and herbs make an attractive 'park lawn' type landscape.

Above the highland forest is the alpine zone, an often narrow, thinly vegetated area extending up as far as the bare rock almost to the permanent snowline. Tundra species, including many alpine wildflowers, are found here.

The highland zone merges with the semiarid continental zone on the Patagonian Andes' lower eastern sides. Here, sparse steppe-like vegetation, such as tough, slow-growing tussock grasses known as *coirón* and thorny 'saltbush' plants called *mogotes*, is found. Sporadic clusters of low trees (especially *ñirre*) and *calafate* scrub grow in sheltered places and along the river courses.

Spanning 16,800 sq km, the Hielo Continental Sur (southern ice field) is the world's third biggest extension of continental ice after Antarctica and Greenland. Its first north-to-south crossing was accomplished by a Chilean team in 1998 and took a total of 98 days.

SHRUBS & FLOWERS

Woody shrubs grow as heaths, and form thickets or stand on slopes and meadows.

Thickets of thorny **calafate** grow most commonly in the far south. Its bright-yellow flowers turn into sweet purple berries by late February.

The original species of all the world's fuchsia cultivars, bright red and purple **chilco** grows in the cool, humid rainforest, typically by waterfalls or streams. These distinctive flowers are a major source of nectar for hummingbirds.

Reaching up to 3m in a single growing season, **nalca** (also called *pangue* in Mapundungun) thrives in wet locations. The end of its 1m-wide 'elephant ear' leaf produces a half-dozen thorny succulent stems that can be eaten (see Wild Food, p233).

A distant relative of Australia's *waratah*, the **notro,** or Chilean firewheel (*ciruelillo*), is a large bush with spidery red flowers.

Separate species of native bamboo grow in temperate rainforest. Vigorous opportunist **quila** spreads out horizontally to colonize the opening left by fallen trees. This is normally the first stage of regeneration after a forest fire or landslide, when quilla can form impenetrable thickets up

A good website to gather general information on Chile's and Argentina's big ski resorts is www.andesweb.com, which has photo essays, reviews and trail maps.

THE BACKYARD PHARMACY

A remarkable variety of wild plants are used in Mapuche medicine:

- The extract from **quilquil** stems, a giant fern, treats eye problems
- **Notro** leaves and pods contain natural agents to alleviate toothache and inflamed glands
- **Nalca** roots, with a gum rich in tannin, act as a stimulant
- The bark of the **radal** tree is a natural purgative
- Native tobacco, or **petrem**, is used as medicine and a ceremonial fix

to 6m high. The thicker **colihue** is used to make traditional Mapuche trumpets (*trutruca*), baskets and furniture.

December is the best month for viewing Patagonian wildflowers. Look for **añañucas** in the volcanic soils of the Araucanía and Lakes District – large pink or red goblet-shaped flowers at the end of a long succulent stem.

For detailed stats, route descriptions and inspirational photos of mountaineering, volcaneering and ice-climbing throughout Chile, visit www.escalando.cl.

Orange **amancays** (known to gardeners as *alstroemerias*) typically grow in drier sunny clearings or along roadsides. *Amancay* means 'eternal love' in Mapundungun; according to indigenous folklore it is the reincarnation of a Mapuche girl who sacrificed herself in order to save her lover.

Chile's national flower is the **copihue**, a climbing rainforest plant with delicate pink flowers and a yellow stamen.

TREES

Even when rain obscures mountain views, Patagonia's superb forests offer a fascinating landscape. The primary species are listed below.

Southern Beech

Get a grip on Chilean culture with the dynamic website www.nuestro.cl, from the Chilean Cultural Heritage Corporation, with interviews, rich stories and profiles.

The Andean-Patagonian vegetation is strongly characterized by the (broadleaf) **southern beech** (genus Nothofagus). Seven species are found in the Patagonian Andes and, although many other tree species may also be present, southern beech forms the basis of the forest in virtually all areas.

Three evergreen species of southern beech known as **coigüe** (*coihue* in Argentina) are mostly found at lower elevations. The vigorous and adaptable **common coigüe** (*coigüe común*) has larger and more serrated leaves and grows (often in a distinct 'stratified' form) to well over 50m, often attaining a truly massive girth. Equally widespread is **coigüe de Magallanes** (*guindo* in Mapundungun, especially in Argentina), identified by its smaller leaves. Since the distribution of both these *coigüe* species overlaps considerably, novices may find it difficult to distinguish the two. **Coigüe de Chiloé** has scaly, almost triangular

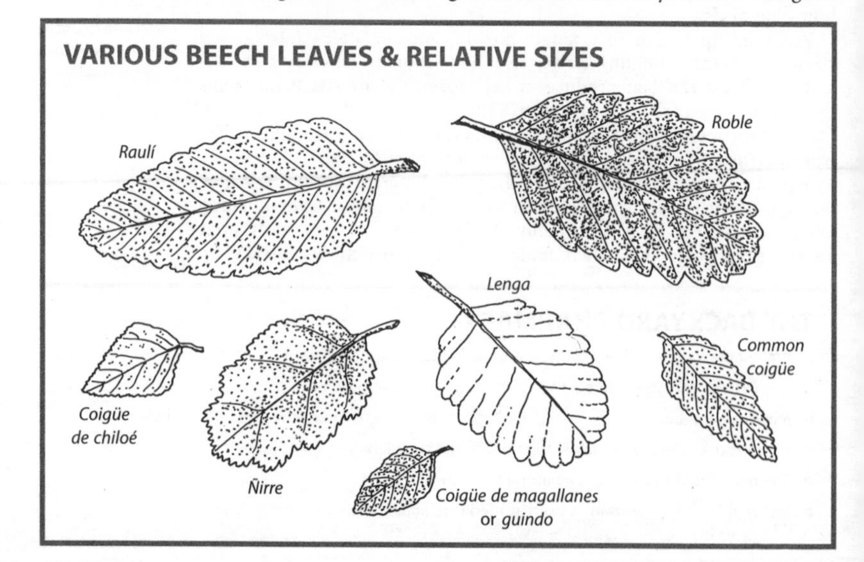

PINING FOR PIÑONES

A dietary staple of dozens of insect species and the *cachaña* (parakeet), **araucaria nuts** also lured native Pehuenche to trek far to harvest them. This native nut, known as *piñon* in Spanish and *ngülla* in Mapundungun, is rich in complex carbohydrates. Mapuche still employ it to thicken stews or bake a nutty loaf.

leaves of a lighter color. It is found on the large island of Chiloé, and the adjacent mainland.

The bonsai-like **lenga** is the most common of the deciduous species of southern beech. Its 3cm-long leaves have neat, rounded double-indentations. It is commonly found right up to the tree line, forming low impenetrable thickets. In fall (autumn) the leaves turn a burnished red. In the mountains of the Araucanía and Lakes District, *lenga* is rarely found below 1000m, but in the far south of Patagonia and Tierra del Fuego, *lenga* often grows as low as sea level, where it may grow up to 40m in height.

Get your fix on Patagonian news (in English) at www.patagonia times.cl.

A small southern beech species found throughout Patagonia, **ñirre** (*ñire* in Argentina) occupies difficult sites, from dry semi-steppe to waterlogged *mallín* country. When large enough to be considered a proper tree it is easily mistaken for *lenga* – particularly in fall when its leaves turn the same golden-red hue. *Ñirre* is easily distinguished from *lenga* by its crinkled, irregular leaves and much coarser bark.

Travel delays can be a good thing...The planned two-year expedition of the *HMS Beagle* actually lasted five, giving Darwin ample fodder for his later-developed theory of evolution.

Another deciduous southern beech species found only in Araucanía and northern Lakes District forests, **raulí** has leathery, almost oval-shaped leaves of up to 15cm and reaches a height of up to 40m. Relatively fast-growing, it is an ideal species for reforestation programs. Found in similar areas and also further south, **roble** has distinctive 'oaklike' leaves with serrations.

Other Broadleaf Trees

The **arrayán** thrives in wet coastal rainforests or along lakes and rivers. Covered with smooth almost luminescent cinnamon-red bark that peels off leaving strips of white, the *arrayán* typically produces multiple trunks and beautiful, dimpled, twisted branches. In January the tree is covered in white flowers that develop into edible purple berries.

Sacred to the Mapuche people, **canelo** (*fuñe* in Mapundungun) is a stunning rainforest tree belonging to the magnolia family. It grows in moist areas throughout the Patagonian Andes, reaching a height of 30m and a diameter of 1m. Canelo has thick, light-green elongated leaves that grow out radially around the branchlets, and in November it is covered with fragrant white flowers. The bark of the *canelo* (meaning 'cinnamon') is rich in vitamin C, mineral salts, essential oils and natural antibacterial substances.

Handy to tell *hierba buena* from *hierba mala*, field guide *Flora Nativa* from Editorial Andres Bellow, is a comprehensive plant guide, found in Chilean bookstores.

Tepa (a relative of southern Australia's sassafras) is a tall, straight tree with thick, serrated leaves that, when crushed, give off an intense aroma somewhere between eau de cologne and fresh basil.

Conifers

The Dr Seuss–like **araucaria** (*pehuén* in Mapundungun; 'monkey puzzle' tree in English), with its edible nut (see p234) typifies the Araucanía and northern Lakes District, where it grows from an altitude of about 1000m right up to the tree line. Individual trees have been measured at 50m in height and 2000 years of age.

Waterproof and nearly indestructible, the valuable **alerce**, or *lahuén*, ranks among the oldest and largest tree species in the world, with specimens reaching almost 4000 years old. Although it's illegal to cut down living trees, some clandestine felling does occur. This protected species is seen within national parks such as Alerce Andino and Los Alerces.

For field guides, check out the fantastic bilingual selection from Editorial Fantástico Sur (www.fantasticosur.cl), available online, in Chilean bookstores and Fantastic Sur-run refugios in Parque Nacional Torres del Paine.

Several species of **mañío** (often spelt *mañi*), members of the coniferous *Podocarpus* genus, grow in the forests of the Lakes District. *Mañío* is recognizable by its distinctive waxy elongated leaves and unpalatable red fruit. It grows to be a very large, attractive tree with a reddish-brown trunk that is often deeply twisted, although it yields excellent timber.

The hardy but slow-growing **Cordilleran cypress** (*ciprés de la cordillera*) produces male and female flowers on separate flattened, scaly branchlets, and when the trees are in bloom (in October) large puffs of pollen blow around the forests. Preferring a drier 'continental' climate, Cordilleran cypress is most widespread in the Argentine Araucanía and Lakes District, where it forms glorious tall, pure-stand forests fringing the eastern foothills of the Andes.

The world's most southerly conifer, **Guaitecas cypress** (*ciprés de las Guaitecas*) – in stark contrast to the related Cordilleran species – thrives in waterlogged ground in the intensely wet coastal areas of western Patagonia. The tree resembles the *alerce*, but is considerably smaller and without the same reddish bark.

NATIONAL PARKS & RESERVES

With the creation of the first South American parks in the early 20th century, Chile and Argentina pioneered continental conservation efforts. If you've ever wondered what kind of a difference one person can make, consider the regional history. The land area of Patagonia's first national park was given to the Argentine explorer Francisco 'Perito' Moreno for his services to the national boundary commission. Perito Moreno promptly donated this land back to the nation to form today's Parque Nacional Nahuel Huapi. At 7580 sq km, it is easily the largest national park on either side of the Andes in northern Patagonia. Today, private efforts again headline the race to keep Patagonia pristine, from Doug Tompkins' Pumalín Park, to other adventurous initiatives (see p131).

Today, 99% of European potatoes can be traced back to the island of Chiloé. In recent years, the island has been actively trying to rescue its some 200 indigenous spud varieties.

The region boasts many dozens of national parks, provincial parks and national reserves in the greater Patagonian Andes (including 22,000 sq km in the Araucanía and Lakes District) with a combined area of well over 100,000 sq km. By far the largest parks are in Chile, whose roughly 26,000-sq-km Parque Nacional Bernardo O'Higgins covers much of the Hielo Sur and the fjords or glaciated islands along the west coast of southern Patagonia. Two adjoining areas, Reserva Nacional Las Guaitecas, which takes in the Península de Taitao, and Parque Nacional Laguna San Rafael, which includes the entire Hielo Norte, are similar in size and character.

Around 7370 BC the Toldense culture made its first hand paintings inside Patagonia's famous Cueva de las Manos.

To the south in Chilean Tierra del Fuego is the 22,000-sq-km Parque Nacional Alberto de Agostini. These stupendously large wilderness areas have savage terrain and weather, however, and are inaccessible by land; there are almost no trails or other infrastructure. Argentina's largest park in southern Patagonia is Parque Nacional Los Glaciares, which abuts the Chilean parks of Bernardo O'Higgins and Torres del Paine.

While complete isolation has kept some parks and reserves out of the hands of predatory interests (such as logging or mining), it also makes

THE ULTIMATE TRAIL: TOP TO BOTTOM CHILE

Conceived as a cross-country adventure on the scale of the USA's Appalachian Trail, Chile's **Sendero de Chile** (www.senderodechile.cl, in Spanish) aims to create one of the longest pathways in the world, approximately 8000km, designated for hiking, mountain biking and horse riding. Starting in the desert north and ending at Cape Horn, it will pass through around 40 watershed systems and encourage a necklace of ecotourism projects along its path. However, not all is rosy with this mega project. Funding appears to be running out, infrastructure is lacking and some stretches follow gravel road instead of beautiful trails – in short, research the part that you wish to undertake. There are updates and maps on the website and in Chile's guidebook series, Turistel.

them almost impossible to visit (as in the case of Parque Nacional Bernardo O'Higgins).

In other cases, national parks have become essential to the economy of rural Patagonia. The Parque Nacional Torres del Paine for example, receives nearly 200,000 visitors per year. But even a few hundred trekkers per year can propel small-scale tourism on the sparsely-populated Isla Navarino, where the Dientes de Navarino circuit remains without reserve status, though it is part of a Unesco World Heritage site.

Argentine parks are run by **Administración de Parques Nacionales** (APN; ☎ 011-4312 0257, 4311 0303; www.parquesnacionales.gov.ar; Santa Fe 690). In Chile, national parks and reserves are administered by Corporación Nacional Forestal, or **Conaf** (☎ 02-696 6677, fax 6715881; www.conaf.cl; 5th Floor, Oficina 501, Av Bulnes 285, Santiago) Before leaving Santiago, visit their **central information office** (☎ 02-390 0282; Av Bulnes 265, Centro; 9.30am-5.30pm Mon-Fri) for basic maps and brochures.

The indigenous Yaghan began populating the southernmost islands of Tierra del Fuego around 4000 BC.

Conaf and the APN have information centers (*centros de informes*) or ranger stations (*guarderías*) at, or close to, popular parks and reserves. Even if you do not speak enough Spanish to converse with staff, it is generally well worth visiting the local information center or ranger office before you set out on your trek.

Most Argentine, and some Chilean, national parks have restricted areas (*reservas naturales estrictas*) where public access is strictly controlled, and generally allowed only under the supervision of national park personnel (see Permits & Fees, p237).

ENVIRONMENTAL ISSUES

For centuries, Patagonia's isolation has been its best defense against environmental degradation, but improved access means those days are coming to an end. With Argentina and Chile striving to compete in the global market, it is inevitable that attentions would fall to the resource-rich south.

In 1865 over 150 Welsh immigrants, traveling aboard the clipper *Mimosa*, landed in Patagonia and established Argentina's first Welsh colony in the province of Chubut.

Dams

Water and energy have been key components of Chile's race toward modernization. Unlike Argentina, which has abundant gas reserves, the country has often had to deal with energy shortages, so successive governments have promoted hydroelectricity. Heavy spring snowmelt in the high Andes feeds raging rivers that pass through narrow canyons, making ideal sites for dams. However, these projects also have major social and environmental drawbacks. High-profile battles are underway over dams on the Río Baker and Pascua, among ten other Patagonian rivers (see the boxed text, p200). The Bachelet administration has come out in favor

RESPONSIBLE TREKKING

Just experiencing Patagonia's magnificent wilderness can inspire you towards its stewardship. And why not? The region's environmental issues may be exasperating but each of us can do our part.

RUBBISH

- Remove packaging from food supplies before hiking to cut down on rubbish
- Buried rubbish is likely to be dug up by curious creatures; it also disturbs soil and ground cover and encourages erosion and weed growth
- Take out all garbage and help pick up any ugly remainders left by others

HUMAN WASTE DISPOSAL

- Always use toilets provided at campsites
- When there are no toilets, bury waste with a trowel or tent peg. Dig a small 15cm hole well away from streams, paths and buildings. Cap it with a good layer of soil
- Keeping your waste out of water sources prevents the transmission of giardia, a human bacterial parasite

CAMPING

- Always seek permission before camping near a farm or house
- Minimize impact by using recognized sites, and camp at least 30m from watercourses and paths
- Do not dig trenches – choose a naturally well-drained site
- Leave sites as you found them

WASHING

- Since even biodegradable soaps and toothpaste can harm fish and wildlife, keep them out of streams or lakes
- Wash at least 50m from the watercourse. Collecting used water and dispersing it widely helps it filter through the soil before it returns to the stream
- Wash cooking utensils with a scrub pad or gritty sand instead of detergent

FIRES

- Campfires are banned completely in many national parks.
- If fires are allowed, use a safe existing fireplace rather than making a new one. Clear away all flammable material for at least 2m. Keep the fire modest and use a minimum of dead, fallen wood
- Never leave a fire unattended
- Don't light fires in areas of highly flammable peat soils
- Extinguish your fire by spreading the embers and drowning them with water. Scatter the charcoal and cover the fire site with soil and leaves

of the dams, although, officially, approval depends upon the results of environmental impact studies.

Global Warming

Nowhere is global warming more apparent than in the world's glaciers, and Patagonia's abundant glacial reserves are at stake. Scientists have documented many glaciers doubling their thinning rates in recent years while the northern and southern ice fields continue to retreat. In particular, the Northern Patagonian Ice Field is contributing to rising

TRIAL BY FIRE

When colonists in the 1930s and 1940s set out to farm densely forested southern Chile, clear land was requisite for gaining its title. Government-sanctioned burning destroyed some 20,000 sq km of virgin forest in the southern Andes. With strong winds fanning the flames, some fires burned for entire summers, laying waste vast tracts of native forest. The results can still be seen today – a landscape radically altered from its origins, with dead trees and scarred mountains as enduring landmarks of the colonization.

Fires are still problematic in Patagonia, where fire fighting is volunteer-only, with scant resources for planes or fire jumpers. As a result, slow regeneration post-fire makes soil erosion a severe problem in Patagonia. The resulting loss of habitat is also responsible for an alarming decline in some species, including *pudu* and endangered *huemul*.

ocean levels at a rate one-quarter higher than formerly thought. In fact, reports suggest that glaciers are thinning more rapidly than can be explained by warmer air temperatures and decreased precipitation. While tour operators count the sunny days with a smile, this change also stands to impact plant and animal life, water levels in lakes and rivers, and overall sustainability.

Magellanic penguins, native to Patagonia and Tierra del Fuego, have approximately 27 feathers per sq cm – now that's a down jacket!

Farmed Salmon

When a 2007 *New York Times* article revealed widespread virus outbreaks in Chilean salmon, Chile's $2.2 billion salmon industry was rocked to the core. Though the species is not native, Chile had become the world's second-largest producer of farmed salmon. Responsible for polluting water, devastating underwater ecology, and depleting other fish stocks, the industry remains under questioning by regulatory agencies. Some areas, such as the Lakes Region Seno de Reloncaví, have become too polluted for sustainable production; sadly, farming operations are just skirting further south to Aisén.

With a special focus on Latin America, Ron Mader's Planeta (www.planeta.com) is the most comprehensible online resource for exploring ecotourism and environmental reporting.

Other Issues

Forests, fish stocks, water and soil have all been overexploited and continue to be so. Livestock grazing on fragile topsoil contributes to erosion and, ultimately, desertification. In times of economic hardship, these issues can take a back seat but they remain everpresent. The growing hole in the ozone layer over Antarctica has become such an issue that medical authorities recommend wearing protective clothing and heavy sunblock to avoid cancer-causing ultraviolet radiation in Patagonia.

On a positive note, environmental consciousness is rapidly growing in Chile and Argentina, and a number of conservation groups organize campaigns in opposition to over-the-top development or vandalistic forestry practices as well as positive campaigns to save native species. Most of these organizations welcome volunteers and can offer useful suggestions on how to help.

Chile's warm but powerful easterly winds are known as *puelches*. Southern wind (*viento sur*) presages stable weather.

Environmental Organizations

Ancient Forest International (AFI; ☎ 707-923 4475; www.ancientforests.org) US-based organization with close links to Chilean forest-conservation groups.

Codeff (Comité Pro Defensa de la Fauna y Flora; ☎ 02-777 2534; www.codeff.cl, in Spanish; Ernesto Reyes 035, Providencia, Santiago) Campaigns to protect the country's flora and fauna, especially endangered species. Trips, seminars and work projects are organized for volunteers. **Conservación**

According to Greenpeace, Patagonian glaciers are shrinking, as a whole, at a rate of 42 cu km annually – faster than anywhere else on the planet.

Patagónica (in USA ☎ 415-229 9340; www.conservacionpatagonica.org) An NGO dedicated to preserving unique Patagonian ecosystems, such as Valle Chacabuco, with opportunities for volunteers.
Defensores del Bosque Chileno (☎ 02-2041914; www.elbosquechileno.cl, in Spanish; Diagonal Oriente 1413, Ñuñoa) Defending the native forests through education, lobbying, promoting the planting of native species over exotics, and taking legal action against logging interests.
Fundación Vida Silvestre Argentina (☎ 011-43313631; fax extension 24; www.vidasilvestre.org.ar) Defensa 251 Piso 6 'K' (C1065AAC) Buenos Aires. Argentina's leading nongovernment conservationist organisation; owns nature reserves throughout Argentina.
Greenpeace Argentina (☎ 011-45518811; www.greenpeace.org.ar in Spanish; Zabala 3873 (C1427DYG) Buenos Aires. Focuses on forest conservation, ocean ecology and dealing with toxic waste.
Greenpeace Chile (☎ 02-6342120; www.greenpeace.cl in Spanish; Agromedo 50, Centro, Santiago). Focuses on forest conservation, ocean ecology and dealing with toxic waste.
Patagonia Sin Represas (Patagonia Without Dams; www.patagoniasinrepresas.cl) A coalition of Chilean environmental groups supporting the anti-dam movement in Patagonia.
Terram (☎ 02-2694499; www.terram.cl; Bustamente 24, Providencia, Santiago) One of the biggest-hitting pressure groups at the moment.
WWF (☎ 063-244590; www.wwf.cl; Carlos Andtwander 624, Casa 4, Valdivia) Involved with the preservation of the temperate rainforests around Valdivia, conservation in southern Patagonia, and protection of the native wildlife.

The Araucanía

HIGHLIGHTS

- Peering down into Volcán Copahue's Tolkeinesque crater lake at the steaming **Laguna Termal** (p41)
- Glissading down, down, down **Volcán Antuco** (p45) toward the green valleys below
- Navigating the misty skirts of **Volcán Lonquimay** (p50)
- Dissolving all those aches in the rustic thermal pools of the **Termas de Río Blanco** (p57) on the Huerquehue Lakes circuit
- Stargazing from the tundra under the snowcapped **Volcán Villarrica** (p61)

From jade lakes to the frozen cone of Volcán Villarrica (2847m), the Araucanía heralds the start of the great south. The region offers a fascinating brew of natural phenomena, including many hot springs and active volcanoes. The territory starts south of the Río Biobío, and shares many of the typical features of the more southerly Lakes District, but with milder temperatures and more sunshine.

In summer, this region becomes saturated with holiday-makers who come to tourist centers for their lakeside retreats, luxurious spas, casinos and nightlife. But even if you are planning your nights under starry skies, you can take advantage of the excellent outdoor infrastructure, including cheap and frequent public transport to trails, with the occasional five-star thermal pool to blow the camper's budget.

The Chilean side of the Araucanía is the stronghold of the Mapuche, now numbering around 620,000, a resilient culture known as the only ethnic group to have successfully fought off Inka invasion. Here, in the most ethnically driven region of Patagonia, visitors should take advantage of opportunities to explore Mapuche culture, whether it be through a visit to a rural farm or an *empanada* (pie) spiced with the smoked peppers known as *merquen*.

Look for the inverted umbrella shape of araucarias, a regional symbol that stamps logos and landscapes alike. Resembling something out of a Dr Seuss book, these glorious conifers, also known as monkey-puzzle trees, still grow throughout the region, protected by many national parks and reserves.

GATEWAY

See Temuco (p76).

PARQUE PROVINCIAL COPAHUE

The 105-sq-km Parque Provincial Copahue lies in the remote northwest of Argentina's Neuquén province. It takes in the eastern slopes around the Volcán Copahue (2928m), an exploded volcano cone with two new side craters. Since pre-European times, the Mapuche have trekked up to Volcán Copahue to collect its lake water, known for its healing properties. Copahue's hot springs and mineral waters continue to be held in highest esteem, though their source has proved less than stable. In June 2000 the volcano shot a plume of smoke 600m high, sending a layer of grey ash to the nearby villages of Caviahue and Copahue. The eruption turned Lago Caviahue (also called Lago Agrio) green with sulfur-rich material.

Though light araucaria forest covers the slopes above Caviahue, the 1500m reserve is mostly above the tree line. While its summers are dry and hot, winters are cold with heavy snowfalls (about 5m in Copahue). In summer, sheep graze on the sparse, mostly unfenced highland pastures surrounding the park.

The Araucanía

THE ARAUCANIA – MAPS

LAGUNA TERMAL

Duration 6½–8¼ hours
Distance 25km
Difficulty moderate
Start/Finish Copahue
Nearest Town Caviahue
Transport bus
Summary A circuit up to a remarkable warm, steaming lake that fills the small eastern crater of Volcán Copahue.

Surrounded by small glaciers, fumaroles and hot springs, Laguna Termal is unusually acidic and rich in trace minerals. Its temperatures fluctuate between 20°C and 40°C, depending on the season and the level of volcanic activity. The water drains subterraneously as the source of the Arroyo Caviahue (Río Agrio).

This trek involves an ascent/descent of 700m. Don't miss an excellent side trip up to Volcán Copahue and two very interesting alternative route options. Basic *refugios* (mountain huts) along the route could be useful for bad weather, though their condition is extremely poor.

PLANNING

When to Trek

Conditions are ideal between mid-January and mid-April. Earlier, much of the route may be snow-covered (and possibly impassable without ice axe and crampons).

Maps

The only available topographical map that covers the area at any useful scale is the Chilean IGM 1:50,000 map *Volcán Copahue* (Section G, No 44). Although this map shows detail well, it has some topographical errors and outdated information, including the position of most foot tracks and minor roads.

> **WARNING**
>
> Particularly on windy days, acrid fumes rising from Laguna Termal can be overpowering due to sulfur dioxide gas, which attacks your airways. Approach the lake cautiously, beware of sudden wind changes and don't even consider swimming in it. Less experienced trekkers are advised to go with an organized tour (see Caviahue p71).

Permits & Regulations

Trekkers do not require permits, but should register with the **Gendarmería Nacional** (☎ 02948-495055) at the park entrance. Camping is not permitted in Parque Provincial Copahue apart from in the upper Arroyo Caviahue (Río Agrio).

THE TREK

From the Hotel Valle del Volcán at the upper (southwest) edge of the village, cross the little footbridge and climb briefly past a life-size statue of the Virgin. The well-worn foot track leads across a sparsely vegetated plain toward the exploded cone of Volcán Copahue. Continue straight, ignoring a well-worn left-hand turn-off.

Use cairns to keep track of the path as it dips down to lush, green lawns by the northern shore of the **Lagunas Las Mellizas**' western 'twin'. From here, it's worth making a 200m detour northwest to the **Paso de Copahue** (2013m), where an orange marker (*hito*) indicates the Argentina–Chile border. The pass looks down into the headwaters of the Río Queuco, a tributary of the Río Biobío.

Follow a path along the lake's north side past black-sand beaches and gushing springs on its opposite shore to reach the start of a steam pipeline, one to 1¼ hours from the village. The roaring of steam from the subterranean Copahue Geothermal Field (see p43) entering the vapoducto (pipeline) and irregular explosive blasts of discharging steam can be heard along much of the trek.

Cross the lake outlet to reach a yellow metal cross, then follow the trail up over a ridge to eventually meet a 4WD track. Turn right and follow this rough road up around left. The 4WD track continues westward up through a barren volcanic moonscape to end under a tiny glacier on the east flank of Volcán Copahue, one hour from the pipeline. (Guided treks usually begin from here.)

Ascend southwest over bouldery ridges, crossing several small mineral and meltwater streams. To the northwest, in Chile, there are views of the ice-smothered Sierra Velluda and the near-perfect snowy cone of

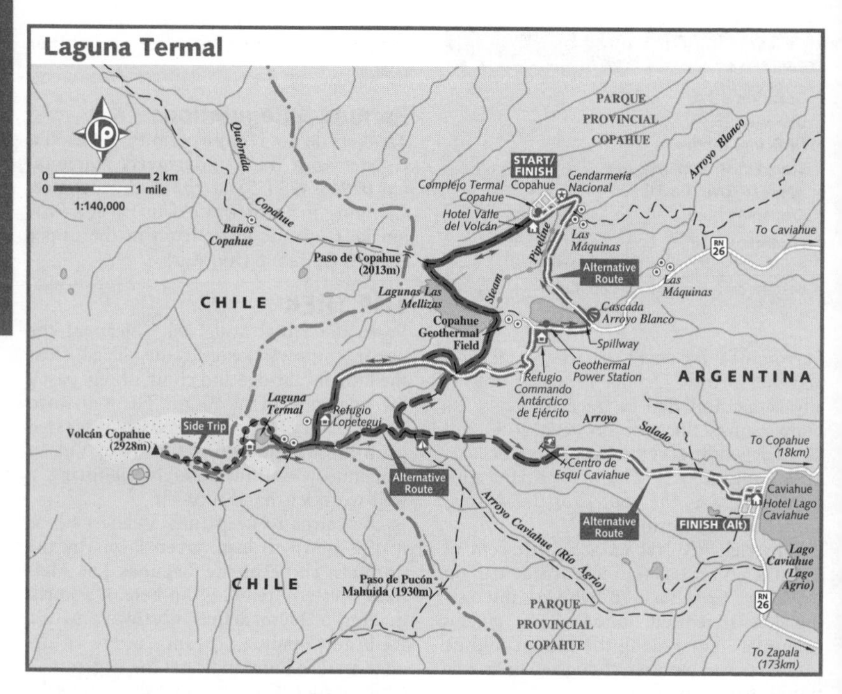

Volcán Antuco. From the third streamlet (with yellowy, sulfur-encrusted sides), cut along the slope below a hot spring then climb to the top of a prominent grey-pumice spur that lies on the international border. Ascend the spur until it becomes impossibly steep, then traverse up to your right over loose slopes into a gap to reach **Laguna Termal**, 1¼ to 1½ hours from the end of the 4WD track (3½ to 4¼ hours from Copahue).

Filling Volcán Copahue's eastern crater, this steaming hot lake feeds itself by melting the snout of a glacier that forms a massive rim of ice above its back wall. Sulfurous fumes often force trekkers to retreat from the lake, but these high slopes also give great vistas across the vast basin (where both villages are visible) between the horseshoe-shaped Lago Caviahue (Lago Agrio) and the elongated Lago Trolope to the northeast. From here, more experienced trekkers can continue up to the summit of Volcán Copahue (see Side Trip).

Either return from Laguna Termal via your ascent route (in three to four hours), opt for the Alternative Route back to Copahue via Arroyo Caviahue (Río Agrio) and Ruta 26, or take the Alternative Finish to Caviahue.

SIDE TRIP: VOLCÁN COPAHUE SUMMIT

2¾–3½ hours return, 8km, 200m ascent/descent

This is the normal route to the top of Volcán Copahue – other more difficult ascent possibilities exist from the volcano's south side. The route is demanding and may not be passable without an ice axe (and perhaps crampons) until mid-January.

From Laguna Termal, ascend steeply northwest along the right side of the rim, turning left to reach the edge of the glacier. The route cuts southwest across the (crevasse-free) ice, then heads over left to a gap in the main ridge. At this point, it's worth detouring a short way back north past a dilapidated, A-frame **refugio** (GPS 37° 51.515 S, 71° 09.822 W) to a spectacular lookout high above Laguna Termal. Skirt on around to the left just above the snowy basin (the remains of the ancient, exploded crater), then make a short climb to the small summit of **Volcán Copahue** (2928m), which is marked by a wooden cross with a tiny shrine and an orange border-marker.

From here you get a superb panorama of dozens of distant and closer volcanoes, including Volcán Callaqui directly to the southwest. A round, blue crater lake (usually snow-filled early in the season) sits right below you, above wild Chilean valleys forested with araucarias that contrast sharply with the dry terrain on the Argentine side.

Return via the ascent route.

ALTERNATIVE ROUTE: VIA ARROYO CAVIAHUE & RUTA 26

3–4 hours, 13.5km, 700m descent

From Laguna Termal, drop back via the spur (400m past where you joined it), following along the ridge to reach **Refugio Lopetegui** (GPS 37° 51.508 S, 71° 08.785 W). This tiny, almost completely ruined A-frame hut stands half-buried in the pumice at around 2475m on a little shelf. The dimpled form of Volcán Llaima is recognisable to the southwest, in Chile.

Head down and northeast through a bare basin before cutting to the right over a minor saddle. The trail (marked with cairned stakes) descends on to the right, then turns left at a track junction (see Alternative Finish) to ford the small Arroyo Caviahue (Río Agrio), 50 minutes to 1¼ hours from the lake.

Continue eastward over fine, eroding glacial-volcanic moraines on a shelf above the stream. The route turns northeast again as it skirts a minor depression to cross a waterlogged *mallín* (wet meadow) and intersect with a 4WD track, 25 to 30 minutes from the Arroyo Caviahue (Río Agrio).

Follow this dirt road northeast past the small A-frame **Refugio Commando Antárctico de Ejército** (GPS 37° 50.402 S, 71° 06.326 W) to the east lake of the **Lagunas Las Mellizas**. Continue along its southern shore past the noisy geothermal power station to reach Ruta 26, 50 minutes to one hour from the *mallín*. Turn left and proceed across the outlet spillway bridge above the Cascada Arroyo Blanco and on uphill past the thermal area of Las Maquinitas to arrive back in Copahue after a final 50 minutes to 1¼ hours.

ALTERNATIVE FINISH: CAVIAHUE

3–4 hours, 12km, 1130m descent

From Laguna Termal descend via **Refugio Lopetegui** to the turn-off (GPS 37° 51.147 S, 71° 08.049 W) as described in the Alternative Route. Turn right and head down to spring-fed meadows dotted with *llaretas* (green, lawnlike mounds) along the Arroyo Caviahue (Río Agrio). Follow cairns across the normally small stream (where **camping** is permitted only among the bare rubble), cutting eastward over a broad scoria plain to the left of a boulder field.

After reaching a marker pole by a square rock block, the route drops to the left across a reddish mineral spring. Continue eastward through waterlogged meadows and over a bare ridge, then sidle around southeast above the upper basin of the Arroyo Salado to reach the **Centro de Esquí Caviahue**. From this small ski slope, a road leads 5km down valley through beautiful araucaria forest to Caviahue.

COPAHUE GEOTHERMAL FIELD

Between the Lagunas Las Mellizas, the Copahue Geothermal Field (over 1 sq km in area) acts as a subterranean reservoir of highly pressurized steam. Melting snow replenishes the field each spring as it seeps down through the porous earth to a depth of almost 1300m. As it comes into contact with hot rock (reaching temperatures of up to 200°C), the snowmelt vaporizes, creating an ultra-powerful 'pressure-cooker effect'. The resulting steam is then forced up to the surface.

Nature's big show isn't wasted. A 670kW geothermal power station transmits this energy as far as Loncopué, more than 50km away. In a unique project completed in 1999, steam roars and hisses its way to Copahue along a 3km pipeline known as a *vapoducto*. The village uses a network of coiled pipes laid under each street to heat the pavement and keep it snow-free during winter.

PARQUE NACIONAL LAGUNA DEL LAJA

The great snow cone of puffing Volcán Antuco (2979m) is the centerpiece of Parque Nacional Laguna del Laja. East of the Chilean city of Los Ángeles, the park sits just north of the Río Biobío, almost abutting the border with Argentina. In little more than 100 sq km, the park packs in varied and surprisingly compact Andean wilderness. Highlights include Volcán Antuco, the classic multi-armed highland lake of Laguna de la Laja, and, just outside the park boundary, the biologically rich *bofedal* (high marsh) of Los Barros and the great glaciated Sierra Velluda range.

Volcán Antuco is made up of the Mapuche words *antu*, meaning 'sun', and *co*, meaning 'water'. Antuco is one of the region's many dormant volcanoes, though its caldera still steams and puffs out sulfuric gases. Immediately to the southwest is the Sierra Velluda, a spectacular range that rises to 3585m. Choked by hanging glaciers and icefalls, these nonvolcanic peaks contrast sharply with Antuco's smoother contours.

Laguna de la Laja sits at the eastern foot of Volcán Antuco. This large lake is the source of the Río Laja, the major river of Chile's Chillán region, whose famous Salto del Laja waterfall is far downstream on the Panamerican Hwy – Ruta 5 (*Carretera Panamericana*). The lake's Rorschach form was created by the volcano's 1873 eruption, when masses of lava blocked the Río Laja, impounded its waters and drowned the valleys upstream. Unfortunately, hydroelectric development has disturbed the lake's natural shoreline (which is around 1400m above sea level), but its setting among lofty peaks still makes a dramatic scene.

LAGUNA DEL/DE LA LAJA

It's easy enough to confuse Spanish pronouns, so what's up with the name Parque Nacional Laguna del Laja? While the lake itself is called Laguna de la Laja, the name actually refers to (el) Río Laja. And, though the name *laja* implies 'smooth rock', you won't see too much smooth rock in Parque Nacional Laguna del Laja! It actually describes a section of the Río Laja far downstream.

ENVIRONMENT

Because of its climate, altitude and recent volcanic activity, the park has relatively sparse vegetation, but one notable feature is the Cordilleran cypress (*ciprés de la cordillera*). This small coniferous tree thrives in the dry alpine conditions, like the mountainsides on the approach road to the park. Small evergreen *coigüe* (Southern beech) forests and deciduous *ñirre* scrub are present at higher altitudes.

Hardy wildflowers grow sporadically in the loose volcanic earth in spring and early summer. Look for alpine violets, whose delicate blooms often produce a 'desert-garden' effect. There are also specialized succulents, including the *maihuén*, a rather atypical member of the cactus family. The *maihuén* grows in large spiny mounds that look a bit like closely mown lawns (though you wouldn't want to sit on them), from which clustered, bright-yellow flowers emerge in early summer. The pink-petalled *mutisia volcánica*, the white, vaguely carnation-like *estrella de la cordillera* and several bulbous rhodophilias are rarer .

Visitors can observe the slow regeneration patterns that follow Volcán Antuco's last catastrophic eruption in 1869. Look for islands of original vegetation left untouched within the desolate fields of lava.

Condors and other birds are the most visible native fauna. It's harder to spot the pumas, foxes, vizcachas (rodents from the chinchilla family), lizards and frogs that exist in and around the park.

CLIMATE

Parque Nacional Laguna del Laja, the most northerly area covered in this book, has a climate akin to mountain areas further north. The seasons show a marked annual contrast, with hot, dry summers averaging 13.6°C in January and cold winters. Most of the year's precipitation falls in winter as snow. The average midwinter snow depth at the park information center (approximately 1200m above sea level) is 2m, but this increases with elevation. Skiing is possible at a small ski village at around 1400m on the northwestern slopes of Volcán Antuco.

Spring's warmer weather quickly melts away the snow cover and by late January the largest patches of snow remain only above 2000m. Volcán Antuco and the Sierra Velluda cause a rain shadow on the eastern edge of the volcano, producing drier conditions in that sector of the park.

AROUND VOLCÁN ANTUCO

Duration 3 days
Distance 40.5km
Difficulty moderate
Start/Finish Guardería Chacay
Nearest Town Los Ángeles
Transport bus, walk

Summary Crunch over lava that looks as though it solidified yesterday, see hanging glaciers and cool off in a highland lake on this circuit through the wildest parts of Parque Nacional Laguna del Laja.

This circumnavigation of Volcán Antuco is the park's only trek, crossing bare lava flows and loose volcanic earth for virtually its entire length. It involves a climb from Guardería Chacay (1115m) to a 2054m pass, and the route is largely unmarked, though fairly straightforward. In the central section there is no real track and deep snow may lie well into January. The long final section is along an easily navigable dirt road. Fine summer weather can make the going insufferably hot at lower altitudes.

The trek can be done in two very long days, but parties should plan to take three days. An ascent of Volcán Antuco on either the northern or southeastern side (see More Treks p69) would take an additional day. An easy but spectacular one-hour return trek can also be made from opposite Conaf to the nearby waterfalls of Salto Las Chilcas and Salto El Torbellino on the Río Laja, where in parts the subterranean flow of water from Laguna de la Laja and Volcán Antuco gushes from the porous ground.

The circuit can be walked in either direction, but the recommended way to go is counterclockwise.

For information on accommodations near Guardería Chacay, see Parque Nacional Laguna del Laja & Around (p73).

PLANNING

When to Trek

The best months to trek in Parque Nacional Laguna del Laja are December (when the wildflowers are best) and April (when there is little snow and conditions are not so hot). Before mid-November much of the park, is still snowbound. From mid-December until late January, *tábanos* (horseflies) can be bothersome at lower elevations. On the other hand, trekkers will find the going hot and dusty in January and February. Cooler yet snow-free conditions can generally be expected from late March until early May.

What to Bring

As there are no huts along the route, this trek can only be done safely with a tent. Wide tent pegs such as snow pegs would be useful in the loose volcanic soil, though fallen *quila* (bamboo) canes make a satisfactory substitute.

Maps

The entire park is covered by one Chilean IGM 1:50,000 map, *Laguna de la Laja* (Section G, No 21). Although this map indicates topographical detail very well, some higher areas are left uncontoured and the trekking routes themselves are not shown.

Information Sources

The Corporación Nacional Forestal (Conaf) Centro de Información Ambiental (park information center), 700m uphill from the Guardería Chacay, was not functioning when we researched this edition. However, the *guardaparque* (ranger) at the administration center adjacent to Guardería Chacay is enthusiastic and knowledgeable.

Permits & Regulations

An entry fee of CH$1000 per person is payable at the park entrance gate (Portería El Álamo). No permit is required for this trek, but the standard rules apply regarding signing in and out. Visitors can sign in at the Guardería Chacay or (better) at the adjacent administration center, and must sign out on completing the trek.

The park has few restrictions on camping, but trekkers must give special consideration to sanitation, and carry out all rubbish.

Park authorities may insist that trekkers ascending Volcán Antuco (see More Treks,

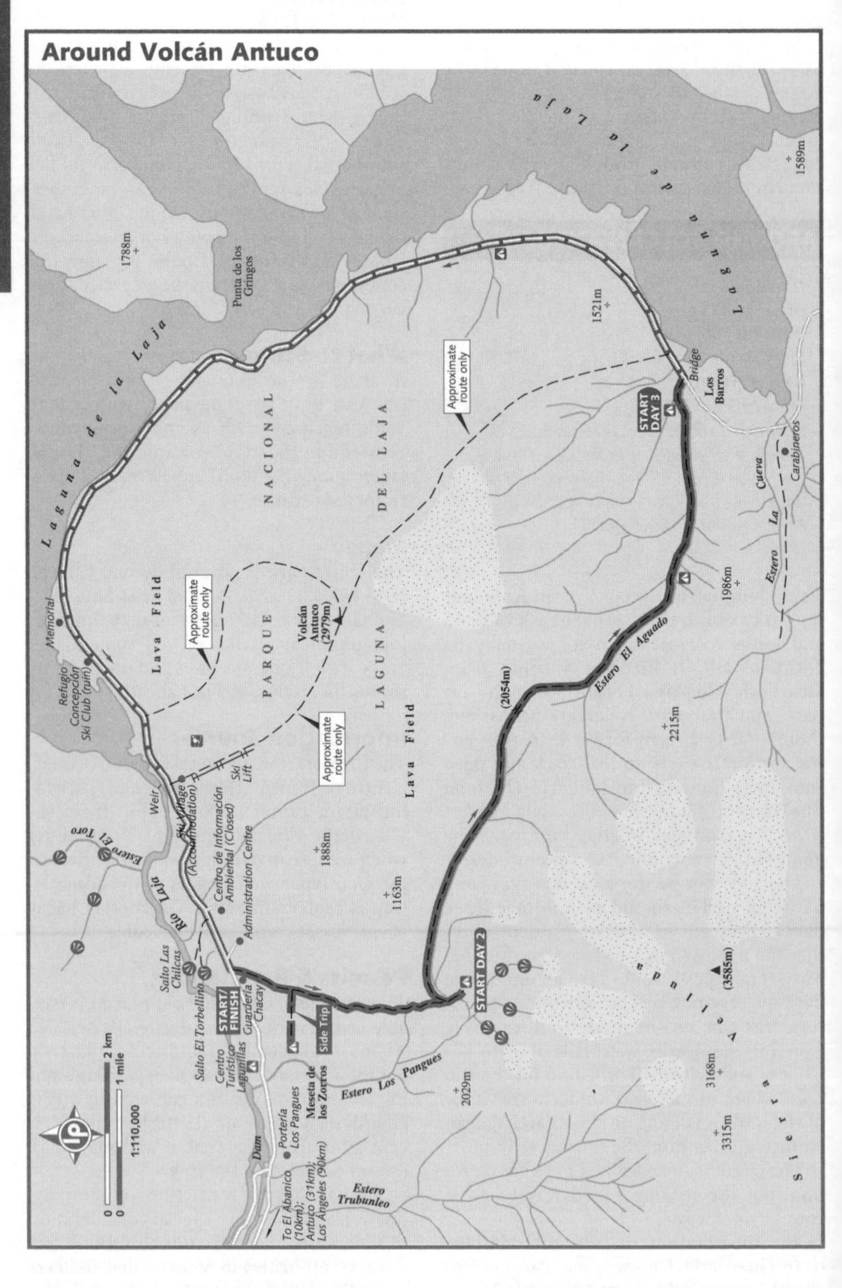
Around Volcán Antuco
Laguna de la Laja
Punta de los Gringos
1788m
1521m
1589m
Bridge
Los Barros
START DAY 3
Approximate route only
NACIONAL
DEL LAJA
PARQUE
LAGUNA
Volcán Antuco (2979m)
Lava Field
Memorial
Refugio Concepción Ski Club (ruin)
Carabineros
Cueva
Estero La
1986m
Estero El Aguado
(2054m)
2215m
Weir
Ski Village (Accommodation)
Centro de Información Ambiental (Closed)
Administration Centre
Ski Lift
1888m
1163m
Estero El Toro
Río Laja
Salto Las Chilcas
Salto El Torbellino
START/ FINISH
Guardería Chacay
Centro Turístico Lagunillas
Side Trip
START DAY 2
(3585m)
Sierra Velluda
3168m
3315m
Estero Los Pangues
2029m
Meseta de los Zorros
Portería Los Pangues
Dam
To El Abanico (10km); Antuco (31km); Los Ángeles (90km)
Estero Trubunleo
0 2 km
0 1 mile
1:110,000

p69) be accompanied by a local guide, but this is not really enforced.

GETTING TO/FROM THE TREK

Parque Nacional Laguna del Laja is 90km by road east of Los Ángeles. There is no public transport the whole way to the park, but there are regular buses from Los Ángeles' central bus station, Terminal Santa Rita, via Antuco to El Abanico, a village near the turn-off to the park (CH$1600, 1½ to two hours, up to six daily). These stop at the turn-off. Buses run between 7am and 7pm. On Sunday the buses leave from La Vega, about one block away from Terminal Santa Rita.

From the El Abanico turn-off, the road leads 11km up beside the Río Laja to the Guardería Chacay, a minor ranger station adjacent to the park administration center at Chacay. This stretch can be walked in three or four hours, but there is enough friendly traffic during the busy tourist season to make successful hitchhiking reasonably certain. The trek described here begins at the guardería.

THE TREK

Day 1: Guardería Chacay to Estero Los Pangues Camp

1¾–2½ hours, 4.5km

Follow the path (signposted 'Sendero Meseta Los Zorros y Sierra Velluda') just above Guardería Chacay due south up the slope past clusters of Cordilleran cypresses. Head up a steep, eroding, reddish ridge to reach a signposted junction at the edge of a tiny plateau overlooking the Río Laja after 30 to 45 minutes. From here an easy side trip goes to Meseta de los Zorros (see Side Trip).

To continue, take the left branch (marked 'Sierra Velluda') up over the low, sparsely vegetated ridges until you come to a lava flow. The path first skirts left along the edge of the lava, then follows a scrubby lead amid the mass of solidified slag before heading across broken rock, marked by cairns and *quila* wands, directly toward a prominent hanging glacier high up on the Sierra Velluda. Eventually the rock ends, and the trail continues across volcanic sand to reach the small but fast-flowing Estero Los Pangues after one to 1½ hours. Here you meet another foot track coming up the north bank of the stream.

Go briefly downstream until you find a place to cross the Estero Los Pangues, then head toward tall *lenga* trees at the foot of a ridge coming down from the Sierra Velluda to **camp** after a further 15 minutes or so. The ground is loose and sometimes dusty, but water is close by and the views directly up to the Sierra Velluda, which towers above a wide grassy bend in the stream, are spectacular.

SIDE TRIP: MESETA DE LOS ZORROS

40 minutes–1 hour return, 2.5km

From the signpost at the edge of the plateau, take the right branch (marked 'Meseta Los Zorros') and follow the track down through light forest to the lovely grassy meadow of Meseta de los Zorros (shown on IGM maps as Los Pangues), set among moss-draped Cordilleran cypress and *coigüe* trees. There are good views across the valley toward the adjacent rocky range. Just below, the spectacular torrent of the Estero Los Pangues washes black volcanic scoria out from the mountains. **Camping** is possible on the grass, and a track continues down into the lower Estero Los Pangues valley. Retrace your steps to the signpost.

Day 2: Estero Los Pangues Camp to Los Barros

3¾–5½ hours, 13km

Backtrack to cross again to the north side of the Estero Los Pangues, then head upstream, tending southeast, across the scoria toward the obvious low point between the Sierra Velluda to your right and the majestic cone of Volcán Antuco. Marked only by occasional cairns, the track stays within earshot of the Estero Los Pangues, for the most part avoiding the vast expanse of broken volcanic rock. After you pass a steep ridge descending from the Sierra Velluda, the tiny upper valley widens to reveal more glaciers up to the right.

Make your way across a broad, rusty-red alluvial wash to the head of the now tiny stream. From here on, winter avalanches have mostly erased any markings leading up to the pass, but the best option is probably to ascend a loose-rock ridge that goes up steeply between two eroded gullies. Where this peters out, sidle rightward to arrive at the **pass** (2054m), two to three hours from camp.

The pass affords stunning views ahead down the valley to the southern arm of Laguna de la Laja and the ranges along the Chile–Argentina frontier. Hidden behind a bluff from the pass itself is the impressive glacier-clad eastern face of the Sierra Velluda's 3585m main summit.

The pass is likely to be snowed over and corniced well into January, so it may be necessary to traverse leftward along the ridgetop for 500m or so before dropping down into the small basin below the pass. Snowdrifts here in early summer provide good glissading. Later in the season a faint trail sidles to the left before directly descending the steep, loose-earth slopes to the banks of the milky **Estero El Aguado** after one to 1¼ hours.

If coming in the other direction, look out for a large cairn opposite a chasm with a waterfall before you reach the head of the valley. This points directly to the pass. In the upper Valle El Aguado, occasional grassy patches among *ñirre* thickets on the true right (south) bank of the stream (which is easily waded) make nice alternative **campsites**.

Proceed downstream through the sparsely vegetated Valle El Aguado. Away from the moister ground near the stream, the growth consists only of low shrubs and small vegetated mounds.

The dusty path follows the northern bank, crossing several clear streams that emanate from the snow on Volcán Antuco's southern slopes. As you approach a lone araucaria, stay close to the stream to avoid a boggy area over to the left, then continue a short way to reach a small wooden bridge at **Los Barros** after 45 minutes to 1¼ hours. Here, the flat shoreline of Laguna de la Laja is periodically inundated when the lake rises. Just upstream of the bridge, by a ford in the broad, shallow Estero El Aguado, is a good **campsite**. Goats and cattle graze hereabouts, so you may wish to treat the water, which is best taken from a clear tributary stream that crosses the dirt road between the ford and the bridge.

Strong trekkers may want to push on a few extra kilometers and thus trim off a bit from the trek's long third day. A stream flowing off the volcano passes the road just after the 20km marker. Good **campsites** with an excellent lake view can be found approximately 200 meters upstream.

ANTUCO TRAGEDY

In 2005 one of the biggest tragedies of Chilean military history occurred on the slopes of Volcán Antuco. In total, 40 Chilean soldiers died. The victims, mostly teenagers, were performing training exercises on the mountain when they were caught off guard by a fierce late fall snowstorm with whiteout conditions.

Day 3: Los Barros to Guardería Chacay

4¾–7 hours, 23km

There are no permanently running streams along this hot and sandy section, so it's advisable to carry water from camp. (The lake itself is not always easily accessible, though its water is generally safe to drink.) There is modest traffic along the rough, narrow road – mostly sport fishers or the odd truck from the summer-only *estancia* (farm or ranch) at the southern end of the lake – so it may be possible to hitch a ride.

Head off northward around the western side of Laguna de la Laja, through a volcanic desert caused by the eroding sand and the rain shadow of Volcán Antuco and the Sierra Velluda. In the heat of the late afternoon occasional meltwater streams may flow down from the volcano's upper slopes. Across the turquoise waters of Laguna de la Laja impressive bare eroding crags drop straight down to the shore, while mountains further to the north and south are heavily forested. The road dips and rises constantly, passing the curiously named narrow of **Punta de los Gringos** after two to three hours. There is reasonably good **camping** and opportunities for a cooling swim around the shore, although the ground is quite muddy in places.

From here the trek takes on a more sombre note as the road is marked periodically by memorials to 2005's Antuco Tragedy. Make your way round northwest into an enormous lava flow (responsible for damming the Río Laja to create the lake) and on past the derelict Refugio Concepción Ski Club. The road continues through this raw landscape, soon bringing the peaks of the Sierra Velluda back into view, and passes a weir built over the lake outlet just before reaching the Volcán Antuco **ski village**, 1¾ to 2½ hours on. This small winter sports center consists of 20 chalets scattered around the base of a ski lift. Summer accommodation options are detailed on p74.

Follow the road as it winds steadily down into the upper Valle Laja. Just after crossing a small brook the road passes a signposted turn-off, which leads a few minutes left through *coigües* to the Centro de Información Ambiental – closed when we researched this edition. The main trail arrives back at the Guardería Chacay after a final one to 1½ hours.

RESERVA NACIONAL MALALCAUELLO-NALCAS

The jewel of Northern Araucanía, Reserva Nacional Malalcahuello-Nalcas is a combined reserve of 313 sq km, 120km northeast of Temuco. Though off the main park circuit, it offers one of the most dramatic landscapes in all of Sur Chico, a charcoal desertscape of ash and sand. It consists of two, jointly managed reserves that border on the summit of Volcán Lonquimay (2726m).

The area has seen abuse. Although a large forest reserve was originally established around the volcano in 1931, much of this land was later given to colonists, whose land clearing sparked uncontrolled forest fires (see p37) until the mid-1940s, ravaging a quarter of Malalcahuello-Nalcas. In the 1950s the area was extensively logged, partly for sleepers used in the construction of the now disused rail line to Lonquimay. In the early 1960s exotic conifers were planted.

In spite of the fact that almost half this forest was once burnt or logged, today the reserve is a surprisingly wild – but easily accessible – wilderness with some outstanding shorter and multiday treks and plenty of challenging terrain to explore.

ENVIRONMENT

The superb araucaria tree most typifies the local vegetation, and at higher elevations it is the dominant tree species. Also well represented among the forest trees are a number of Nothofagus species, including the common *coigüe, coigüe de Magallanes, lenga* and *raulí*. Unfortunately, exotic Douglas firs (introduced from North America) are gradually supplanting native forest in some areas on the reserve's periphery.

Growing in the sandy volcanic soil among the araucarias you'll find the *quellén*, a native wild strawberry whose yellow-white flowers mature into edible berries by March. The striking, deep-red flowers of the *notro* (Chilean firewheel) bush grow on sunny sites. Common mountain wildflowers found in the reserve include the añañuca, which has several pink flowers in an elongated goblet form growing from a single succulent stem; the *violeta del monte*, a yellow subalpine violet species; and *capachitos*, attractive yellow, white or pink flowers of the genus *Calceolaria*. Tough native tussock grasses endure in less exposed places above the tree line.

The local fauna includes the elusive puma and its much smaller feline cousin, the *huiña*, as well as the pudu (native South American deer) and the tree-dwelling mouse oopossum (*monito del monte*). At times trekkers may sight falcons or even Andean condors circling the ridgetops, and native ducks like the red shoveller (*pato cuchara*) and the Chiloé wigeon (*pato real*) around the lakes and rivers. The black Magellanic woodpecker (*carpintero negro*) inhabits the forests.

CLIMATE

Annual precipitation levels in Malalcahuello-Nalcas average almost 3000mm, mostly falling in winter as snow. Normal midwinter (July–August) snow cover is around 2m near the base of Volcán Lonquimay, but down the valley of the Río Cautín snow does not normally remain for much longer than a week. The warmer weather of spring (October–November) quickly melts away the snow cover, however, and by late January few areas below around 2300m have any snow. Summer weather is typically pleasantly hot, though long periods of dry weather are fairly uncommon.

LONQUIMAY CIRCUIT

Duration 6 days
Distance 95.5km
Difficulty moderate–demanding
Start/Finish Malalcahuello
Nearest Town Curacautín
Transport bus
Summary A varied round-the-mountain trek through a fascinating volcanic landscape formed by very recent eruptions.

Largely following long-disused logging roads dating from the 1950s, this trek crosses several minor saddles and two passes to make a circumnavigation of Volcán Lonquimay. The route leads through beautiful araucaria and *lenga* forests, skirts a vast scoria field and passes small lakes dammed by a lava flow before climbing past a crater that formed in the volcano's 1989 eruption.

The route is marked by steel stakes in various colors, which distinguish each trail section. It is probably best done in a clockwise direction. Combined with Day 1 only, the Alternative Route (p55) forms a much shorter (19.5km) circuit suitable as a day trek.

Another option is to start – or better end – the trek on Day 4 at the Hostal Lonquimay Extremo (p54), from where it may be possible to get a ride back down to Malalcahuello (13km).

PLANNING

When to Trek

The trek is best undertaken between mid-December and late April. Early in the season the route may be severely snowed over and tricky to cross without an ice axe and crampons. The trails are virtually snow-free by mid-January.

What to Bring

You will need to bring a tent for this trek as accommodation is only available on Day 4. Campfires are prohibited, so pack a camping stove.

Maps

Two Chilean IGM 1:50,000 maps, *Malalcahuello* (Section G, No 64) and *Lonquimay* (Section G, No 65) cover the trek but do not indicate any of the tracks. Conaf has produced a 1:80,000 color-contoured map available free from the Malalcahuello office. It shows official tracks accurately and is good enough for basic navigation. (Note that it gives only UTM – Universal Transversal de Mercator – coordinates, so you may have to reset your GPS receiver.)

Permits & Regulations

Permits are not required to trek in the reserve, though there is an admission fee (CH$3000) and all parties should inform staff at the **Conaf office** (☎ 045-5452224), 200m east of the Malalcahuello village entrance, of their intended route. Camping is permitted at existing sites but, due to high fire danger, campfires are prohibited.

THE TREK

Day 1: Malalcahuello to Upper Rio Coloradito

4–5½ hours, 11km, 950m ascent

Carry some water, as the central part of this section (although well shaded) has no running water.

Walk to the Conaf administration center, 200m east of the village entrance. After signing in, pick up a clearly marked path that begins from the upper left side of the Conaf office and pass through three turnstiles. Following signs marked Sendero Piedra Santa, turn right and head up into roble forest that goes over into stands of *raulí* and fragrant *tepa* as you climb steadily higher beside a rushing little stream. The trail, marked by blue-tipped stakes, leads on round to the northwest through exotic Douglas firs and moss-covered araucaria. It ascends past two lookout points, eventually reaching an open hillside, 2½ to three hours from the Conaf office. A large sign and map indicate the end of the Piedra Santa trail and the beginning of the Laguna Blanca section.

Pick up yellow paint markings and stakes guiding you diagonally across the eroding slope, then cut up right to gain the ridgetop fringed by *lenga* forest after 15 to 20 minutes. There are clear views southward to the snowcapped Sierra Nevada and Volcán Llaima as well as ahead to Volcán Lonquimay. The track rises and dips northward along the 1700m contour line between sparse grassy tundra and the uppermost *lengas* and araucarias, before dropping away

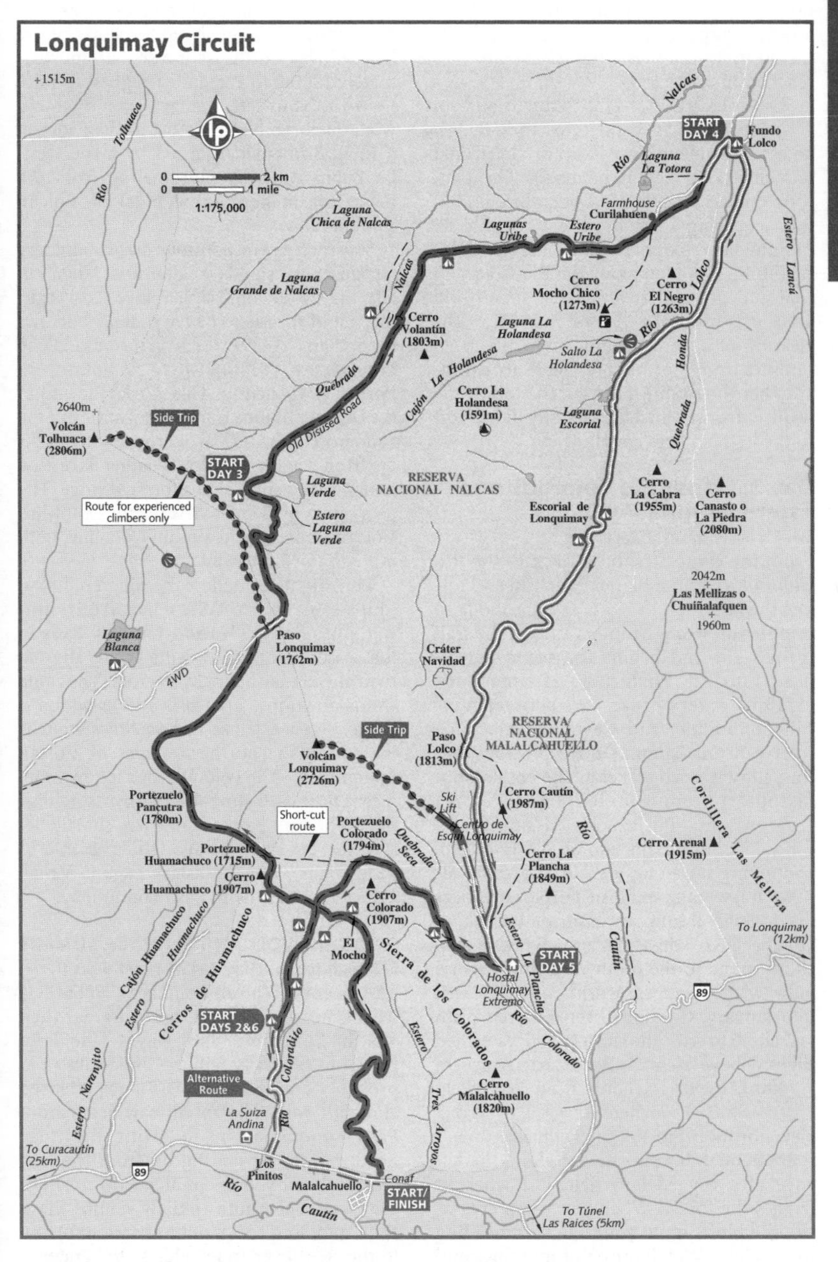
Lonquimay Circuit
1:175,000
2 km
1 mile
START DAY 4
Fundo Lolco
Laguna La Totora
Farmhouse Curilahuen
Lagunas Uribe
Estero Uribe
Laguna Chica de Nalcas
Laguna Grande de Nalcas
Cerro Volantín (1803m)
Cerro Mocho Chico (1273m)
Cerro El Negro (1263m)
Laguna La Holandesa
Salto La Holandesa
Cajón La Holandesa
Cerro La Holandesa (1591m)
Laguna Escorial
Old Disused Road
Volcán Tolhuaca (2806m)
2640m
Side Trip
START DAY 3
Route for experienced climbers only
Laguna Verde
Estero Laguna Verde
RESERVA NACIONAL NALCAS
Cerro La Cabra (1955m)
Cerro Canasto o La Piedra (2080m)
Escorial de Lonquimay
2042m
Las Mellizas o Chuiñalafquen
1960m
Laguna Blanca
4WD
Paso Lonquimay (1762m)
Cráter Navidad
RESERVA NACIONAL MALALCAHUELLO
Paso Lolco (1813m)
Volcán Lonquimay (2726m)
Ski Lift
Centro de Esquí Lonquimay
Cerro Cautín (1987m)
Portezuelo Pancutra (1780m)
Short-cut route
Portezuelo Colorado (1794m)
Quebrada Seca
Cerro La Plancha (1849m)
Cerro Arenal (1915m)
Cordillera Las Melliza
Portezuelo Huamachuco (1715m)
Cerro Huamachuco (1907m)
Cerro Colorado (1907m)
El Mocho
Sierra de los Colorados
To Lonquimay (12km)
Hostal Lonquimay Extremo
START DAY 5
Estero La Plancha
Río Colorado
Cerros de Huamachuco
Cajón Huamachuco
Estero Huamachuco
START DAYS 2&6
Coloradito
Estero Tres Arroyos
Cerro Malalcahuello (1820m)
Alternative Route
La Suiza Andina
Estero Naranjito
To Curacautín (25km)
Los Pinitos
Malalcahuello
Conaf
START/ FINISH
Río Cautín
To Túnel Las Raices (5km)
89
+1515m
Río Tolhuaca
Río Nalcas
Quebrada Nalcas
Río Lolco
Estero Lancú
Quebrada Honda
Río Cautín

left into a broad bamboo gully. Continue on down into the forest past **campsites** around a tiny, soggy meadow grazed by timid cattle, 30 to 45 minutes from where you first reached the ridgetop.

Rise over a minor embankment and on across spring-fed streamlets to a fork. Follow an obvious yellow blaze to bear right (Conaf has closed the left-hand trail). The path soon crosses two small wooden bridges before emerging from the trees, roughly 25 minutes later, to juncture with the Río Colorado trail. Head left along the Río Colorado trail and descend steadily past superb old araucarias to meet a disused road below the clearing of an old logging camp, 15 to 20 minutes from the juncture. There are **campsites** here on sloping lawns or (better) by the nearby stream, which lies slightly hidden off to the left. No fires are allowed.

Day 2: Upper Rio Coloradito to Estero Laguna Verde

5½–6¾ hours, 17km, 750m ascent

From the campsites, head back to the Río Colorado/Laguna Blanca junction and follow the latter left to reach a gorge about 20 minutes on from the intersection. The trail turns right and begins to ascend as you head into the **Portezuelo Huamachuco** (1715m), a very broad pass between Volcán Lonquimay and Cerro Huamachuco (cerro means 'summit'). Keep a look out for yellow-tipped stakes as the path all but disappears heading up to the pass.

From the Portezuelo Huamachuco, drop down and right into an old lava field, continuing on along a shelf covered in alpine grasses and pinkish-purple añañucas overlooking the upper basin of the Estero Huamachuco. Dip across a small ravine then climb round to the north via a broad scoria gully where large snowdrifts often lie well into January. Continue over a barren plain and climb to cross the lava-choked watershed slightly above (right of) **Portezuelo Pancutra** (1780m), 1¼ to 1½ hours from Portezuelo Huamachuco. From here you get a first direct view northward to Volcán Tolhuaca.

Descend 1.2km northwest along the left edge of a rugged lava field just where it fringes the forest. When you reach cream-colored bluffs up to your left, start heading to the right. Watch for paint markings and sporadic orange-tipped marker stakes that guide you through narrow sections of sandy scoria between the broken black rocks. The route moves diagonally up the slope before beginning a northeast traverse at approximately 1800m to avoid the roughest terrain. Down to your left, the lava extends into a wild, enclosed basin almost to the shore of a small, unnamed lake fed by a spectacular 300m waterfall plummeting from the névés (permanent snowfields) of Volcán Tolhuaca.

Stay high as you continue across bouldery terrain above stands of araucarias, then cut left slightly downhill over sparse scoria tundra full of *tucotuco* (native rodent) burrows to meet an old 4WD track on the broad **Paso Lonquimay** (1762m), two to 2½ hours from Portezuelo Pancutra. This marks the end of the **Laguna Blanca** trail and beginning of the Sendero Tolhuaca. The old road switchbacks up from Laguna Blanca, a larger lake that remains unseen behind a forested ridge. The pass opens up a great view northeast toward Volcán Callaqui and Volcán Copahue, both more than 40km away.

Turn right and follow the rough old road (impassable even to 4WD vehicles) on northward into Reserva Nacional Nalcas. Early in the season, large snowdrifts across the old road ahead may be tricky to cross. The route winds down into araucaria and *lenga* forest above a vast expanse of lava flows stretching across the northern slopes of Volcán Lonquimay. (The younger rock left by more recent flows is distinguishable by its reddish tint.) The trail passes **campsites** shortly before the old road bridge (still passable to pedestrians) over the Estero Laguna Verde, 1¼ to 1½ hours from Paso Lonquimay.

SIDE TRIP: VOLCÁN TOLHUACA SUMMIT

6–8 hours return, 15km, 1045m ascent/descent

The ascent of Volcán Tolhuaca (2806m) via its southeast side is not much harder than Volcán Lonquimay (see Day 4 Side Trip, p54), but generally requires an ice axe (and probably crampons). It is for experienced climbers only. The ascent can begin from Paso Lonquimay by following the ridge northwest or by cutting up from the first hairpin bend you encounter 3km north of the pass. The route initially climbs via a spur, avoiding rocky outcrops as it cuts up to the right over snowfields to the crater.

Descend by the same route.

Day 3: Estero Laguna Verde to Río Lolco–Estero Lancú Confluence

4¾–6¼ hours, 21km, 300m ascent

Contour high above Laguna Verde, a tarn at the edge of the lava – glimpsed through the trees but difficult to reach. Then rise gently over the scenic Portezuelo Nalcas watershed (1660m) after 25 to 30 minutes. The often heavily eroded old road makes a long downward traverse northeast toward distant snowy ranges on fire-cleared slopes high above the roaring Quebrada Nalcas. When you reach the first hairpin bend (marked by a large cairn and stake No 29) after 50 minutes to 1¼ hours, continue straight ahead, leaving the road behind. Take care, as the path is easy to miss. (The road itself winds down 15 to 20 minutes to attractive **campsites** by the Quebrada Nalcas.)

A graded but sometimes overgrown foot track now rises briefly before descending into mixed forest, gradually turning eastward as it crosses side streams and **campsites** in occasional tussock-grass clearings. Head on smoothly down beneath bluffs to your right, through *ñirre* scrub dotted with anemones, purple-flowered vetches and yellow *capachitos*, crossing a minor watershed 1¾ to 2½ hours after leaving the old road. Jump across the small Estero Uribe and climb along a minor ridge, then drop back right to reach a small bridge over the (now larger) Estero Uribe, 25 to 30 minutes on. There are pleasant **campsites** along the stream's southern bank.

Head on through meadows beside the cascading stream toward the striking, pyramid-shaped Cerro Maravilla (2178m) in the Cordillera Lancú to the east. The path drops gently into roble forest scattered with pineapple-like bromeliads. It continues over slopes that look out north across the marshy plains of the Río Nalcas then cuts down to the lush boggy pastures of **Curilahuen** (an enclave of private land in the reserve), 30 to 40 minutes from the second Estero Uribe crossing.

Continue eastward through 2m-high spiny *chacay* bushes to the right of a wire fence (marking the boundary of this enclave). The route passes a small corral and old farm shacks (from where a blue-marked trail leads off southwest for 3km to the 1273m lookout peak of **Cerro Mocho Chico**). Follow the path along the fence line northeast across a scrubby stream and past a homestead to meet a 4WD track (the access to Curilahuen) after 25 to 30 minutes.

Turn right and follow the rough road (directly past the left trail turn-off going 1.2km to Laguna la Totora) to meet the Río Lolco near its confluence with the Estero Lancú, after 15 to 20 minutes. Excellent **campsites** can be found in daisy meadows a short way upstream along the west bank of the Río Lolco, but fires are not allowed.

Day 4: Río Lolco–Estero Lancú Confluence to Hostal Lonquimay Extremo

6–8 hours, 26km, 880m ascent, 180m descent

This rather long section follows a road proper for the entire distance. It can be broken into two leisurely days by making a camp lower down on the northern approach to Paso Lolco.

Follow the road across the Río Lolco out of the reserve – an iron gate on the east side of the bridge blocks public vehicle access – to reach the Malalcahuello–Lolco road after five to 10 minutes. (If coming from the other direction, this turn-off is about 100m up valley from a blue farmhouse on the north side of the Estero Lancú.) You are now within the private property of the **Fundo Lolco**, where camping is prohibited.

Turn right and follow the often rough dirt road steadily up through roble and *coigüe* forest above the rushing river to re-enter Reserva Nacional Nalcas after one to 1½ hours. The gradient eases as you continue five to 10 minutes past a short turn-off to **campsites** on moist clover lawns near the **Salto la Holandesa**, a waterfall at the edge of a recent red lava flow.

Continue up opposite the enormous expanse of lava fringing the Río Lolco, which has been forced into a narrow course between the raw, broken-up rock and the valley's steep, forested eastern slopes. In places the lava has dammed the (now small) river to create tarns in whose clear, greenish waters submerged trees are still visible. Parts of the old road itself may be flooded early in the season (though construction of a basic road slightly higher up is planned), but sections of foot track generally allow easy passage. Head on up valley to reach **Laguna Escorial**, a larger and deeper lake, also hemmed in by the lava, 30 to 45 minutes on from the Salto la Holandesa.

Climb on into *lenga* forest past **campsites** lying by a shallow tarn down to the left. Cross a final streamlet (your last water for some time) flowing down from the bare ridges. At a sharp curve, ignore an older road that continues off right, alongside the lava, and ascend left through the last araucarias. The road winds its way up through the desolate moonscape, granting good views across the volcanic basin to Volcán Tolhuaca and up to the northeastern face of Volcán Lonquimay. It finally curves slightly downward into **Paso Lolco** (1813m), three to four hours from Laguna Escorial.

From the pass, a rough and poorly marked route (1½ hours, 4km return) leads round to the northwest up over loose blacksand slopes above a deep scoria basin to the rim of Cráter Navidad (see the boxed text Christmas Crater below), from where you can peer into the raw core of this very young crater. Another high-level route cuts up left over Cerro Cautín to rejoin the road lower down.

The road drops south over heavily eroding volcanic ash into the basin of the Río Colorado, passing the (right) turn-off to the tiny Centro de Esquí Lonquimay by a short driveway to an upscale lodge (only open during the winter), one to 1¼ hours from the pass. A good end point for the day's trek is **Hostal Lonquimay Extremo** (☎ 099-7440919; camping per person CH$3000, r per person from CH$7000), about 1km down the road toward Malalcahuello. The hostel is messy at times but can be a welcome (and warm) respite for weary trekkers. Trekkers may choose to end the trek here, either hitchhiking or negotiating with staff for a ride back down to Malalcahuello (13km).

CHRISTMAS CRATER

On 25 December 1988 Volcán Lonquimay celebrated Christmas by blasting ash and smoke 8000m into the atmosphere. Vulcanologists were less surprised by the eruption itself than by its creation of a new 'parasitic' crater on the volcano's northeast side. Promptly dubbed Cráter Navidad, the side crater continued expelling volcanic debris for over a year, building a 100m cone. This was the first time in Chile that the full birth-to-extinction cycle of a volcano had been observed. Cráter Navidad – though certainly not the volcano as a whole – is now thought to be extinct. Considering the size of the eruption, its impact on the local ecology was relatively minor.

SIDE TRIP: VOLCÁN LONQUIMAY SUMMIT

6–8 hours return, 16km, 1100m ascent/descent

This route up the southeast side of the volcano that has dominated and at times blocked your views is the highlight of the circuit. Although rated moderate–demanding, the climb is surprisingly uncomplicated, but early in the season (before January) snow higher up may make it advisable to carry an ice axe. Follow the road up to the Centro de Esquí Lonquimay and head up beside the ski lift. The route continues up the ridge northwest over a snowdrift before ascending a steeper spur that leads to the summit. The sensational panorama takes in dozens of key peaks in the Araucanía, including the now familiar Sierra Nevada, Volcán Llaima and Volcán Tolhuaca, as well as more distant landmarks like Volcán Lanín to the south.

Descend by the same route.

Day 5: Hostal Lonquimay Extremo to Upper Río Coloradito

2½–3 hours, 9.5km, 175m ascent

From the hostel, follow the road back toward the volcano and take a (left) trail turn-off by a Conaf information board and map. Head northwest onto a sparse scoria plain and cross (normally dry) stream gullies of the upper Río Colorado to reach the tree line, 30 to 40 minutes from the *refugio*. Attractive **campsites** can be found nearby among the araucarias.

As Conaf no longer manages this part of the trail, it can be very difficult to follow. The easiest way to proceed is to follow the tree line northward until reaching a deeply eroded gully. Head left into the woods to locate a half-hidden yellow-tipped marker (stake No 29). Follow an overgrown trail north up onto a hillside above the gorge. Make your way back down toward the now much shallower gorge and follow it toward the obvious pass between Volcán Lonquimay and the low, pinkish summit of Cerro Colorado to reach **Portezuelo Colorado** (1794m), roughly two hours from the hostel. This pass gives views east to the bare ridges of Cerro Cautín and southwest to Volcán Llaima. A short-cut route traverses west across the slope to Portezuelo Huamachuco.

Descend southwest through a broad dry gully toward Cerro Huamachuco. Treading carefully, as burrowing tucotucos have created ground hollows that sink under your weight, head left down around an old lava field. The route (confused in places by diverging cattle pads) cuts down across a stream gully among the grassy alpine herbage, recrossing the stream some way down. Continue right to meet the small upper Río Coloradito, which splashes over lava slabs as you follow it down to reach the trail junction (see Day 1), 40 to 50 minutes from Portezuelo Colorado. See the end of Day 1 for possible **camping** options.

Day 6: Upper Rio Coloradito to Malalacahuello

3–4½ hours, 11km, 950m descent

Retrace your steps as on Day 1 or opt for the Alternative Route described below. Both variants could be combined with Day 5 for a longer day's trekking.

ALTERNATIVE ROUTE: VIA LOS PINITOS

2¼–3¼ hours, 9.5km, 600m descent

This is a quicker and less steep variant back to Ruta 181 (R-89). Combined with Day 1 only, the Alternative Route forms a shorter circuit suitable as a day trek.

Head down into the forest from the Río Colorado/Laguna Blanca junction along the true left (east) bank of the river to meet the old road (see Day 1). Follow it directly right to ford the small stream, then drop smoothly past excellent **campsites** (but no fires allowed) around a grassy clearing among araucarias on your left. The rough road descends through *coigüe* and *raulí* forest logged and/or burnt decades ago. It then reaches another attractive clearing just uphill from a locked gate (marking the reserve boundary), 50 minutes to 1¼ hours from the upper Río Coloradito. There is a Conaf information board and map here. This is also an attractive spot for **camping** (no fires permitted).

The road continues down past the first farmhouses (watch out for dogs!) to cross the river on a bridge, levelling out before it intersects with Ruta 181 (R-89) at **Los Pinitos**, a further 50 minutes to 1¼ hours on. There is a bus shelter here, and the recommended hostel **La Suiza Andina** (see p73 for details) is 400m to the right (west).

Turn left and walk along the highway directly past the Restaurante-Hostería Piedra Santa, through rich dairy pastures picked over by honking flocks of black-necked ibis to reach Malalcahuello after 35 to 50 minutes.

PARQUE NACIONAL HUERQUEHUE

Old growth forest and green lakes characterize the lovely Parque Nacional Huerquehue (where-kay-way). East of Lago Caburgua and 35km northeast of Pucón, this 125-sq-km park encompasses a gentle landscape of numerous lovely lakes on small plateaus (averaging 1300m) under almost 2000m peaks. The lowest point in the park is the eastern shore of Lago Tinquilco, a deep, 3km-long glacial lake with sliver-like beaches.

Visitors shouldn't miss the trekking, but also take along a rod and swimsuit, essential for this lake paradise. Lago Tinquilco reaches around 20°C in summer, and the higher lakes in the central part of Huerquehue are generally a few degrees cooler. Several developed hot springs surround the park, including the Termas de Río Blanco (visited on the Huerquehue Lakes trek, p57).

ENVIRONMENT

The park's Mapuche name means 'place of the thrushes', a reference to the austral thrush, or *zorzal*, which inhabits this densely forested area. But there is also the ubiquitous *chucao*, whose chuckling calls resound throughout the undergrowth; the large Magellanic woodpecker, or *carpintero negro;* and its smaller relative *carpintero chico*. You can occasionally spot the tiny native deer, or pudu, scurrying through the underbrush.

As in much of the Araucanía, the araucaria tree, or *pehuén*, dominates the more elevated areas, often forming pure stands. These beautiful conifers fringe the shores of the higher lakes, and their distinct umbrella-like form stands out on the ridgetops. Southern beeches *lenga* and *coigüe* are also present. Lower down, the forests are dominated by *tepa*, identifiable by its serrated, deliciously fragrant leaves, and the coniferous *mañío*. Lower elevations also favor *boldo*, whose oval-shaped, leathery leaves make a fine tea. A parasitic plant called the *quintral* lives on *boldo*, and unsuspecting observers might mistakenly assume its more flamboyant white, red-tipped blooms belong to the **plant's host** (whose flowers are actually pale yellow).

Wherever the forest is fully mature, the understorey is quite open and surprisingly sparse, featuring epiphyte species such as the *botellita* and *estrellita*. Typically seen growing on tree trunks, these two climbing

A WAR FOR LIFE

Chile's largest indigenous group, the Mapuche (che meaning 'people' and mapu meaning 'of the land'), is unique in the Americas as the first and only indigenous nation on the continent whose sovereignty and independence was legally recognized, but they have exhausted generations in fighting to keep it that way.

The Mapuche, born of modern-day La Araucanía, first successfully fought off the marauding Inka empire, only to take on a sustained 300-year attack by the Spanish empire and, to this day, the Chilean state. The Mapuche used the Río Biobío as a natural frontier against the intruders and resisted colonization until the 19th century. It was the longest and hardest-fought indigenous defense in the Americas. By its end, the nation's once vast territory of 10 million hectares was reduced to a mere half a million hectares of communal *reducciones* (settlements).

Despite signing the Treaty of Killin with the colonizing Spaniards in 1641 (the document solidified the territorial autonomy of the Mapuche and 28 others over two centuries of diplomatic relations), the Mapuche remained, and still remain, under threat of physical and cultural extinction. In the late 1800s, 100,000 Mapuche were massacred by the Chilean and Argentine military. From 1965 to 1973 land reform improved the situation for the Mapuche, but the military coup of 1973 reversed many of these gains. Between the restoration of democracy in 1989 and 2009, the Mapuche people made limited progress in their continuing fight for reparations and the return of their lands although most of the court rulings granting them land were effectively overturned by powerful business interests.

These days, due to overcrowding and population growth of the dominant Chilean society, the majority of the Mapuche now live in large urban centers. Those that have steadfastly remained in their historical ancestral territory (known as *Wallmapu*) are organized into four geographical regions or *Meli wixan-mapu*. Each *wixan-mapu* is made up of *aylla rewe* (eight districts), which, in turn, are made up of communities known as *lof*.

Various human rights organizations, as well as the Special Rapporteur of the UN, have widely reported the imposition of assimilation policies and protests in Temuco are nearly a daily affair. Even tourists, filmmakers and foreign journalists aren't immune: it's not uncommon for people to be harassed by police after being seen among Mapuche communities where there exists ongoing land-dispute conflicts, and two French filmmakers were arrested in March 2008 for talking to a Mapuche leader.

Deprived of most of their ancestral lands, the Mapuche now earn a precarious livelihood from agriculture and handicrafts. Still, they soldier on, managing to preserve their traditional language (Mapudungun, the 'language of the land'), their religion and their socio-political structure. Whether they will win the ongoing war of freedom and independence from the greater country at large remains the question.

For more on modern Mapuche culture and issues, check out the five-language Mapuche international link (www.mapuche-nation.org), created with foreign collaboration.

vines produce fine red flowers that brighten up the shady forest floor.

Quila grows in small clusters anywhere that receives even a few stray rays of direct sunlight. Around the shores of Lago Tinquilco you will also see the graceful *arrayán*, a water-loving myrtle species with smooth, almost luminescent orange bark.

CLIMATE

Huerquehue is in a climatic transition zone between the warm temperate lowlands and the cooler Andes. The Lago Tinquilco area has a moderate climate with a mean annual temperature of 11.5°C. Precipitation is concentrated between the winter months of May and September – when the upland area above 1300m receives heavy snowfalls – and annual levels reach a relatively moderate 2000mm in the ranges of central Huerquehue.

HUERQUEHUE LAKES

Duration 4 days
Distance 38.5km
Difficulty easy–moderate
Start/Finish Guardería Tinquilco
Nearest Town Pucón
Transport bus
Summary This trek explores a delightful lakeland plateau on the way to remote hot springs.

The subalpine lake basin above Lago Tinquilco can be visited fairly easily as a day trek. This multiday out-and-back route takes trekkers beyond the most visited routes. Tracks are well maintained, marked with yellow and (later) blue stakes and signposts at important junctions. Fast trekkers may opt to reach Termas de Río Blanco in a single day, then return the next day.

For details of accommodations on the lake, see p76.

PLANNING

When to Trek

The trek can normally be done from mid-November at least until the end of April. Note, however, that *tábanos* (horseflies) are out in full force from late December to early February.

Maps

The entire park area is covered by the Chilean IGM's 1:50,000 *Nevados de Caburgua* (Section G, No 96). Although topographically very accurate, this map does not show any trekking routes. Conaf has produced a simpler contoured map at a scale of 1:38,000, *Parque Nacional Huerquehue*, which is available free when you pay your entry fee. The Conaf map indicates the main paths with a fair degree of accuracy, and most trekkers will find it good enough.

Permits & Regulations

The entrance fee to Parque Nacional Huerquehue is CH$4000 for foreigners and CH$2500 for Chileans, payable at the Guardería Tinquilco, about halfway around the lake's southeastern shore.

There is a ban on camping in Parque Nacional Huerquehue, except at the Conaf campsite on Lago Tinquilco and at Camping Renahue, at the end of Day 1. All other nearby campsites are outside the park boundaries. Fires are not permitted anywhere in the park.

GETTING TO/FROM THE TREK

The trek begins and ends at Guardería Tinquilco, 35km from Pucón. **Buses Caburgua** (☎ 099-8389047; Uruguay 540; CH$1900, 40 minutes) runs three buses daily from Pucón to Guardería Tinquilco, leaving Pucón at 8.30am, 1pm and 4pm, and returning from Guardería Tinquilco at 9:40am, 2:10pm and 5pm.

There are also several daily buses from Pucón that run (via Caburgua) only as far as Paillaco (CH$1000, 40 minutes). From here it's a 7km (two-hour) mostly uphill walk to Guardería Tinquilco.

Campers can park cars for free near the Guardería Tinquilco, but vehicles must otherwise be left at the private parking area near Refugio Tinquilco (CH$800 per day) at the northern end of the lake.

THE TREK

Day 1: Guardería Tinquilco to Camping Renahue

3¾–5¼ hours, 11km, 640m ascent

Follow the dirt road past the Guarderia Tinquilco information center to **Camping & Hospedaje El Rincón** (see p72 for details). Proceed around the northern side

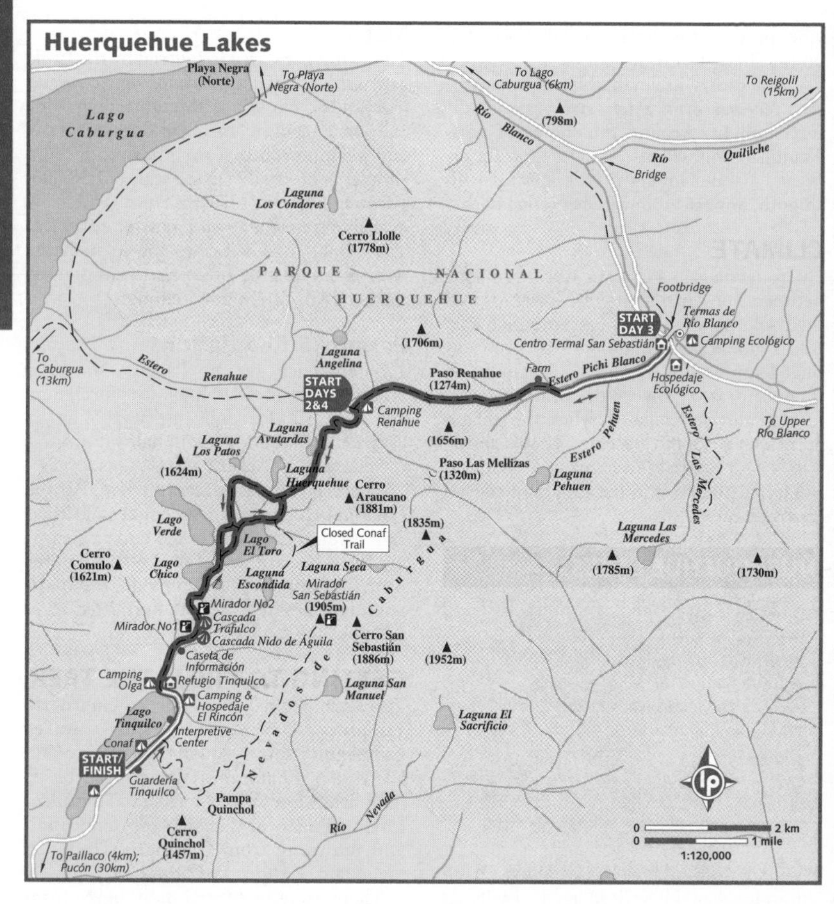

of Lago Tinquilco to reach a small parking area where the navigable road ends. Here, cross the lake's main inlet stream on a little footbridge into the clearing where **Refugio Tinquilco** (p72) stands, 25 to 30 minutes from the guardería. **Camping Olga** (p72) is five minutes' walk past Refugio Tinquilco.

Cut up rightward to rejoin the (now rougher) vehicle track, and climb mostly gently to the **Caseta de Información**. This is a Conaf checkpoint on the national park boundary, where a friendly *guardaparque* will register your details. The track continues up quickly past the turn-off leading 400m to the **Cascada Nido de Águila**, 30 to 45 minutes from the *guardería*. This mossy-laden waterfall lies within a lovely forest of *mañío* and *tepa* smothered by *estrellitas* and *botellitas*.

Continue up to the minor lookout point known as the **Mirador No 1**, where Lago Tinquilco comes back into view below, then on past the turn-off down to the more spectacular **Cascada Trafulco**, a long cascade splashing over smooth granite rocks. The stepped path begins a steeper winding ascent past the **Mirador No 2** (1094m) to finally reach **Lago Chico**, 50 minutes to 1¼ hours from the Cascada Nido de Águila.

Cross the outlet of Lago Chico on a footbridge, then walk around the eastern shore through stands of *coigües* and araucarias to an intersection just after crossing the lake's first inlet (flowing down from Lago El Toro).

Take the right branch to pass by a tiny pebble beach on the southwest tip of **Lago El Toro**, a few minutes on. The path rises and dips gently along the western side of Lago El Toro (past a connecting trail left to Lago Verde and short right turn-offs to several scenic points by the lake) to reach a picturesque little inlet at its northern shore, 45 minutes to one hour after crossing the Lago El Toro outlet. Ignore an old trail here (now closed by Conaf) that leads off right to Laguna Seca and Laguna Escondida.

Head up northeast through the forest to reach a trail junction on a tiny, flat shelf among stands of graceful old araucarias, after 15 to 20 minutes. Just 50m along this left (northwest) branch is **Laguna Huerquehue**. Although not one of its prettier lakes, this shallow tarn has at least given the park its name.

Follow the (now blue-marked) trail northeast along the edge of a long, thin *mallín*, then drop gently through a saddle past the tiny, murky Laguna Avutardas and come onto fire-cleared slopes high above the Estero Renahue. This spot grants a sudden (and the only) glimpse down valley to the blue waters of Lago Caburgua before you begin a steep winding descent through regenerating *notro* and *colihue* scrub. The route then eases right into the forest to reach a track intersection by a little stream, 50 minutes to 1¼ hours from Laguna Huerquehue.

Head down across the stream to arrive at **Camping Renahue** (Mar-Dec two-night campsite CH$7000, Jan-Feb two-night campsite CH$10,000) after 10 minutes. Beneath high ridges, Camping Renahue lies on a grassy lawn between the two small branches of the upper Estero Renahue. This is the only place on the trail where camping is permitted within the national park, apart from the Conaf campsite at Lago Tinquilco. Pay the camping fee at Guardería Tinquilco before departure.

An easy three-hour return side trip can be made up to **Laguna Angelina** by following a path across the stream and climbing gently northwest.

Day 2: Camping Renahue to Termas de Río Blanco

2½–3 hours, 7.5km, 540m ascent, 215m descent

From Camping Renahue follow the path through alternating fire-damaged and intact forest, ascending gradually to **Paso Renahue** (1274m). The trail then descends, first gently through mature araucarias, then steeply along an often heavily eroded path. The path continues east until reaching a farmhouse. Continue through the farm, crossing a right-hand side stream. Look for the remnants of tire tracks to pick up the path, now a road, and continue east, following the Estero Pichi Blanco. The valley narrows as you proceed through *mañío* and fragrant *tepa* to meet the road along the Río Blanco, immediately above **Termas de Río Blanco** (see p76 for accommodation details).

Day 3: Termas de Río Blanco to Camping Renahue

2½–3 hours, 7.5km, 540m ascent, 215m descent

Retrace your steps to return via the route as described on Day 2.

Instead of returning to Guardería Tinquilco from the Termas de Río Blanco, some trekkers choose to continue 18km on along the little-transited road to Reigolil (via the turn-off 4km down valley), where there are bus connections to take you back to Pucón.

Day 4: Camping Renahue to Guardería Tinquilco via Laguna Los Patos & Lago Verde

3¾–5 hours, 12.5km, 640m descent

Retrace you steps to the junction near Laguna Huerquehue as described on Day 1. Go right, following this somewhat less trodden trail for 15 to 20 minutes northwest to a (right) turn-off. This leads in a few minutes to the **Laguna Los Patos**, another tiny tarn surrounded by araucarias.

The main trail continues around southward, sidling down along the left side of a ridge. It passes a left turn-off to Lago El Toro (signposted 'Renahue') to reach a little beach on the southeast shore of **Lago Verde**, after 25 to 30 minutes. Surrounded by forested ridges crowned by the umbrella-like outlines of araucarias, this tranquil lake is perfect for a hot weather dip. Continue across the outlet footbridge and make your way down to the junction at Lago Chico, 10 to 15 minutes on. Now retrace the route described on Day 1 to the trek's starting point at Guardería Tinquilco.

PARQUE NACIONAL VILLARRICA

Crowned by the snowy dome of Volcán Villarrica (2847m), one of Chile's most popular parks is the 610-sq-km Parque Nacional Villarrica. It features a stark lunar landscape crafted of lava flows, scoria and pumice, and scattered with alpine lakes. About 30km southeast of the tourist resort of Pucón, it was created in 1925 from a forest reserve originally set aside in 1912. Among the most accessible national parks in Chile, it stretches along a broad volcanic range running southeast from Volcán Villarrica as far as the 3776m summit of Volcán Lanín on the Chile–Argentina border. This extensive plateau was created several thousand years ago with the explosion of Volcán Quetrupillán.

Recent and older lava flows on Volcán Villarrica tell of a battle of natural forces, as the local vegetation struggles to survive against recurring, intense volcanic activity. Névés and glaciers cover Volcán Villarrica's upper slopes, and its northern slopes have been developed for winter skiing.

ENVIRONMENT

The lower slopes of Parque Nacional Villarrica are clothed in rich virgin forests, where montane southern beech species such as *raulí*, roble and the evergreen *coigüe* predominate up to an elevation of approximately 1000m. Above this altitude *lenga* and *ñirre*, alpine species of southern beech, coexist with superb forests of araucaria trees.

The araucaria is often found in pure stands that form the tree line (at around 1600m above sea level).

Typical southern Andean wildflowers, such as the añañuca and the Chilean field orchid, or *orquídea del campo*, are well represented. Hardy shrubs, including the *michai*, a thorny member of the *Berberis* genus (similar to *calafate*) with yellow flowers, and *chauras* thrive on the upper slopes of these volcanic mountains. Usually present in alpine herb fields of the Araucanía are numerous species of yellow groundsels, or *senecios*. The volcanic soils also favor *brecillo*, a small shrub that produces edible purple berries (often seen in the scat of native foxes).

With the exception of birds, which are relatively easy to spot, the shy native fauna is seldom seen in Parque Nacional Villarrica. A bird common in the park is the Chilean pigeon, or *torcaza*, a large grey bird that the Mapuche call *conu*. Although this species seemed dangerously close to extinction in the early 1960s, populations of Chilean pigeon have recovered dramatically in recent decades. The austral parakeet, or *cachaña*, feeds largely on araucaria nuts, splitting them open with its sharp beak. The luxuriant forests also provide an ideal habitat for the Magellanic woodpecker, often seen tapping about the tree trunks.

VOLCÁN VILLARRICA

The indigenous Mapuche people knew Volcán Villarrica by the name of Rucapillán, meaning 'house of the spirits', and believed the mountain to be the abode of their ancestors. The volcano is extremely active and unpredictable. From the crater rim, molten magma is visible deep down in the core, and at times red-hot lava spurts up. Its smouldering volcano smoke is visible from all over the northern Lakes District.

The volcano has experienced repeated catastrophic eruptions over the centuries, most recently in 1971, when a 4km-wide fracture opened, releasing massive lava flows that destroyed the small township of Coñaripe and only just spared Pucón. Smaller eruptions are even more common – such as in September 1996, when Volcán Villarrica shot out columns of thick gaseous smoke that covered its northwest slopes in a fine layer of ash.

Both despite and due to its continuing activity, Villarrica is the most climbed – and studied – mountain in Chile. Seismic and volcanic activity are now carefully monitored, and any increase can result in 'closure' of the mountain until activity subsides. Residents surrounding the volcano live in a permanent state of alert, ready to evacuate their homes with little notice.

The **Proyecto de Observación Villarrica** (www.povi.cl) is a scientific organization that studies Volcán Villarrica.

CLIMATE

Parque Nacional Villarrica's elevated topography ensures that it has higher average precipitation levels and lower temperatures than the surrounding Araucarían lowlands. Summer temperatures generally range between 9°C and 23°C. Reaching nearly 4000mm annually (concentrated between May and early September), precipitation is highest on the western slopes of Volcán Villarrica, which lie directly in the path of the moist Pacific airstream. The winter period brings frequent and heavy snowfalls above 1000m.

VILLARRICA TRAVERSE

Duration 6 days
Distance 81km
Difficulty demanding
Start Refugio Villarrica (Centro de Ski Pucón)
Finish Puesco
Nearest Town Pucón
Transport bus

Summary A classic longer trek along the rugged volcanic spine of Parque Nacional Villarrica.

This incredibly scenic, high-level trek traverses virtually the whole length of the national park, giving constantly changing views. The route first leads around Volcán Villarrica's glacier-shrouded southern sides, then along a complex volcanic plateau of alpine lakes, small calderas and lava flows that extends as far as Volcán Lanín. The mostly rocky, open terrain provides sensational vistas, although the route dips repeatedly into beautiful highland araucaria and *lenga* forests.

Most trekkers complete a three-day section of the traverse starting at Guardería Chinay or Termas de Palguín (see the Day 3 Alternative Start). The Villarrica Traverse is marked by colored – yellow, red and then green – stakes that identify various sections of the trail. The guided ascent of Volcán Villarrica (see More Treks, p70) is itself an unforgettable experience, and can be done on the first day of the trek.

Note that early in the day and late in the season, only larger streams can be relied on to have running water so you may have to plan to bring your own.

PLANNING

When to Trek

Early in the season, snow may still cover large areas of the route. Summer (December–February) can be surprisingly hot. From about late December until early February, bothersome *tábanos* are out in force, although they are almost absent above the tree line.

What to Bring

Trekkers should bring a tent, warm clothing, food supplies and camp stove. Bring enough water for a full-day hike, it can be replenished at campsites. (Ice axe and crampons are not necessary for the traverse). The box below talks about weather conditions.

Maps

Conaf has produced a 1:110,000 color-contoured map of Parque Nacional Villarica that, for the most part, shows routes correctly. Most trekkers will find it detailed enough for the Villarrica Traverse.

Otherwise, four 1:50,000 Chilean IGM maps cover the trek: *Pucón* (Section G, No 104), *Curarrehue* (Section G, No 105), *Liquiñe* (Section G, No 113) and *Paimún* (Section G, No 114). An additional map, *Villarrica* (Section G, No 103) is optional. These maps do not show the track (or Laguna Blanca) but they are topographically accurate.

Permits & Regulations

Visitors to Parque Nacional Villarrica pay a daily admission (foreigner/Chilean CH$3000/1500) or for an indefinite longer

WARNING

Although the Villarrica Traverse is well marked and well trodden, it is a long, high-level route almost entirely above tree line. There are no *refugios* (huts), so all trekkers must carry a sturdy tent. The central section is very exposed. Deep winter snow often remains well into January, but among the extensive fields of lava the going can be very hot. Bad weather or low cloud can quickly move in to make navigation difficult. Finding water is often hard as the earth is very porous and streams tend to flow underground (and/or streams stop running overnight because of the cool night temperatures).

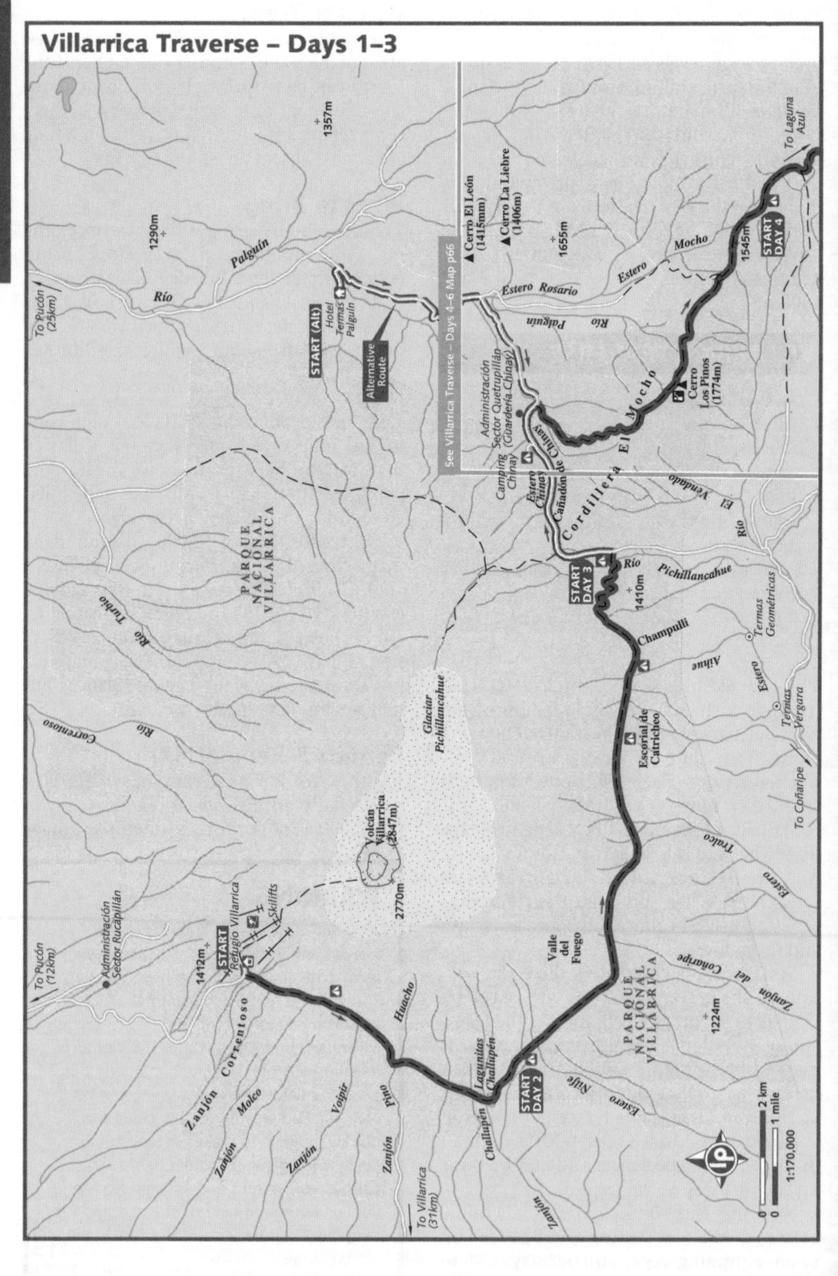
Villarrica Traverse – Days 1–3
See Villarrica Traverse – Days 4–6 Map p66
To Pucón (25km)
To Pucón (12km)
To Villarrica (31km)
To Coñaripe
To Laguna Azul
START (Alt)
Hotel Termas Palguín
Alternative Route
START
Refugio Villarrica
Skilifts
Administración Sector Rucapillán
START DAY 2
START DAY 3
START DAY 4
Administración Sector Quetrupillán (Guardería Chinay)
Camping Chinay
Cerro El León (1415mm)
Cerro La Liebre (1406m)
Cerro Los Pinos (1774m)
Volcán Villarrica (2847m)
Glaciar Pichillancahue
PARQUE NACIONAL VILLARRICA
Cordillera El Mocho
Cañadón de Chinay
Estero Chinay
Estero Rosario
Estero Mocho
Río Palguín
Río Turbio
Río Correntoso
Río Pichillancahue
Río El Venado
Champulli
Escorial de Catricheo
Termas Geométricas
Termas Vergara
Estero Aihue
Valle del Fuego
Lagunitas Challupén
Challupén
Huacho
Zanjón Correntoso
Zanjón Molco
Zanjón Voipir
Zanjón Pino
Zanjón del Coñaripe
Estero Trafco
Estero Ñilfe
1290m
1357m
1655m
1545m
1410m
1412m
2770m
1224m
0 2 km
0 1 mile
1:170,000

stay (foreigner/Chilean CH$7000/5000). Pay fees at Administración Sector Rucapillán, 8km from Pucon on the road to the ski area or Guardería Chinay (Day 3). Apart from several Conaf-organized campsites, camping is only permitted in the park at least one hour's trek from the nearest road. Trekkers are strongly encouraged to carry a stove rather than light fires.

GETTING TO/FROM THE TREK

The trek begins at Refugio Villarrica (also known as Centro de Ski Pucón), a ski lodge (closed in summer) roughly 18km from Pucón on the northwest side of Volcán Villarrica. There is no public transport, but taxis can be chartered up to Refugio Villarrica for – depending on your bargaining skills – around CH$12,000. You can walk to Refugio Villarrica from Pucón in around five hours.

Many local outdoor-adventure companies (see p74 for details) organize guided ascents of Volcán Villarrica. In fine weather in the main tourist season (January and February), several guided parties are likely to make the climb each day. These trips include transport by the companies' own minibuses to and from Refugio Villarrica, and if there is extra space, a ride may be negotiable.

The trek ends in Puesco.

ALTERNATIVE START

It is also possible to start the trek roughly midway on Day 3 at the Termas de Palguín (see p65), on the Palguín Bajo–Coñaripe road. From Pucón, you can either take a taxi (CH$$20,000), or a shuttle (CH$5000) with **Sierra Nevada** (☎ 045-444210; Av O'Higgins 524), with daily 7am departures in summer. The taxi can leave you at the Administracion Sector Quetrupillan (Guarderia Chinay). Alternatively, a local bus from Pucón to Curarrehue or Puesco goes past the turn-off at Palguín Bajo, from where it is a pleasant 3½-hour trek up the valley to the Termas.

For those wanting to continue further up the valley, it is also possible to join the Villarrica Traverse from the Guardería Chinay, another 3.5km up the Palguín Bajo–Coñaripe road from Termas de Palguín. This alternative start is described later in this chapter.

THE TREK

Day 1: Refugio Villarrica to Estero Ñilfe

4½–6¼ hours, 11.5km, 350m ascent

The road ends at a parking lot beside Refugio Villarrica (a winter ski lodge that's closed in summer), a short way above the tree line at around 1500m. Walk 200m back down the road to the start of the track, which begins just beside the first ski-lift post on the first bend near a large tin shed. The first several meters are marked off in stones. Follow yellow-tipped, metal marker-stakes south across the first eroded gully, the **Zanjón Correntoso**. The route rises over mostly dry streambeds on the open slopes of hardy Andean heath and wildflowers to cross the **Zanjón Molco**, 25 to 30 minutes from the *refugio*. There is fair **camping** by this stream among the bare rock.

The well-formed track climbs on steadily leftward through lava fields and occasional snowdrifts and on to sparse tussock-grass ridges. The shining blue waters of Lago Calafquén gradually move into view down to the southwest. Cut back down through a rocky gully between the lava, into the scrub, to reach the **Zanjón Voipir**, 1¾ to 2¼ hours from the Zanjón Molco. There is a good view up this sediment-filled stream (flowing underground in places) to the snowy crown of Volcán Villarrica.

Head on across another trickling gulch into mature *lenga* and araucaria forest, whose *quila* understorey has perished (a curiosity of its life cycle; see the boxed text The Quila Cycle, p87). The trail passes a signposted turn-off going down to the Villarrica township (33km – a useful exit route in bad weather) just before it drops into the **Zanjón Pino Huacho**, 50 minutes to 1¼ hours from the Zanjón Voipir. A deteriorated wooden pipe ducts water from a tiny spring trickling out of the sandy embankment at the base of the canyon.

On the other side, continue left (ignoring a minor path along the left bank) and begin an undulating traverse through more beautiful forest and pockets of red-flowered *notro* scrub. The route passes a signposted trail turn-off (leading down 28km to the town of Lican Ray) to reach the **Zanjón Challupén** after 30 to 40 minutes. Cut 300m left, diagonally up through this wide streamway that (when flowing) washes scoria down from the slopes of Volcán Villarrica.

Pick up the trail on the other side and head 200m through lava rock before you cut away to the right up a steep embankment (ignoring a rough, paint-marked route going off left to a glacier). Stay to the right as you continue to climb. Eventually the path turns left into the trees to reach the ponds known as the **Lagunitas Challupén** (approximately 1250m), 30 to 40 minutes on.

Climb on southeast over a minor forested ridge, descending across a dry gully to jump an unnamed stream (with reasonable **campsites** on tiny terraces along its south side). The trail continues briefly through *ñirres* to arrive at the **Estero Ñilfe** (GPS 39° 27.486 S, 71° 58.712 W), a glacial stream 25 minutes from the Lagunitas Challupén. These open slopes give a clear view south toward the snowcapped double summit of Volcán Choshuenco and Volcán Mocho, rising behind forested ranges. The best **campsites** are sheltered by low lengas on the stream's north bank.

Day 2: Estero Ñilfe to Río Pichillancahue

4–5½ hours, 16.5km, 330m ascent, 35m descent

Follow yellow marker-stakes across a broad tundra basin scattered with *chaura*, yellow groundsels and other tiny wildflowers under glaciers on Villarrica's southwest face. Traverse past recent lava flows in the area known as the **Valle del Fuego** (Valley of Fire), over a minor crest, then cut across an upper channel of the Zanjón del Coñaripe.

Well defined by stone borders, the trail climbs slightly north of east to reach a saddle (1516m) between a reddish side crater (2006m) and another smaller cone (1646m), 1¼ to 1¾ hours from the Estero Ñilfe. From here you get the first clear views southeast toward the exploded crater of Volcán Quetrupillán and Volcán Lanín's 3776m ice-encrusted cone behind it.

Descend via a ridge leading around to the right and cross a trickling stream, then climb over a steep grassy ridge to meet the **Estero Tralco**, after 15 to 25 minutes. Cut up left across the stream through a deep, sometimes snow-filled trench. Head toward a rock marked with a white-paint circle, then continue eastward into the **Escorial de Catricheo**. The trail avoids the worst of this large field of black scoria, following an easy route through gaps in the coarse, gnarled rock that resembles petrified tree trunks. Past the lava the trail passes a large boulder called *Piedra de la Junta*. Down to the right, araucarias stand silhouetted against the outline of Volcán Lanín.

Climb to a ridgetop under crevassed icefalls on the southern side of Volcán Villarrica, descending on rightward through sparse alpine tundra strewn with tiny yellow, starlike *quinchamalí* to meet a grassy stream near a basalt bluff. The route continues quickly over a crest (marked by a pole) to cross the **Estero Aihue** (GPS 39° 28.630 S, 71° 53.149 W), one to 1½ hours from the Zanjón del Coñaripe. A scenic but unsheltered **camp** could be made downstream on grassy flats within the canyon.

Sidle left round past a prominent red ridge coming off Villarrica to reach a cluster of araucarias just above the normal tree line at **Champulli** (wrongly shown on the IGM map), after 20 to 30 minutes. These slopes overlook the wild upper valley of the Río El Vendado. Disregarding trails that descend right, traverse around northeast, slightly upward over grassy mountainsides scattered with pink añañucas opposite Volcán Quetrupillán. The foot track crosses a series of small, steep stream gullies (usually snow-filled at least until mid-December) before finally cutting down into the *lenga* scrub (GPS 39° 28.239 S, 71° 52.122 W), 35 to 45 minutes on.

A steep, switchbacking descent through tall forest leads to the **Río Pichillancahue** after a final 30 to 40 minutes. There is no bridge here, but this large stream can usually be forded with little difficulty a short way upstream. There are excellent **campsites** among *coigüe* forest on the true left (east) bank of the river, but be particularly careful with campfires as large amounts of dead *quila* here could set the whole area ablaze. Glaciar Pichillancahue is visible through the trees at the head of the valley.

Day 3: Río Pichillancahue to Upper Estero Mocho

5½–7 hours, 16.5km, 1150m ascent, 700m descent

The path leads five minutes downstream along the east bank, then climbs left over a low ridge to come out at the Palguín

Bajo–Coñaripe road after 15 to 20 minutes. The trail turn-off is signposted 'Challupén' (GPS 39° 28.284 S, 71° 51.221 W). Turn left and follow this often-rough – almost 4WD-standard – road up through araucaria forest (past a left trail turn-off leading 3km northwest to a lookout under Glaciar Pichillancahue) to cross a pass at 1264m on the top of the main Villarrica range after 30 to 40 minutes.

Follow the winding road down for 30 to 40 minutes past a Conaf picnic area and **Camping Chinay** (Palguín Bajo–Coñaripe road; CH$7000 per person, paid at the *guarderia*/admin center). This is an alternative start point for the trek. About 1km up valley from the Guardería Chinay, this Conaf campsite has 10 organized sites with tables and fireplaces among lovely araucarias and *lengas*; there is also a toilet block with cold showers. The road descends through rich forests of mixed southern beech species, crossing and recrossing the rushing **Estero Chinay** to reach Conaf's Administración Sector Quetrupillán (**Guardería Chinay**), near the park boundary, after a further 25 to 35 minutes. Advise the officious *guardaparque* of your arrival. Park fees can be paid here.

Walk 50m past a swing gate on the road and turn off right at a red-marker stake. This trail quickly crosses the stream on a footbridge, then heads rightward over a minor crest to ascend slopes ablaze with red *notro* bushes. The gradient eases only briefly as you pass a short side trail down to a fresh spring (your only source of water for some time). Climb on steeply southward, through regenerating fire-cleared forest high above the Cañadón de Chinay, to finally reach grassy alpine slopes that give welcome views across the upper valley of the Río El Vendado to araucaria-clad ranges and volcanoes. The path traces the scrub line along the right side of the ridge, then cuts up left along a streamlet to a rocky gap (1688m) in the Cordillera El Mocho, 2¼ to three hours from Guardería Chinay.

Don't descend from the gap, but climb 15 to 20 minutes along the bare ridge to a flat **lookout** at 1758m that gives a fantastic panorama of the five surrounding volcanoes – Villarrica, Quetrupillán, Lanín, Mocho and Choshuenco – as well as many more distant summits. The route traverses left below Cerro Los Pinos (1774m), following the scrubby ridge down into forest to intersect with an unsigned trail coming up from the Fundo El Mocho on a broad saddle (around 1435m) among araucarias, 1½ to two hours from the lookout.

Climb gently on for 25 to 30 minutes until the ridge finally ends by a small stream at the edge of the gently tilted plateau on the western side of Volcán Quetrupillán. Here, pleasant **campsites** can be found a short way right along the stream among the shelter of the scrub. The familiar puffing summit of Volcán Villarrica dominates the skyline to the northwest.

ALTERNATIVE START: TERMAS DE PALGUÍN

4½–6 hours, 12km, 880m ascent

This route is easier and shorter (but less scenic) than the track via the Cordillera El Mocho. This route can also be driven in a taxi from Pucon (see p62).

The **Termas de Palguín** (☎ 045-441968; baths CH$5000; 9.30am-7.30pm) are 12km along the Palguín Bajo–Coñaripe road from the turn-off on Ruta 119. A good place for a meal, **Hotel Termas Palguín** (r per person with full board CH$41,400) was reconstructed after the historic building burnt down in 1998. Camping is possible nearby. (Trekkers coming down valley from the Guardería Chinay – 3.5km and one to 1¼ hours – should turn right just after crossing the Río Palguín.)

From the Termas de Palguín, follow the Palguín Bajo–Coñaripe road up valley for 1¼ to 1½ hours to a Y-fork (recognisable by the signpost 'Al Parque 3km') and take a right toward the park. Walk all the way to the **Quetrupillán administrative center**, where the track begins.

Day 4: Upper Estero Mocho to Laguna Blanca

3¾–5 hours, 13.5km, 150m ascent

Head out over the open plateau to the left of a rounded rock bluff (an old volcanic plug). The track leads southeast over alpine grassland and raw volcanic scoria through a stream gully (filled with snow early in the season, but dry later in the summer) to cross the tiny source of the Río Llancahue after 30 to 40 minutes.

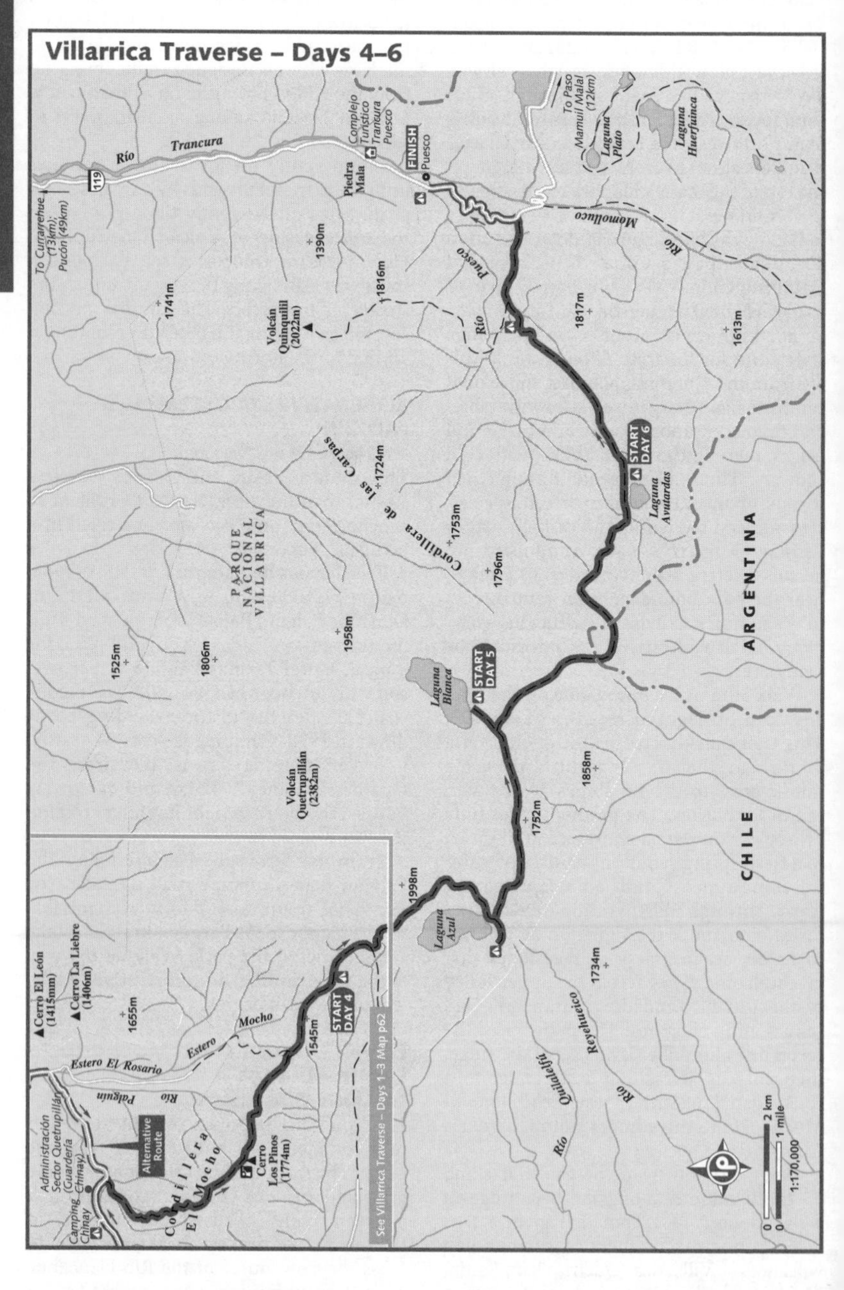
Villarrica Traverse – Days 4–6
Río Trancura
119
To Curarrehue (13km); Pucón (49km)
Complejo Turístico Trancura Puesco
FINISH
Puesco
Piedra Mala
To Paso Mamuil Malal (12km)
Laguna Plato
Laguna Huerfuinca
Río Momolluco
Río Puesco
1741m
1390m
1816m
Volcán Quinquilil (2022m)
1817m
1613m
START DAY 6
Laguna Avutardas
Cordillera de las Carpas
1724m
1753m
1796m
PARQUE NACIONAL VILLARRICA
ARGENTINA
1525m
1806m
1958m
START DAY 5
Laguna Blanca
1858m
Volcán Quetrupillán (2382m)
1752m
CHILE
1998m
Laguna Azul
1734m
Río Reyehueico
Río Quillalelfú
Cerro El León (1415mm)
Cerro La Liebre (1406m)
1655m
Estero Mocho
Estero El Rosario
Río Palguín
START DAY 4
1545m
See Villarrica Traverse – Days 1–3 Map p62
Alternative Route
Administración Sector Quetrupillán (Guardería Chinay)
Camping Chinay
Cerro Los Pinos (1774m)
Cordillera El Mocho
0
2 km
0
1 mile
1:170,000

Follow the path five to 10 minutes downstream to where a marker stake (GPS 39° 30.763 S, 71° 45.181 W) indicates the point from which to begin climbing left. (Ignore another path that continues downstream (southwest) and eventually meets the Palguín Bajo–Coñaripe road.) Markings guide you up roughly south over tussock-grass ridges with sporadic clusters of wild orchids, then to the right up sparsely vegetated slopes into a rocky gap, 40 to 50 minutes on. From here there are more fine volcanic vistas toward the north.

Sidle southwest to get your first glimpse of the dark-blue lake directly below to your right, then cut back up southeast (left) on to the ridge. Here, the giant of the region, Volcán Lanín, and the lower, double cone of Volcán Choshuenco and Volcán Mocho (off to the south) come back into view, while Andean condors drift around above you. Maintain a high route over the coarse slopes and snowdrifts that persist well into summer, then drop down to the right in zigzags along a loose-earth ridge to reach the southeast shore of **Laguna Azul** (shown on IGM maps as Laguna de los Patos), 50 minutes to 1¼ hours from the gap. This impressive lake lies in a deep trough whose outlet stream was dammed by the large lava flow nearby. There are **campsites** here among the *lenga* scrub, but unconscientious campers have left them in pretty poor condition. Less sheltered spots exist across the small outlet on the grassy saddle a short way below the ruins of a *refugio*.

From the southeastern shore of Laguna Azul, head east between the broad band of lava and the ridge you descended. Occasional paint markings and small tree branches propped up with cairns lead easily through the broken rock. Climb over a minor crest, then cut through another regenerating lava field and continue northeast along a broad, barely vegetated ridge to a barren, rocky area. Edge down to the right of this into a silt-filled streambed before making your way left for 500m. (Winter snow tends to accumulate here, its meltwater temporarily forming a shallow lake.)

At this point head up northeast, immediately left of a tiny stream, to reach a narrow sandy gap, 1½ to two hours from Laguna Azul. From here you get a view across the desolate moonscape to Laguna Blanca, a small lake lying at just above 1600m. Drop down the eroding slopes into the barren basin (if the gap is dangerously corniced, climb briefly around left), then head directly northeast across the raw, undulating plain to arrive at **Laguna Blanca**, 15 to 20 minutes on. Scenic, but only semisheltered, **campsites** can be found among boulders on the southern shore of this starkly beautiful alpine lake.

Day 5: Laguna Blanca to Laguna Avutardas

3½–4¼ hours, 11km, 400m ascent

Return to the main trail and head on around to the right into a dry gully. Follow the gully until it turns eastward, then climb away around the eastern rim of a small extinct crater. Continue on generally south toward the distant twin peaks of Volcán Choshuenco and Volcán Mocho, before crossing to the left over a small spur marking the Chile–Argentina frontier. The path sidles around slopes overlooking the wild, forested valley of the Río Blanco in Argentina, dips into a bare bowl-like basin, then ascends northeast to reach a pass (GPS 39° 34.191 S, 71° 40.280 W) back on the international border, 1½ to two hours from Laguna Blanca. The Conaf map puts this section of the route inside Chilean territory!)

At 1838m, this often-windy ridgetop is the highest point on the traverse, and looks out northeast (into Chile) toward 2022m Volcán Quinquilil, the major summit of the jagged Cordillera de las Carpas. Beyond the valley of the Río Puesco, further over to your right, stands an impressive saw-shaped range, which locals call La Peineta (literally, 'the Comb'). You can also enjoy the last clear views of Volcán Lanín over to your right.

Drop to the right, and then ease down leftward beside the stream on to a wet shelf of shallow pools and alpine bogs, vegetated by water-loving plants such as native yellow buttercups known as *madecos*. Pick up the path at the northernmost edge of the shelf, where the stream tumbles over a low escarpment, before descending in a few quick switchbacks. The route doubles back right to cross the stream below the waterfall.

Continue upward under the cliff face across another waterlogged area into *lenga* scrub to reach an open ridgetop separating two branches of the upper Río Puesco, 50 minutes to 1¼ hours from the pass. Up to your right, more small cascades tumble over the escarpment, while there are enticing glimpses of a welcoming lake down in the valley below you.

Follow the ridge to just before a rock knob, then watch out for markings on the right that indicate where the trail starts its steep descent to the southeast. Drop via narrow snow chutes down into taller forest to finally come out on a marshy meadow grazed by noisy flocks of black-necked ibis at the western corner of **Laguna Avutardas** (shown on IGM maps as Laguna Los Patos), after 25 to 30 minutes.

Make your way directly east, bounding across babbling brooks to pick up the trail again at the edge of the trees. This sometimes-indistinct track sidles through the forest above the lake's north side, before cutting through to **campsites** on an open grassy clearing at the eastern end of Laguna Avutardas, a final 20 to 30 minutes on.

Laguna Avutardas lies at around 1450m, and is enclosed on three sides by steep forested ranges. It has a narrow sandy beach, and in hot weather the water is just right for a leisurely dip (a welcome respite from the voracious *tábanos* of late December and January). Visitor impact has been high here; please light fires only in existing fireplaces and carry out all rubbish.

Day 6: Laguna Avutardas to Puesco

3¾–5 hours, 12km, 775m descent

Rejoin the trail and continue gently northeast down through tall *lenga* forest and *quila*, crossing a small stream to reach a *mallín* after 20 to 30 minutes. Make your way 500m through the middle of this scrubby strip before moving rightward to where the route re-enters the trees (GPS 39° 34.109 S, 71° 37.047 W). Continue northeast, rising and dipping over low ridges, before you drop down through *coigüe* forest scattered with *quellén* (wild strawberries) and long-abandoned farm clearings to meet a disused old road, 1½ to two hours from the *mallín*.

(From here, a 4km orange-marked route leads off left to ford the Río Puesco before it climbs to the summit of Volcán Quinquilil. It is possible to **camp** near the crossing, although sites are less than ideal unless you wade the knee-deep river.)

Turn right and follow this rough track through *ñirre* and *notro* scrub. The old road (closed to all motorized vehicles) sidles gently down in an almost easterly direction above the raging Río Puesco, crossing through a remnant cherry orchard to pass a small house just before it intersects with Ruta 119 (the international road between Pucón and Junín de los Andes), one to 1½ hours on. (This junction is signposted 'A Quetrupillán'.) Go left here and descend northward through the forest of *raulí* and roble, watching out for unmarked short-cut trails that lead down more directly between the road's numerous hairpin bends to arrive at Puesco after a final 40 to 50 minutes. The Conaf office now has free **camping** here, with fire pits and toilets.

As a courtesy, present your papers at the Puesco customs office. Make sure the staff realise that you have not just crossed from Argentina (although they may want to inspect your gear anyway).

MORE TREKS

CORDILLERA DEL VIENTO (ARGENTINA)

Ascent of Volcán Domuyo

By strict definition, the 4709m summit of Volcán Domuyo, in the Cordillera del Viento in the remote northern corner of Argentina's Neuquén province is the highest point in the Patagonian Andes. It is one of the few volcanoes entirely within Argentina that has significant geothermal activity, including fumaroles, geysers and thermal springs.

Volcán Domuyo can be climbed in around five days return from its south side. Although technically straightforward, this remote, high-alpine ascent, with the associated dangers of altitude sickness (see Health & Safety, p258), requires proper experience, equipment (including ice axe and crampons) and planning.

Albus (☎ 02942-432108) runs daily buses from Zapala to Chos Malal, roughly 110km south of Domuyo, but access to the volcano itself is by private (preferably 4WD) vehicle only. Some outdoor-adventure companies (eg Alquimia in Junin, see the Lakes District, p126) organize guided ascents.

Unfortunately, to date no topographic map of the area has been published at a useful scale.

PARQUE NACIONAL LAGUNA DEL LAJA (CHILE)

Ascent of Volcán Antuco

The 2979m cone of Volcán Antuco ends in a crater just 40m in diameter, which sometimes emits gases and steam. This summit grants a superb panorama that includes the upper Valle Laja to the west and the Sierra Velluda to the south. Across Laguna de la Laja, there is Volcán Chillán (3122m), to the north, and the ranges extending into Argentina to the east.

Volcán Antuco can be climbed from several points. One route starts 4km past the ski village on the volcano's northern slopes, beyond the lava flow. It is steep and direct, and takes around eight hours return. A less steep and somewhat faster route goes up the southeastern slopes from Los Barros. There is no trail to follow on this route.

Beware of a dangerously crevassed glacier on the volcano's upper southern slopes. Depending on snow conditions, crampons and an ice axe are generally advisable (sometimes essential) before about mid-January, and cannot be hired at the park.

The ascent is more strenuous when there is no snow covering the loose earth. Inexperienced trekkers should inquire at the park administration center or the Centro Turístico Lagunillas (p74) for a guide.

PARQUE NACIONAL CONGUILLÍO (CHILE)

The 612-sq-km Parque Nacional Conguillío (con-gee-yo) lies east of Temuco. Its key features are Volcán Llaima's distinctive twin summits at 2920m and 3125m, and spectacular Laguna Conguillío, a large lake below the towering Sierra Nevada. Unusual animals, like the *monito del monte*, pudu and vizcacha, as well as diverse bird species, call Conguillío home.

The **park administration center** (☎ 045-1970860) is on the southern shore of Laguna Conguillío, where there is also a **campsite** (☎ 045-841710; camping per site CH$15,000, three-/seven-person cabins CH$45,000/55,000). Park visitors must pay an entrance fee (foreigner/Chilean CH$4000/3000).

There is no public transport to Laguna Conguillío, meaning visitors have the option of either hiring a vehicle, chartering a taxi or taking an organized tour. Taxis from Curacautín (CH$30,000) can be arranged through the city's **oficina de turismo** (☎ 045-464858; Av Manuel Rodríguez), facing the main plaza.

The lack of public transport, the park's policy of prohibiting camping anywhere except at Laguna Conguillío and the relative difficulty of (longer) routes generally makes the park less attractive for trekking. However, several interesting treks are described below.

La Baita (☎ 045-581253, 099-7332442; www.labaitaconguillio.cl), at the park boundary on the Melipueco–Conguillío road, organizes guided treks, climbs and transportation in the area.

Laguna Captrén

The easy 3½-hour trek to the lovely Laguna Captrén begins a short way west of the park administration center. The trail leads 5km northwest through beautiful forest then skirts the shore of Laguna Captrén. The lake was created when a lava flow dammed a stream, and drowned trees are still visible in its waters.

Use the Chilean IGM's 1:50,000 map *Volcán Llaima* (Section G, No 75).

Sierra Nevada

The 18km, 6½- to 8½-hour return trek up to the Sierra Nevada leaves from Playa Linda, on the southeast shore of Laguna Conguillío. A well-graded track climbs a broad spur through araucaria and *lenga* forest to the base of the Sierra Nevada, then ascends along a rock ridge before cutting left to a lookout that gives wonderful views across the lake to Volcán Llaima.

Use the Chilean IGM's 1:50,000 map *Volcán Llaima* (Section G, No 75).

Ascent of Volcán Llaima

Volcán Llaima's distinctive double-cone summits present few technical difficulties and are a popular goal for local andinists (Andean mountaineers). Following two eruptions in 2008, the volcano was temporarily closed to trekkers. It has since been reopened. Emergency updates appear on www.onemi.cl in Spanish, Chile's Oficina Nacional de Emergencia. Llaima is best climbed from its western side, where the **Centro de Ski** (☎ 045-562313; www.skiaraucarias.cl; dm CH$7500, four/six-person apt (CH$30,000/40,000) offers summer dorm accommodation, and can organize two-day guided tours to the volcano's crater. Use the Chilean IGM's 1:50,000 map *Laguna Quepe* (Section G, No 74).

PARQUE NACIONAL HUERQUEHUE

Pampa de Quinchol & Mirador San Sebastián

From the road 500m north of the Guardería Tinquilco, a well-graded, 3km path winds up steep slopes to the grassy alpine ridgetop known as the Pampa Quinchol (three hours return). From here an easy 1km loop cuts around clockwise along the southern side of the ridge through a smaller grassy saddle to meet the main track again lower down. A more demanding 6km (3½ hours return) route leads northeast up a craggy ridge to the Mirador San Sebastián (1905m). This lookout offers tremendous views across Huerquehue's lakes to numerous summits of the Araucanía. Carry plenty of water on the Mirador climb.

PARQUE NACIONAL VILLARRICA

Ascent of Volcán Villarrica

Volcán Villarrica is Chile's most climbed high summit, despite the fact that Conaf now requires everyone – apart from properly trained mountaineers and guides, who must present adequate proof of their qualifications – to make the ascent with an approved guide. Almost a dozen outdoor-adventure companies in Pucón (see p74 for several examples) organize guided ascents of Volcán Villarrica from around CH$35,000 (which covers equipment, lunch and transfers).

The climb begins from Refugio Villarrica (Centro de Ski Pucón) at 1420m. A well-trodden track ascends to the upper chairlift station (1882m). The route leads up a steep ridge past the minor outcrop of Piedra Negra and a rocky rib known as the Pingüinera (2247m). It continues up over broad snowfields to make a final steep ascent to the 2847m summit. Approach the rim cautiously to avoid noxious fumes and be alert to sudden changes in wind direction.

The 1:50,000 Chilean IGM map *Pucón* (Section G, No 104) covers Volcán Villarrica but the summit area is omitted (due to clouds on the aerial photographs!). Conaf's 1:110,000 free color map of the park shows the route.

Santuario Cañi

Created in 1991 to thwart logging interests in this spectacular swathe of native forest, the nature sanctuary **El Cañi** (www.santuariocani.cl; Pinchares; admission with/without guide CH$6000/3000) protects some 500 hectares of ancient araucaria forest, with an emphasis on education and scientific research. Located 21km along the road to Huife, the sanctuary is now maintained by a local guide association, **Cañi Guides Group** (☎ 099-837 3928; santuariocani@chile.com).

A hiking trail (three hours one way, 9km) ascends the steep terrain (the first 3km very steep) of *lenga* and araucaria to arrive at Laguna Negra. On clear days the 1600m lookout – another 40 minutes – allows for spectacular views of the area's volcanoes. Guests can overnight at a huge **rustic refuge** at the Sanctuary entrance (1100m), or **camp** below the Mirador. All trekkers must go with a guide, except in summer when the trail is easier to find. Make arrangements to visit El Cañi at the park entrance or at ¡École! in Pucón (p74), which also has transport information. Self-guiding maps are available from rangers.

PARQUE NACIONAL LANÍN

Lago Quillén to Lago Ñorquinco

This trek explores the remote northern sector of Parque Nacional Lanín, crossing two high passes that connect three beautiful lakes. As camping is not permitted between each stage, it requires two very long days.

The route leads north from the eastern end of Lago Quillén, crossing the Arroyo Malalco and switchbacking up through a pass (at around 1850m) on the eastern side of the Cordón de Rucachoroi. It then descends to meet a road on the south shore of Lago Rucachoroi, where there is a **campsite**. From here the route heads northwest up the Arroyo Calfiquitra and across a watershed at Mallín Chufquén before again descending to Lago Ñorquinco via the Arroyo Coloco. There is another **campsite** here.

It is possible to extend the trek by continuing along the scenic, lightly transited Ruta 11 (either hitchhiking or walking) to Moquehue, then trekking on around the south side of Lago Moquehue to Villa Pehuenia. In summer there are several daily buses from San Martín de los Andes (see The Lakes District, p128) to Zapala via Aluminé, from where there are connections to Villa Pehuenia and Moquehue.

Two old Argentine IGM 1:100,000 maps, *Lago Ñorquinco* (Neuquén, No 3972-23) and *Quillén* (Neuquén, No 3972-29), cover the area (but not the track). Sendas y Bosques' 1:200,000 map *Parque Nacional Lanín* shows the route clearly.

TOWNS & FACILITIES

CAVIAHUE (ARGENTINA)

☎ 02948 / pop 500 / 1600m

Ski village Caviahue flanks the western shore of Lago Caviahue at the foot of Volcán Copahue. Though both villages are going through a construction boom, it's a more attractive alternative to nearby Copahue. Popular day treks go to **Laguna Escondida** via the waterfall of the same name and to a series of four waterfalls known as **Cascadas Agrio**.

Information

The **oficina de turismo** (☎ 02948-495036; www.caviahue-copahue.com.ar has an excellent map showing these and other treks around the area. It can be hard to change money here, so bring plenty of cash.

Supplies & Equipment

Outfitter **Caviahue Tours** (☎ 02948-495138; www.caviahuetours.com; Av Bialous Centro Comercial local 11) organizes treks, including to Laguna Termal and Volcán Copahue. **La Huella** (☎ 02948-495116; viatursur@yahoo.com.ar; Bungalow Alpino Sur 2) rents mountain bikes and offers dog-sledding trips in winter.

Sleeping & Eating

Alpine-style **Hebe's House** (☎ 02948-495237; lacabanadehebe@ciudad.com.ar; Mapuche & Puesta del Sol; dm/d AR$35/100; Dec-Sep) has laundry facilities, kitchen access and plenty of tourist information.

The rambling **Hotel Caviahue** (☎ 02948-495044; hotelcaviahue@issn.gov.ar; 8 de Abril s/n; s/d AR$130/200) is open year-round, with a restaurant (mains AR$15-$20). Rates drop around 30% in the off-season.

Getting There & Away

BUS

Cono Sur (☎ 02948-421800) runs a bus service daily between Zapala and Caviahue (AR$30, three hours). Buses for Zapala leave Caviahue at 5am, 10am and 2pm.

COPAHUE (ARGENTINA)

☎ 02948 / 2030m

Small thermal springs resort Copahue (2030m) stands on the northeastern side of its namesake volcano among steaming, sulfurous pools. The popular **Laguna del Chancho** (8am-6pm; admission AR$6) is one such bubbling mud pool. Due to snow cover, the village is only open from the start of December to the end of April.

The village centers on the large, modern **Complejo Termal Copahue** (☎ 02948-495049; www.termasdecopahue.com; Ortiz Velez; baths AR$8), which offers a wide range of curative bathing programs.

Sleeping & Eating

Near the trailhead, **Camping Pino Azul** (☎ 02948-495111; camping per person AR$15) is by far the most affordable option in town.

Residencial Codihue (☎ 02948-495151; codihue@futurtel.com.ar; Velez s/n; s/d with full board AR$60/100) is the best budget option, just down the road from the thermal baths complex.

The modern **Copahue Hotel** (☎ 02948-495117; www.copahuehotel.com.ar; Bercovich s/n; s/d from AR$200/250) boasts atmospheric common areas and an excellent traditional Argentine restaurant.

Parrillada Nito (☎ 02948-495040; Zambo Jara; mains AR$15-35; lunch & dinner) is the most frequently recommended *parrilla* (mixed grill) restaurant in town.

Getting There & Away

Copahue is on Ruta Provincial 26, 139km from Zapala and 19km from Caviahue. There are no buses to Copahue, which can be reached from Caviahue by taxi (☎ 02948-495032; Remises Caviahue; AR$45) or by **Caviahue Tours** (see Caviahue, earlier) on its shuttle service (AR$12 per person).

CURACAUTÍN (CHILE)

☎ 045 / pop 16,995

Curacautín is the northern gateway to Parque Nacional Conguillío and Reserva Nacional Malalcahuello-Nalcas. The **tourist office** (☎ 045-464858; Plaza de Armas; 8am-6.30pm Mon-Fri, 9am-4.30pm Sat) has brochures and information on the parks and accommodation in town.

Sleeping & Eating

Overnight options are slim. **Hostal Rayén** (☎ 099-0014421; Manuel Rodríguez 104; r per person without bathroom CH$8000) isn't the nicest or the quietest, but its hospitality speaks volumes.

Hospedaje María del Carmen (☎ 099-0966365; Iquíque & Manuel Rodríguez; r per person incl breakfast CH$10,000) offers immaculate rooms.

There are simple restaurants around the Plaza de Armas.

Getting There & Away

BUS

The bus terminal (cnr Arica & Manuel Rodríguez) is directly on the highway to Lonquimay. **Buses Bio Bio** (☎ 045-881123) heads to Temuco via Victoria (CH$2400; 1½hrs, seven daily Monday to Saturday), and via Lautaro (CH$1600; 2hrs, four times daily Monday to Friday). **Buses Curacautín Express** (☎ 045-258125) goes to Temuco all day long via Lautaro.

Tur-Bus (☎ 045-881596; Serrano 101) has four direct buses per day to Santiago in summer and two in winter (CH$18,100; 10hrs). Buses running between Temuco and Zapala via Paso de Pino Hachado pass through Curacautín.

LAGO TINQUILCO

☎ 045

Conaf's Guardería Tinquilco, about halfway around the lake's southeastern shore, administers the park. The interpretation center in the caseta de informacion, 300m past the guardería, has exhibits on local flora and fauna.

Sleeping & Eating

The 24-site **Conaf campsite** (camping per site Jan-Feb CH$15,000, camping per site Mar-Dec CH$10,000) sits among beautiful *arrayán* trees along the lakeshore near the Guardería Tinquilco.

At the northeast corner of Lago Tinquilco is **Camping & Hospedaje El Rincón** (☎ 099-6463025; camping per site CH$8000, r per person CH$7000). Prices include firewood for campers and hot showers. El Rincón has a small restaurant (breakfasts CH$1500).

In a clearing next to the lake's inlet stream, 25 to 30 minutes walk from the guardería, **Refugio Tinquilco** (☎ 099-5392728; www.tinquilco.cl; dm CH$7000, r with shared/private bathroom CH$19,900/24,900) is a superb wooden hut among tall *tepa* and *mañío* trees. A trail leads down past the sauna to a beachlet on the lake.

Camping Olga (☎ 045-441938; campingolga.com; camping per site CH$6000), five minutes walk past Refugio Tinquilco, has secluded lakeside sites and offers hot showers for CH$500.

LOS ÁNGELES (CHILE)

☎ 043 / pop 145,000

This unassuming regional capital lies north of the Río Biobío, just outside Chile's Araucanía region. It's a jumping-off point for Laguna del Laja and Tolhuaca national parks as well as many other potential trips into the nearby Cordillera. The city is just west of the Panamerican Hwy, is well serviced and is easily reached from the north or south.

Information

A good source of information is the **oficina de turismo** (☎ 043-408643; 2nd fl Edificio O'Higgins, Colón 185). **Inter Bruna** (☎ 043-313812; Caupolicán 350) changes money and travelers checks.

Sleeping & Eating

Much of Los Ángeles' accommodation is along the Panamerican Hwy, but the most reasonable options are in town. **Residencial El Angelino** (☎ 043-325627; Colo Colo 335; r per person CH$8000) is a great place with clean, cheerful rooms.

Only a few doors down is **Hotel Oceano** (☎ 043-342432; Colo Colo 327; s/d with bathroom CH$22,000/26,000, s with shared bathroom CH$13,000).

Supermarkets for provisions include **Lider Express** (Av Sor Vicenta 2051), attached to the Terminal Santa Maria bus station. **Julio's Pizza** (Colón 452; pizzas CH$7000-10,000) serves good pizzas, pasta and other dishes. **Bife Sureño** (Lautaro 681; mains CH$6000) is a pleasing option for carnivores.

Getting There & Away

BUS

In the center of town, **Terminal Santa Rita** (Villagrán & Rengo) serves local destinations. For long-distance destinations, passengers can taxi to **Terminal Tur-Bus** (☎ 043-363135; Av Sor Vicenta 2061) or **Terminal Santa María** (Av Sor Vicenta 2051) for about CH$2000. *Colectivos* (shuttle taxis) are an even more affordable option (CH$350).

Terminal Santa María has frequent buses to Puerto Montt (CH$10,000, eight hours), Temuco (CH$4000, four hours) and Santiago (CH$10,000, eight hours). Bus companies operating on these routes all have offices at the terminal, and include **Biobío** (☎ 043-534699), **Igi Llaima** (☎ 043-363100), **Cruz del Sur** (☎ 043-363050), **Inter** (☎ 043-363220) and **Jota Be** (☎ 043-533181). Jota Be also runs to Angol, the gateway to Parque Nacional Nahuel Buta, via Renaico (CH$1300, 1½ hours).

MALALCAHUELLO (CHILE)

☎ 045

Pronounced mal-al-ka-way-yo, its Mapuche name means 'horse corral'. The access point for Reserva Nacional Malalcahuello-Nalcas, Malalcahuello lies on Ruta 181 (R-89), 31km east of Curacautín and 15km west of Lonquimay.

Termas de Malalcahuello (☎ 045-197-3558; www.malalcahuello.cl, in Spanish; Ruta Biooceánica 181-CH; admission CH$10,000; Mon-Sat 9am-9pm, Sun 9am-7pm) has spa services and one large hot spring (in need of a refinishing) behind large bay windows with views to Volcán Lonquimay. It is within walking distance of the town center.

For information on the reserve, **Conaf** (☎ 045-5452224) lies 200m east of the village entrance.

Sleeping & Eating

Cut left from the disused rail line for **Residencial Los Sauces** (☎ 099-8911130; camping per site CH$5000, cabins CH$25,000), which, along with **Hostal La Nahuelcura** (☎ 045-1970311; Balmaceda 320; r per person CH$6000, cabins CH$35,000), has modest rooms and a restaurant.

Three kilometers out of town, the recommended Swiss-run **Suizandina** (☎ 045-1973725; www.suizandina.com; Camino Internacional km83; camping per person CH$4000, dm CH$12000, s/d from CH$26,000/37,000) features extra cozy comforters, big breakfasts and organized treks.

Getting There & Away

BUS

Erbuc buses (☎ 045-272204) running between Curacautín (p72) and the village of Lonquimay pass by Malalcahuello roughly every two hours in either direction. The last bus back to Curacautín (CH$800, 40 minutes) passes at approximately 6.30pm.

TAXI

It is possible to get a taxi (CH$10,000) directly to the reserve from Curacautín.

PARQUE NACIONAL LAGUNA DEL LAJA & AROUND (CHILE)

☎ 043

This area is the launch pad for trekking Volcán Antuco. The nearest stores are in El Abanico and Antuco, and there are kiosks beside the turn-off to the park for limited last-minute purchases, but Los Ángeles is by far the best option for buying supplies.

Sleeping & Eating

Near the village of El Abanico, just before the turn-off, are the **Hotel Malalcura** (☎ 043-1972720; r per person CH$10,000) and **Hosteria el Bosque** (☎ 043-1972719; r per person CH$10,000).

About 3km along the road toward the park, **Antucalhue Cabanas** (☎ 096-8496340; www.antucalhue.cl; cabins per person from CH$15,000) is a brand new facility with pristine and rustic cabins.

Within the park itself, on the banks of the Río Laja about 1km up the road from the Portería El Álamo, is the **Centro Turístico Lagunillas** (camping per site CH$10,000, six-person cabins CH$30,000). This privately run campsite offers good self-contained cabins and sheltered, rather dusty campsites. There are hot showers and a kitchen for guests. For information and reservations, call Lili (☎ 097-4542184) or Ricardo (☎ 099-3354285).

Higher up at the small ski village of Volcán Antuco is the **Casino Club de Esquí/Refugio Antuco** (dm CH$5000). Although much busier in winter, the refugio is open year-round and serves meals and drinks.

Also here is **Refugio Digeder** (☎ 098-3458989; CH$5000; summer only), operated by the city of Concepción's Dirección General de Deportes y Recreación.

PUCÓN (CHILE)

☎ 045 / pop 17,000

If you can walk it, jump off of it, ride it or climb it, you can do it in Pucón (www.chile-pucon.com). This adventure hub flanks Lago Villarrica, at its back is the smouldering volcano of the same name. Once a summer playground for the rich, Pucón is becoming a year-round destination catering to all incomes, especially in February (a time to avoid, if possible).

For a list of the best thermal soaks in the area, see boxed text below.

Information

For information, the **oficina de turismo** (☎ 045-293002; cnr Av O'Higgins & Palguín; 8.30am-10pm Dec-Feb, to 7pm Jun-Aug) has stacks of brochures and usually an English speaker on staff. Try also www.chile-pucon.com for an online guide to Pucón.

Conaf (☎ 045-443781; Lincoyán 336) can advise on trekking and climbing in the area. **TravelAid** (045-444040; www.travelaid.cl; Ansorena 425) serves up hiking advice, maps and GPS rental.

Supplies & Equipment

More than a dozen companies in Pucón run guided climbing, trekking and other outdoor-adventure tours in the surrounding mountains. A couple of good options are **Sol y Nieve** (☎ 045-463860; www.solynievepucon.cl; Lincoyán 361b; 9am-midnight Jan-Feb, 11am-7pm Mar-Dec) and **Aguaventura** (☎ 045-444246; www.aguaventura.com; Palguín 336; 8.30am-9pm).

For ethnotourism, check out **Patragon** (☎ 045-444606; www.patragon.net), connecting visitors with local Mapuche culture.

Sleeping & Eating

If not camping, book lodgings weeks ahead in the high season.

Camping Parque La Poza (☎ 045-444982; campinglapoza@hotmail.com; Costanera Roberto Geis 769; camping per

TOP THREE SOAKS AROUND PUCÓN

To get to these *termas* you must arrange group transportation through an agency, taxi or hostel in Pucon. You can also drive yourself if you have a rental car.

Termas Geométricas (☎ 099-4425420; km16 Camino de Coñaripe; www.termasgeometricas.cl; adult/child CH$14,000/6000; 10am-10pm Jan-Feb, 11am-8pm Mar-Dec) With waterfalls, cold plunge pools and a maze of 17 slate hot springs, you might think you've died and gone to a better place. But no, it's 16km north of Coñaripe.

Termas de Panqui (☎ 045-442039; on an offshoot of the road to Curarrehue; panquihotsprings@hotmail.com; day baths CH$6000, camping per person CH$8100) Panqui, 58km east of Pucón, caters to a New Age crowd and can get overrun in the summer, but the numerous baths here are still quite good and are set in a tranquil mountain location.

Termas Los Pozones (☎ 045-1972350; km37; day baths adult/child CH$3500/1500, night baths adult/child CH$4500/2500; 11am-6am) Lively and sometimes crowded, these six natural-stone pools sit next to the rushing Liucura river. Transportation from Pucón (CH$10,000) is included in the admission price.

person CH$3000) has about 82 sites on shady grounds, and a fair amount of noise from the busy road.

The HI-affiliated **¡École!** (☎ 045-441675; www.ecole.cl; Urrutia 592; dm from CH$7000, d with shared/private bathroom CH$20,000/30,000) has a range of rooms and cosy common spaces; the restaurant serves excellent vegetarian fare.

A friendly Dutch–Chilean couple runs **El Refugio** (☎ 045-441596; www.hostalel refugio.cl; dm/d CH$8000/18,000), a snug place to rest. Ask here for excellent trip advice.

A British–Chilean venture, the **Tree House** (☎ 045-444679; www.treehouse chile.cl; General Basilio Urrutia 660; dm/d CH$10,000/24,000) has attractive dorms and common spaces with hammocks.

La Tetera (☎ 045-441462; www.tetera .cl; Urrutia 580; d with/without bathroom from $37,000/29,000) caters to couples, with hearty breakfasts.

For homemade ice cream or gourmet salads, try **Cassís** (☎ 045-444715; Fresia 223; sandwiches CH$2000-4500).

Pizza Cala (☎ 045-463024; Lincoyán 361; pizzas CH$2700-9900; year-round) serves pizzas straight from a brick oven.

Meat specializts should visit the popular Uruguayan steakhouse **La Maga** (☎ 045-444277; Fresia 125; mains CH$5900; Mar-Dec) for a mean *bife de chorizo* (steak) with house-cut fries.

Getting There & Away

AIR

In summer only, both **Lan** (☎ 600-5262000 in Chile; www.lan.com; CH$74,900) and **Sky Airlines** (☎ 600-6002828 in Chile; Gerónimo de Alderete 203) offers twice-weekly flights between Pucón and San Martín de los Andes.

BUS

Buses JAC (☎ 045-443326; cnr Uruguay & Palguín) goes to Puerto Montt (CH$5900, five hours). For Temuco, Buses JAC goes every 20 minutes (CH$2000, one hour). From the same bus station, **Minibuses Vipu-Ray** and **Trans Curarrehue** (Palguín 550; CH$800, 45 minutes) have frequent services to Villarrica (30 minutes, CH$700) and Curarrehue. The Curarrehue bus stops at Puesco and Reigolil.

Buses JAC and **Buses Caburgua** (☎ 099-8389047; Uruguay 540) have services to Caburgua and Parque Nacional Huerquehue (CH$1000, 45 minutes).

For San Martín de los Andes, Argentina, **Buses San Martín** (☎ 045-443595; Av Colo Colo 612) offers departures Tuesday to Sunday at 10:35am (CH$10,000, five hours), stopping in Junín de los Andes (CH$8000, four hours) on the way. **Igi Llaima** (☎ 045-444762; cnr Uruguay & Palguín) departs Monday, Wednesday, Friday and Saturday at 9:25am.

PUESCO (CHILE)

☎ 045

The Villarrica Traverse finishes at the tiny village of Puesco, which has an altitude of 700m and is the last Chilean settlement on Ruta 119 (the international road across Paso Mamuil Malal) before the border. Conaf's Guardería Puesco, just down from the *aduana* (customs post), is responsible for the park's eastern sector.

Sleeping & Eating

Puesco has no hotels or stores. Conaf's Guarderia Puesco offers free **camping** with fire pits and toilets. **Complejo Turistico Trancura Puesco** (Piedra Mala; camping per person CH$2000; two-/three-person cabins CH$10,000/15,000), 2km north of Puesco below the peak known as La Peineta, has a riverside campsite and cabins with gas stove and hot showers.

Getting There & Away

BUS

From the Puesco Conaf office, buses run to Pucón on Monday, Wednesday and Friday at 6am and 5pm (CH$1000). From Curarrehue, local buses travel every half-hour to Pucón. Complejo Turistico Trancura Puesco (see details above) also offers transportation to Curarrehue (CH$18,000), Pucón (CH$30,000) and San Martín de los Andes, Argentina (CH$50,000).

Buses run daily in both directions between Junín de los Andes and San Martín de los Andes in Argentina, and Pucón and Temuco in Chile. International buses arriving from Argentina (at around 10.30am) can be boarded if there are vacant seats. Buses heading into Argentina (generally arriving in Puesco around noon) only take pre-booked passengers – although it's certainly worth asking.

TEMUCO (CHILE)

☎ 045 / pop 259,102

The largest city in the Araucanía, Temuco is a workhorse town on the Panamerican Hwy, 675km south of Santiago. Though it has important links to Mapuche culture, Temuco does not have a lot of attractions in itself. However, it is a quick trip to the national parks of Villarrica, Huerquehue, Conguillío and Nahuel Buta, as well as Reserva Nacional Malalcahuello-Nalcas. The small Conaf-administered Cerro Ñielol nature reserve borders the town (access via Calle Prat), and is ideal for a short 'urban trek'.

Information

Opposite the Plaza de Armas, **Sernatur** (☎ 045-211969; Bulnes 586) offers tourist information. The regional headquarters of **Conaf** (☎ 045-298100, 298210; temuco@conaf.cl; 2nd fl, Bilbao 931) are in Temuco. Anglers can buy a Chilean fishing license (CH$15,000) at the regional office of **Sernap** (Servicio Nacional de Pesca; ☎ 045-278522; Balmaceda 795).

Sleeping & Eating

Lodging options aren't outstanding. **Hopsedaje Tribu Piren** (☎ 045-985711; www.hospedajetemuco.cl; Prat 69; r per person CH$8000) is tidy and amicable, with an English-speaking owner.

The quaint, nonsmoking **Hostal Austria** (☎ 045-247269; www.hostalaustria.cl; Hochstetter 599; s/d with bathroom CH$15,400/23,500) is also a winner.

The dynamic **Feria Libre** (Barros Arana; 8am-5pm) churns out cheap *cazuelas, sopaipillas con queso, empanadas* and other tasty dishes.

Affordable and delicious, **Tradiciones Zuny** (Tucapel 1374; meals CH$2000) is perhaps the city's best-kept secret.

Popular **Pizzería Madonna** (☎ 045-329393; Av Alemania 660) serves Italian staples (CH$6000-9000), including to-die-for tiramisu.

Getting There & Away

AIR

Numerous flights to Santiago (CH$60,000) are offered by **Lan** (☎ 045-744823; Bulnes 687) and **Sky** (☎ 045-747300; Bulnes 655).

BUS

Temuco is a major transport hub. Long-distance buses use **Terminal Rodoviario** (☎ 045-225005; Pérez Rosales 1609) at the northern approach to town.

Bus lines serving main cities along the Panamerican Hwy include **Tur-Bus** (☎ 045-278161; cnr Lagos & Manuel Montt) and **Pullman Bus** (☎ 045-212137; Claro Solar 611), both with frequent services to Santiago; **Cruz del Sur** (☎ 045-730320; Claro Solar 599, Manuel Montt 290), which also serves the island of Chiloé and Bariloche via Osorno; and **Igi Llaima/Nar-Bus** (☎ 045-407777; Miraflores 1535), which also heads to Argentina.

International buses run several times weekly to the Argentinian destinations of Zapala and Neuquén (via Paso de Pino Hachado), and Junín de los Andes and San Martín de los Andes (via Paso Mamuil Malal). **Buses JAC** (☎ 045-465465; cnr Av Balmaceda & Aldunate), with its own terminal, offers the most frequent services to Villarrica and Pucón.

Buses to other regional destinations leave from the **Terminal de Buses Rurales** (☎ 045-210494; Balmaceda & Pinto), including to Curacautín.

Sample travel times and costs are as follows (prices fluctuate with the quality of the bus):

Destination	Fare (CH$)	Duration (hr)
Curacautín	2400	2
Osorno	3500	4
Pucón	2000	2
Puerto Montt	4500	5
Santiago	11,000	9
Villarrica	1500	1½
Zapala & Neuquén (AR)	14,000	10
San Martín de los Andes (AR)	10,000	7

TERMAS DE RÍO BLANCO

On the Huerquehue Lakes circuit, **Termas de Río Blanco** (per person CH$4000), is an isolated and almost undeveloped hot springs beside the small, icy Río Blanco.

As accommodation is extremely limited (less than a dozen beds), it is advisable to carry a tent. The fee includes the *piscina* (swimming pool) and *pozos* (a concrete tub and makeshift rock pools of varying warmth). There is one (public) telephone at the Termas.

Centro Termal San Sebastián (☎ 02-1968546; camping per person CH$6000, 6-person cabins CH$60,000), on the river's left (southern) side, has an open, steaming *piscina* in a streamside meadow. Meals are available, including a wild boar barbeque for CH$5000.

A short way up the road, across the Estero Las Mercedes, is the simple **Hospedaje Ecológico** (d per person CH$6000). Across a footbridge from the *piscina*, on the opposite (right) bank, are the *pozos*. Just upstream lies **Camping Ecológico** (camping per site CH$5000).

ZAPALA (ARGENTINA)

☎ 02942 / pop 31,800

Dusty Zapala lies on the dry, windswept steppes, 186km west of Neuquén at the junction of Ruta Nacional 22 and Ruta Nacional 40. Dubbed the 'Dead Swamp' by Mapuche, this place has unsurprisingly little to offer apart from the 112-sq-km Parque Nacional Laguna Blanca, an outstanding bird refuge 30km southwest of town.

Information

Zapala's helpful **tourist office** (☎ 02942-424296; www.zapaladigital.com.ar, in Spanish; Ruta Nacional 22; 7am-9pm) is on the opposite side of the city from the bus terminal but can be reached easily by taxi.

The **Laguna Blanca APN** (☎ 02942-431982; lagunablanca@zapala.com.ar; Av Ejercito Argentino 260; 8am-3pm Mon-Fri) can advise on Parque Nacional Laguna Blanca.

Sleeping & Eating

Free camping can be found at **Camping Municipal** (El Bosque Comunal, Ruta 13). Conveniently near the bus terminal, **Hotel Pehuén** (☎ 02942-423135; Etcheluz & Elena de la Vega; s/d AR$55/100) is the best deal in town.

With outdoor tables, **El Chancho Rengo** (☎ 02942-422795; Av San Martín & Etcheluz) is popular for espresso and sandwiches. Restaurant-bar **Mayrouba** (☎ 02942-421315; Etcheluz & Luis Montt) serves up tasty fare with shades of Middle Eastern influence, as well as Patagonian faves like smoked trout (AR$20).

Getting There & Away

BUS

The **bus terminal** (Etcheluz & Uriburu) is about four blocks from Av San Martín. Westbound buses from Neuquén en route to Junín de los Andes (AR$30, three hours), San Martín de los Andes (AR$34, 3½ hours) and Temuco, Chile (AR$60, six hours), pass through Zapala. Most services to Buenos Aires (AR$150, 18 hours) require changing buses in Neuquén (AR$23, three hours), the nearest major hub. There is a daily service to Laguna Blanca (AR$10, 30 minutes) and Aluminé (AR$18, three to 3½ hours). In summer, buses depart for Caviahue (AR$30, three hours) at 9am, 4pm and 11pm and there are frequent departures for Copahue (AR$36, four hours).

Lakes District

HIGHLIGHTS

- Getting high on the craggy **Nahuel Huapi Traverse** (p103)
- Crunching over scoria dunes amidst geysers and bubbling mud pools on the **Baños de Caulle** trek (p89)
- A remote farmland trek to a thermal soaking in the hardwood tubs at **Termas de Callao** (p97)
- Summiting the snow-covered **Volcán Lanín** (p81) for a gaping Lakes District panorama
- Worshipping the natural cathedral of alerces on the trek to **Laguna Fría** (p118)

This is the south at its greenest. Rain rears grasses and temperate rainforest into a palette of emerald, olive, lime and sage. This lush, mud-spattered backdrop sets the stage for the star attractions: the undulating hills, craggy peaks and snowcapped volcanoes.

Water, taking the form of huge glacial lakes, hot springs and clear streams, is another defining feature. And where there's water, there is life. In the Lakes District, hikers will find the greatest diversity of plants and animals found anywhere in Patagonia. Even if you travel to the end of the continent, it is more likely that in these dense forests you'll spot a miniature pudu (deer), marvel over an ancient alerce (one of the world's oldest trees) or trace the shape of a fresh puma track.

From volcanic plateaus to wild mountain passes there's a diversity of landscapes that makes this area a real delight to explore. Trekkers may be drawn to the well-structured refugio treks around Bariloche or the wilder, overgrown trails on the Chilean side. Given the ready accessibility of this region, it's not hard to understand why the Lakes District has become the premier trekking region of Chile and Argentina.

GATEWAYS

See Bariloche (p124), Osorno (p126), Puerto Montt (p127).

PARQUE NACIONAL LANÍN

A skyscraper over the Andean wilderness, the snowcapped cone of Volcán Lanín (3776m) is the centerpiece of Parque Nacional Lanín, a 3790-sq-km park that stretches 150km from Parque Nacional Nahuel Huapi in the south to Lago Ñorquinco in the north. The volcano effectively splits the park into northern and southern zones.

The northern zone – theoretically in the Araucanía – covers about one-third of the park's area. It centers around the elongated, fjord-like Lago Quillén. To the south, a much larger and broader zone forms a band of rugged mountains dispersed with the major glacial lakes of Lago Huechulafquén, Lago Lolog and Lago Lácar splayed eastward almost as far as the Patagonian steppes.

Until the late 19th century this vast area of the park was inhabited by the Pehuenche people. The lifestyle of this large Mapuche tribe was integrally linked with the annual harvest of nuts from the region's extensive montane forests of coniferous araucaria trees. The Mapuche reservations of Curruhuinca and Rucachoroi are located within the park, fittingly called *reducciones*.

ENVIRONMENT

Argentina's richest southern beech forests grow in the park. The evergreen *coigüe* (spelt *coihue* in Argentina), is present mainly at the lowest elevations. Two deciduous species of southern beech dominate these subalpine forests: *raulí* and roble (or *pellín*). *Raulí* has long leathery, almost oval-shaped leaves, while its close relative roble has oaklike leaves with deep serrations.

The alpine zone (roughly above 1000m) features two other deciduous southern beech species, *ñirre* (spelt *ñire* in Argentina) and *lenga*. The two trees are easily distinguishable: *lenga* leaves have rounded double notches, while those of the *ñirre* have irregularly crinkled edges. *Lenga* grows right up to the tree line in low, weather-beaten scrub. In fall the mountainsides are aflame with color as these forests turn golden red.

Various parasitic plants attack the southern beech. Common parasites are the *liga*, native mistletoes, the *quintral*, whose red nectar-filled flowers attract hummingbirds, and the *llao-llao*, a fungus that deforms the wood into a large, knotted growth on which round spongy balls form.

Extensive forests of umbrellalike araucaria cloak the northern zone of Parque Nacional Lanín. Particularly in the park's southern zone, forests of Cordilleran cypress, with occasional stands of *maitén* (a native willowlike species), spread across the less watered Andean foothills.

Numerous species of native wildflowers can be identified. The bright spots of yellow scattered around the floor of montane forests could be the delicate *violeta amarilla*, or perhaps the yellow *topa topa*, which resembles a large pea flower. Two pretty white species are the *centella*, a native anemone, and the *cuye eldorado*, an oxalis species that has long been a favorite of gardeners in the British Isles.

Parque Nacional Lanín is one of the last habitats of the *tunduco*, an extremely rare species of native rat. A member of an ancient rodent family (the so-called octodontids), the *tunduco* typically inhabits *quila* and *colihue* thickets, feeding on the roots and shoots. Other mammals found in the park include the *monito del monte* (or mouse oopossum), pudu, *coipo*, *viscacha* and the rare Andean deer known as the *huemul*. These animals are variously preyed on by the puma, the Patagonian red fox, the *huillín* and *huiña*.

There are many small ground-dwelling birds, including the *chucao*, the *huet-huet* and the *churrín*, or Andean *tapaculo*, which all find shelter in bamboo thickets, forest underbrush or alpine heathland. Unmistakable because of its absurdly long tail – about double the length of the bird's body – is Des Murs' wiretail, or *colilarga*.

CLIMATE

Parque Nacional Lanín has a continental climate ranging from subalpine to alpine, with a relatively low proportion of rainfall outside the spring-to-fall period. Summers are warm to hot, particularly in the park's northern (Araucanía) sector, while winters are crisp and white, particularly on the higher ranges. The areas immediately east

Lakes District

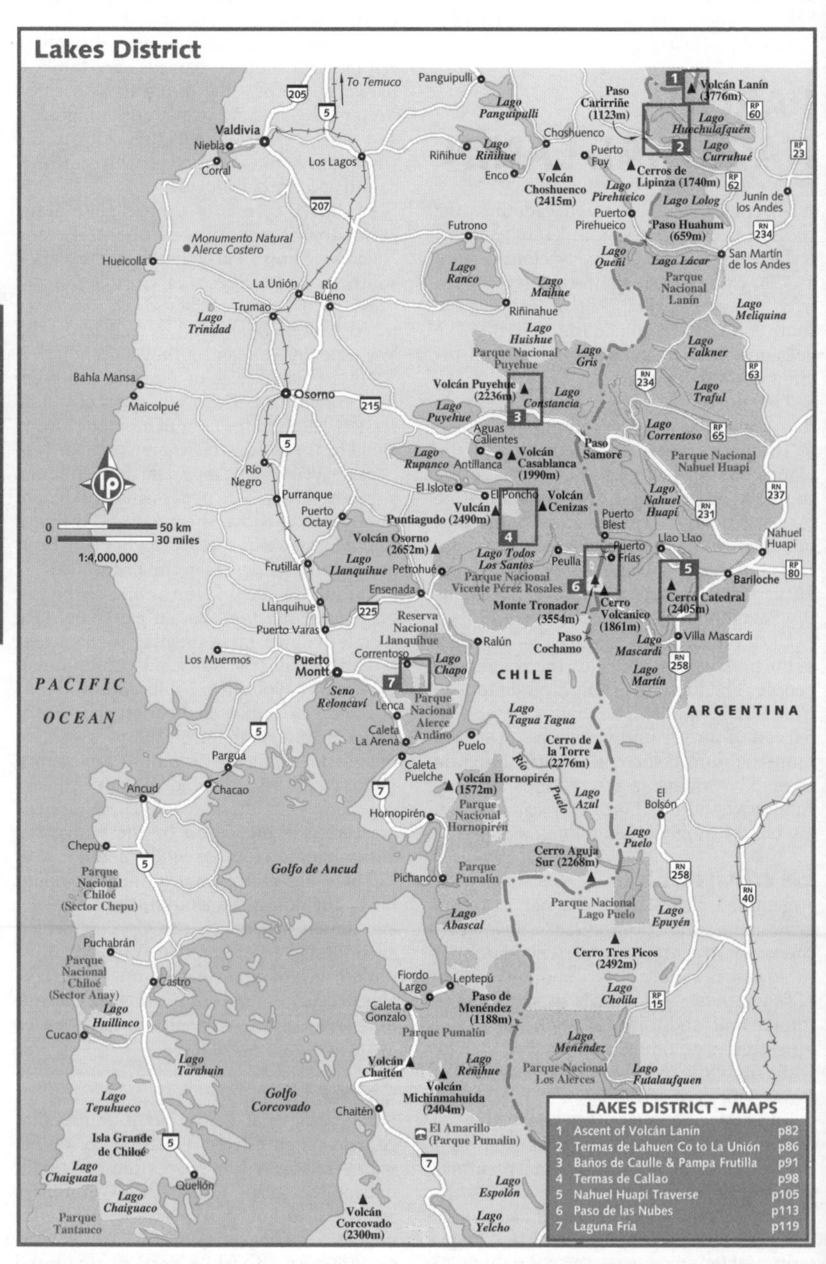

LAKES DISTRICT – MAPS

and north of Volcán Lanín lie in a marked rain shadow created by the volcanic range extending east from Volcán Villarrica. From an annual maximum rainfall of 4500mm on the snowy upper slopes of Volcán Lanín, precipitation levels drop away sharply to well under 1000mm near the dry plains bordering the eastern fringes of the park. Towards the south, in the moist temperate forests of the park's mountainous western sectors, annual precipitation is around 2500mm. The temperature averages 20°C in summer and 4°C in winter.

PLANNING

The APN Intendencia in San Martín de los Andes (p128) can give up-to-date advice and information (including weather forecasts) on trekking and climbing.

An entry fee of AR$9 applies but is payable only when you enter via an APN *portada* (entrance gate). Camping is not permitted outside organized campsites and established en route campsites.

Maps & Books

A 1:200,000 trekking map titled *Parque Nacional Lanín* and published by **Sendas y Bosques** (www.sendasybosques.com.ar) covers the entire park. It shows most official trails and, although its scale is small for comfortable navigation, it is the only widely available quality map. Sendas y Bosques also publishes *Parques Nacionales Lanín y Nahuel Huapi*, a Spanish-language trekking guidebook to the Argentine Araucanía that includes some information in English.

ACCESS TOWNS

See San Martín de los Andes (p128) and Junín de los Andes (p125).

ASCENT OF VOLCÁN LANÍN

Duration 3 days
Distance 25km
Difficulty demanding
Start/Finish Guardería Tromen
Nearest Towns Junín de los Andes San Martín de los Andes
Transport (international) bus

Summary A climb to the top of a majestic volcanic cone that gives a tremendous panorama of the Lakes District and Araucanía.

Towering over the northern Lakes District, Volcán Lanín rises from a base plain of around 1100m to a height of 3776m. Viewed from any other direction than the east, Volcán Lanín's thick cap of heavily crevassed glacial ice makes it look almost impossible to climb, but up its eastern side is a strenuous, though straightforward ascent route. In fact, Lanín is probably the highest summit in Patagonia safely attainable without ropes.

Lanín's Mapuche name means 'Dead Rock', as the Mapuche people believed that anyone who climbed the mountain would be killed by evil spirits (although, today, freezing winds and glacier crevasses are generally a greater danger).

PLANNING

When to Trek

Although winter ascents of Volcán Lanín are not unheard of, the summit is normally tackled between November and February. All climbers must carry an ice axe and crampons. Ascents early in the season are generally easier because the remaining snowpack provides a more stable surface than the often loose volcanic earth underneath. An early start is imperative, since after midday the snow often becomes soft and slushy, making the going tiring uphill and hazardous on the descent.

The volcano's exposed, steep slopes are definitely no place for tents, so all trekkers must stay at one of the three unstaffed *refugios* on Lanín, which are all roughly halfway up the mountain.

The *refugios* provide good, basic shelter – free of charge – but it is essential to carry your own means of cooking and a warm sleeping bag. The ascent of Volcán Lanín is a popular excursion, and in the peak holiday season (January to mid-February) the number of climbers on the mountain may exceed the huts' comfortable capacity.

With good weather, very experienced climbers in top shape may make the climb in one day with day packs.

What to Bring

It is now mandatory for all trekkers to carry an ice axe and crampons, waterproof jacket, mountain sunglasses, sleeping bag, stove, sturdy boots (suitable for snowy conditions), headlamp and a medical kit.

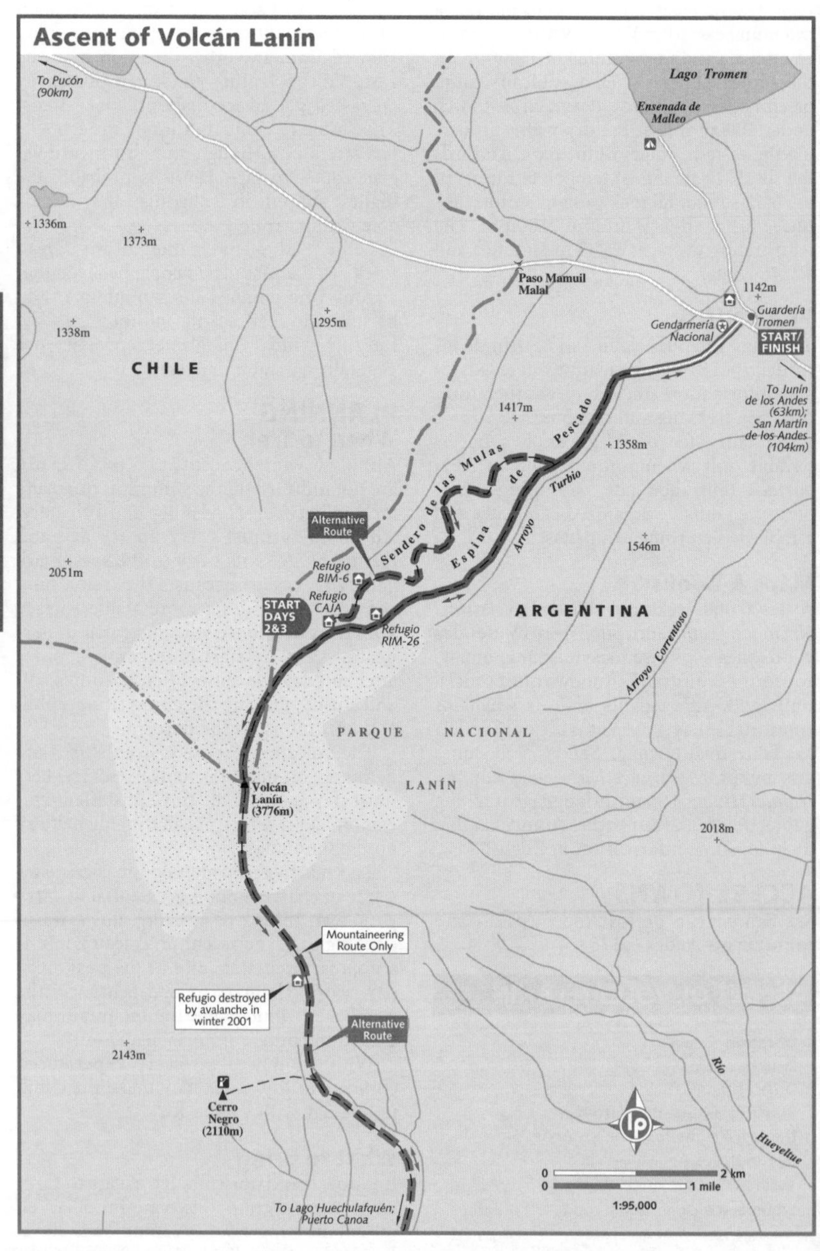

Ascent of Volcán Lanín
To Pucón (90km)
Lago Tromen
Ensenada de Malleo
1336m
1373m
Paso Mamuil Malal
1142m
Guardería Tromen
Gendarmería Nacional
START/ FINISH
1338m
1295m
CHILE
To Junín de los Andes (63km); San Martín de los Andes (104km)
1417m
1358m
Sendero de las Mulas
Espina de Pescado
Arroyo Turbio
Alternative Route
Refugio BIM-6
Refugio CAJA
Refugio RIM-26
START DAYS 2&3
2051m
1546m
ARGENTINA
Arroyo Correntoso
PARQUE NACIONAL LANÍN
Volcán Lanín (3776m)
2018m
Mountaineering Route Only
Refugio destroyed by avalanche in winter 2001
Alternative Route
2143m
Cerro Negro (2110m)
Río Hueyeltue
To Lago Huechulafquén; Puerto Canoa
0 2 km
0 1 mile
1:95,000

You can hire an ice axe and crampons (each around AR$30 per day) in San Martín or, less reliably, in Junín. Trekking poles can be useful for balance. Climbing ropes are of little use and not required, but wearing gaiters to protect your shins and keep rocks and snow out of your boots is advisable. Charting your route with a compass and altimeter or GPS unit can be a tremendous advantage if visibility becomes poor upon the return.

Maps

The best map available is the Chilean IGM 1:50,000 map, *Paimún* (Section G, No 114). This map provides good topographical information on Volcán Lanín, but does not show huts, ascent routes or the correct position of glaciers. JLM Mapas 1:250,000 map, *Pucón – San Martín de los Andes* (No 07), includes an inset scaled at 1:65,000 that accurately shows the route and *refugios*.

Permits & Regulations

All parties must receive authorization to climb the volcano from the *guardaparque* (national-park ranger) at the Guardería Tromen. Trekkers without proper ice-climbing gear (see What to Bring, above) will not be permitted to make the ascent. Be sure to inform the ranger upon your return.

Camping is not permitted anywhere on or around the base of Volcán Lanín apart from at the Guardería Tromen and the campsite at the southern shore of Lago Tromen. For details on accommodation in this area, see p126.

Guides

See under Information for San Martín de los Andes (p128).

GETTING TO/FROM THE TREK

This trek begins and ends at Guardería Tromen. A number of bus companies, including Empresa San Martín, Igi-Llaima and JAC, run buses almost daily to/from Temuco and Bariloche, San Martín or Zapala.

In January and February, there may be public transportation to Tromen, which was unavailable at the time of research, check with Junín's tourism office. Otherwise, **Julio Villanueva** (☎ 02972-491375) in Junín runs shuttles to Tromen (four passengers one-way AR$140).

After clearing customs, trekkers arriving directly from Chile can disembark at Tromen. It might be worth reserving a seat with the bus company for the trip back out, even if you have to pay a bit extra, to ensure an onward seat when you return.

Trekkers intending to cross the border after the climb should note that they are not normally permitted to board a Chile-bound bus in Tromen unless their names are on the official passenger list. It's important that you have a ticket to Chile – with a definite arrangement to join that bus – before you get to Tromen; this can be organized in San Martín de los Andes or Junín de los Andes. The road is remote and carries only light traffic, so hitching is an unreliable transport option and we don't recommend it as a rule.

THE TREK

Day 1: Guardería Tromen to Refugio CAJA

4½–5½ hours, 7km, 1518m ascent

As there is unlikely to be any running water for most of today's sweaty climb, fill up at the campsite when you sign in at Guardería Tromen (1142m). Pick up the trail behind the Gendarmería Nacional building and

WARNING

The trek involves a total ascent of almost 2700m (from around 1100m to 3776m) over loose earth and/or snow slopes. Trekkers should be physically fit, carry basic ice-climbing gear (see What to Bring, p81) and have some experience in mountainous terrain. Although the ascent route itself (apart from the summit) is not exposed to the worst of the westerlies, strong, freezing winds can pick up at any time and with little warning. Attempt the summit only in perfect weather. As you climb, watch for changing conditions and be prepared to descend if conditions deteriorate. Lanín is high enough to cause altitude sickness (p258), so be alert to symptoms in yourself and your companions. Although the route does not cross glaciers, there are dangerous, heavily crevassed glaciers near the summit – keep to the route.

follow this roughly southwest through attractive *lenga* forest, then across a plain of volcanic sand to cross the **Arroyo Turbio** after 30 to 45 minutes. (Early in the day this stream may carry little or no water, but Lanín's melting névés and glaciers normally produce a steady flow by late afternoon.)

You will notice the **Espina de Pescado**, a long, lateral moraine ridge that snakes around to the right above the stream. Climb this 'spine', following the narrow ridgetop as it steepens and curves slightly rightward past an old secondary crater on the left to reach the **Sendero de las Mulas** turn-off going off to the right (see Alternative Route, p84), one to 1½ hours from the Arroyo Turbio.

Keep to the craggy ridge line, where unstable rock calls for careful footwork, minor detours are necessary to negotiate small outcrops. The route climbs up alongside a long, broken-up glacier down to your left to arrive at the red- and orange-painted **Refugio RIM-26**, two to 2½ hours on. Built at 2450m along the Espina de Pescado route by the Regimiento de Infanteria de Montaña, the *refugio* is on a flat razed by a receding glacier. It has capacity for up to 10 people. Afternoon meltwater can be collected from the glacier, but take care not to get too close to where the ice falls away abruptly. Tread cautiously on dirt-covered ice, and save enough water for the next day.

Just above the *refugio*, pick up a vague trail leading up beside the glacier, following this up to where the rock rib disappears. The route continues up for 100m, before leaving the ridge line and heading right through an area of broken-up rock rubble to reach the much more rustic **Refugio CAJA** after 25 to 35 minutes. The rustic tin-roofed hut stands at 2660m on a low, flat ridge. Built and owned by the Club Andino de Junín de los Andes, this smaller civilian *refugio* has space for up to eight people. Collect water from a small névé just around to the west.

ALTERNATIVE ROUTE: VIA SENDERO DE LAS MULAS

5½–7 hours, 9km, 1518m ascent

The Sendero de las Mulas (litreally 'mule track') is a longer but less strenuous route that follows a trail proper (rather than the much steeper Espina de Pescado). It is a better option for slower or less fit trekkers.

From the turn-off, the trail turns away westward, winding and switchbacking up repeatedly through the scoria to finally reach **Refugio BIM-6** after two to three hours. This comfortable *refugio* (built by the Batallon de Ingenieros de Montaña) is situated at 2350m and sleeps up to 15 people. The path continues its serpentine course, rising around slightly leftward to arrive at **Refugio CAJA** after a further one to 1½ hours.

Day 2: Refugio CAJA Return (via Summit of Volcan Lanín)

7–11 hours, 11km, 1116m ascent/descent

When not snowbound, this final section climbs over extremely unstable scoria slopes. The steep and loose earth makes a frustratingly unstable trekking surface, and you need to step very carefully to avoid slipping. Allow yourself plenty of time and do not try for the summit unless the weather is good. There is no running water higher up, so carry plenty (at least a litre per person).

Head up the initially gentle slope over large patches of snow, passing between the two larger permanent snowfields (about 400m over from the glacier), where the gradient begins to steepen. As the ground becomes looser, often giving way as you step, keep an eye out for marker stakes and paint splashes on rocks. Layers of volcanic rock have weathered unevenly to produce very low ridges that lead up the slope. These are much more stable and, if winds are not too strong, they may make for easier climbing.

Although strenuous, the route is now straightforward. In the last stages before you reach the summit, a scramble over rock ledges leads up past the impressive seracs of a glacier that descends westward. Follow a few rock cairns left on to the small névé leading up to the summit of **Volcán Lanín,** which – atypically for a volcano – is not topped with a wide caldera. The relatively small summit is capped by glacial ice which falls away sharply on the south side. You should be extremely careful here. Small crevasses sometimes open up.

Llaima, Villarrica, Tronador and many major peaks of the Lakes District and Araucanía regions are visible from the summit of Lanín. Directly north and south are the large lakes Tromen and Huechulafquén, and a number of beautiful smaller lakes lie on the northwestern slopes of the volcano. In clear conditions you might even be able to make out Chile's Pacific coast far to the west.

Retrace your way back to Refugio CAJA.

Day 3: Refugio CAJA To Guardería Tromen

4–7 hours, 7km, 1518m descent

Retrace your steps as on Day 1. Fit and fast trekkers often prefer to descend the whole way from the summit to Guardería Tromen on their – long – second day. Despite the slope's steepness, the loose volcanic earth breaks your fall. This often makes the going easier. If the sustained descents are painful for your knees, opt for the Sendero de las Mulas route.

ALTERNATIVE ROUTE: PUERTO CANOA

9–12 hours, 17km, 2850m descent

Experienced climbers can opt for an alternative and more difficult descent route leading southeast to the ruins of a *refugio*. At an elevation of 2400m, it was destroyed by an avalanche in the winter of 2001. From there, a path goes on southward down the Arroyo Ruc Leufu to Puerto Canoa, near La Unión on Lago Huechulafquén. Once down, be sure to report back to the Guardería Tromen or the Guardería Puerto Canoa.

TERMAS DE LAHUEN CO TO LA UNIÓN

Duration 2 days
Distance 26km
Difficulty easy
Start Termas de Lahuen Co
Finish La Unión
Nearest Towns San Martín de los Andes · Junín de los Andes
Transport guided tour and/or taxi
Summary An uncomplicated trek from remote hot springs to the scenic shores of Lago Paimún under the spectacular cone of Volcán Lanín.

This A-to-B style 'destination' route leads from the Termas de Lahuen Co along abandoned roads (last used in the 1960s), over abandoned pastures and past an old sawmill to the last remaining farmlets on the southern shore of Lago Paimún. Trekkers will see the gradual regeneration of vegetation cleared by settlers in the early decades of the last century. Introduced wild boar and red deer (known to North Americans as elk) are abundant along this route but, being wary of humans, they are seldom seen.

PLANNING

When to Trek

This relatively low-level trek is normally passable from mid-November until mid-May, although seasonal weather conditions may compromise road access to the trailheads (especially to Termas de Lahuen Co).

Maps

The best available topographical map is the Chilean IGM 1:50,000 map *Paimún* (Section G, No 114), which does not show the route and is not available locally. The Argentine IGM 1:100,000 map, also titled *Paimún* (Neuquén, No 3972-34), is extremely out of date but still shows the route fairly accurately. The Sendas y Bosques 1:200,000 *Parque Nacional Lanín* map also covers the trek and is sold locally.

Permits & Regulations

Permits are not necessary, but all trekkers should register with the appropriate APN office (either in San Martín or at Guardería Carilafquen). Camping is permitted only at the park-authorised Camping Libre Aila on Lago Paimún.

ACCESS TOWNS

See San Martín de los Andes (p128) and Junín de los Andes (p125).

GETTING TO/FROM THE TREK

Termas de Lahuen (start)

The trek begins at Termas de Lahuen Co. These remote hot springs (once known as the Baños de Epulafquen) lie at 930m, just off Ruta Provincial 62, 350m past (ie west of) the APN's Guardería Carilafquen. The now privately run **Lahuen Co Spa Termal de Montana** (www.lahuenco.com) is upscale but expensive and not particularly friendly. Camping is not allowed in the area.

Termas de Lahuen Co is an 80km, 2½-hour drive northeast from San Martín de

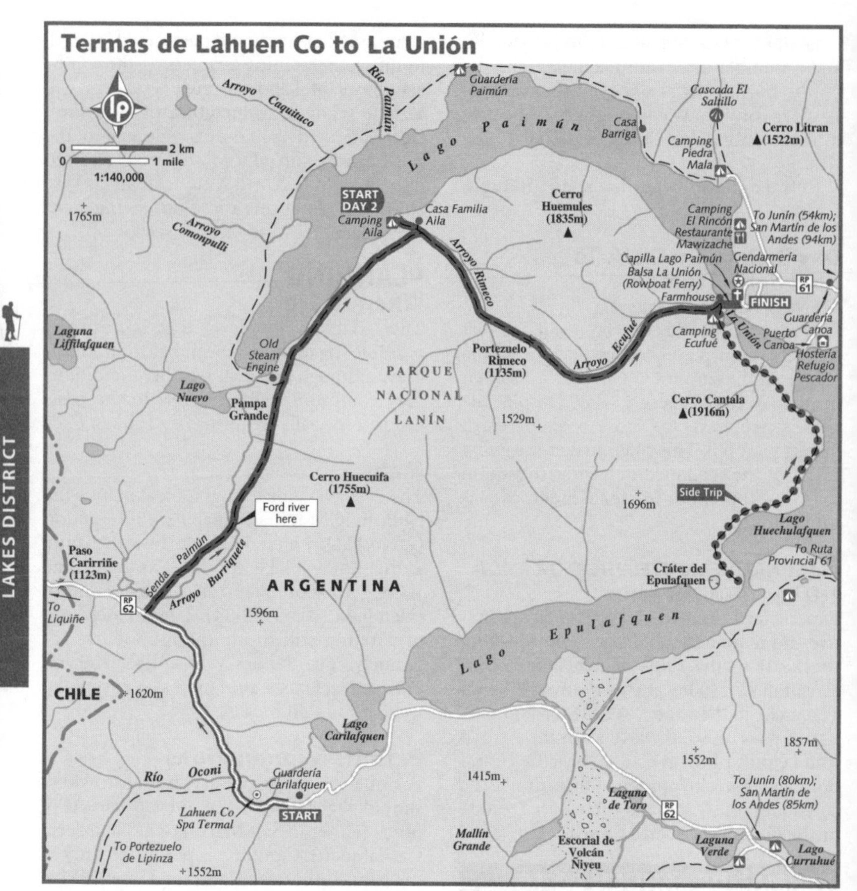

los Andes (p128) via Ruta Provincial 62 (which continues 7km over Paso Carirriñe into Chile). The last 20km of road is narrow and sometimes rough, but passable for non-4WD vehicles except in wet or snowy conditions.

Termas de Lahuen Co is not accessible by public transport, but throughout the summer season (from mid-December until mid-March) travel agencies in San Martín de los Andes run organized tours to both the Termas and to the eastern end of Lago Paimún (which make a stop at the chapel in La Unión, where the trek ends). Most agencies are quite happy to drop off trekkers by arrangement, but their normal practice is usually to charge trekkers the full price for each tour.

La Unión (finish)

The trek ends at the chapel in La Unión. La Unión is the name given to the picturesque narrows where Lago Paimún drains into Lago Huechulafquén, at the western end of Ruta Provincial 61.

Transporte Castelli (☎ 02972-491557) runs buses between La Unión and Junin de los Andes (AR$16), leaving the APN *guarderia* at 10.15am, 3pm and 7.45pm. La Unión-bound buses leave Junin de los Andes at 8am, 12.45pm and 5.30pm.

THE TREK

Day 1: Termas de Lahuen Co to Camping Aila

4–5¼ hours, 16km, 350m ascent/descent

From the Termas, follow the road across

THE QUILA CYCLE

Numerous species of native bamboo of the *Chusquea* genus grow in the moist, temperate Valdivian rainforests of Patagonia. Even for botanists, these species are difficult to differentiate, although most are commonly known by the Mapuche name of *quila*. An extremely vigorous and aggressive plant, *quila* often smothers smaller trees as it spreads out to monopolize sunnier sites in the forest.

Like bamboo world-over, *quila* flowers only at the end of its reproductive cycle. In a given area, up to 90% of the *quila* may be on the same cycle – approximately 25 years for most species – which results in big simultaneous blooms. These events are a party for mice and rats, which thrive from gorging on this nutritious fruit, causing rodent population booms. Once their food source is exhausted, the rodents leave the forest for surrounding farms and villages. Later, dry canes present a fire hazard that lasts for many years.

Quila can barely survive in a mature, closed rainforest because too little sunlight reaches the ground, yet its regrowth is particularly vigorous after fires, which destroy the shade of the forest canopy and release nutrients. This has led some botanists to theorise that *quila* may actually have evolved its die-back cycle as a way of 'provoking' fires, in order to create new openings in the forest.

the **Río Oconi** uphill through lush, tall rain forest to where the **Senda Paimún** (GPS 39° 47.821 S, 71° 39.222 W) departs on your right after one to 1¼ hours. Quite overgrown, the path drops directly northeast to ford the very small **Arroyo Burriquete**, then continues smoothly downvalley (often on an old road) to recross the stream (via a huge fallen tree trunk) after 45 minutes to one hour. Views are few apart from glimpses of the bald ridgetops around Cerro Huecuifa up to your right, but trekking is pleasant through mixed stands of *ñirre*, araucaria, *lenga* or *raulí* with a – largely dead – *quila* understorey (see boxed text).

Continue on through the forest to reach **Pampa Grande** – cleared farmland that is gradually regenerating. Guided by occasional blue or yellow markings where stock trails confuse the route, head along the right (eastern) side of these scrubby meadows to encounter a rusted old locomotive (once used to power a local sawmill) near the southeastern corner of **Lago Paimún**, one to 1¼ hours from the second stream crossing.

The track climbs rightward, passing below a square of living poplars (the former site of a farmhouse) before it begins an undulating traverse along Lago Paimún's southeastern side, where pink *mutisias* and orange *amancays* grow.

Do not descend at a small sloping shelf dotted with *calafate* and rose bushes (from where there are the first clear views across the lake to Cerro Caquituco and ahead to the stunning glacier-capped southwest face of Volcán Lanín), but contour directly along the slope, eventually reaching another *pampa* (about an hour from the old locomotive) that features a lone araucaria. Continue straight another 10 minutes until you see a sign marked 'camping' pointing left toward the lake.

You can then either short-cut down left across cattle pastures (in places infested by *pega-pega*, whose annoying prickly seeds attach to clothing) to reach **Camping Aila** on the lake shore, 1¼ to 1½ hours from the old locomotive, or continue a short way on to **Arroyo Rimeco** and follow the stream's left (west) bank down, which takes five to 10 minutes longer.

The idyllic campsite (AR$5) sits under araucarias beside a tiny beach, from where you can admire Volcán Lanín's red alpenglow.

Day 2: Camping Aila to La Unión

2¼–2¾ hours, 10km, 255m ascent/descent

Follow a trail up the stream past a short turn-off that crosses to the **house of Don Aila**, whose family established this small farm in the 1940s, before beginning a steeper southeastward ascent. The gradient eases as you head through a series of pretty tussock-grass meadows among low *ñirres* to cross the now tiny **Arroyo Rimeco**. Climb gently across – probably without noticing it – the broad, flat, forested saddle of **Portezuelo Rimeco** (around 1135m), one to 1¼ hours from the lake shore. Virtually the only views around here are of black

Magellanic woodpeckers tapping about the highland *lenga* forest (where the *quila* understorey has also largely died back).

The path dips gradually through mature stands of araucarias, where wild pigs plough up the ground as they forage for *piñones*, then traverses the valley's right (southern) slope well above the rushing Arroyo Ecufué, opposite Cerro Huemules. Descend more steeply through *coigüe* forest into little meadows (frequented by mountain *caracaras* spying small prey) under the rugged ridges of Cerro Cantala. Views emerge of the southern face of Volcán Lanín. Finally, the route switchbacks down to arrive at a **farmhouse** on the west side of **La Unión**, 1¼ to 1½ hours from Portezuelo Rimeco.

From here, a worthwhile 18km, four- to five-hour side trip leads south around the shore of Lago Huechulafquén to **Cráter del Epulafquen**, a tiny extinct volcano.

Near the farmhouse on Lago Paimún's western shore is the rustic but popular **Camping Ecufué** (camping per person AR$10), without facilities. The owners run the Balsa La Union 'ferry', and will row you across the 50m-wide narrow for AR$8 per person, including pack.

On the eastern shore of La Unión, you can summon the ferry by ringing the makeshift gong beside the picnic area, about 200m south of a rather incongruous Austrian-style chapel and **Gendarmería Nacional** post. Near here, a road turn-off goes 3km north past **Restaurante Mawizache**, serving quality meals, and **Camping El Rincón** (camping per person AR$16), which has no facilities, to **Camping Piedra Mala** (camping per person AR$16) on a black-sand beach.

At nearby Puerto Canoa is an APN *guardería* and the **Hostería Refugio Pescador** (☎ 02972-491132; r with full board AR$315 per person).

PARQUE NACIONAL PUYEHUE

Volcán Puyehue (2236m) blew its top the day after southern Chile's major earthquake in 1960, turning a large chunk of dense, humid evergreen forest into a stark landscape of sand dunes and lava rivers. Situated to the east of the Chilean provincial city of Osorno, Parque Nacional Puyehue (pooh-**yay**-way) consists of 1070 sq km of forested wilderness stretching from the eastern shores of Lago Puyehue and Lago Rupanco as far as the Chile–Argentina frontier. Its Mapuche name translates as 'place of the *puye*', after a small native fish abundant in the freshwater lakes and rivers of the Lakes District.

Volcán Puyehue and a fascinating broad volcanic plateau stretching out to its northwest are the park's central features. The volcano has remained dormant since the 1960 eruption, and vulcanologists suspect that the center of geothermal activity may be shifting north to nearby Volcán Carrán, a much younger and lower volcano that has erupted a number of times in recent decades. The combination of intense volcanic activity and high precipitation levels gives rise to numerous hot springs, including Chile's premier spa resort, Aguas Calientes/Termas de Puyehue at the park's western extremity. There are also numerous other small, undeveloped thermal springs in the area.

ENVIRONMENT

Luxuriant temperate rainforest – the most species-rich ecosystem found anywhere in the Lakes District – blankets the slopes surrounding Volcán Puyehue and Volcán Casablanca. The chief botanical features of these so-called Valdivian forests are several southern beech species, the three *maňíos* as well as *ulmo* and fragrant *tepa*. *Tineo*, which has attractive fernlike branchlets with serrated opposing leaves, is also common, and there are even examples of the coniferous alerce and Guaitecas cypress. The often very thick forest understorey nurtures species such as the *chilco* – the progenitor of countless fuchsia cultivars grown in gardens throughout the world – whose nectar attracts the green-backed firecrown, a tiny hummingbird.

Half a dozen or so species of the genus *Baccharis* grow as small upright bushes that produce fluffy, pale-yellowish flowers, including the *pañil*. Bushes of *murta*, whose five-petalled, bell-shaped, pinkish-white flowers develop into yummy edible red berries in March, are found at the edge of forest clearings.

The flowering trees and shrubs support an abundance of insects. Two native beetles are the beautiful, multicolored *coleóptero* and the carnivorous *peorro*, a large carabid whose black, shell-like abdomen has a luminescent, reddish-green sheen. The *peorro* crawls about tree trunks sniffing out ants and other tiny prey. Also remarkable is the *neuroptera*, a well-camouflaged predatory insect with pale-green wings that resemble the leaves of *quila*. One extraordinary butterfly is *Eroessa chilensis*, a living fossil whose evolutionary development has remained almost static for millions of years; it is found in close association with the thorny *tayu*, or *palo blanco*, an ancient tree species that has also changed little over time.

Often seen in the park is the house wren, known locally as the *chercán*, which has a yellow underbody and coffee-colored, black-striped wings and tail. Also quite common is the austral thrush, which migrates up from the Pacific coast to spend the summer foraging for insects, seeds and berries in the rainforests of Puyehue. It has a brownish head and wings, a white breast and its beak and legs are yellow. The black-winged ground dove, or *tórtol cordillerana*, lives in the forests of the montane zone above 600m.

The less conspicuous mammalian wildlife includes the vizcacha, *monito del monte* (mouse oopossum), pudu, puma and the small, grey Azara's fox.

CLIMATE

The park's proximity to the high mountains along the continental divide produces a very wet climate, even by the standards of the southern Lakes District. Precipitation levels start at around 4000mm annually in Anticura and Aguas Calientes on Puyehue's western edge, rising progressively towards the east. At elevations above 1000m, winter snows begin to accumulate after May, when skiing is possible at the alpine resort of Antillanca on Volcán Casablanca. By early summer (December) snow cover is mostly confined to areas above 2000m, although large wind-blown drifts remain in many places. The temperature averages 14°C in summer and 5°C in winter.

ACCESS TOWN

See Osorno (p126).

BAÑOS DE CAULLE

Duration 4 days
Distance 50km
Difficulty moderate
Start/Finish Anticura
Nearest Town Osorno
Transport bus
Summary A marvellous trek to a thermal field with fumaroles, geysers and undeveloped hot springs on a high, barren volcanic plateau.

This trek takes you into a stark, but spectacular landscape of dunelike ridges of pumice and enormous black lava flows to the northwest of Volcán Puyehue, where steaming fumaroles (volcanic steam vents) break through the ground in places, depositing sulfurous crystals over the bare earth. Geysers gush out among pools of perpetually boiling water and bubbling mud pits, and thermal springs provide naturally heated bathing high above the tree line.

PLANNING

Although described below as an out-and-back route, this trek can be done as a circuit via the Ruta de los Americanos or as a one-way traverse by continuing north to Riñinahue (see Alternative Finish: Riñinahue, p93).

When to Trek

The trek can be done from December to mid-April, although this can vary somewhat depending on seasonal (snow) conditions and the impact of this on access into the area.

Maps

Two Chilean IGM 1:50,000 maps cover this trek: *Volcán Puyehue* (Section H, No 27) and *Riñinahue* (Section H, No 17), but do not show the route of the trek. Fundo El Caulle has produced a quality 1:40,000 – not 1:50,000 as it claims – map based on the IGM maps (although it does not show grid coordinates), which is available at the El Caulle entrance.

Permits & Regulations

Permits are not required, but all trekking parties should register at Conaf's Guardería Anticura before setting out.

See also Fundo El Caulle (below).

GETTING TO/FROM THE TREK

Anticura (start/finish)

The trek starts and finishes in Anticura. In summer, Expreso Lago Puyehue, at the company's terminal at the eastern end of Mercado Municipal in Osorno, runs two daily buses to/from Anticura (CH$4500, 1½ hours). These leave Osorno at 10.30am and 3pm, and return at 12.10pm and 4.30pm. International buses running from Osorno's main bus terminal, via Paso Puyehue to Bariloche, will normally carry passengers travelling only as far as Anticura (or back) if there are spare seats.

THE TREK

Day 1: Anticura to Refugio El Caulle

3¼–4½ hours, 10.5km, 1070m ascent

After signing in at the *guardería*, walk for 25 to 30 minutes northwest along the highway and across the Río Golgol bridge to reach the entrance gate to **Fundo El Caulle** (See boxed text, below), where trekkers must sign in and pay an entry fee. Here, you can also buy maps and basic supplies (including homemade bread and cheese).

> ## FUNDO EL CAULLE
>
> The start and finish of the Baños de Caulle trek leads through **Fundo El Caulle** (www.elcaulle.com). A peculiarity of land ownership in Chile, the area of this 270-sq-km private property overlaps extensively with national park territory. El Caulle now operates mainly as an ecotourism business and runs regular guided (especially horse-riding) trips in the Puyehue area.
>
> At the El Caulle entrance gate on Ruta 215, 2km west of Anticura, trekkers pay a fee of CH$10.000 with CH$3.000 refunded once they have packed out their trash. As El Caulle built and/or maintains most of the infrastructure (including tracks, picnic tables, signposts and a free *refugio*), this payment is not unreasonable. The complex includes a high-end restaurant.

> ## WARNING
>
> The trek crosses an exposed and unvegetated plateau well above the tree line where it is surprisingly easy to become disoriented during bad weather or misty conditions. The loose pumice is shifted constantly by wind, rain and snow, making the trodden path harder to follow. Wooden stakes marking the route are often pushed over by the elements – please firmly re-erect any fallen marker stakes you encounter.

Head along the dirt road directly past a (left) trail turn-off (signposted 'Miradores') near the new **hostería**, before turning around to the right through the pastures past the El Caulle administration building. The road passes a (right) trail turn-off (signposted 'Saltos del Río Golgol') to reach a trail junction immediately before **Campamento Los Ciervos**, 15 to 20 minutes from the entrance gate. There are idyllic campsites with tables and fireplaces here on grassy meadows by a small stream.

Turn left and climb gently along a rougher bulldozed track through the forest to reach a large flat clearing scattered with blackberry bushes and fringed by *ulmos*, 20 to 25 minutes on. Follow white-tipped wooden posts past **Campamento de Perdida** to briefly glimpse a gushing waterfall in the rainforest up to the left before you cut right into the trees.

A foot track leads up steadily northeast to cross a trickling streamlet under high cliffs, continuing up across a second streamlet (the last water until the end of Day 1) after one to 1½ hours. Contour briefly around eroded gullies before beginning a steep, strenuous and sustained ascent over slopes of unstable volcanic earth. Make a final climb through pleasant, open *lenga* forest to emerge onto grassy alpine meadows, and sidle 300m ahead to arrive at **Refugio El Caulle** (also called Refugio Volcán Puyehue), 1¼ to 1¾ hours after crossing the second streamlet.

The *refugio* (GPS 40° 36.904 S, 72° 08.525 W) stands at the tree line, just under 1400m, in a very scenic spot at the base of Volcán Puyehue. This new but very basic hut sleeps

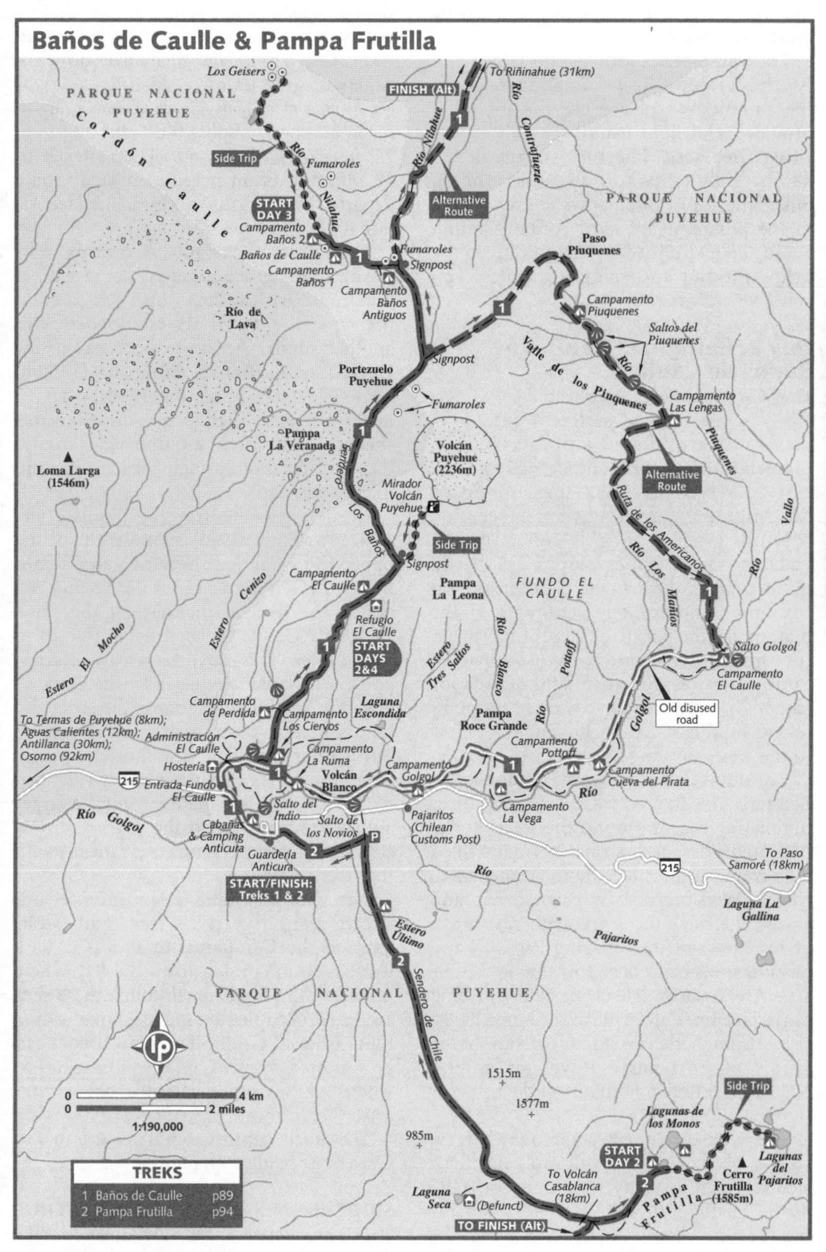

LAKES DISTRICT

up to 16 people and has a wood stove (the nearby wood shed is regularly stocked by Fundo El Caulle).

The **campsites** (with picnic tables and benches) receive heavy usage throughout the summer, so please use the pit toilet provided and light campfires only in existing fireplaces. The tiny stream in the nearby gully tends to flow underground, but higher up it often stays running. Due to the possibility of fecal contamination, avoid collecting water from anywhere below the hut and campsites unless you can properly treat it.

Day 2: Refugio El Caulle to Baños de Caulle

3¼–4½ hours, 14.5km, 350m ascent

Head to the right of a stream gully over grassy meadows dotted with daisy bushes, following staked cairns moderately northeast to reach the track turn-off up to the Mirador Volcán Puyehue (see side trip, this page) at roughly 1600m on the volcano's bare upper slopes, 35 to 45 minutes from the *refugio*. From here, you can enjoy an excellent panorama of the major volcanic peaks to the south: Osorno (the magnificent cone to the southwest), Puntiagudo, Casablanca and Tronador (the high, irregular, ice-covered mountain to the southeast). Lago Puyehue is below to the west.

Continue left (northwest) along the **Sendero Los Baños**, which makes a long, undulating ascent around the steep, rocky mountainsides, across ravines (many filled with snow until late summer) and small ridges. Well-marked by cairned bamboo stakes, the track turns gradually northeast, giving views of the amazing Río de Lava, an enormous black lava flow that looks like a petrified glacier. Head on below puffing fumaroles on Volcán Puyehue's northwest side, through the broad, snow-smothered saddle of **Portezuelo Puyehue** (around 1730m), 1½ to two hours from the mirador (lookout) turn-off.

The route dips northeast into the barren, rolling plateau on the volcano's northern side to reach a sturdy steel signpost (GPS 40° 33.545 S, 72° 07.439 W) at 1635m marking the fork where Ruta de los Americanos departs right (see Alternative Route, p93), 15 to 20 minutes on.

Continue left along the Sendero Los Baños, which leads gently down slightly northwest (towards Volcánes Mocho and Choshuenco in the distance), over dunelike slopes of grey pumice, skirting the right (east) side of a deep, green stream gully to reach another signpost (GPS 40° 32.526 S, 72° 07.556 W) at around 1525m after 25 to 30 minutes. From here, a multiday route departs right (north) to Riñinahue (see Alternative Finish, p93).

The Sendero Los Baños now turns westward, winding around past some extinct fumaroles. It then cuts down left to cross the stream gully at its confluence with another similar stream a short way below **Campamento Baños Antiguos** (1430m; GPS 40° 32.374 S, 72° 08.117 W) after 15 to 20 minutes. There are secluded, semi-sheltered campsites just upstream around these former hot springs (which dried up many years ago).

Head northwest over the desolate terrain, crossing a (cold) side stream of the upper Río Nilahue to reach **Campamento Baños 1** (GPS 40° 32.113 S, 72° 08.964 W), beside the river at the start of the small **Baños de Caulle** thermal field after 20 to 25 minutes. This tiny, flat area has a few poorly sheltered campsites by the track. A dug-out 'bath' hidden among the ferns and *nalcas* here is often uncomfortably tepid but bathers regulate the hotter springs emerging directly from the rocky river bed by building shallow pools. (Avoid a larger and very warm hot spring slightly downstream, however, as it mixes erratically with the river water.)

The path continues a few minutes upstream along the river's true right (west) bank to the **Campamento Baños 2**, by a warm stream coming from the left. There is better camping here, although these sites are often occupied by guided horse-riding tours from El Caulle. This side stream can be followed for five or 10 minutes up to where various other bathable hot springs arise.

The track continues northward to Los Geisers (see side trip, p93).

SIDE TRIP: MIRADOR VOLCÁN PUYEHUE

2½–3½ hours return, 3.5km, 630m ascent/descent

This side trip continues from the junction above the *refugio* signposted simply 'Crater' and cuts up northeast to the left of a spur. The most popular route climbs (virtually straight up) across snowdrifts in a minor basin, then curves around to the left to gain a ridge leading to the highest point (2236m) on the volcano's rim overlooking the ice-filled crater. Snow-corniced cliffs drop away into the crater, so be careful where you tread. From the rim there is a superb view of the surrounding countryside, with the double summit of Volcán Choshuenco now also visible towards the northeast, as well as Lago Rupanco to the southwest.

SIDE TRIP: LOS GEISERS

3–4 hours return, 11km, 120m ascent/descent

This easy trek to a small field of bubbling mud tubs, effervescent pools and geysers is a must.

From the Baños de Caulle, trek a short way upstream along the true right (west) bank of the Río Nilahue, briefly following then crossing a side stream. The route heads northwest through a pumice gully, before cutting across a sparse plain to make a (sometimes knee-high) wade through a larger spring-fed side stream, 25 to 30 minutes from Campamento Baños 2.

The main path – evidently routed more for the convenience of horse-riders – crosses and recrosses the now very small Río Nilahue several times as it leads on upstream past fumaroles on the slopes over to the right. A less-prominent track saves trekkers either time or wet feet by continuing along the true right (ie west) bank until crossing at the shallow, uppermost ford (GPS 40° 30.741 S, 72° 09.943 W), after 20 to 25 minutes.

Ascend away right (northwest), where the river emerges in several clustered cold springs to the top of a minor ridge overlooking an undrained depression normally filled by a shallow, murky lake. Follow the ridge rightward (north) then cut down to the far end of the boggy basin. There, make a quick, steep climb to the right high above the lake, continuing northeast to a point (GPS 40° 29.770 S, 72° 09.556 W) directly above the steaming, sulfurous thermal field of **Los Geisers**, 45 minutes to one hour from the final upper Río Nilahue crossing. For your own safety, and to preserve the delicate formations, be careful where you tread while exploring the area. Return via the same route.

Days 3 & 4: Baños de Caulle to Anticura

5½–8 hours, 25km

Retrace your steps as on Day 2 and Day 1. Fitter and faster parties can opt to do both sections in one long day.

A worthwhile short trek from Anticura goes to **Salto del Indio**, a churning, 6m-high waterfall on the Río Golgol (where legend has it that a Mapuche fleeing slavery in a gold mine eluded the colonial Spaniards by hiding behind the cascading curtain of water).

ALTERNATIVE ROUTE: VIA RUTA DE LOS AMERICANOS

3 days, 49km

Although it is 24km longer, the Ruta de los Americanos is an excellent alternative to backtracking via Refugio El Caulle. (It is also more interesting and challenging than the other alternative route to Riñinahue.) The route receives only light use and is not always well marked, so careful navigation and route-finding are needed. Fundo El Caulle is establishing well-spaced campsites along the way.

Retrace your steps (as per the description Day 2) to the signposted trail junction just northeast of Portezuelo Puyehue, then head northeast via a narrow, snowy gap and a broad ridge to **Paso Piuquenes** (around 1425m). The route then drops southward along the western side of the Río Piuquenes, climbing high above the **Saltos del Piuquenes** (several waterfalls spilling over escarpments), before turning southwest to cross a series of stream gullies on the tundra-covered eastern slopes of Volcán Puyehue.

Watch for where a foot track enters the largely dead upper scrub (GPS 40° 35.537 S, 72° 03.711 W) and descend through the forest to meet a disused road on the northern side of the Río Golgol. The old road continues west through superb tall rainforest that gradually gives way to cow pastures before you reach **Campamento Los Ciervos** (see Day 1).

ALTERNATIVE FINISH: RIÑINAHUE

3 days, 36km

This easier alternative is more straightforward, although generally less scenic, than the Ruta de los Americanos. From Baños de Caulle retrace your steps (as on Day 2) to the signposted trail junction east of Campamento Baños Antiguos, then head northward between two branches of the Río Nilahue. The route drops steeply right to cross the eastern branch before climbing to join a disused road. Continue along a broad ridge separating the Río Nilahue from the Río Contrafuerte, before fording and refording the latter river several times due to recent landslides. The often muddy trail continues through the wet rainforest to meet a rough road shortly before reaching a farmhouse (the owner here charges a 'transit fee' of CH$2000 – watch out for aggressive dogs).

The road steadily improves as it crosses the Río Nilahue (not far above its confluence with the Río Contrafuerte) and the Río Los Venados, passing dairy farms and patches of forest. Campsites can be found in attractive meadows scattered with wild blackberry bushes. Proceed past the picturesque Laguna Pocura, from where there are daily buses to Riñinahue. Otherwise, continue through the scattered settlement of Quirrasco to intersect with the Futrono–Lago Ranco road, then turn left and head a short way on to Riñinahue. This village has two hosterías and several daily buses to the town of Lago Ranco. At Riñinahue, free **camping** is possible on the southeastern shore of Lago Ranco – ask permission before camping on private property.

PAMPA FRUTILLA

Duration 2 days
Distance 44km
Difficulty easy–moderate
Start/Finish Anticura
Nearest Town Osorno
Transport bus

Summary A straightforward out-and-back trek up to one of the Chilean Lakes District's most extensive *coirones*, or natural highland pastures.

Pampa Frutilla, whose lowest point lies at just over 1200m, is an attractive subalpine plateau at the northeastern foot of Volcán Casablanca. Its Spanish name (meaning 'strawberry field') refers to the native Chilean strawberry, or *quellén*, found among the tussocky grasses of Pampa Frutilla. These scrumptuous little red berries begin to ripen in late January.

The trek follows an old road originally built by the Chilean military in the late 1970s during the period of confrontation with Argentina. Now quite impassable to motorized vehicles, the road forms a section of the Sendero de Chile, or the Chilean Trail (see boxed text, p35) – a planned trail extension will eventually take it from Pampa Frutilla up to Volcán Casablanca.

PLANNING

When to Trek

The trek can normally be done between late November and late April. In January, *tábanos* (native horseflies) are likely to be out in force at lower elevations, but you will leave most of them behind as you climb through the damp, dim forest.

Maps

Two Chilean IGM 1:50,000 maps, *Volcán Puyehue* (Section H, No 27) and *Volcán Casablanca* (Section H, No 36) cover the trek.

Permits & Regulations

Trekkers are required only to sign in before they depart and sign out after they return. Although Pampa Frutilla receives a moderate number of visitors, practice 'leave-no-trace' principles to keep it pristine.

GETTING TO/FROM THE TREK

See Anticura (p124).

THE TREK

Day 1: Anticura to Lagunas de los Monos

7-8½ hours, 22km, 875m ascent

After signing in at the Guardería Anticura, enter the complex on foot, passing the sign for Salto Pudu on your right and bearing slight left to join the trail signposted 'Sendero de Chile.' The 2.5km section goes east, parallel to Ruta 215 for 40 to 50 minutes to a hanging footbridge. Cross the bridge and head left 50m to join the main trail. The left branch goes to a parking area on Ruta 215 (GPS 40° 39.679 S, 72° 08.634 W) near waterfall **Salto de los Novios**; go right for Pampa Frutilla.

Continue along the old road (not passable for vehicles) fringed by stinging nettles, elephant-ear *nalcas* and red-flowered *escallonia* bushes. The track leads southeast, rising only very gently up through moist forest of *tiaca* and fragrant *tepa*. After one to 1½ hours you reach an open grassy field offering views of the snowy tops of Volcán Casablanca to the south as well as to Volcán Puyehue back north – a welcome respite from the temperate jungle. Ideal **campsites** can be found here.

Cross the **Estero Ultimo** as you re-enter the forest – this stream is the last water source for some time – and begin a steady but moderate climb through well-spaced stands of common *coigüe* with a dense understorey of fuchsias and *quila*. In places, the scarlet flowers of creeping *estrellitas* light up the dark, mossy trunks, but there are no views until the track leads up under a jagged ridge over to your left. The track rises into stands of *coigüe de Magallanes* that gradually give way to highland *lenga*, passing an unmarked turn-off (shortly after the route makes a rightward curve) that goes off southwest down to *refugio* ruins by the aptly named **Laguna Seca**, two to 2½ hours from Estero Ultimo.

The old road cuts up around to the left, skirting the side of the ridge as it ascends through *ñirre* scrub into grassy rolling tundra dotted with *chaura*. There are great vistas southeast along the wild, densely forested basin of the Río Negro as far as the mighty Monte Tronador massif. Make your way around eastward across a broad pass (1350m), before short-cutting down left to rejoin the old road. There are new views across the alpine meadows of **Pampa Frutilla** immediately below to Cerro Frutilla and further southeast to the remarkable horn of Cerro Pantojo.

Continue left across a normally dry, eroding stream bed to reach scenic, semi-sheltered **campsites** at the forest fringe by the upper lake of the **Lagunas de los Monos**, two to 2½ hours from the Laguna Seca turnoff. The larger, lower (northeast) lake can be reached in five minutes by cutting over in a northeasterly direction; its southeastern shore is suitable for **camping**. Pairs of Andean gulls frequent these lakes.

SIDE TRIP: LAGUNAS DEL PAJARITOS

2–3 hours return, 10km, 120m ascent

From the upper of the Lagunas de los Monos, cut 1km southeast across the open meadows, then turn around left and follow a narrow extended clearing within the *lenga* forest (GPS 40° 44.774 S, 72° 02.027 W) until it ends. Here, pick up the sometimes slightly overgrown track leading northeast over a crest to reach a small stream (which drains into the lower of the Lagunas de los Monos), crossing and recrossing the stream as it heads up into an eroding, gravelly canyon. At a small, isolated stand of *lengas*, cut up steeply rightward then traverse well above the stream, past where it divides into several branches to a ridgetop. From the ridgetop the nearby Cerro Frutilla (1585m) can be climbed in around two hours return.

The route skirts around to the left into a minor pass (around 1335m) covered with *brecillo*, 45 minutes to one hour from Lagunas de los Monos. Head around left onto a scoria embankment, then cut down southeast through the forest to reach the **Lagunas del Pajaritos** after 25 to 30 minutes. These beautiful aqua-blue lakes offer excellent **camping** on grassy meadows (which extend well to the southeast of the lakes). Return via the same route.

Day 2: Lagunas de los Monos to Anticura

5–6½ hours, 22km, 875m descent

Retrace your steps as on Day 1.

ALTERNATIVE FINISH: ANTILLANCA VIA VOLCÁN CASABLANCA

6½–9 hours, 18km, 1020m ascent

This difficult traverse across Volcán Casablanca is suited only to trekkers with excellent navigational and route-finding abilities. Before January, an ice axe (and perhaps also crampons) is advisable.

Return to the small pass above Pampa Frutilla (see Day 1), then cut down southwest through the light forest and across the uppermost streamlets of the Río Negro basin. The route climbs westward via open volcanic ridges to the summit of Volcán Casablanca, whose views do not disappoint. The descent normally leads via Crater Rayhuén (a small side crater) then along a dirt road to reach the tiny ski village of **Antillanca** (www.skiantillanca.cl, in Spanish) on the volcano's western slopes, 18km by road from the hot-springs resort of Aguas Calientes. In summer, you can stay at Antillanca's **Refugio Buschmann** (contact in Osorno; ☎ 65-235114; s/d from CH$17,000/24,000).

Alternatively, trekkers can follow an 11km trail from Crater Rayhuén northwest via Conaf's rustic Refugio Bertin to Aguas Calientes.

PARQUE NACIONAL VICENTE PÉREZ ROSALES

Featuring a great emerald lake ringed by steep Valdivian rainforest and volcanoes, Chile's oldest national park protects 251,000 hectares. The vegetation is lush and the scenery stunning. The largest park in the Chilean Lakes District, it reaches the Argentine border, connecting with Parque Nacional Nahuel Huapi. These two parks, together with the adjoining Parque Nacional Puyehue, form the largest tract of trans-Andean wilderness in the Lakes District. The park's name pays homage to the Chilean businessman and mining magnate Vicente Pérez Rosales, who was also an accomplished writer and the founder of Puerto Montt.

Lago Todos Los Santos, at only 184m above sea level, is the park's lowest point. This 221-sq-km lake is ringed by some of the highest and most prominent volcanic peaks of the southern Lakes District: the snowtipped volcanoes Osorno (2652m), Puntiagudo (2190m) and Monte Tronador (3554m). Apart from Lago Pirehueico, some distance to the north, Lago Todos Los Santos is the only major low-level lake on the Chilean side that stretches deep into the Andes.

The lake lies deep within a glacial trough, not at the termination of a former glacier's path (like nearby Lago Llanquihue). Immediately following the last ice age, Lago Todos Los Santos was joined with Lago Llanquihue in an enormous body of water, but subsequent eruptions of Volcán Osorno and Volcán Calbuco divided them into separate lakes. Apart from the access road to Petrohué at its outlet and the isolated road between Peulla and Puerto Frías at its eastern tip, no roads penetrate its wild, densely forested shoreline.

Todos los Santos, which means 'All Saints Lake', was christened by early-17th-century Jesuit missionaries, who took this route from Chilé to Argentina, seeking an Andean passage to form missions with hostile Mapuche tribes around Lago Nahuel Huapi.

ENVIRONMENT

The heavy rainfall and mild weather of Vicente Pérez Rosales support dense, lush Valdivian rainforest whose predominant trees are *coigüe*, *tepa*, *mañío*, *ulmo*, *canelo*, *olivillo* (or *teque*), *lingue* and *avellano*. Less common tree species include the *lleuque*, a podocarp that grows on moist slopes above 600m. The *lleuque*'s small yellow fruit have the appearance of tiny lemons. The *maqui* is a very small tree typically found in stands (so-called *machales*) at the edge of the forest. It has oval leaves on a reddish stem and produces seedy edible purple berries, from which the Mapuche made an alcoholic drink called *tecu*.

The rainforest understorey harbors great botanical diversity. The park is an important refuge for the *ciprés enano*, an extremely rare dwarf member of the podocarp family that is almost identical to the pygmy pine of New Zealand. This tiny, prostrate conifer grows in montane swamps, often largely hidden by other nearby plants. More common is the *quilquil*, a species of tree fern typically found growing in stream gullies. Its palm-like appearance earned it the common name of *palmilla*. In small clearings you'll find several species of *ñipa*, recognisable by their red or pinkish tubular flowers that end in five out-turned petals. Found along streams or wetlands, the distinctive *chaquihue* (also called *polizonte*) produces bright-red, rounded, podlike flowers on its large, leafy twigs.

The park's lush vegetation makes it a veritable paradise for birds, of which parrots and nectar-eating hummingbirds are especially plentiful. The *choroy*, a large green parakeet most easily identified by its long curved beak, dwells in these forests. The *run run* is a species of tyrant flycatcher that typically frequents wetlands, lake shores and riverbanks; apart from its yellow beak the male is black, while the female has a coffee-colored upper body and a pale-yellow breast with dark longitudinal stripes.

The *yeco*, also called *bigua*, a large black cormorant common throughout the moist coastal areas of southern South America, often visits Lago Todos Los Santos, to feed on its abundant fish and small amphibians. This large waterbird is an excellent diver and can often be seen perched on a log or rock with its wings outstretched.

The tiny brown *monito del monte*, or mouse oopossum, inhabits these temperate rainforests along with its marsupial cousin, the *rincholesta*. The *rincholesta* is a rare nocturnal insectivore that was only discovered by science – although the indigenous Mapuche people certainly knew about it – in the 1950s. Other mammals common to the forests of Vicente Pérez Rosales include the pudu, *coipo*, *huiña*, Patagonian red fox and puma.

Numerous native fish live in the park's lakes and rivers. The main species are *pejerrey*, *puyen*, Patagonian perch and *peladilla*. More plentiful are introduced salmon and trout. The peculiar Darwin's frog (*sapo partero* as it's known in Spanish or midwife frog), first zoologically classified by Charles Darwin, also inhabits the park's ponds, lakes and rivers. After fertilization, the male frog incubates and hatches the eggs inside his own mouth, from which the fully developed froglets – not tadpoles – emerge after three weeks.

CLIMATE

In this extremely wet coastal climate, annual rainfall averages 2500mm at Ensenada on the park's western extreme, and rises steadily towards the east. Precipitation levels around Paso de Pérez Rosales on the Chile–Argentina frontier reach over 5000mm – the highest levels in the Lakes District. Moderated by the lake's low elevation and proximity to the Pacific coast, average annual temperatures around the shore of Lago Todos Los Santos are a relatively high 12°C. The hottest summer days rarely exceed 30°C. Conditions are less mild at higher altitudes in the surrounding ranges, where winters regularly bring heavy snowfalls.

PLANNING

When to Trek

Unless you're planning to go above the tree line, treks in Parque Nacional Vicente Pérez Rosales can generally be done between early November and early May. The hot weather between mid-December and late January usually brings out the *tábanos*, which can be a particular nuisance in locations below the tree line.

Permits & Regulations

There are few restrictions on trekking in Parque Nacional Vicente Pérez Rosales. No permit is required but, where possible, inform the park authorities of your intended route and the names of all members in the party. There are a number of small enclaves of freehold land within the park, and although the trekking routes are public rights of way, trekkers should respect private property. Some recognized campsites are also on private land and an increasing number of property owners levy a small charge for camping. Wild camping is permitted, but use discretion when choosing your site.

ACCESS TOWN

See Petrohué (p127).

TERMAS DE CALLAO

Duration 3 days
Distance 40km
Difficulty easy
Start El Rincón
Finish El Poncho
Nearest Towns Petrohué, Osorno
Transport boat, bus
Summary Trek through dense temperate rainforest and farmland with volcano views and soak in a wooden hot tub on this traverse between two major lakes.

Relatively remote, Termas de Callao lies hidden behind Volcán Puntiagudo in the Valle Sin Nombre. These luxuriant natural hot springs sit just beside the small Río Sin Nombre, which flows into Lago Todos Los Santos. The forest banking the river is dotted with small farms. The trek reaches its highest point at a forested pass around 800m, then descends to finish along the shore of tranquil Lago Rupanco.

The trek generally follows horse trails kept in condition by the local inhabitants, and all larger streams are bridged. Along the central section of the route between the Termas de Callao and Laguna Los Quetros, however,

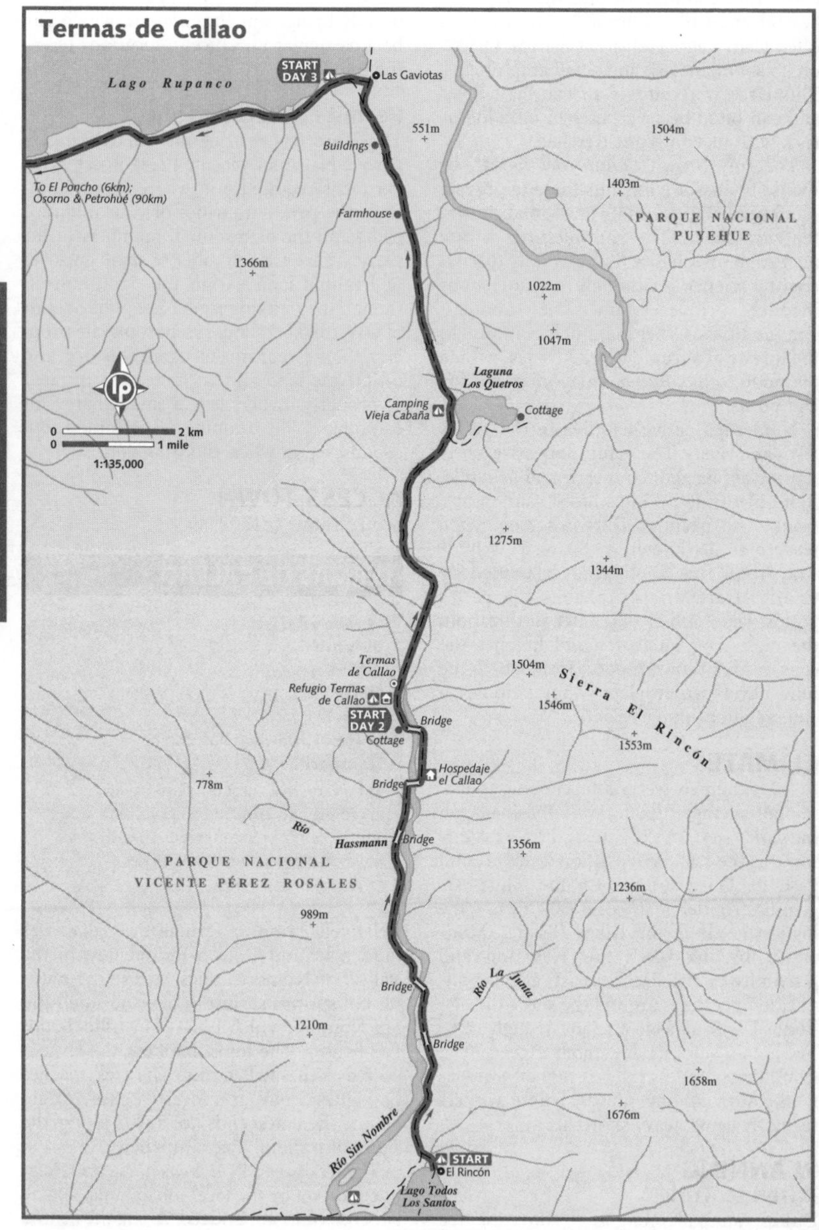
Termas de Callao
Lago Rupanco
START DAY 3
Las Gaviotas
551m
1504m
Buildings
1403m
To El Poncho (6km); Osorno & Petrohué (90km)
Farmhouse
PARQUE NACIONAL PUYEHUE
1366m
1022m
1047m
Laguna Los Quetros
Camping Vieja Cabaña
Cottage
0 2 km
0 1 mile
1:135,000
1275m
1344m
Termas de Callao
Refugio Termas de Callao
1504m
Sierra El Rincón
1546m
START DAY 2
Bridge
Cottage
1553m
Hospedaje el Callao
778m
Bridge
Río Hassmann
Bridge
1356m
PARQUE NACIONAL VICENTE PÉREZ ROSALES
1236m
989m
Bridge
Río La Junta
1210m
Bridge
1658m
1676m
Río Sin Nombre
START
El Rincón
Lago Todos Los Santos

fallen trees obscure the way in places, so careful route-finding is occasionally required. Throughout this trek, where the earth is composed of friable pumice, the path rapidly erodes to form deep trenches, revealing the history of previous local volcanic eruptions in the layers of the soil. In places where the trenches have become too deep the path has been rerouted or reinforced with logs.

Trekkers are strongly advised to walk in a south-to-north direction, as there is no reliable way of getting out from El Rincón (on the remote northern shore of Lago Todos Los Santos).

PLANNING

When to Trek

Because of their low elevation and relatively sheltered aspect, the Termas de Callao can be visited from late spring until late fall (late October to early May) when other walks may be out of condition. However, summer (December to February) is the best time to do the trek. An additional day could be spent enjoying the lovely valley around the springs.

What to Bring

There is only one area with lodging along the route. Although it is possible for fit and fast parties to do the trek without carrying a tent, this is not recommended.

Puerto Montt or Puerto Varas are the logical places to buy supplies before the trek. Farms along the trek often sell home-baked bread, honey and other produce.

Maps

The JLM *Mapas Ruta de los Jesuitas* map (No 15) includes a 1:50,000 (approximately) map of the Termas de Callao sector of Parque Nacional Vicente Pérez Rosales. It and the two Chilean IGM maps on which it appears to be based – *Volcán Casablanca* (Section H, No 36) and *Peulla* (Section H, No 44) – show the walking track but suffer from omissions and errors regarding the exact route.

GETTING TO/FROM THE TREK

El Rincón (start)

Trekkers must bus to Petrohué, then charter a boat to the trailhead. The trek begins at El Rincón (also known as Puerto Callao) in an inlet on the northern shore of Lago Todos Los Santos, about halfway across the lake.

BUS

You can get to Petrohué from Puerto Montt by catching a minibus to Puerto Varas on Lago Llanquihue – these leave throughout the day from the eastern end of Puerto Montt's main bus terminal (CH$1000, 30 minutes) – changing in Puerto Varas for Petrohué (CH$2000, one hour). In summer, buses run between Puerto Varas and Petrohué about every half hour from 8.30am to 6pm.

BOAT

In summer, boats wait for passengers at the dock in Petrohué. The starting price for a boat to El Rincón is CH$70,000, so try to find other trekkers to share the cost. The trip takes between one and two hours, depending on the type of boat as well as the direction and speed of the winds. It should also be possible to charter a boat to El Rincón from Peulla, a village on the lake's remote eastern shore. Remember, once you reach El Rincón the only way out is the trek described below.

El Poncho (finish)

The walk finishes at El Poncho, a small scattering of holiday houses on the southern shore of Lago Rupanco. Buses leave El Poncho for Osorno (CH$2300, 2½hours) at 6am Monday through Saturday and at 1pm on Sundays.

THE TREK

Day 1: El Rincón to Termas de Callao

3–4 hours, 12km

The boat lands on the sandy beach of El Rincón. Make your way uphill past the beach, through a clearing (a pleasant **campsite**), and over a minor crest with views of Lago Todos Los Santos. (You can also find good camping on the scenic flats where the Río Sin Nombre enters Lago Todos Los Santos, 15 to 20 minutes west around the lakeside via a good trail.) Continue through semicleared fields. A good horse track sidles down northward through *ulmo* forest above the **Río Sin Nombre**, which rushes through a deep gully on your left, to cross the **Río La Junta** side stream after 40 to 50 minutes. If you don't trust the rickety suspension bridge, wade the shallow water slightly downstream.

Follow the sometimes muddy path for 20 to 25 minutes to cross the Río Sin Nombre itself on another precarious suspension bridge and continue upstream. The path dips and rises along the river's steep-sided western bank before it climbs away to the left past a farm (with produce for sale) and crosses another suspension bridge over a large side stream, the **Río Hassmann**, after a further one to 1¼ hours. Here, the trail goes briefly left, upstream, then climbs back to the right and proceeds on through the rainforest. 'Termas' signs direct you through a bamboo-scattered clearing and back across the Río Sin Nombre to reach a farmhouse 35 to 45 minutes on.

The farmhouse **Hospedaje el Callao** (in Puerto Varas ☎ 065-252998; r per person with dinner and breakfast CH$16,000, lunch CH$7000) boasts full views of the majestic summit of Volcán Puntiagudo to the west. You can pick up the keys to the *refugio* and hot springs, and pay your dues, at the farmhouse. It may be wise to arrange to leave the keys at the *refugio* to save backtracking to the farm.

The route now leads along the eastern bank of the Río Sin Nombre, crossing once more before it passes an abandoned, shingled, wooden cottage and arrives after a final 30 to 40 minutes at **Termas de Callao** (camping per tent CH$3500, *refugio* per person CH$6000). This excellent hut, built from native timbers, stands on private land and has a wood stove, a sink, bamboo furniture and space for six people.

There is very attractive camping just below the *refugio*. The **thermal baths** (CH$2500) are just down by the river in a little shed with two tubs inside. The water is piping hot, moderated with a hose coming from the cold stream. The valley sits enclosed by high, densely rainforested granite peaks on either side, well-worth a day of exploring.

Day 2: Termas de Callao to Las Gaviotas

4–5¼ hours, 16km

From the *refugio* make your way up valley through scrubby pastures along the river's western bank before rising into the rainforest. Bear left at the second (probably dry) major side stream you come to, carefully following the route through an area of fallen trunks, then on through tiny grassy patches.

After 40 to 50 minutes the well-maintained path turns away from the Río Sin Nombre and begins climbing gently northwestward beside a cascading stream, through a forest of gnarled *mañío* and fragrant-leafed *tepa*.

Cross the stream and ascend along a steep spur through dense thickets of bamboo until the gradient eases, 50 minutes to 1¼ hours on. The path briefly follows the ridgetop northward through montane *coigüe* and *ulmo* forest, dropping down steeply to cross a stream, then climbing again, before it makes a proper descent northeast into fire-cleared pastures where the southwestern corner of **Laguna Los Quetros** comes into view.

Continue for 40 to 50 minutes around the lake's reedy western shore to reach **Camping Vieja Cabaña** (camping per tent CH$3500), which has a pit toilet, beside a small stand of alerce trees. There is a picturesque farm cottage on the opposite side of Laguna Los Quetros, which lies in a basin that drains underground through the porous volcanic soil. The lake and campsite are on private land attached to the cottage, and the owner rows across the lake to collect fees.

Follow the prominent horse track, in places massively reinforced with logs, up around the northwest side of the tranquil lake into the forest and over a low watershed. Make your way down beside a stream (a small tributary of the Río Gaviotas) towards the snowy cap of Volcán Casablanca. The path descends steadily through clearings, giving way to open hillsides, to pass the first farmhouse at the edge of a broad green bowl after 1¼ to 1½ hours. Horses, cattle and flocks of noisy black-necked ibis graze on these choice Lakes District pastures.

Skirt northwestward through a series of gates in the middle of the fields into a minor saddle high above Lago Rupanco. With the volcano and shimmering lake ahead of you, drop down past wooden cottages, neat vegetable gardens and a rural school to reach a trail fork on grassy slopes scattered with blackberry bushes after 30 to 40 minutes. Five minutes further down, the left-hand branch meets a wide track along the black-sand shore of **Lago Rupanco**, while the right-hand path goes down almost to the village of Las Gaviotas at the lake's southeastern corner.

Las Gaviotas has no accommodation or store, and there is no particular reason to go right into the village unless you need a public telephone, which it does have. There is a nice **campsite** (camping per tent CH$3000), with picnic tables and firewood provided, a 10- to 15-minute walk west, near where a stream enters the lake; a landowner collects the fee. Other camping possibilities exist along the black-sand beach a short way from where you meet Lago Rupanco.

Day 3: Las Gaviotas to El Poncho

2¼–2¾ hours, 12km

Follow the dark, sandy shore west through the front yards of lake-side holiday houses. The wide, graded track rises and dips around the often very steep banks of Lago Rupanco, past rustic shacks and through patches of forest fringed by blackberry bushes. Cross a large, dry gully and head up to the left, past the remains of a suspension footbridge, just before you come out above a lovely lakeside pasture after one to 1¼ hours.

The trail climbs away left over scrubby slopes high above the lake, bringing into view the bare volcanic ridges surrounding Volcán Puntiagudo to the south. Drop down behind more holiday houses around a broad tranquil bay, its western side now scarred by an unsightly road extension, to cross a major stream on a sturdy log bridge, 30 to 40 minutes on. On the far side of this bridge the dirt road begins. Follow this around the bay, past a *kiosco* (store) and across the Puente Río Blanco, then past the exclusive Bahía Escocia Fly Fishing Lodge, to reach the tiny settlement of **El Poncho** after a final 40 to 50 minutes. El Poncho itself has a small store and a bus stop but little else.

PARQUE NACIONAL NAHUEL HUAPI

With craggy ranges, deep forested valleys and big lakes, the great Parque Nacional Nahuel Huapi (nah-**well-wah**-pee) is the largest national park on either side of the northern Patagonian Andes. One of South America's finest climbing destinations, it lies to the west of the popular tourist hub of Bariloche in the Argentine Lakes District. Nahuel Huapi's rugged interior is accessible via an extensive network of well-maintained trails – as well as numerous rougher, unmarked routes – supported by many excellent alpine *refugios*.

HISTORY

Formally established in 1934, Nahuel Huapi is the oldest of Argentina's national parks. The original park (whose title was Parque Nacional del Sur) was first granted to the pioneering explorer Francisco Perito Moreno for his services to the Argentine Boundary Commission. Perito Moreno donated it back on the condition that it be turned into a national park.

Today's park once formed a large part of the Mapuche heartland, with tribes inhabiting the eastern shores of the great lake. Several low Andean passes in the park, such as Paso Vuriloche (near Pampa Linda) and Paso de Pérez Rosales, linked the many Mapuche tribes on either side of the Cordillera. Christian missionaries later used these passes as a safe route to Chilé.

The name Nahuel Huapi is usually translated from the Mapuche as 'island of the tiger'. This refers to the spotted South American jaguar, or *yaguarete*, whose vast range once included northeastern Patagonia.

ENVIRONMENT

Parque Nacional Nahuel Huapi's northern boundary fronts Parque Nacional Lanín. The park includes 7580 sq km of prime wilderness, whose heart is the 557-sq-km Lago Nahuel Huapi itself. With its numerous fjordlike branches, Lago Nahuel Huapi is unquestionably the finest example of a major glacial lake anywhere in northern Patagonia. This enormous lake lies at 765m above sea level – the lowest point within the northern four-fifths of the park, which is drained by the Río Limay and is therefore part of the Atlantic basin.

Approximately 20% of the park's area is covered by water. Numerous sizable lakes lie in the park's deep valleys. The largest of these are Lago Traful and Lago Espejo to the north, and Lago Mascardi in the park's most southerly zone; this drains westward via the Río Manso and Río Puelo into the Chilean Pacific.

The other dominant feature of Parque Nacional Nahuel Huapi is the icy crown of Monte Tronador. At 3478m above sea level, Monte Tronador is the highest point within the entire Lakes District, and stands almost 1500m above its nearest rivals. The loftiest of Monte Tronador's four summits, Pico Internacional, marks the Argentina–Chile frontier. This massif is smothered by some 60 sq km of névés, glaciers and icefalls, and is the only significant glacially active area found in the park.

Parque Nacional Nahuel Huapi is one of the few areas in Patagonia where the Andes are more extensive and rugged on the Argentine side than on the Chilean side. (Although individual volcanoes do form higher summits in Chile, the ranges surrounding them are relatively low.) This is particularly evident in the mountains to the south of Lago Nahuel Huapi, where the 2405m Cerro Catedral – the highest nonvolcanic peak in the Lakes District – rises up in craggy, steeple-like columns of granodiorite, favored by climbers. Many other peaks in the area surpass 2000m. There are no real glaciers left on this eastern side of the park, but in many places intense frost shattering has formed large scree slides on the higher slopes.

Flora

Three main types of forest are found in Parque Nacional Nahuel Huapi: wet temperate (Valdivian) rainforest in the park's most westerly valleys, deciduous alpine forest at higher elevations, and coniferous forest in the drier eastern sectors of the park.

Of these, the rainforest is easily the most species diverse, with several dozen different types of trees forming the canopy, including alerce (or *lahuén*), *arrayán*, *avellano*, *canelo*, *ciprés de las Guaitecas*, *coigüe*, laurel, *mañío*, *olivillo* (or *teque*), *tineo* and *ulmo*. The deciduous forest of the highland valleys is dominated by *lenga* mixed with *ñirre* and occasional *luma blanca*, a bush of the myrtle family. The *lenga* forest is interspersed with areas of *mallín* (wet meadow) country where the local drainage is poor, but the mountainsides are barren and sparsely vegetated above 1700m.

Parque Nacional Nahuel Huapi has some of the best-preserved coniferous forests in the southern Andes. These are composed of *ciprés de la cordillera*, a graceful cypress species that forms pure stands on the dry and exposed ranges around the eastern side of Lago Nahuel Huapi.

Alpine and subalpine wildflowers are abundant. One of the most lovely and widespread species is the *amancay*, or *liuto*, found in forest clearings, where its orange blooms carpet the ground. Various members of the *Mutisia* genus, collectively known by the popular name of *clavel del campo* (carnations of the countryside), are climbing opportunists that produce orange, pinkish-white or purple daisy-like flowers. They often grow along sunny roadsides or where the forest has been disturbed.

Hidden among the rocks on drier slopes, you may spot the *estrellita de la cordillera*, a small composite perennial whose flowers have numerous white clustered petals. *Capachitos*, various herblike plants with yellow flowers, are also found here. The *cuye colorado* is a small alpine shrub with clam-like leaves; its white flowers have pink-tipped petals around a yellow center. Other common wildflowers include the *coxinea*, an annual that grows as a single reddish stalk crowned by a clustered head of tubular yellow flowers with five crimson petals, and a ground orchid whose flowers have a bluish tinge. The *chupa sangre* (litreally 'bloodsucker') is a spiky cushion-like plant, found still further to the east where the park fringes the semiarid Patagonian steppes.

Fauna

Ground-dwelling birds, such as the *chucao*, *churrín* and *huet-huet*, inhabit the forest floor, where hummingbirds flutter madly around nectar-yielding flowers. The forests also provide the habitat for the *carpintero negro*, or black woodpecker, often seen hammering tree trunks; the *torcaza* (or *conu*), a large grey pigeon; and the austral parakeet *cachaña*. Countless waterbirds, including native ducks such as the *quetru*, *pato cuchara* and *pato real*, live in the park. Mammals sometimes spied in the rainforest are the shy pudu and the *monito del monte*. The puma and the far smaller *huiña* are the main terrestrial predators, while the amphibious *coipo* and the carnivorous *huillín* inhabit the waterways of the park. North American red deer have multiplied greatly since their introduction early in the 20th century, and this is a major factor in the increasing rarity of the *huemul*, or Andean deer.

Parque Nacional Nahuel Huapi is the only place where the rare tucotuco colonial, which was only discovered in 1983, is known to exist. A small ratlike creature, it lives in big colonies, unlike other members of this genus. On the rare occasions when it leaves the warren, the tucotuco colonial gives out a peculiar cheeping call that sounds more like that of a bird than a mammal. Two other species of tucotuco also inhabit the park.

CLIMATE

The park's relatively high elevation and isolation from the Pacific means that a cool and dry 'continental' climate prevails. At low elevations, mean temperatures in winter are around 2°C and in summer they're around 18°C. Summers tend to be relatively dry and most of the annual precipitation occurs in winter and spring, when areas above 1000m are covered by a thick mantle of snow.

The high ranges on the international frontier – most of all, Monte Tronador – cause a typical rain-shadow effect, with steadily diminishing precipitation levels towards the east. It is very wet close to the main continental divide, and the eastern sectors of Parque Nacional Nahuel Huapi are semiarid. For example, Puerto Frías, on the border with Chile, has an annual average rainfall of around 4000mm, while the Cerro Catedral area receives less than 2000mm and the eastern outskirts of Bariloche less than 800mm.

PLANNING

When to Trek

As most scenic routes in Parque Nacional Nahuel Huapi take you well up into the mountains, there's not much scope for trekking before mid-November or any later than early May. The period from December to April offers the best chance of encountering favourable conditions. Early- and late-season trekkers are cautioned that if there is any breakdown in the weather it is likely to bring snowfalls on the ranges. In January the trails and *refugios* are crowded with trekkers.

Books

Spanish-reading trekkers can find the locally-produced guidebook *Las Montañas de Bariloche,* by Toncek Arko & Raúl Izaguirre, in Bariloche book stores.

Permits & Regulations

Nahuel Huapi visitors entering through an official park entrance gate pay a fee of AR$15. This fee does not apply if the road is a public right of way, as in the case of the Villa Catedral and Llao Llao roads, but visitors to the park's Pampa Linda, Río Manso or Lago Steffen sectors will have to pay it.

Camping within the park is allowed only at designated campsites. In most cases these are clearly indicated on trekking maps and by official signs at the park-approved campsites themselves. Away from the more travelled trails, however, wild camping is generally tolerated as long as trekkers take care of their surroundings (see boxed text, p36). Lighting fires is prohibited throughout the park.

ACCESS TOWN

See Bariloche (p124).

NAHUEL HUAPI TRAVERSE

Duration 5 days
Distance 36.5km
Difficulty moderate–demanding
Start Villa Catedral
Finish Puente López
Nearest Town Bariloche
Transport bus
Summary A classic trek with a challenging middle day that hops over passes and mountain ridges amid some of the finest scenery in the Argentine Lakes District.

This spectacular route offers ever-changing scenery of craggy mountain summits, lovely alpine lakes, waterfalls and forests. Not surprisingly, it's one of the most popular treks in Argentina.

PLANNING

Most parties opt for a shorter version of the full traverse presented here, which can be done in four to five days. An additional day or two allows for rest or short side trips. Popular shorter variations include:

- the three-day Circuito Chico, which combines Day 1 (or the Alternative Route via

Arroyo Van Titter), Day 2 and the Alternative Route: Refugio San Martín (Jakob) to Ruta Nacional 79
- a shorter circuit that combines Day 1 and (in reverse) the Alternative Route via Arroyo Van Titter, either as a long day walk or in two short days
- a combination of Days 1 to 3, exiting via Arroyo Goye (Alternative Route: Refugio Segre (Italia) to Colonia Suiza), for a 3–4 day trek

Most sections of the route are well marked and well trodden, and route-finding is relatively straightforward. The exceptions to this are Day 3, between Refugio San Martín and Refugio Segre, where trekkers must navigate extremely carefully, and on Days 2 and 4, where the terrain is too rocky and/or steep to hold a proper path.

Many other tracks intersect with the traverse route, allowing you to shorten or vary the walk as you like. On all stages of the trek it is possible to walk out in one day. Less experienced parties are advised to opt for the Circuito Chico mentioned above.

Apart from Day 3, which is rated demanding, and Day 4 (moderate–demanding) all sections are of a moderate level of difficulty.

When to Trek

Many sections of this trek are well above the tree line. The route's relatively high altitude generally makes it unsuitable for inexperienced parties until around the beginning of December, although in places snow may remain right through the summer. The area is somewhat sheltered by the mountains to the west (chiefly Monte Tronador), and bad weather tends to be slightly less extreme than on the other side of the Andes. Nevertheless, many parts of the route are very exposed to the elements, so if conditions are poor you should wait for the weather to improve.

What to Bring

The four *refugios* along the route make it possible to do the trek without carrying a tent. Nevertheless, trekkers are advised to carry a tent and stove for greater safety. Huts also become overcrowded in January and February, particularly in spells of bad weather. *Refugios* are generally open from early December until mid-April.

Bring a sleeping bag. The *refugios* offer basic bunks, with little or no bedding apart from, perhaps, a mattress. With the exception of Refugio López, the *refugios* belong to CAB, although they are generally run by a private concessionaire who acts as a *refugiero* (hut keeper). Guests pay a fee to overnight and an additional charge to use the cooking facilities. Simple meals, refreshments and supplies are available from all of the *refugios*.

The deep and steep-sided valleys often require heavy climbs and descents through loose rock or scree; it's most comfortable to wear gaiters or long pants that cover the tops of your boots.

Maps

Recommended is the contoured 1:50,000 *Trekking 1* map in the Refugios, Sendas y Picadas series, which is an extract (with additional topographical information) from the larger-format 1:100,000 *Refugios, Sendas y Picadas Parque Nacional Nahuel Huapi* color map. This latter map covers a much wider area and is perhaps a better alternative if you plan further treks elsewhere in the park. All are available from the CAB in Bariloche. Unfortunately, these maps are inaccurate in a few short (but very important) sections of the route.

Permits & Regulations

Trekkers attempting Day 3 from Refugio San Martín (Jakob) to Refugio Segre (Italia) are asked to fill out a form at Refugio San Martín before they leave and hand it in on arrival at Refugio Segre. The *refugiero* at San Martín will advise staff at Segre by radio to expect you. At the same time, trekkers are strongly advised to view the photos of the day's route held at Refugio San Martín.

GETTING TO/FROM THE TREK

Villa Catedral (start)

The trek begins at Villa Catedral, a ski village about 20km by road from Bariloche.

BUS

Throughout the trekking season, **Ómnibus 3 de Mayo** (☎ 02944-425648; Perito Moreno 480) goes from Bariloche to Villa Catedral (AR$1.10, 30 to 40 minutes, hourly). Buses depart from the bus

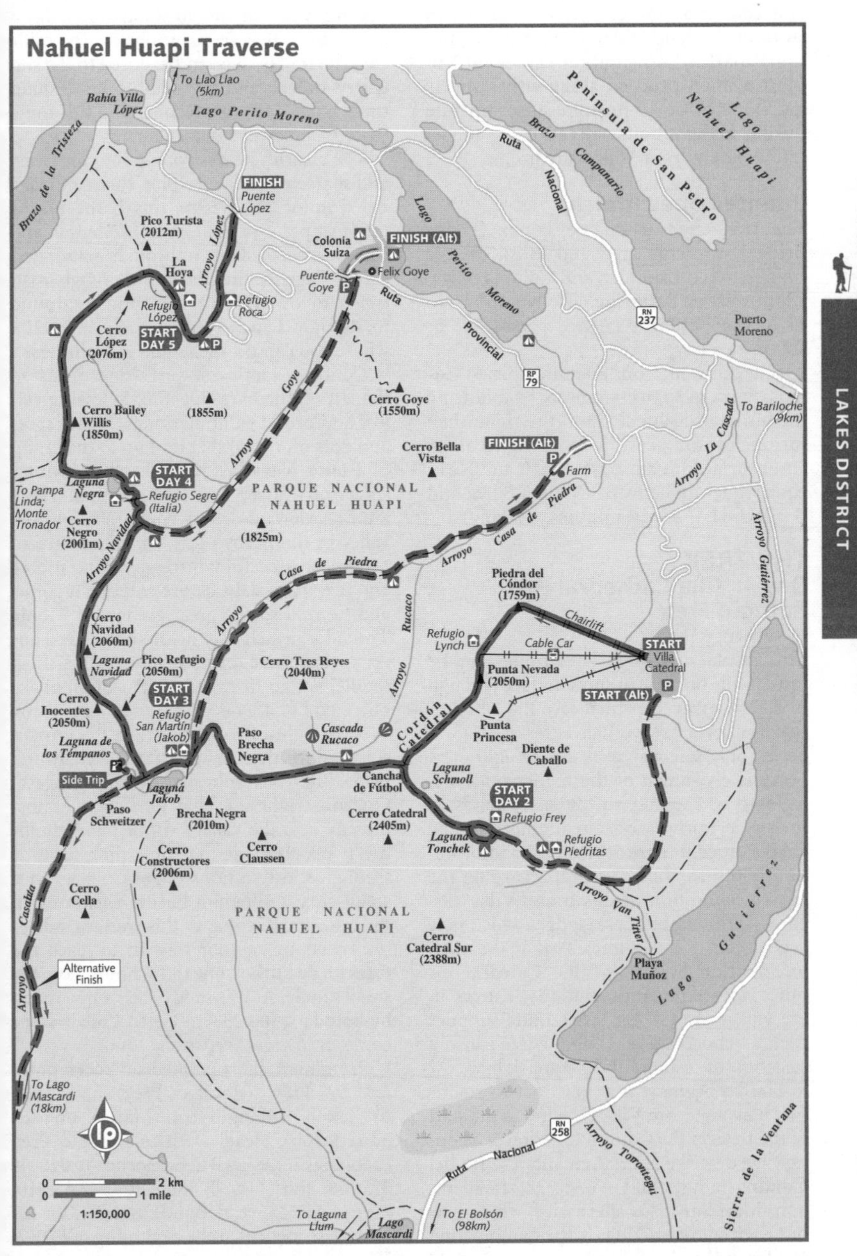
Nahuel Huapi Traverse
To Llao Llao (5km)
Bahía Villa López
Lago Perito Moreno
Brazo de la Tristeza
Península de San Pedro
Lago Nahuel Huapi
Brazo Campanario
Ruta Nacional
FINISH
Puente López
Pico Turista (2012m)
Arroyo López
Colonia Suiza
FINISH (Alt)
Lago Perito Moreno
La Hoya
Puente Goye
Felix Goye
Ruta Provincial
Refugio López
Refugio Roca
RN 237
Puerto Moreno
Cerro López (2076m)
START DAY 5
RP 79
Arroyo Goye
Cerro Goye (1550m)
To Bariloche (9km)
Cerro Bailey Willis (1850m)
(1855m)
Arroyo La Cascada
Cerro Bella Vista
FINISH (Alt)
Farm
START DAY 4
To Pampa Linda; Monte Tronador
Laguna Negra
Refugio Segre (Italia)
PARQUE NACIONAL NAHUEL HUAPI
Arroyo Casa de Piedra
Cerro Negro (2001m)
(1825m)
Arroyo Navidad
Arroyo Gutiérrez
Arroyo Casa de Piedra
Piedra del Cóndor (1759m)
Chairlift
Cerro Navidad (2060m)
Refugio Lynch
Cable Car
START
Villa Catedral
Laguna Navidad
Pico Refugio (2050m)
Cerro Tres Reyes (2040m)
Arroyo Rucaco
Punta Nevada (2050m)
START (Alt)
START DAY 3
Cerro Inocentes (2050m)
Refugio San Martín (Jakob)
Cordón Catedral
Punta Princesa
Laguna de los Témpanos
Paso Brecha Negra
Cascada Rucaco
Diente de Caballo
Side Trip
Laguna Jakob
Cancha de Fútbol
Laguna Schmoll
Paso Schweitzer
Brecha Negra (2010m)
Cerro Catedral (2405m)
START DAY 2
Refugio Frey
Laguna Tonchek
Refugio Piedritas
Cerro Constructores (2006m)
Cerro Claussen
Cerro Cella
Arroyo Casalata
Arroyo Van Titter
PARQUE NACIONAL NAHUEL HUAPI
Cerro Catedral Sur (2388m)
Playa Muñoz
Lago Gutiérrez
Alternative Finish
To Lago Mascardi (18km)
RN 258
Ruta Nacional
Arroyo Torrontegui
Sierra de la Ventana
0 2 km
0 1 mile
1:150,000
To Laguna Llum
Lago Mascardi
To El Bolsón (98km)

terminal at the eastern edge of Bariloche and call in at the center, including two stops on Moreno and one opposite the national park administration center on San Martín, then proceed along either Av de los Pioneros or Av Bustillo. Buses operate during daylight hours, all returning almost immediately from Villa Catedral.

Puente López (finish)

The trek ends at Puente López (López Bridge), a picnic area and kiosk on the road between Llao Llao and Colonia Suiza, 22km west of Bariloche. The No 10 or No 11 bus to Bariloche (AR$3) passes five or six times a day.

You can walk from Puente López to Colonia Suiza in 30 to 40 minutes by following the bitumen 150m along to the right, then turning off southeast (ie to the right) along an unsurfaced road. Buses No10 and No11 run frequently between Colonia Suiza and Bariloche (AR$3, 50 minutes, 14 daily).

THE TREK

Day 1: Villa Cathedral to Refugio Frey

2¾–4 hours, 8.5km

This exhilarating high-level route may be impassable because of snow and ice through mid-December, in which case the Alternative Route via Arroyo Van Titter (p107) will be the only safe way to reach Refugio Frey. Fortunately, much of the higher option is exposed to the sun so the snow tends to melt away fairly early. If in doubt, ask in the CAB's office in Bariloche or at its information booth in Villa Catedral regarding the current condition of this route. Villa Catedral has a number of ski lodges which may accept guests in summer. Ask at the CAB information booth in Villa Catedral for other accommodation options. Kiosks in the village are OK for last-minute supplies such as chocolate and film. There's also a selection of restaurants and snack bars.

The day begins with a choice of two ski lifts that haul you from Villa Catedral to the start of the trek on the Cordón Catedral. The option we describe is the **Aerosilla Piedra del Cóndor** (adult/child AR$40/28; 10.30am-6pm Mon-Sun). An alternative, which cuts out even more walking, is the combination **Cablecarril y Aerosilla Lynch** (adult/child AR$40/28), which goes to Refugio Lynch. If the fares, or the very idea of chairlifts, put you off, you can trek to Refugio Lynch on a foot track that spirals up below the cable car. The trail is steep and exposed to the sun (carry water), and the climb takes around three hours. We only recommend this route to save money or build character.

The chairlift heaves you up into the stony and sparsely vegetated alpine zone to **Piedra del Cóndor**. At 1759m, this is the northernmost point of the Cordón Catedral, and offers an excellent unbroken panorama across Lago Nahuel Huapi. A rough road can be followed for 30 to 35 minutes around to **Refugio Lynch** (year-round), at 2042m, where you can get meals and refreshments.

Continue southwestward along, or just to the left of, the bare ridgetop, following yellow and/or red paint markings (lots of spots and dots on rocks) that lead up to the hump of **Punta Nevada** (2050m), where winter snowdrifts linger well into summer. There are fine views down to your right into the valley of the Arroyo Rucaco, whose stream meanders peacefully through alpine moors and over rock slabs before entering a gorge, and beyond to the great glaciers of Monte Tronador, which rises up on the western horizon. The route dips down to reach a small saddle, not far from the upper station of another ski lift, after 45 minutes to one hour.

Sidle rightward off the ridge to cross a scree slide, then make your way around below the rock spires of **Punta Princesa**. On your right the land falls away almost directly into the valley. Minor hand climbing is necessary as the route picks its way through short sections of rock blocks with small chrysanthemum bushes sheltering in the crevices. Keeping to this western side of the range, make your way on to reach the **Cancha de Fútbol**, one to 1¼ hours from the small saddle. At this sandy shelf surrounded by boulders, the 2388m Cerro Catedral Sur comes into view over to the south.

Prominent signs painted on rocks point left to 'Frey' (Refugio Frey) and right to 'Jakob' (Refugio San Martín on Laguna Jakob). Head down to **Refugio Frey** (bookings at the CAB in Bariloche; ☎ 02944-527966; dm AR$30; kitchen use AR$10; dinner AR$25; year-round) as described (in reverse sequence) at the beginning of Day 2. Walking time from the Cancha de Fútbol to the *refugio* is 40 to 50 minutes.

The *refugio* stands at 1700m in a particularly scenic location on the eastern shore of **Laguna Tonchek**, looking out across the lake to the craggy spires of Cerro Catedral (Cathedral Mountain). The lake takes its name, which you may also see spelt 'Toncek', from the late Slovene andinist and CAB member Toncek Pangrec. The neat two-storey hut is built of local stone, and has sleeping space for 40 people upstairs. It can get very crowded, particularly during periods of poor weather in the main tourist season. There are sheltered but cramped and uneven **campsites** in the *lenga* scrub just across the outlet creek on the southern side of the lake, and less sheltered but more spacious and level sites on open ground further round the southern shore.

ALTERNATIVE ROUTE: VIA ARROYO VAN TITTER

3½–4½ hours, 12km

This stage is longer than Day 1 and has no lifts to haul you up the mountain, but ascends at a more leisurely rate and is more sheltered. It is the only safe route when the high-level option is snowed over or icy.

From the CAB lodge at the southern edge of Villa Catedral, cut across the parking lot below a minor ski tow and take an old road up left to a signpost at the trailhead. The broad foot track goes southward through *ñirre* and *quila* scrub on a kind of wide terrace above Lago Gutiérrez, then rises gently into the forest below overhanging cliffs to a fork 1½ to two hours from the village.

Continue up, heading right (the left-hand route leads down to the lake), turning up northwest through moist forest, and cross the **Arroyo Van Titter** on a footbridge. The first authorised **campsites** along the route are by the stream just after you cross this bridge. Ascend at a leisurely pace through the tall *lenga* forest with an understorey of herbs and wildflowers to pass **Refugio Piedritas** after 50 minutes to 1¼ hours. This quaint little *refugio* belongs to the local Club Andino Esloveno and has been constructed by building a log wall across the opening of a large overhanging boulder just to the right of the path. Refugio Piedritas only has space for about eight people and is basic. You can find numerous good **campsites** in the forest nearby.

Climb on through the forest, which soon changes into lower and denser *lenga* scrub, granting views of the peaks on the Cordón Catedral. The route crosses the now much smaller stream on stepping stones shortly before you reach **Refugio Frey**, beside Laguna Tonchek, after a final 50 minutes to 1¼ hours.

Day 2: Refugio Frey to Refugio San Martín (Jakob)

5-6½hours, 8.5km

Make your way easily around either shore of Laguna Tonchek to its northwestern side, then begin ascending to the right (northwest). The path winds up the loose-rock slopes beside a splashing stream to **Laguna Schmoll**, a smaller and shallower lake that occupies a sparsely vegetated terrace opposite the impressive craggy columns of Cerro Catedral. Cross the tiny outlet and climb on more steeply into a rock gully. Early in the season, snow here may make this section dangerous. Look back for a final view of the lovely upper valley behind you, then continue up through a small sandy basin to reach the **Cancha de Fútbol** after one to 1½ hours.

A sign ('Jakob') and an arrow painted on a boulder indicate where the route descends into the next valley. Follow red splashes on rocks down a short way to the right, then traverse back briefly leftward. Now begin a long and very steep descent more or less straight down through dusty, raw talus, continuing down via a dry gully into the scrub. As the gradient eases, head off to the left along a good trail where the beautiful *lenga* forest fringes the grassy valley floor. The path ducks in and out of the trees to cross a stream below a tiny cascade at an excellent official **campsite**, 50 minutes to one hour from the Cancha de Fútbol.

Make your way on gently up valley through the forest, avoiding the soggy open area to the right. The route soon moves out into sporadic *ñirre* scrub, then crosses a stream coming down from the left. The **Cascada Rucaco** waterfall comes into sight on the slopes of Cerro Tres Reyes to the north, and red markings guide you up onto a flat, stony ridge dividing the upper valley. Behind you, on the adjacent range, the now familiar multisteepled form of Cerro Catedral rises up, looking just as spectacular from this angle.

The track leads across the broad ridgetop to a well signposted rock, then makes a final strenuous, but short climb west up through steep, loose rock to reach **Paso Brecha Negra** after one to 1½ hours. This is the broad ridge that connects Cerro Tres Reyes with Brecha Negra. There are superb views from here (better from a few paces downhill), with the *refugio* on Laguna Jakob clearly visible below to the southwest.

Sidle down towards the lake as far as a small outcrop, then descend steeply via (or beside) a loose chute of coarse gravel until below the scrub line. Turn left where the route meets the main trail coming up through the valley, and follow this through a few boggy areas to cross the small **Arroyo Casa de Piedra** on stepping stones just below where it leaves Laguna Jakob.

A short way on, the route intersects with the main path coming up through the valley. Follow this briefly to the left to **Refugio San Martín (Jakob)** (dm AR$30; kitchen use AR$20; dinner AR$40; Nov-Apr), beside Laguna Jakob at 1650m, 45 minutes to one hour from Paso Brecha Negra. This timber and stone *refugio* stands near a tiny peninsula. It has a wood stove, toilet and sleeps up to 100 people. You can buy a few basic provisions and sweet luxuries from the hut warden. **Camping** is permitted in clearings in the *lenga* above the *refugio*; collect water from the spring water tap at the hut.

SIDE TRIP: LAGUNA DE LOS TÉMPANOS

1–1½ hours return, 3.5km

This easy side trip from Refugio San Martín should not be missed. From the campsite head up the steep ridge, then sidle on around westward over polished limestone slabs (note the scratch marks left by ice age glaciers) to reach Laguna de los Témpanos after 25 to 30 minutes. This spectacular little lake lies within a south-facing cirque with sheer rock walls that tower above its icy, blue waters. Return the way you came.

Day 3: Refugio San Martín (Jakob) to Refugio Segre (Italia)

5–7 hours, 8.5km

This section of the trek, following a high-level route, is harder and more hazardous than other stages. Ideally for very experienced trekkers, it should not be attempted unless the weather is very good. At any time – most commonly, early in the season (until about mid-December) – crampons and an ice axe may be needed to do the route safely. The hut warden at Refugio San Martín (who has photographs that clarify the route) can give further advice, and will ask you to fill in a form and hand it in on arrival at the other end.

Follow the side trip to Laguna de los Témpanos (above) as far as a rocky spur that comes down from Pico Refugio, just before Laguna de los Témpanos comes into view. After carefully studying the route from this point, follow occasional cairns northeastward, with some scrambling as the ridge steepens, to meet a narrow ledge. Head left along the ledge for about 50m, then move up with care diagonally rightward through a steep couloir (rocky chute), which may be wet or snow-filled. After another 50m or so, ease back left across snowdrifts – or, if possible, below them – to gain the top of the ridge.

Taking care when negotiating more patches of old snow, head northwest along the ridge. After a short distance, a rocky pinnacle blocks the way. Avoid this by descending around to the right and traverse the slopes below the rock face. Continue through a stony area of gully cracks, where more snow may lie, towards an obvious narrow gap in the craggy range ahead, two to three hours from Laguna de los Témpanos. From here, move over onto the loose scree slopes on the eastern side of the range above Laguna Navidad. These lead to a low point in the main ridge line between Cerro Inocentes and Cerro Navidad. From here, make your way 500m up a spur on scree to the summit of **Cerro Navidad** (2060m).

Head 400m down the ridge on the northern side of Cerro Navidad. From here a rough route can be followed northeast down more steep and unstable slopes into the narrow canyon at the head of the **Arroyo Navidad**. Late-lying snow may make this section tricky to negotiate. Crossing the cascading stream wherever necessary, follow it down to meet the main path coming up the **Arroyo Goye**, two to three hours on.

Follow red-paint markings up through *lenga* scrub, before beginning a steep, spiralling ascent adjacent to waterfalls where the Arroyo Goye spills over 300m cliffs. The path sidles on around westward over a low rock crest, from where Laguna Negra comes into view. Laguna Negra lies in a little trough directly below Cerro Negro (2001m), and was evidently named for its proximity to the black-rock mountain as its water is blue. To the north lies the paler-brown shale rock of Cerro Bailey Willis (1850m).

Cut down leftward across the lake outlet to arrive at **Refugio Segre (Italia)** (dm AR$25; use of kitchen AR$8; dinner AR$30; Nov-Apr) after a final 60 to 80 minutes. This two-storey concrete construction (whose bunkerlike design can withstand heavy snows and small avalanches) lies at 1650m and has bed space for 60 trekkers. There are numerous sheltered **campsites** hunkering in the scrub as you come over the rock crest just before arriving at Refugio Segre.

ALTERNATIVE FINISH: REFUGIO SAN MARTÍN (JAKOB) TO RUTA PROVINCIAL 79

2¾–4½ hours, 13km

This is the normal access to Refugio San Martín and is the quickest exit route from the hut. It is also the final stage of the three-day trek known as the Circuito Chico.

Follow the well-travelled path down the true left (west) side of the **Arroyo Casa de Piedra**, crossing the stream just above a waterfall. Descend steeply in a series of switchback curves (known as Las Serpentinas) into the *lenga* forest, then more gently on past a side valley that ends in a large cirque at Laguna Navidad. From here, the route enters the drier central part of the valley (which apparently lies in the rain shadow of ranges to the west). The path leads through *mogotes*, *calafate* bushes and *ñirres* – typical dryland vegetation – to cross the stream on a rickety suspension bridge, 1½ to 2½ hours from the *refugio*.

Continue down the stony riverflats past where the Arroyo Rucaco flows into the main stream, then climb away left and drop back to the riverbank several times to avoid steeper banks before sidling gradually down into pleasant stands of *coigüe* trees, and some good **campsites**, by the Arroyo Casa de Piedra after 50 minutes to 1¼ hours. The route soon leaves the riverside again, ascending briefly through the forest onto slopes covered by thickets of *retama* as it goes over into a 4WD track. Ahead of you, across Lago Nahuel Huapi, are the snowcapped mountains of the Sierra Cuyin Manzano. Pass by a tiny car park and a kiosk beside a farm, after which a proper road brings you down to intersect with the Ruta Provincial 79 after 30 to 45 minutes.

Those travelling in the reverse direction should watch out for a sign marking the start of the track beside Ruta Provincial 79; going uphill the trekking time is around six hours.

It's possible to walk from here to the holiday village of **Colonia Suiza** (p125) in 1½ to two hours (turn left and follow the road), but easier to wait for the No 11 bus from Bariloche, which passes this point five times daily (between 9.30am & 8.30pm) on the way to Colonia Suiza.

ALTERNATIVE FINISH: REFUGIO SAN MARTÍN (JAKOB) TO LAGO MASCARDI

8-9hrs, 24kms

Use a compass or GPS unit to hike this little-used trail linking two of the region's finest trekking areas. The **Arroyo Casalata trail** requires good route finding skills and is best attempted when river levels are low, since there is one tricky crossing.

Following the trail to Laguna Los Tempanos, take the left side of the lake valley to **Paso Sweitzer**. On the pass the trail drops straight into the valley (west). Once you reach the valley floor, follow the trail south. The trail mostly takes the east bank (river left), with some river crossings. The trail is poor and overgrown, with swampy parts. Just before Lago Mascardi, there is a junction that follows the lake's northern shore; follow the indications to eventually get to a hanging bridge over the Río Manso.

Pass **Arroyo Casalata** and head west-northwest for at least 30 minutes until the trail meets the Rio Claro. It can be crossed when the river is low by the facing hill where some abandoned measurement instruments lie. In high water, good jumpers only could go 100m upstream to a rocky gully (2.5m wide) to cross. Walk southwest on the main track, headed toward a pair of *álamos* (poplars) to arrive at Rio Manso's hanging bridge. Cross to the road to Pampa Linda, 17kms away. From here buses pass for both Pampa Linda (around 10am) and Bariloche (around 5.30pm) in summer.

Day 4: Refugio Segre (Italia) to Refugio López

4–5½ hours, 7.5km

Head along the eastern lake shore, dotted with chrysanthemum bushes and yellow daisies, making your way on around the northern side of **Laguna Negra** over cracked rock and perhaps some snowdrifts. There is a short section of rock here (probably with a fixed rope to hang on to) that requires some careful downclimbing. From the far end of Laguna Negra, climb a short distance up to the right beside the small inlet stream, then cross to its true right side and head up a broad open rocky slope towards the low point in the ridge between Cerro Negro and Cerro Bailey Willis.

Head up right along the ridge (guided by a few cairns, canes and paint markers), over a knob and down to reach a gap on the southern side of Cerro Bailey Willis (where snow may lie well into the summer), 45 minutes to one hour from Refugio Segre. From here, the now familiar form of Cerro Catedral can be made out to the southeast beyond Laguna Negra. Sidle northward for a further 15 to 20 minutes, across a slope of coarse *talus* above a snow basin, to reach another small pass.

From the slopes of **Cerro Bailey Willis** (1850m) you get an unobstructed panorama of the magnificent mountain scenery along the Chile–Argentina frontier. The great white rump of Monte Tronador, smothered by sprawling glaciers, completely dominates the views of the western horizon. The pointed peak visible to the north of Monte Tronador is Volcán Puntiagudo in Chile, and the highland lake perched in a depression to the southwest is Laguna Lluvú (see More Treks, p123).

Drop down north from the pass, descending briefly rightward through loose rock before you sidle along the left side of a green, boggy gully. In places the foot track is less definite, but the route is marked with cairns and occasional red-paint splashes on rocks. Follow these down left on to moist grassy meadows to cross a brook at the head of a tiny valley (the northern branch of the Arroyo Goye), 40 to 50 minutes from the pass. There is a small park-approved **campsite** here among low *lenga* forest.

Head on over a marshy clearing and up out of the *ñirre* scrub. The indistinct path leads northeast gently up the sparsely vegetated slopes to cross a small stream coming from an obvious rocky gap to the north. From this point, begin a very steep ascent up to the right via a gully of frost-shattered rock, whose large, loose, sharp fragments make the going strenuous (and slightly dangerous). Pass to the right of a rocky knob to reach a small dip in the range some way north of Cerro López's principal summit, 1½ to two hours from the campsite.

A short way northwest along the top of this ridge is a trig marker on the slightly lower summit of **Pico Turista** (2012m). This point offers another great panorama, which now includes Volcán Osorno (the perfectly symmetrical snowcapped cone visible beyond Monte Tronador in Chile), while to the north there are sweeping views across the islands, peninsulas and isthmuses that separate Lago Perito Moreno from Lago Nahuel Huapi. Condors often soar around these mountain tops.

Following paint arrows, drop down east from the dip in the ridge to skirt along the left side of a small glacial cirque known as **La Hoya**. A shallow tarn forms here once the snow melts, but by fall this basin is normally dry and snow-free. Descend more steeply towards the *refugio*, visible far below you, downclimbing repeatedly at short sections of rock, to arrive at **Refugio López** (☎ 02944-527966 in Bariloche for reservations; info@activepatagonia.com.ar; dm AR$30; mid-Dec–mid-Apr), after 50 minutes to 1¼ hours.

The privately owned Refugio López is the most popular and accessible hut on this trek, and sits at around 1600m in a very scenic location overlooking Lago Nahuel Huapi. This two-storey red-brick building has modern amenities (but no hot showers) and there is sleeping capacity for 100 people. There are poor **campsites** near the hut, or you can camp on a grassy area below a waterfall about 15 minutes down beyond the *refugio*. Refugio López stays open for the entire trekking season.

ALTERNATIVE FINISH: REFUGIO SEGRE (ITALIA) TO COLONIA SUIZA

2½–3¼ hours, 12km

This is the usual access to Refugio Segre (Italia). It's also an easier alternative route out for trekkers who don't feel confident enough to tackle the high-level traverse of Day 4.

Head back down the switchbacks as described at the end of Day 3 to cross the Arroyo Goye and the Arroyo Navidad just above their confluence. The path dips down into the *lenga* forest beside the cascading stream to an official campsite after 40 to 50 minutes. Head gently downstream below high rock walls fronting the opposite side of the valley, crossing through a small area of *ñirre* and *quil*a before you pass a side valley of the Arroyo Goye (barely visible through the trees).

Continue along the true-right bank, gradually moving down into evergreen forest dominated by *coigüe* to where the route joins a rough, disused road, one to 1½ hours down from the official **campsite**. At this point you'll see a signpost ('Picada a Laguna Negra/Refugio'), which indicates the way back up to the hut. Another trail branches off right (southeast) from here up to the 1550m lookout peak of **Cerro Goye** (1550m), a return side trip of 3½ hours.

Sidle down above the rushing stream through patches of exotic North American fir trees, then turn right off the vehicular track at a gate and make your way along the right-hand side of a fence. The first part of this route ascends steeply; the last section takes you through stands of *ciprés de la cordillera* before dropping steeply through the *coigüe* forest to reach Ruta Provincial 79 at a parking area and a signpost ('Refugio de Montaña Laguna Negra…6 horas') after 35 to 45 minutes. Go left along this road, turning right into Felix Goye to arrive in **Colonia Suiza** (p125) a further 10 to 15 minutes on. Trekkers hiking up to Refugio Segre will find the signpost indicating the trailhead beside a black gate 400m east of the road bridge over the Arroyo Goye.

Day 5: Refugio López to Puente López

1½–2 hours, 3.5km

From just below the terrace of the *refugio* take a path that winds down through low scrub before joining a broad track that comes in from the right. This crosses two small streams at the source of the **Arroyo López** and meets the end of a road after 15 to 20 minutes. Follow the road past a small car park, then turn off left on to a signposted foot track leading steeply down into the forest. The route twice crosses the road at hairpin bends, then leads down through previously fire-cleared slopes, now regenerating with *lenga* scrub and thickets of spiny *crucero*. It leads to **La Roca**, a *refugio* offering meals and snacks. Here, avoid picking up trails which diverge rightward back on to the road, and continue down north into the forest. (If you follow the road, you'll end up about halfway along Ruta Provincial 79 between Puente López and Colonia Suiza).

The last section of the route follows the right side of the Arroyo López before coming to a picnic area and kiosk at **Puente López** after a final 1¼ to 1¾ hours.

Trekkers who do this stage in reverse order should reckon on taking two to three hours to reach Refugio López from Puente López because of the steepness of the trail.

PASO DE LAS NUBES

Duration 2 days
Distance 23km
Difficulty moderate
Start Pampa Linda
Finish Puerto Frías
Nearest Town Bariloche
Transport bus, boat
Summary Links two river valleys through saturated rainforest and below hanging glaciers at the foot of the mighty four-summit massif of Monte Tronador.

The aptly named 1435m Paso de las Nubes (Pass of the Clouds) lies on a continental watershed, sending its waters into the Pacific on its southern side, via the Río Manso and Río Puelo, and into the Atlantic on its northern side, via Lago Nahuel Huapi. The route over Paso de las Nubes can be done as a trans-Andean trek by continuing over Paso de Pérez Rosales to the isolated village of Peulla on Lago Todos Los Santos in Chile (see the Alternative Finish, p117).

PLANNING

The trek follows a much travelled and generally well-marked path for most of the way. Apart from a short section on top of Paso de las Nubes and the side trip to Refugio Otto Meiling, the route is completely within the shelter of the forest. Snow often lies on the pass well into January. On the section between the upper camp near Glaciar Frías and Laguna Frías, fallen logs and *colihue* canes sometimes lie across the path; here the going may be slippery after rain.

From Puerto Frías many trekkers continue into Chile via a good dirt road to Peulla on Lago Todos Los Santos (see the Alternative Finish, p117). This isolated 26km section across Paso de Pérez Rosales is inaccessible to outside traffic, and is traveled only by a regular bus service and occasional border-control vehicles.

The usual trekking time from Pampa Linda to Puerto Frías is two full days, but the recommended side trips to the Salto Garganta del Diablo or Piedra Pérez and Refugio Otto Meiling will lengthen the trek by one day each. These side trips begin and end in Pampa Linda, and so need to be done before you set out on Day 1 of the trek. Continuing to Peulla requires at least one additional (very long) day. Those continuing on to Chilean towns will need a second day to boat across Lago Todos los Santos and reach a transport hub by bus.

The walk can be done in either direction, although for transport reasons south-to-north will probably be the most convenient.

When to Trek

This trek is best done between December and April.

What to Bring

Some form of alternative footwear suited to wet terrain, such as sport sandals, makes negotiating the *mallín* north of the Upper Río Alerce campsite less of a drama. As this is a frontier area, be sure to carry proper identification.

Permits & Regulations

All trekkers must register before the trek at the Intendencia (administration center) in Pampa Linda, and return their registration stub to the office at Puerto Blest on the way back to Bariloche after the end of the trek, or to Argentine Gendarmeria if crossing into Chile.

Maps

Recommended is the contoured 1:50,000 *Trekking 2* map in the Refugios, Sendas y Picadas series, which is an extract (with additional topographical information) from the larger-format color 1:100,000 *Refugios, Sendas y Picadas Parque Nacional Nahuel Huapi*. This latter map covers a much wider area and is perhaps a better alternative if you plan further treks elsewhere in the park. Both are available from the CAB in Bariloche.

The Argentine IGM 1:100,000 map *Llao Llao* (Neuquén, No 4172-22) covers this area completely. However, this map (also used for the Nahuel Huapi Traverse) gives poor topographical detail and doesn't shown the trekking route correctly.

A Chilean IGM 1:50,000 map, *Monte Tronador* (Section H, No 46), includes a good part of the frontier area on the Argentine side and is especially useful for trekkers who continue on to Peulla. Maps can be found at Bariloche's CAB.

GETTING TO/FROM THE TREK

Pampa Linda (start)

The trek begins at Pampa Linda, 77km by road from Bariloche via Villa Mascardi.

Through summer, **Express Meiling** (☎ 02944-529875; reservations at the CAB) runs regular buses to Pampa Linda and Cerro Tronador (AR$40, 2½ hours), leaving throught the morning from outside the CAB in Bariloche. Daily return buses leave Pampa Linda starting at 5pm. Charter service can also be arranged.

Puerto Frías (finish)

The trek ends at Puerto Frías. From here a tourist boat across Laguna Frías to Puerto Alegre connects with a bus to Puerto Blest on a branch of Lago Nahuel Huapi. Or trekkers can trek or take a catamaran to Peulla, Chile.

BOAT/BUS COMBINATION

Those continuing on to Bariloche in Argentina can book a boat-bus-boat combination (AR$150), followed by a public bus to Bariloche. Always check prices and departure times at the CAB in Bariloche or the CAB's *campamento móvil* (a kind of base camp) at

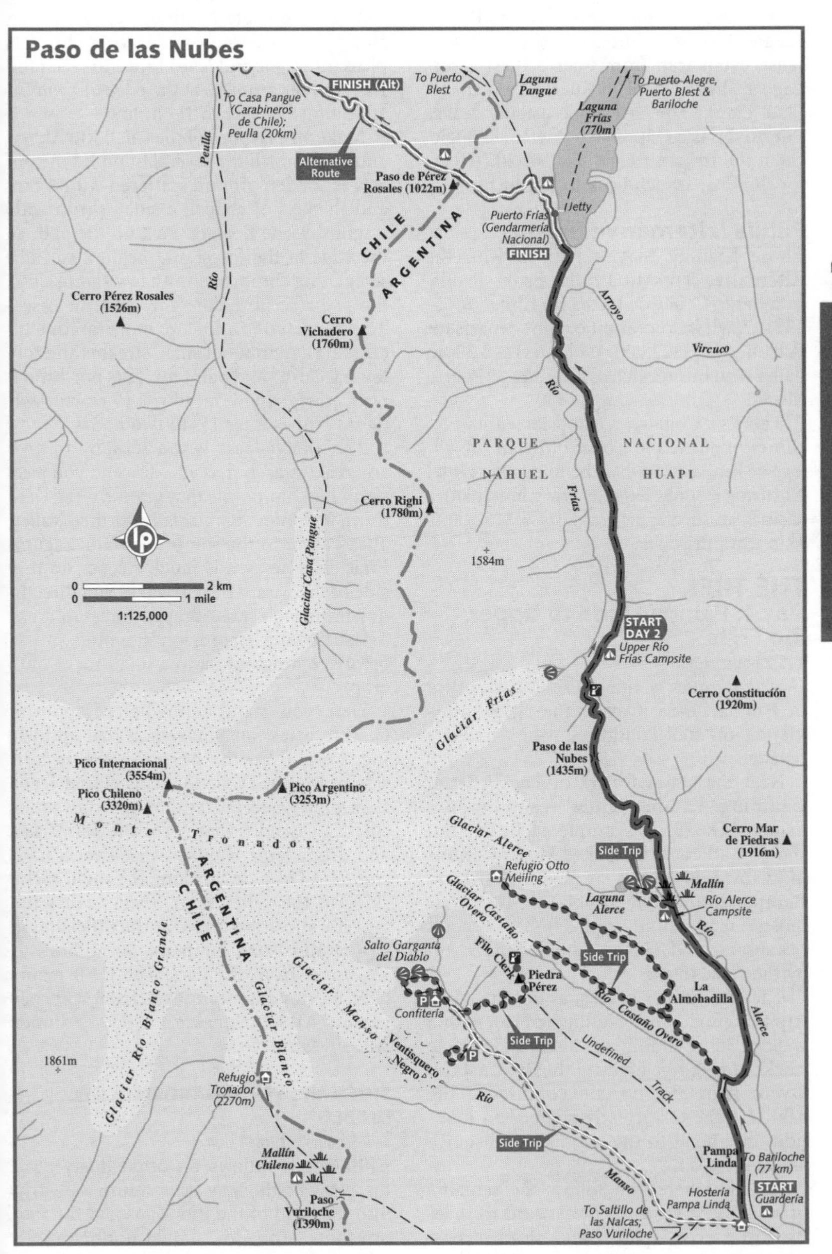
Paso de las Nubes
FINISH (Alt)
To Puerto Blest
Laguna Pangue
To Puerto Alegre, Puerto Blest & Bariloche
Laguna Frías (770m)
To Casa Pangue (Carabineros de Chile); Peulla (20km)
Alternative Route
Paso de Pérez Rosales (1022m)
Jetty
Puerto Frías (Gendarmería Nacional)
FINISH
CHILE
ARGENTINA
Río Peulla
Cerro Pérez Rosales (1526m)
Cerro Vichadero (1760m)
Arroyo Vircuco
Río Frías
PARQUE NAHUEL NACIONAL HUAPI
Cerro Righi (1780m)
1584m
Glaciar Casa Pangue
0 2 km
0 1 mile
1:125,000
START DAY 2
Upper Río Frías Campsite
Cerro Constitucíón (1920m)
Glaciar Frías
Paso de las Nubes (1435m)
Pico Internacional (3554m)
Pico Chileno (3320m)
Pico Argentino (3253m)
Monte Tronador
Glaciar Alerce
Cerro Mar de Piedras (1916m)
Side Trip
Refugio Otto Meiling
Mallín
Laguna Alerce
Río Alerce Campsite
Glaciar Castaño Overo
Salto Garganta del Diablo
Filo Clerk
Piedra Pérez
La Almohadilla
Río Castaño Overo
Confitería
Glaciar Manso
Ventisquero Negro
Undefined Track
Glaciar Río Blanco Grande
Glaciar Blanco
1861m
Refugio Tronador (2270m)
Río Manso
Mallín Chileno
Paso Vuriloche (1390m)
Pampa Linda
To Bariloche (77 km)
START
Guardería
Hostería Pampa Linda
To Saltillo de las Nalcas; Paso Vuriloche
LAKES DISTRICT

the upper Río Frías campsite. The combination runs: boat from Puerto Frias to Puerto Alegre, bus from Puerto Alegre to Puerto Blest, catamaran from Puerto Blest across Lago Nahuel Huapi to Puerto Pañuelo (at Llao Llao). The last boat usually leaves Puerto Frías at 3pm. At Puerto Pañuelo, catch the frequent local bus No 20 (AR$4) for the final stretch back to Bariloche.

Peulla (alternative finish)

Those heading to Chile finish with the Alternative Trek to Peulla. From Peulla, catamaran **Cruce de Lagos** (in Chile; ☎ 65-437127; www.cruceandino.com) departs for Petrohué (CH$22,000, 1¾ hours) at 3.30pm daily, with bus service continuing to Puerto Montt.

There's a Conaf-run campsite without facilities opposite the Conaf office in the village of Peulla, as well as the upmarket **Hotel Natura** (☎ 065-560483; www.hotelnatura.cl, in Spanish, d with breakfast CH$132,000), 1km from the dock.

THE TREK

Day 1: Pampa Linda to Upper Río Frías

4–5½ hours, 13km

Guardaparques at the national park office in Pampa Linda provide the latest information on trail conditions when trekkers register.

Near the national park office, CAB-run **Camping Pampa Linda** (camping per person AR$15) has ample facilities, hot showers and a well-stocked kiosk. Continuing towards Monte Tronador, **Hostería Pampa Linda** (☎ 02944-490517; www.hosteriapampalinda.com.ar) has a good restaurant, and Hostel Pampa Linda, run by the same outfit.

The trek proper begins, as does the side trip to Refugio Otto Meiling (p115), with a walk of 30 to 40 minutes along the vehicle track from Pampa Linda to the **Río Castaño Overo**. Cross the river and continue up the vehicle track to a clearly signposted junction on a bend to the left a short distance above the river.

Go right here and follow the remains of an ancient road northeastward to meet the **Río Alerce**. Apart from a short section where you have to climb over fallen logs at a tight bend in the river (while the old road simply fords and re-fords the milky waters), the route continues on gently up along the western bank. It goes through pleasant *coigüe* and *lenga* forest to reach the **Río Alerce campsite** at the edge of a *mallín* after a further one to 1½ hours.

Make an easy ford of the small Río Alerce and wade north for several hundred meters across sodden ground scattered with *ñirres* and thickets of chapel, a small shrub with fragrant white flowers. Pick up the path at the edge of the forest and begin a steadily steepening climb, making a few zigzags into the *lenga* scrub before the gradient eases. The route continues up more gradually, crossing a number of small streams and following cairns and paint markers northward over grassy alpine meadows to reach **Paso de las Nubes** after 1½ to two hours.

The 1435m pass is too scrubby to give any real vistas, but as you descend you pass small lookout points that grant a clear view down through the glacially formed valley ahead as far as the sombre-looking Laguna Frías. The descent is much steeper on this side of the pass. The path takes you directly down through moss-draped forest to cross a fast-flowing stream on stepping stones before coming out on to a small rocky outcrop.

Here you stand immediately opposite Glaciar Frías, an amazing icefall sprawling down from the névés on the eastern side of Monte Tronador. This glacier feeds a surging waterfall and numerous other smaller cascades that form the Río Frías, and drops large chunks of ice over a high cliff face. Drop down along the small rocky ridge to the valley floor, then recross the gravelly stream to arrive at the official, free **Upper Río Frías campsite**, 50 minutes to 1¼ hours from the pass. The CAB maintains a **campamento móvil** (fixed tents per person AR$30; breakfast AR$25; dinner AR$30) here.

SIDE TRIP: SALTO GARGANTA DEL DIABLO

3–4½ hours return, 17km

Although it follows an often dusty road for most of the way, this return side trip into the head of the Río Manso, at the foot of Monte Tronador, should not be missed (although you might consider hitching). For safety reasons the road is open only to upward traffic until 2pm and to downward traffic after 4pm. If you arrive with a return-day bus tour from Bariloche, the trip up to the Salto Garganta del Diablo will probably be included.

From Pampa Linda, walk northwest along the road past the *guardería* and *hostería*. Five minutes on, you pass the signposted path that's the turn-off to the Saltillo de los Nalcas (which is also the trail head for the route to Refugio Tronador – see More Treks, p122). The road rises steadily beside the upper Río Manso, crossing the northern branch of the river shortly before it comes to a car park at a lookout point, one to 1½ hours on.

From here you get a sensational view up to Glaciar Manso, which ends abruptly at a hanging icefall above a 750m-high precipice on Monte Tronador. Blocks of ice that periodically drop off the icefall are smashed to pieces as they hit the ground, where the pulverized ice re-forms as another glacier. It's known as the Ventisquero Negro (Black Glacier) since large quantities of moraine and broken rock mixed in with the ice give it a dark hue. A short trail leads down to the murky lake where the Ventisquero Negro ends.

Head on for 10 to 15 minutes to the **confitería** (cafe) at the end of the road; snacks and refreshments are available here. A foot track from the upper end of the car park here continues for a further 15 to 20 minutes up to the stream at the base of an impressive cirque at the head of the valley. Up to your left the long and spectacular waterfall known as the **Salto Garganta del Diablo** shoots down from the side of Glaciar Manso, while numerous other high cascades emerge from the icefalls up to the right. The agile can climb up to where the Salto thunders into a tiny chasm, spraying out mist that settles on the mossy rocks.

Trekkers who visit the Salto Garganta del Diablo should be mindful that there is a risk, although it is relatively low, of ice breaking off the hanging glaciers directly above and falling into the upper valley.

SIDE TRIP: PIEDRA PÉREZ/FILO CLERK

1¾–2½ hours return, 3km

If you don't mind a strenuous climb, this 'side trip on a side trip', to a lookout point up on the ridge to the north of the route to the waterfall, is even more rewarding than the original.

From behind the *confitería* (see side trip: Salto Garganta del Diablo, p114), head 50m right and downstream, crossing several small channels in the glacial stream. Pick up a graded foot track at the edge of the *coigüe* forest, and follow it as it snakes its way upward with the odd fallen trunk to clamber under or over. The route steepens as it rides a narrow spur covered with *lengas* up to the top of a broad ridge known as **Filo Clerk** (sometimes used by andinists as a route to the summits of Monte Tronador). Follow white paint markings a few hundred meters left (northwest) along the scrubby ridge above **Piedra Pérez**, a small but prominent tooth-shaped pinnacle visible from down in the valley, to reach a lookout point one to 1¼ hours from the *confitería*.

This part of the ridge offers a classic close-up view of Glaciar Castaño Overo. The crevasses and seracs of the glacier terminate in an impressive icefall that – like Glaciar Manso – hangs over a mighty precipice. Numerous meltwater cascades spill out from the edge of the ice. Visible on the ridge beyond the glacier is the path going up to Refugio Otto Meiling (see Side Trip: Refugio Otto Meiling, below), while to the southwest you should just be able to make out the old Refugio Tronador (see More Treks, p122) on a high rock ridge just left of the Glaciar Manso icefalls. You also get an excellent view back into the upper valley of the Río Manso.

Return to the *confitería* via the ascent route.

SIDE TRIP: GLACIAR CASTAÑO OVERO & REFUGIO OTTO MEILING

5–6¾ hours return, 18km

This is another highly scenic return day or overnight side trip that is recommended to all trekkers. Note that the 4WD road above the Río Castaño Overo has been affected by landslides; the *guardaparques* at Pampa Linda have the latest information on the route.

After signing in at the *guardería*, take the vehicle track heading roughly north past a signposted trail diverging rightward up to Laguna Ilón (see Pampa Linda to Refugio López under More Treks, p122). This 4WD road brings you through *coigüe* forest and small clearings intermittently strewn with the striking orange flowers of the *amancay* to reach the Río Castaño Overo after 30 to 40 minutes. Cross the small glacial river on a footbridge and continue a short way upstream to rejoin the 4WD road.

Bear left briefly along the road, which soon begins a steady winding ascent through attractive mature *coigüe* forest. Follow the vehicle track only for short sections (it has been cut by landslides further east), cutting between the long switchback curves on foot tracks to reach a signposted turn-off to Glaciar Castaño Overo. The return side trip to this glacier, which ends in a spectacular icefall, takes around one hour. After a longish switchback in the road, continue up a steep network of often eroded foot tracks through *lenga* forest to reach the top of the ridge at an area known as **La Almohadilla**, 1¼ to 1¾ hours from the Río Castaño Overo.

Make your way gently up along this broad ridgetop until the 4WD track ends at a grassy clearing near the upper limit of the *lenga* scrub. A well-marked path sidles on around to the left above high bluffs on the southern side of the ridge, giving wonderful views across to the adjacent Glaciar Castãno Overo and the various summits of Monte Tronador behind it. Cross back up to the right over a small snowfield before following large cairns and marker stakes up the bare, rocky ridgetop to arrive at **Refugio Otto Meiling** (dm AR$30; use of kitchen AR$15; dinner AR$42) after one to 1½ hours.

Refugio Otto Meiling stands at an altitude of around 2000m, a short way below the permanent snowline, and has a loft with sleeping capacity for 60 people. Its location offers a superb panorama taking in Pampa Linda, Paso de las Nubes and Cerro Catedral to the east. There is space for several tents in the shelter of rocks near the *refugio*, where trekkers may camp with the permission of the warden in reasonable weather. This side of Monte Tronador is relatively sheltered from the westerlies, but it's still a windy site.

Descend by the same route.

SIDE TRIP: LAGUNA ALERCE

2 hours return, 2km

From the Upper Río Frías campsite, head up the south (true right) bank of the Río Alerce to the base of a cliff on the left side of the gushing meltwater cascade. A steep climb over rock slabs leads into a tiny moraine-filled upper valley, which is followed (crossing the stream where necessary) to this impressive glacial lake lying directly under the hanging glacier known as Glaciar Alerce. When crossing the river, move between the rocks, not over them, since they are extremely slippery. Return the same way.

Day 2: Upper Río Frías to Puerto Frías

3¼–4½ hours, 10km

Pick up the trail below the campsite and begin the trek downvalley. This route avoids the open, waterlogged ground near the banks of the river by maintaining a slightly higher course along slopes on the eastern side of the valley through wet temperate rainforest dominated by *coigüe*, *mañío* and laurel. The moist conditions favour climbing epiphytes such as the *botellita* and the *estrellita*, whose delicate crimson flowers stand out on trunks.

The foot track is quite well maintained, with logs laid across boggy sections, as it leads through dense thickets of *colihue* cane and negotiates numerous trees that have fallen across the way. The going is slow but not tedious, despite there being only the occasional glimpse through the trees of the range (usually snowcapped until midsummer) on the adjacent side of the valley. The path meets the Río Frías 2¼ to three hours from the campsite.

Follow the true right (eastern) bank of the river for 10 to 15 minutes, then cross its deep, murky waters on a large fallen log to halfway, then the rest of the way on a log bridge with handrails. Head on, close to the true left bank of the Río Frías at first, then leaving the river and coming on to a long-abandoned road just before you pass a memorial to members of the Argentine Gendarmería Nacional, who died in a plane crash here in 1952.

The route soon skirts the southwestern side of **Laguna Frías** to arrive at a small boat landing, a shelter with toilets and an outpost of the Gendarmería Nacional at **Puerto Frías** after a final 30 to 40 minutes. Laguna Frías is a superb example of a glacial trough and is surrounded by sheer-sided mountains that rise directly from the shore, giving it a dramatic fjordlike appearance. Trekkers continuing to Peulla in Chile pass through customs here (if you want to leave early it's possible to have your passport exit-stamped the night before). Be aware that you can't take fruit, meat or dairy products across the border. Those not going on to Chile begin the long trip back to Bariloche here by catching a boat to Puerto Alegre (see Getting to/from the Trek, p112).

There is a small **campsite** at Puerto Frías, just up from the jetty, but no roofed accommodation.

ALTERNATIVE FINISH: PEULLA (CHILE)

6–9 hours, 26km

Be sure to have your passport exit-stamped at the *gendarmería* building before setting out.

Follow the good dirt road around the southwest side of Laguna Frías. The road climbs steadily in switchbacks to reach **Paso de Pérez Rosales** (1022m) after 45 minutes to one hour. The pass lies in lush rainforest on the Argentina–Chile border.

Begin the descent into Chile past tiny pampas and an abandoned farmhouse on your left. There are excellent **campsites** on little meadows 10 to 15 minutes down from the pass. The road gradually winds down through more dense forest of *coigüe* and *arrayán* to reach Casa Pangue after two to three hours. This post of the Carabineros de Chile looks up the valley towards the spectacular snowbound northern slopes of Monte Tronador. From here trekkers can opt to do the long (20km return) day trek up the gravelly east bank of the Río Peulla to the snout of the receding Glaciar Peulla.

Follow the road 3km downstream and cross to the southern side of the Río Peulla on a suspension bridge. The road heads west across the flat valley floor for two to three hours, before swinging around through a wide expanse of soggy grassland. Continue south for another 1½ to two hours to the Chilean customs post just outside Peulla (p114). Passports must be presented here and luggage may be inspected.

While in Peulla, stroll around to the Cascada de los Novios waterfall, or do the threehour return trek up to Laguna Margarita. The tiny harbor is 1km on from the village.

INDESTRUCTIBLE, ETERNAL ALERCE

Waterproof and nearly everlasting, the valuable alerce shingle once served as currency for the German colonists in Chile's south. Known as *lahuán* in Mapuche, *Fitzroya cupressoides* ranks among the oldest and largest tree species in the world, with specimens reaching almost 4000 years old. This 40m to 60m jolly evergreen giant plays a key role in temperate rainforests, though its prime value as a hardwood (and surefire shelter in a rainy climate) means it was logged to near-extinction. It is no longer legal to harvest live trees, but you can see alerce shingles on Chilote houses and the real deal deep in Lakes Region and Northern Patagonian forests.

PARQUE NACIONAL ALERCE ANDINO

Few venture to the rugged emerald forest of 40,000-hectare Parque Nacional Alerce Andino, despite its 40km proximity to Puerto Montt. The park was created in 1982 to protect some of the last remaining stands of alerce, found primarily 400m to 700m above sea level. An extremely slow-growing native conifer (known to the Mapuche as *lahuén*), the now-endangered alerce was logged to near extinction up until the mid-20th century.

Those who brave the mud and frequent rain will be rewarded by forest vistas ranging from sea level to 900m, a thick twisting medley of *coigue* and *ulmo*, ferns, climbing vines and dense thickets of *quila*. Pumas, pudus, foxes and skunks are about, but you'll have better luck glimpsing condors, kingfishers and waterfowl.

The park occupies precordillera, or Andean foothills, between the broad bay of Seno Reloncaví and its elongated eastern arm known as the Estuario de Reloncaví. At its hub, two small valleys (of the upper Río Lenca and the Río Chaica) run between granite ranges with summits surpassing

1500m. Intensive glaciation marks this rugged landscape, notable with its dozen or so beautiful glacial lakes. On its northeastern side the park almost touches Lago Chapo, a natural lake whose water level has been raised as part of a hydroelectricity project.

ENVIRONMENT

Luxuriant montane rainforest grows – at an almost visible speed – at all but the highest elevations. Two trees particularly favoured by Andino Alerce's moist and mild climatic conditions are the *tiaca*, with elongated, serrated leaves, and the *ulmo*, found up to an altitude of 500m. In January and February, the *ulmo* is easy to identify by its many fragrant white blossoms, producing delicious honey.

Hummingbirds, or *picaflores*, thrive on such nectar-bearing flowers, and because of their surprising lack of timidity, you can observe these delicate birds from close range. Unfortunately, *tábanos* also gain strength feeding on nectar, but soon start to crave the protein-rich blood of passing trekkers.

Other common tree species found in Alerce Andino include *coigüe de Chiloé, tepa, tineo, canelo, arrayán, avellano, ciprés de las Guaitecas* – and, of course, the majestic alerce. The area's relative inaccessibility has prevented major exploitation of its stands of giant alerces. The species is now protected, its most ancient and massive specimens may exceed 4m in diameter and reach several thousand years of age.

Among the numerous creepers and vines of the rainforest understorey are the *copihue*, whose beautiful crimson flowers are the floral emblem of Chile. The related *coicopihue* has somewhat less exuberant red flowers, which are nevertheless quite lovely. Less discreet climbers are the *pilpil de canasta*, recognisable by its pinkish, tubular flowers, and the *voqui*, or *lilinquén*, a small bushy plant with alternate tear-shaped leaves that yields clusters of tiny (but unpalatable) deep-purple, cherrylike fruit.

Native fauna is much less conspicuous, but the shy pudu and the marsupial *monito del monte* are occasionally spotted in the forest. The vegetarian *coipo* and the carnivorous *huillín* are thought to inhabit Andino Alerce's lakes and streams. Cat cousins, the puma and the far smaller *huiña*, are the largest terrestrial predators.

CLIMATE

Close to the coast, the area has a mild maritime climate and high annual rainfall. Precipitation ranges from 3300mm in the lower sectors to maximum levels of 4500mm on the highest ranges, usually falling as snow down to 800m (or lower) in winter.

PLANNING

Information Sources

There are three ranger stations in Parque Nacional Alerce Andino. The administrative office is at Guardería Correntoso, on the park's northern boundary; and Guardería Sargazo is 10km further along the road at the main entrance gate. The southern sector of the park is managed from Guardería Chaica.

Permits & Regulations

There is a CH$1000 entrance fee to Parque Nacional Alerce Andino, payable when you sign in at Guardería Sargazo. The only official campsite is Camping Correntoso. The only other place to stay is Refugio Sargazo, at the park entrance.

LAGUNA FRÍA

Duration 2 days
Distance 17km
Difficulty easy–moderate
Start/Finish Guardería Sargazo
Nearest Town Puerto Montt
Transport bus, walk
Summary Trek into the heart of the park, where massive and ancient alerces grow and solitary lakes nestle in the cool, temperate forest.

Although the *guardaparques*, with the help of volunteers, do their best to keep Alerce Andino's foot tracks open, the ferocious growth rate of the southern Lakes District vegetation makes this a difficult task. This trek takes advantage of those tracks on which most attention is lavished. Even so, occasional fallen tree trunks have to be ducked or climbed over, and vigorous *quila* leans over the route in many places. Heavy winter snowfalls can flatten the *quila* canes, completely obscuring the path, and the trek's level of difficulty will depend largely on how recently track-clearing work has been done.

The difficulty of keeping tracks open means that an additional section between Guardería Correntoso and Guardería Sargazo, and an alternative to that route via Refugio Pangal (closed), are closed for an undetermined period. If these tracks are eventually reopened, they would offer a worthwhile three-day trek beginning and ending in Correntoso, which is accessible by bus from Puerto Montt.

PLANNING

When to Trek

You are best to trek in Parque Nacional Alerce Andino between late November and mid-April. In January the *tábanos* are a nuisance.

What to Bring

Carry a tent or do the trek in one longish day from a base at Refugio Sargazo. *Refugios* within the park are derelict. Hikers should avoid them due to the presence of hanta virus, spread by rodents, in the region.

Maps

Two IGM 1:50,000 maps cover the central part of the park: *Correntoso* (Section H, No 52) and *Lenca* (Section H, No 61). These maps do not accurately show local roads or trekking routes, but are otherwise reasonably accurate (note that on these maps the Río Lenca is incorrectly given as the Río Chaica and vice versa). The same is true of the JLM *Mapas Ruta de los Jesuitas* map (No 15), which includes a 1:50,000

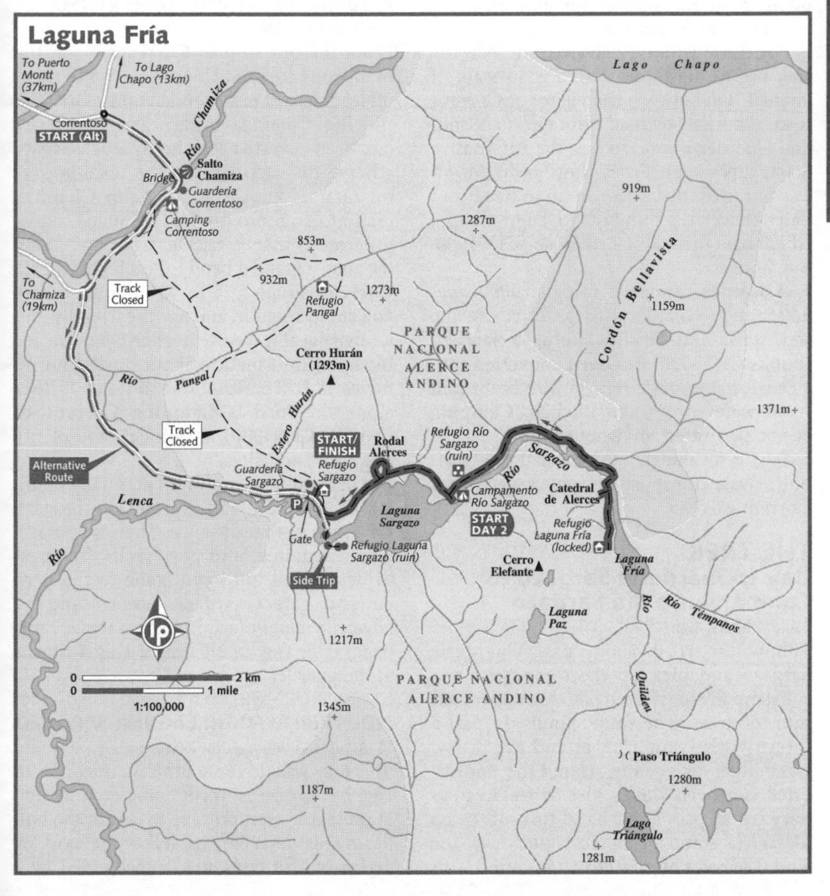

(approximately) partial map of Parque Nacional Alerce Andino.

ACCESS TOWNS

Puerto Montt (p122) is the logical base for the trek and has the nearest well-stocked supermarkets. The village of Correntoso has a small grocery store selling basic provisions, which is likely to be your last option after leaving Puerto Montt. In the park itself there's nowhere to buy anything.

GETTING TO/FROM THE TREK

To get there in a private vehicle, follow Ruta 7 – the Carretera Austral – east from Puerto Montt across the Río Chamiza to Chamiza, then head left up the Chamiza valley to the park. Vehicles can be left at the end of the public road, just outside the park entrance at Guardería Sargazo.

For those without private transport, the trek begins and ends with a road walk of about 13km between the village of Correntoso, 37km east by road from Puerto Montt, and Guardería Sargazo (see the Alternative Start, this page). From the Puerto Montt bus terminal, Buses JB run up to five buses daily (fewer on Sunday) to Lago Chapo, which pass through Correntoso (CH$1000, one hour).

A former residence for *guardaparques* adjacent to Guardería Sargazo, where the trek starts and finishes, **Refugio Sargazo** (bunks CH$5000) has been converted into a comfortable, basic *refugio* with bathroom (cold water only) and kitchen. Camping is not permitted anywhere nearby, so the *refugio* is a valuable option for those without private transport who must walk from Correntoso.

THE TREK

Day 1: Guardería Sargazo to Campamento Río Sargazo

1¾–2¼ hours, 4km

Follow the road 500m past Guardería Sargazo and pick up the signposted and substantially reinforced path leading off left into the trees. The route climbs up past a forestry observation tower and over a low ridge, then dips gently around the rainforested northern slopes just above **Laguna Sargazo** to pass a left-hand turn-off to an *alerzal* (a stand of alerces) known as the **Rodal Alerces** after 40 to 50 minutes. This is a rewarding short side trip to a small stand of particularly massive ancient alerces.

Make your way on through damp groves of leafy *tiacas*, which grant only the occasional unobstructed glimpse of the lake, and cut down across a small wash full of boulders. After finding the trail again in the scrub just up from the tiny rocky beach, climb on some way above the lake before you drop down again to a small, unofficial campsite and the reedy eastern shore of Laguna Sargazo after one to 1¼ hours.

Pick up the path in the scrub on the far side of this flat, boggy area and continue northeastward to the remains of an old orchard and the free **Campamento Río Sargazo**, with pit toilets, after 10 minutes or so.

ALTERNATIVE START: CORRENTOSO

2¼–3 hours, 13km

From the bus stop in Correntoso (on the main road to Lago Chapo), take the turnoff leading east past wooden houses to cross the Río Chamiza bridge. Because water has been diverted for the hydroelectricity scheme on Lago Chapo, the once-powerful cataract known as the **Salto Chamiza** (Salto Correntoso on the JLM map) is now little more than a trickle. Continue along the road around a bend to reach **Guardería Correntoso** after 20 to 25 minutes, where you should sign in and ask the friendly and knowledgeable resident *guardaparque* for the latest information about tracks and *refugios* in the park. A few minutes further along the road is **Camping Correntoso** (per site CH$3000), with toilets and plenty of grassy campsites.

The road now continues gradually uphill for about 10km, and lies outside the park for much of that distance. There's no navigation required, and not much of interest to detain you until you come to the park entrance gate, **Guardería Sargazo** and the adjacent *refugio* (see Refugio Sargazo, this page) after two to 2½ hours. Day 1 begins at the guardería.

SIDE TRIP: REFUGIO LAGUNA SARGAZO

50 minutes–1 hour return, 2km

This easy walk to the southwestern corner of Laguna Sargazo is worth doing even though at present it's not possible to stay at the hut. From Guardería Sargazo follow the road for 1.5km until it ends at a tunnel sealed by a locked gate. A path leads off right to meet the **Río Lenca** after a minute or two. Cross the river a short way downstream from here – an easy ford, since a weir just upstream diverts most of its water into the nearby tunnel. The path climbs up roughly eastward through the damp forest of *tepa* and *mañío*, then descends to the *refugio* after 25 to 30 minutes. This dilapidated shingled wooden shack stands just above a tiny beach on Laguna Sargazo.

Return by the same route.

Day 2: Campamento Río Sargazo to Guardería Sargazo

4¼–5 hours, 13km

The continuation of the trek as far as Laguna Fría could be done at the end of Day 1 or even omitted (although it's hard to imagine why you'd come here and not go on).

Leaving your packs at camp, continue northeast and almost immediately pass the largely demolished **Refugio Río Sargazo**. Built by a long-since evicted local settler, this shelter awaits rebuilding.

Proceed gently upvalley along the northern bank of the Río Sargazo through *quila* thickets, crossing several small side streams before a log bridge over the Río Sargazo after 35 to 45 minutes. The foot track, valiantly maintained in the face of overgrowth by vigorous bamboo, leads on up past a signpost pointing east towards another fine *alerzal*, the **Catedral de Alerces**, accessible just a short distance off the main track. Continue upstream to reach the lovely **Laguna Fría** 40 to 50 minutes after the Río Sargazo crossing.

Refugio Laguna Fría, closed to trekkers, is 300m on around the western side of the lake. Despite its name 'Cold Lake', Laguna Fría is actually fine for swimming, enclosed by various granite peaks visible only from the middle of the lake.

Return the same way to Campamento Río Sargazo to collect your packs, then reverse Day 1 to reach **Guardería Sargazo**, three to 3½ hours from Laguna Fría.

MORE TREKS

PARQUE NACIONAL LANÍN

Around Lago Lácar

For trekkers based in San Martín de los Andes, this easy and convenient three-day route (two days if you get picked up in Pucará) leads around the southern shore of Lago Lácar. From the trailhead 2km south of Quila Quina (accessible in summer by regular buses and organized tours), a broad path climbs gently southwest to the eastern shore of Lago Escondido, where there is a park-authorised campsite. From a turn-off 1.5km before (east of) Lago Escondido, a trail climbs away north across a pass past Laguna Vizcacha and on down to Lago Lácar. The route then follows the lake's southern shore via Ruca Ñire and Pucará to Hua Hum, from where there are daily tourist boats and buses back to San Martín in summer. Trekkers can also arrange to be picked in Pucará by one of the organized tours that explore Lago Lácar (including the nearby Termas de Queñi) in summer. Sendas y Bosques' 1:200,000 trekking map *Parque Nacional Lanín* shows the route.

PARQUE NACIONAL VICENTE PÉREZ ROSALES

Volcán Puntiagudo Lookout

Puntiagudo is a spectacular sharp volcanic plug whose distinctive form makes it easily recognisable from many places in the southern Lakes District. A long return day walk from Bahía Escocia (near the southern shore of Lago Rupanco – see Day 3 of the Termas de Callao trek, p97) follows a path south via a steep spur to a lookout point on the prominent volcanic ridge coming down from Puntiagudo's northeastern side. Two Chilean IGM 1:50,000 maps, *Cerro Puntiagudo* (Section H, No 35) and *Volcán Casablanca* (Section H, No 36), cover this trek but do not show its route.

Volcán Osorno to Rufugio Picada

This short one- to two-day trek from Petrohué on Lago Todos Los Santos follows a trail around the northeastern slopes of Volcán Osorno (2652m) to the ruins of Refugio Picada. Markings are minimal; for more information, consult the *casa de expediciones* (guide services) of Hotel Petrohue. Ascents of Osorno are usually made from the ski area on the other side of the mountain. The Chilean IGM 1:50,000 map *Petrohué* (Section H, No 44) covers this area of the trek but does not show the path.

Ralún to Ensenada Cayutúe

This easy return trek to Ensenada Cayutúe, an isolated southern arm of Lago Todos Los Santos, takes around three days. The route begins at a prominent road turn-off 2km east of the village of Ralún on Seno Reloncaví. The road passes farms before it terminates at a logging camp, from where a path climbs northward through the valley of the Río Reloncaví to the low pass of Portezuelo Cabeza de Vaca. From here, you descend to the lovely Laguna Cayutúe, then continue down the Río Concha to Ensenada Cayutúe. The recommended place to camp is at Laguna Cayutúe, on the other side of the inlet stream. The land fronting Ensenada Cayutúe is private property and camping there is not permitted.

Two Chilean IGM 1:50,000 maps, *Petrohué* (Section H, No 44) and *Cochamó* (Section H, No 53), cover the route. Ralún is about 95km east of Puerto Montt by road and can be reached by daily bus or ferry.

PARQUE NACIONAL NAHUEL HUAPI

For further suggestions, consult CAB and the staff at the APN Intendencia in Bariloche.

Refugio Tronador (Refugio Viejo)

Refugio Tronador was the CAB's first *refugio* on Monte Tronador. Today, this small, arched-stone building (with room for 10 people) is also known as Refugio Viejo (Old Refuge), and has largely been superseded by Refugio Otto Meiling.

Standing on a high ridge of the main Cordillera, Refugio Tronador offers superb views of both sides of the Lakes District. Five minutes west of Pampa Linda, the path (signposted 'Cascada de las Nalcas') leads off the road and across the young Río Manso. The route follows the Río Cauquenes up across Paso Vuriloche on the Argentina–Chile frontier to Mallín Chileno, a beautiful alpine meadow, then follows a rocky ridge northwest to the *refugio*, just a few paces inside Argentine territory at 2270m. The best map is the 1:50,000 *Trekking 2* map. The trek is recommended as an overnight trip. If the hut is full, Mallín Chileno is a good place to camp.

Cerro Volcánico

The climb to the 1861m summit of Cerro Volcánico is another excellent long day (or overnight) return trek from Pampa Linda. The route fords the Río Cauquenes where it leaves the path to Refugio Tronador (described previous) and follows a large side stream southward. A gentle climb eastward leads to Laguna La Rosada, from where the trail continues southwest through *mallín* meadows then on steeply through lenga forest on to a flat, windy ridge that gradually brings you up to the summit. Cerro Volcánico offers a fine view down to Lago Fonck and Lago Hess in the upper basin of the Río Manso between Cerro Cretón and Cerro Granítico. Use the 1:50,000 *Trekking 2* map.

Refugio Neumeyer

This easy and sheltered area makes a good option for two or three days trekking if the weather looks unstable. From Ruta Nacional 258 on the way to El Bolsón, a turn-off heads southwest up the Arroyo Ñirecó, before entering the broader side valley of the Arroyo Challhuaco. The road leads to **Refugio Neumeyer** (general use AR$5; dm AR$25; kitchen use AR$10), a well-equipped CAB hut, from where you can do a variety of nice day walks. Where the road crosses the Arroyo Ñirecó a foot track turns off to the right (west). A path continues along the eastern bank of the stream to Refugio Ñirecó, beside a *mallín* at the head of the valley. From here, a more difficult route leads west to a pass and follows the range north before descending via the Arroyo Melgurejo to Lago Gutiérrez. The best map is the 1:50,000 *Trekking 3* map. Refugio Neumeyer is accessible from Bariloche by private vehicle or tour bus (ask at the CAB office); you can walk to the trailhead in half a day.

Pampa Linda to Refugio López

This excellent four- or five-day trek is similar to the Nahuel Huapi Traverse, but much wilder. An old road leads from Pampa Linda across the Río Alerce, then climbs up between Cerro del Viento and Cerro Punta Negra to a minor pass. The descent dips north to Laguna Ilón, with a basic *refugio* on its northern shore. The route continues eastward between Cerro Capitán and Cerro Punta Negra, then descends past Laguna

Jujuy to Laguna Callvu (Azul). From Laguna Callvu you go northeast via another gap south of Cerro Cristal, before dropping down to Laguna Lluvú (or CAB) and another basic *refugio*. From here the route descends to the Arroyo Lluvuco and crosses the Bailey Willis range to connect with Day 4 of the Nahuel Huapi Traverse (p103). Another possibility is to continue down the Arroyo Lluvuco to meet an old road leading northeast along the southern shore of Brazo Tristeza to Bahía López on Lago Nahuel Huapi. See the Paso de las Nubes trek (p111) and the Nahuel Huapi Traverse for transport details. The 1:50,000 *Trekking 1* and *Trekking 2* maps cover the route.

Around Lago Mascardi

Lago Mascardi has a rough 'U' shape formed by two arms on either side of a peninsula. From the northeastern side of Lago Mascardi, a path leads around the lake's western shore, cutting off the peninsula as it climbs to Laguna Llum, a tranquil lake surrounded by rainforest. The route continues over the main ridge north of Cerro General Justo, then drops back down to the lakeside. The route follows this western arm (Brazo Tronador) around to cross a footbridge over the Río Manso 1.5km before meeting the Pampa Linda road. Alternatively, trekkers can make their way up the Arroyo Callvuco (or Azul) to Laguna Callvu (or Azul) to meet the Pampa Linda to Refugio López route described previously. Use the 1:100,000 *Refugios, Sendas y Picadas Parque Nacional Nahuel Huapi* color map. This is a two-day trek with a camp at Laguna Llum. For access, take one of the daily buses between Pampa Linda (see Paso de las Nubes, p111) and Bariloche.

Ascent of Volcán Osorno (Chile)

One of the great landmarks of the southern Chilean Lakes District, the perfect white cone of Volcán Osorno attracts considerable attention from serious mountaineers. Volcán Osorno's last major eruption occurred in 1835, and released a series of catastrophic floods and lahars (mud avalanches). The volcano has been more or less dormant since then, allowing extensive glaciers to re-accumulate around its upper slopes.

The climb to the summit takes one long day and should be started at dawn. It is normally undertaken from the *refugio* at 1180m on the western slopes of Volcán Osorno (outside Parque Nacional Vicente Pérez Rosales). At all times of the year crampons and an ice axe are required, and inexperienced climbers are strongly urged to make the ascent of the volcano with a professional local mountain guide.

A paved road leads off the main Puerto Octay–Puerto Varas road, 2km north of Ensenada on the eastern shores of Lago Llanquihue, up to Refugio Teski and the Centro de Esqui. The Chilean IGM 1:50,000 map *Las Cascadas* (Section H, No 43) covers the west side of Volcán Osorno and most of the ascent route. The adjoining map *Petrohué* (Section H, No 44) is also very useful.

RESERVA NACIONAL LLANQUIHUE (CHILE)

The roughly 300-sq-km Reserva Nacional Llanquihue forms a narrow band of wilderness stretching southeast from the southeastern corner of Lago Llanquihue along the north side of Lago Chapo almost as far as Seno Reloncaví. The 2015m Volcán Calbuco, in the north of the reserve, can be climbed in a two-day return trek from the Guardería Chapo, which is at the northern end of Parque Nacional Alerce Andino. The trek follows a path up the Río Blanco to a rustic Conaf *refugio* on the volcano's southern side. From here experienced climbers can tackle the relatively easy Volcán Calbuco. The 1:50,000 Chilean IGM map *Correntoso* (Section H, No 52) covers the trek.

PARQUE NACIONAL ALERCE ANDINO

Lago Triángulo

Lago Triángulo lies in a deep fjordlike trough fronted by massive smooth granite walls in the southern (Chaica) sector of Parque Nacional Alerce Andino. It can be visited in an easy three-hour return trek through the rainforest from the parking lot at Lago Chaiquenes. The path leads briefly around the northern shore of Lago Chaiquenes, then follows the east bank of the Río Triángulo northward to the southern end of Lago Triángulo. Lago Chaiquenes is 17km by road from Lenca, a scattered village on Seno Reloncaví; there is a Conaf *guardería* 4km before Lago Chaiquenes. Lenca is on the Carretera Austral, and can be reached from Puerto Montt by several daily buses. There is no public transport to Lago Chaiquenes, which makes a pleasant but long 4½-hour uphill walk from Lenca. The 1:50,000 Chilean IGM map *Lenca* (Section H, No 61) covers the route.

PARQUE NACIONAL CHILOÉ (CHILE)

The 430-sq-km Parque Nacional Chiloé, on the windswept western side of the large island of Chiloé, offers two excellent treks with wonderful coastal scenery of sandy beaches and estuarine lagoons set before a backdrop of densely forested hills. Due to the mild coastal climate, these treks can be undertaken at virtually any time apart from winter (June to September).

A two-day return trek leaves from the village of Chepu, in the park's northern sector, accessible by daily bus from Ancud. A good foot track can be followed south to a Conaf *guardería* and *refugio* by the Río Lar, where seal colonies inhabit the numerous rocky islets just offshore. The Chilean IGM 1:50,000 map *Chepu* (Section H, No 75) covers this route.

A more popular three-day return trek (25km) leads from the village of Cucao in the park's southern sector. Cucao is accessible by up to six daily buses from Castro. The route leads along lovely sandy beaches, past isolated farmlets and through wet rainforests as far as the Río Anay (which can be crossed to reach a wild surf beach). Wild camping is free. Two renovated Conaf *refugios*, at Río Cole Cole and Río Anay, are planned for 2010. For updates, contact **Conaf** (☎ 065-532502) in Castro.

Use two 1:50,000 Chilean IGM maps: *Río Anay* (Section H, No 86) and *Cucao* (Section H, No 95).

TOWNS & FACILITIES

ANTICURA (CHILE)

☎ 064

Meaning 'rock of the sun' in Mapundungun, Anticura is 94km east of Osorno on the international highway Ruta 215 (which runs via Paso de Puyehue to Bariloche in Argentina). The **Guardería Anticura** (☎ 064-374572) is on the south side of Ruta 215. Opposite, north of the highway, are Conaf's information center and **Etnoturismo Anticura** (☎ 099-1774672; www.etnoturismoanticura.blogspot.com), a Mapuche-run *albergue* (dm CH$6,000 per person) with **camping** (campsites with hot showers CH$3,000 per person), two person cabins with gas cooking & hot water (CH$25,000) and a snack kiosk. Overnight parking is CH$800.

BARILOCHE (ARGENTINA)

☎ 02944 / pop 98,000

The Breckenridge of South America, Bariloche is a ski town of city proportions, sprawled out on southeastern shores of cobalt Lago Nahuel Huapi. This dose of urban Andes is as dedicated to mountain culture as its main strip is to chocolate shops and the sale of carved gnomes. Local andinist tradition started with its Swiss settlement, and is evident today in various mountain refuges and a near constant cycle of outdoor events. Bariloche is also the gateway to Argentina's superb Parque Nacional Nahuel Huapi.

Information

All trekkers should visit **Club Andino Bariloche** (CAB; ☎ 02944-422266; www.clubandino.com.ar; 20 de Febrero 30; 9.30am-1pm & 4.30-8.30pm Mon-Sat, 4.30-8.30pm Sun), which sells trekking maps and is a great source of information. The **administration center** (☎ 02944-423121; pnint@bariloche.com.ar; San Martín 24; 9am-2pm Mon-Fri) for Parque Nacional Nahuel Huapi is uphill from the Centro Cívico and one block downhill from CAB. The city website is www.bariloche.com.

Supplies & Equipment

For used gear, try the sale board at CAB. The biggest outdoor retailer is **Scandinavia** (☎ 02944-433170; Mitre 219). Mountain store **RAID** (☎ 02944-522178; Neumeyer 60) has new and used equipment, plus does repairs. Try **Grupo García Pinturería** (cnr Gallardo & Rolando), a paint shop, for *solvente* (white gas), and outdoor-gear suppliers for gas canisters.

Supermarkets include **Todo** (San Martín 281), which has several branches around town.

Sleeping & Eating

The **oficina de turismo** (☎ 02944-423022, 423122; www.barilochepatagonia.info; Centro Cívico; 8am-9pm daily) has accommodations listings.

Party hostel **Periko's** (☎ 02944-522326; www.perikos.com; Morales 555; dm AR$45, d AR$150; i) has large six-bed dormitories and rents bikes. Immaculate **Albergue El Gaucho** (☎ 522-464; www.hostelelgaucho.com; Belgrano 209; dm AR$56; ni) is plain but spacious. The penthouse panoramas at **Hostel 1004** (☎ 02944-432228; 1004hostel@ciudad.com.ar; 10th floor, San Martín 127; dm AR$45) beat any hotel views in town. There's no sign; enter the Bariloche Center, take the elevator to the 10th floor, and look for room 1004. Or get a free transfer to the hostel's mountain property **La Morada**, just out of town. The restored **Hostería El Ciervo Rojo** (☎ 02944-435241; www.elciervorojo.com in Spanish; Elflein 115; s/d AR$130/160) has slate floors, sloped ceilings and homey touches.

The best licks are at **Helados Jauja** (Perito Moreno 14; cone AR$5), with ice creams that incorporate local berries and honey. **Días de Zapata** (☎ 02944-423128; Morales 362; mains AR$25-35; lunch & dinner) is a warm and inviting little Mexican restaurant with happy hour specials on margaritas. For creative pastas, **La Trattoria de la Famiglia Bianchi** (Av Bartolomé Mitre 240; mains AR$20-35; lunch & dinner) fully satisfies. Cozy pub/restaurant **Map Room** (Urquiza 248; mains AR$20-30; 11am-1am) promises a good range of beers and real American breakfasts.

Getting There & Away

Bariloche is the Patagonian Andes' best connected city for air services, with flights to/from Buenos Aires (AR$500, 2¼ hours, several daily), El Calafate (AR$305, 1¾ hours, nine weekly) and many other large cities throughout Patagonia. The main local carriers are **Aerolíneas Argentinas** (☎ 0810-2228-6527; Mitre 185) and **LADE** (☎ 02944-423562; Quaglia 238/242, Via Firenze center).

The **bus terminal** (☎ 02944-426999; Ruta Nacional 237) is out of town to the east; serving local and long-distance destinations. Numerous daily buses run south along Ruta 258 to El Bolsón (AR$15, two hours) and Esquel (AR$32, 4½ hours), as well as north to San Ma[...] hours) and Buenos Aire[...] hours). There are also dai[...] orno (AR$60, five hours) an[...] (AR$60, seven hours) in C[...] Tas-Choapa (☎ 02944-426663; Moreno 138).

COLONIA SUIZA (ARGENTINA)

☎ 02944

Colonia Suiza, near the end of the Nahuel Huapi Traverse, was originally settled by Franco-Swiss farming families in the first decades of the 20th century and is today a modest lake-side holiday village. A number of the original houses remain, and the locals sell homemade fruit preserves and chocolates.

Colonia Suiza has two public campsites, both with hot showers: the cramped and dusty **Camping Goye** (☎ 02944-448627; www.campinggoye.com.ar, in Spanish; camping per person AR$20), near the No 10 bus stop, and the more spacious **Camping Hueney Ruca**, with sites right on the shore of Lago Perito Moreno (closed at the time of research). **Restaurante Heidi** (☎ 02944-448492; beds AR$38) offers basic lodging and a restaurant.

Campsites

The road to Llao Llao has several campsites, **La Selva Negra** (☎ 02944-441013; Av Bustillo km2.9; per site AR$25) is the nearest. Further down is **Camping El Yeti** (☎ 02944-442073; Av Bustillo km5.8; per site AR$24) and **Camping Petunia** (☎ 02944-461969; Av Bustillo km13.5; per site AR$24).

JUNÍN DE LOS ANDES (ARGENTINA)

☎ 02972 / pop 11,000

Humble Junín is popular with fly-fishers but has less happening than other Lakes District towns. Its location 41km north of San Martín makes it a good base for trips to the north of Parque Nacional Lanín.

Information

Junín's helpful **tourist office** (☎ 02972-491160; turismo@jandes.com.ar; Padre Milanesio 596; 8am-11pm Nov-Feb, 8am-9pm Mar-Oct) is on Plaza San Martín. The local **APN office** (☎ 02972-491160; Domingo Milanesio at Coronel Suárez;

...-8.30pm Mon-Fri, 2.30-8.30pm Sat & Sun) gives information on Parque Nacional Lanín. **Alquimia** (☎ 02972-491355; www.alquimiaturismo.com.ar; Padre Milanesio 840) rents climbing gear and does two-day guided volcano ascents. Recommended **Tromen Turismo** (☎ 02972-491469; Coronel Suárez 445) does trips into Parque Nacional Lanín and tours of Mapuche communities. Rentals include mountain bikes and climbing gear.

Sleeping & Eating

The fully-equipped **Camping Laura Vacuña** (Ginés Ponte s/n; sites per person AR$5) occupies a sublime location, perched on an island in between two burbling creeks. A beautiful spot minutes from the center, **Hostería Chimehuín** (☎ 02972-491132; www.interpatagonia.com/hosteriachimehuin, in Spanish; Coronel Suárez & 25 de Mayo; s/d AR$130/150) has big, comfortable rooms and a tranquil air. For pasta, try **El Preferido de Junín** (General Lamadrid 20; mains AR$20-30; lunch & dinner), also offering takeout.

Getting There & Away

From Junín's **bus terminal** (☎ 02972-492038) there are frequent departures to all of the region's major centers, including San Martín de los Andes (some via Aluminé) and Zapala. Empresa San Martín, Igi-Llaima and JAC all have (almost) daily buses to Pucón and Temuco, which run via Tromen and Paso Mamuil Malal.

THROUGH THE ANDES BY BOAT

One of the Andes' classic journeys is the Cruce de Lagos, an ultra-scenic 12-hour bus-and-boat trip over the Andes between Bariloche, Argentina and Puerto Montt, Chile. Aimed at package tourists, all this scenery comes with a price tag. The total fare is US$238, and those who try to book ahead may be told that segments cannot be purchased at a discount. Ferry segments can be purchased on-site though, given availability.

Service is daily in the summer and weekdays the rest of the year. **Cruce de Lagos** (www.crucedelagos.cl) runs the trip. You can book in Puerto Montt with **Turistur** (☎ 065-437127) or in Bariloche with **Catedral Turismo** (☎ 02944-425444; www.crucedelagos.cl; Palacios 263). In winter (mid-Apr to Sep), the westbound trip takes two days.

MAMUIL MALAL/TROMEN AREA (ARGENTINA)

☎ 02972

The remote locality of Tromen consists of a Gendarmería Nacional customs post and the APN's **Guardería Tromen** (☎ 02972-427204, 427210; laningparque@smandes.com.ar) on Ruta Provincial 60, which continues 4km across Paso Mamuil Malal into Chile. Free camping is allowed near the *guardería* (ranger station), but much better is the beautiful free campsite 3km away on the southern shore of Lago Tromen. There is no nearby store or accommodation.

OSORNO (CHILE)

☎ 064 / pop 149,443

Agricultural hub Osorno, 910km south of Santiago, is an access point to Parque Nacional Puyehue and a convenient bus-transfer point for crossing into Argentina. While mild-mannered and pleasant, there's little to seduce a visitor into dawdling here. **Sernatur** (Servicio Nacional de Turismo; ☎ 237575) has a tourist office on the west side of the Plaza de Armas. **Conaf** (Corporación Nacional Forestal; ☎ 234393; Martínez de Rozas 430; 10am-5pm, Mon-Fri) has park information.

Sleeping & Eating

The best budget option, the basic **Hospedaje Sánchez** (☎ 064-422140; Los Carrera 1595; r per person CH$5000) is run by a nice older couple. Upgrade with **Hostal Reyenco** (☎ 064-236285; reyenco@surnet.cl; Freire 309; s without bathroom CH$12,000, d CH$16,000) with a nice living room and breakfast area. The alluring **Clube de Artesanos** (☎ 064-230307; Juan Mackenna 634; mains CH$2600-5200; lunch & dinner Mon-Sat, lunch Sun), a former union house, serves traditional *pastel del choclo* and *Märzen*, a local homebrew. On the plaza, the busy **Café Central** (☎ 064-257711; O'Higgins 610; mains CH$1250-6100; breakfast, lunch & dinner) offers colossal burgers and breakfast.

Getting There & Away

There are daily flights to/from Santiago (from CH$141,000) with **Lan** (☎ 600-5262000; Eleuterio Ramírez 802) and **Sky Airlines** (☎ 064-230186; Galeria Centro Osorno, Cochrane).

Long-distance buses use the **main bus terminal** (☎ 064-234149; Errázuriz 1400), near Angulo. Companies include **Pullman Bus** (☎ 064-318529), **Tas Choapa** (☎ 064-233933), **JAC** (☎ 064-553300), **Tur-Bus** (☎ 064-201526), **Igi Llaima** (☎ 064-234371) and **Cruz del Sur** (☎ 064-232777). **Bus Norte** (☎ 064-233933) and **Andesmar** (☎ 064-233-050), reach the Argentine Lakes District. Sample travel times and fares follow:

Destination	Fare (CH$)	Duration (hr)
Ancud	$4500	4
Bariloche (AR)	$12,000	5
Coyhaique	$30,000	20
Puerto Montt	$1500	1½
Punta Arenas	$40,000	27
Santiago	from $1800	12
Temuco	$4000	4½
Zapala-Neuquén (AR)	$14,000	17

Buses leave from the **Terminal de Buses Rurales** (☎ 064-232073; Mercado Municipal, Errázuriz & Prat), two blocks west. **Expreso Lago Puyehue** (☎ 064-243919) goes to Termas Puyehue/Aguas Calientes (CH$1700) and Anticura (CH$4000) from the northeast corner.

PETROHUÉ (CHILE)

☎ 065

At the western end of Lago Todos Los Santos, Petrohué has a dock, trails and beach access. Conaf has a **park administration center** (☎ 065-486115) here and a small **campsite** (four-person site CH$8000) on the beach, usually smoked-out with family barbecues. In summer, vendors sell last-minute snacks at the boat dock.

On the other side of the Río Petrohué, **Camping Küschel** (camping per tent CH$4000) has noisy waterfront sites. Boats from the dock at Petrohué shuttle backpackers across the river (CH$1000). The upscale **Hotel Petrohué** (☎ 065-258042; www.petrohue.com; s/d CH$99,000/130,000) has the feel of a luxuriant lodge but the small restaurant (mains CH$5000-8000) maintains leisurely service.

PUERTO MONTT (CHILE)

☎ 065 / pop 168,242

Puerto Montt has grown up from the ho-hum provincial capital of Los Lagos to a grinding hub of commerce and industry. Chile's salmon industry is based here and it's also the springboard to a number of national parks, the Island of Chiloé and Patagonia.

Information

On the plaza, Puerto Montt's **municipal tourist office** (☎ 065-261823; Antonio Varas 415; 9am-9pm) offers plenty of national park information. **Conaf** (☎ 065-486130; Ochagavía 464) can provide details on nearby national parks.

Sleeping & Eating

Hospitality makes family lodging **Casa Perla** (☎ 065-262104; www.casaperla.com; Trigal 312; campsites per person CH$5000, dm & r per person CH$7000) worth the uphill walk. Boutique hotel **Tren del Sur** (☎ 065-343939; www.trendelsur.cl; Santa Teresa 643; s/d from CH$21,800/29,900) offers high style with cozy rooms, central heating and a sky-lit hallway.

The ecologically-minded **Camping Anderson** (☎ 099-5177222; www.chipsites.com/camping/; Panitao; campsites per person CH$3000) is worth the short trip. Fresh food provisions are available on site. Buses Bohle makes the 20km trip from Puerto Montt's bus terminal to Panitao (nine times daily, CH$750).

Supermarket **Santa Isabel** (Diego Portales 1040) faces the bus station. A choice spot for Chilean junk food, **Tablón del Ancla** (☎ 065-367554; Antonio Varas 350; mains CH$1900-5900; lunch & dinner) serves *chorillana*, a mixture of fries, cheese and sausage, and typical fare with beer on tap. It's on the main plaza. The fancy **Fogón del Leñador** (☎ 065-489299; Rancagua 245; mains CH$6000-9500; lunch & dinner) has the best steak in town, served with hot *sopaipillas*.

Getting There & Away

Lan (☎ 600-5262000; O'Higgins 167, Local 1-B) flies daily to Punta Arenas (from CH$105,350), Balmaceda/Coyhaique (from CH$62,100) and Santiago (from CH$108,100). Competitor **Sky Airlines** (☎ 065-437-555; www.skyairline.cl, in Spanish; cnr San Martin & Benavente; 9am-6.45pm Mon-Fri, 10am-1pm Sat) flies to Punta Arenas and Santiago (from CH$32,300) with slightly cheaper fares.

Puerto Montt's waterfront **bus terminal** (☎ 065-253143; cnr Av Diego Portales & Lillo) is the chaotic transportation hub for the region – watch your belongings or leave them with the *custodia*. In summer, trips to Punta Arenas and Bariloche can sell out, so book in advance.

Minibuses to Puerto Varas (CH$800, 25 min), from where there are connections to Petrohué, leave frequently from the eastern side of the terminal. **Buses Fierro** (☎ 065-289024) leaves for the villages of Ralún (CH$1500, two hours) and Cochamó (CH$2000, 2½ hours) five times daily, two of which carry on to Río Puelo (with ferry and bus connections to Llanada Grande).

With offices at the terminal, bus companies include **Cruz del Sur** (☎ 065-252872), with frequent services to Chiloé; **Tur-Bus** (☎ 065-259320), **Igi Llaima** (☎ 065-254-519); and **Pullman Bus** (☎ 065-254399). All go to Santiago, stopping at various cities along the way. For long-haul trips to Coyhaique and Punta Arenas via Argentina, try Cruz del Sur.

For Bariloche, Argentina, Tur-Bus/Tas-Choapa, **Andesmar** (☎ 065-312123) goes daily via the Cardenal Samoré pass east of Osorno. Cruz del Sur goes on Thursday and Sunday only. For information on the popular bus-boat combination trip to Bariloche, see the boxed text, p126.

Some sample travel times and costs are as follows:

Destination	Fare (CH$)	Duration (hr)
Ancud	$3300	2½
Bariloche (AR)	$13,000	6
Castro	$4700	3½
Coyhaique	$30,000	24
Osorno	$1500	1¾
Pucón	$5900	6
Punta Arenas	$35,000	30
Santiago	$20,900	12
Temuco	$8000	5½

The **Terminal de Transbordadores** (Av Angelmó 2187) hosts **Navimag** (☎ 065-432360; www.navimag.com), a commercial transporter that runs the popular three-night journey through Patagonia's canals. Navimag's M/N Magallanes sails each Monday to Puerto Natales. If you reserve via the internet, confirm your booking pre-departure. Fares (which include meals) vary according to season, class of accommodation and view, but in high season (November to March), the cheapest one-way fares start at CH$202,800 per person.

Navimag also sails the Ferry *Puerto Eden* to Puerto Chacabuco on Wednesdays in high season. Prices range from CH$143,000 for the AA single to CH$38,000 for the C berth.

SAN MARTÍN DE LOS ANDES (ARGENTINA)

☎ 02972 / pop 26,000

This mountain town, a tourist attraction in its own right, is the kind of place you would see a local biking with skis on their shoulder and perhaps a dog running alongside. Known as San Martín, it occupies the east end of Lago Lácar in Parque Nacional Lanín's southern sector. Cerro Chapelco is the local hub of alpine skiing.

Information

San Martín's **tourist office** (☎ 02972-425500; www.smandes.gov.ar; San Martín & Rosas; 8am-9pm, until 10pm Dec-Mar), across from Plaza San Martín, is well organized and sells fishing licenses. Across the plaza, the **APN Intendencia** (☎ 02972-427233; www.parquenacionallanin.gov.ar, in Spanish; Emilio Frey 749; 8am-2pm Mon-Fri, daily Jan & Feb) administers Parque Nacional Lanín and offers some maps.

For guided Volcán Lanín ascents, check out **Cerro Torre** (☎ 02972--429162; cerrotorre@smandes.com.ar; San Martín 960) a reputable outfitter with retail and rentals of mountain gear. Recommended guide service **Andestrack** (☎ 02972-420588; www.andestrack.com.ar; Perito Moreno 722) also does volcano climbs.

Sleeping & Eating

Spacious **Camping ACA** (☎ 02972-427332; Av Koessler 2640; sites per person with two-person minimum fee AR$10) sits on the eastern outskirts of town. For a hostel, try the HI-affiliated **Puma Youth Hostel** (☎ 02972-422443; www.pumahostel.com.ar; A Fosbery 535; dm AR$35, d AR$95) with spacious dorms and ski transfers; or shiny newcomer **Secuoya Hostel** (☎ 02972-424485; Rivadavia 411; dm AR$33, d with shared bathroom AR$80; i), offering welcoming spaces. The alpine-style **Hostal del Lago** (☎ 02972-427598; hostallago@hotmail.com; Coronel Rhode 854; s/d AR$120/150) offers six super-cozy rooms and friendly management.

For homemade pastas, **Trattoria Mi Viejo Pepe** (Villegas 725; mains AR$15-25) makes outstanding dishes. Vegetarian **Pura Vida** (☎ 02972-429302; Villegas 745; mains AR$10-18; lunch & dinner daily, closed lunch Sun) serves tasty pizzas, savory pies and heaping salads, with a couple of meat options.

Getting There & Away

Aerolíneas Argentinas (☎ 02972-427003, 427004; Capitán Drury 876) flies to Buenos Aires (AR$700 one-way) daily except Wednesday.

The **bus terminal** (☎ 02972-427044; Villegas & Juez del Valle) is a block south of the highway and 3½ blocks southwest of Plaza San Martín. To get to Aluminé you must first change buses in Zapala (AR$39, four hours). Departures south to Bariloche (AR$40, 4½ hours via Seite Lagos) are also frequent. **Igi Llaima** (☎ 02972-428100) has three departures weekly via Paso Mamuil Malal to Temuco AR$50, six hours), in Chile. **Buses Lafit** (☎ 02972-427422) runs several times weekly, via Paso Huahum to Puerto Pirehueico in Chile (AR$9), from where there are sporadic ferry/bus connections on to Puerto Fuy and Panguipulli.

In addition to serving Bariloche via the Seite Lagos route, **Ko-Ko** (☎ 02972-427422) travels from January through March to Puerto Arturo (AR$4) on Lago Lolog; from here hikers can do a two-day trek north via Portezuelo Auquinco to Lago Curruhue.

To access treks in Parque Nacional Lanín, the only form of public transport are tour agencies, including **Huemul Turismo** (☎ 02972-422903; www.huemulturismo.com.ar; San Martín 881), with service on most summer days. Destinations include Quila Quina, Termas de Lahuen Co, Termas de Queñi and Lagos Huechulafquén and Paimún. **Andes** (☎ 02972-429110; Villegas 944) shuttles trekkers to trailheads for reasonable rates.

Central Patagonia

HIGHLIGHTS

- Exploring the wild back country around the cathedral peaks of **Cerro Castillo** (p145)
- Exclaiming 'Futalaufquen!' as you plunge into the icy lake in **Parque Nacional Los Alerces** (p140)
- Tracing the towering trunks of ancient alerces in **Parque Pumalín** (p131)
- Braving the rickety bridges and cruising through the hush *lenga* forests of the **Comarca Andina** (p135)

Wild and isolated, central Patagonia is the untamed heart of the region, less feted and crowded than other famous hotspots. Few visitors arrive at these remote outposts. For starters, just getting here is work. On the Chilean side, heavy rains wash out roads, and big rivers and thick undergrowth slow progress on the trail. On the Argentine side, Ruta 40 challenges travelers with scant transport, whipping winds and sometimes snow. But hey, the rewards always fit the challenge.

Those who brave this backwater can plot a course through dense forests, clear streams, unnamed peaks and sprawling glaciers. Isolation has kept the local character self-reliant and tied to nature's clock. In Chile, the Carretera Austral (Hwy 7) was the first road to effectively link these remote regions in the 1980s. The Argentine side moves (a touch) faster. Pavement may be coming to the mythical Ruta 40, but big sky landscapes still rule over its dusty settlements.

With the potential to transform the region, a dozen hydroelectric dams on major Chilean waterways have been proposed. These would inundate virgin forest, disrupt wildlife and require massive tree clearing to create the longest transmission lines in the world. While the Chilean government's priority is to avert a looming energy crunch without the dams, the proposals herald sad tidings for the great Patagonian wilderness.

It may be wise to see it while you can. This section runs north to south, with the hub of Coyhaique also useful to trekkers accessing Southern Patagonia treks around Villa O'Higgins.

GATEWAYS

See Coyhaique (p155) and Esquel (p157). For the latest on Chaitén, in the path of Volcán Chaitén's latest series of eruptions, see boxed text p133.

PARQUE PUMALÍN

Verdant and pristine, this 3300-sq-km park encompasses vast extensions of temperate rainforest, clear rivers, seascapes and farmland. A remarkable forest conservation effort, Parque Pumalín attracts 10,000 visitors yearly (no small number, considering that tourist season is a three-month period) to explore these tracts of forest stretching from near Hornopirén to Chaitén. Owned by American Doug Tompkins (see boxed text, below), it is Chile's largest private park and one of the largest private parks in the world. For Chile it's a model park, with well-maintained roads and trails, extensive infrastructure and minimal impact. Concessions are local businesses a boost.

Agricultural use goes on alongside forest preservation in a park model that's 'unique in the world'. according to Dagoberto Guzmán, park manager. Staff participate in projects that range from bee-keeping and organic farming to animal husbandry and ecotourism. Private *fundos* (small farms) within the park boundaries continue to operate, but with an emphasis on sustainable living. The park maintains a free *refugio* (rustic shelter) for the local workers, and it doesn't charge admission. Tompkins' goal is to allow visitors to immerse themselves in pristine nature and come out with a deeper appreciation for the natural environment.

There are three short but rewarding treks, which all begin quite close together from the Carretera Austral, and can be done either individually, together over a long day, or over two days by camping at Cascadas Escondidas or Tronador.

With the recent activity of Volcán Chaitén (see boxed text p133), Parque Pumalín has closed its infrastructure for a time and may relocate services to El Amarillo, south of Chaitén. Given the unpredictability of volcanoes, visitors should check the region's most recent status before traveling. You can check the park website (www.pumalínpark.org) or contact the Centro de Visitantes Parque Pumalín office (☎ 02945-465-250079; www.pumalínpark.org; Klenner 299, Puerto Varas; 8.30am-6.30pm Mon-Fri, 9am-1pm Sat) for the latest details.

For more treks in this area, see p151.

THE TOMPKINS' LEGACY

Ecobarons – the wealthy philanthropists recycling their greenbacks into green causes – have become a powerful force in the push for Southern Cone conservation, and none more so than US entrepreneur Douglas Tompkins. The founder of Esprit clothing and North Face outdoor-equipment stores, along with his wife Kris Tompkins (a former CEO of Patagonia-brand clothing), started by creating Parque Pumalín, a Rhode Island–sized conservation project cobbled together from small Patagonian farms abutting ancient forest. Donated to the Fundación Pumalín in 2005, it will eventually become a national park.

This gift, however, hasn't left the dynamic duo empty-handed. Today the couple's holdings have burgeoned into an impressive 5180 sq km in Chile and 2924 sq km in Argentina. Kris Tompkins' *Conservación Patagónica* (www.conservacionpatagonica.org) has added important wildlife corridors like Valle Chacabuco and Estancia El Rincón to the region.

More importantly, the couple's hands-on approach has inspired similar contributions, such as Chilean presidential candidate Sebastian Piñera's Parque Tantauco in Chiloé (p124).

Not surprisingly, Douglas Tompkins' interventionist style has attracted its share of controversy. After decades of clamoring by locals for a more convenient road alternative to the Hornopirén–Caleta Gonzalo ferry, the Chilean government proposed a direct route through the heart of Pumalín. Despite local support for the project, Tompkins has opposed the current plan, proposing instead a less-costly coastal route that would more closely follow the settlement pattern.

Beyond the politics, however, many Chileans have found the parks to be a worthwhile contribution. Are the Tompkins environmental visionaries or part of a wave of wealthy foreigners with designs on Patagonia? One thing is for sure: it's not easy being green.

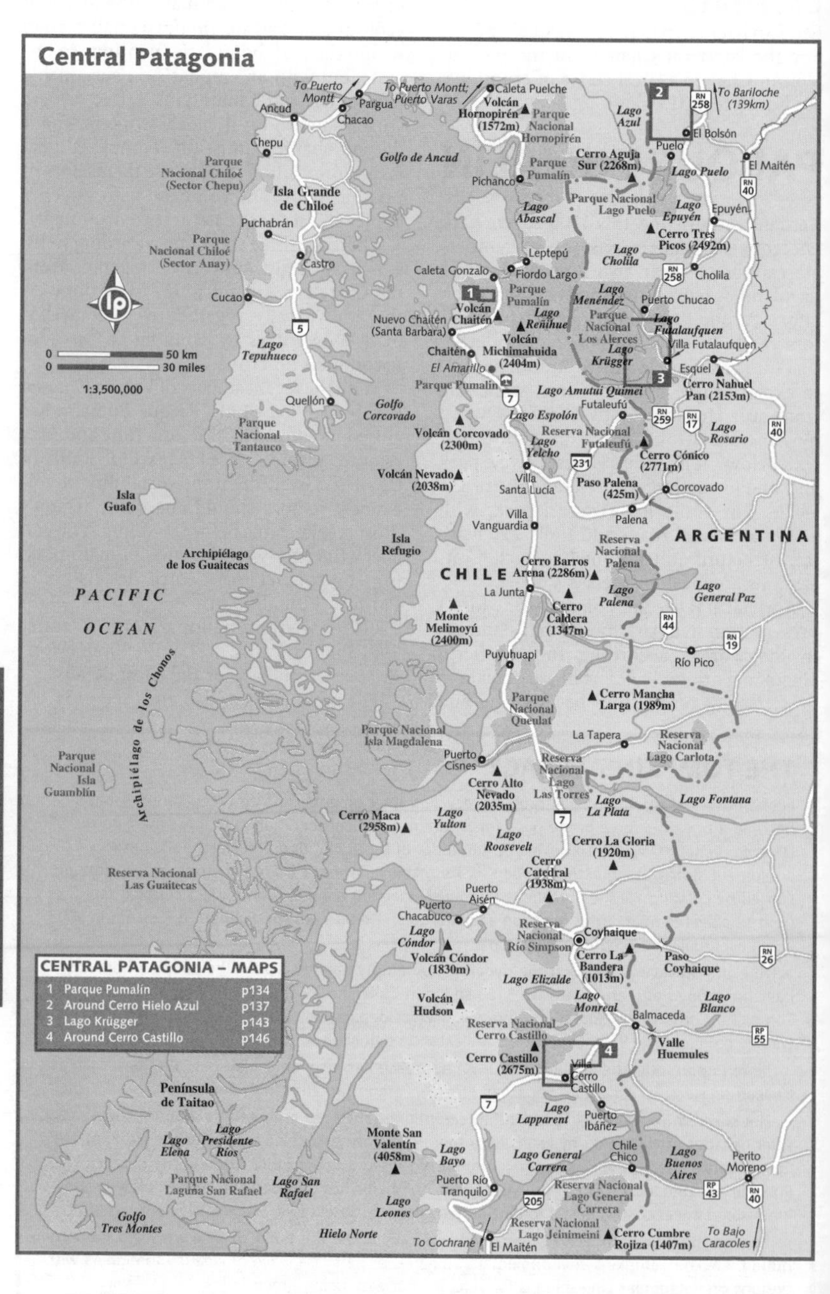
Central Patagonia
To Puerto Montt
To Puerto Montt; Puerto Varas
Caleta Puelche
Ancud
Pargua
Chacao
Volcán Hornopirén (1572m)
Parque Nacional Hornopirén
Lago Azul
To Bariloche (139km)
El Bolsón
Puelo
Chepu
Golfo de Ancud
Cerro Aguja Sur (2268m)
Lago Puelo
El Maitén
Parque Nacional Chiloé (Sector Chepu)
Pichanco
Parque Pumalín
Parque Nacional Lago Puelo
Isla Grande de Chiloé
Lago Abascal
Lago Epuyén
Epuyén
Puchabrán
Cerro Tres Picos (2492m)
Parque Nacional Chiloé (Sector Anay)
Castro
Leptepú
Lago Cholila
Caleta Gonzalo
Fiordo Largo
Cholila
Cucao
Parque Pumalín
Lago Menéndez
Puerto Chucao
Volcán Chaitén
Lago Reñihue
Parque Nacional Los Alerces
Lago Futalaufquen
Nuevo Chaitén (Santa Barbara)
Villa Futalaufquen
Volcán Michimahuida (2404m)
Lago Krügger
Lago Tepuhueco
Chaitén
El Amarillo
Esquel
50 km
30 miles
1:3,500,000
Parque Pumalín
Cerro Nahuel Pan (2153m)
Lago Amutui Quimei
Quellón
Golfo Corcovado
Futaleufú
Lago Espolón
Lago Rosario
Parque Nacional Tantauco
Volcán Corcovado (2300m)
Reserva Nacional Futaleufú
Lago Yelcho
Cerro Cónico (2771m)
Volcán Nevado (2038m)
Villa Santa Lucía
Paso Palena (425m)
Corcovado
Isla Guafo
Palena
Villa Vanguardia
ARGENTINA
Isla Refugio
Reserva Nacional Palena
Archipiélago de los Guaitecas
Cerro Barros Arena (2286m)
CHILE
Lago General Paz
La Junta
Lago Palena
PACIFIC OCEAN
Cerro Caldera (1347m)
Monte Melimoyú (2400m)
Archipiélago de los Chonos
Puyuhuapi
Río Pico
Cerro Mancha Larga (1989m)
Parque Nacional Queulat
Parque Nacional Isla Magdalena
La Tapera
Reserva Nacional Lago Carlota
Parque Nacional Isla Guamblín
Puerto Cisnes
Reserva Nacional Lago Las Torres
Cerro Alto Nevado (2035m)
Lago La Plata
Lago Fontana
Cerro Maca (2958m)
Lago Yulton
Lago Roosevelt
Cerro La Gloria (1920m)
Reserva Nacional Las Guaitecas
Cerro Catedral (1938m)
Puerto Aisén
Puerto Chacabuco
Lago Cóndor
Reserva Nacional Río Simpson
Coyhaique
Volcán Cóndor (1830m)
Cerro La Bandera (1013m)
Paso Coyhaique
CENTRAL PATAGONIA – MAPS
1 Parque Pumalín p134
2 Around Cerro Hielo Azul p137
3 Lago Krügger p143
4 Around Cerro Castillo p146
Lago Elizalde
Volcán Hudson
Lago Monreal
Lago Blanco
Balmaceda
Reserva Nacional Cerro Castillo
Valle Huemules
Cerro Castillo (2675m)
Villa Cerro Castillo
Península de Taitao
Lago Lapparent
Puerto Ibáñez
Lago Elena
Lago Presidente Ríos
Monte San Valentín (4058m)
Lago Bayo
Lago General Carrera
Chile Chico
Lago Buenos Aires
Perito Moreno
Parque Nacional Laguna San Rafael
Lago San Rafael
Puerto Río Tranquilo
Reserva Nacional Lago General Carrera
Lago Leones
Golfo Tres Montes
Hielo Norte
Reserva Nacional Lago Jeinimeini
Cerro Cumbre Rojiza (1407m)
To Bajo Caracoles
To Cochrane
El Maitén

ENVIRONMENT

Parque Pumalín has an extremely wet, but relatively mild climate that nourishes some of the richest old-growth rainforests found anywhere in the southern Andes. All three *coigüe* (southern beech) species are present, and often dominate the forest canopy along with moisture-loving *arrayán* (native myrtle), *avellano*, *luma*, *ulmo* and *tineo*.

More than 100 bird species inhabit the park (sometimes seasonally), including many species of aquatic ducks and geese, and marine birds such as native herons.

PLANNING

Maps

The Chilean Instituto Geográfico Militar's (IGM) 1:50,000 *Fiordo Reñihue* (Section H, No 101) covers the treks but does not show trails (or even the Carretera Austral).

Information Sources

Parque Pumalín has offices in Puerto Varas (☎ 065-250079; www.pumalínpark.org Klenner 299; 8.30am-6.30pm Mon-Fri, 9am-1pm Sat). The excellent Parque Pumalín website is full of practical travel information.

Permits & Regulations

Permits are not required to visit Parque Pumalín and there is no entry fee. Fires are prohibited outside campsites. Camping is not permitted in the backcountry apart from at park-designated sites.

ACCESS TOWNS

See Caleta Gonzalo (p155). For the latest on the town of Chaitén, unfortunately located in the path of the 2008 volcanic eruption, see boxed text below.

LAGUNA TRONADOR

Duration 2½–3½ hours
Distance 5km
Difficulty easy–moderate
Start/Finish Puente Tronador
Nearest Town Caleta Gonzalo
Transport bus, tour
Summary An energetic up-and-down trek (415m ascent/descent) to a jewel of a lake among luxuriant rainforest.

GETTING TO/FROM THE TREK

The trek begins and ends at the trailhead at Puente Tronador, a bridge on the Carretera Austral, 13km south of Caleta Gonzalo (35km north of Chaitén). There is limited parking space nearby.

Chaitur (☎ 097-4685608; www.chaitur.com) does tours of Parque Pumalín that usually stop at one or more of the trailheads for these treks.

VOLCÁN CHAITÉN WAKES UP

It wasn't even ranked among Chile's 120 volcanoes, but that changed quickly on May 2, 2008. Volcán Chaitén, 10km northeast of its namesake town, began a month-long eruption. Its ashen cloud rose 20km in the air. The rampage caused flooding and severe damage to homes, roads and bridges, decimated the area's livestock and spewed ash as far as Buenos Aires. Luckily, 8000 inhabitants successfully evacuated.

A year on, activity continues under close monitoring. As the 1112m volcano evolves, vulcanologists from Chile's Mining and Geology Service fear that a new dome complex could collapse, sending a pyroclastic flow into Chaitén in minutes. Rain also may loosen large flows of ash and debris, and explosions are a third danger, since the magma contains high concentrations of dense silicon dioxide. While many locals have resisted abandoning their properties, the Chilean government has declared the area untenable.

It is likely that regional transport and services will relocate 10km north to Santa Barbara. In the meantime, barring emergency status, ferries come in and out of Chaitén's port, coordinated with regional buses, but there are no hotels or services.

Please check the current status of the region and services before traveling to the area. For updates, contact *Parque Pumalín* (www.pumalínpark.org) or local tourist offices. At the time of research, the park administration was in the process of transferring the majority of its infrastructure to El Amarillo, 35km south of Chaitén.

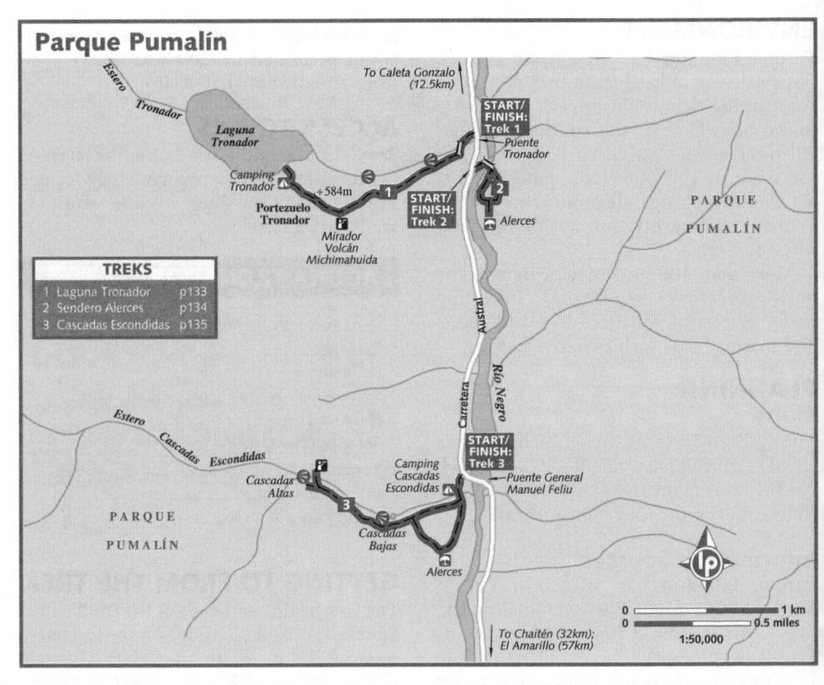

THE TREK

Follow a stepped boardwalk up past cascades plunging into pools in the Estero Tronador. Soon you'll cross the stream on a suspension bridge over a spectacular little gorge. The well-routed track climbs steeply through fern forest of *canelo,* over mossy roots, under trunks and up short ladders in places. Climb away left to a minor ridgetop, and then head rightward through stands of *mañío* and fragrant *tepa* to cross a small stream in a tiny open area.

Another steep climb brings you up to **Mirador Volcán Michimahuida,** one to 1½ hours from Puente Tronador. From here, the volcano's domed snowy expanse is visible to the southeast. The route continues up gently past superb thick-trunked alerces (one is 1.3m in diameter) and through the **Portezuelo Tronador**, a gap (around 545m) to the south of Point 584m.

Rest a while on the log benches here before you drop steeply down northwest to reach a tiny beach at the southern shore of **Laguna Tronador** (around 450m), after 15 to 20 minutes. The *huala,* or great grebe, is sometimes spotted on this beautiful lake, which is surrounded by almost sheer-sided ridges blanketed by rainforest. Hot weather – and possibly bothersome biting *tábanos* (horseflies) – will quickly tempt you to take a cool dip in the deep water. **Camping Tronador**, about 50m round to the left, has two sites with tables and a pit toilet. Campfires are strictly prohibited.

Return via the same route.

SENDERO ALERCES

Duration 30–40 minutes
Distance 1.1km
Difficulty easy
Start/Finish Carretera Austral, 200m south of Puente Tronador
Nearest Town Caleta Gonzalo
Transport bus, tour
Summary A brief return trek to stands of glorious old alerces.

GETTING TO/FROM THE TREK

The trek starts 200m south of Puente Tronador (see Getting to/from the Trek for

Laguna Tronador p133). There is limited parking space near the trailhead.

THE TREK

This short trek goes to what is probably the closest *alerzal* (stand of alerces) to any roadway – mainly because the road was built so recently. The path leads leftward from the road across a footbridge over the Río Negro, then cuts downstream to a first stand of tall alerces. Sadly, one of these superb trees has been partially stripped of its bark (used in an old method of caulking boats) and is unlikely to survive.

Continue on to a particularly enormous alerce, whose gently tapering trunk has a diameter of almost 4m at the base. A short way on, a little side trail leads over the trunks of long-fallen alerces to another small stand. When you're through marveling at these wondrous trees, follow the trail around left, back over the footbridge and return to the Carretera Austral.

CASCADAS ESCONDIDAS

Duration 1½–2 hours
Distance 3.5km
Difficulty easy
Start/Finish Camping Cascadas Escondidas
Nearest Town Caleta Gonzalo
Transport bus, tour
Summary A short rainforest trek up to several 'hidden cascades' spouting into green rock pools.

GETTING TO/FROM THE TREK

The trek leaves directly from Camping Cascadas Escondidas, 14.5km south of Caleta Gonzalo, at the end of a short access road just north of the Puente General Manuel Feliu road bridge.

For transport to/from the trailhead, see Getting to/from the Trek for Laguna Tronador (p133).

THE TREK

At the trailhead, **Camping Cascadas Escondidas** (camping per site CH$5000) features covered platform sites. It has picnic tables, toilets and cold showers.

Take the signposted track (opposite the campsite toilet block) and cross the Estero Cascadas Escondidas on a footbridge. The trail climbs through the ferny, moss-draped forest on the left of the stream to a right turn-off. This leads down right via a ladder to a spectacular viewing platform at the base of the **Cascadas Bajas**, where the stream spouts through a crack in the rock and tumbles 25m down into a deep pool.

Climb on past sitting benches above the waterfall to a left turn-off (which loops down for 15 to 20 minutes through stands of medium-sized alerces and back to the campsite) and continue right. The gradient eases as you continue smoothly through thickets of *quila* (bamboo) and fragrant *tepa* forest to reach another right turn-off. This leads down across the stream and climbs briefly to the **Mirador Cascadas Altas**, a tiny lookout 'box' above a second waterfall that spills into a green, mossy pool. The main trail follows numerous ladders up until it ends at a final **cascade** that splashes over rocks into a smaller pool.

Return the same way (but via the alerces loop this time) to the campsite.

COMARCA ANDINA

With summits topping 2000m, this band of rugged snowcapped ranges features cascading glaciers and long lateral canyons that tumble to the eastern steppes. The Argentine region known as the Comarca Andina del Paralelo 42 (42°S) straddles the border with Chile. It delimits Río Negro from Chubut, passing several kilometers south of El Bolsón. Those traveling in late spring to early summer are treated to bursts of wildflowers.

For more treks in this area, see p152.

ENVIRONMENT

Tall evergreen forest dominated by *coigüe* grows in the moister valleys of the Comarca Andina, which becomes increasingly species-rich the closer it gets to the Chilean frontier. The ranges' drier eastern slopes are covered by fragrant stands of Cordilleran cypress, and the understory in these areas consists largely of thickets dominated by scrubby species.

Beautiful open deciduous forests of *lenga* mixed with *ñirre* (spelt *ñire* in Argentina) are found above 1100m. The *lenga* forest provides an ideal habitat for the Patagonian red fox (called *zorro colorado* in Argentina), and Geoffroy's cat (*gato montés*), a shy wild cat that measures up to 1m from head to tail.

Two adaptable bird species, the small silvery-grey diuca-finch (*diuca*) and the rufous-collared sparrow, or *chinchol*, also dwell in these highland forests. The austral pygmy owl, or *chuncho*, makes up for its small size by its audacious and occasionally aggressive temperament. Larger birds of prey are the Andean condor and the black-chested buzzard-eagle, or *águila mora*.

CLIMATE

Visitors arriving from the nearby Argentine Lakes District will notice the dry, crisp continental climate. The high range of the Cordón Nevado acts as a surprisingly effective climatic barrier, filtering out much of the Pacific moisture carried by the westerly winds. Except for the loftier peaks close to the frontier, where rain and snowfall may exceed 3000mm annually, precipitation levels are relatively modest. Beyond the mountains annual precipitation drops dramatically – in the valley of El Bolsón, to as little as 700mm. Summer temperatures can be hot, historically averaging between 12–20°C, though recent years have been much warmer.

In winter snow covers all areas above 800m.

PLANNING

Books

Spanish-language guidebook *Montañas de la Comarca*, by Gabriel Bevacqua, describes the best treks in the region.

AROUND CERRO HIELO AZUL

Duration 3 days
Distance 35km
Difficulty moderate
Start Doña Rosa
Finish Warton
Nearest Town El Bolsón
Transport bus, taxi
Summary An excellent trek linking two of the Comarca Andina's loveliest alpine valleys in the ranges visible from El Bolsón.

This route takes you into a cirque at the headwaters of the Río Teno, surrounded by craggy ridges with small glaciers, and traverses into the Cajón del Azul, a deep gorge of the wild upper Río Azul. In addition to a recommended side trip, the trek can be lengthened by several days by continuing up the Río Azul from the Refugio Cajón del Azul.

Trails are well marked so route finding should not be a problem. It is much easier in the direction described (ie south to north).

PLANNING

When to Trek

The trek can normally be done from mid-November until late April. January and February can be hot and the *refugios* crowded, but, unlike in areas with moister climates, there are few or no *tábanos* then.

What to Bring

With three refugios on this trek, it can be done without a tent – although it's not advisable during peak season in January. Bring your own sleeping bag. Simple meals are available, as well as luxuries such as chocolate and beer. Some areas are scrubby or dusty, and wearing protective gaiters, or long trousers, will make your trek more comfortable.

Maps

Although it does not show the trekking route itself, the Argentine IGM's 1:100,000 map *El Bolsón* (Río Negro, No 4172-34) is relatively new and covers the area of the trek.

Information Sources

Online hut information can be found at www.bolsonweb.com/aventura under *Refugios*.

Permits & Regulations

No permits are necessary. Camping is not permitted apart from at designated areas near the *refugios*. (If you do make an illicit camp, at least refrain from lighting a fire.) The route crosses private properties where trekkers should be particularly respectful.

GETTING TO/FROM THE TREK

Doña Rosa (start)

The trek begins at **Doña Rosa**, a landmark for taxi drivers. Walking from El Bolsón,

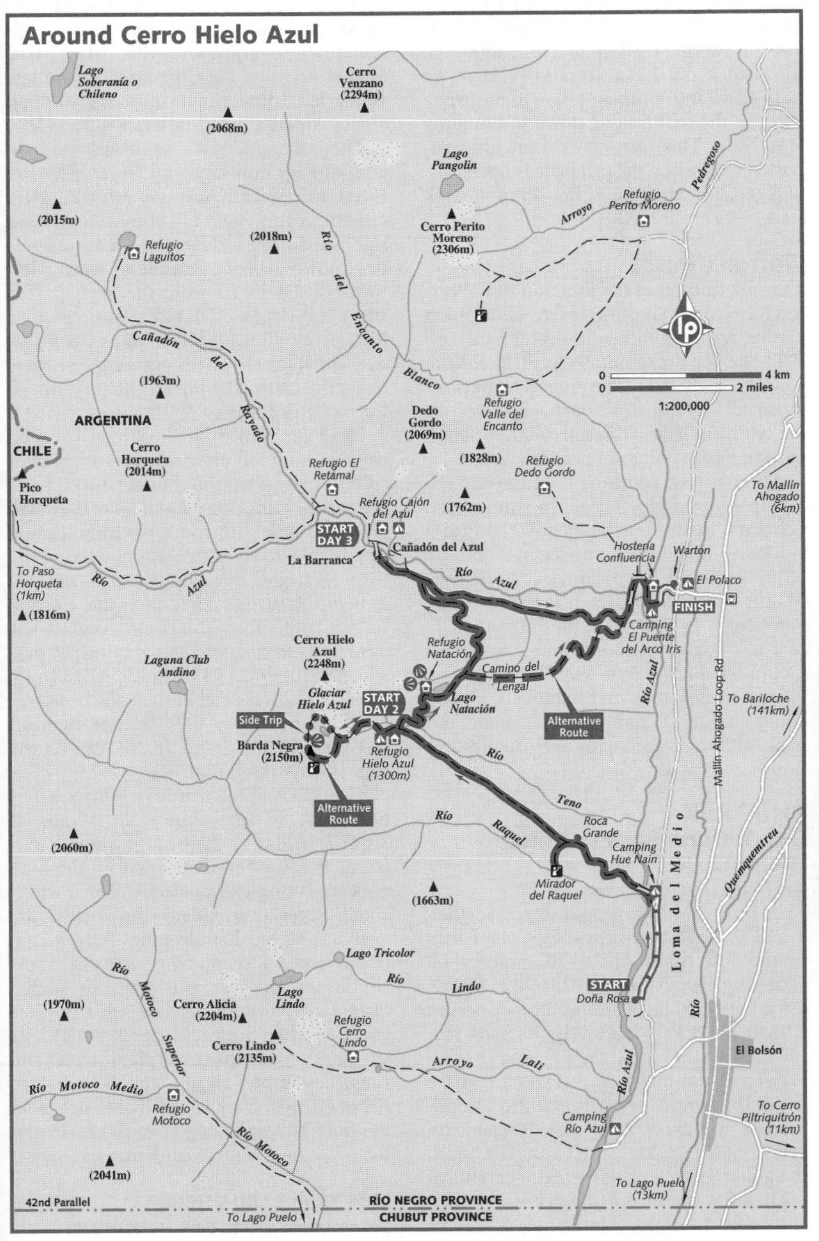

CENTRAL PATAGONIA

it's about 1½ hours (7km). Trek west along Calle Azcuénaga and across the Río Quemquemtreu bridge. Turn right and follow the curving road up to a fork above the Río Azul, about 2.2km from town. Here, go right again and continue 4.8km to the driveway (on the left) leading down to Camping Hue Nain. This turn-off is normally signposted only when the campsite is open.

A *remís* (taxi) from El Bolsón to the trek start costs around AR$26.

Warton (finish)

The trek finishes at the junction near Warton (also spelt Wharton), a farmstead 10km further north along the Río Azul road.

Phone for a prompt *remís* at **El Polaco** (☎ 02944-498026; camping per person/dorm AR$15/35), an all-purpose pit stop on the northeast side of this intersection. Showers and basic rooms are available here.

Alternatively, continue 1.4km east to the Mallín Ahogado loop road. In January and February, up to four buses daily run (in a clockwise direction only) from El Bolsón (AR$8) around the 37km circuit road via Mallín Ahogado. Buses leave from Calle San Martín in El Bolsón, on the south side of Plaza Pagano. For information, call **La Golondrina** (☎ 02944-492557).

Locals often pick up hitchhikers, so you could also try thumbing a ride there and back, although the roads are usually very dusty.

THE TREK

Day 1: Doña Rosa to Refugio Hielo Azul

4–6 hours, 13km, 985m ascent

Trek upstream following a dirt road then a trail through the campsite on the banks of the Río Azul. About 20 minutes in, **Camping Hue Nain** (☎ 02944-1563 8490; www.huenain.com.ar; camping per person AR$10; Jan & Feb) has lovely sites with picnic tables right beside the Río Azul.

After 20 minutes trekking, you will arrive above the confluence with the Río Raquel. There's a rickety (but safe) suspension bridge. Short trekkers won't be able to reach the guide wires, so balance extra carefully!

Go a few paces left (downstream), then cut back up right. Marked with yellow arrows on red-painted tin-tops nailed to trees, the track begins a long, often steep northwesterly ascent through *coigüe* to cross through a gate at a grassy shelf scattered with wild roses. Climb on through meadows overgrown with blackberry bushes across a trickling stream (the last water for some time) into dusty, steep slopes covered in Cordilleran cypress.

The gradient eases somewhat as you continue up into highland *lenga* and *ñirre* forest mixed with scrubby *retama*. After crossing a tiny *mallín* (wet meadow), head rightward along a ridge past the large boulder known as **Roca Grande** to reach a left turn-off, 2½ hours from the bridge. This short trail leads off for five minutes to a high precipitous bluff known as the **Mirador del Raquel**, which grants a fine view along the canyon of the Río Raquel toward Cerro Piltriquitrón.

Head on gently up the broad forested ridge among tall alpine *lenga* with a light *colihue* (native bamboo) understory, crossing through another gate to meet the small Río Teno. The path continues up smoothly beside this lovely little stream, passing the turn-off (right) to Cajón del Azul (see Day 2) before it turns off left alongside a brook to reach the **Refugio Hielo Azul** (www.refugiohieloazul.com.ar; camping per person AR$10, dm AR$35, meals AR$30-35), with hot showers and homemade beer, two to 2½ hours from the Mirador turn-off (GPS 41° 53.292 S, 71° 38.346 W). As the sign says: *Animo!* (Spirit!)

This CAP (Club Andino Piltriquitrón) hut, built in log-cabin style, stands at around 1300m in the beautiful upper valley of the Río Teno, enclosed by the high rock walls of a glacial cirque, above which small névés (permanent snowfields) are visible. The hut has sleeping space for up to 30 people. Depending on seasonal snow conditions, the *refugio* is generally staffed from early November to late April, but it is left open when the hut keeper is absent. The surrounding **campsite** has picnic tables and fireplaces among *lenga* – collect your own firewood well away in the forest, not from the hut's supply. Patagonian red foxes and the occasional puma visit here.

SIDE TRIP: BARDA NEGRA

4–6 hours return, 7km, 850m ascent/descent

Fine weather is essential for this moderate–demanding day trek from the hut to a lookout summit opposite 'blue ice' glaciers on Cerro Hielo Azul. Only parties with mountaineering experience and ice-climbing equipment should ascend Cerro Hielo Azul itself. Although technically straightforward, it involves crossing a small glacier with dangerous crevasses.

Cross a tiny wooden bridge over a streamlet at the edge of the *lenga* forest, just a few paces on from the *refugio*. Head out directly into the amphitheatre through alluvial rubble and cross a second, somewhat larger stream, following this up until red markings on rocks lead off to the right through a gravelly chute. The route leads on up a rocky moraine ridge to the base of cliffs rounded and smoothed by the action of glaciers. Here trekkers may spot the white *estrella de la cordillera* and the red bottle-shaped *voqui*, two hardy Andean wildflowers on these otherwise bare slopes.

Sidle briefly left, back to the now cascading stream, and climb on steeply through the rock. Make your way over polished slabs littered with glacial debris to a milky-green meltwater lake at the snout of the small **Glaciar Hielo Azul**. Cross the turgid stream (the nascent Río Teno) to reach a waterfall spilling down from the left, one to 1½ hours from the *refugio*. From here the summit of Cerro Hielo Azul (2248m) is more clearly visible up to the right, above the broken-up ice on the upper part of the glacier.

Skirt the left-hand side of the Glaciar Hielo Azul, then cut up over the ice around a rock outcrop (marked by a prominent cairn) and climb on via the minor spur behind it into a snowy basin. (Alternatively, you can head directly up to the left of the waterfall through steep scree, but this is a route better taken on your way down.) The route ascends beside the small stream, crossing and recrossing as it rises steeply through (probably snow-filled) gullies and over loose rock. Where the stream ends, move rightward over persistent snowdrifts to gain the ridgetop (about 500m to the right of white veins of rock in the reddish-brown ridge forming a cross). Continue northwest along the snowy ridge to reach the 2150m summit of **Barda Negra**, after one to 1½ hours.

Barda Negra offers a superb alpine panorama that takes in Cerro Piltriquitrón to the east beyond El Bolsón; Monte Tronador almost directly to the north; the perfect cone of Volcán Osorno to the northwest in Chile; and the distinctive triple summits of Cerro Tres Picos – the major landmark of the Comarca Andina – to the south. Laguna Club Andino can be seen in a deep glacial hollow to the northwest, and another, unnamed lake is visible to the southwest. Trekkers also have an excellent chance of seeing condors swooping around the nearby mountaintops.

Return via the same route or take the alternative descent.

Day 2: Refugio Hielo Azul to Refugio Cajón del Azul

4–6 hours, 10km, 135m ascent, 865m descent

Go back to the turn-off (signposted 'Lago Natación') 600m downstream from the refugio (see Day 1), then follow this rougher path across the Río Teno on a fallen-log bridge. Yellow-and-red marker plates lead up the slope to a shallow grassy lagoon. Drop gently northwest, just left of a long *mallín*, to reach a signpost (GPS 41° 52.887 S, 71° 37.497 W) in a grassy clearing near a snow-fed waterfall splashing over high cliffs on your left, 50 minutes to 1¼ hours from the *refugio*. From here, a brief side trip leads off northwest (left) 350m through *ñirre* scrub to **Lago Natación**, a tarn with a rocky islet and muddy shores.

The new **Refugio Natación** (camping per person AR$10, dm AR$35, meals AR$30-35), 1½ hours from Refugio Hielo Azul, occupies the far eastern shore of the lake. From here it's 2½ to 3½ hours to Refugio Cajón del Azul. Continue around northeast just above Lago Natación before descending through *lengas* mixed with bamboo to cross the cascading lake outlet (your last water for some way). The path leads up diagonally left over a minor crest onto high, open slopes overlooking the broad valley north of El Bolsón, 50 minutes to 1¼ hours from Lago Natación.

Begin the long, hot and dusty descent into the deep canyon, alternating between long leftward (northwest) sidles and short, sharp switchbacks. The path drops through fragrant stands of Cordilleran cypress toward the 2014m Cerro Horqueta and Dedo Gordo – the 2069m 'fat finger' peak on the opposite side of the valley – to meet a rough old 4WD track after one to 1¼ hours. This inconspicuous junction (GPS 41° 51.150 S, 71° 36.530 W) is marked only with a laconic 'H. A.' visible from upvalley. Taking this right will put you on Camino del Lengal (see Alternative Route below), shortcut to Warton.

Proceed left through tall *coigüe* forest for five minutes to meet the Río Azul again. The road fords the river here, but a good foot track continues 15 to 20 minutes upstream along its wild southern bank past small alerces and turquoise pools to cross the impressive 3m-wide, 40m-deep gorge known as the **La Barranca** on a footbridge.

The path leads on for five minutes through an orchard to the popular, recently extended, 45-bed **Refugio Cajón del Azul** (camping per person AR$10, dm AR$35, meals AR$30-35). This homey hut stands at around 620m in a small opening in a valley corralled by steep rock walls. Hearty meals, like roast lamb with garden vegetables, fresh bread and home-brew, are available. Notify the friendly hut keeper of your safe arrival, even if you are not staying at the *refugio*.

A popular two-day side trip from here leads upvalley to the rustic Refugio Laguitos at the head of the Cañadón del Rayado.

ALTERNATIVE ROUTE: VIA CAMINO DEL LENGAL

3-3½ hours, 12km

After stocking up with water at Refugio Natación, follow the trail to Cajón de Azul, taking the above-mentioned junction (GPS 41° 51.150 S, 71° 36.530 W). The Camino del Lengal starts as an easy descent through *lenga* forest following a narrow trail with red and yellow markers. After an hour, the trail widens considerably and follows an old 4WD logging road, dusty and sun-exposed, with little water. It joins the trail to Warton before the hanging bridges for Rios Azul and Blanco.

Day 3: Refugio Cajón del Azul to Warton

2½–3¼ hours, 12km, 150m descent

Retrace your steps to the 4WD track and follow it on downvalley past campsites and occasional shacks along the Río Azul. After fording a cool side stream, the road climbs away rightward through low *maitén* trees to a high, dusty crest, then winds down to the Río Azul. Cross the river on a suspension footbridge just above its confluence with the smaller Río del Encanto Blanco, then cross the latter river on a second (equally rickety) bridge to reach the basic **Hostería Confluencia** (closed during research), just downstream.

From here a road winds up past the pleasant **Camping El Puente del Arco Iris** (☎ 02944-15558330; elpuentedelarcoiris@hotmail.com; camping per person AR$15) to meet a four-way intersection on the Río Azul road near the farm of **Warton**. The small store **El Polaco** is on the northeastern side of the intersection.

For trekkers going the other way, there are several signs at the turn-off – the most prominent reads 'Confluencia del Río Azul y Blanco'.

PARQUE NACIONAL LOS ALERCES

This collection of spry creeks, verdant mountains and mirror lakes resonates as unadulterated Andes. The real attraction, however, is the alerce tree (*Fitzroya cupressoides*), one of the longest-living species on the planet, with specimens that have survived up to 4000 years. Following the acclaim of well-known parks further north and south, most trekkers miss this gem, which makes your visit here all the more enjoyable.

Resembling California's giant sequoia, the alerce flourishes in middle Patagonia's temperate forests, growing only a centimeter every twenty years. Individual specimens of this beautiful tree can reach over 4m in diameter and exceed 60m in height. Like the giant sequoia, it has suffered overexploitation because of its valuable timber. West of Esquel, this 2630-sq-km park protects some of the largest alerce forests that still remain.

Three major glacial lakes, which form a natural division between the dry, almost steppe-like eastern fringe of the park and the increasingly wet sector toward the west, dominate the northern half of the park. Since the park's interior is closed to public access, overnight treks are limited.

ENVIRONMENT

Parque Nacional Los Alerces, like Chile's Parque Nacional Alerce Andino (p117), conserves some of the southern Andes' most majestic stands of giant alerces. The most eminent representative of the so-called Valdivian rainforest, the alerce grows throughout the southern Lakes District, but only occasionally reaches the enormous size for which it is so famous. The main prerequisites for this – mild conditions, deep and perpetually wet soil, absence of fire and lots of time – are fulfilled by several locations in the remote interior of the park. On the extreme northwest arm of Lago Menéndez, alerces are aged well over 2000 years, but a single ancient specimen found on the lake's southwest arm is believed to be more than 4000 years old.

Alerces are typically found growing in association with other rainforest trees. One species is the *olivillo*, or *teque*, which has pointed oval leaves whose undersides are lighter and often red-speckled, and produces small, round fleshy fruit. Also present are *avellano*, with shiny serrated leaves and white-spotted ash-grey bark, and *tineo*, instantly recognisable by its serrated, paired leaves. The holly-leafed *taique*, *traumén* and *tepú*, a myrtle bush with small white flowers, are typical plants of the Valdivian forest understory.

Los Alerces' lakes provide a habitat to an extensive array of water birds. Visitors with their wits about them may spy the great grebe, or *huala*. Brownish-grey with a long reddish neck and white underbelly, it feeds on a rich diet of fish, mollusks and aquatic insects in freshwater lakes. It's often found with the red-gartered coot, or *tagua*, a black, yellow-beaked bird that builds a floating nest on lakes and still-water streams. The torrent duck, or *pato de torrentes*, is well adapted to fast-flowing rivers and streams, occasionally seen diving into white water in search of food. The colorful bronze-winged duck, or *pato anteojillo*, builds its nest on small islands.

In the forest, trekkers will hear the warble of the *chucao*, hiding in *colihue* bamboo, and may see the green-backed firecrown, or picaflor, a hummingbird that gorges itself on the nectar of the *notro* and fuscia flowers. The green austral parakeet, or *cachaña*, is usually observed in pairs.

Predators found in the park include the puma, kodkod (or *huiña*) and two native foxes, the bluish-grey Azara's fox (*zorro gris*) and the brownish-colored Patagonian red fox (*zorro culpeo*). The very lucky might even chance to spot the amphibious southern river otter, or *huillín*, which lives along the banks of the larger rivers and lakes.

CLIMATE

Parque Nacional Los Alerces is in a rain shadow, which is typical for areas in the lee of the Andes. Annual precipitation peaks at almost 4500mm in the ranges along Argentina's frontier with Chile, but declines progressively to a minimum of just under 800mm at the park's northeast boundary near Lago Rivadavia. A continental climate prevails, with occasional hot summer weather and crisp winters that can bring heavy snowfalls. Summer temperatures at Lago Krügger average around 20°C.

Permits & Regulations

Throughout Parque Nacional Los Alerces, camping is permitted only at organized campsites and the free park-authorized campsites. Even for short treks, it is compulsory to sign in at one of the Administración de Parques Nacionales (APN) *guarderías* (ranger stations) before you set out. Set out before 10am on all routes to arrive safely before nightfall.

LAGO KRÜGGER

Duration 3 days
Distance 44km
Difficulty moderate
Start/Finish Villa Futalaufquen
Nearest Town Esquel
Transport bus
Summary A pleasant trek past lakeside beaches fringed by luxuriant forests on the southern shores of Lago Futalaufquen and Lago Krügger.

This is an out-and-back route leading over a windy pass (around 1050m), then down via a lovely little beach at the wild western end of Lago Futalaufquen to Lago Krügger. You can shorten the trek by traveling by launch between Refugio Lago Krügger (see Getting to/from the Trek p142), at the end of Day 2, and Punta Mattos on the other side of the lake.

Fallen logs and thickets of *colihue* may slow you down in places, especially on Day 2, between Playa Blanca and Lago Krügger.

For trekkers wishing to spend more time on the lake, there are numerous accommodation possibilities along the northeastern edge of Lago Futalaufquen (see Lago Futalaufquen p158 for details).

PLANNING

When to Trek

The trail is usually open from mid-December until mid-April. Call or email infoalerces@apn.gov.ar (in Spanish) to check on trail closures.

What to Bring

You will need to bring a tent for camping on Day 1 of the trek. Refugio Lago Krügger has only limited beds available, so camping on Day 2 may also be your only option.

Maps

Two Argentine IGM 1:100,000 maps, *Lago Rivadavia* (Chubut, No 4372-10) and *Villa Futalaufquen* (Chubut, No 2372-16), cover the trek, but do not accurately show the route.

Permits & Regulations

Before leaving for Lago Krügger, all trekking parties are required to register and obtain a permit at the Administración de Parques Nacionales (APN) *centro de informes* in Villa Futalaufquen (p159), or at Guardería Punta Mattos.

Camping is permitted only at Playa Blanca (see Day 1) and at Refugio Lago Krügger (Day 2). Due to overcrowding, return parties are no longer allowed to camp at Playa Blanca, requiring a long (but manageable) trek out on Day 3.

GETTING TO/FROM THE TREK

The trek begins and ends at the village of Villa Futalaufquen (p159).

You can shorten the trek by taking a boat to/from **Refugio Lago Krügger** (☎ 011 1544-247964; info@lagokrugger.com.ar; www.lagokrugger.com.ar). The refugio runs a boat on demand to/from Punta Mattos (one way/return per person AR$60/90), 21km north of Villa Futalaufquen. Charter it by telephone, email or two-way radio – ask at ranger stations or at Fiunque Osuzt in Puerto Limonao, north of Villa Futalaufquen.

In summer, **Transportes Esquel** (☎ 453529) goes through Parque Nacional Los Alerces (AR$9, 1¼ hours) to Lago Futalaufquen daily at 8am and 4pm. The first bus goes all the way to Lago Puelo (AR$23, six hours), stopping at points along the way, including Lago Verde (AR$13) at 10.30am. An open ticket (AR$30) allows passengers to make stops along the way. Service is reduced off-season.

THE TREK

Day 1: Villa Futalaufquen to Playa Blanca

4¾–6¼ hours, 14km, 450m ascent/descent

It's best to set out from Villa Futalaufquen before 9.30am. After signing in at the APN information center, follow the road (or a path slightly closer to the lake) round the southwest side of Lago Futalaufquen. Go left at a short road turn-off several hundred meters before Puerto Limonao. It soon ends at a small car park by the Arroyo de los Pumas, after 30 to 40 minutes. Cross the small stream on a footbridge and head into the forest past a signposted trail leading off left to the **Cinco Saltos** (a series of waterfalls that can be visited in around 30 minutes return).

Continue trekking behind the exclusive and elegant **Hostería Futalaufquen** (see p159 for details). The trail then begins an undulating traverse up along the steep-sided lake through stands of Cordilleran cypress that are gradually replaced by *coigüe*. The path then begins a steady winding climb away to the left through clustered thickets of overhanging *colihue* flowers, sidling on rightward over high slopes of *ñirre*, and *notro* scrub with its seasonal flamboyant red flowers, giving good views of Cerro Alto El Petiso and other peaks on the northern side of Lago Futalaufquen.

After turning northwest to cross a small stream, head up through a hollow covered with low, weather-beaten *coligue*. The route skirts the *lenga* forest on the right-hand side of this shallow basin to reach the portezuelo (*saddle*) (at roughly 1050m). With the best views of the trip, the scrubby saddle

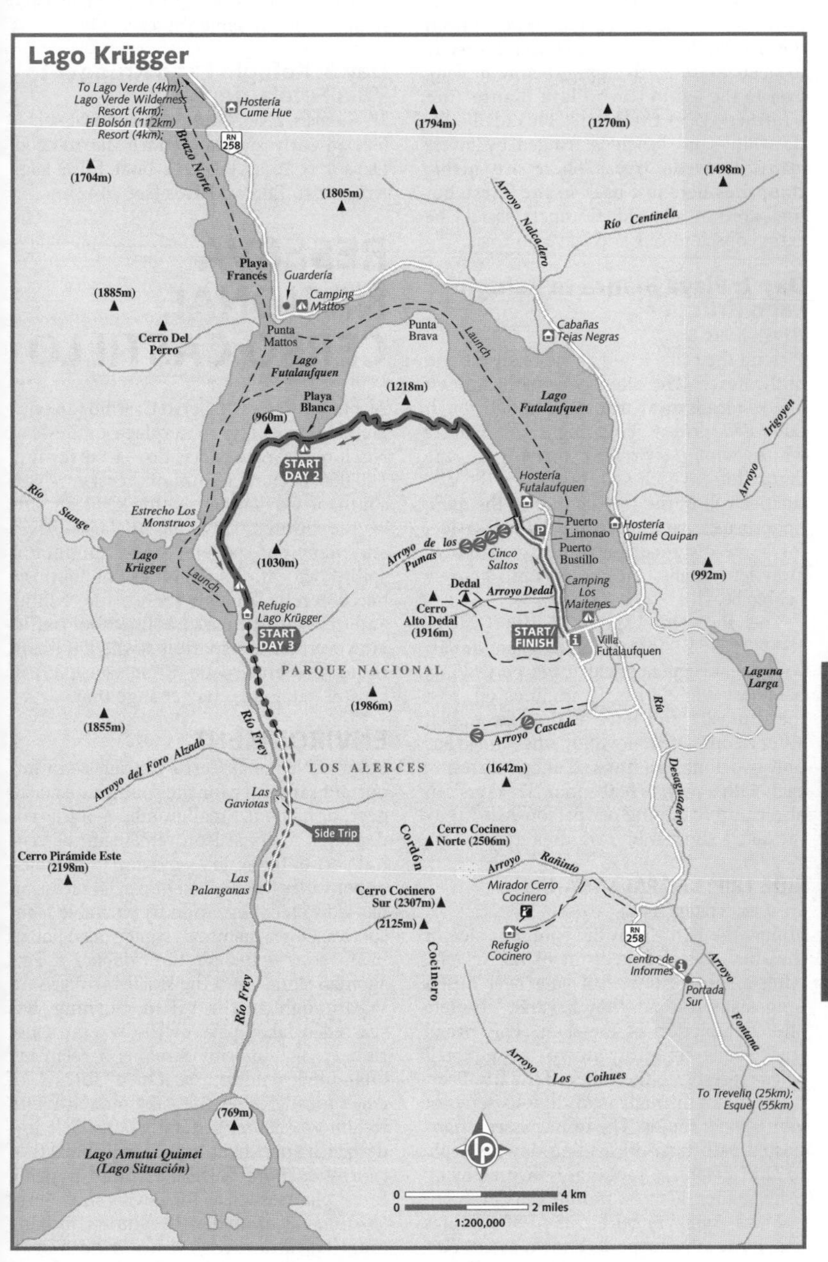

CENTRAL PATAGONIA

overlooks a small cove in the lake immediately below to the west, 2¾ to 3½ hours from the Arroyo de los Pumas. Descend directly in steep, loose-earth zigzags before moving over to the left to reach **Playa Blanca** after a further 1½ to two hours. This idyllic little white-sand beach is fringed by lovely *arrayán* myrtle trees. There are idyllic **campsites** here just back in the forest, but fires are not allowed. Campers should be extra conscientious and leave no trace.

Day 2: Playa Blanca to Refugio Lago Krügger

2½–3¼ hours, 8km

Pick up the route again at the reedy far end of the beach. The often-poor path through *arrayán* leads away from the shore through tall *coigüe* forest. You might see delicate white *palomita* orchids thriving in the damp, humus-rich soil. Listen for the distinctive call of the tiny *chucao* in the *quila* underbrush. After returning to the lakeside, for some distance the route again moves away left, finally coming out onto a lovely pebble beach at Lago Krügger.

The **Refugio Lago Krügger** (☎ 011 1544-247964; info@lagokrugger.com.ar; www.lagokrugger.com.ar; r per person incl breakfast AR$200) is 10 minutes on, past the campsite and jetty at the lake outlet. After a complete renovation, the *refugio* has only two double rooms and one triple room, each with a private bathroom. Trekkers can also **camp** (camping per person AR$15) by the lake a short way from the refugio.

SIDE TRIP: LAS PALANGANAS

5½–7 hours return, 14km

Follow the path from the southern side of the small clearing in front of the *refugio*. After a short distance, it goes over into a long-disused road that became obsolete after completion of the dam. This broad track leads smoothly down through tall *coigüe* forest into the valley of the **Río Frey**, which flows through a continuous series of white-water rapids. The route passes a signposted path turn-off leading down steeply to *Las Gaviotas*, a spot that is favored by fly fishers, after 40 to 50 minutes.

Make your way on for 25 to 30 minutes past more anglers' pools known as *Las Palanganas*, proceeding smoothly through tiny meadows dotted with raspberry bushes and wild strawberries. Return to Refugio Lago Krügger via the same route.

Day 3: Refugio Lago Krügger to Villa Futalaufquen

7½–10 hours, 22km, 450m ascent/descent

Get an early start to retrace the route of Days 1 & 2, or take the boat from Lago Krügger to Punta Mattos (see p142).

RESERVA NACIONAL CERRO CASTILLO

The basalt spires of Cerro Castillo (2675m) are the crowning centerpiece of Reserva Nacional Cerro Castillo, a sprawling 180,000-hectare mountain reserve 75km south of Coyhaique on the Chilean side of the border. Covered by large névés and hanging glaciers, these mountains spill down into lovely valleys of southern beech forest. Though there's fine fishing and trekking, the park has little foot traffic. However, its designation as the landmark route for Sendero de Chile (see p35) in central Patagonia may change that.

ENVIRONMENT

Reserva Nacional Cerro Castillo is an important sanctuary for the southern Andean deer, or *huemul*. Small numbers of this endangered national icon remain in the central part of the reserve, grazing in secluded upper valleys where recent glacial recession has led to recolonization by palatable plant species. Other mammals sometimes spotted in the reserve include the *chingue*, or Patagonian skunk, and the small *zorro gris*.

Although uncontrolled burning has scarred a large part of the reserve's periphery, the interior remains a relatively unspoiled wilderness. Open forests of *lenga* mostly cover the subalpine areas up to almost 1200m, generally with little underbrush apart from occasional thickets of thorny *calafate* bushes. Ground-hugging forest plants, such as the devil's strawberry (*frutilla del diablo*), the similar-looking Magellan strawberry (*frutilla de Magallanes*), with pinkish edible berries, and *brecillo*, whose purple berries are a favored food of foxes and other native fauna, can be found on moister places.

The Chilean flicker, or *pitío*, is an endemic Patagonian woodpecker seen in the drier *lenga* forests of the eastern sector of the reserve. The *pitío* has a greyish crown and brownish-black bands, but its yellow face and upper neck make it easy to recognize. The great-shrike tyrant of Aisén, or *mero austral aiseño*, is a coffee-grey-colored subspecies endemic to the region.

CLIMATE

Situated well inland and largely sheltered from the far wetter coastal climate by high ranges to the west, Reserva Nacional Cerro Castillo has a continental climate. Annual precipitation levels are relatively moderate by regional standards, generally not exceeding 3000mm on the higher peaks. In the Valle Ibáñez to the south, the reserve borders abruptly on the drier monte terrain so typical of the Andes' eastern fringes, where rainfall is generally under 1000mm. Summers are generally mild, with January temperatures only occasionally rising above 30°C. Winter can bring locally heavy snowfalls above 500m, and the first patches of permanent snow are encountered at a little over 1200m.

AROUND CERRO CASTILLO

Duration 4 days
Distance 62km
Difficulty moderate–demanding
Start Las Horquetas Grandes
Finish Villa Cerro Castillo
Nearest Town Coyhaique
Transport bus
Summary A route through a raw alpine landscape where glaciers cling to craggy mountainsides and waterfalls tumble into the valleys.

Towering over the Río Ibáñez and the Carretera Austral, Cerro Castillo is the most prominent peak of the compact Cordillera Castillo. The mountain's Spanish name comes from its many striking basalt turrets and craggy ridges, which resemble a medieval castle. A striking landmark of the Aisén region, this peak regularly attracts international climbers.

This trek leads along the principal section of the Sendero de Chile in the Aisén region. Although it's an increasingly well-trodden route, it requires a high level of fitness and careful navigation. The trek crosses glacier-fed streams in several places, although they are normally manageable and can usually be forded without difficulty. Exposed sections, fallen branches and loose rock must also be negotiated.

An alternative start near Lago Monreal (see Alternative Start p149) is being developed as part of Sendero de Chile – it already exists but lacks adequate signposting. This attractive alternative adds one to two very pleasant days to the trek.

Trekkers uncomfortable with the long, unstable and exposed descent required to reach Campamento Neozelandés on Day 3 should take the Alternative Route (see p150) down to Villa Cerro Castillo, finishing the trek in three rather than four days.

It is possible to camp 6km from the trailhead on the small lake of Laguna Chiguay (see p158 for details).

PLANNING

When to Trek

The trek is best done from mid-November to the end of March. Snow covers steep scree on the passes until January, making early crossings preferable, if you don't mind fording bigger rivers.

What to Bring

There are no *refugios* for trekkers (although Sendero de Chile has plans to construct several along the route). In the meantime a tent is essential.

Maps

The Chilean IGM 1:50,000 series covers the area of the trek in three maps: *Lago Elizalde* (Section I, No 132), *Balmaceda* (Section I, No 133) and *Villa Cerro Castillo* (Section J, No 10). Although most of the route described here is not shown on these maps, they are still very useful.

Permits & Regulations

Permits are not required. Trekkers should leave their route details at the guardería at Laguna Chiguay (p158) or at the Conaf office in Coyhaique (p155). Conaf charges a CH$3000 entry fee at the guardería at

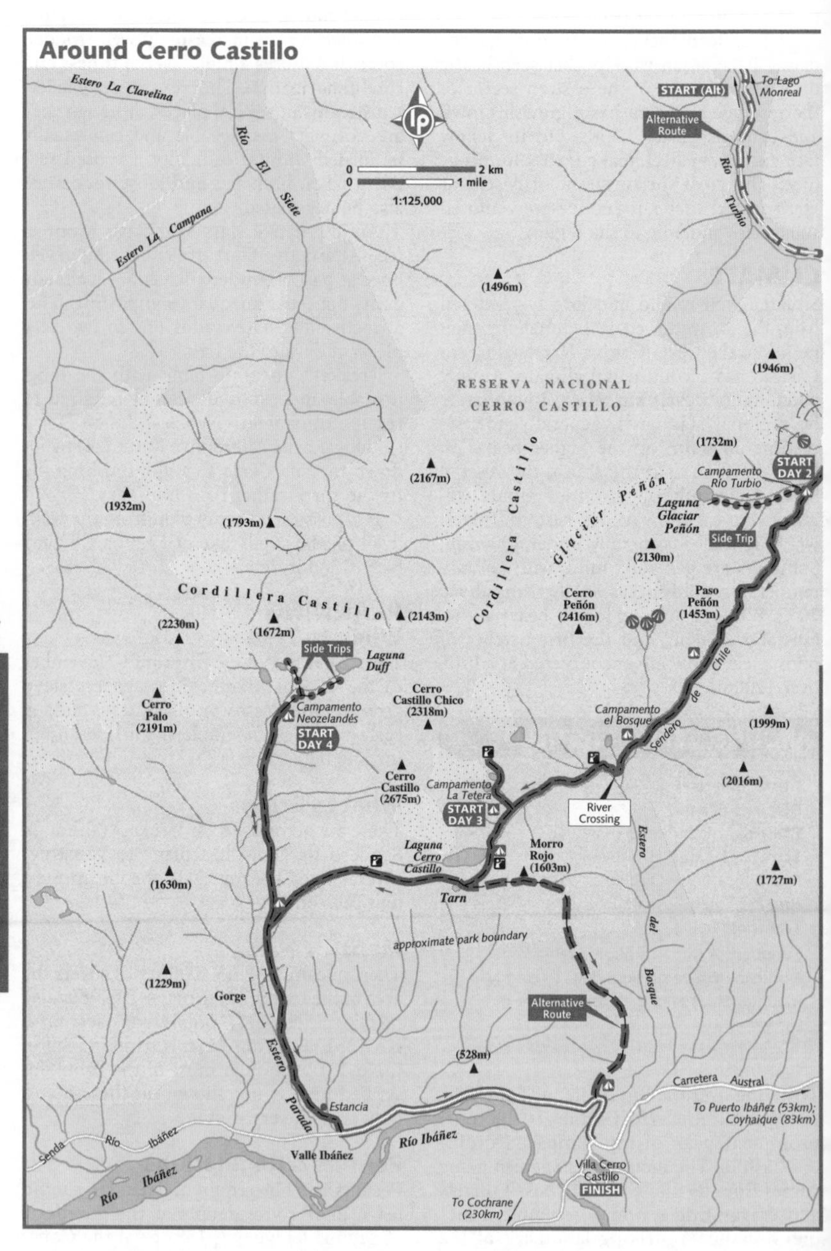
Around Cerro Castillo
Estero La Clavelina
Río El Siete
Estero La Campana
0 2 km
0 1 mile
1:125,000
START (Alt)
To Lago Monreal
Alternative Route
Río Turbio
(1496m)
(1946m)
RESERVA NACIONAL CERRO CASTILLO
(1732m)
Campamento Río Turbio
START DAY 2
Laguna Glaciar Peñón
Glaciar Peñón
Side Trip
(2167m)
(1932m)
(1793m)
Cordillera Castillo
(2130m)
Cordillera Castillo
(2143m)
Cerro Peñón (2416m)
Paso Peñón (1453m)
(2230m)
(1672m)
Side Trips
Laguna Duff
Cerro Palo (2191m)
Campamento Neozelandés
START DAY 4
Cerro Castillo Chico (2318m)
Sendero de Chile
Campamento el Bosque
(1999m)
Cerro Castillo (2675m)
Campamento La Tetera
START DAY 3
River Crossing
(2016m)
Laguna Cerro Castillo
Morro Rojo (1603m)
Estero del Bosque
(1630m)
Tarn
(1727m)
approximate park boundary
(1229m)
Gorge
Alternative Route
Estero Parada
(528m)
Estancia
Carretera Austral
To Puerto Ibáñez (53km); Coyhaique (83km)
Senda Río Ibáñez
Río Ibáñez
Valle Ibáñez
Río Ibáñez
Villa Cerro Castillo
FINISH
To Cochrane (230km)
CENTRAL PATAGONIA

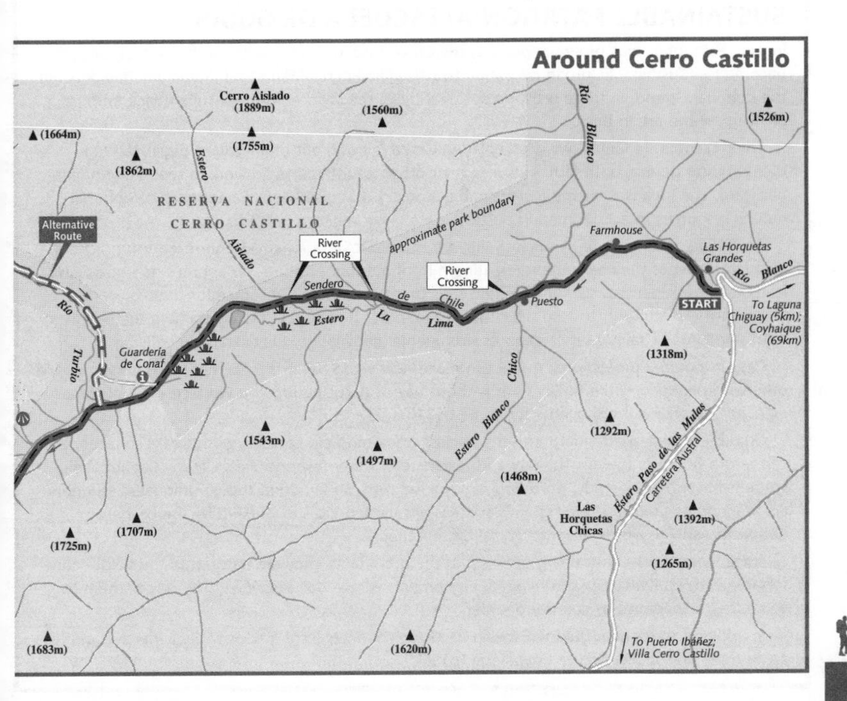

Laguna Chiguay. A final optional section of the trek cuts through private property (fee CH$5000 per person), where trekkers should be on their best behavior.

Due to an increasing number of visitors to this fragile area, please be especially mindful of your impact on the environment (see Responsible Trekking, p36). In particular, avoid campfires in areas without fire pits and be sure to carry out all your garbage – and perhaps that left by less responsible trekkers.

GETTING TO/FROM THE TREK

The trek begins at Las Horquetas Grandes, 75km south of Coyhaique. Las Horquetas Grandes is little more than a bend in the Senda Río Ibáñez (the name given to this section of the Carretera Austral), where two minor streams flow together. The Dirección de Vialidad has a small roadworks depot here on the west side of the road.

If arriving from Coyhaique, you can take buses going to either Cochrane (five services weekly), departing around 8am, or Puerto Ibáñez (CH$6000, under two hours from Coyhaique to Las Horquetas Grandes). The road is relatively good and the journey takes less than two hours. Private minibuses to Puerto Ibáñez often pick up passengers along Arturo Prat in Coyhaique.

Trekkers arriving at the trailhead from Cochrane or Puerto Ibáñez will disembark shortly after crossing the scenic Paso Las Mulas – but note that Las Horquetas Grandes is after (ie downvalley from) Las Horquetas Chicas.

For those starting at Lago Monreal, **Don Dario** (☎ 099-3562138) can shuttle passengers from Coyhaique or Balmaceda (one way CH$50,000) in a private charter for up to 10 passengers.

Alternatively, you can access the trail driving from El Blanco (40km south of Coyhaique) via the gravel road to La Paloma. Take a left-hand turn-off (3km) onto the Lago Monreal road. A 4WD vehicle is recommended in low season.

The trek ends at Villa Cerro Castillo (p158).

SUSTAINABLE PATAGONIA: ESCUELA DE GUIAS

In rural Patagonia, kids grow up working the great outdoors, not playing in it. As rural ranches become less sustainable, urban migration to cities like Puerto Montt and Coyhaique has become the dominant trend. In these growing regional hubs, the children of rural subsistence farmers grow up as the urban poor.

Enter **Escuela de Guias** (www.escueladeguias.cl), a nonprofit organization dedicated to training local guides, both farm kids and their urban counterparts, to work in their Patagonian backyard. The idea is to create a sustainable industry that also keeps Patagonia's exceptional natural resources intact. Women in particular are encouraged to participate.

According to its founder, Francisco Vio, a former NOLS (National Outdoor Leadership School) instructor, part of the challenge is 'creating a local outdoors culture', an appreciation of which leads toward wilderness stewardship. Vio sees tourism as a great resource for the region. 'We don't want our students to lose their *campesino* roots,' he assures, 'but by training them with high standards of safety, service and environmental knowledge, they can make a living.'

Case in point: a professional guide can make nearly US$100 in a day. That same person would otherwise be working the family farm without pay or participating in a work crew – *trabajando en la pala* (working the shovel) – for some US$10 a day.

Guides-in-training attend 18 months of classroom and field courses, with breaks so attendees can return home to harvest the hay and take care of other responsibilities. Many pay for their studies through work-study, portering real guided trips. So far, 50 of the 60 graduated students are working as guides. The program's success has earned Vio sponsorship by the US-based nonprofit Ashoka, which supports social entrepreneurs.

Since many guides-in-training grew up in the mountains, they are naturals in the field – comfortable with bad weather and minimal equipment. 'All we do,' says Vio, 'is try to get them to value their experience as country people.'

In addition to training guides, Escuela de Guias connects local guides with clients and guides some trips, principally around Coyhaique (p155).

THE TREK

Day 1: Las Horquetas Grandes to Upper Río Turbio

3¾–5 hours, 18km, 240m ascent

Cross the bridge over the Estero Paso de Las Mulas just above where it enters the Río Blanco, and follow a dirt road down the true left bank of the river. The road soon turns away westward past a farmhouse, winding on through open *lenga* forest before it drops gently down onto grassy flats beside the **Estero La Lima**, after one to 1¼ hours. Make your way past a rustic **puesto** (outbuilding) and cross the small side stream of the Estero Blanco Chico, heading on upvalley through streamside pastures to easily ford the shallow Estero La Lima itself, after a further 30 to 40 minutes.

After crossing the Estero Aislado, which drains another tiny side valley to the north, the increasingly rough vehicle track skirts above a reedy lagoon frequented by black-necked swans to reach a fork after one to 1¼ hours. To the right, the **Guardería de Conaf** post charges a park entry fee. After paying, take the left-hand branch, which avoids a *mallín* stretching along the poorly drained valley floor, before it (almost imperceptibly) crosses a watershed to meet the **Río Turbio**, another 30 to 40 minutes on. This roaring white-water torrent flows through a wild upper valley below the Cordillera Castillo, its towering peaks visible along much of the approach route.

Follow an indistinct 4WD track southwest along the broad gravelly valley floor below waterfalls spilling over sheer cliffs from hanging glaciers up to your right. Where the vehicle track finally peters out, after 30 to 40 minutes, pick up a trail that continues into the *lenga* forest. The route crosses a clear brook before climbing gently rightward onto an open field of old glacial debris now covered by tussocky alpine grasses and *chaura* berries, a further 10 to 15 minutes on. There is scenic *Campamento Rio Turbio* around this pretty head of the Río Turbio valley, where *huemul* deer sometimes graze.

ALTERNATIVE START: LAGO MONREAL TO CAMPAMENTO EL TURBIO

12–16 hours / 2 days, 20.7km

Day 1 (six to eight hours, 11.2km) begins on an old logging road that crosses a wooden bridge over the outlet stream for Lago Monreal. The road crosses gates (always close behind you), heading uphill over exposed terrain, arriving at an old logging camp with a steam engine. Here a Conaf sign marks the trail, which veers off right from the logging road. Continue for 30 minutes until you reach a sign for the Cerro Castillo Reserve and a gate.

Continue on a logging trail, which arrives in one hour at a picnic table near a large boulder (site of a future Conaf post). Equipped with an outhouse, it's a good spot for camping. Cross a small stream on a bridge improvised out of logs, and then continue through a *mallín* marked by stakes. Enter a *lenga* forest and climb to Mirador La Paloma, a right turn-off veering 10 minutes from the main trail, where condors dive over the spectacular Lago Monreal. Watch the steep banks for grazing *huemul*.

The trail continues through lovely forest, descending to a small stream (a good place to fill up on water) and rising again to an open scree field known as *el carreo*. Be careful on the loose sand; it's quite exposed. Crossing this section, always maintaining the same elevation, takes one to two hours. Trekking poles come in handy if conditions are windy.

Re-enter the forest for a half-hour, coming to a small bridge and red-and-white trail markings. Cross Río El Salto to reach Campamento El Salto, with a bathroom, table and fire pit, adequate for a few tents.

On the second day (six to eight hours, 9.5km), start a steep climb through the *lenga* forest above camp, coming to a stream that rises vertically to open alpine terrain. Climb the stream bank, staying true left of the river, until you reach a high alpine meadow above the tree line surrounded by snowy peaks. The total climb should take about two hours. This spectacular location has southeast headwalls perfect for winter ski turns. Follow the relatively flat valley south for another 1½ hours, passing cairns and snow patches. Stay left of the stream.

Arrive at the saddle known as **El Portazuelo**. Descend directly over the snow and follow the cairns that lead left, descending uncomfortably through scree. A cairn marks the forest entry just past a small stream crossing. The well-defined forested trail eventually widens into a logging road and descends. Follow the road to the **Guardería de Conaf** to register and pay the park entry fee (CH$3000).

Use the Day 1 route directions from the **Guardería de Conaf** post to arrive at Campamento el Turbio, 40 minutes on.

SIDE TRIP: LAGUNA GLACIAR PEÑÓN

3 hours return, 6km

Receding at an alarming pace, the Glaciar Peñón curls down from the heart of the Cordillera Castillo as the source of the Río Turbio. Follow the river's boulder-strewn south bank west from the clear brook (see Day 1) for 20 to 30 minutes to a murky meltwater pool below Glaciar Peñón. Beware of the ice.

Day 2: Upper Río Turbio to Campamento La Tetera

4¼–5¾ hours, 14km, 775m ascent

Follow the trail on up southwest as the terrain steepens and the forest goes over into scrub. Higher up the path is less distinct, but the going is relatively easy close to the cascading stream. The route climbs on higher into a rocky gully, passing streamlets splashing down from a small névé up to the right before reaching **Paso Peñón** (1453m), after 1½ to two hours. Paso Peñón is a long, narrow gap filled by frost-shattered rock and accumulated winter snow (which may remain well into February). From the southern end of the pass, the high, turquoise lake visible roughly southwest indicates the way ahead.

Descend cautiously onto steep and unstable scree-covered slopes, directly opposite spectacular icefalls gripping the raw eastern flank of Cerro Peñón that produce numerous meltwater cascades. Cut left across the glacial wash below to pick up random trails leading down the stream's forested left bank. After making a sometimes uncomfortable ford (which is easier where the stream briefly divides into two channels) you reach some reasonable unofficial **campsites**.

Continue on downstream to arrive at the Estero del Bosque junction, just 1½ to two hours from Paso Peñón. Here, the eastern branch of the Estero del Bosque merges with the somewhat larger western branch before racing through a narrow canyon. Winter avalanches sweeping off the southern side of Cerro Peñón have flattened much of the forest around this stream junction. Slightly uphill you will find **Campamento El Bosque**, with picnic tables and a primitive toilet.

Head up along embankments on the true left (ie northwestern) side of the west branch of the Estero de Bosque to meet a rocky streamway, after 50 minutes to 1¼ hours, then move a short way up right where the trail ducks back into the weather-beaten scrub. The path continues upvalley for 10 or 15 minutes to the sheltered campsites of **Campamento La Tetera**. Conaf plans to install primitive toilets here in the future.

After making camp, it's well worth climbing either moraine ridge to reach **several tarns** on the shelf behind the waterfall; more adventurous and energetic trekkers can climb the loose bare slopes on the right for more spectacular views.

Day 3: Campamento La Tetera to Campamento Neozelandés

6–8 hours, 11km, 650m ascent

Continue upvalley, crossing a side stream that spills down in a large cascade fed by an icefall on Cerro Castillo Chico. Ascend 15 to 20 minutes through streamside meadows interspersed with *lenga* thickets to arrive at **Laguna Cerro Castillo**. A stunning sight, the lake lies at 1275m above sea level in a deep glacial basin directly under the imposing Cerro Castillo (2675m). Hanging glaciers periodically drop ice blocks onto the rock cliffs below, where they shatter and occasionally hit the water. The open stony ground around the lake offers scenic views but it's too exposed for camping.

Cross the lake's outlet stream on steppingstones. Climb diagonally left along coarse, bare moraines to a very narrow shelf high above the lake and follow this around to reach a broad, flat saddle just west of Morro Rojo after one hour. This spot offers a fine view to Cerro Castillo directly opposite (although you'll need a 28mm lens to get it all in one shot!). Trek a short way left across the saddle to a tarn, from where you can see Villa Cerro Castillo and, down along the Valle Ibáñez, as far as Lago General Carrera. The Alternative Route (see below) leaves the main trail here.

Continue westward along a shelf opposite the basalt turrets of Cerro Castillo, before climbing easily over boulder rubble to reach a rocky gap after one hour. This ridgetop overlooks the wild, forested valley of the Estero Parada, which is enclosed by interesting jagged peaks. This section requires some care. Most trekkers drop directly into the steep, scree-filled gully ahead, following its right side as it curves leftward into the trees to meet a prominent path coming up through the valley, 1½ hours on. A longer but less rough option is to climb north to a forested ridge, then follow it down to meet the path after one to 1½ hours on.

Head upvalley through the *lenga* forest, passing **campsites** by the Estero Parada (not far downstream from where a large glacial tributary enters from an adjacent side valley). The path rises steadily onward, skirting soggy bogs close to the stream to arrive at **Campamento Neozelandés**, 1½ to two hours on. This is where a small mountaineering party from New Zealand established its base camp in 1976, making a number of first ascents in the area. This beautiful valley head is a great place to pitch your tent, but dry and level sites are limited.

SIDE TRIP: UPPER VALLE PARADA

2–3 hours return, 2–3km

The upper valley is enclosed on three sides by jagged summits of the Cordillera Castillo, and half a day or so might be spent exploring this area. **Laguna Duff**, a small tarn set in bare surroundings under Cerro Castillo Chico, can be visited from Campamento Neozelandés by heading up beside the narrow eastern branch of the Estero Parada. After the path peters out, continue over mossy slopes and glacial debris to the lake. On the west side of the valley, two more lakes formed by end moraines are best reached by crossing the east stream and heading round underneath the cliff face.

ALTERNATIVE ROUTE: LAGUNA CERRO CASTILLO TO VILLA CERRO CASTILLO

3½–4½ hours, 11km, 1100m descent

A more direct (although not particularly rewarding) route down to Villa Cerro Castillo leaves from the saddle west of Morro

Rojo (see Day 3). First contour eastward around Morro Rojo's southern side, before descending 1km along a steep spur to a prominent cairn. Here, move rightward and pick up an initially vague trail. The route improves as it leads down roughly southeast through regenerating forest into a fire-cleared area, then past a corral and a private property gate to meet a 4WD track. Follow this track down past a farmhouse to the meet the Río Ibáñez road at the Estero del Bosque bridge. Continue as described on Day 4.

Day 4: Campamento Neozelandés to Villa Cerro Castillo

4–5 hours, 19km, 870m descent

Backtrack downvalley to the rocky stream gully where you first encountered the trail (see Day 3). After climbing over a minor ridge, follow the path across burnt-out slopes scattered with wild strawberries, above where the Estero Parada races through a deep chasm. The route descends gently through pockets of *lenga* forest, before dropping rightward to the banks of the stream on the wide, open **Valle Ibáñez**. Now on the private property of an *estancia* (large cattle or sheep property), cut down left across rocky pastures past a homestead sheltered by graceful poplars, 2¼ to three hours after you left Campamento Neozelandés.

Head slightly south of east along a farm track across rich grassy flats grazed by sheep and *bandurrias* (black-necked ibis), then take a graded road on through *ñirre* scrub and *calafate* bushes to meet the Río Ibáñez after 40 to 50 minutes. The glacial waters of this large, swift-moving river flow through deep channels. Proceed on over a sandy plain to cross the Estero del Bosque on a bridge (where the Alternative Route rejoins the route), then continue a short way down the road to arrive at **Villa Cerro Castillo** after a final one to 1½ hours.

MORE TREKS

PARQUE NACIONAL HORNOPIRÉN

This 482-sq-km Chilean national park lies southeast of Puerto Montt near the village of Hornopirén on the Carretera Austral. The park centers on the 1572m cone of Volcán Hornopirén, whose name (a curious mixture of Mapuche and Spanish) means 'oven of snow'.

Buses Fierro (☎065-253022; Plaza de Armas) has three buses daily between Hornopirén and Puerto Montt (CH$3500, three hours); schedules change, so ask around. The bus trip includes a ferry crossing between Caleta Puelche and Caleta La Arena on Estuario/Seno Reloncaví. The ferry runs on a two- or three-hourly schedule in either direction.

Lago Cabrera

A two-day return trek from Hornopirén follows a good horse trail through the forest along the western side of Volcán Hornopirén to the eastern shore of Lago Cabrera, from where there are good views across the lake to the superb 2111m Volcán Yates. Volcán Hornopirén can be climbed from its eastern side.

The Chilean IGM's 1:50,000 map *Volcán Hornopirén* (Section H, No 72) covers virtually all of the park; the adjoining map *Volcán Apagado* (Section H, No 71) is also useful.

PARQUE PUMALÍN

Valle Ventisquero

A large tributary of the Río Puelo, the Río Ventisquero (Glaciar River) drains the northeasternmost area of Parque Pumalín. This beautiful river valley can be visited in a four-day return trek from the village of Llanada Grande, about halfway up the Río Puelo. **Hospedaje El Salto** (☎02-196-9212; agroturelsalto@gmail.com; r per person without bathroom CH$21,000) can arrange local guides.

From Llanada Grande, it's a long day's trek upriver via El Portón to the hanging bridge known as La Pasarela, which you cross before continuing in another long day up the Río Ventisquero to Fundo Rincón Bonito, an isolated farm belonging to Parque Pumalín. Since this trek crosses mostly private property, trekkers should be on their best behavior. Leave all livestock gates as is and always ask the nearest farmhouse if it's OK before setting up camp. Nothing is signposted, but local guides can also take visitors to Lago Azul, Lago Las Rocas and Segundo Corral. A new road leads up the river to (eventually) connect with Segundo Corral, the last town before the Argentine border.

Buses Fierro has several buses daily from Puerto Montt (CH$6000, three hours), passing Puerto Varas, to the small town of Puelo at the mouth of the Río Puelo. Passengers can take the ferry *Don Felipe* (CH$800) to cross Lago Tagua Tagua, then take local transport (CH$4000, two hours) to Llanada Grande or further upvalley to Los Álamos (to get a head start on trek).

Three Chilean IGM 1:50,000 maps cover the trek: *Llanada Grande* (Section H, 74), *Lago Las Rocas* (Section H, 84) and *Arroyo Ventisquero* (Section H, 83).

Lago Reñihue

Lago Reñihue is a large, remote lake at the headwaters of the Río Reñihue, which flows into Fiordo Reñihue near Caleta Gonzalo (p155). A six-day, 60km return trek from Caleta Gonzalo follows a foot track upriver past campsites and excellent fishing spots to Lago Reñihue. The start of the route crosses private property, where trekkers should be on their best behavior.

Two Chilean IGM maps cover the route: *Fiordo Reñihue* (Section H, No 101) and *Pillán* (Section H, No 102).

Ventisquero Amarillo

The largest of several glaciers descending from the large névé on Volcán Michimahuida, the spectacular Ventisquero Amarillo can be visited in a two- or three-day trek from the village of El Amarillo, 25km south of Chaitén (p133). From Parque Pumalín's guardería (just 60m along the road to the Termas del Amarillo), a road turn-off goes to a campsite. From here, a foot track makes a long sidling climb over a saddle and down past an old puesto to the upper Río Amarillo. A route leads upvalley along the wide, gravelly flood plain to the snout of Ventisquero Amarillo, but it requires a serious wade of one of the river's several fast-flowing channels – a planned foot track would avoid any crossings.

Use the Chilean IGM's 1:50,000 map *Volcán Michimahuida* (Section H, No 111).

COMARCA ANDINA

Cerro Perito Moreno

This five-hour return trek begins from **Refugio Perito Moreno** (☎ 02944-483433; free camping, shelter AR$25, dm AR$40, meals AR$25). This hut at 950m belongs to the local CAP, and is 25km by road north of El Bolsón (p156). The route first climbs to the upper end of the winter ski lifts. It then heads westward into the *lenga* scrub and crosses a plateau (at around 1600m) to reach the snout of the glacier on the side of Cerro Perito Moreno. The 2206m summit can only be reached by experienced climbers with proper mountaineering equipment, but from a lookout point on a spur a short way over to the left, trekkers get an excellent view southward across the valley of the Río Encanto Blanco to the peaks around Dedo Gordo.

The 1:100,000 Argentine IGM map *El Bolsón* (Río Negro, No 4172-34) covers this area, but does not properly show the route itself; see also the 'Around Cerro Hielo Azul' map (p137).

Cerro Piltriquitrón

Another of the Comarca Andina's key landmarks, the rump ridge of Cerro Piltriquitrón (pill-tree-key-**tron**) rises up directly east of El Bolsón. This panoramic 2260m peak can be climbed in a day trek from Plataforma del Piltriquitrón, at the end of the 11km access road (a taxi to here costs around AR$30).

A one-hour climb brings you to the **Refugio Cerro Piltriquitrón** (☎ 02944-498843, 1569-0044; free camping, dm AR$25, meals AR$20), a CAP hut at 1450m. A marked trail ascends on beside a disused ski lift, skirts away eastward, then climbs steeply through loose scree to the summit, giving superb views across Lago Puelo to Cerro Tres Picos and northward to Volcán Osorno and Monte Tronador.

The Argentine IGM's 1:100,000 map *Cuesta del Ternero* (Río Negro, No 4172-35) covers the trek.

Cerro Lindo

The glacier-crowned 2135m Cerro Lindo, which stands just less than 15km directly west of El Bolsón, can be climbed in a moderate three-day return trek. In the near future it's possible that climbers will only be allowed with guides. The path crosses the suspension bridge near the free **Camping Río Azul** (☎ 1531-2228) and climbs northwest through the forest. After descending steeply to cross the small Arroyo Lali (the last water until the *refugio*), continue up westward to reach the **Refugio Cerro Lindo** (radio contact only; free camping, beds AR$30, meals AR$15), a CAP hut that can get crowded in January. From here a rougher trail leads up to the summit of Cerro Lindo; the return trip takes around three hours. Recommended maps are as for the Around Cerro Hielo Azul trek (p137).

PARQUE NACIONAL LAGO PUELO

Surrounding the 40-sq-km Lago Puelo, this small, 237-sq-km national park is 15km southwest of El Bolsón in the province of Chubut. The park administration center, or **intendencia** (☎/fax 02944-499064/499232), is at the village of Lago Puelo on the lake's northeastern shore.

Camping Lago Puelo (☎ 02944-499186; camping per person AR$8) is in the village. **Juana de Arco** (☎ 02944-493415; www.interpatagonia.com/juanadearco) takes passengers across the lake, including to Río Turbio on the south shore (see Río Turbio & Cerro Platforma below), and to the Chilean border (AR$60, three hours).

For hard-core trekkers heading to Chile, it's possible to continue on foot or on horseback. This trek involves crossing the border, then continuing along the north shore of Lago Las Rocs and inland to Lago Azul. After crossing the lake by boat, trekkers continue to Llanada Grande (see p152), from where buses take passengers to Puelo, with a ferry crossing, and on to Puerto Montt.

In summer there are buses approximately every hour to Lago Puelo from El Bolsón and regularly from Esquel.

Two Argentine IGM 1:100,000 maps, *Cordón del Pico Alto* (Chubut, No 4372-3) and *Lago Puelo* (Chubut, No 4372-4), cover the entire park.

Cerro Currumahuida

You can climb this peak (about 1200m) in around six hours return from the *intendencia* (park administration center). The route sidles along slopes on the eastern side of Lago Puelo, then climbs through stands of *coigüe* and Cordilleran cypress (higher up the forest has been largely destroyed by the fires of 1987) to the top of the range. A trek along (or near to) this ridgetop to the summit of Cerro Currumahuida offers great views across Lago Puelo to Lago Inferior (in Chile), to Cerro Tres Picos to the southwest and Cerro Piltriquitrón to the northeast.

Río Turbio & Cerro Plataforma

The day trek to the Río Turbio leaves from the free campsite at El Desemboque, where the Río Epuyén runs into Lago Puelo; this is some 16km from El Hoyo, which is roughly 14km south of El Bolsón. The trail begins at the southern end of the beach, sidling up through burnt forest on the western slopes of Cerro Durrumbe before descending again to an APN *guardería* at the southeastern corner of Lago Puelo. From here launches run back across the lake to the jetty near the intendencia on the northeast shore.

Cerro Plataforma, a flat-topped mountain well outside the park boundaries, where ancient marine fossils are found, can be reached in a three-day return trek from the guardería. The route turns southwestward, crosses the Arroyo Durrumbe and climbs steadily up past little farms high above the valley of the Río Turbio; a final climb following red paint markings leads to the Cerro Plataforma. There are two rustic *refugios* along the route.

Two Argentine IGM 1:100,000 maps, *Lago Puelo* (Chubut, No 4372-4) and *Lago Rivadavia* (Chubut, No 4372-10), cover this trek.

PARQUE NACIONAL LOS ALERCES

For all these routes, trekkers must begin climbing at least before 10am in order to return safely by nightfall.

The 1:100,000 Argentine IGM map *Villa Futalaufquen* (Chubut, No 2372-16) covers the area but does not show the routes.

Cerro Alto Dedal

The trek up to Cerro Alto Dedal (1916m) is the most popular in the park, and takes around seven hours return from Villa Futalaufquen.

The signposted foot track leaves from the museum and soon crosses the Arroyo Dedal (carry water from this stream as it is the last) as it climbs steeply out of the forest and follows a spur over Dedal (a minor point at around 1600m) to Cerro Alto Dedal. The summit offers great views northward across Lago Futalaufquen, east to Laguna Larga, south along the range to Cerro Cocinero (Situación) and southwest to the Cordón de los Pirámides.

Refugio Cocinero

The trek up to this lookout point, which gives excellent views of a small glacier in the cirque between the northern and southern summits of Cerro Cocinero (Situación), is best done as an overnight trip.

An unsignposted foot track leaves from the road 10km south of Villa Futalaufquen, first following the southern side of the Arroyo Rañinto. Head up left at the first large side stream you meet, crossing this several times as you climb steeply to reach **Refugio Cocinero**. This small hut has a fireplace and sleeping space for up to six people.

Cerro Alto Petiso

The 1790m Cerro Alto El Petiso is the best lookout point in the park's northern sector, and you can visit it in a full-day trek of moderate difficulty taking around seven hours return. The trailhead is at Puerto Mermoud (where there is a historic wooden farmhouse built by the first settler in this area) on the western shore of Lago Verde. As a rule, trekkers must set out before 9am so that they have enough time to return safely by nightfall.

The path climbs over a ridge, then follows the Arroyo Zanjón Honda up to its source at two tiny streamlets (the last running water). A final steep ascent along a spur leads to the summit, from where you get a superb panorama that includes Lago Menéndez, Lago Futalaufquen, Lago Rivadavia and the glacier-clad peak of Cerro Torrecillas.

RESERVA NACIONAL FUTALEUFÚ

The 120-sq-km Reserva Nacional Futaleufú is directly southeast of the attractive village of Futaleufú, 160km from Chaitén in Chile. The reserve protects one of Chile's most northerly populations of *huemul.*

A three-day circuit can be done from the bridge over the Río Futaleufú, 3km east of the Plaza de Armas in the village center.

The route leads up the Río Chico, then crosses a pass and descends along the Arroyo Quila Seca to meet the Río Futaleufú, following the river upstream back to the bridge. Another route goes up to the superb lookout summit of Cerro Cónico (2271m) on the Chile–Argentina border.

There are daily buses to Futaleufú from Esquel. For more information, contact Futaleufú's **tourist office** (O'Higgins 536).

Two Chilean IGM 1:50,000 maps cover the reserve: *Futaleufú* (Section I, No 11) and *Río Futaleufú* (Section I, No 24).

PARQUE NACIONAL QUEULAT

The 154-sq-km Parque Nacional Queulat lies southeast of the tiny town of Puyuhuapi on Chile's Pacific coast. Its wet, maritime climate has produced vast glaciers and ice fields in the interior of the park, while the lower areas are vegetated by dense coastal rainforest. The administrative *guardería* for the park is at the end of a 2km turn-off, 25km south of Puyuhuapi along the Carretera Austral.

The *guardería* looks out toward the Ventisquero Colgante, a spectacular hanging glacier that drops great blocks of ice over a precipice several hundred meters high. There's a better lookout about 15 minutes on past the Conaf campsite.

A harder return day trek continues across the suspension bridge and follows an increasingly overgrown path along the Río Ventisqueros to Laguna Témpanos, a small lake directly below the Ventisquero Colgante.

The Chilean IGM 1:50,000 map *Puyuhuapi* (Section I, No 61) covers the central part of the park around Ventisquero Colgante.

RESERVA NACIONAL RÍO SIMPSON

Reserva Nacional Río Simpson is a small reserve taking in the mountains to the west and northwest of Coyhaique. A two-day return trek from the Guardería Correntoso takes you to the **Bosque Petrificado**, where small petrified stumps of ancient Guaitecas cypress are found. The trek begins and ends at the Guardería Correntoso, accessible from 500m east of the Puente Correntoso, a bridge on the Coyhaique–Puerto Aisén road (Ruta CH 245), 22km from Coyhaique. Also check for the possible reopening of a marvellous three-day trek to a small lake under craggy Cerro Catedral.

One Chilean IGM 1:50,000 map *Río Correntoso* (Section I, No 108) covers the area.

TOWNS & FACILITIES

CALETA GONZALO (CHILE)

☎ 065

Within the park, this tiny village occupies a scenic cove of Fiordo Reñihue, 60km north of Chaitén, where the Carretera Austral terminates at a ferry crossing to Hornopiren. Parque Pumalín has an information center and store here. There are short nature trails and an organic farm nearby. Due to the recent activity of Volcan Chaiten, some of these services may be affected. Always check ahead through the offices of Parque Pumalín (p133)

Sleeping & Eating

Overlooking the fjord, **Caleta Gonzalo Cabañas** (☎ 065-232300; s/d CH$25,000/35,000, extra person CH$5000) are crisp and attractive, though without kitchen facilities.

For fireside meals, **Café Caleta Gonzalo** (lunches CH$7500; breakfast, lunch & dinner) has organic vegetables, as well as local honey and fresh bread.

Getting There & Away

BOAT

The summer-only **Naviera Austral** (☎ 065-270430) ferry sails daily from Caleta Gonzalo to Hornopirén (five to six hours), departing at 9am. Passengers pay CH$10,000 (cars CH$64,000).

BUS

Buses Fierro (☎ 065-253022; Plaza de Armas) has three buses daily between Hornopirén and Puerto Montt (CH$3500, three hours); schedules change, so ask around. The bus trip includes a ferry crossing between Caleta Puelche and Caleta La Arena on Estuario/Seno Reloncaví. Those arriving from Puerto Montt will first take a bus to Hornopiren (which includes a ferry between Caleta Puelche and Caleta La Arena), followed by the Naviera Austral ferry to Caleta Gonzalo.

Chaitur (☎ 097-4685608; www.chaitur.com) runs a bus to Caleta Gonzalo (CH$5000) for the ferry at 7am. Reservations are required.

COYHAIQUE (CHILE)

☎ 067 / pop 45,000

Outsized cow town Coyhaique is an urban center plunked amidst an undulating range, with rocky humpback peaks and snowy ranges in the backdrop. Pronounced coy-**aye**-kay, its name means 'landscape of lakes' in Tehuelche. Its location marks the transition from northern Patagonia's rainforest to drier southern steppes. Day treks in the scenic **Reserva Nacional Coyhaique**, 5km north of town, are worthwhile.

Information

Near the Plaza de Armas, **Sernatur** (Servicio Nacional de Turismo; ☎ 067-233949; sernatur_coyhaiq@entelchile.net; Bulnes 35; 8.30am-8pm Mon-Fri, 10am-6pm Sat & Sun in summer) has general tourist information. Also visit the city website at www.coyhaique.cl.

Conaf (Corporación Nacional Forestal; ☎ 067-212125; Av Ogana 1060; 9am-8pm Mon-Sat, 10am-6pm Sun) is on the southern road out of town. Rural homestays and guides (see p227) can also be arranged in Coyhaique.

Supplies & Equipment

Sodimac (☎ 067-231576; Baquedano 421) hardware store sells white gasoline (*bencina blanca*).

Condor Explorer (☎ 573634; www.condorexplorer.com; Dussen 357) sells topographic maps, gear and Patagonia-brand clothing. It also offers recommended trips and expeditionary logistical support.

Sleeping & Eating

Only 1km from the city, **Camping Alborada** (☎ 067-238868; camping per person CH$2500) has exceptionally clean and sheltered sites. Take Av General Baquedano north out of town, it's on the right, on the way to Reserva Nacional Coyhaique.

Woodsy guesthouse **Albergue Las Salamandras** (☎ 067-211865; www.salamandras.cl; Teniente Vidal km1.5; dm/d/cabins CH$7000/19,000/32,000) offers comfortable dorms and cabins in a rural setting 2km south of town.

The family-run **Doña Herminia** (☎ 067-231579; 21 de Mayo 60; r per person without bathroom CH$8000) is shipshape and comfortable.

Upscale **El Reloj** (☎067-231108; www.elrelojhotel.cl; Baquedano 828; s/d CH$38,000/56,000) blends rustic elements with a smart, clean design. The restaurant is recommended.

Serving greens, fresh rolls and healthy meals, **Café Confluencia** (☎067-245080; 25 de Mayo 548; mains CH$3000-5000; breakfast, lunch & dinner) is a chic eatery focused on fresh food.

For deep-fried goodness, **Casino de Bomberos** (☎067-231437; General Parra 365; fixed-price lunches CH$3500; lunch) serves classics like steak and eggs.

The popular **Café Ricer** (☎067-232920; Horn 48; mains CH$5000-7500; 9.30am-midnight) is always open but somewhat overpriced.

Getting There & Away

AIR

Balmaceda airport is 50km southeast of town. For the door-to-door shuttle service (CH$4000), call **Transfer Coyhaique** (☎067-210495).

Lan (☎067-231188; General Parra 402) has several daily flights (most leaving in the morning) to Puerto Montt (CH$94,000) and Santiago (CH$125,000 return) from the Balmaceda airport.

Sky Airline (☎067-240827; www.skyairline.cl; Arturo Prat 203) has flights to Punta Arenas (CH$89,000).

Transporte Aéreo Don Carlos (☎067-231981; www.doncarlos.cl; Cruz 63) flies small craft to Villa O'Higgins (CH$35,000) on Monday and Thursday.

BOAT

Ferries to Puerto Montt leave from Puerto Chacabuco, two hours west of Coyhaique by bus, but the closest regional offices are in Coyhaique. **Navimag** (☎067-223306; www.navimag.com; Paseo Horn 47-D) sails several times per week (high season CH$38,000 to CH$143,000, 18 hours); see the website for the current departure schedule.

BUS

Most buses leave from the **Terminal de Buses** (☎067-258203; cnr Lautaro & Magallanes). Schedules change frequently; check with Sernatur (p239) for the latest information. Check also on the status of Chaitén-bound buses, which may be suspended due to volcanic activity (see boxed text p60).

Companies serving destinations north include the following:

Buses Becker Eirle (☎335050; Ibañez 358) Twice a week to Puyuhuapi, La Junta, Villa Santa Lucía and Chaitén.
Buses Daniela (☎067-231701, 099-512 3500; Baquedano 1122) Four times a week to Puyuhuapi, La Junta, Villa Santa Lucía and Chaitén.
Buses M&C Tours (☎067-242626; General Parra 329) Three times a week to Puyuhuapi, La Junta, Villa Santa Lucía and Chaitén.
Buses Suray (☎067-238387; Arturo Prat 265) Hourly to Puerto Chacabuco.
Queilen Bus (☎067-240760; cnr Lautaro & Magallanes) Osorno, Puerto Montt and Chiloé via Argentina.

Companies serving destinations south include the following:

Acuarío 13 (☎067-240990) Cochrane
Buses Don Carlos (☎067-231981; Cruz 63) Villa Cerro Castillo, Puerto Murta, Puerto Río Tranquilo, Puerto Bertrand and Cochrane.
Buses Interlagos (☎067-240840; www.turismointerlagos.cl, in Spanish; cnr Lautaro & Magallanes) Cochrane and Chile Chico.
Colectivos Puerto Ibáñez (cnr Arturo Prat & Errázuríz) Door-to-door shuttle to Puerto Ingeniero Ibáñez (CH$3500, 1½ hours).
Transporte Bellavista (☎067-244855) Puerto Río Tranquilo (CH$7500, five hours) with connections to Chile Chico (CH$6000). Picks up passengers from lodgings.

Destination	Fare (CH$)	Duration (hr)
Osorno	28,000	20
Puerto Montt	30,000	24
Chaitén	15,000	12
La Junta	8000	7–10
Puyuhuapi	8000	6
Chile Chico	13,500	12
Cochrane	10,000	7–10

EL BOLSÓN (ARGENTINA)

☎ 02944 / pop 18,000

The 'ecological municipality' of El Bolsón attracts outdoor types, back-to-nature folk and out-of-work circus acts (mostly in summer). In a broad basin between two high ranges, its name translates as 'handbag'. With trekking within easy reach, homemade beers *and* ice cream, it's an ideal spot to kick back.

El Bolsón's **oficina de turismo** (☎ 02944-492604, 455336; www.bolsonturistico.com.ar, in Spanish; Av San Martín & Roca; 9am-9pm, until 10pm summer) is near Plaza Pagano, the town's central park.

Club Andino Piltriquitrón (☎ 02944-492600; Sarmiento; Dec-Mar only), almost directly west of the tourist office between Roca & Feliciano, operates a number of the *refugios* in the surrounding mountains.

Online hut information can be found at www.bolsonweb.com/aventura/refugios.htm#lista (in Spanish).

Sleeping & Eating

Camping Refugio Patagónico (☎ 15-635463; Islas Malvinas s/n; camping per person AR$8) has field camping next to a pleasant stream with barbecues and a clean, modern toilet block.

If you've got a sleeping bag, **Albergue Sol del Valle** (☎ 02944-492087; 25 de Mayo 2485; dm/d AR$40/100) has good-value dorm rooms with kitchen access.

El Molinito (☎ 02944-493164; 25 de Mayo & Dorrego; dm/s AR$45/90) boasts firm beds, squeaky clean bathrooms and kitchen use.

Rustic **La Posada de Hamelin** (☎ 02944-492030; www.posadadehamelin.com.ar, in Spanish; Granollers 2179; s/d AR$140/200) has four comfortable rooms but breakfast is extra.

Dine at *coniíitería* **Jauja** (Av San Martín 2867; mains AR$15-30), a cafe with excellent homemade ice cream, trout and pastas; or **Las Brasas** (☎ 02944-492923; Av Sarmiento & Pablo Hube; mains AR$18-30; lunch & dinner), a lauded Patagonian grill.

Getting There & Away

AIR

Lade (☎ 02944-492206; Perito Moreno at Plaza Pagano) flies weekly to Bariloche (AR$68), Comodoro Rivadavia (AR$206) and Esquel (AR$68). Flights leave from the small airport (☎ 02944-492066) at the north end of Av San Martín.

BUS

Andesmar (☎ 02944-492178; Av Belgrano & Perito Moreno) goes to Bariloche (AR$15, two hours) and Esquel (AR$20, two to three hours), and to points further north.

TAC, represented by **Grado 42** (☎ 02944-493124; Av Belgrano 406), goes to Bariloche (AR$15) and Neuquén (AR$58, nine hours).

Don Otto (☎ 02944-493910; cnr Av Sarmiento & Roca) goes to Bariloche and Esquel (prices as above).

Transportes Nehuén (☎ 02944-491831; Sarmiento), near Roca, goes to Bariloche and Parque Nacional Los Alerces AR$30.

TAXI

Remis company **Patagonia** (☎ 02944-493907) has competitive taxi fares to trailheads.

ESQUEL (ARGENTINA)

☎ 02945 / pop 36,000

Set in western Chubut's dramatic foothills, the dusty town of Esquel is an easygoing and exceedingly friendly base camp. It's just off Ruta Nacional 40.

Information

The **oficina de turismo** (☎ 02945-451927; www.esquel.gov.ar, in Spanish; Av Alvear 1220) offers multilingual assistance.

The **Asociación de Guías de Montaña** (☎ 02945-450653; Ameghino 98) organizes mountain guides and can give advice on trekking and climbing in the area.

Sleeping & Eating

Run with dedication and affection, **Casa del Pueblo** (☎ 02945-450581; www.grupoepa.com, in Spanish; San Martín 661; dm/d/tr AR$33/80/111) has comfortable dorms, as well as books, adventure trips and mountain bikes for rent. It is associated with EPA, an adventure tour operator offering hikes, rafting and more.

Affable family home **Casa de Familia Rowlands** (☎ 02945-452578; Rivadavia 330; r per person AR$35) offers basic rooms seven blocks from the center.

Hospitable and polished, **Hostería Angelina** (☎ 02945-452763; www.hosteriaangelina.com.ar; Av Alvear 758; s/d standard AR$120/160, superior AR$140/180) follows international standards, with professional service and a good breakfast buffet.

Rock 'n' roll restaurant-bar **La Luna** (☎ 02945-453800; www.lalunarestobar.com.ar, in Spanish; Rivadavia 1080; mains AR$15, pizzas AR$30; noon-4pm & 7pm-1am) serves tasty spinach pizzas and heaping portions of steak and fries.

Artsy **Dionisio** (☎ 15-507749; Av Fontana 656; mains AR$24) specializes in crepes, both savory and sweet.

Getting There & Away

AIR

Esquel's **airport** (ESQ; ☎ 02945-451676) is 20km east of town off Ruta Nacional 40. **Aerolíneas Argentinas** (☎ 02945-453614; Av Fontana 406) flies to Bariloche (AR$1539) and Buenos Aires (AR$1256) several times a week. **Lade** (☎ 02945-452124; Av Alvear 1085) reaches those destinations and El Calafate (AR$411).

BUS

Esquel's **bus terminal** (☎ 02945-451477/9; cnr Av Alvear & Brun) is an easy trek from the center. There are daily buses to all major destinations, including Bariloche (AR$37, 4½ hours), Neuquén (AR$100, 10 hours) and Buenos Aires (AR$203, 30 hours).

Transportes Jacobsen (☎ 02945-453528) goes to Futaleufú (AR$15, 1½ hours), in Chile, Monday and Friday at 8am and 6pm. In summer, *Transportes Esquel* (☎ 02945-453529) goes through Parque Nacional Los Alerces (AR$9, 1¼ hours) to Lago Futalaufquen daily at 8am and 4pm. The first bus goes all the way to Lago Puelo (AR$23, six hours), stopping in Lago Verde (AR$13) at 10.30am and Cholila at 12pm. If you plan on exploring the area by bus, purchase an open ticket (AR$30), which allows passengers to make stops along the way between Esquel and Lago Puelo or vice-versa. Service is reduced off-season.

LAGO FUTALAUFQUEN (ARGENTINA)

☎ 02945

The eastern shores of Lago Futalaufquen have 11 free campsites without facilities, in addition to campsites (camping per person AR$16-20) and cabins with amenities and lodgings. Among the best are **Hostería Quime Quipan** (☎ 02945-471021; www.cpatagonia.com/quimequipan, in Spanish; d with/without views AR$300/270, six-person cabins AR$350; Nov-Apr), **Cabañas Tejas Negras** (☎ 02945-471012, 471046; tejasnegras@ciudad.com.ar; four-/five-person cabins AR$400/500; year-round), **Lago Verde Wilderness Resort** (☎ 011-4312 7415 in Buenos Aires; www.hosteriaselaura.com; camping per person AR$14-28, per car AR$6, two-/three-/four-person cabins AR$942/1224/1507) and the basic **Hostería Cume Hue** (☎ 02945-450503; www.cumehue.com.ar; per person with full board AR$210; year-round).

See Villa Futalaufquen (p159) for transport information to/from the lake.

LAGUNA CHIGUAY (CHILE)

Laguna Chiguay is a small lake surrounded by exotic conifers beside the Carretera Austral, 6km north of Las Horquetas Grandes and 64km south of Coyhaique. Here, Conaf's Guardería Chiguay can give advice on the trekking route and you can pay the park entry fee (CH$3000).

The Conaf-run **Camping Laguna Chiguay** (camping per site CH$3000) has six sites with tables, fire pits, bathrooms and hot showers.

VILLA CERRO CASTILLO (CHILE)

☎ 067 / pop 300

On the Carretera Austral 98km south of Coyhaique, the hamlet of Villa Cerro Castillo – not to be confused with its namesake further south on the Torres del Paine road – lies almost below the majestic mountain itself. Near the village is an ancient **Tehuelche rock-art site**.

Sleeping & Eating

Cabañas Don Niba (public phone ☎ 067-419200; Los Pioneros 872; camping per person CH$7000) serves big breakfasts and the company of Don Niba, horse-riding guide, storyteller and grandson of pioneers.

About 1.5km from the crossroads of the Carretera Austral and Puerto Ibañez (toward Ibañez), **La Casona** (public phone ☎ 067-419200; camping per person CH$4000, r per person CH$8000) offers friendly farmhouse lodgings, ideal for cyclists or trekkers who need some space to air out their gear.

La Querencia (☎ 067-411610; O'Higgins 460) serves up typical Patagonian fare.

Getting There & Away

BUS

In Coyhaique, **Buses Don Carlos** (☎ 067-231981; Teniente Cruz 63) runs buses to Villa Cerro Castillo (CH$3500, 2¼ hours) several days per week. Buses running between Cochrane and Coyhaique (see p155 for details) call in at Villa Cerro Castillo; going north, they generally pass Villa Cerro Castillo at around 1pm.

VILLA FUTALAUFQUEN (ARGENTINA)

☎ 02945

At the southern end of Lago Futalaufquen, the village has a grocery store with a museum and APN's **centro de informes** (information center; ☎ 02945-471020, 471015, ext 23), where you can obtain a fishing license.

Sleeping & Eating

Camping Los Maitenes (☎ 02945-471006; camping per person AR$16), 200m from the Intendencia, offers lovely water views. Sites include shade, electricity and fire pits.

Exclusive and elegant, **Hostería Futalaufquen** (☎ 02945-471008/9; www.brazosur.com.ar/hosteria.htm, in Spanish; d with half-pension low/high season AR$587/800, four-/five-person apt AR$1200/1600) has nine well-appointed doubles, three log cabins and a restaurant. It's along the route of Day 1, 3km from the village at the end of the road (500m on from Puerto Limonao).

For camping options around the lake, see Lago Futalaufquen (p158).

Getting There & Away

BUS

Villa Futalaufquen is most easily accessible from Esquel (p157). In summer, **Transportes Esquel** (☎ 02945-453529) goes through Parque Nacional Los Alerces to Lago Futalaufquen (AR$9, 1¼ hours) daily at 8am and 4pm. The first bus goes all the way to Lago Puelo (AR$23, six hours), stopping in Lago Verde, just beyond Lago Futalaufquen (AR$13) at 10.30am. Purchasing an open ticket (AR$30) allows you to make stops along the way between Esquel and Lago Puelo, or vice-versa. Service is reduced in the off-season.

Southern Patagonia

HIGHLIGHTS

- Coming off John Gardner Pass to face the colossal **Glaciar Grey** (p182)
- Scrambling to the lookout for **Monte Fitz Roy** (p172) and its satellite peaks
- Ice trekking across the blue contours under **Cerro Torre's chiselled tower** (p171)
- Spying on *huemules*, the **endangered Andean deer** (p168), near Glaciar Tigre
- Following de Agostini's footsteps on the secluded approach to **Monte San Lorenzo** (p163)

Wind drives all here. It razes the barren plains, whittles granite monoliths and ripples long sheaths of ice. Glaciers also had a hand in forming these fine landscapes. Their presence continues: two vast continental icecaps known as Hielo Norte and Hielo Sur make this region the most intensely glaciated part of South America. Stretching from Lago Carrera/Buenos Aires to the Straits of Magellan, Southern Patagonia encompasses the renowned national parks of Torres del Paine and Los Glaciares, as well as many extraordinary little-known reserves.

For many, these landscapes represent the distilled essence of Patagonia. This selection takes trekkers in the wake of famous climbers and mountaineers, from Padre Agostini to Ferrari, to explore around Cerro Torre, San Lorenzo and Torres del Paine. Remote regions on the Carretera Austral and Ruta 40 also have their treasures. Here nature, long left to its own devices, grows wild, barren and beautiful. Spaces are large, as are the silences that fill them.

Southern Patagonia's celebrity attractions receive massive visitation. Please be aware of your impact on the area, practice 'leave-no-trace principles' and keep the community spirit alive on the trail.

FITZ ROY OR PAINE?

These two truly spectacular destinations are occasionally pitted against each other when travelers find themselves strapped for time. How do you choose just one?

The budget breakdown is ever-changing with these two flip-flopping economies. Some years one country is cheaper – so do your homework. If you plan to camp, the point might be moot, but if you're done with foam mattress nights, you will probably find the hostels in El Chaltén cheaper than the *refugios* in Torres del Paine. That's right, most of the treks in the Fitz Roy area can be done as day trips. The area is more compact; its glaciers are smaller yet still spectacular. What does this mean for you? Easy. If the weather turns grizzly, in hours you'll be in a warm pub with a cold pint.

But if you want a world-class trek of a week or more, the Paine Circuit is the clear choice. You will get to see a landscape that's diverse and magnificent, with great glaciers, big turquoise lakes and iconic peaks. In Paine you can trek for a week without retracing your steps. It doesn't have to be Woman/Man vs. Wild. Paine's *refugios* and catamaran services offer a level of backpacking comfort not found in Fitz Roy's *campamentos*.

There's one more consideration: what else do you want to do? El Chaltén isn't far from the massive Glaciar Moreno. On the other hand, Chile has penguins nearby.

The choice, if you must make it, is yours. A final word of caution, though. If you need guaranteed sunshine, we hear Aruba is nice.

GATEWAYS

See Coyhaique p155, Calafate p195 and Punta Arenas p199.

SAN LORENZO MASSIF

A colossal complex of towers and glaciers, the San Lorenzo massif straddles the Chile–Argentina border. Monte San Lorenzo's coveted 3706m summit is the second- or third-highest summit in the Patagonian Andes – depending on who's keeping score. Reminiscent of the Macizo Paine far to the south, this more isolated range sits a few dozen kilometers southeast of Cochrane.

Monte San Lorenzo, called Monte Cochrane in Chile (at least on government documents), is most accessible from its western (Chilean) side via private farms along the Río Tranquilo. However, the eastern side of the San Lorenzo massif enjoys much better environmental protection. It lies couched within Argentina's Parque Nacional Perito Moreno (see More Treks, p194) and the 154-sq-km Estancia El Rincón, protected by the private **Conservación Patagónica** (www.conservacionpatagonica.org).

ENVIRONMENT

Although rock and ice often block the way, the existence of several key passes and lower ridges in the San Lorenzo massif facilitates biological communication between flora and fauna on each side.

The vegetation cover is determined mainly by microclimatic variations in precipitation along with exposure to the sun and savage drying winds. The upper valleys are largely covered by light Magellanic (southern Patagonian) forest of deciduous *ñirre* and *lenga*, with an understorey of *brecillo* and *chaura*. The daisylike *chilca* grow in the forest or on moist sunny sites. On the lower or exposed slopes, sparse vegetation more typical of the Patagonian steppes predominates, including tussock grasses and saltbushlike *mogotes*.

Although grazing cattle are the most dominant herbivore, *huemul* and occasionally even guanaco are seen on the Chilean side, stalked by the furtive puma. Trekkers may also be lucky enough to spot the shy *piche* (Patagonian armadillo), which digs its burrow in soft earth.

The gregarious *bandurria* (black-necked ibis) is often seen in the lower valley and around moister areas, usually in flocks of a dozen or more, picking over the grassy areas with its long curved beak. The diminutive *rayadito* (thorntail) lives and nests

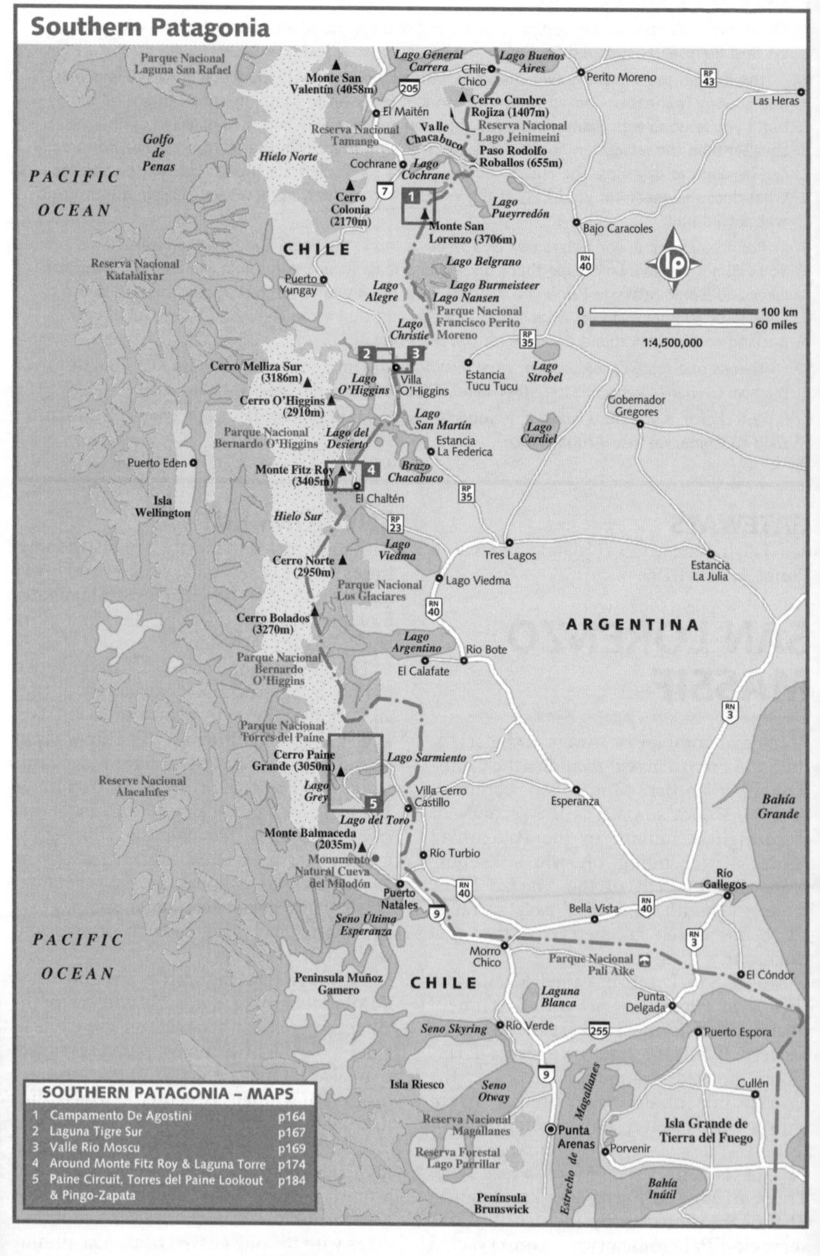
Southern Patagonia
Parque Nacional Laguna San Rafael
Monte San Valentín (4058m)
Lago General Carrera
Chile Chico
Lago Buenos Aires
Perito Moreno
RP 43
Las Heras
205
El Maitén
Cerro Cumbre Rojiza (1407m)
Reserva Nacional Lago Jeinimeini
Valle Chacabuco
Reserva Nacional Tamango
Paso Rodolfo Roballos (655m)
Golfo de Penas
Hielo Norte
Cochrane
Lago Cochrane
PACIFIC OCEAN
Cerro Colonia (2170m)
7
1
Monte San Lorenzo (3706m)
Lago Pueyrredón
Bajo Caracoles
CHILE
Lago Belgrano
RN 40
Reserva Nacional Katalalixar
Puerto Yungay
Lago Alegre
Lago Burmeisteer
Lago Nansen
Parque Nacional Francisco Perito Moreno
0 100 km
0 60 miles
1:4,500,000
Lago Christie
RP 35
2
3
Cerro Melliza Sur (3186m)
Lago O'Higgins
Villa O'Higgins
Estancia Tucu Tucu
Lago Strobel
Cerro O'Higgins (2910m)
Lago San Martín
Gobernador Gregores
Parque Nacional Bernardo O'Higgins
Lago del Desierto
Estancia La Federica
Lago Cardiel
Puerto Eden
Monte Fitz Roy (3405m)
4
Brazo Chacabuco
RP 35
El Chaltén
Isla Wellington
Hielo Sur
RP 23
Lago Viedma
Tres Lagos
Estancia La Julia
Cerro Norte (2950m)
Lago Viedma
Parque Nacional Los Glaciares
RN 40
ARGENTINA
Cerro Bolados (3270m)
Lago Argentino
Rio Bote
El Calafate
Parque Nacional Bernardo O'Higgins
RN 3
Parque Nacional Torres del Paine
Cerro Paine Grande (3050m)
Lago Sarmiento
Reserve Nacional Alacalufes
Lago Grey
5
Villa Cerro Castillo
Esperanza
Bahía Grande
Lago del Toro
Monte Balmaceda (2035m)
Río Turbio
Monumento Natural Cueva del Milodón
Puerto Natales
RN 40
Río Gallegos
9
Seno Última Esperanza
Bella Vista
RN 40
RN 3
PACIFIC OCEAN
Morro Chico
Parque Nacional Pali Aike
El Cóndor
Peninsula Muñoz Gamero
CHILE
Laguna Blanca
Punta Delgada
Seno Skyring
Río Verde
255
Puerto Espora
9
Estrecho de Magallanes
Isla Riesco
Seno Otway
Cullén
Reserva Nacional Magallanes
Punta Arenas
Porvenir
Isla Grande de Tierra del Fuego
Reserva Forestal Lago Parrillar
Bahía Inútil
Península Brunswick
SOUTHERN PATAGONIA – MAPS
1 Campamento De Agostini p164
2 Laguna Tigre Sur p167
3 Valle Río Moscu p169
4 Around Monte Fitz Roy & Laguna Torre p174
5 Paine Circuit, Torres del Paine Lookout & Pingo-Zapata p184

among the *lenga* forests, feeding on the plentiful insects that hide in the trees' flaky bark. The cinnamon-bellied tyrant (called *dormilona rufa* in Spanish) inhabits the drier scrubland. Upland geese and flying steamer ducks visit the lakes and waterways. Andean condors are regularly seen circling high above the ridges.

CLIMATE

Exposed to westerly winds, unusually high and located in a 'gap' between the two great continental icecaps (the Hielo Norte and the Hielo Sur), the San Lorenzo massif is known for changeable weather and sudden storms. Precipitation exceeds 4000mm on the higher summits and ridges – falling almost entirely as snow – feeding the major glaciers that splay down in all directions. So-called ice mushrooms are created as the moist airstream deposits crystals of ice in bizarre formations. Although too low to attract significant precipitation, the valleys surrounding the massif are buffeted by strong, dry winds, producing conditions similar to the steppes further east.

ACCESS TOWN

See Cochrane (p195).

CAMPAMENTO DE AGOSTINI

Duration 4 days
Distance 54km
Difficulty easy–moderate
Start/Finish Fundo Olivieo Paillacar
Nearest Town Cochrane
Transport bus
Summary A little-travelled route into a wild and remote upper valley from where De Agostini made his legendary first ascent.

Not to be confused with its namesake in Parque Nacional Los Glaciares, the classic route to Campamento De Agostini sees little traffic beyond andinists on their hopeful way to the summit. Following old roads, it's generally a well-formed trail with few difficulties – unless you want to continue to the summit of Monte San Lorenzo.

Trekkers can contract a guide (see 'Guides' p234) to do the difficult one-day extension to Glaciar Cochrane via Paso del Comedor, which requires crampons. The extension loops to Laguna del Tranquilo.

PLANNING

When to Trek

The trek can normally be done from early November until late April.

Maps

The route of the trek spreads over four Chilean IGM 1:50,000 maps, but, unfortunately, only two of these are published: *Cochrane* (Section J, No 66) and *Lago Brown* (Section J, No 67). Fortunately, the area of the unpublished Chilean IGM maps is covered by one Argentine IGM 1:100,000 map: *Cerro Pico Agudo* (No 4772-27).

Permits & Regulations

As the San Lorenzo massif is a somewhat sensitive border area, both climbers and trekkers are required to fill out a form detailing their intended route at **Carabineros** (☎ 067-522313; Esmeralda 522) in Cochrane. While this wild frontier is only sporadically patrolled, those crossing the border without official permission are violating the law and, if caught, certain to be forcibly expelled and/or fined.

As the trek is entirely within private property, do not camp anywhere other

THE MOUNTAINEER PRIEST

In the late 1930s and the early 1940s, the ecclesiastical andinist Father Alberto De Agostini reconnoitred the San Lorenzo massif in search of a viable route to the 3706m summit. After years of exploration, De Agostini returned with two companions (Heriberto Schmoll and Alex Hemmi of the Club Andino Bariloche) for a last attempt. It was late 1943 and the priest was 60 years old.

With luck (or divine intervention), De Agostini established a base camp in the upper Arroyo San Lorenzo. The climbing party headed southwest via Paso del Comedor and the Brecha de la Cornisa, then traversed across glaciers and over the northern summit to reach the main summit of Monte San Lorenzo on 17 December. This remote mountain with near-mythic status now sees yearly attempts by dedicated mountaineers.

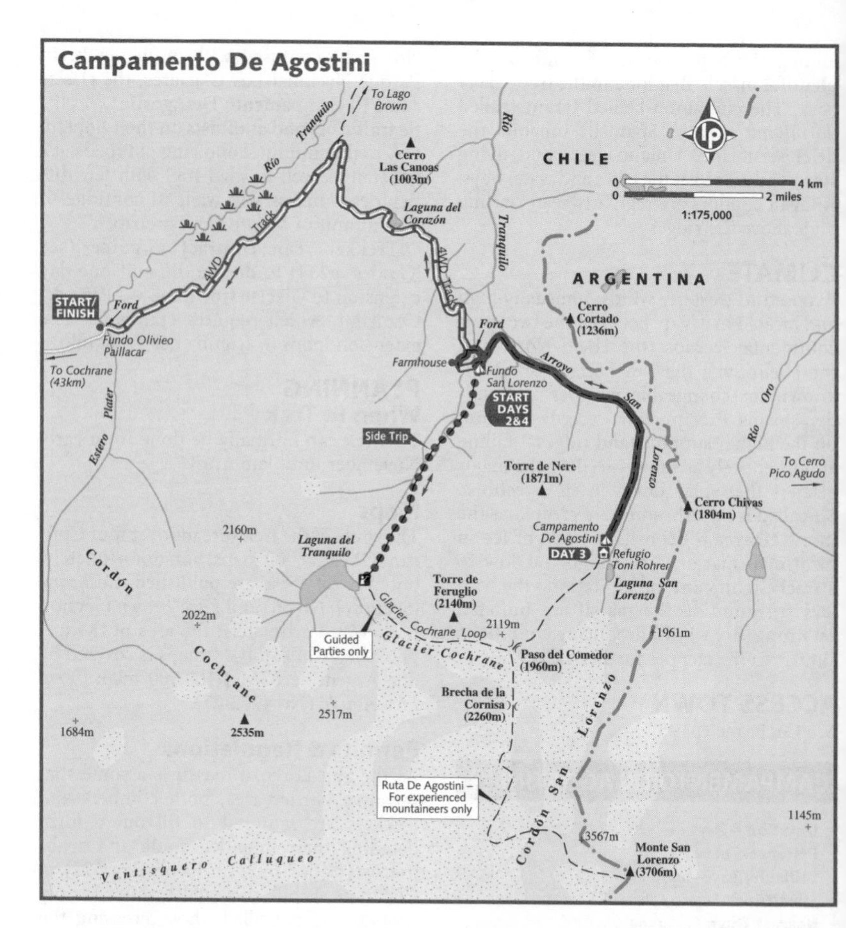

than at the campsite near the Fundo San Lorenzo farmhouse (see The Trek, Day 1) or at Campamento De Agostini (see The Trek, Day 2).

Guides

See Condor Explorer (p155) or Escuela de Guias (p148) in Coyhaique.

GETTING TO/FROM THE TREK

For those using public transportation, the trek begins and ends in the valley of the Río Tranquilo at Olivieo Paillacar, a farm 43km from Cochrane. Local transport **Buses Acuario 13** (☎ 067-522143; Río Baker 349) goes on Mondays and Thursdays at 10.30am to Fundo Olivieo Paillacar (CH$5000), returning same day at 1pm.

Those with private transportation can take a 4WD road to start at Fundo San Lorenzo, effectively cutting two days off. The farm's owner, Luis Soto, is in regular two-way radio contact with Cochrane's municipality, and can order trekkers a *flete* (shuttle CH$50,000, one-way).

THE TREK

Day 1: Fundo Olivieo Paillacar to Fundo San Lorenzo

4–5½ hours, 16km, 420m ascent

The bus stops beside tall poplars sheltering the farmhouse. Here, cross the Estero Plater (which flows through several stream channels that can often be jumped individually). Follow a rough 4WD track that makes a long upward traverse northeast to high above the swampy, meandering Río Tranquilo under the sharp towers of the Cordón Cochrane, a lateral range of the San Lorenzo massif. Across the valley are the less angular summits of the Cordón Esmeralda.

After two to 2½ hours, the old road turns abruptly around to the right away from the river, bringing the first direct views of Monte San Lorenzo, whose gleaming dome resembles an enormous cake smeared with thick icing. Continue up southeastward among low *ñirres* and clearings scattered with *calafate* bushes to reach **Laguna del Corazón**, a small tranquil lake visited by flying steamer ducks, 50 minutes to 1¼ hours on.

Head up around the southwest shore then cut on southeast across a broad plain strewn with *mogotes*. The 4WD track climbs through *lenga* forest to a ridgetop before it sidles down left and fords the frigid, milky Río Tranquilo to terminate at the **Fundo San Lorenzo**, 1¼ to 1¾ hours from the lake. Particularly after midday, the river tends to be too high and fast-flowing for a comfortable wade, so about 50m before reaching the river, head right 400m upstream through the scrub to cross on a sturdy (but makeshift) bridge over a narrow gorge.

The beautiful Fundo San Lorenzo (radio contact via Cochrane Municipality) is owned by Luis Soto and Lucy Gomez. No accommodation is available at the farmhouse itself, but there is scenic **camping** nearby (CH$2000 per person). Simple meals are served, and bread, pies and fruit conserves are sold – otherwise bring all supplies. Washing facilities are basic (cold!). Horses can be hired (per day CH$20,000 plus guide).

The scenic **campsite**, just upvalley from the farmhouse under *ñirres* among moist meadows, looks south to hanging glaciers on jagged peaks at the head of the Río Tranquilo (see side trip below). From here a six-hour side trip can be made up to Torre de Nere (1871m), a lookout that gives great views of the San Lorenzo massif and the distant Monte San Valentín.

SIDE TRIP: LAGUNA DEL TRANQUILO

3½–4½ hours return, 13km, 475m ascent/descent

This trail may be very muddy in November and December. Head upvalley past the campsite along a rough road across wet pastures. This 4WD track cuts up left to slightly higher ground, passing through two fence gates among *calafate* meadows before it peters out at a 100m-wide gravel wash choking the *lenga* forest. Proceed along cattle trails across a small gully, then cut up rightward out of the trees through stabilising rubble to the end of a lateral moraine, one to 1½ hours from the farmhouse. Look up to spot circling condors.

Climb steeply, either along the crest of the moraine ridge or just left of it, to high above the raging Río Tranquilo, continuing well past where the forest begins to fringe the moraine until good views of Laguna del Tranquilo emerge, one to 1½ hours on. The grey waters of this bleak lake fill a deep trough ringed by half-a-dozen glaciers clinging to the sheer walls of the valley. Slabs of ice and waterfalls crash down from the glaciers. After enjoying the view, return via the ascent route.

Day 2: Fundo San Lorenzo to Campamento De Agostini

3½ hours, 9.5km, 325m ascent

From the farmhouse, head northeast across open fields to the right of a stand of exotic pines, then cut back up steeply right over a ridge into lovely grassy meadows along the **Arroyo San Lorenzo**. Follow a foot track upvalley over beautiful grassy flats along the stream's true left (southern) bank towards Cerro Pico Agudo, a lone spiked peak across the border in Argentina. After passing through a narrow gap, the route continues past the Portezuelo Arroyo San Lorenzo, an unobtrusive, scrubby saddle directly across the arroyo. (Estancia El Rincón, owned by Conservación Patagónica, sits on the Argentine side).

Begin an initially gentle rise that steepens as you turn southward past where the stream races through a deep chasm. The gradient moderates again as you head on through several small meadows towards the looming colossus of Monte San Lorenzo to arrive at **Campamento De Agostini** (camping CH$2500 per person). Here among the *lenga* stands the basic shelter built by Father De Agostini during his determined attempts on the summit. Modified by generations of climbers, it sits at around 1000m. More enticing, however, is the excellent **Refugio Toni Rohrer** (CH$4000 per person). This wooden hut is dedicated

to a Swiss mountaineer who died climbing Monte San Lorenzo in 2000. It has a stove and a dining area with benches and tables; the loft has sleeping space for 12 people. Pay at the farmhouse; the *refugio* is left unlocked. Campers may use the outdoor picnic tables.

A path leads five to 10 minutes on upvalley to peter out among gravelly moraines overlooking Laguna San Lorenzo, a murky tarn fed by a glacier sprawling down from the northern summit of Monte San Lorenzo. From here, intrepid mountaineers continue southwest to the summit via the classic Ruta De Agostini (see the boxed text, p163). Guided trips may also loop to Laguna del Tranquilo via Paso Del Comedor.

Days 3 & 4: Campamento De Agostini to Fundo Olivieo Paillacar

5½–7½ hours, 27km, 745m descent

Retrace your steps of Day 2 and Day 1, descending to Fundo San Lorenzo (two to three hours), then to Fundo Olivieo Paillacar (another 3½ to 4½ hours). If you want to camp at Fundo Olivieo Paillacar, ask permission first.

LAGO O'HIGGINS AREA

Among the wildest and most thinly settled parts of the Patagonian Andes, the region around Lago O'Higgins occupies the northeast edge of the Hielo Sur. At 836m, Lago O'Higgins is the deepest lake in the Americas, but it is also fascinatingly complex, with a half-dozen arms and mountainous peninsulas. The lake is shared fairly evenly between Chile and Argentina (where it is called Lago San Martín). Since the Carretera Austral's completion in Villa O'Higgins in 2000, the area has lost some of its isolation. Moreover, hydroelectric dams proposed for the remote outflowing Río Pascua (see boxed text, p200) would have a tremendous impact on the region and its biodiversity.

ENVIRONMENT

Fashioned by enormous glaciers that once extended from the Hielo Sur far out into the Patagonian steppes, today this intensely glaciated landscape is largely covered by Magellanic forest of southern beech species, especially the deciduous *lenga* and *ñirre*. At lower elevations the forest is mixed with *canelo* and other evergreen understorey species. The area is one of the last strongholds of the *huemul* and breeding pairs are often encountered feeding on alpine grasses and mosses above the tree line. Also commonly sighted is the great Andean condor, which nests on high inaccessible cliff ledges.

CLIMATE

Chilled by the winds blowing off the Hielo Sur and/or Lago O'Higgins, average summer temperatures in this area do not exceed 15°C. The mountains of the continental icecap catch much of the moisture in the westerly winds, however, leaving the Lago O'Higgins area with modest rain and snowfalls. Annual precipitation levels at Villa O'Higgins are only 850mm, but rise to over 2500mm in surrounding mountains.

ACCESS TOWN

See Villa O'Higgins, p201.

LAGUNA TIGRE SUR

Duration 2 days
Distance 8km
Difficulty moderate
Start/Finish Carretera Austral km 25.58
Nearest Town Villa O'Higgins
Transport bus, taxi
Summary A simple trek that explores a wild, heavily glaciated upper valley frequented by *huemul*.

This short trek follows a rough, steep route to high tarns under small glaciers in the Cordón Nevado, whose snowcapped almost 200m peaks are visible to the northwest from Villa O'Higgins. The Cordón Nevado is exposed to severe winds and frequent rain or snowfalls (even in summer), so come well prepared.

Currently, a lack of trail markings on the initial part of the trail, coupled with lots of confusing animal paths, make this route best undertaken with a local guide referred from Hielo Sur or Camping & Albergue El Mosco (p201).

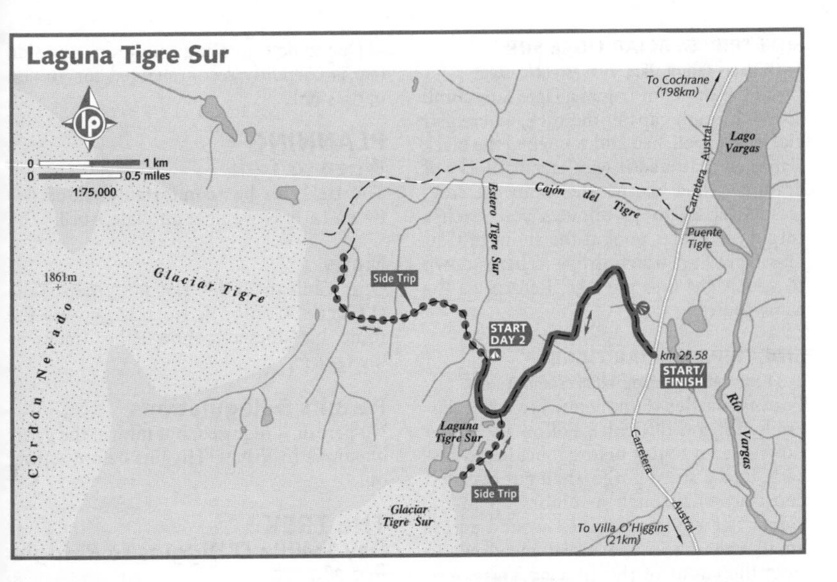

PLANNING

When to Trek

The trek can normally be done from early December until at least mid-April.

Maps

One Chilean IGM 1:50,000 map, *Río Ventisquero* (Section J, No 112), covers the area but shows neither the Carretera Austral nor the trekking route itself.

Permits & Regulations

No permit is required, but trekkers should be mindful that the lower route crosses private property.

GETTING TO/FROM THE TREK

The trek starts and ends near Puente Tigre on the Carretera Austral, 25.58km from Villa O'Higgins. The only public transport is a bus which runs twice weekly between Cochrane (p195) and Villa O'Higgins on Wednesdays and Saturdays (at the time of research). A taxi from Villa O'Higgins will charge CH$40,000–60,000 round-trip.

THE TREK

Day 1: Carretera Austral km 25.58 to Laguna Tigre Sur

2¾–4 hours, 3km, 565m ascent

Start at km 25.58 (marked in paint by road workers) on the Carretera Austral. Cross a tiny stream and head up northwest through forest of *coigüe de Magallanes* mixed with *canelo* and Guaitecas cypress. The route continues rightward up the slope out of the trees to cross a small stream above its cascading waterfall. Wind your way on more directly up through small scrubby cliffs and over tiny terraces in the steep slope, before cutting back southwest (to the left of an obvious boulder on the ridge high above). The route ascends even more steeply to reach an isolated band of weather-beaten *ñirre* forest, 1¾ to 2½ hours after leaving the road. (There are plans to remark the trail, which is obscured by confusing animal tracks).

Skirt southward below a rocky, glaciated ridge that climbs up to your right via an undulating ledge. There are great views southeast along the swampy lower Río Mayer to Lago O'Higgins and across the valley to Lago Briceño, in a superb glaciated plateau.

The route cuts up rightward (roughly west) over moraines past a tarn to reach the outlet of Laguna Tigre Sur, 45 minutes to one hour on from the *ñirre* forest. Scenic **campsites** occupy the moist, scrubby meadows downstream along the lake outlet, with views of the glacier-shrouded peaks to the north (climbable by experienced parties).

SIDE TRIP: GLACIAR TIGRE SUR

1–1½ hours return, 2km, 70m ascent/descent

From the outlet of Laguna Tigre Sur, climb south through gaps in the rock, where glacial ice has polished and scratched the black slab then scattered it with erratic blocks of granite. Yellow daisies shelter in the crevices. After 30 to 40 minutes you reach a turgid meltwater pool at the snout of Glaciar Tigre Sur, which drops icebergs down to your right into the lake. Return via the same route.

SIDE TRIP: GLACIAR TIGRE

2–3 hours return, 5.5km, 140m ascent/descent

Ford the outlet 400m below the lake (generally not too difficult). Follow the outlet downstream to just before it begins to cascade into a steep gorge, then cut over left (northwest) through a minor gap in the ridge. The route continues around across small streams in the moist meadows to near the snout of the **Glaciar Tigre**. The glacier's surging meltwater stream, which flows into the Cajón del Tigre, is usually too dangerous to cross.

Day 2: Laguna Tigre Sur to Carretera Austral km 25.58

2¼–3 hours, 3km, 565m descent

Return via the route described in Day 1, taking precautions on the long, steep descent.

VALLE RÍO MOSCU

Duration 2 days
Distance 13km
Difficulty easy
Start/Finish Villa O'Higgins
Transport bus or plane
SummaryA short trek that explores a wild, glaciated valley drained by a spectacular roaring torrent.

In the proposed 60-sq-km Reserva Nacional Shoen (whose name means *huemul* in Tehuelche), this area takes in the ranges stretching east from Villa O'Higgins to the Argentine border. Most locals know the trek by its river and valley – Moscu. Since this pleasant out-and-back trek leads up the glacier-fed Río Mosco to a free Conaf *refugio*, it can be done without a tent.

Due to deteriorating conditions, the side trip is currently recommended for guided parties only.

PLANNING

When to Trek

The trek can be (comfortably) done between early November and late April.

Maps

One Chilean IGM 1:50,000 map *Villa O'Higgins* (Section J, No J113) covers the route, but does not show either tracks or the *refugio*.

Permits & Regulations

No permit is required, but inform the *guardaparque* in Villa O'Higgins before setting out.

THE TREK

Day 1: Villa O'Higgins to Refugio Río Mosco

2¼–3 hours, 6.5km, 250m ascent

We recommend getting an early start to reach the river crossing at low water. From the Conaf *guardería*, follow left around picnic tables, climbing a path rightward to reach the **mirador** after five minutes. This lookout shelter (about 315m) has views across the village to the Cordón Nevado and Lago Ciervo. Red-white markings and arrowed posts lead southeast gently up through *canelo*, *lenga* and *coigüe de Magallanes* to a fork, 15 to 20 minutes on. (The yellow-orange marked left turn-off goes up to a lookout.)

Bear right and skirt a green, fire-cleared pasture above a small corral. Head rightward through scattered *calafate* bushes (with edible berries in late February), then ascend a steep ridge overlooking the lower Río Mosco and the Brazo Norte Oriental (northeast arm) of Lago O'Higgins. The route begins a long, undulating traverse under the Cordón de Villa O'Higgins high above the roaring river, passing a second marked turn-off (that climbs to another lookout peak) just before it re-enters the unburnt forest, 30 to 45 minutes from the first turn-off.

Continue upvalley past a misty, mossy viewing point, where the torrential Río Mosco churns through a little gorge, to cross a narrow glacial side stream (sometimes

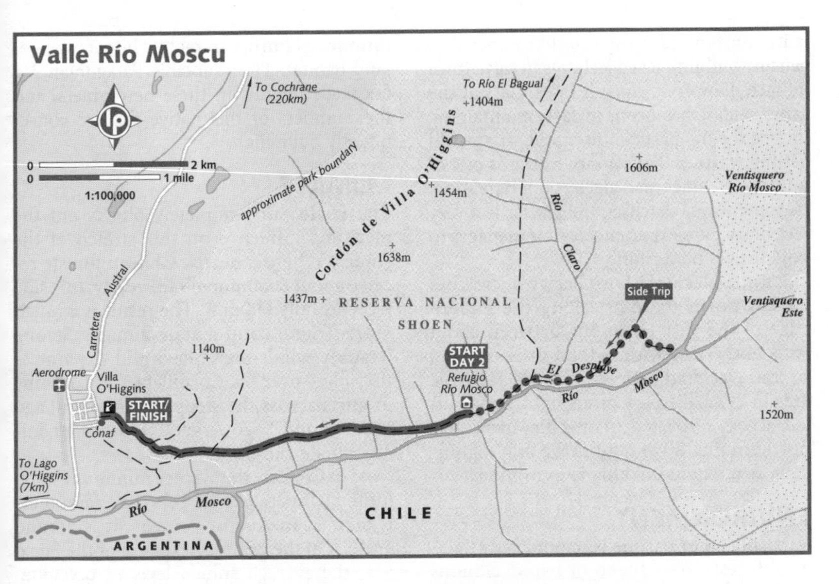

tricky by midafternoon or after rain), 1¼ to 1½ hours on. Check out the views of a waterfall and a gleaming glacier in a side valley to the southeast, specifically look for pairs of condors circling above. If you're lucky enough o be in the right place at the right time, it can make for a unique photo opportunity. The path first hugs the furious, milky river, but soon climbs away left to arrive at the **Refugio Río Mosco** (GPS 48° 28.190 S, 72° 29.298 W) after a final 15 to 20 minutes. At around 485m, this hut, with fireplace and bunk space for six people, is surrounded by lovely *lengas* – partly cut to build it! Get water from the stream 30m upvalley.

SIDE TRIP: VENTISQUERO RÍO MOSCO

3–4 hours return, 8km, 200m ascent/descent

This moderate–demanding route leads into a raw glacial landscape at the head of the valley. Unfortunately, a recent landslide has made the approach untenable and somewhat dangerous until it is repaired. Check with Conaf, Hielo Sur or Camping & Albergue El Mosco for current status; it may be possible to do as a guided trip.

Day 2: Refugio Río Mosco to Villa O'Higgins

2¼–2¾ hours, 6.5km, 250m descent

Retrace your steps from Day 1.

PARQUE NACIONAL LOS GLACIARES

The vast Parque Nacional Los Glaciares is Argentina's greatest single tract of wilderness. The park owes its pristine conditions to geography: it straddles the Hielo Sur, the largest icecap outside the earth's polar regions. The Fitz Roy Range, with its rugged wilderness and shark-tooth summits, is easily the de-facto mountaineering mecca of Patagonia. Cerro Torre (3102m) and Monte Fitz Roy (3405m) provide epic ascents for world-class climbers. This sector occupying the northern half of Parque Nacional Los Glaciares offers numerous, well-marked trails for trekking and jaw-dropping scenery – that is, when the clouds clear.

Created in 1937 to protect this unique glacial landscape, Los Glaciares continues to exhibit spectacular glacial phenomena. Among the earth's most dynamic and accessible ice fields, its Glaciar Perito Moreno is the stunning centerpiece of the southern sector of Parque Nacional Los Glaciares. Locally referred to as Glaciar Moreno, it measures 30km long, 5km wide and 60m high, but what makes it exceptional in the world of ice

is its constant advance – up to 2m per day, causing building-sized icebergs to calve from its face. However, since it loses mass at the same rate, it has been, in fact, maintaining its size for the past century. Still, in a world getting warmer that's a rare feat: it is one of only three Patagonian glaciers not retreating. In some ways, watching the glacier is a very sedentary park experience, but it manages to nonetheless be thrilling.

Parque Nacional Los Glaciares stretches 200km north to south along the eastern edge of the vast Hielo Sur between about 48°S and 51°S, with a total area of 4460 sq km. Declared a Unesco World Heritage area in 1982, the park offers tightly controlled access restricted to specific areas. The northern Fitz Roy sector is the only significant area where trekking is permitted.

ENVIRONMENT

Virtually all of Parque Nacional Los Glaciares' forests are a blend of two deciduous beech species, *lenga* and *ñirre*. Playing the role of postglacial colonizers, they have moved into new terrain left vacant by the receding glaciers. This so-called 'Magellanic' forest forms a thin strip close to the Cordillera. Towards the east, the terrain recedes into dry steppeland due to the drying westerly winds that whip across the valleys and plains, carrying off moisture even as it falls as rain.

Scattered around the steppes are woody bushes, native Patagonian cactus and the *maihuén*, a more atypical member of the cactus family that grows in small mounds like spiny lawns.

Parque Nacional Los Glaciares boasts bountiful bird life, including Patagonia's two largest bird species. The flightless, ostrich-like *ñandú* streaks across the steppes and the great Andean condor glides around the summits. On the steppes you'll also find partridge, *loica* (a meadowlark; the male sports a flashy red breast) and grey-hooded finch which nest in thorny *calafate* bushes. The *tucúquere* is a species of forest owl with twin crests above its eyes that look like feathery horns. Flocks of *cachañas* also visit Los Glaciares over the summer. This colorful and boisterous Patagonian parakeet feeds on seeds, fruit and shoots. Gravely endangered, the mara, or Patagonian hare, manages to survive despite the steady encroachment of introduced European rabbits into its steppeland habitat. The adaptable Patagonian red fox feeds mainly on these newcomers, and the numbers of this native fox are consequently quite high.

CLIMATE

The Hielo Sur completely blocks out the maritime influence on this stretch of the Andes. Whereas nearby Chilean forests receive about 8000mm of rain yearly, this side receives only 600mm. The result is a much more frigid continental climate. Strong westerly winds are chilled and dry out as they blow over the Cordillera and continue in gusts across the steppes. Closer to Lago Viedma and Lago Argentino a milder microclimate exists.

At El Chaltén, the average minimum/maximum temperature in February (summer) is 5/22°C. In August (winter), it is around 1/9°C. On the great icy expanse of the Hielo Sur, the average annual level of precipitation (falling almost entirely as snow) reaches 5000mm in places; this figure drops to little more than 1500mm on the forested Andean foothills, and to less than 400mm on the steppes at the park's eastern fringe.

Except for minor 'wind shadows' at the foot of the Cordillera, blustery winds blow almost incessantly throughout the summer. These cool, windy conditions prevent summer thunderstorms from developing, and the infrequent rain that falls often quickly evaporates in the wind. Though weather is notably unstable, winter conditions are not as severe as you might think, since these pervasive winds drop away from around May to early September.

PLANNING

When to Trek

Since large parts of Parque Nacional Los Glaciares receive heavy winter snowfalls, the recommended time to visit the park is during the summer season from November to April. Trails often become overcrowded in January and early February.

Maps

Most recommended is Zagier & Urruty's 1:50,000 *Monte Fitz Roy & Cerro Torre Trekking-Mountaineering Minimap* or the same map with a Lago del Desierto map at 1:100,000, titled *Monte Fitz Roy & Cerro*

Torre Trekking-Mountaineering, Lago del Desierto Trekking-Travel Map; both are available in El Calafate and many other cities in Argentine Patagonia. Less detailed but also useful is the Chaltén Outdoor 1:100,000 *El Chaltén, Fitz Roy – Torre* trekking map, which includes a rough El Chaltén map and some trekking information.

Permits & Regulations

There is no charge to enter Los Glaciares' Fitz Roy sector, and trekkers do not require a permit, yet they may not stay longer than seven days at Campamento De Agostini or Campamento Poincenot. Commercial tour groups must be accompanied by a certified Argentine guide booked in advance.

In order to protect the park's delicate environment, public access to Parque Nacional Los Glaciares is restricted. Only the northernmost Fitz Roy sector is open for trekking. Apart from supervised tourist launch excursions across Lago Argentino, venturing into the heart of Los Glaciares is not encouraged. Those who want to trek in remote areas or on the glaciers must preregister at the parks office.

Climbing permits (for mountaineers) are available without charge at the national park visitor center in El Calafate and are valid for 30 days (renewable only once).

ACCESS TOWN

See El Chaltén (p197).

LAGUNA TORRE

Duration 2 days
Distance 19km
Difficulty easy
Start/Finish El Chaltén
Transport bus
Summary A pleasant trek that gets you up close to the classic granite spire of Cerro Torre, one of mountaineering's most sought-after prizes.

This recommended short trek takes you to an exhilarating viewpoint opposite the 3102m Cerro Torre, which was for decades considered impossible to climb.

It is often done as a long return day trek, but a more leisurely two days are recommended with a night at Campamento De Agostini. The Sendero Madre e Hija alternative route (p176) provides a short cut between Campamento De Agostini and Campamento Poincenot and makes it possible to segue into the Around Monte Fitz Roy trek without returning to El Chaltén.

THE TREK

Day 1: El Chaltén to Campamento De Agostini

1¾–2¼ hours, 9.5km

The trek starts at the northwestern edge of El Chaltén. From a signpost on Av San Martín just south of a sign for Monte Fitz Roy, head west on Eduardo Brenner and then right to find the signposted start of the track. (Another signposted starting point in the middle of town is behind Hotel Los Cerros).

The Laguna Torre track winds up westwards around large boulders on slopes covered with typical Patagonian dryland plants, then leads southwest past a *mallín* (wet meadow) to a junction with a trail coming in from the left (see Alternative Start) after 35 to 45 minutes.

Continue up past a rounded bluff to the **Mirador Laguna Torre**, a crest giving you the first clear view of the extraordinary rock spire of Cerro Torre above a sprawling mass of intersecting glaciers. The trail dips down gently through stout stands of ancient *lengas* before cutting across open scrubby riverflats and old revegetated moraines to reach a signposted junction with the Sendero Madre e Hija, a short-cut route to Campamento Poincenot, approximately two hours on (see Alternative Route, p197).

Continuing upvalley, bear left at another signposted fork and climb over a forested embankment to cross a small alluvial plain, following the fast-flowing glacial waters of the Río Fitz Roy, and arrive at **Campamento De Agostini** (formerly Campamento Bridwell), after a further 30 to 40 minutes. This free campsite (with pit toilet) is the only park-authorised place to camp in the vicinity. It sits riverside in a pleasant grove of *lengas* below Cerro Solo.

SIDE TRIP: MIRADOR MAESTRI

1½–2 hours return, 5km

This trek leads to a lookout with grandstand views of Cerro Torre and its companion peaks and glaciers. It can comfortably be combined with either Day 1, 2 or both).

First head up northwest through barely vegetated glacial rubble to the top of the moraine wall damming Laguna Torre, a stark lake fed directly by Glaciar Torre, which sporadically drops blocks of ice that slowly skate across the water.

Make your way northwards along the narrow crest of the moraine until about halfway around Laguna Torre, then begin zigzagging up and diagonally leftwards. A few logs that indicate the former **Refugio Maestri** come into view on a small terrace of dwarf *lengas*.

The route emerges from the trees and climbs a short way up a moraine ridge to reach the unmarked **Mirador Maestri**, 50 minutes to 1¼ hours from Campamento De Agostini. Enjoy the enhanced views of the Cordón Adela, a serrated ridge that includes half a dozen snowcapped peaks between Cerro Grande (2751m) and Cerro Torre (3102m).

Retrace your steps to camp.

Day 2: Campamento De Agostini to El Chaltén

1¾–2¼ hours, 9.5km

Reverse Day 1 to El Chaltén.

HACKING A WAY TO THE TOP

In 1959 the Italian alpinist Cesare Maestri reported that he and his Austrian companion Toni Egger had reached the summit of Cerro Torre. Egger, however, had been swept to his death by an avalanche on the descent – along with him went a camera with summit photos. Since Maestri's claim aroused widespread scepticism, he returned in 1970 with another party hoping to squash doubts. Instead he provoked perhaps the most bitter controversy in mountaineering history. After fixing hundreds of bolts with a portable compressor drill to reach the top of the rock, he then neglected to climb the unstable 'snow mushrooms' to the mountain's highest point. Many credit a subgroup of the Italian Alpine Club, the Ragni de Lecco, led by Casimiro Ferrari with the first undisputed ascent of Cerro Torre in 1974.

AROUND MONTE FITZ ROY

Duration 3 days
Distance 38km
Difficulty easy–moderate
Start/Finish El Chaltén
Transport bus
Summary View one of the world's finest mountain landscapes – mighty Fitz Roy and its spectacular satellites – from many angles while exploring the beautiful surrounding valleys.

Easily the highest peak in the area, Monte Fitz Roy was first climbed in 1952 by a French expedition based at Campamento Poincenot. Even by today's climbing standards, its summit is still a highly prized objective. This trek takes you into the valleys surrounding Monte Fitz Roy for close-ups of this classic Patagonian peak.

El Chaltén is Cerro Fitz Roy's Tehuelche name, meaning 'peak of fire' or 'smoking mountain,' an apt description of the cloud-enshrouded summit. The Tehuelches venerated this mountain, probably a key landmark in their migrations from the Atlantic to the mountains. Perito Moreno and Carlos Moyano later named it after the *Beagle's* Captain Fitz Roy, who navigated Darwin's expedition up the Río Santa Cruz in 1834, only coming within 50km of the cordillera.

The trek can be done in three days, either as described or by returning to El Chaltén along Ruta Provincial 23 (see Alternative Route: via Ruta Provincial 23, p109).

To combine this trek with Laguna Torre, complete Day 1 of this trek (not missing Laguna Los Tres) and follow the Alternative Route: Sendero Madre & Hija before joining the Laguna Torre description.

The enjoyable detours described here deserve at least one additional day and probably more, in case weather obscures mountain views in the early part of the trip.

The well-trodden path up to Campamento Poincenot is marked with yellow-painted stakes and occasional red splashes on rocks. Except for the short section leading out of the Río Blanco into the Valle Eléctrico, the trek is easy to follow. Trekkers may also opt to start behind Hostería El Pilar (p177), the 5.6km trek is a shuttle ride from town, preferable for its considerably easier and more straightforward route.

THE TREK

Day 1: El Chaltén to Campamento Poincenot

1¾–2¾ hours, 8km

The trek starts at the northern end of El Chaltén, at a signpost just beyond the (currently closed) Campamento Madsen. Climb to the right of a large rock outcrop onto open slopes of *mogotes* and tussock grasses giving fine views of the adjacent Cordón de los Cóndores. The route sidles on steadily upwards high above the braided gravelly channels of the Río de las Vueltas through pockets of *lenga* and occasional *coigüe de Magallanes*. After swinging around northwestwards through a minor saddle, head up beside the ravine of the Chorrillo del Salto to reach the signposted turn-off to Laguna Capri (see side trip: Campamento Laguna Capri, below) after one to 1½ hours.

Make your way on upvalley through heathland scattered with *ñirre* scrub past the signposted Sendero Madre e Hija, a short cut from Campamento De Agostini, diverging left (see Alternative Route: Sendero Madre & Hija, p176). Skirt along the left side of a broad boggy *mallín*, hopping across the tiny clear stream and following yellow-tipped marker stakes northwestwards through a band of Magellanic *lenga* forest. You will arrive at **Campamento Poincenot**, a free campsite with pit toilet, 45 minutes to 1¼ hours from the turn-off to Laguna Capri.

Named in memory of a French mountaineer who died in 1952 while attempting to cross the Río Fitz Roy, this charming spot flanks the grassy (eastern) bank of the Río Blanco and the forested terrace above the river. It looks up directly to the Fitz Roy massif (if views are obscured, wait to hike to Laguna Los Tres). Campamento Río Blanco, on the opposite side of the river from Campamento Poincenot, is a base camp exclusively for mountaineering parties.

SIDE TRIP: CAMPAMENTO LAGUNA CAPRI

20 minutes return, 1.5km

A tranquil lake with lovely little beaches, Laguna Capri sits before the jagged backdrop of the Fitz Roy massif. This recommended short side trip leads south from the signposted turn-off in the Chorrillo del Salto valley, up to the lake's northern shore, then dips left through the forest to reach the free campsite of **Campamento Laguna Capri** after just 10 minutes. Other than Campamento Poincenot, this is the only place trekkers are permitted to pitch tents along Day 1. Although Laguna Capri has no outlet, its water is considered safe to drink. Please don't pollute the lake with detergents or soap, and use the pit toilet provided. To return to the main track, retrace your steps to a signpost, then take the left fork.

SIDE TRIP: LAGUNA SUCIA

1½–2 hours return, 5km

This spectacular lake can be reached on a track which begins 40m northwest of the footbridge over the Río Blanco and ends up following the river's bouldery bed. Laguna Sucia lies in a deep cirque under the towering granite 'needles' of Cerro Poincenot and Aguja Saint Exupery. Frozen white chunks periodically peel off the Glaciar Río Blanco icefall and plummet into the lake. The return journey follows the same route.

SIDE TRIP: LAGUNA DE LOS TRES

2–3 hours return, 5km, 450m ascent/descent

The obligatory trek up to this lake at the foot of Monte Fitz Roy is a highlight of any Patagonian trip. A predawn start gets you there for the scenic sunrise. However, if visibility is poor from Campamento Poincenot, it's unlikely you'll have views at the *laguna*.

From Campamento Poincenot, cross the small river on a substantial footbridge to the mountaineers' base camp of **Campamento Río Blanco**, where you can pick up a signposted trail leading left. Try to stick to the cairned route, which steeply spirals west-southwest out of the trees and on over loose rocky ground to reach a low crest.

From here there is a sudden and stunningly close-up view of Monte Fitz Roy towering more than 2000m above the turquoise Laguna de los Tres, which lies in a glacial hollow immediately in front of you. Away to the southeast, beyond the nearby Laguna Madre and Laguna Capri, the enormous Lago Viedma sprawls on the dry steppes. Another wonderful lookout can be easily reached by heading west around

Laguna Torre & Around Monte Fitz Roy

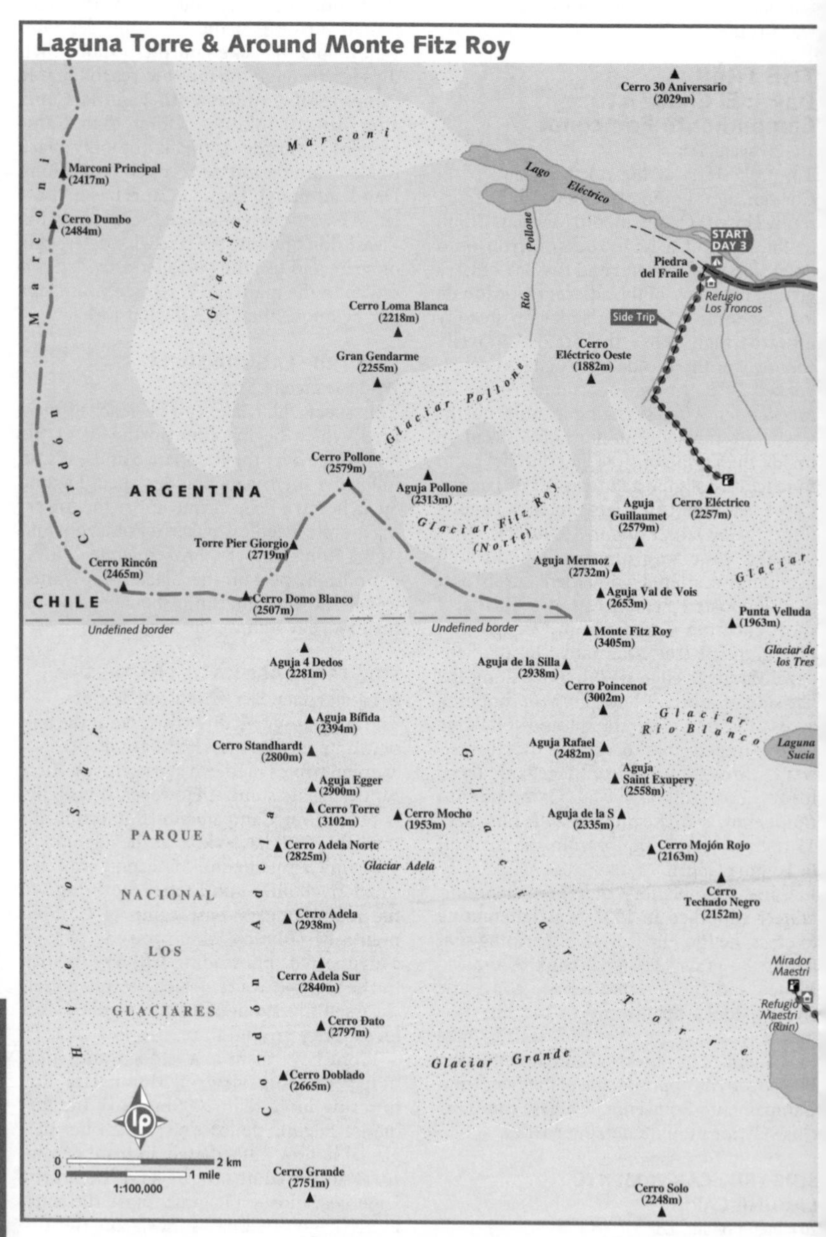

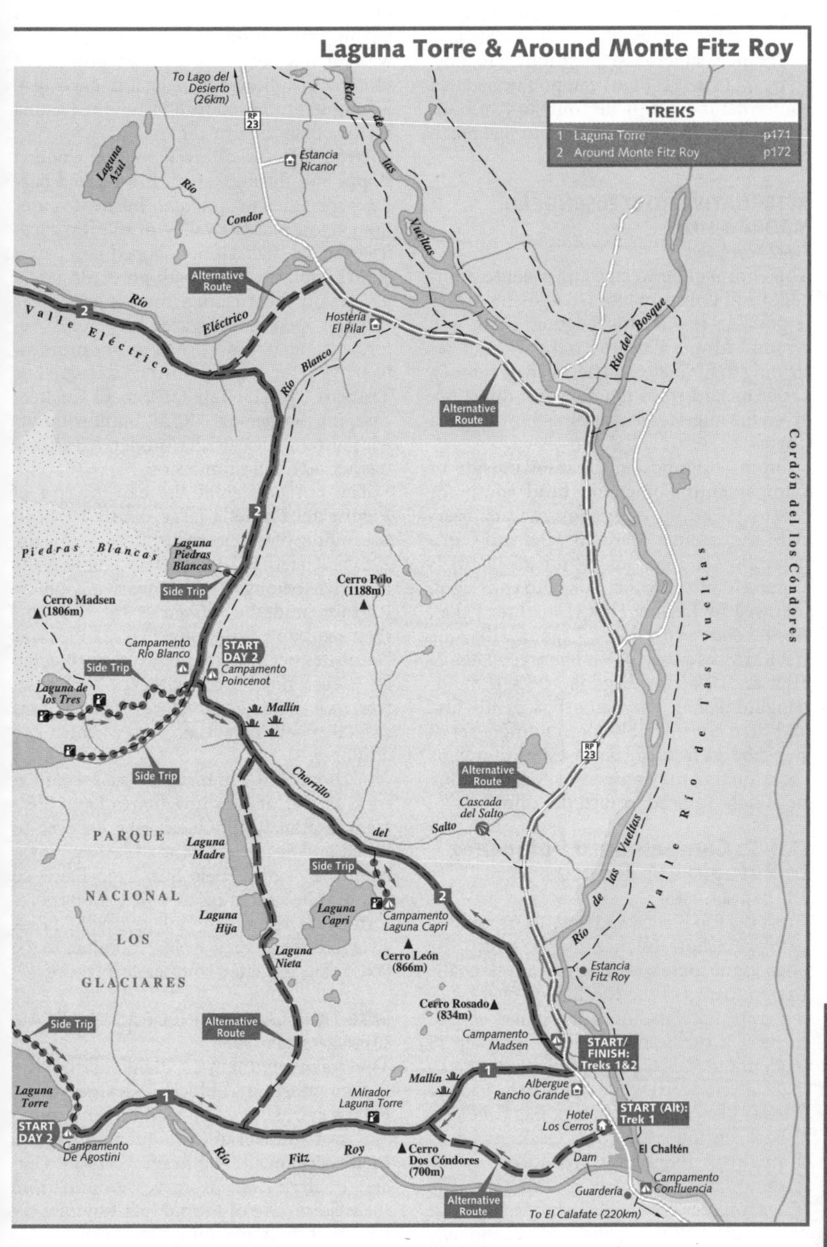
Laguna Torre & Around Monte Fitz Roy
TREKS
1 Laguna Torre p171
2 Around Monte Fitz Roy p172
To Lago del Desierto (26km)
RP 23
Laguna Azul
Estancia Ricanor
Río Condor
Río de las Vueltas
Alternative Route
Río Eléctrico
Valle Eléctrico
Hostería El Pilar
Río Blanco
Río del Bosque
Cordón del los Cóndores
Piedras Blancas
Laguna Piedras Blancas
Side Trip
Cerro Polo (1188m)
Cerro Madsen (1806m)
Campamento Río Blanco
START DAY 2
Campamento Poincenot
Laguna de los Tres
Mallín
Chorrillo del Salto
Cascada del Salto
Valle Río de las Vueltas
PARQUE NACIONAL LOS GLACIARES
Laguna Madre
Laguna Hija
Laguna Nieta
Laguna Capri
Campamento Laguna Capri
Cerro León (866m)
Cerro Rosado (834m)
Estancia Fitz Roy
Campamento Madsen
START/ FINISH: Treks 1&2
Albergue Rancho Grande
Hotel Los Cerros
START (Alt): Trek 1
El Chaltén
Laguna Torre
Mirador Laguna Torre
Campamento De Agostini
Cerro Dos Cóndores (700m)
Río Fitz Roy
Dam
Guardería
Campamento Confluencia
To El Calafate (220km)

the shore of Laguna de los Tres to its outlet stream, then leftwards to a high precipice far above the cloudy-green Laguna Sucia.

For more superb vistas of Monte Fitz Roy, Cerro Madsen (1806m) can be climbed in a somewhat more difficult four- to five-hour return route that follows the spur just north of Laguna de los Tres.

ALTERNATIVE ROUTE: SENDERO MADRE & HIJA

1½–2 hours, 6km

This short cut between Campamento Poincenot and Campamento De Agostini makes it possible to link the Laguna Torre and Around Monte Fitz Roy treks without returning to El Chaltén in between. It is much easier to start from the northern direction, given the huge descent approaching Laguna Torre.

From a signposted junction outside of Campamento Poincenot, head south for one to 1¼ hours. A signposted track veers right for Lagunas Madre & Hija and Campamento De Agostini. The trail parallels Laguna Madre (Mother Lake), to your right, followed by Laguna Hija (Daughter Lake). At the southern end of Laguna Hija, the track crosses a strip of land between Laguna Hija and the tiny Laguna Nieta (Granddaughter Lake). The trail drops, gently first and then considerably, descending a set of switchbacks headed southwest until it joins the main trail for Campamento de Agostini. Bear right to head toward the camp.

Day 2: Campamento Poincenot to Refugio Los Troncos

2½–3½ hours, 11km

Cross the Río Blanco and find the signposted path just a short distance into the forest. The often vague route goes downstream along the western banks of the Río Blanco over eroding embankments and small gravel washes to meet a rubble-filled side valley after 35 to 45 minutes. From here, agile trekkers can make a very worthwhile side trip to Laguna Piedras Blancas (see side trip, this page).

Back on the main route, pick your way through the moraine debris and cross the gushing lake outlet stream with care. The trail continues downvalley, skirting the edge of the rocky alluvial plain and occasionally dipping briefly left into the forest, and leaves Parque Nacional Los Glaciares at a stile over a wire fence. Where the valley fans out at its mouth, move away from the river towards hanging glaciers on mountains to the northwest to intersect with a more prominent foot track (indicated by red paint markings), 50 minutes to 1¼ hours on from the Laguna Piedras Blancas turn-off.

Head left (west) over rolling wooded slopes and through small fire-cleared pastures sprinkled with *calafate* bushes to enter the enclosed upper valley of the Río Eléctrico below high glacier-shaped cliffs after 30 to 40 minutes. The path proceeds gently up beside the rushing, murky-grey river through open, cattle-grazed *lenga* forest before cutting across a broad grassy meadow to arrive at the privately-owned **Refugio Los Troncos** (☎ 02962-493312, in El Chaltén; camping per person AR$25, bunk without/with sheets AR$70/120, dinner AR$30), a further 40 to 50 minutes on.

The *refugio* lies at the eastern end of **Piedra del Fraile**, a large erratic block in the middle of the flat valley floor below the 2257m Cerro Eléctrico. The whole Valle Eléctrico belongs to the nearby Estancia Ricanor, and the *refugio* is the only authorized campsite along Day 2. Pleasant campsites occupy watered lawns protected by Piedra del Fraile, with cooking shelters, toilets and a hot shower. The resident caretaker sells essentials such as chocolate and beer.

A short path climbs up to the top of the rock for a great view upvalley to **Lago Eléctrico**, a dramatically bleak lake exposed to fierce and incessant winds blasting down from the nearby Hielo Sur. Lago Eléctrico can also be visited in around 1½ hours return by taking an easy trail across the moist river flats then over wavelike moraines to the lake's raw, glaciated southeastern shore.

SIDE TRIP: LAGUNA PIEDRAS BLANCAS

30 minutes return, 800m

The track on the west bank of the Río Blanco meets a rubble-filled side valley. Follow cairns here that lead up left around and over white granite boulders to **Laguna Piedras Blancas**. The heavily seraced **Glaciar Piedras Blancas** curves around from the eastern face of Monte Fitz Roy in a series of icefalls reaching this impressively bleak meltwater lake. Retrace your steps to the main track.

SIDE TRIP: CERRO ELÉCTRICO LOOKOUT

7½–9 hours return, 8km, 1500m ascent/descent

This much longer and more difficult side trip (rated moderate–demanding) takes you well into the realm of the mountaineers, and should only be attempted during stable weather. Take the well-worn foot track southwest across the river flats, then up the steep southern side of the valley beside two streams that cascade down in the shape of a Y. When the gradient moderates, continue ascending steadily southwards to a rock bivouac on the lip of an impressive cirque filled by a small glacier after 1½ to two hours. Monte Fitz Roy can be seen towering above the back wall of this cirque.

The path leads slightly left, but after passing over a small spur it finally peters out. Head south along the bottom of reddish scree slopes with the glacier to your right for 30 to 45 minutes, bearing left where the cliffs up to your left suddenly change into black rock. Make your way up to the right of the red rock over steep loose scree slopes into a small col, another 1½ to two hours on. Head east from the col and traverse the steep boulder slopes below a huge wedge-shaped rock, then ascend gradually to reach the lowest point of the main ridge of Cerro Eléctrico, 45 minutes to one hour on. From here there are utterly stupendous views towards Fitz Roy, Cerro Pollone and southwest over the Hielo Sur.

Return the same way.

Day 3: Refugio Los Troncos to El Chaltén

5–7 hours, 19km

Backtrack to El Chaltén via Campamento Poincenot (ie Days 1 and 2 in reverse order). Without detours, this is comfortably done in a single day; alternatively, an additional night at Campamento Poincenot or Campamento Laguna Capri allows you to do side trips you missed on the outward journey or to spend more time in favorite places.

ALTERNATIVE ROUTE: VIA RUTA PROVINCIAL 23

4¼–5½ hours, 20km

Retrace your steps towards the Río Blanco and bear left at the trail junction, following signs eastwards through boulders and regenerating *ñirres*, and crossing several tributaries of the Río Eléctrico. The route swings northwest to meet Ruta Provincial 23, the main road through the Valle Río de las Vueltas. This is at the Río Eléctrico road bridge 1¾ to 2¼ hours from the *refugio*.

Follow the gravel southeastwards across the Río Blanco after 1km, and past the turn-off to **Hostería El Pilar** (☎ 02962-493002; www.hosteriaelpilar.com.ar; s/d AR$390/470), suitable to splurgers or honeymooners, then around a tight, cliffed bend beside the river, edging on along a wide plain – your pace accelerated by gusty tailwinds – back into the national park. After two to 2½ hours the road passes the signposted trail to the Cascada del Salto, a waterfall spurting out of the gorge up to your right (reached in around one hour return). Proceed for another 30 to 40 minutes to reach the northern end of El Chaltén.

PARQUE NACIONAL TORRES DEL PAINE

Soaring almost vertically more than 2000m above the Patagonian steppe, the granite pillars of Torres del Paine dominate the landscape of what may be South America's finest national park. Most people visit the park for its one greatest hit, but once here realize that there are other (less-crowded) attractions with equal wow power. We're talking about vast open steppe, azure lakes, trails that meander through emerald forests, roaring rivers with rickety bridges and one big, radiant blue glacier.

Parque Nacional Torres del Paine is 112km north of Puerto Natales. The park takes in 1814 sq km at the southeastern end of the Hielo Sur, connected to Argentina's Parque Nacional Los Glaciares to the north, and the ultra-remote Parque Nacional Balmaceda to the west. Before its creation in 1959, the park was part of a large sheep *estancia*, and it's still recovering from nearly a century of overexploitation of its pastures, forests and wildlife. Since 1978, it has been a Unesco Biosphere Reserve.

HISTORY

No one is exactly sure how Torres del Paine got its name. The word *paine* (pie-nee) means 'pale blue' in Tehuelche and may refer to the intense colors of the area's half-dozen or so large glacial lakes. Local Andean nomenclature often uses the names of andinists who achieved first ascents, and another theory names Paine as an early Welsh climber.

ENVIRONMENT

Back in the Pleistocene ice age, the glaciers of the Hielo Sur covered all but Torres del Paine's highest ground and most easterly areas. The ice has largely receded, but four major appendages – glaciers Dickson, Grey, Pingo and Tyndall/Geikie – remain. The 17km-long Glaciar Grey is the largest.

Surrounded by glacial lakes, the great Macizo Paine (Paine Massif) forms core of the park. At its southwestern end, the main summit of Cerro Paine Grande (3050m) is the park's highest point and its only peak over 3000m. Ice mushrooms or *hongos de hielo* cap the peak—a phenomenon mostly unique to Patagonia. These features form only at high elevations in subpolar regions, where extremely intense winds freeze moisture directly onto alpine rock. Just east of Cerro Paine Grande are the Cuernos del Paine, jagged turrets of resistant layer of sedimentary black shale cover the granite base. At the eastern end of the Macizo Paine are three magnificent frost-polished 'towers' of granite, the Torres del Paine.

In this southern forest, *lenga* cover the moist interior, while *coigüe de Magallanes* can also be found at lower elevations, although it rarely challenges the dominant *lenga*. *Ñirre* covers drier and well-drained slopes in the central part of the park. Daisy bushes including the *romerillo*, which resembles rosemary, grow where moist natural pasture meets the drier steppeland. *Chilco de Magallanes* is another daisy species found in this transition zone, it differs from the common native species of fuchsia known simply as *chilco*.

The easternmost third of the park is covered by vegetation characteriztic of the lee of the Patagonian Andes. These plants are well adapted to dry and extremely windy conditions, such as *mogotes* (tumbleweeds), spinifexlike *maihuén*, the world's most southerly cactus, *cacto patagónico* or *yerba del guanaco*, and clumps of native tussock grasses known as *coirón*. A subspecies of butterfly, *Etcheverrius chilensis magallanicus*, lives among these steppeland plants, somehow managing to avoid being blown away.

Bird life is abundant and diverse. The park's lakes (particularly the saltwater ones such as Lago Sarmiento and Laguna Amarga) provide an ideal habitat for the Chilean flamingo. The sole flamingo species found in Patagonia, it eats aquatic insects and small mollusks, whose pigments make its plumage a striking pink. Even more common is the *cisne de cuello negro*, a large white swan with a black neck.

Look for ducks, such as the *quetru volador* (flying steamer duck), and the *caiquén* (upland goose), on lakes. In fast-flowing rivers (such as the Río de los Perros), the now rather rare *pato de torrentes* (torrent duck), may be spotted swimming up current in search of its prey, chiefly invertebrates and their larvae. Several species of heron, including the *garza grande*, are found in lagoons and rivers. In the drier eastern sectors of the park, there are several species of *chorlos* (plovers). These dry steppes are also the home of the *ñandú*, which sprints in a fast, zigzagging gait to escape predators.

Look up to spot condors gliding effortlessly around the peaks and the inaccessible cliffs on the eastern side of the park where they nest. They can be identified by their enormous size and distinctive splayed wing tips and white collar. Condors prefer to feed on carrion, though they will sometimes take small live mammals or attack a dying guanaco. Other birds of prey to look for are the *águila mora*, a handsome species of eagle, and hawks, harriers and falcons such as the *peuquito* and the *traro*.

Guanaco graze on the grasslands in the eastern sector of Torres del Paine, and the park's less accessible western interior provides a refuge for small numbers of *huemul*. Such rich game sustains the puma, although trekkers are rarely lucky enough to catch even a fleeting glimpse of this discreet predator.

Torres del Paine's ranching past is clearly visible in old fences and the occasional *puesto* (herder's hut). Some of the land used by trails is owned by one local *estancia*, which still runs some cattle outside of peak season. The graziers' past use of fire to clear forest has greatly modified the landscape, and regeneration is occurring only slowly – a reminder of fire's destructive effect in the Patagonian Andes.

CLIMATE

Abutting the Hielo Sur, the western sectors of Parque Nacional Torres del Paine experience extremely unstable and often localized weather. Precipitation levels vary enormously over relatively short distances, and it is not uncommon to experience heavy downpours in areas closer to the icecap while sunshine warms the steppes just a few kilometers to the east. The highest precipitation levels, exceeding 4000mm, occur on the Hielo Sur (slightly west of the park's borders), dropping to about 2000mm around Mountain Lodge Paine Grande and under 800mm at Laguna Amarga. The mean annual temperature at Lago del Toro is only around 6°C, and summer days never rise much above 20°C. From October to April, but particularly from December to February, winds are almost unremitting and often extremely strong. The chilling effect of the freezing winds that blow off the great glaciers should not be underestimated.

PLANNING

Trekkers should reserve *refugios* well in advance. **Vertice Patagonia** (☎ 061-412742; www.verticepatagonia.cl) runs Mountain Lodge Paine Grande and also manages *refugios* and campsites Lago Grey, Dickson and Perros. **Fantastico Sur** (☎ 061-614184; www.fantasticosur.com; Esmeralda 661, Puerto Natales; 9am-5pm Mon-Fri, 10:30am-1.30pm & 3-5pm Sat & Sun) owns *refugios* Torres, Chileno and Los Cuernos, their associated campsites and Campamento Serón. Campsites do not require reservations.

When to Trek

December to late March is peak season for trekking in Parque Nacional Torres del Paine, with most visitors arriving from January to mid-February. However, the park is open year-round, subject to your ability to get there. Transportation connections are less frequent in the low season and winter weather adds additional challenges to hiking. Shoulder seasons of November and March are some of the best times for trekking, with fewer crowds and windy conditions usually abating in March. Winter visits should be limited to low-level routes.

What to Bring

Trekking poles are recommended. Not only will they help with stream crossings and long descents, but they can be useful to brace yourself against Paine's epic gusts. If you want complete independence, your best bet is bringing all camping equipment including tent, sleeping bag and stove. That way you can always stay at a free campsite (without equipment rentals) if desired. Yet, the park's eight *refugios* and paying campsites rent all gear, so in theory, campers can travel light. In practise, equipment may run out during the busiest months. Those hiking without gear should note that the trek from Los Perros to Refugio Grey is long and arduous in good weather. Completing this long stretch in one day is only recommended for fit and experienced parties.

Maps

The two best maps for all treks in the park are the JLM Mapas 1:100,000 *Torres del Paine Trekking Map* and the similar Luis Bertea Rojas 1:100,000 *National Park Torres del Paine Trekking Map*. Neither map is perfect – in particular, the Rojas map has

AVOID THE MULITITUDES

- Most trekkers go up to the Torres towers around 8am and down at 4pm. With full summer light, you can go against traffic by starting a couple of hours earlier or later (inquire about the times of sunset/sunrise at your refugio or *guardaparques*)
- Trek less crowded routes like Glaciar Zapata or the Full Circuit
- Try joining a multiday trip kayaking Río Serrano or horseback riding; you'll get a completely different perspective and incredible views
- Trek in the shoulder season, when the weather is still warm enough but the crowds are gone: March is an excellent time in the park; for the hearty, winter can be too

inaccuracies in contours shown – but both show adequate topographical detail, trekking routes with average times and the location of *refugios* and park-authorised campsites. Both are easily found in Puerto Natales. Park administration distributes a detailed map to all visitors and the same map is available as a download on the official park website.

Information Sources

Internet resources include the official park website for **Parque Nacional Torres del Paine** (www.pntp.cl), **Torres del Paine** (www.torresdelpaine.com) and **Erratic Rock** (www.erraticrock.com), with a good backpacker equipment list.

Permits & Regulations

All visitors to Parque Nacional Torres del Paine pay an entry fee (high/low season CH$15,000/5000) and must register with Conaf upon entry. Trekkers must stay on official trails and camp only at designated campsites. The lighting of open fires is prohibited throughout the park. Given the impact of growing numbers of visitors to Torres del Paine it is important to follow these simple rules.

Climbers must obtain a climbing permit (CH$60,000) at park headquarters. The application requires climbers to submit a climbing résumé, emergency contact numbers and authorization from their consulate.

Climbers must also get permission from the **Dirección de Fronteras y Límites** (Difrol; ☎ 02-6714110; www.difrol.cl, in Spanish; 4th fl, Bandera 52, Santiago), which takes about an hour to get if in Santiago and up to five days if requested from Puerto Natales. Ask for plenty of time for the permission to avoid paying a separate fee each time you enter the park. Avoid delays by arranging the permissions with a climbing outfitter, such as **Antares Patagonia** (☎ 061-414611; www.antarespatagonia.com; Bories 206, Puerto Natales) before arrival in the country.

Accommodations

CAMPING

Camping at the *refugios* costs CH$4000 per site, hot showers included. *Refugios* rent decent equipment – tent (CH$7000 per night), sleeping bag (CH$4500) and mat (CH$1500) – but potential shortages in high season make it prudent to pack your own gear. Small kiosks sell expensive pasta, soup packets and butane gas.

Sites administered by Conaf are free and very basic (rain shelters and pit toilets). Many campers have reported rodents lurking around campsites; don't leave food in packs or in tents; hang it from a tree instead.

REFUGIOS

Refugio rooms have four to eight bunk beds each, kitchen privileges (for lodgers and during specific hours only), hot showers and meals. A bed costs CH$12,500 to CH$17,500, sleeping-bag rental CH$4500 and meals CH$4000 to CH$7500. Should the *refugio* be overbooked, staff provides all necessary camping equipment. Most *refugios* close by the end of April. Mountain Lodge Paine Grande is the only one that stays open year-round, but it has very limited operations.

GETTING THERE & AWAY

Parque Nacional Torres del Paine is 112km north of Puerto Natales via a decent but sometimes bumpy gravel road, partially paved at the time of writing.

At Cerro Castillo there is a seasonal border crossing into Argentina at Cancha Carrera. The road continues 40km north and west to **Portería Sarmiento**, the main entrance where user fees are collected. It's another 37km to the Administración (park headquarters) and the Centro de Visitantes.

Book your transportation a day ahead, especially for morning departures. For more information on buses. Within the park, it takes 45 minutes from the entrance gate to reach the Pudeto boat landing and another hour to Administración. The earliest bus leaves Administración at 12.15pm.

The recent opening of an alternative park approach that enters via Lago Toro may provide shorter travel times and drop-off options in the future. These schedules are in constant flux, so double-check them before heading out.

GETTING AROUND

Buses drop off and pick up passengers at Laguna Amarga, the catamaran launch at Pudeto and park headquarters.

Hielos Patagónicos catamaran (one way/round-trip per person CH$11,000/17,000) leaves Pudeto for Mountain Lodge Paine Grande at 9.30am, noon and 6pm December to mid-March, noon and 6pm in late March and November, and at noon only in September, October and April. Another launch travels Lago Grey between Hostería Lago Grey and Refugio Lago Grey (CH$70,000 round-trip, 1½ to two hours) a couple of times daily; contact the *hostería* for the current schedule.

ACCESS TOWN

See Puerto Natales (p198).

TORRES DEL PAINE LOOKOUT

Duration 4½–6 hours
Distance 19km
Difficulty easy–moderate
Start/Finish Hotel Las Torres
Nearest Town Puerto Natales
Transport bus
Summary The postcard view – Torres del Paine's most spectacular lookout at the base of the granite towers the park is named after.

Don't miss this short trek to the park's centerpiece: the towers are toothy pinnacles of hard Andean batholith rock in a deep valley of the Paine massif. They are what remain of a great cirque sheared away by forces of glacial ice. The tallest is 2850m Torre De Agostini, towering over the intensely glaciated and barren surroundings 1500m below.

Apart from some minor rock-hopping on the final climb, this return trek follows a good and well-marked path for the whole way. The trek is easily combined with the Paine Circuit. If you can spare the time and the weather is favorable, spend a night close enough to visit the lookout at dawn.

GETTING TO/FROM THE TREK

For details of how to reach the park entrance at Guardería Laguna Amarga see Getting There & Away (p180). Las Torres shuttle buses meet buses from Puerto Natales at Laguna Amarga and ferry trekkers and guests to Hotel Las Torres, where the trek begins (CH$2.500, 15 minutes, five daily). Trekkers staying here can ask permission to leave private vehicles.

THE TREK

Follow the signposted road uphill past the Hotel Las Torres before dropping down to cross the **Río Ascensio** on a sturdy suspension footbridge. Continue across a small alluvial plain to where the 'Los Cuernos' path diverges left (see Paine Circuit, Day 8, p191). From here begin climbing northwestwards up an ancient heath-covered moraine ridge that lends a fine view south across Lago Sarmiento. Down to your right, the stream rushes through a gorge of layered black shale. The path traverses into the valley along steep slopes high above the Río Ascensio, before moving down to meet the river again opposite the Fantástico Sur-operated **Refugio El Chileno** (camping per person CH$4000, bunks CH$19,000), one to 1¼ hours from the hotel.

Cross to Chileno and continue up the western bank for 20 minutes then cross the river again to join the eastern bank, gradually rising away from the river. Crossing several streams on log bridges and stepping stones, the trail brings you up through lovely stands of dwarf *lenga* to arrive at **Campamento Torres** after 50 minutes to 1¼ hours. The main campsite for trekkers and mountaineers in the valley, this site has the best and most abundant campsites in the valley of the Río Ascensio. There's a toilet behind the national park *guardería*.

Take the signposted path from the southern side of the small gully just before you reach the campsite. First follow the tiny clear stream up the left side of the regenerating glacial rubble, then follow orange paint spots leading rightwards over bare boulders to arrive at the **Torres del Paine Lookout** at the top of the moraine wall after 40 to 50 minutes. Often windy, this spot sits immediately below the Torres del Paine, a set of mighty granite columns ringed by shelf glaciers – one of the Patagonian Andes' classic scenes.

Return downvalley by the same route.

SIDE TRIP: CAMPAMENTO JAPONÉS

2–2½ hours return, 8km

This side trip takes you into the wild upper valley of the Río Ascensio. Pick up the initially vague trail at the lower edge of Campamento Torres. Follow cairns leading out over boulder rubble and across several channels of the cloudy glacial stream that descends from the lake at the foot of the Torres. The route ascends almost gently along the western side of the Río Ascensio before reaching an attractive forested flat after 50 minutes to 1¼ hours. Here you'll find **Campamento Japonés**, an old climbers' camp with a small, makeshift hut and various improvised plaques made from tin lids nailed to trees. From here a much less distinct route swings west to the head of the evocatively name Valle del Silencio.

PAINE CIRCUIT

Duration 8 days
Distance 101km
Difficulty moderate–demanding
Start/Finish Hotel Las Torres
Nearest Town Puerto Natales
Transport bus
Summary Circumnavigate the Paine massif, from dry steppes through moist forests to highland moors and back again, with constantly changing views of peaks, lakes and enormous glaciers.

Truly one of the world's classic treks, the Paine Circuit is the longest and wildest route in the park, following the course of the Río Paine up to Paso John Gardner, descending the Río Grey and skirting several of the park's spectacular lakes.

PLANNING

The full Paine Circuit as described takes eight days, although side trips and rest days might stretch it out to 10 days or more. Do not underestimate trekking times with a full pack. It's important to bring sufficient supplies for a safe, comfortable trip. If you are unable to do the entire circuit, a shorter trek known as the W, taking around five days, is a popular alternative (see boxed text, p186).

If you are not sure that you are in physical condition to do the full circuit, or if you have doubts about your equipment, it may be wise to start the circuit counterclockwise at Mountain Lodge Paine Grande (Day 7); that way you can warm up with the highlights of the W with better access to roads. Otherwise, you may find yourself at the remotest part of the park when things get difficult.

In most places the Paine Circuit is well enough marked (with orange stakes and paint) and trodden that serious navigational difficulties should not arise. The trail is less well maintained along the central section of the route, however, where fallen logs and boggy terrain can make the going slower and more strenuous. Reliable bridges now provide safe crossings of all larger streams.

The 1241m Paso John Gardner is located in the most remote central section of the Paine Circuit. Conaf does not allow solo trekkers to pass (those hiking solo should join up with other trekkers at the Campamento Los Perros). Although technically very straightforward, this pass is exposed to strong, frigid westerly winds that bring sudden snowfalls. Snow may close the pass completely, even in summer, but particularly between March and December. In recent years, inexperienced and poorly prepared trekkers have come to grief on Paso John Gardner, so the crossing must be taken very seriously. Less dangerous but extremely bothersome (particularly in December and January) are the plagues of mosquitoes at some of the campsites along the circuit – carry insect repellent.

Most parties trek the Paine Circuit in a counterclockwise direction, as it is described here. While this requires a steep, slippery descent from Paso John Gardner, it also avoids the arduous climb up Gardner from the opposite direction. Also, climbing from the east permits staggering views over Glaciar Grey for an extended period of time.

What to Bring

Thanks to *refugios* and rental equipment available at paying campsites, it's possible to trek the Paine Circuit without carrying a tent. However, this means covering the most difficult and remote stretch of the circuit—between Campamento Los Perros and Refugio Grey, including the crossing of Paso John Gardner—in one long day. For some parties, this arrangement is too demanding and, since *refugio* accommodation must be booked in advance, their itineraries may be disrupted as a result.

In January and February *refugios* are often very full. Campers should note that park authorities prohibit lighting campfires along the entire Paine Circuit; trekking parties must use a camping stove.

GETTING TO/FROM THE TREK

The trek begins at Camping Las Torres, the main entrance point to Torres del Paine. It ends at Hotel Las Torres (p198), from where Las Torres shuttle buses ferry trekkers to Guardería Laguna Amarga (CH$2500, 15 minutes, five daily). Days 7 and 8 of the trek can be avoided by taking the catamaran from Mountain Lodge Paine Grande to Pudeto (see Getting Around, p181).

THE TREK

Day 1: Camping Las Torres to Puesto Serón

3¼–4 hours, 16.5km

Take a 4WD track five minutes up the eastern side of the stream opposite Camping Las Torres past **Refugio Las Torres**. Just beyond the *refugio* a signposted path leads off to the right over grassed-over moraine mounds and through a tiny canyon, then climbs on gently across mostly open slopes scattered with *notro* bushes. Follow wire fences running below the steeper forested slopes up to your left, traversing high above the valley of the Río Paine as the route gradually swings from a north to a northwestward direction.

As you approach a broad flat plain beside the river, begin a northward descent to join with the other path from Laguna Amarga (which comes in on your right) at a signpost after 2½ to 2¾ hours.

Cut over left and through a gate to ford a shallow stream, then make your way approximately northwest across broad grassy riverflats scattered with *ñirre* woodland to arrive at **Puesto Serón** after a final 50 minutes to 1¼ hours. This pleasant private campsite has toilets, hot showers and good sites corralled at the edge of a large, often windy pasture. Meals are available.

ALTERNATIVE START: GUARDERÍA LAGUNA AMARGA

4–5¼ hours, 20km

You will probably have the trail to yourself on this little-transited, slightly longer but flatter start. Trek down to cross two road bridges over the Río Paine and continue for a few minutes along to the right until a signpost indicates where the path leaves the road. Marked with orange-painted stakes and rocks, the trail moves well away from the Río Paine as it heads roughly north-northwest across the rolling grassy floor of the valley. After 1¼ to 1½ hours you pass a route leading off right. (This side trip takes less than 1½ hours return and leads almost directly east to the Cascada Paine, where the cloudy waters of the Río Paine drop 4m.)

The main path meets the Río Paine again 2km on, then continues upstream some distance above the river's steepening banks to reach a signposted trail junction (where the Day 1: Camping Las Torres intersects) after two to 2½ hours.

Day 2: Puesto Serón to Refugio Lago Dickson

4¼–5½ hours, 18.5km

From the old *puesto* building head right beside a fence before you continue upvalley. The path first skirts above broad waterlogged riverflats, where *caiquenes* and other water birds congregate in the marshy overflow ponds. It leads on immediately beside the swift-flowing milky-blue river, then starts climbing away northwestwards through *ñirre* woodland to reach **Laguna Alejandra** after 45 minutes to one hour.

Make your way around the southern shore of this tiny horseshoe lake, then continue up in a few wide switchbacks. A more gentle westwardly climb brings you to an indistinct saddle after 30 to 45 minutes. This gusty spot gives a panorama of Lago Paine, several hundred meters below and the arc of jagged peaks along the Chile–Argentina frontier that is behind Lago Dickson at the head of the valley.

Begin descending through a gradual traverse high above Lago Paine. The trail alternately climbs and dips as views emerge of the glacier-crowned summit of Cerro Paine Chico, 20km to the west. Continual exposure to wind and sun make well-anchored plants such *calafate* bushes and *mogotes* prominent on these steep north-facing slopes. Sidle down gently through a light forest above boggy *mallin* where Río Paine enters the lake. The trail arrives at Campamento Coirón (now closed), one to 1¼ hours on. This area is recovering from a 2005 fire.

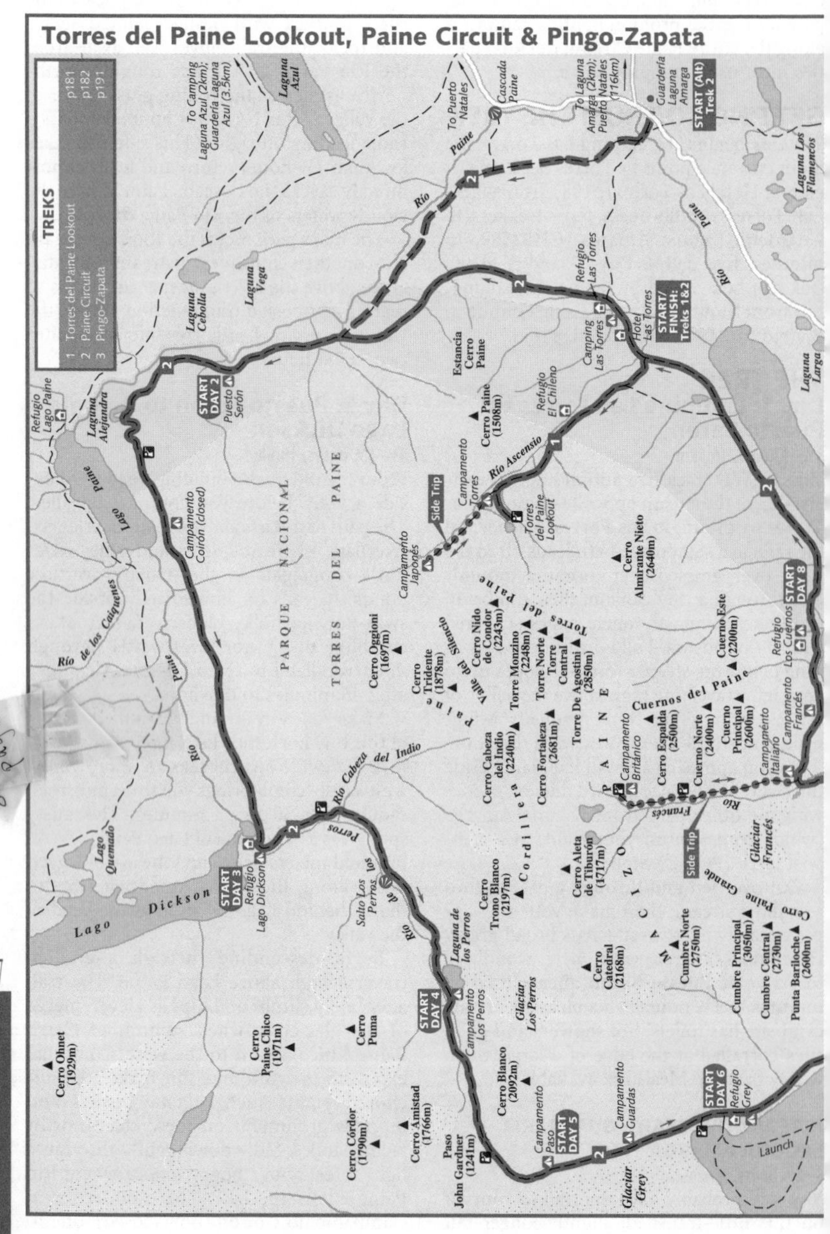

SOUTHERN PATAGONIA

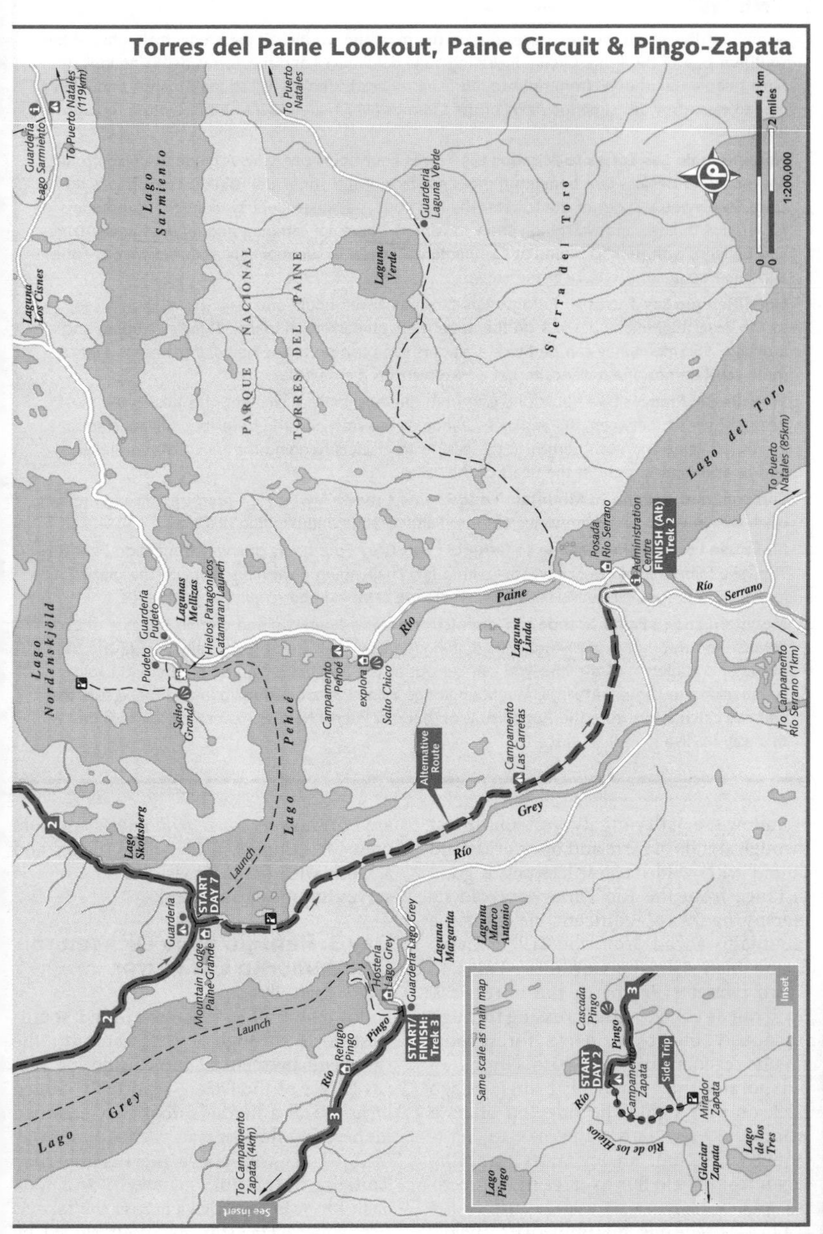
Torres del Paine Lookout, Paine Circuit & Pingo-Zapata
Lago Sarmiento
Guardería Lago Sarmiento
To Puerto Natales (119km)
To Puerto Natales
Laguna Los Cisnes
PARQUE NACIONAL TORRES DEL PAINE
Laguna Verde
Guardería Laguna Verde
Sierra del Toro
Lago del Toro
To Puerto Natales (85km)
Posada Río Serrano
Administration Centre
FINISH (Alt) Trek 2
Río Serrano
To Campamento Río Serrano (1km)
Lago Nordenskjöld
Lagunas Mellizas
Guardería Pudeto
Pudeto
Hielos Patagónicos Catamaran Launch
Salto Grande
Lago Pehoé
Launch
Campamento Pehoé
explora
Salto Chico
Río Paine
Laguna Linda
Alternative Route
Campamento Las Carretas
Río Grey
Lago Skottsberg
START DAY 7
Guardería
Mountain Lodge Paine Grande
Laguna Margarita
Laguna Marco Antonio
Hostería Lago Grey
Guardería Lago Grey
START/ FINISH: Trek 3
Refugio Pingo
Río Pingo
Lago Grey
To Campamento Zapata (4km)
See Inset
Same scale as main map
Inset
Cascada Pingo
START DAY 2
Campamento Zapata
Side Trip
Mirador Zapata
Río de los Hielos
Lago Pingo
Glaciar Zapata
Lago de los Tres
0 4 km
0 2 miles
1:200,000

THE 'W'

Named for the shape the trek traces out on the map, the 'W' hits all the scenic highlights of the southern side of the Paine Circuit, including Valle del Francés and the Torres del Paine lookout. Most people trek the 'W' from right to left (east to west), starting at Laguna Amarga, and hiking east to west provides superior views of the Cuernos (which are otherwise more often to your back).

Hotel/Refugio Las Torres to Mirador Las Torres Four hours one way. A moderate hike up Río Ascencio to a treeless tarn beneath the eastern face of the Torres del Paine proper. This is the closest view you will get of the towers. The last hour is a knee-popping scramble up boulders (covered with knee and waist-high snow in winter). There are camping and *refugios* at Las Torres and Chileno, with basic camping at Campamento Torres. In summer stay at Campamento Torres and head up at sunrise to beat the crowds.

Hotel/Refugio Las Torres to Refugio Los Cuernos Seven hours one way. Hikers should keep to the lower trail (many get lost on the upper trail, unmarked on maps). There's camping and a *refugio*. Summer winds can be fierce. Campers can push on to the new Campamento Francés (between Cuernos and Italiano) to get a headstart on the next day.

To Valle del Francés Five hours one way from Cuernos. In clear weather, this hike is the most beautiful stretch between 3050m Paine Grande to the west and the lower but still spectacular Torres del Paine and Los Cuernos to the east, with glaciers hugging the trail. Camp at Italiano and/or at Británico, right in the heart of the valley.

Campamento Italiano to Mountain Lodge Paine Grande A windy 2.5 hour trek through rolling, open terrain with immediate views of Cerro Paine Grande and hanging glaciers.

Mountain Lodge Paine Grande to Refugio Lago Grey Four hours one way from Lago Pehoé. This hike follows a relatively easy trail with a few challenging downhill scampers. The glacier lookout is another half-hour's hike away. There are camping and *refugios* at both ends.

Mountain Lodge Paine Grande to Administración Five hours. Up and around the side of Lago Pehoé, then through extensive grassland along Río Grey. This is not technically part of the 'W,' but after completion of the hike you can cut out to the Administración from here and avoid backtracking to Laguna Amarga. Mountain Lodge Paine Grande can radio in and make sure that you can catch a bus from the Administración back to Puerto Natales. You can also enter the 'W' this way to hike it west to east.

Follow the path roughly west-southwest through stands of *ñirre* and open grassland dotted with wild daisies, keeping a good distance from the Río Paine to avoid its marshy banks. Magnificent views of the mountains ahead, from the 2197m Cerro Trono Blanco in the Cordillera Paine to Cerro Ohnet (1929m) to the northwest, open out as you go. After crossing through previously burnt-out *lenga* forest now slowly regenerating, the path climbs an old moraine ridge, suddenly bringing Lago Dickson into sight. The ridgetop offers a wonderful view across the lake to Ventisquero Dickson, an icy mass tumbling down from Hielo Sur to calve in its greenish-grey waters.

On a lakeside meadow immediately below stands **Refugio Lago Dickson**, about two to 2½ hours from Campamento Coirón. There are hot showers for *refugio* guests and cold ones for campers, flush toilets, tables and a kiosk with basic provisions. The *refugio* serves hot meals and drinks.

Day 3: Refugio Lago Dickson to Campamento Los Perros

3¼–4¼ hours, 9km

Follow the trail as it loops around southwestwards through low forest onto the steep embankment of the **Río de los Perros** (River of the Dogs), reportedly named in honor of a herder's dogs that drowned in these fast-flowing waters. Make your way on upwards well above the rushing river (initially heard but not seen), and look back for your last views across the lake to Ventisquero Dickson, its snout ringed by floating ice debris. Shortly after passing a tiny peat bog, from where you get the first

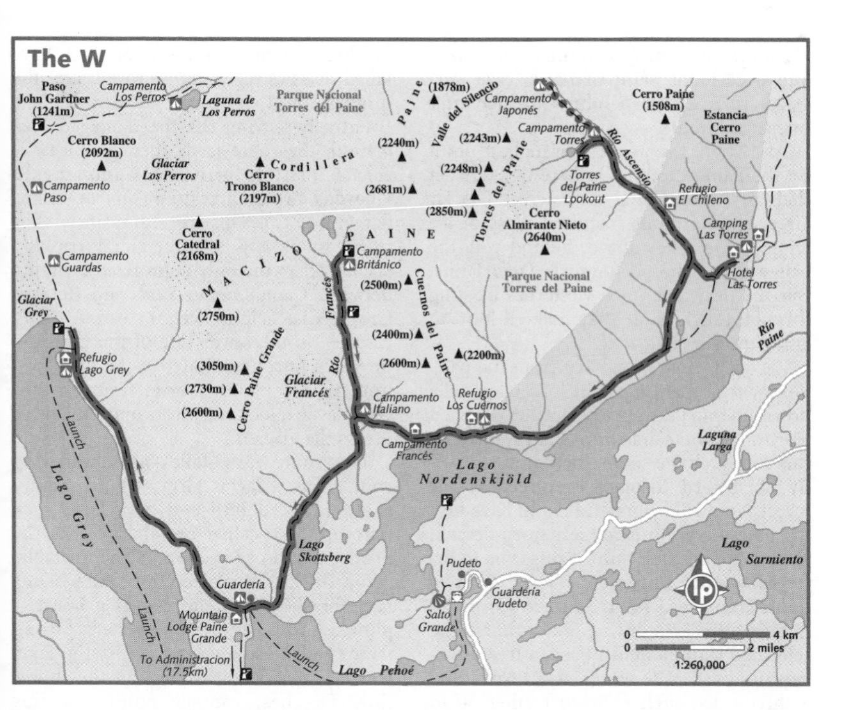

views upvalley into the wildest and least accessible section of the Paine Circuit, the route comes to the Río Cabeza del Indio. Cross this large side stream on a log bridge 1¼ to 1¾ hours from the *refugio*.

The path undulates southwestwards through stands of *coigüe de Magallanes* to pass **Salto Los Perros** in a thunderous chasm after 20 to 25 minutes. Delicate ground orchids such as the tiny white *palomita* (little dove) thrive here in rich, moist humus. Continue upvalley through open *lenga* forest in long, virtually flat stretches interrupted only by very short steeper climbs to cross a suspension bridge spanning the Río de los Perros some 1¼ to 1½ hours on.

Head up through regenerating glacial debris, then climb left up the end-moraine that dams **Laguna de los Perros**. A small glacier calves directly into the lake, and blocks of ice float in its frigid waters. The route now follows the top of the moraine wall before leading off rightwards across river flats to arrive at **Campamento Los Perros**, 30 to 40 minutes on from the suspension bridge. This forest campsite sits near the confluence of the valley's two uppermost stream branches. Operated by Vertices, it has toilets, cold showers and a large cooking shelter. Meals are available, there is camping equipment for hire, and a small (and expensive) food store.

Day 4: Campamento Los Perros to Campamento Paso

3¾–5½ hours, 12km, 680m ascent, 800m descent

Today's terrain is very exposed and well above the tree line with a potential for visibility problems or whiteouts. Avoid crossing the pass alone or in poor weather.

Staying on the true right bank (an older trail crosses the stream), make your way upvalley along an often very muddy path through stunted forest, one to 1¼ hours from the campsite.

Follow the stream briefly to the tree line, then pick up cairns leading away to the left (roughly west-southwest) up over sparse alpine grasses. The route then ascends more steeply to cross a tiny tumbling brook, climbing on over barren rock slopes. To the north a small crevassed glacier, the source of the valley's uppermost stream, descends from Cerro Amistad

(1766m). Watching carefully for stakes and occasional paint markers, ease leftwards to reach **Paso John Gardner** after one to 1½ hours.

At 1241m, the pass is the highest point on the Paine Circuit. Up here trekkers get their first astonishing view across Glaciar Grey, an enormous fractured mass of ice choking the valley ahead. Behind you, the valley drops sharply towards Lago Paine. But the near gale-force westerlies blasting through this keyhole may make it hard to enjoy the views for long.

Zigzag a short way down from the pass. Follow trail markings that lead diagonally down left into the uppermost wind-whipped *lengas*. The route first drops sharply through this robust alpine scrub, then moves steadily downward through evergreen *coigüe* forest. You will be grateful if you have hiking poles here. An extremely steep descent – very slippery after rain – brings you to the former site of Campamento Paso, 1¼ to two hours from Paso John Gardner. *Cachañas* frequent this area during the summer. The relocated **Campamento Paso**, a free, park-approved campsite with a squat toilet and a three-sided shelter, lies a further 30 to 40 minutes south, just beyond a log bridge over a substantial stream. As there is no supervision at this campsite it can get quite filthy; please be conscientious with your trash and use the toilet.

Day 5: Campamento Paso to Refugio Grey

2¾–4 hours, 10km

It's best to get an early start for stream crossings to avoid high water from glacial melt. Contour roughly southeast through the forest to reach a ravine heavily eroded by a small torrent. Metal railings and ladders have been erected here to help trekkers cross, but these aids occasionally get blown out by flash floods, so you might have to negotiate this somewhat dangerous obstacle using your own wits.

Continue on, rising and dipping along the steep slopes high above Glaciar Grey to enter a second ravine, which should be easier to cross than the first. On the bottom of the ravine, snow and other material suspended over the rushing water can be unstable and dangerous so try to move along.

Along much of this section fires have killed most of regenerating forest after the original forest was burnt out decades ago. Eventually leaving the fire-damaged area behind, the route leads through pleasant *coigüe* forest to arrive at **Campamento Guardas**, two to three hours on from Campamento Paso. This free campsite with a squat toilet and a three-sided cooking shelter offers the only authorized camping between Campamento Paso and Refugio Grey. Please help to keep it clean. A pretty cascade on the lower side of the campsite provides uncontaminated water. A short, unmarked trail leads from Campamento Guardas to a lookout with wonderful views across the glacier.

The route now takes an undulating course past Glaciar Grey, whose mighty snout (divided into two by a large rock outcrop, a so-called nunatak) forms the northern end of Lago Grey. The unstable, 200m-thick wall of ice continually sends large blocks – some as big as a house – plunging into the freezing waters. Strong winds sail these icebergs across the lake, leaving them stranded around the shoreline. The best vantage points for this spectacle are reached via short side trails passed just before the main path cuts up behind a minor peninsula.

Descend gently to a signposted path junction and proceed briefly right to arrive at **Refugio Grey** (camping per site CH$3500, bunks CH$15,000), 45 minutes to one hour down from Campamento Guardas. Run by Vertices, this *refugio* looks out towards Glaciar Grey from a lovely little lakeside meadow with its own pebble beach. It has toilets, hot showers and meals available. Though it may be just the thing for a whisky cocktail, please don't remove the floating glacial ice nearby.

If you want to hike on the glacier, contact **Rutas Patagonia** (☎ 061-613874; www.rutaspatagonia.com), the sole company with a park concession for ice treks (CH$70,000; Oct-May) on Glaciar Grey. You can also visit their operations base in a corner of the campsite. There's a tourist launch (CH$40,000 one-way, twice daily) that travels between the dock near the Hostería Lago Grey (at the southern end of the lake) and Glaciar Grey, calling in at Refugio Grey. On occasion, strong winds,

THE ERASURE OF GLACIERS

Ribbons of ice, stretched flat in sheets or sculpted by weather and fissured by pressure, glaciers' raw magnificence is boggling to behold. During the ice age nearly a third of the planet sat under glaciers, now they only cover about 10%.

Yet hundreds dot the Patagonian landscape. The most accessible are in Argentina's Parque Nacional Los Glaciares (home of the famous Perito Moreno glacier), Chile's Torres del Paine and Bernardo O'Higgins National Parks, along the Beagle Channel and Chile's Patagonian fjords. Consider now as the time to see them. While manmade greenhouse gases turn up the heat on the planet (about 0.7°C this century), most northern Patagonian glaciers are thinning at a rate of 2m per year. In the past decade some are retreating hundreds of meters per year.

You can see the global trend for yourself at the **Extreme Ice Survey** (www.extremeicesurvey.org), with stunning photographs and a page on how to reduce our carbon footprint.

Carolyn McCarthy with contributions by Ursula Rick

icebergs or mechanical problems suspend operations.

Day 6: Refugio Grey to Mountain Lodge Paine Grande

3–4 hours, 11km, 300m ascent/descent

Return to the junction a few minutes up from the *refugio* and follow the main path on behind a long rock rib. After descending slightly past a large waterfall and crossing its raging torrent on a bridge over a tiny gorge, the route continues leftwards up a steep, muddy slope equipped with handrails. Accompanied by the sharp ice-shrouded peaks of Cerro Paine Grande jutting up to the left, you now begin a steady upward traverse via narrow glacial terraces covered with the prostrate, heatherlike *brecillo* high above Lago Grey to cross a saddle after two to 2½ hours.

Make your way on around the left side of a little lake perched scenically above Lago Grey, then descend southeastwards through a broad dry gully vegetated with *maihuén* and *mogote* bushes to reach an attractive grassy plain at the northwestern shore of **Lago Pehoé**, one to 1½ hours on. The national park *guardería*, with weather forecasts posted on the door, occupies the old *refugio*. Away to the right, looking out across the brilliant turquoise lake, stands **Mountain Lodge Paine Grande**. This enormous *refugio* has a bar, expensive cafeteria and small food store. Campsites spread out behind the lodge, where there are boardwalks leading to a round cooking shelter and bathrooms with running water.

Except when strong winds or mechanical breakdowns stop it from operating, a motorized catamaran runs between Mountain Lodge Paine Grande and Pudeto (one way/round-trip per person CH$11,000/17,000, about 40 minutes, three daily). The boat landing is to the right, beyond the *refugio*.

ALTERNATIVE FINISH: LAGO DEL TORO

4–5½ hours, 17.5km

Climb over a minor ridge at the western edge of the grassy plain, beyond the *refugio*, sidling up and down around the mostly steep lakeside to reach a tiny bay opposite some islets after 45 minutes to one hour. Stop to catch the stunning view of the Cuernos del Paine rising up from the brilliant turquoise waters of Lago Pehoé.

Cut southeastwards away from the lake, first over ancient moraine mounds now covered with grasses and light scrub, then across a broad *pampa* to meet the broad, cloudy-green **Río Grey** (the outlet of Lago Grey). Follow the undulating path downstream along often steep banks, climbing high to avoid cliffs before you drop down to the riverside to reach **Campamento Las Carretas**, a free campsite in a slight depression (giving shelter from winds), after 1¾ to 2¼ hours. Past fires have killed off the *ñirres* here.

The route now breaks away from the Río Grey, turning gradually east as it crosses a wide expanse of windy steppes, where flocks of *bandurrias* and occasional groups of *ñandú* may be observed. (Trekkers heading in the other direction are almost certain to encounter strong northwesterly headwinds along this section.) The path arrives

at a road (to Lago Grey); turn left and trek along trails not far to its left to arrive at the **administration center at Lago del Toro** after a final 1½ to 2¼ hours. Buses from Puerto Natales terminate here (see Getting There & Away, p192).

Day 7: Mountain Lodge Paine Grande to Refugio Los Cuernos

3½–4½ hours, 13km

Pick up the path near the *guardería*, rising around the steepening lakeside before you break away north-northeast to reach **Lago Skottsberg**. The route gently rises and dips around the western side of this windswept lake, with views of small hanging glaciers slipping down the southern flank of Cerro Paine Grande.

Climb over a minor crest with stretches of boardwalks, and continue past a smaller lake on your right to meet the **Río Francés** on its true right bank. Head upstream to cross the river in two bites, on a footbridge across a secondary braid, then a suspension bridge over the main branch, and enter the popular free campsite **Campamento Italiano** after two to 2½ hours. Level sites and a pit toilet are just a couple of minutes downstream. Visitor impact has been particularly high here. If you camp, please do so conscientiously.

Continue downstream and swing to the east below the imposing Cuernos del Paine with fine views back up the Valle del Francés. About midway between Campamento Italiano and Refugio Los Cuernos, you will come to a right hand turn-off (marked) for **Campamento Francés** (camping per person CH$4000). A five-minute walk takes you to this new campsite with full facilities (including showers and toilets). Run by Fantástico Sur, it is slated to open in late 2009.

After rounding a shoulder to bring the *refugio* ahead into view, the track descends to the rocky northern shore of Lago Nordenskjöld. Ignoring an unmarked branch that heads into the forest, take the lakeshore trail, crossing a couple of small streams, to reach **Refugio Los Cuernos** (camping per person CH$4000, bunks CH$19,000, 2-person cabins with hot tub CH$69,000) after 1½ to two hours. This can be a very windy spot and sheltered campsites are few. Campers may use the toilets and showers in the Fantástico Sur–operated *refugio*, and meals and hot drinks are available.

SIDE TRIP: VALLE DEL FRANCÉS

3–4 hours return, 12km, 520m ascent/descent

This superb side trip into the awesome valley between the Cuernos del Paine and Cerro Paine Grande should not be missed – not even if you're knackered and near completing the Paine Circuit! One good option is to combine Day 6 with the first part of Day 7; after a night at Campamento Italiano or Francés either spend an entire day exploring the Valle del Francés, or visit the valley and continue to Refugio Los Cuernos the same day.

Head upstream through Campamento Italiano, then follow paint markings leading through boulder rubble up to your right to gain a lateral moraine ridge. The route traces this forested ridgetop, then drops down leftwards past where the Río Francés shoots through a cool water slide, before climbing on through the woods to reach an opening that's a **natural lookout.**

Enjoy the exciting views of the **Glaciar Francés**. Hanging icefalls cling to the sheer black-rock east face of Cerro Paine Grande where whopping hunks of ice dislodge and crash into the valley. Their shattered fragments then re-form into a small glacier that finally melts into two murky pools. Looking southwards, the view stretches beyond Lago del Toro on the park's southern periphery.

Head on into the upper valley, rising at a more gentle grade beside the stream through a bonsai forest of lovely alpine *lenga*. After crossing a waterlogged grassy area with fine views of the Cuerno's ice-formed 'horns' up to your right, the path enters the forest to reach **Campamento Británico**, without facilities, after 1½ to two hours.

From Campamento Británico a foot track continues for 10 to 15 minutes to a **mirador** with grandstand views of the peaks surrounding the head of the valley. Backtrack down the Río Francés to Campamento Italiano. Really eager trekkers can follow rough tracks beyond the mirador to the northeast, up a gully past another fine viewpoint, and northwest, up to two attractive tarns near the tree line at the head of the valley.

Day 8: Refugio Los Cuernos to Hotel Las Torres

2¾–4 hours, 11km, 160m ascent, 100m descent

Behind the *refugio*, cross the stream on a substantial bridge and head east over a headland. After climbing steadily above Lago Nordenskjöld, the track levels out and passes alongside a compact cliff line, then through a gap after 40 minutes to one hour.

Continue roughly northeast, crossing an eroded stream gully and another headland before coming to Río Arrieros, a large stream in a wide stony gully, after 35 to 45 minutes. Go upstream if necessary to wade across several minor braids, then back down to track level to cross the major branch. This can be a daunting prospect after rain or warm weather (which increases the melt rate of the small glacier that feeds the stream). If you are alone, cross with another group, using a point-person to spot.

Continue past a short cut to Refugio El Chileno on the left. Use the stepping stones to cross the tiny outlet stream of a little lake. After a 'El Chileno' signpost just past the little lake, the route winds through a small valley beside a sizable stream hidden in *lenga* on the left. Splash across the stream where it emerges into the open and regain the track, which leads around a moraine and across a grassy plain to cross the Río Ascensio suspension bridge. Continue to **Hotel Las Torres** (p198) after 1½ to 2¼ hours.

PINGO-ZAPATA

Duration 2 days
Distance 28km
Difficulty easy
Start/Finish Guardería Lago Grey
Nearest Town Puerto Natales
Transport
Summary Head up a tranquil forested valley to view two glaciers right on the edge of the Hielo Sur.

This trek takes you into the wild western sector of Parque Nacional Torres del Paine, beyond Lago Grey through the Pingo Valley. Spilling down from the edge of the Hielo Sur. Here, Glaciares Pingo and Zapata give rise to Río Pingo and its tributary, Río de los Hielos. Magellanic forest lines the valley and *calafate* bushes fill the undulating riverbanks, their edible berries ripe in February and March. Small numbers of *huemul* thrive in this isolated region.

PLANNING

The simple return trek to Campamento Zapata follows a marked and very well- trodden path – if anything, too well-trodden by horses – and presents little route-finding difficulty. The gradient rises gently along the course of the river, and there are no really strenuous sections. Mosquitoes can be a problem in late December and January.

At the time of writing, a crucial footbridge over the Río de los Hielos had still not been replaced several years after a flood destroyed it. The park authorities have no immediate plans to rebuild this bridge, and in its absence – although some intrepid trekkers wade the icy waters – the Río de los Hielos is unsafe to cross. This means that Lago Pingo, into which Glaciar Pingo calves in spectacular fashion, must be viewed from a distance. Easily visited on a side trip, though, is the smaller but still impressive unnamed lake, fed by Glaciar Zapata, that is the source of the Río de los Hielos.

The trek takes two days, but an extra day spent exploring this lovely area is time well spent. Trekkers should sign in and out at the beginning and end of the trek at Guardería Lago Grey.

GETTING TO/FROM THE TREK

The trek begins and finishes at the parking lot of Guardería Lago Grey at the southern end of Lago Grey. It's 18km beyond the park administration center at Lago del Toro, where buses to the park from Puerto Natales terminate (see Getting There & Away, p198), and about 1km beyond Hostería Lago Grey (p198). The only sure way to get here is to hike the road, drive yourself or contract a private transfer in Puerto Natales. With luck, you may be able to order a transfer here via radio contact from a *refugio*, if you ask nicely and are lucky. Otherwise, you can check to see if there is an available driver at the administration center or Hostería Lago Grey.

THE TREK

Day 1: Guardería Lago Grey to Campamento Zapata.

3¾–4¾ hours, 14km, 330m ascent, 230m descent

From the parking lot below the *guardería*, take the signposted foot track upstream along the western side of the river to reach **Refugio Pingo** after 30 to 40 minutes. This basic tin hut has a pit toilet and sleeping space for eight trekkers. Continue upvalley, climbing away from the Río Pingo through grassy meadows with views of Cerro Paine Grande to the northeast. The trail passes thickets of thorny *calafates* and patches of mature forest before returning riverside just before passing the signposted turn-off to the Cascada Pingo, 2½ to 3¼ hours on from Refugio Pingo. This waterfall can be visited as a 15-minute side trip.

Make your way on for 30 to 40 minutes to **Campamento Zapata** at the edge of a grassy open riverflats. The only park-approved campsites are here and at Refugio Pingo.

SIDE TRIP: MIRADOR ZAPATA

1½–2 hours return, 4km, 100m ascent/descent

Marked by signs and cairns, this rewarding return trek goes southwest from Campamento Zapata across a bare stony valley. The route swings south into *lenga* and climbs to a lookout after 35 to 45 minutes. Here Glaciar Zapata ends above a meltwater cascade feeding a small unnamed lake that drains into Río Pingo via the short-lived Río de los Hielos. For more extensive views, which include Glaciar Pingo and Lago Pingo to the northwest, follow a faint track marked with cairns south above the lake, reaching the crest of a moraine in 20 minutes. Retrace your steps to Campamento Zapata.

Day 2: Campamento Zapata to Guardería Lago Grey

3¼–3¾ hours, 14km, 230m ascent, 330m descent

Retrace the route of Day 1. With mostly downhill gradient, the going is easier.

MORE TREKS

RESERVA NACIONAL LAGO JEINIMEINI

Turquoise lakes and the rusted hues of the steppe mark the rarely visited **Reserva Nacional Jeinimeini** (admission CH$1000), 52km southwest of Chile Chico. Its unusual wonders range from cave paintings to foxes and flamingos. In the transition zone to the Patagonian steppe, it covers 1610 sq km. North of the *guardería* on the northern end of Lago Jeinimeini, **Sendero Lago Verde** takes visitors on a three-hour, 10km-round-trip hike to a gemstone lake enclosed by high glaciated cliffs. Through-hikers can link to Valle Chacabuco via a two-day mountain traverse on **Sendero La Leona**; for information contact **Estancia Valle Chacabuco** www.conservacionpatagonica.org.

The Chilean IGM 1:50,000 map *Lago Verde* (Section J, No 49) covers the key area around Lago Jeinimeini. There is no regular public transport up to Reserva Nacional Lago Jeinimeini, although in summer hitching a ride may be possible (ask at the Conaf office in Chile Chico).

RESERVA NACIONAL TAMANGO

Tamango Circuit

Boasting Chile's largest population of endangered *huemul* deer, **Reserva Nacional Tamango** (admission CH$3000) protects a 70-sq-km transition zone to the Patagonian steppe. *Huemul* are notoriously shy, but chances of sighting one are better here than anywhere. A three-day (33km), easy–moderate circuit leads from Laguna Tamango (from where more experienced trekkers can climb the 1722m Cerro Tamango in a six-hour side trip) to Lago Elefantita. From here, you can either traverse southwest high above Lago Cochrane to back to the Guardería El Hungaro or follow the shore to the Guardería Embarcadero, just 3km from Cochrane. **Camping Las Correntadas** (Embarcadero, Playa Paleta; 6-person campsites CH$8000, 4-person cabins CH$25,000) provides large campsites (ask about individual rates) with potable water, washbasins and toilets. Cabins have toilets but not showers. The reserve is 6km northeast of Cochrane; there is no public transportation to the entrance. At the corner of Colonia and San Valentín, hikers can take Pasaje No 1 north and then east to access trails to the entrance. Cochrane's Conaf (p195) may have trail maps.

Valle Chacabuco (Future Patagonia National Park)

Initiated in 2004 with the purchase of the 175,000-acre Estancia Valle Chacabuco by private foundation Conservación Patagónica (see boxed text, p131), the future Patagonia National Park occupies the core area of Chilean national parks' number one conservation priority for over 30 years. All of its original species are still intact – including thousands of guanacos, *huemul* deer, the rare mountain vizcacha, puma, culpeo fox, and many species of birds, rare orchids and an extraordinary array of wildflowers.

Trekkers will find diverse landscapes from high alpine and glacial peaks to southern beach forests, the Patagonian grasslands, lakes, lagoons, rivers and many wetlands rarely found within the Patagonia landscape.

Park infrastructure is currently under construction to include a visitors center, restaurant, campsites, volunteer bunkhouses, trails and signage. The visitors center and restaurant should be completed by 2011. While trails are still under construction, visitors can get hiking information at the *guardería* or *centro de administración* on site. Trails are planned to connect with Reserva Nacional Lago Cochrane and Reserva Nacional Lago Jeinimeini. Check for updated information at www.conservacionpatagonica.org.

Valle Chacabuco is accessible by road on the Carretera Austral, about 20 km north of Cochrane or via the Paso Roballos frontier crossing to Argentina.

PARQUE NACIONAL PERITO MORENO

Wild and windblown, Parque Nacional Perito Moreno is an adventurer's dream. Approaching from the steppe, the massive snowcapped peaks of the Sierra Colorada rise like sentinels. Guanacos graze the tufted grasses, condors circle above and wind blurs the surfaces of Technicolor aquamarine and cobalt lakes. If you come here you will be among 1200 yearly visitors – that is, mostly alone. Solitude reigns and, save for services offered by local *estancias*, you are entirely on your own.

Its name honors the park system's founder, the park encompasses 1150 sq km, 310km southwest of the town of Perito Moreno. For more information, contact the **national parks administration office** (☎ 02962-491477; San Martín 882; 9am-4pm Mon-Fri) in the small town of Gobernador Gregores, 225km from the *guardería* near the east end of Lago Belgrano.

An easy overnight trek goes to Lago Azara from the end of the road near Cerro Mie. The track leads five hours around the southern side of Lago Belgrano to Puesto del Nueve, a rustic hut that serves as a good base for exploring the area. A four-day return trek from Estancia El Rincón, owned by Conservación Patagónica (www.conservacionpatagonica.org), leads up via the Río Lácteo (shown on IGM maps as 'Río Late') to a *refugio* at around 1000m. From here, a more difficult route climbs to two high glacial lakes known as Lagunas Los Tempanos.

From October to March both Estancia **La Oriental** (☎ 02962-452196, in Buenos Aires, 011-4343 2366/9568; gesino@fibertel.com.ar; s/d/t/q AR$204/267/314/393, camping per person AR$47), which lies inside the park, and the hospitable **Estancia Menelik** (satellite ☎ 011-4152 5500, in Buenos Aires 011-4836 3502; www.cielospatagonicos.com; s/d/q AR$188/251/377, *refugio* per person AR$63) offer accommodation.

The Argentine IGM's 1:100,000 maps *Lago Belgrano* (Santa Cruz, Nos 4772-33 & 4772-32) and *Monte Tetris* (Santa Cruz, No 4972-3) cover the park. There is no public transportation but tour agency **Las Loicas** (☎ 02963-490272, 15-4213194; http://lasloicas.com) provides transport from Perito Moreno.

PARQUE NACIONAL LOS GLACIARES

For more backcountry routes in the park, consult the extremely helpful *guardaparques* at the park ranger office in El Chaltén (p197).

Lago Toro

Lago Toro's raw setting makes it a worthy objective for this two-day trek. Hikers must register first at the park office. The route begins behind the park ranger office, leading southwards across a footbridge then southwest to a shallow lake on a little plateau looking out towards Cerro Huemul. Pass the sign for Lomo de Peigue Tumbado (a four-hour ascent with views of Cerros Torres and Fitz Roy) on your right. Continue traversing straight with views of the valley below. Only camp at the marked campsite with latrine.

Experienced trekkers with appropriate gear can continue up to Paso del Viento at the edge of the Hielo Sur, a trackless route that takes another long day. Cross a short section of the lower Glaciar Río Tunel (there are no crevasses on this part of the glacier), continuing around a tiny lake at the snout of a second glacier before you ascend steeply southwest over scree slopes to the pass.

El Chaltén (Argentina) to Villa O'Higgins (Chile)

Trekkers can skirt the Southern Ice Field to get from Argentina's Parque Nacional Los Glaciares to Chile's Villa O'Higgins. The one- to three-day trip can be completed between November and March. Bring all provisions, plus your passport and rain gear. The trek starts at Lago del Desierto, 37km north of El Chaltén. Check Chilean ferry schedules pre-departure.

Shuttle service **Las Lengas** (☎ 02962-493044; Viedma 95) goes to Lago del Desierto (AR$80, one hour), leaving El Chaltén at 7am daily. From there, either take the tour boat run by **Patagonia Aventura** (☎ 02962-493110; www.patagonia-aventura.com.ar, in Spanish; per person AR$90) or hike along the eastern shore (15km, five hours) to the north end of the lake. Camping is allowed here. Continue through Argentine customs and immigration, 1½ hours to Laguna Larga. The route becomes a well-worn vehicle track, passing Laguna Redonda. After three hours you will reach **Candelario Mansilla** and Chilean customs and immigration.

In Candelario Mansilla a family offers meals, camping and basic farmhouse accommodations; bring Chilean pesos, if possible. If you leave El Chaltén first thing in the morning, it's possible to cross the Chilean border and reach Candelario Mansilla in one long day.

Chilean excursion boat **Hielo Sur** (www.villaohiggins.com, in Spanish) goes from Candelario Mansilla to Puerto Bahamondez (CH$33,000). From Puerto Bahamondez, there is bus service to Villa O'Higgins (CH$1500), 7kms away. The boat travels two to three times per week.

The most useful map is Zagier & Urruty's *Monte Fitz Roy & Cerro Torre Trekking-Mountaineering, Lago del DesiertoTrekking-Travel Map*, with a 1:100,000 insert showing the route.

PARQUE NACIONAL TORRES DEL PAINE

Laguna Verde

This is a longish one-day trek to a large shallow lake where bird life and guanacos can be observed. Just north of the Río Paine bridge (2.5km north of the administration center) a foot track climbs northeast and leads across the windy steppes to Laguna Verde. At the southeastern corner of the lake are a *hostería* and a Conaf guardería open from October until March. There's nowhere to stay other than the *hostería*, and camping is not permitted.

Salto Paine & Cuernos Lookout

From the Pudeto boat landing a 1½- to two-hour return trek leads via the nearby surging falls of Salto Grande (where the Río Paine enters Lago Pehoé), to a lookout point from where there are classic views across Lago Nordenskjöld to the imposing Cuernos del Paine immediately north of the lake.

TOWNS & FACILITIES

CARRETERA AUSTRAL LODGINGS

The following are recommended lodgings on the road between Coyhaique and Cochrane.

La Casa del Río Konaiken (www.konaiken.blog.com; 2-person cabins CH$40,000) These stylish cabins on the forested shores of the Baker River, 6km south of Puerto Bertrand, dish out tranquility. There's plenty of personalized attention if you want it, including reiki and massage, as well as treats like woodstove fires, wholegrain pies and homemade jams.

Terra Luna (☎ 067-431263; www.terra-luna.cl; two-person huts CH$30,000, d/tr/q incl breakfast CH$80,000/90,000/110,000) Anglers and mountaineers hunker down at these attractive cabins with a hot tub tucked into the woods. Budget travelers should check out the rustic huts with kitchen. They are run by Azimut, a French-owned guide service with glacier trips, and are 1.5km from Puerto Guadal toward Chile Chico.

El Puesto (☎ satellite 02-1964555; www.elpuesto.cl; Pedro Lagos 258; Puerto Rio Tranquilo; s/d CH$45,000/55,000) This modern wood home pampers guests with woollen slippers, hand-woven throws and rockers. English-speaking owners Francisco and Tamara also have a reputable professional guide service offering ice trekking on Glaciar Exploradores and other services.

COCHRANE (CHILE)

☎ 067 / pop 3000

This old ranching outpost is the southern hub of the Carretera Austral. Not much is going on here, but if the dams proposals push through there will be an onslaught of workers and construction. Residents are currently very divided.

Open only in summer, the **tourist kiosk** (☎ 067-522326; turismo@cochranepatagonia.cl; Plaza de Armas; 10am-1pm & 2-9pm Jan-Feb) has information on camping and lodging. **Conaf** (☎ 067-522164; Río Nef 417; 10am-6pm Mon-Sat), at the uphill edge of town, can give advice on treks in the area. On the plaza, **Melero Ferreteria-Tienda** (☎ 067-522197; Golondrinas 148) sells supplies and white gasoline.

Sleeping & Eating

With warm hospitality, **Latitude 47** (☎ 067-522280; Lago Brown 564; r per person without bathroom CH$8000) has a selection of narrow upstairs rooms with single beds. Front rooms are superior. The frilly **Hospedaje Rubio** (☎ 067-522173; Sargente Marino 871; s/d CH$14,000/24,000) has comfortable, well-furnished doubles. **Ñirrantal** (☎ 067-522760; Av O'Higgins 650; mains CH$5000; lunch & dinner) serves salmon or meat and mashed potatoes with homemade cherry compote.

Getting There & Away

Bus schedules change frequently; check companies for their most current schedule. Buses to Coyhaique (CH$10,000, seven to 10 hours) typically leave between 8am and 9.30am. The following have services several days per week: **Buses Don Carlos** (☎ 067-522550; Prat 334), **Buses Acuario 13** (☎ 067-522-143; Río Baker 349) and **Buses Interlagos** (☎ 067-522606; San Valentín 599).

For Villa O'Higgins (CH$12,000, six hours), **Buses Los Ñadis** (☎ 067-522448; Los Helechos 490) departs at 2:30pm on Monday and Thursday. Don Carlos buses also go twice weekly.

Chile Chico (CH$12,000, six hours), near Reserva Nacional Jeinimeini (p192), is served by **Transportes Ale** (☎ 067-522448; Las Golondrinas 399) at 10am on Sunday and Thursday.

EL CALAFATE (ARGENTINA)

☎ 02902 / pop 600

Named for the berry that, once eaten, guarantees your return to Patagonia, El Calafate hooks you with another irresistible attraction: Glaciar Perito Moreno, 80km away in Parque Nacional Los Glaciares. On the southern shore of Lago Argentino, El Calafate lives almost entirely off the hubbub over that big, beautiful hunk of ice. While the town's intrinsic attractions are limited, there are far worse places to spend a day.

Information

Parque Nacional Los Glaciares office (☎ 02902-491005/755; Av Libertador 1302; 8am-7pm Mon-Fri, 10am-8pm Sat & Sun) offers brochures and a decent map of the southern part of Parque Nacional Los Glaciares. El Calafate's **tourist office** (☎ 02902-491090; www.elcalafate.gov.ar, in Spanish; 8am-10pm daily) is at the bus station.

The town website is www.calafate.com.

Supplies & Equipment

Stock up here for treks in Parque Nacional Los Glaciares. Two of the biggest supermarkets are **La Anónima** (Libertador 902), at the east end of town, and **Alas** (9 de Julio 59); both open daily until late. **La Leyenda** (Libertador 1180; 10am-1pm & 5-10pm daily) sells white gas (*solvente*) for stoves. **Paralelo 53** (☎ 02902-492596; 25 de Mayo 38) sells quality outdoor clothing, footwear, backpacks and accessories.

Various shops along Av del Libertador sell trekking maps.

INTERNATIONAL TREKKING FESTIVAL

The first Argentine attempt on Fitz Roy was on March 18, 1948 and each year, El Chaltén honors the date with the **International Trekking Festival**. Held around the third weekend of March, it's not just an excuse to drink beer; it has events like the *trekkatlon*, climbing competitions and live ska-punk. Find details at the local APN or municipal tourist office.

Sleeping & Eating

Lodgings are plentiful but book ahead if you're picky. Most places can do airport pickups.

Camping El Ovejero (☎ 02902-493422; campinglovejero@hotmail.com; José Pantín; sites per person AR$20; dm AR$35) has woodsy, well-kept, secure sites by the creek just north of the bridge into town and a newly added hostel. There is 24-hour hot water.

America del Sur (☎ 02902-493525; www.americahostel.com.ar; Puerto Deseado 151; dm/d AR$50/220) boasts top-tier service and big views. One thing you won't find here is solitude – it's bustling at every hour.

Traveler-run **Albergue Lago Argentino** (☎ 02902-491423; www.losglaciares.com/lagoargentino; Campaña del Desierto 1050; dm/d without bathroom AR$40/120, s/d with bathroom AR$160/180) boasts good-vibe, basic dorms and bike rentals. Its annex has quiet garden rooms geared towards couples. Megalodging **Calafate Hostel** (☎ 02902-492450/2; www.calafatehostels.com; Moyano 1226; dm AR$50, s/d/t standard AR$120/160/190, superior AR$140/180/240) has double-bunk dorms and tidy brick doubles, cafe service, tours and bilingual desk staff. The very friendly **Hospedaje Familiar Las Cabañitas** (☎ 02902-491118; lascabanitas@cotecal.com.ar; Valentín Feilberg 218; d/t/q AR$180/210/240) has storybook A-frames and a sheltered dining patio brimming with plants. There's hot-beverage service, kitchen use and meals upon request.

Café fare is exquisite at **Viva la Pepa** (☎ 02902-491880; Amado 833; mains AR$21-40; 10am-midnight, closed Wed), with gourmet sandwiches (blue cheese and roasted apples with chicken), crepes and even *maté*. Grill house **La Tablita** (☎ 02902-491065; Coronel Rosales 24; mains AR$30-50) serves perfect steaks, add a fresh salad or garlic fries, but you must reserve ahead. **Pura Vida** (☎ 02902-493356; Av Libertador 1876; mains AR$30-50; dinner Thu-Tue) does wholegrain fare and abundant vegetarian dishes with candlelight style, it's a ten-minute walk west of the center.

Upstairs in the gnome village, **Librobar** (☎ 02902-491464; Av Libertador 1015) serves coffee and beers alongside poetry chapbooks. There's good occasional live music.

Getting There & Away

The modern **Aeropuerto El Calafate** (ECA; ☎ 02902-491220/30) is 23km east of town off RP 11; the departure tax is AR$54. **Aerolíneas Argentinas** (☎ 02902-492814/16; 9 de Julio 57) flies daily to Bariloche (AR$879), Ushuaia (AR$350) and Buenos Aires (AR$380 to AR$675). **LADE** (☎ 02902-491262; at bus terminal) flies a few times a week to Ushuaia (AR$280), Esquel (AR$412), Buenos Aires (AR$336) and other smaller regional airports.

El Calafate's hilltop **bus terminal** (Av Roca s/n) is easily reached by a pedestrian staircase from the corner of Av Libertador and 9 de Julio. Book ahead in high season, as outbound seats can be in short supply. For El Chaltén (AR$60, three hours), several companies share passengers and leave daily at 7.30am, 8am and 6.30pm. For Puerto Natales (AR$50, five hours), **Cootra** (☎ 02902-491444) departs daily at 8.30am.

Freddy (☎ 02902-452671) and **Interlagos** (☎ 02902-491179) offer connections to Bariloche and Ushuaia that require leaving in the middle of the night and a change of buses in Río Gallegos.

From mid-October to April, **Chaltén Travel** (☎ 02902-492212/480; www.chaltentravel.com; Av Libertador 1174) goes to El Chaltén (AR$70, three hours) four times daily. It also runs shuttles north along RN 40 to Perito Moreno and Los Antiguos departing on odd-numbered days at 8am, to connect with onward service to Bariloche the next morning. See prices under El Chaltén (p197).

EL CHALTÉN (ARGENTINA)

☎ 02962 / pop 600

This ragtag village serves the thousands of visitors on summer pilgrimages to explore the range. Unpolished but appealing, it's Argentina's youngest town (created in the 1980s) and hiker services continue to evolve rapidly; the recent paving of RP 23 may improve them, even as it makes way for large-scale tourism.

Information

All incoming buses stop at the **park ranger office** (☎ 02962-493004/024; park admission free, donations welcome; 8am-7pm) for a short orientation and free map. Register here for uncommon routes in the park; the staff is gracious and knowledgeable. The **municipal tourist office** (☎ 02962-493270; comfomelchalten@yahoo.com.ar; Av MM De Güemes 21; 8am-8pm) is extremely helpful, with an informative town website at www.elchalten.com.

Gas canisters are available at **Viento Oeste** (☎ 02962-493200; Av San Martín 898), where camping gear is also rented. Friendly and professional guide services include **Casa de Guias** (☎ 02962-493118; www.casadeguias.com.ar; Av San Martín s/n) and **Fitz Roy Expediciones** (☎/fax 493-017; www.fitzroyexpediciones.com.ar; Av San Martín s/n), with English-speaking AAGM (Argentine Association of Mountain Guides) certified guides. Both offer worthwhile ice-trekking trips below Cerro Torre.

Sleeping & Eating

Across from the park ranger office and visitor center, **Campamento Confluencia** (sites free) is without extra amenities, register at the office. Visitors are limited to a seven-day stay.

The homey **Condor de Los Andes** (☎ 02962-493101; www.condordelosandes.com; cnr Río de las Vueltas & Halvor Halvorsen; dm/d AR$40/180; Oct-Apr) has the feel of a ski lodge, with worn bunks, warm rooms and a roaring fire. Attentive **Nothofagus B&B** (☎ 02962-493087; www.nothofagusbb.com.ar/; cnr Hensen & Riquelme; s/d with shared bathroom AR$130/140 s/d/t with bathroom 200/210/260; Sep-Apr) is tidy, comfortable and green, They are among few Patagonian lodgings to separate organic waste and replaces towels only when asked.

Known for its congenial atmosphere, **Albergue Patagonia** (☎ 02962-493019; www.elchalten.com/patagonia; Av San Martín 493; dm AR$50, d with shared/private bathroom AR$140/230; Sep-May) has spacious, modern dorms and common areas. Doubles with bathroom are worth coveting. Backpacker factory **Rancho Grande Hostel** (☎ 02962-493092; www.ranchograndehostel.com/chalten; Av San Martín 724; dm/d AR$50/220) churns out clean bunkrooms, adventure tours, reservation services and a cafe.

Get groceries at **La Tostada Moderna** (San Martin 36; 9am-10pm). **Patagonicus** (☎ 02962-493025; cnr Av MM De Güemes & Andreas Madsen; pizzas AR$21) bakes 20 kinds of pizza, in addition to salads and wine served at sturdy wood tables. The memorable **El Bodegón Cervecería** (☎ 02962-493109; Av San Martín s/n; snacks AR$12) brews authentic Czeck pilsner to popular acclaim. Don't miss the heavenly locro (a spicy stew of maize, beans and pork). **Fuegia Bistro** (☎ 02962-493019; Av San Martín 493; mains AR$18-34) serves savory mains and ethnic veggie options with a reasonable wine list. It's among few spots open for breakfast.

Getting There & Away

El Chaltén is located 220km from El Calafate via newly paved roads.

Chaltén Travel (☎ 02962-493005/092; www.chaltentravel.com; cnr San Martín 724) has four daily departures for El Calafate (AR$70, 3½ hours) in summer from Rancho Grande Hostel. **Cal-tur** (☎ 02962-493079; San Martín 520) and **Taqsa** (☎ 02962-493068; Av Antonio Rojo 88) also make the trip. Service is less frequent off-season.

Las Lengas (☎ 02962-493-023/227; Antonio de Viedma 95) runs minivans at 5.30am to coastal destinations on RN 3 and transport to Lago del Desierto. **El Huemul Transfer** (☎ 02962-493312; www. elchalten.com/elhuemul) goes to trailheads at Hostería El Pilar and the Río Electrico bridge for AR$35 per person.

Chaltén Travel heads north via RN 40 to Perito Moreno, Los Antiguos (up to 15 hours, both AR$190) and Bariloche

(AR$380, two days) on odd-numbered days at 8am.

PARQUE NACIONAL TORRES DEL PAINE LODGINGS (CHILE)

The following are highlights of Parque Nacional Torres del Paine's ever-expanding lodging offerings. Prices are high season.

Posada Río Serrano (☎ 02-1930338, 061-613-531 in Puerto Natales; www.baqueanozamora.com; dm CH$19,000, d with shared/private bathroom CH$52,000/70,000) This 19th-century ranch house is a boon to bargain hunters. While fixtures are dated, the 13 rickety rooms with central heating are pretty cozy. Groups can order a traditional *asado* (lamb barbecue).

Mountain Lodge Paine Grande (☎ 061-412742; www.verticepatagonia.cl; camping per person CH$3500, dm CH$20,000, full board CH$36,000, two-person dome CH$20,000; year-round) Its scale is decidedly not sustainable for a mountain *refugio*, but guests do love the bar's daily happy hour and the sublime Cuernos views. All beds are dorms, for greater privacy, there's deluxe camping in domes.

Hotel Las Torres (☎ 061-710050; www.lastorres.com; Magallanes 960, Punta Arenas; s/d US$267/305; closed Jun) A hospitable and well-run hotel with international standards and good guided excursions. Most noteworthy, the hotel recycles and donates a portion of package fees to the nonprofit park-based environmental group AMA (Agrupación Medio Ambiental Torres del Paine).

Hostería Lago Grey (☎ 061-712100; www.lagogrey.cl; s/d/tr incl breakfast US$301/348/398) Open year-round, this tasteful hotel has 30 well appointed rooms. It is snug and elegant, with clusters of white cottages linked by raised boardwalks. Zodiac boat tours (three hours, CH$40,000) are available on the lake, but not to the glacier.

explora (☎ 02-2066060 in Santiago; www.explora.com; four nights d per person US$2920) With otherworldly luxury, this elite retreat spoils sophisticated travelers taking a stab at adventure. Rates include airport transfers, full gourmet meals and a wide variety of excursions led by assuredly handsome bilingual guides.

PUERTO NATALES (CHILE)

☎ 061 / pop 18,000

Hunkered on the windy eastern shore of Seno Última Esperanza (Last Hope Sound), Puerto Natales is the gateway to Parque Nacional Torres del Paine. It's a Gore-Tex mecca, but there is appeal in its corrugated tin houses and granny-style lodgings.

Information

In the Museo Histórico, the **Municipal tourist office** (☎ 061-411263; Bulnes 285; 8.30am-12.30pm & 2.30-6pm Tue-Sun) has region-wide lodgings listings. **Conaf** (Corporación Nacional Forestal; ☎ 061-411438; O'Higgins 584) has national parks information. **Fantástico Sur** (☎ 061-614184; www.fantasticosur.com; Esmeralda 661) manages Las Torres, El Chileno and Los Cuernos *refugios* and campsites in Parque Nacional Torres del Paine. **Vertice Patagonia** (☎ 061-412742; www.verticepatagonia.cl) runs *refugios* and campsites Mountain Lodge Paine Grande, Lago Grey, Dickson and Perros in Torres del Paine. **Erratic Rock** (☎ 061-410355; Baquedano 719) aims to keep Torres del Paine sustainable with good visitor advice, alternative options, informative talks and gear rentals.

Supplies & Equipment

Buy supplies for Torres del Paine treks in Puerto Natales. Supermarket **Abugosh** (Bulnes 742) has the biggest selection of foodstuff. Wine and cheese shop **Emporio de la Pampa** (☎ 061-413279; Eberhard 302; 9am-10.30pm Sep-Apr) has trail goodies including fresh coffee, hearty brown bread and regional goat cheese. Get camping gear and gas at **La Maddera** (☎ 061-413318, 24hr emergency ☎ 099-418-4100; www.lamadderaoutdoor.com; Prat 297; 8am-11.30pm) sells gas and camping gear and also fixes damaged camping equipment. You can call after-hours if you need something for an early departure. Bookstores and souvenir shops sell trekking maps of Torres del Paine.

Sleeping & Eating

For a small town, Puerto Natales brims with lodgings, many guesthouses also store bags and rent camping gear. Family-run **Hospedaje Nancy** (☎ 061-410022; www.nataleslodge.cl; Ramírez 540; r per person without bathroom CH$5000) offers lived-in rooms with kitchen privileges and internet access. On the plaza, **Patagonia Aventura** (☎ 061-411028; www.apatagonia.com; Tomás Rogers 179; dm/d without bathroom CH$9000/21,000) is a comfortable full-service hostel with an attached gear shop. Ideal for couples, **Erratic Rock II** (☎ 061-412317; www.erraticrock2.com; Benjamin Zamora 732; d CH$30,000) offers spacious decked-out doubles and tidy new bathrooms. With a focus on environmental education and recycling, the eccentric **4Elementos** (☎ 099-5246956; www.4elementos.cl, Esmeralda 813; s/tw/d CH$15,000/30,000/45,000) has simple, comfortable rooms and amazing breakfasts. A pampered finale to your trip, **Hotel Indigo** (☎ 061-418718; www.indigopatagonia.com; Ladrilleros 105; d/std/ste US$260-350) is a stunner, with fresh, modern design and rooftop Jacuzzis.

A sacred post-trek ritual, **La Mesita Grande** (Prat 196; pizzas CH$5000; lunch & dinner) serves scrumptious thin-crust pizzas, quality pastas and organic salads at a community table. Locals like **La Picada de Don Carlitos** (☎ 061-414232; cnr Blanco Encalada & Esmeralda; menú del día CH$2500) for hearty Chilean fare. Well worth the splurge, **Afrigonia** (☎ 061-412232; Eberhard 343; mains CH$5000) serves spicy and fresh dishes inspired by African delicacies.

Getting There & Away

Commercial flights to Puerto Natales are not currently available.

Buses to Torres del Paine (CH$8000, 2½ hours) leave two to three times daily at around 7am, 8am and 2.30pm. If you are headed to Mountain Lodge Paine Grande in the off-season, take the morning bus (CH$8000) to meet the catamaran (CH$11,000 one way, two hours). Double-check schedules before heading out. To El Calafate, Argentina (CH$11,000, five hours), Turismo Zaahj, Cootra and Bus Sur have the most services. Companies and destinations include:

Bus Sur (☎ 061-614221; www.bus-sur.cl, in Spanish; Baquedano 658) Punta Arenas, Torres del Paine, Puerto Montt, El Calafate, Río Turbio and Ushuaia.
Buses Fernández/Pingüino (☎ 061-411111; www.busesfernandez.com; cnr Esmeralda & Ramirez) Torres del Paine and Punta Arenas (CH$4000, four hours).
Buses Gómez (☎ 061-411971; www.busesgomez.com, in Spanish; Arturo Prat 234) Torres del Paine.
Cootra (☎ 061-412-785; Baquedano 456) Goes to El Calafate daily at 7.30am.
Turismo Zaahj (☎ 061-412260/355; www.turismozaahj.co.cl, in Spanish; Arturo Prat 236/70) Torres del Paine and El Calafate.

For many travelers, a journey through Chile's spectacular fjords aboard Navimag's car and passenger ferry (p245) becomes a highlight of their trip. This four-day and three-night northbound voyage has become so popular it should be booked well in advance. You can also try your luck. To confirm when the ferries are due, contact **Turismo Comapa** (☎ 061-414300; www.comapa.com; Eberhard 555; 9am-1pm & 3-7pm Mon-Fri, 10am-2pm Sat) a couple of days before the estimated arrival date.

PUNTA ARENAS (CHILE)

☎ 061 / pop 130,136

A strange combination of the ruddy and the grand, Punta Arenas is a sprawling metropolis on the edge of the Strait of Magellan. Though central to the easy treks on Península Brunswick, it is less base camp than regional transport hub. Among the interesting stops, the **Museo Salesiano** (☎ 061-221001; Av Bulnes 374; admission CH$1500; 10am-12.30pm & 3-6pm Tue-Sun) has outstanding material on indigenous groups and the mountaineer priest Alberto De Agostini.

Information

Sernatur (☎ 061-241-330; www.sernatur.cl; Lautaro Navarro 999; 8.15am-8pm Mon-Fri Dec-Feb, 8.15am-6pm Mon-Thu, 8.15am-5pm Fri rest of year), off Plaza Muñoz Gamero, publishes a list of accommodations and transport options. **Conaf** (☎ 061-230681; Bulnes 0309) has details on the nearby parks.

Sleeping & Eating

Generous with insider tips, **Hostal La Estancia** (☎ 061-249130; www.backpackerschile.com/en/hostel-estancia.php; O'Higgins 765; dm/d without bathroom CH$8000/25,000) has big rooms with vaulted ceilings and tidy shared bathrooms.

PATAGONIA'S RIVER DEBATE

Patagonia boasts one of the world's great water reserves, with deep glacial lakes, two of the planet's largest non-polar ice fields and powerful, pristine rivers rushing from the Andes to the Pacific. It's a dream if you're a salmon, a nature lover or kayaker. Or a hydroelectric company.

It's a hot topic in Chile, where the cost of energy is much higher than in neighboring countries. Spurred by fears of a pending national energy crisis, Spanish–Italian multinational Endesa and Chile-based conglomerate HydroAysén are laying plans for large-scale dams on the Baker and Pascua rivers. By some estimates, 12 Patagonian rivers, including the Futaleufú, Manso and Puelo, are threatened. A study by the University of Chile found that tourism, the region's second-largest industry, would take a severe hit if the dams are built. While the dams would provide a short-term energy solution, in the long term they would transform one of the greatest wildernesses on earth into an industrial engine.

Popular views construe the project as necessary to protect the nation's energy reserves, but in fact the public sector uses only a third of Chile's energy – over half is consumed by the mining industry. Pristine ecosystems and rural farms are at stake, but an even greater issue is building the world's longest transmission lines. Thousands of high-voltage towers would run 2415km to bring power to Santiago and mining operations in the north. In addition, these lines would make damming other rivers feasible.

Global warming is expected to exacerbate the planet's freshwater crisis. 'Chile has an opportunity to protect sources of freshwater that are immensely valuable,' contends Gary Hughes of International Rivers, 'perhaps even priceless.'

In the Puelo Valley, the flood zone would put the farm and family burial ground of third-generation subsistence farmer Segundo Cardenas underwater. A century ago, the government gave citizens incentives to populate this remote region. In a reversal, it's now asking Patagonians to give up their waterways and in some cases their livelihood. Some feel that the country is pillaging its resource-rich south to feed the energy-hungry north.

'It doesn't make sense,' Cardenas wondered. 'When you build a house, would you take a board from one wall to patch another? That's what Chile's doing.'

For more information, contact Patagonia Sin Represas (Patagonia Without Dams; www.patagoniasinrepresas.cl), the US-based International Rivers (www.internationalrivers.org/patagonia) or the US-based NRDC (National Resources Defense Council; www.nrdc.org). For information about dams and development, check out the website at World Commission on Dams (www.dams.org).

Hip recycled bunkhouse **Imago Mundi** (☎ 061-613115; www.imagomundipatagonia.cl; Mejicana 252; dm with/without bathroom CH$10,000/8000) hosts live music, shows arthouse films and teaches climbing. There are a few snug bunks too. The on-site cafe serves homemade treats and sandwiches. If it's full, try **El Conventillo** (☎ 061-242311; www.hostalelconventillo.com; Pje. Korner 1034; dm CH$8000) an appealing brick hostel in the reviving waterfront district. The slightly upscale **Hostal Terrasur** (☎ 061-247114; www.hostalterrasur.cl; O'Higgins 123; s/d CH$28,500/38,500) offers rooms with flowing curtains and flower patterns and a miniature green courtyard.

Supermarket **Abugosh** (Bories 647) sells provisions. Chile's answer to the sidecar diner, **Lomit's** (☎ 061-243399; José Menéndez 722; mains CH$3000; 10am-2.30am) serves made-to-order burgers. Unbeatable for ambiance, **La Marmita** (☎ 061-222056; Plaza Sampaio 678; mains CH$6000-8000) prepares fresh salads and hearty, home-cooked creations.

Getting There & Away

AIR

Book ahead online for the best **Lan** (☎ 061-241100, toll free ☎ 600-5262000; www.lan.com; Bories 884) deals on national flights . Lan flies several times daily to Santiago (CH$194,000) with a stop in Puerto Montt (CH$124,000). Flights reach Ushuaia (CH$107,500) three times per week. **Sky Airline** (☎ 061-710645; www.skyairline.cl; Roca 935) flies daily between Santiago and Punta Arenas, with a stop either in Puerto Montt or Concepción.

From November to March **Aerovías DAP** (☎ 061-223340, airport ☎ 061-213776; www.dap.cl; O'Higgins 891) flies to Puerto Williams (CH$52,000) Wednesday through Saturday and Monday. Luggage is limited to 10kg per person.

BOAT

Ferry operator **Transbordador Austral Broom** (☎ 061-218100; www.tabsa.cl, in Spanish; Av Bulnes 05075), sails from the Tres Puentes ferry terminal to Puerto Williams (p223), on Isla Navarino. Departures run almost weekly, Wednesday only, returning Saturday, both at 7pm (reclining seat/bunk CH$65,250/78,000 including meals, 38 hours).

BUS

Punta Arenas has no central bus terminal. The **Central de Pasajeros** (☎ 061-245811; cnr Magallanes & Av Colón) is the closest thing to a central booking office. Destinations include Puerto Montt (CH$35,000, 36 hours), Puerto Natales (CH$4000, three hours) and Ushuaia (CH$25,000, 10 hours). Companies include:

Buses Fernández/Pingüino (☎ 061-221429/812; www.busesfernandez.com; Armando Sanhueza 745) Puerto Natales, Torres del Paine.
Buses Ghisoni/Queilen Bus (☎ 061-222714; Lautaro Navarro 975) Ushuaia and Puerto Montt.
Bus Sur (☎ 061-614-224; www.bus-sur.cl; José Menéndez 552) El Calafate, Puerto Natales, Ushuaia and Puerto Montt.
Bus Transfer (☎ 061-229613; Pedro Montt 966) Puerto Natales and airport transfers.
Turíbus (☎ 061-227970; www.busescruzdelsur.cl, in Spanish; Armando Sanhueza 745) Puerto Montt, Osorno and Chiloé.

VILLA O'HIGGINS (CHILE)

☎ 067 / pop 500

The last stop on the Carretera Austral, the isolated Villa O'Higgins boasts mythic status. The road didn't reach here until 1999. Alluring in its isolation, O'Higgins provides spectacular country to explore on horseback or foot, and it has world-class fishing.

Conaf (☎ 067-211834; Lago Cisnes 101) is right below the lookout tower (mirador). Outfitter and transporter **Hielo Sur** (☎ 067-431821/822; www.villaohiggins.com; 9am-1pm & 3-7pm Mon-Sat) has the inside scoop on just about everything: check out the website for information about town. Guided horse riding or trekking trips are available with advance booking. Bike rentals (CH$900 per hour) are also available.

Hielo Sur runs catamaran tours from Bahía Bahamondes to Candelario Mansilla (CH$25,000), from where you can go on foot to El Chaltén in Argentina, and Glaciar O'Higgins (one way/round-trip CH$33,000/40,000). The trip leaves at 8.30am on Wednesdays and Saturdays in summer, with some extra dates. The border is closed in winter, starting May 1.

Sleeping & Eating

Friendly and full-service **Camping & Albergue El Mosco** (☎ 067-431819, 098-983-9079; www.patagoniaelmosco.com; Carretera Austral Km1240; camping/dm CH$5000/10.000) has kitchen and bathroom privileges for campers; the friendly host Jorge (known around town as el Español) has information on local hikes.

Getting There & Away

Transporte Aéreo Don Carlos (☎ 067-231981, in Coyhaique; www.doncarlos.cl) flies from Coyhaique (CH$36,000, 1½ hours) on Monday and Thursday. **Buses Los Ñadis** (☎ 067-522196) goes to Cochrane (CH$12,000, six hours) at 10am on Tuesday and Friday; buy your return ticket in advance. **El Mosco** bus, leaving from the Carretera Austral, goes to Tortel (CH$10,000, four hours) at 8.30am on Sunday.

For information on connecting to Argentina by catamaran, see above.

Tierra del Fuego

HIGHLIGHTS

- Navigating the naked wilderness of the **Dientes Circuit** (p217), the world's most southerly trek
- Condor-spotting under the **Cordón Vinciguerra** (p209) on Paso de la Oveja
- Tramping through reddish moors and finding wild strawberries on the way to **Lago Windhond** (p222) on the remote Isla Navarino
- Gazing out on the Fuegian Andes on the high windy gap of **Paso Mariposa** (p207) on the Sierra Valdivieso Circuit
- Trading yarns with the sailors at **Club de Yates Micalvi** (p224), a long-grounded German cargo-boat-turned-bar

Cruel weather may make it a less than welcoming host; nevertheless, Tierra del Fuego is a wild prize for hale explorers. Its appeal is singular. At this latitude, the sun sets so late in summer that each day practically counts for two. Drawn by landlocked glaciers, chilled forests, talus (rock-scree) scrambles and burnt orange bogs, trekkers court the challenge of this mad geography at the end of the world.

The largest of South America's islands, politically Tierra del Fuego (73,753 sq km) is split between Argentina and Chile. On Isla Grande, the barren northern steppe transitions to peat bogs and moss-draped lenga forests that rise into the snow-covered Darwin Range in the south. The Argentine Fuegian Andes dip toward the city of Ushuaia, before the island ends in a sea of lapping currents.

Isla Grande's remote west side of Chile is mostly lonely sheep ranches and a roadless expanse of forest, lakes and nameless mountains. In contrast, the Argentine half practically pulses with activity – namely tourism, commerce and industry. The Beagle Channel separates Ushuaia from Chile's Isla Navarino and uninhabited groups of glacier-bound islands that peter out at Cabo de Hornos, the southern terminus of the Americas.

From the off-the-map feel of Isla Navarino to the well-worn trails around Ushuaia, trekking options are diverse. Yet for all the wonderful, rugged terrain, trekkers often find the defining feature of their visit is actually the weather. Come fully prepared, or when it howls you'll howl back.

ARGENTINE FUEGIAN ANDES

Forming an arc of rugged wilderness around the regional capital of Ushuaia, the Argentine Fuegian Andes resemble scaled-down versions of far higher mountain massifs. Deeply carved glacial valleys and passes separate jagged peaks ringed with glaciers. The upper limit of alpine vegetation reaches around 600m, with the permanent snowline only several hundred meters above this. Numerous excellent off-track routes make exciting possibilities for experienced trekkers.

This range is sandwiched between Lago Fagnano (also known by its indigenous Ona name, Lago Kami) to the north and the Beagle Channel to the south. Sunsets at this austral extreme are simply sublime.

ENVIRONMENT

The moist Fuegian forests tend to be less dense than those further north, with numerous kinds of low herblike plants but little real underbrush. The southern beech species *lenga* is dominant higher up, where soils tend to be shallower, but *coigüe de Magallanes*, known locally as *guindo*, is more common lower down.

A typical herblike plant of these subantarctic forests is the devil's strawberry (*frutilla del diablo*), which grows close to the ground and produces miniature, but inedible, bright-red berries on tiny brushlike branchlets. The

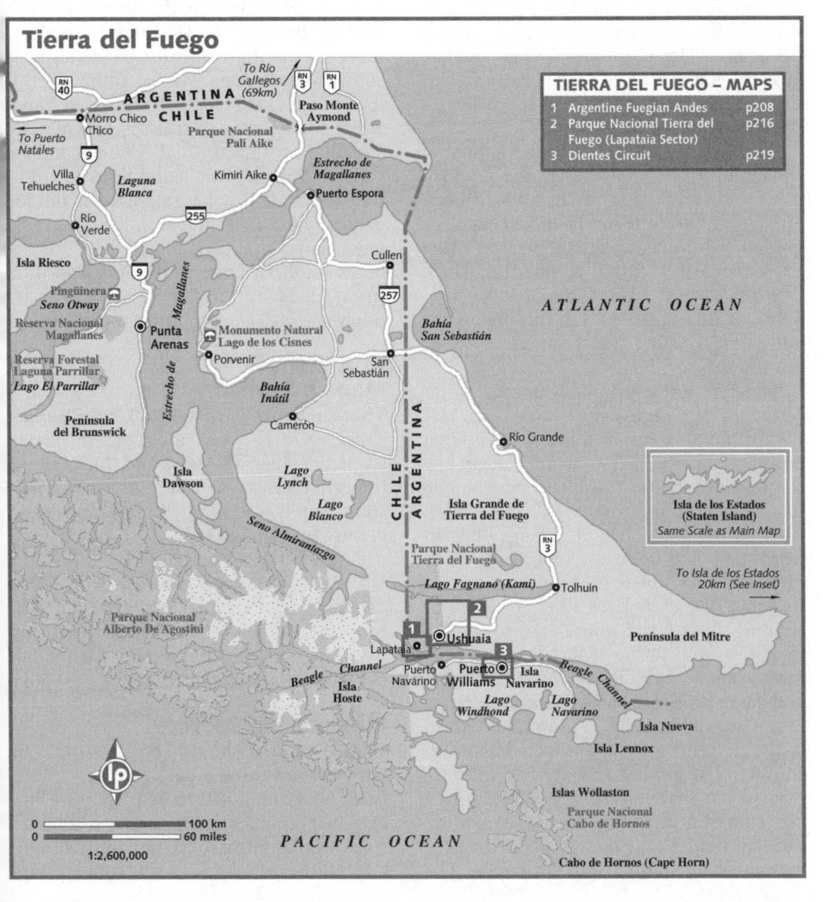

tiny Magellan strawberry (*frutilla de Magallanes*) is most easily distinguished by its 'real' berries, whose look and taste is actually more akin to that of raspberries.

Thickets of thorny *calafate* and miniature ferns cover the ground in open, well-drained areas. Sundews grow in the acidic soils low in nutrients, but these delicate plants are able to supply their needs by trapping small insects with their sticky, tentaclelike branchlets. Another carnivorous plant is the *flor del pantano*, which has violet flowers.

Numerous species of lichens and mosses grow on tree trunks, including the parasitic *cabello de ángel*, a relative of mistletoe. The *llao-llao*, or Indian bread (*pan del indio*), a parasitic fungus, produces spongy yellow clustered balls on the branches of southern beech species, and was traditionally eaten by the indigenous peoples of Tierra del Fuego. The luminous orange jellylike growths you may see on fallen trees are another interesting fungus, which accelerates the rotting of the dead wood.

Poor drainage favors the development of sphagnum bogs, known as *turbales*, which cover extensive areas of the valley floors. Sphagnum bogs form beautiful, spongy golden-red peat mounds that are often dry enough (but tiring) to walk on. Thick deposits of peat have accumulated – to a depth of 5m in places – and this material is cut commercially (chiefly for use as plant potting mix).

Trekkers are most likely to see water birds on the numerous lakes and rivers. Although more at home on the open plains of northern Tierra del Fuego, the ashy-headed goose (*cauquén*, or *canquén* in Chile) is found in the Fuegian Andes. This native goose has an orangey-brown head and upper neck, and bluish-grey body plumage interrupted by brown stripes on its breast. Trekkers have a better chance of sighting the upland goose (*caiquén*). The female upland goose looks similar to the ashy-headed goose but is somewhat larger and darker, while the male has a white head, breast and underbelly. A common seabird is the dolphin gull, a species endemic to southern Patagonia and Tierra del Fuego.

Guanaco (native relatives of the camel) are common throughout the Argentine Fuegian Andes and their trails often provide excellent natural walking routes. The Fuegian fox (*zorro fueguino*) is a subspecies of the Patagonian red fox (now also introduced from the mainland). It is the only fox native to Tierra del Fuego, and lives its furtive existence in field and forest.

Regrettably, North American beavers now inhabit most forested streams all over Tierra del Fuego. The gnawed tree stumps and the animals' often surprisingly high dams are a constant hindrance and eyesore. Reindeer have also been introduced to the Fuegian Andes, but their numbers have stayed low enough to keep them a novelty.

CLIMATE

Somewhat sheltered by the much higher mountains to the west and by other, lower ranges on the Chilean islands of Isla Hoste and Isla Navarino to the south, the Argentine Fuegian Andes have a relatively moderate maritime climate considering their subantarctic latitude. Average annual precipitation levels in the Argentine Fuegian Andes are 1500mm, though there is considerable variation between the higher ranges and the valleys. Subantarctic conditions concentrate the climatic zones into narrow altitude bands, which are reflected in the local vegetation and low permanent snowline. Because of the southerly latitude, the Fuegian winter (from late May until early September) brings heavy snowfalls – even down to sea level.

PLANNING

Maps & Books

The Zagier & Urruty 1:50,000 *Ushuaia Trekking Map* covers most of the eastern Argentine Fuegian Andes and shows all the important routes quite accurately. This new color map is sold locally in bookstores and at the Club Andina Ushuaia (CAU) in Ushuaia (see Information p224).

Guía de Sendas & Escaladas de Tierra del Fuego, by Luis Turi and Carolina Etchegoyen (available in local bookstores and from the CAU), includes treks throughout the Argentine Fuegian Andes.

Information sources

Club Andino Ushuaia (☎ 02901-422335; www.clubandinoushuaia.com.ar; Juana Fadul 50; 10am-12.30pm & 2-9.30pm Mon-Fri, 10am-2pm Sat) sells a map and bilingual trekking, mountaineering and mountain-bikingguidebook with rough maps and plenty of trail descriptions. The club occasionally organizes hikes and can recommend hiking guides. Unguided trekkers are strongly encouraged to register with the club or the tourist office before heading out – and check in after a safe return.

SIERRA VALDIVIESO CIRCUIT

Duration 4 days
Distance 48.5km
Difficulty demanding
Start Ruta Nacional 3 (16km from Ushuaia)
Finish Posada del Peregrino
Nearest Town Ushuaia
Transport minibus or taxi
Summary An adventurous trek through the heart of the Argentine Fuegian Andes, crossing superb rugged wilderness in splendid isolation.

Extending eastward along the southern side of Lago Fagnano (Kami) from the boundary of Parque Nacional Tierra del Fuego to the landmark summit of Monte Falso Carbajal (1250m), the Sierra Valdivieso arguably offers the most scenic wilderness trekking in the Argentine Fuegian Andes. The numerous (now mostly quite small) glaciers and névés (permanent snowfields) of this jagged range are remnants of far larger glaciers that reshaped the landscape during past ice ages, gouging out countless alpine lakes and tarns. Connecting many of its tiny valleys are gentle passes that serve as convenient crossing routes between the raw ice-clad peaks.

A variant on Day 3, not described in detail, takes trekkers north to Bahía Torito on the stunning Lago Fagnano (Kami). Descending this valley, trekkers could take a new ferry service to the village of Tolhuin, 100km northeast of Ushuaia on Ruta 3. Contact **Nunatak Turismo** (☎ 02901-492364; Pedro Olivia 614, Tolhuin) for schedules and ticket prices. Confirm that tickets can be purchased directly on board.Be sure to confirm boat itineraries with operator **Fernández Campbell** (www.fernandezcampbell.com) ahead of your trip.

This route is mainly open trekking – through clearings and moors or above the tree line – where markings are minimal (though they are more reliable at crucial junctions).

For information on staying at the Hostería Kauyeken, 500m south of the trek's finish, see p223.

PLANNING

When to Trek

The trek can normally be done between early December and late March, although in some years the trekking season is longer. Conditions in April can also be quite mild, but any breakdown in the weather so late in the season is likely to bring snowfalls down to at least 300m.

What to Bring

Apart from Refugio Bonete, a few hours from the start, there are no huts or any other reliable shelter along the trek, so it is essential that all parties carry a good tent and clothing for all weather conditions. There is waterlogged ground (caused in part by the vandalistic work of introduced North American beavers), so wear waterproof boots.

See also Warning in relation to carrying sufficient food supplies.

Permits & Regulations

No permit is required to trek the Sierra Valdivieso Circuit. Trekkers are permitted to camp where the route transits the eastern fringe of Parque Nacional Tierra del Fuego – despite a general ban on overnight trekking in the park – but should be mindful of their impact on the environment at all times (see Responsible Trekking, p36).

WARNING

The Sierra Valdivieso Circuit follows a largely unmarked and little-trodden route through rugged and challenging country. It is therefore suitable only for fit and self-reliant parties with good navigational skills.

Even summer weather is highly erratic, with sudden southerly storms – be alert to changes in the weather. Streams (especially the Río Olivia) become difficult to cross safely after rain. Parties should carry at least two extra days of supplies in order to wait for better weather and/or for stream levels to fall. See p264 for information on safe river crossings.

The final section of the route crosses private land, where camping is not allowed.

GETTING TO/FROM THE TREK

Both trailheads can be reached from Ushuaia by (irregular) minibus. **Transporte La Paloma** (☎ 02901-443756; lapalomatransfer@hotmail.com.ar; cnr Maipu & Juana Fadul) takes passengers (AR$20 per person); at least three are required for a departure. Arrange your trip in advance.

Remises Carlitos (☎ 02901-422222; San Martín 891) charges around AR$35 for a taxi (up to three people) in either direction.

Traffic is busy enough to make hitchhiking along the Ruta Nacional 3 also a reasonable proposition.

Ruta Nacional 3 (start)

The trek starts on Ruta Nacional 3, right where the gas pipeline (*gasoducto*) crosses under the road, approximately 16km northeast from Ushuaia (or 3km from Altos del Valle, at the start of the Laguna Esmeralda trek, see p210). Yellow '*Peligro*' (danger) signs on both sides of the road indicate this point. (Also look for a blazing mark with yellow paint on a tall *lenga* tree.) There is plenty of parking space beside the road.

Posada del Peregrino (finish)

The trek finishes back on Ruta Nacional 3, near the Posada del Peregrino, a youth rehabilitation center at the turn-off to the Turbera Valle Carbajal, 13km northeast of Ushuaia. From Tolhuin, there are frequent buses to Ushuaia (AR$30).

If no public transport is available, you may be able to telephone for a taxi (*remís*) at the Posada, back at the Turbera (see Day 4) or at the Hostería Kauyeken (p223).

The 13km walk back to Ushuaia takes around three hours.

THE TREK

Day 1: Ruta Nacional 3 to Refugio Bonete

1½–1¾ hours, 4.5km, 140m ascent

Especially if you set out early, this section may be too short for one day, so trekkers may opt to continue into the upper Río Beban.

From where the route leaves Ruta Nacional 3 (GPS 54° 43.465 S, 68° 10.071 W), head down 50m past a rustic tin shelter to meet a muddy, eroded 4WD track. Follow it through a little meadow to cross the small Río Esmeralda on a ruined old bridge (made passable by stacked logs) after 10 minutes. Walk northwest along a grassy old road through regenerating *lenga* into a *mallín* (wet meadow), 25 to 30 minutes on. Head 200m through this wet bog before cutting left, back into the forest. The route continues through more forest and soggy areas, turning gradually northeast toward the dominant 1118m summit of Cerro Bonete to cross a small open stream basin with a large beaver dam after 40 to 50 minutes. (Here a rough trail goes off eastward to Altos del Valle.

A gentle climb north brings you to **Refugio Bonete** (GPS 54° 42.048 S, 68° 10.070 W), 10 minutes on, at around 320m on a minor ridge under its namesake mountain. This simple hut has a potbelly stove – the gas stove is only for emergencies – and one two-berth bunk plus a loft with sleeping space for about four people. There is no charge to use the *refugio*. There is no toilet, so please 'go' well downhill, and collect water upstream from the brook 100m north of the hut. A local Fuegian fox passes the *refugio* on its regular patrols.

Day 2: Refugio Bonete to Salto del Azul

4½–6 hours, 14km, 510m ascent

Make your way northwest – from here on there will often be no real track, just a rough route – toward the 1039m 'sentinel' peak of Punta Navidad. Skirt small moors (avoiding *coigüe*-covered ridges up to the right), following an undulating terrace above the Río Beban past a waterfall into a flat valley basin. Continue for 500m until you are under high bluffs on Cerro Bonete's west side, then ford the small river and head into *lenga* forest. The route cuts rightward, back to the stream, rising on past a large broken beaver dam to cross a side stream (GPS 44° 40.709 S, 68° 10.648 W). (A route variant climbs its true left (north) bank of the side stream to a crest and then drops to meet the main route above the campsites.)

Proceed toward Monte Falso Carbajal (1250m), at the head of a superb side valley completely enclosed by craggy rock walls with hanging glaciers. Where the stream divides, climb away via its northwestern branch (with fine views south to the jagged 1331m Monte Olivia) to reach some excellent **campsites** in an isolated clump of *lenga* forest, 1¾ to 2¼ hours from the *refugio*. Here the stream flows through tiny tarns hidden in a field of bouldery moraine debris.

Continue up along the often-marshy true right (south) bank of the stream to a flat slab on a gravelly wash. From here, cut up steeply left through an obvious chute of brittle white shale and ease back right to reach **Paso Beban Este** (around 830m) after 50 minutes to 1¼ hours. This eastern pass gives a good view south down a wild little valley to Laguna Paso Beban, a small lake perched slightly above the tree line under the craggy Tres Picos. Traverse on round to the right over the coarse scree and snowdrifts, then cut up directly into **Paso Beban Oeste** (around 850m) after 15 to 20 minutes.

Apart from a large cairn, you can't see much from this western pass. Descend northwest into the valley of the **Río Torito**, mostly along the boggy right-hand side of the small stream (but crossing where necessary), until you meet a side stream coming down from the north (right). Here, it is probably best to cross the Río Torito and climb through open areas in the scrub on its true left side (although a route also continues down through wet forest on the stream's right bank) to reach a large beaver pond (GPS 54° 38.738 S, 68° 15.223 W).

Follow a minor ridge until it peters out at some more beaver dams, then make your way around through trees killed by the resulting inundation to reach the **Salto del Azul**, a waterfall spilling down from the left, 1½ to two hours from the (western) pass. **Campsites** can be found around attractive meadows here.

Day 3: Salto del Azul to Central Valle Carbajal

5½–7¾ hours, 14km, 550m ascent, 700m descent

This is a long day that can be broken by camping en route – the sites above Laguna Capullo are recommended.

Hop across the **Arroyo Azul** on rocks and head 1.25km downvalley to the end of the higher of two boggy terraces, just before the Río Torito curves right (GPS 54° 38.021 S, 68° 17.525 W). Climb steeply roughly southward through *coigüe* scrub and tiny shelves covered in heathlike *brecillo* to a prominent boulder (marked by a cairn), from where views open out down along the marshy lower valley to Bahía Torito, a remote bay without services, on Lago Fagnano (Kami). Descending this valley 10km, trekkers with good navigational skills could bushwhack and could arrive at Bahía Torito to take a high-season ferry to the village of Tolhuin (see p206), but be sure to check boat itineraries ahead.

Continue round rightward up through sloping clearings on a broad spur to reach a tiny cascade near a beaver pond. From here, cut up directly over a rocky crest to reencounter the Arroyo Azul at a small grassy plateau. The route follows the splashing stream up to **Laguna Azul**, a blue lake in a raw basin below rugged glaciated peaks, 1½ to 2¼ hours from Salto del Azul. Scenic semi-sheltered **campsites** can be found here.

Walk around to lawns along Laguna Azul's southwest inlet, then head up this stream into a rocky gully. The route climbs briefly left onto a broad rock rib, which it follows up west before ascending directly into **Paso Mariposa** (GPS 54° 38.543 S, 68° 19.171 W), one to 1½ hours from the lake. Marked by another large cairn, this high, often windy gap (not much under 1000m) lies between bands of white and grey shale rock. It offers wonderful vistas east and west across the surrounding Argentine Fuegian Andes, including Laguna Azul Superior behind and Laguna Mariposa ahead. (Note that there is a slightly lower pass 600m to the south, which is a better route alternative only if you are doing the trek in the opposite direction.)

Make an initially steep descent across a raw scree basin, then drop left beside a streamlet to reach the (rather uninteresting) elongated **Laguna Capullo** after 30 to 45 minutes. Crossing several inlets, head briefly around the lake's southern shore before you cut up left to a grassy shelf with nice **campsites** among the boulders. The route climbs on steeply southwest over green carpets of *azorella* and on up left via a grassy chute to a high rocky crest. From here there is a wonderful view north across four lakes, including Laguna Mariposa (almost 200m directly below you), to the picturesque Bahía de los Renos on Lago Fagnano (Kami).

Now above the tree line, head southward over an undulating panoramic terrace past

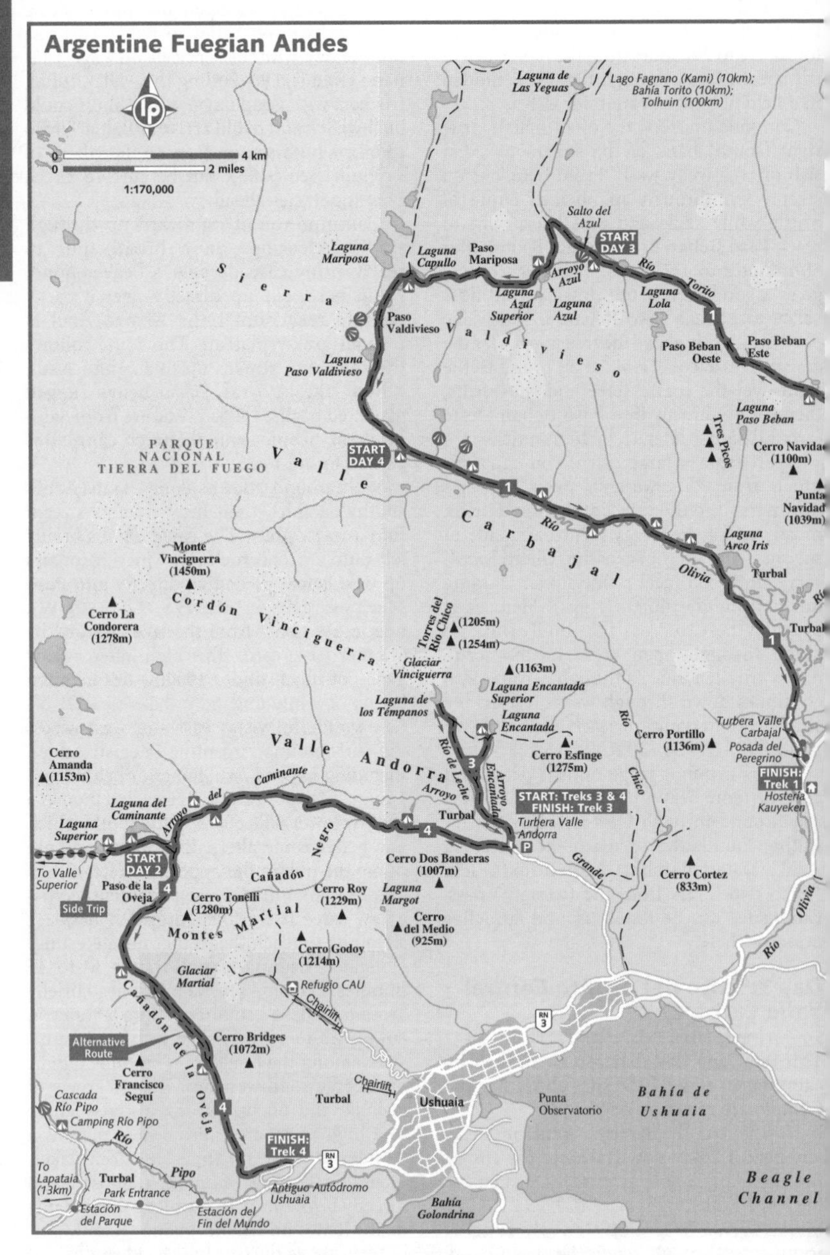

Argentine Fuegian Andes
0 4 km
0 2 miles
1:170,000
Laguna de Las Yeguas
Lago Fagnano (Kami) (10km); Bahía Torito (10km); Tolhuin (100km)
Salto del Azul
START DAY 3
Laguna Mariposa
Laguna Capullo
Paso Mariposa
Arroyo Azul
Río Torito
Sierra Valdivieso
Laguna Azul Superior
Laguna Azul
Laguna Lola
Paso Valdivieso
Paso Beban Oeste
Paso Beban Este
Laguna Paso Valdivieso
Laguna Paso Beban
Tres Picos
Cerro Navidad (1100m)
Punta Navidad (1039m)
PARQUE NACIONAL TIERRA DEL FUEGO
START DAY 4
Valle Carbajal
Río Olivia
Laguna Arco Iris
Turbal
Monte Vinciguerra (1450m)
Cerro La Condorera (1278m)
Cordón Vinciguerra
Torres del Río Chico
(1205m)
(1254m)
Glaciar Vinciguerra
(1163m)
Laguna Encantada Superior
Laguna de los Témpanos
Laguna Encantada
Río Chico
Cerro Portillo (1136m)
Turbera Valle Carbajal
Posada del Peregrino
FINISH: Trek 1
Hostería Kauyeken
Valle Andorra
Río de Leche
Arroyo Encantada
Cerro Esfinge (1275m)
Cerro Amanda (1153m)
Arroyo del Caminante
Laguna del Caminante
START: Treks 3 & 4
FINISH: Trek 3
Turbera Valle Andorra
Laguna Superior
START DAY 2
To Valle Superior
Side Trip
Paso de la Oveja
Cañadón Negro
Cerro Dos Banderas (1007m)
Río Grande
Cerro Cortez (833m)
Cerro Tonelli (1280m)
Cerro Roy (1229m)
Laguna Margot
Cerro del Medio (925m)
Montes Martial
Cerro Godoy (1214m)
Glaciar Martial
Refugio CAU
Chairlift
Río Olivia
Cañadón de la Oveja
Alternative Route
Cerro Bridges (1072m)
Cerro Francisco Seguí
RN 3
Turbal
Ushuaia
Punta Observatorio
Bahía de Ushuaia
Cascada Río Pipo
Camping Río Pipo
Río Pipo
FINISH: Trek 4
To Lapataia (13km)
Park Entrance
Antiguo Autódromo Ushuaia
Estación del Parque
Estación del Fin del Mundo
Bahía Golondrina
Beagle Channel

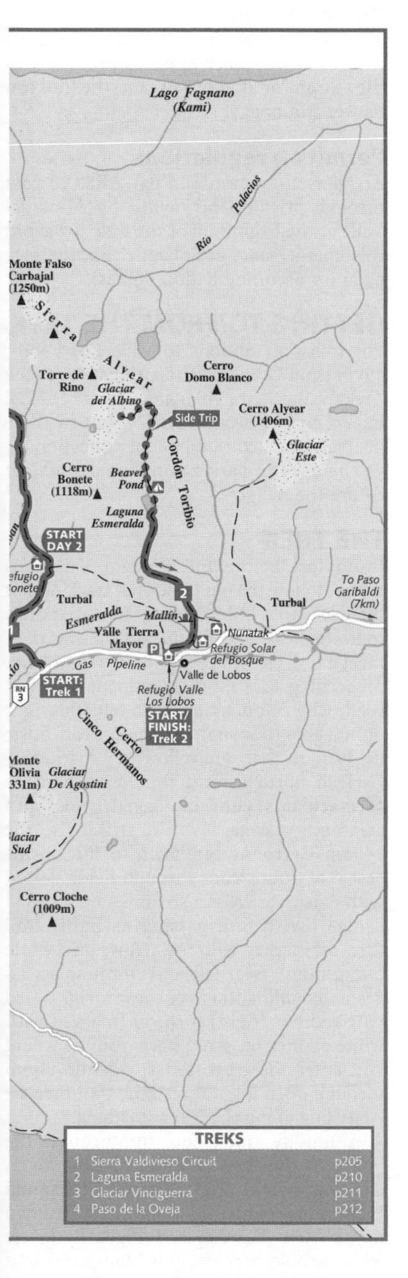

two deep pools, then follow the outlet of the second pool down into the upper valley. The route cuts up past tarns in scrubby alpine meadows to cross **Paso Valdivieso** (also known as Paso de las Cinco Lagunas), 1¼ to 1¾ hours from Laguna Capullo. The cairn (GPS 54° 39.268 S, 68° 21.422 W) is at roughly 700m, although the lowest point is actually some way over to the right. The pass lies directly below a long shelf glacier whose tumbling meltwater streamlets flow both north and south of the watershed. To the southwest, Monte Vinciguerra can be identified beyond the Valle Carbajal.

Walk down past a rocky outcrop, then descend steeply rightward to Laguna Paso Valdivieso. Follow a well-defined trail around the lake's eastern shore, making your way down beside the cascading outlet stream. Cross to the true right bank when you come to the first patches of taller scrub before dropping into the light forest to meet the **Río Olivia** about halfway along the Valle Carbajal, 1¼ to 1½ hours from Paso Valdivieso. Extending from near Lago Alto in the heart of Parque Nacional Tierra del Fuego, this deep wild valley separates the Sierra Valdivieso from the Cordón Vinciguerra.

Campsites can be found around here, although sites along the forested river flats further downvalley are even more pleasant. (Trekkers coming the other way should turn up northwest where the glacier above the pass comes into sight at GPS 54° 40.792 S, 68° 20.908 W.)

Day 4: Central Valle Carbajal to Posada del Peregrino

5½–7 hours, 16km, 100m ascent, 180m descent

Begin the long stretch down through the lovely wild Valle Carbajal. Avoiding occasional areas of beaver activity, follow rough trails through the *lenga* forest (with abundant *chauras* and the native Magellan strawberry) along the northern bank of the meandering river. Excellent **campsites** are passed almost continually. The route leads into an increasingly extensive belt of moors (*turbales*) toward the valley mouth, crossing five larger side streams (which often meet the main valley in high waterfalls as they gush down from 'hanging' side valleys up to your left), before it finally turns away along a forested lateral moraine (GPS 54° 41.995 S, 68° 14.809 W) after three to four hours.

This low ridge ends at the large peaty pond of **Laguna Arco Iris** after 25 to 30 minutes. (Trekkers going the other way should look for a large marker pole where the path enters the forest.) Head around the spongy western shore, from where there are great views across the lake to the majestic 1331m Monte Olivia, then make a (usually knee-deep) ford of the Río Olivia (GPS 54° 42.480 S, 68° 13.711 W), 20 to 25 minutes on.

A muddy path (often confused by cattle trails) now takes an up-and-down southeastward course. It avoids the vast rusty-red moorland dotted with little ponds that stretches along the broad valley junction by staying in the forest. The route continues as a rough road after passing a (locked) gate, crossing through drying racks stacked with cut peat to reach buildings of the **Turbera Valle Carbajal**, a peat-cutting operation, 1½ to two hours from the ford. Watch for unfriendly dogs here. Recross the Río Olivia on the road bridge and continue through another locked gate on Ruta Nacional 3 at the **Posada del Peregrino** youth rehabilitation center after a final 10 minutes.

LAGUNA ESMERALDA

Duration 3–4 hours
Distance 9km
Difficulty easy
Start/Finish Refugio Valle Los Lobos
Nearest Town Ushuaia
Transport minibus or taxi
Summary An excellent day trek (or a short overnight trek) to a lovely subalpine lake below the tiny 'icecap' of the Glaciar del Albino.

One of the most popular day treks near Ushuaia, the trek up to Laguna Esmeralda involves a minimal ascent and descent. It makes a medium-length day trek from a base in Ushuaia or one of the nearby *refugios*. The trek could also be done as a short overnight trek (with a camp at the lake and a side trip to the glacier).

The first section of the route leads over several converging cross-country skiing and dog-sledding runs. Note that sled dog teams are trained on these trails even in summer; if you encounter a team of dogs, step off the trail and let them pass.

PLANNING

When to Trek

The trek is normally easily passable at least from late November to mid-April. Early in the season (or after heavy rain) the trail can be wet and boggy.

Permits & regulations

Trekkers are required to pay AR$8 to pass through private land owned by Altos del Valle at the beginning of the trek. To avoid this charge, start at Solar del Bosque (see p223 for accommodation details).

GETTING TO/FROM THE TREK

For transport options to Valle Los Lobos, 19km from Ushuaia, see Getting to/from the Trek for the Sierra Valdivieso Circuit (p205). Expect to pay around AR$58 (up to three people) for a taxi ride in either direction.

There is free parking on the turn-off just before the *refugio*.

THE TREK

From just before the Refugio Valle Los Lobos, follow the old bulldozed track off left directly into a little clearing. Blue markings indicate the trail. Continue off rightward, to meet a trail crossing the path. Go right here, proceeding to a more prominent unsealed road, where you should turn left (the right option goes to Solar del Bosque). From Solar del Bosque, there are yellow trail markings.

Head north toward the Sierra Alvear's spectacular skyline of jagged peaks and gleaming glaciers – most strikingly, the 1406m Cerro Alvear itself, to the north-east. The route leads through fields dotted with daisies to cross a streamlet on a broad bridge just before passing a (right) trail turn-off marked with red arrows on a white background. Bear left and continue across a small *mallín*, then cut away rightward past another (right) turn-off (marked with white arrows on a red background) where you enter the trees. After a gentle climb through open *lenga* forest, the trail meets a peaty bog along the Río Esmeralda.

A muddy track cuts up through the bog into the tiny valley beside the river, climbing over a crest to arrive at **Laguna Esmeralda** (Emerald Lake), 1½ to two hours from the *refugio*. Fringed by lovely white-pebble beaches, this blue-green lake sits under Glaciar del Albino (see Side Trip).

Ashy-headed geese can sometimes be spotted around the north shore. You can find secluded **campsites** at the northeast end.

Return via the same route.

SIDE TRIP: GLACIAR DEL ALBINO

3½–5 hours return, 7km, 600m ascent/descent

This moderate–demanding route is for trekkers with extra time and energy.

Head on for 10 minutes around Laguna Esmeralda's eastern shore, continuing into the upper valley past a large beaver pond. This unmaintained but generally well-trodden foot track leads alongside the stream past excellent campsites on small flats in the *lenga* forest. Continue to a large bivouac rock immediately below the scrub line. Ascend directly into this moraine-filled gully via a usually decent path, past the point where the stream cascades down over slabs up to your left.

When you reach the grey rock (GPS 54° 40.344 S, 68° 07.840 W), climb steeply west through loose rock beside a streamlet to reach a somewhat larger stream on a rocky shelf. Cross this stream, then head 50m along the shelf and find your way up over the red rock slab. Some minor hand climbing may be required. Although there is no serious exposure to a fall, this calls for some care. The route cuts up to a rock outcrop at the edge of the Glaciar del Albino, 1¾ to 2½ hours from the lake. This small glacier lies between impressive peaks and offers a mountaineer's perspective on the Esmeralda valley far below.

The ice near the rim is not crevassed, and it is safe to walk about 50m up for a view across the glacier to an iceberg-filled lake created by a high moraine wall. Only properly equipped and/or guided trekkers should venture beyond this point.

Return via the same route.

GLACIAR VINCIGUERRA

Duration 5–6½ hours return
Distance 13km
Difficulty moderate
Start/Finish Turbera Valle Andorra
Nearest Town Ushuaia
Transport minibus or taxi
Summary A short jaunt to stunning glacial lakes.

This trek can be done in one long day or as an overnight combination – by camping at Laguna Encantada, then trekking to Laguna de los Témpanos the next day. Alternatively, the route could be broken into two separate day treks. Although not too demanding in terms of distance, it does involve 730m of ascent and descent.

GETTING TO/FROM THE TREK

The trek starts near the Turbera Valle Andorra, 9.5km from Ushuaia in the lower Valle Andorra. The left turn-off is 5km from the center of town on Ruta Nacional 3.

For transport options to the Turbera Valle Andorra, see Getting to/from the Trek for the Sierra Valdivieso Circuit (p205). Expect to pay around AR$25 (up to three people) for a taxi ride in either direction.

Otherwise, it's at least a three-hour walk from Ushuaia.

THE TREK

The trek starts at a parking area at the locked road gate into the Turbera Valle Andorra (a peat-cutting operation). Walk through the pedestrian gate on the right – the sign warning you not to enter does not apply to foot traffic – and follow the road for five minutes to some shacks by the Arroyo Grande.

Walk to the end of the *turba* (peat bog), staying parallel to the river for 15 minutes until you reach a bridge. Cross and continue on the other side.

Continue up northeast into a tiny side valley. The gradient remains fairly steep as you ascend on through highland *lengas* past a left turn-off (marked with a split yellow arrow). The climb then eases as you rise through scrubby meadows to reach **Laguna Encantada**, 45 minutes to one hour from the trail fork. This 'enchanted' lake lies at around 550m. It is perched in a grassy bowl headed by a horned peak (1163m) above high cliffs with a long cascade streaming down (from the unseen Laguna Encantada Superior). On the lake's east side stands the 1275m Cerro Esfinge, which can be climbed (by first following the lake's southeast inlet, then cutting up to the right) for sensational views.

There are scenic (unlevel and only semi-sheltered) **campsites** on the west side of the outlet, and sheltered sites in the scrub a little over halfway around the lake's west side.

Return to the trail fork at around 335m, 30 to 40 minutes from Laguna Encantada. From here, go right and head northwest through tall *lenga* forest. This muddy but initially well-graded path sidles gently upward, gradually turning northward as you climb over a spur to enter a tiny side valley. Make a rising traverse below occasional cliffs to meet the **Río de Leche** (at about 530m), following the cascading stream up briefly before you cross it on a flat grassy shelf, 40 to 50 minutes from the fork. The route climbs through moraine rubble well above the stream to reach **Laguna de los Témpanos** (around 715m), 20 to 30 minutes on.

Alternatively, from Laguna Encantada descend a short way past the streamside meadows to the turn-off noted on the way up. A short cut climbs 250m from here to Laguna de los Témpanos over a distance of 2km, in 45 minutes to an hour. Turn up right (west) and climb steeply over the grassy ridgetop. The route traverses northwest up the ridge's left side, high above glowing red moors in the Valle Andorra, to reach a cairn on a minor rock outcrop at 680m (GPS 54° 44.426 S, 68° 19.413 W). It then cuts down to rejoin the main route at the grassy shelf by the Río de Leche.

Although – despite its Spanish name – there are no icebergs in the lake's cloudy waters, the smooth snout of **Glaciar Vinciguerra** creeps right down into this awesome meltwater tarn from the ice-smothered mountain above. Climbers have built low rock shelters where **camping** is possible. The ice can be reached by heading around the lake's east side past a large polished slab.

When you're done, head down to the trail fork at 335m and retrace your steps to the Turbera Valle Andorra.

PASO DE LA OVEJA

Duration 2 days
Distance 31.5km
Difficulty moderate
Start Turbera Valle Andorra
Finish Antiguo Autódromo Ushuaia
Nearest Town Ushuaia
Transport minibus or taxi
Summary A trek around the Montes Martial through idyllic valleys covered by beautiful forests and areas of Fuegian moor.

This popular trek over Paso de la Oveja connects the two valleys that surround the Montes Martial. Rising abruptly from the Beagle Channel directly behind Ushuaia, this short range offers a shot of wilderness just outside Ushuaia.

Trekkers with extra time should combine this with the Glaciar Vinciguerra trek (p211).

PLANNING

When to Trek

The route is normally in condition from mid-November until mid-April. Early or late in the season, heavy snow may lie on the pass.

Permits & Regulations

Although a ban on overnight trekking applies elsewhere in Parque Nacional Tierra del Fuego, the Paso de la Oveja route is permitted as only a short section of the circuit transits the park's eastern fringe. Trekkers must obtain a permit from the Administración Parques Nacionales (APN) office in Ushuaia (see p225 for details).

In addition, be particularly mindful of your impact on this fragile environment (see Responsible Trekking, p36). Fires are prohibited and all trash must be carried out. The final part of the route crosses private land.

GETTING TO/FROM THE TREK

Turbera Valle Andorra (start)

The trek starts near the Turbera Valle Andorra, 9.5km from Ushuaia in the lower Valle Andorra. The left turn-off is 5km from the center of town on Ruta Nacional 3.

For transport options to the Turbera Valle Andorra, see Getting to/from the Trek for the Sierra Valdivieso Circuit (p205). Expect to pay around AR$25 (up to three people) for a taxi ride in either direction.

Otherwise, it's at least a three-hour walk from Ushuaia.

Antiguo Autódromo Ushuaia (finish)

The trek finishes near the Antiguo Autódromo Ushuaia, a former car-racing track just north off Ruta Nacional 3, 6km west of Ushuaia's center. Buses running from Parque Nacional Tierra del Fuego pass by the autódromo approximately every hour between 8am and 8pm on their way to Ushuaia and can be flagged down.

Otherwise, it's an easy walk back to town.

THE TREK

Day 1: Turbera Valle Andorra to Laguna del Caminante

6–7½ hours, 10.4km, 660m ascent, 250m descent

The trek starts at a parking area at the locked road gate into the Turbera Valle Andorra (a peat-cutting operation). Walk through the pedestrian gate on the right – the sign warning you not to enter does not apply to foot traffic – and follow the road for five minutes to some shacks by the Arroyo Grande.

Turn left along an unsigned old 4WD track that leads upvalley through tiny pastures grazed by horses. Continue on through *coigüe* forest. Where the old 4WD track peters out, drop slightly rightward to reach a small meadow (GPS 54° 45.358 S, 68° 21.003 W) just outside the national park boundary, 50 minutes to 1¼ hours from the road. Late-arrival campers can stay here, although strewn refuse curbs the appeal.

Follow the path up left to cross and recross the stream coming from the **Cañadón Negro**. From here, head northwest through a broad gap on the south side of a long forested ridge, periodically marked by yellow posts. The route continues along the edge of the valley, usually just high enough to avoid spongy moors to the right. There are partial views north to the snowy summits of the Cordón Vinciguerra as you continue westward through open *lenga* forest in earshot of the roaring river.

After cutting through small grassy *mallines*, turn slowly southwest and rise, still only very gently, over timbered flats beside the river. Dip over shallow channels to avoid low cliffs. Shortly afterward the trail crosses to the true left bank of the **Arroyo del Caminante**. You are not far upstream from where the arroyo meets a branch draining the valley to the northwest to form the Arroyo Grande (GPS 54° 45.228 S, 68° 25.152 W), 1¾ to 2¼ hours from the national park boundary. Pleasant **campsites** are both before and after this easy crossing.

The gradient steepens gradually as you head around to the south. Recross the small but rushing Arroyo del Caminante (just above its confluence with the smaller stream coming from Paso de la Oveja) on a makeshift log bridge, after 30 to 40 minutes. Follow the often-muddy track upward for 10 to 15 minutes to reach the right turn-off to Laguna del Caminante (GPS 54° 45.765 S, 68° 25.908 W), marked at the forest edge.

This well-trodden route sidles northwest over grassy slopes under cliffs and then climbs above the tumbling Arroyo del Caminante to a grassy shelf. Cut down to the right on a steep, muddy path and cross the main inlet below a waterfall to reach **Laguna del Caminante**. Various excellent **campsites** can be found in the *lenga* forest on the lake's south shore, with views of the top of the Cordón Vinciguerra. An industrious beaver makes his home at the far western side of the lake, where he has laid waste to a fair chunk of native forest. Your best chance for spotting him is around sunset.

Be very conscientious about taking out trash, which has started to accumulate in this otherwise pristine area.

SIDE TRIP: VALLE SUPERIOR

2½ hours return, 3.5km

A visit to this serene valley should not be missed. From the grassy shelf above the lake, you can continue southwest, carefully crossing a snow bridge and heading upvalley parallel to the river on its southern bank. The trail follows a sometimes narrow and exposed ledge to the slightly higher **Laguna Superior** (an additional 35 to 45 minutes and 2km return), which lies under Cerro Amanda and Cerro Tonelli. This lake also offers scenic yet exposed **campsites**.

In good weather, trekkers can spend an entire day wandering upwalley, potentially climbing one of the surrounding lookouts or peaks for views of the idyllic Valle Superior.

Day 2: Laguna del Caminante to Autódromo Ushuaia

5½–7 hours, 10.4km, 840m descent

Retrace your steps to the main route. After reaching the marked trail junction, you will climb for another 15 to 20 minutes through alpine meadows beside the stream to a marker stake under the pyramid-like crags of Cerro Tonelli (1280m).

From this point, you have two options. You can ford the stream and follow its east (true right) bank, staying close to the stream as you rise through the narrowing talus-filled gully into **Paso de la Oveja** (around 800m). Alternatively, continue up the west side of the stream, then climb and make a higher traverse around into the pass. Both routes take 50 minutes to 1¼ hours. Marked by a chest-high cairn, Paso de la Oveja (also known as Paso del Caminante) lies directly under the spires of Cerro Tonelli and brings into view two towering twin peaks (both just over 1200m) in the valley ahead. There are also more fine views back north to the glacier-clad summits of the Cordón Vinciguerra. Look for condors gliding around these ranges.

Descend past a cirque on Cerro Tonelli's western side to cross the tiny stream emerging from the scree. The best route follows the steep left bank of the stream down and round to the left. It reaches a route fork (GPS 54° 47.062 S, 68° 26.846 W) at the scrub line in the upper Cañadón de la Oveja (see Alternative Route, this page), after 35 to 45 minutes. Scenic **campsites** can be found here in the low vegetation under half a dozen cascades spilling over green, grassy cliffs. (If walking the other way, note that this is the last camping until well beyond the pass.)

At the left (east) side of the valley, climb diagonally left up over coarse talus to a minor rocky spur (GPS 54° 47.203 S, 68° 26.227 W) just before a stream gully coming down from a cirque on the south side of Cerro Tonelli. The route now begins a traverse along steep scree slopes (at just over 500m) with good footing, high above the scrubby, waterlogged meadows of the valley floor. Opposite you are craggy 1200m peaks and spectacular 500m walls spouting waterfalls, with views far beyond to the Beagle Channel and Isla Navarino.

At the end of the scree slopes, the trail appears to continue straight into the forest, but trekkers should instead follow the yellow marker posts that lead rightward down the coarse talus field. Just after entering the forest, there is a poorly marked trail junction, one to 1½ hours from the camp in the upper valley. The right branch leads 100m down to the stream, which can be crossed to reach idyllic **campsites** on grassy meadows (GPS 54° 47.983 S, 68° 25.646W) under Cerro Francisco Seguí. The main trail is to the left.

Continue down through *guindo* (*coigüe*) forest above the stream, which here flows within a gully. Despite muddy sections and occasional fallen logs, the going is fairly easy, and you reach a gate marking the boundary of private land at the end of the deep, enclosed canyon (GPS 54° 49.207 S, 68° 24.718 W), one to 1¼ hours on.

Follow a grassy farm track southwest (toward the airport) gently down over pastures scattered with *calafate* and native daisy bushes. The route passes a shack with nervous guard dogs to reach another (locked) gate along the turn-off to the Autódromo Ushuaia, 150m from Ruta Nacional 3, after 30 to 40 minutes.

(Trekkers going the other way should take the turn-off just east of the Club Hípico and climb over the gate marked with blue stripes. Alternatively, you can continue past the former speedway, then follow the stream up to the start of the canyon.)

ALTERNATIVE ROUTE: LOW-LEVEL TRAIL

1½–2 hours, 3.5km

This slower and less scenic route may be a better bad-weather option. It is very boggy and scrubby in places, though generally quite pleasant going.

From the route fork in the upper Cañadón de la Oveja, skirt the talus for 300m, then duck rightward into the brush. The sometimes-indistinct route leads downvalley beside or near the stream (which you should not have to cross). It passes through open *lenga* forest and lovely grassy flats to meet the main high traverse route below a coarse talus field. Now proceed as described in Day 2.

ISLA NAVARINO

With more than 150km of trails, Isla Navarino is a rugged backpacker's paradise of slate-colored lakes, rusty moors, moss-draped forests and the ragged spires of the Dientes de Navarino. Trails lead past beaver dams, bunkers and army trenches as they climb steeply up into the mountains and deeper into forests. Some 40,000 beavers introduced from Canada in the 1940s now plague the island; they're even on the menu, if you can find an open restaurant.

PARQUE NACIONAL TIERRA DEL FUEGO (LAPATAIA SECTOR)

Parque Nacional Tierra del Fuego forms a 630-sq-km strip of rugged mountainous country stretching northward along the Chilean frontier from the Beagle Channel to well beyond Lago Fagnano (Kami). The national park begins just 10km west of Ushuaia and is surrounded by even more expansive areas of Fuegian-Andean wilderness. Only shorter day treks are possible in the park's southernmost (Lapataia) sector.

PLANNING

Maps

Both the Zagier & Urruty 1:50,000 *Ushuaia Trekking Map*, and the simple maps of Parque Nacional Tierra del Fuego, available free of charge from the Administración Parques Nacionales (APN) or tourist office in Ushuaia (p225), are sufficiently accurate for the routes described in this boxed text.

Permits & Regulations

A fee of AR$20 is payable at the park entrance.

Apart from this southernmost (Lapataia) sector of the park and the Paso de la Oveja route (p212), overnight trekking is prohibited in Parque Nacional Tierra del Fuego unless you are accompanied by a park-approved guide (eg from the Compañía de Guías de Patagonia, see p225).

Absolutely no public access is permitted in two biosphere reserves (known as *reservas estrictas*) on the Chilean border – an area on the south side of Lago Fagnano (Kami), and the peninsula between Bahía Lapataia and the Beagle Channel.

NEAREST FACILITIES

The five free, basic campsites (without facilities) become crowded and unreasonably messy in summer. **Camping Ensenada** is 16km from the park entrance and nearest the Senda Costera; **Camping Río Pipo** is 6km from the entrance near the Pampa Alta trail. **Camping Las Bandurrias**, **Camping Laguna Verde** and **Camping Cauquenes** are on islands in the Río Lapataia.

In addition, **Camping Lago Roca** (per person with shower AR$9) at Lago Roca's southern end, has good facilities, including a restaurant and store.

GETTING TO/FROM THE TREKS

Buses leave from the corner of Maipú and Juana Fadul in Ushuaia several times daily from 9am to 6pm, returning from Lapataia approximately every hour between 8am and 8pm. Depending on your destination, a round-trip fare costs AR$50, and you need not return the same day.

The slow-chugging **Tren del Fin del Mundo** (☎ 02901-431600; www.trendelfindelmundo.com.ar; one way/round-trip AR$85/90) takes tourists between Estación del Fin del Mundo, 8km west of Ushuaia, and Estación del Parque, on the Río Pipo near the road to Bahía Ensenada. A one-way taxi costs AR$35.

Remises Carlitos (☎ 02901-422222; San Martín 891) charges around AR$112 (up to three people) for a one-way taxi ride to Lapataia.

THE TREKS

Senda Hito XXIV

From Camping Lago Roca, a flat 10km (four-hour) round-trip trek leads around Lago Roca's forested northeast shore to Hito XXIV – that number is *veinticuatro* in Spanish – the boundary post that marks the Argentina–Chile frontier. Crossing the regularly patrolled frontier is illegal.

From the same trailhead you can reach Cerro Guanaco (973m) via the steep and difficult 8km trail of the same name; it's a long uphill haul but the views are excellent.

Senda Costera

This 8km (four-hour) trek leads west from Bahía Ensenada along the coastline. Keep an eye out for old middens (archaeologically important mounds of shells left by Yaghan inhabitants), now covered in grass. The trail meets Ruta Nacional 3 a short way east of the park administration center (*guardería*) at Lapataia.

Senda Palestra

This 4km (three-hour) round-trip trek from Bahía Ensenada follows a path eastward past an old copper mine to the popular rock-climbing wall of Palestra, near an abandoned *refugio*.

Pampa Alta

The low heights of Pampa Alta (around 315m) grant long views across the Beagle Channel to Isla Navarino and Isla Hoste. Ruta Nacional 3 meets the trailhead 1.5km west of the Río Pipo and Bahía Ensenada road turn-offs (3km from the entrance gate). The 5km round-trip trail first climbs a hill, passing a beaver dam along the way. Enjoy the impressive views at the lookout. A quick 300m further leads to a trail paralleling the Río Pipo and some waterfalls.

Isla El Salmón & Laguna Negra

From the road 2km southwest of Guardería Lapatia, a trail leads north along the western side of Río Lapataia to a fishing spot opposite Isla El Salmón. Laguna Negra, a lovely lake in the forest, is easily accessible via a 1km circuit loop signposted 200m past the trail to Isla El Salmón.

WARNING

Occasional blooms of native marine algae, known as red tide (*marea roja*), contaminate mollusks (such as clams and mussels) with a powerful toxin that is deadly to humans even in small doses. It's best just to avoid shellfish from the shores of the Beagle Channel.

Dividing the island in two unequal halves, the craggy Cordón de los Dientes (with peaks rising over 1000m) shelters the narrow northern coast from southerly storms. The larger southern half of Isla Navarino is a roadless expanse of subantarctic tundra with hundreds of moorland ponds and the large lakes Lago Windhond and Lago Navarino.

ENVIRONMENT

Understanding Isla Navarino's wildlife starts with a look at the island's physical isolation and severe climatic conditions. Where exposure to the elements becomes extreme, vegetation is reduced to beautiful stunted forms. Sheltered north-facing slopes support the only true forests. As a result, there is less tree diversity compared with areas further north, with *lenga* and *coigüe de Magallanes* predominating, and waterlogged peat bogs and mossy lawns competing with the forest at all elevations.

The island has no native land-dwelling predators, although introduced stray and feral dogs are beginning to have a severe impact on the local ecology. Bird life is affected, including the ground-dwelling flightless steamer duck, which forages in flocks near meadows or streams; and the upland goose (*caiquén*), which also lives and nests in open areas close to water. The open alpine scrublands provide a favorable summer habitat for the fire-eyed diucon (*diucón*), an uncommon small grey-breasted bird with blackish-brown wings and red eyes; and an endemic southern subspecies of the yellow-bridled finch (*yal cordillerano austral*).

Isla Navarino's guanacos (ever more rare) are larger and heavier than those found either on the Fuegian or South American mainland. This appears to be the result of the absence of predators – even the indigenous Yaghan (or Yamana) people were essentially seafaring nomads less skilled in hunting agile land-dwelling animals.

Unfortunately, runaway dogs seem to be causing an alarming decline in guanaco numbers, though at least they may also be helping to control Isla Navarino's introduced North American beavers. Andean condors are surprisingly numerous, perhaps because dead beavers supply them with plenty of carrion.

CLIMATE

Isla Navarino has a stark subantarctic climate similar to that of the adjacent Argentine Fuegian Andes, though its mountains are somewhat more exposed to the fierce gales that frequently sweep in from the moody seas immediately south of the island. The Cordón de los Dientes shelters the northern coast of Isla Navarino from these southerlies, receiving up to 2000mm in precipitation annually. This falls fairly evenly throughout the year, but winter brings snowfalls right down to sea level. In the mountains, summer (December, January and February) temperatures average around 8°C – still less extreme than might be expected this far from the equator.

DIENTES CIRCUIT

Duration 5 days
Distance 53.5km
Difficulty moderate–demanding
Start/Finish Puerto Williams
Transport boat or plane
Summary This most southerly trek in the world leads around the spectacular rock towers of the Cordón de los Dientes.

The Dientes Circuit (*Circuito Dientes de Navarino*) leads around the jagged pinnacles known as Los Dientes de Navarino through a spectacular wilderness with raw rock ranges and hundreds of lakes. The Dientes are the highest summits on Isla Navarino, and are identifiable landmarks from around the island and from the Beagle Channel.

There are many naturally boggy areas, but in places beavers have flooded the forested valleys with their (usually shallow) dams.

Cairns, and numbered markers with painted red horizontal stripes on a white background mark the circuit. The numbering corresponds to the route description in the Bienes Nacionales *Circuito Dientes de Navarino* brochure (see Books).

The trek is normally done over four or five days in a clockwise direction. The trekking days laid out here are suggestions only. As good campsites can be found along much of the route, parties can move at their own pace. Numerous possible additional side trips (such as to the Mirador de los Dientes, Lagunas Chevallay, Laguna Alta or even to Lago Windhond) could lengthen the trek by many days.

See also More Treks (p222) for more detail and a description of the trek to Lago Windhond.

PLANNING

When to Trek

The trek is best done from early December to the end of March, although – provided the weather cooperates – more experienced and well-prepared parties can go at least a month earlier or later.

What to Bring

Since there are no *refugios* (or any other constructions) along the route, and only semisheltered campsites, trekkers must carry a good tent and all attendant equipment for an overnight stay

Maps

Two Chilean IGM 1:50,000 maps also cover the Dientes Circuit: *Puerto Williams* (Section L, No 190) and *Lago Windhond* (Section L, No 203). Although these maps fail to show many lakes and do not indicate the circuit route, they are otherwise quite accurate and very useful.

Books

The Chilean Ministerio de Bienes Nacionales (Ministry of National Resources) produced an excellent bilingual (Spanish-English) color brochure titled *Circuito Dientes de Navarino*, with a careful route description and contoured map (at a scale of approximately 1:121,000).

This brochure may be available in Punta Arenas (p199) from the **Bienes Nacionales** office (☎ 061-221651; Av España 981), and online (www.bienes.cl/rutas), but is hard to find on Isla Navarino itself. It is possible that places like Turismo Shila (p223) in Puerto Williams may have a copy that can be photocopied.

Permits & Regulations

Trekkers must leave their details, including expected return date, at the **Carabineros de Chile** (police station; Piloto Pardo). You are expected also to confirm the details of your expected return.

> **WARNING**
>
> This trek into the wild interior of Isla Navarino should not be taken lightly. It is not recommended for solo trekkers. Although somewhat protected by the mountains further to the west, the island experiences constantly unstable and often savage weather, with strong winds and summer snowfalls. The route is extremely isolated and mostly above the tree line in exposed terrain, where careful navigation and route finding is required.

THE TREK

Day 1: Puerto Williams to Laguna del Salto

4–5¼ hours, 12km, 710m ascent

The first section of the trek takes a cleared track up to Cerro Bandera. This is a popular day trek for locals. With light day-packs, the trip to Cerro Bandera can be done in around four hours return (carry water).

Walk along the street (Calle Teniente Andrés Muñoz Henríquez) out of town past the telecommunications station to **Plaza de la Virgen**, a small park at a road junction. Take the road (signposted 'Acceso al Sendero de Chile') and follow it gently up (past a turn-off going to a navy installation) through *canelo* and *coigüe* scrub beside the small **Río Róbalo**. The road reaches a small parking area at a tiny dam, 35 to 45 minutes from Puerto Williams. A short path crosses a footbridge below the spillway cascade to a picnic area with tables and firepits known as the **Mirador Cascada** – some people also camp here.

Do not take the path that follows the river, nor the one that heads east. Take the path into the woods that runs parallel to the river course above the bank. Follow horizontal red stripes on a white background – the markings of the Dientes Circuit – up increasingly steeply southeast through the Magellanic *lenga* forest. Fifty minutes to 1¼ hours on, the trees suddenly give way to wind-battered beech brush. A direct 20- to 30-minute climb straight up the grassy slope leads to **Cerro Bandera** (620m), though topping the peak is strictly extra credit. More a broad ridgetop than a summit, Cerro Bandera (Flag Mountain) was given its name when a large

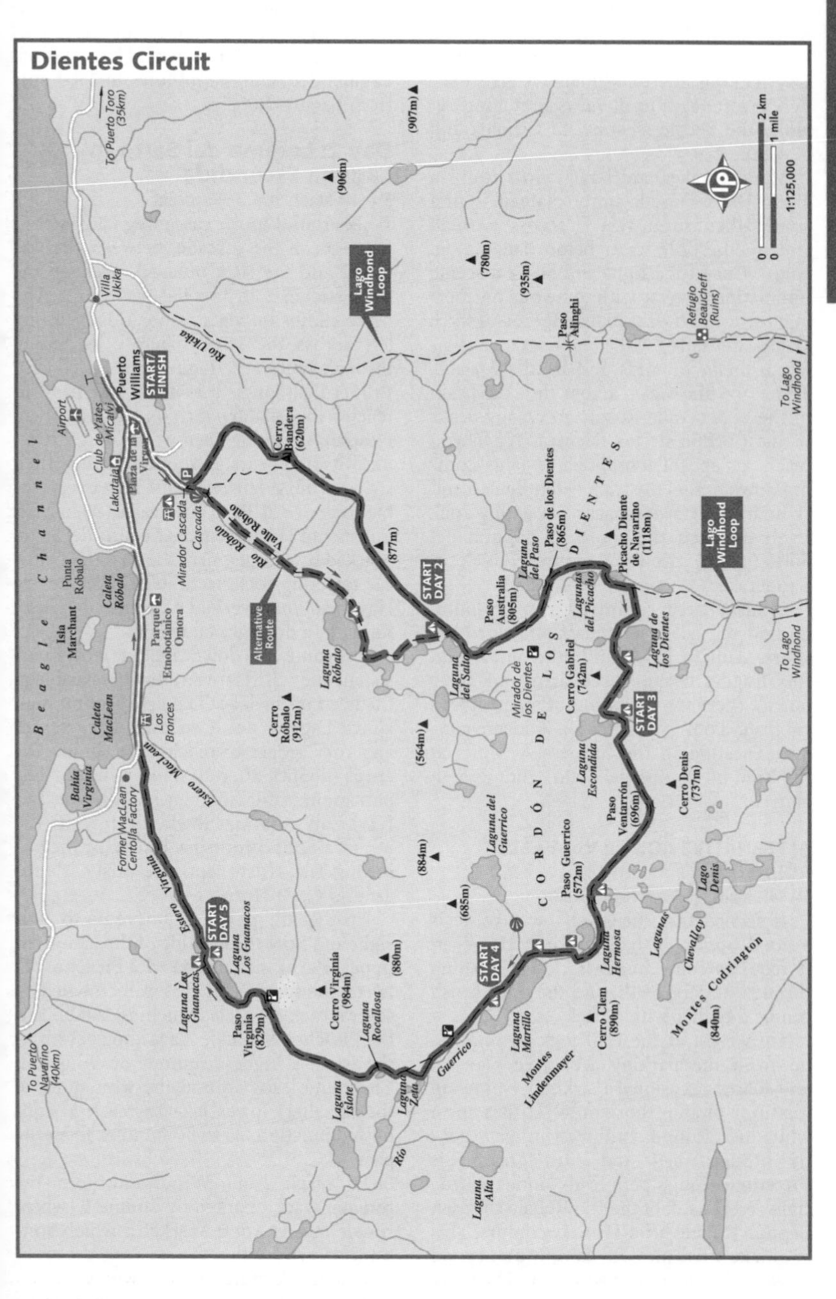
Dientes Circuit
Beagle Channel
To Puerto Toro (35km)
Villa Ukika
Río Ukika
Puerto Williams
START/FINISH
Airport
Club de Yates Micalvi
Plaza de la Virgen
Lakutaia
Mirador Cascada
Cascada
Valle Róbalo
Río Róbalo
Alternative Route
Punta Róbalo
Caleta Róbalo
Isla Marchant
Parque Etnobotánico Omora
Caleta MacLean
Los Bronces
Bahía Virginia
Former MacLean Centolla Factory
Estero MacLean
Estero Virginia
START DAY 5
Laguna Los Guanacos
Paso Virginia (829m)
Cerro Virginia (984m)
Laguna Rocallosa
Laguna Islote
Laguna Zeta
Río Guerrico
Laguna Alta
Laguna Martillo
Montes Lindenmayer
START DAY 4
Laguna Hermosa
Cerro Clem (890m)
Montes Codrington
(840m)
Lagunas Chevallay
Lago Denis
Cerro Denis (737m)
Paso Guerrico (572m)
Paso Ventarrón (696m)
Laguna Escondida
START DAY 3
Laguna de los Dientes
Cerro Gabriel (742m)
Cordón de los Dientes
Mirador de los Dientes
Laguna del Salto
Paso Australia (805m)
Lagunas del Picacho
Picacho Diente de Navarino (1118m)
Paso de los Dientes (865m)
Laguna del Paso
START DAY 2
Laguna Róbalo
Cerro Róbalo (912m)
Laguna del Guerrico
Cerro Bandera (620m)
Lago Windhond Loop
To Lago Windhond
Refugio Beaucheff (Ruins)
Paso Alinghi
To Puerto Navarino (40km)
1:125,000
2 km
1 mile

sheet-metal Chilean flag was erected here in the early 1980s during a tense period of military confrontation with Argentina. Overlooking Puerto Williams, Cerro Bandera gives magnificent views stretching out along the Beagle Channel to Ushuaia and beyond.

Marker stakes and large cairns lead on along the exposed, stony plateau – first south, then southwest – across a small stream (the only water before Laguna del Salto). Cut to the right and begin a scenic undulating traverse with some narrow footing just above the scrub line. It crosses scree slopes alternating with areas of green, lawn-like *azorella* mounds and heathy *brecillo*. There are fine views across the lake basin of the upper Valle Róbalo to craggy peaks in the Cordón de los Dientes. When you reach a slope of loose, coarse talus coming down across the trail, carefully descend right in tight switchbacks via a tiny rock knob to reach the shore of **Laguna del Salto** (474m), two to 2½ hours from Cerro Bandera.

Semisheltered **campsites** can be found around the lake's southeast and northern shore. Aim to have minimum impact on this fragile, heavily used area and carry out all (perhaps including other peoples') rubbish. Look for pairs of Andean condors (nesting in the impressive bluffs at the head of Laguna del Salto) gliding high above.

ALTERNATIVE ROUTE: VIA VALLE RÓBALO

3¼–4¼ hours, 10.5km, 455m ascent

Less scenic, this sheltered lower route is a good option in bad weather. However, it requires some bushwhacking (pushing through undergrowth) and the thick brush can be a bother with a pack.

Turn right at the trail fork 10 minutes up from the parking area (see Day 1), and follow occasional markings (some are missing) of blue horizontal stripes on a white background southwest up very gently through *coigüe* and *lenga* forest. This sometimes-rough path leads along the true right (east) bank of the Río Róbalo to reach **Laguna Róbalo** after 1½ to two hours. This large lake offers pleasant **camping** and good views of the Dientes de Navarino. The route continues around the lake's southeastern shore past another small tarn in the low forest, then climbs slightly southeast past the shore of another unnamed lake to reach Laguna del Salto, 50 minutes to 1¼ hours from Laguna Róbalo.

Day 2: Laguna del Salto to Laguna Escondida

3¼–4¼ hours, 9km, 560m ascent

Walk around to the cascading lake inlet to the right of the cascade, between the waterfall and the rock outcrop. Trek up the steep stream gully to a flat grassy area. The route climbs on via a minor ridge, cutting left across the stream before ascending through a rocky gap (sometimes called Paso Primero, although it is not a true pass) to reach a tiny shallow tarn on a barren shelf. Head up alongside the now trickling stream until it disappears at another tarnlet, then swing around left (eastward) up over rubble to arrive at **Paso Australia** (805m), 50 minutes to 1¼ hours from Laguna del Salto. Marked by a large cairn, the pass lies below the towering rock 'teeth' of the Dientes de Navarino and overlooks Laguna del Paso, filling in a deep glacial trough.

The route cuts down rightward over persistent snowdrifts toward the gap visible at the head of the lake. Traverse around high above Laguna del Paso over scree slopes and rock ledges to reach **Paso de los Dientes** (865m), after 30 to 40 minutes. The pass grants your first views south over Isla Navarino's spongy lowlands toward the mountainous Peninsula Hardy on neighboring Isla Hoste, and the misty islands around Cape Horn.

Drop gently past a tiny névé up to your right and skirt the left side of the elongated upper lake of the **Lagunas del Picacho**, between the spectacular east wall crowned by several rock pinnacles touching 1000m and the Picacho Diente de Navarino (1118m) – the island's highest summit on your left. The route leads around the west shore of the (smaller) lower lake to reach a signposted junction, 25 to 30 minutes from the pass.

To reach Lago Windhond, join the rougher track, marked by Snupie 1 (where *snupie* means 'route marker'), which continues down south.

The circuit route (marked with a red dot and Snupie 16 to the far right) turns away westward, climbing across a minor ridge before it cuts down through *lenga* scrub to reach **Laguna de los Dientes**, after 30 to 40 minutes. Trace the beaver-chewed shoreline for 15 to 20 minutes around to an inlet stream on its northwest side, where you will find scenic **campsites** (GPS 55° 01.044 S, 67° 41.087 W) with views over this sizable lake to the Dientes peaks.

Climb moderately northwest through a tiny side valley past small tarns to a minor watershed under the impressive rock pinnacles of Cerro Gabriel (742m), where the starkly beautiful **Laguna Escondida** suddenly appears. Laguna Escondida (Hidden Lake) is enclosed on three sides by reddish craggy peaks and fringed by scree slides. Descend almost to a rocky bluff, then cut down left and follow the sometimes-bouldery (but always beavered) shore to the lake outlet, 40 to 50 minutes from Laguna de los Dientes. The exposed campsites here are not recommended, but there is sheltered **camping** a few minutes downstream.

Day 3: Laguna Escondida to Laguna Martillo

3–4¼ hours, 8km, 240m ascent

Follow the lake outlet 10 minutes down past small beaver ponds before cutting to the right over the stream. The route sidles on west through low *lenga* forest along the edge of tilted cliffs above more beaver dams and then into the head of a tiny side valley. It then ascends a small ridge to reach **Paso Ventarrón** (GPS 55° 01.350 S, 67° 43.413 W), one to 1½ hours from Laguna Escondida. This very windy saddle (696m) lies on the north side of **Cerro Denis** (737m) and is marked by a high cairn. Paso Ventarrón looks out southwest across the wild enchanting basin of the **Lagunas Chevallay** toward the mildly contoured Montes Codrington (named by Captain Fitz Roy of the HMS *Beagle* after one of his crew, although Fitz Roy almost certainly intended the more striking Dientes).

Do not head directly down the slope, but first walk five minutes along the ridge before you begin a long descending traverse northwest over coarse talus into the *lenga* scrub to reach a first beaver dam. The route circles around the edge of this peaty basin above tarns and past fair **campsites** on occasional drier flat areas to the end of an elongated lake. Here, cut up rightward through a bouldery chute and follow red markings up to **Paso Guérrico** (also called Paso de la Hermosa). This pass (572m) gives a fine view over Laguna Hermosa (Beautiful Lake) to Cerro Clem, the sharp southern summit of the Montes Lindenmayer (see boxed text Patagonian Pioneer Clem Lindenmayer p18).

The path first heads down southwest, traversing some way above the initially steep scrubby sides of Laguna Hermosa before it drops to the lake and continues around to reach the lake's northern shore, 1½ to two hours from Paso Ventarrón. There is scenic semisheltered **camping** in *lenga* scrub on both sides of the outlet. Look for ashy-headed geese (*canquén*) paddling the picturesque islet in this kidney-shaped lake. Make your way on down the stream's true right bank for 20 to 25 minutes to arrive at **Laguna Martillo** (Hammer Lake) with better **campsites** a short way back from this southeastern shore.

Day 4: Laguna Martillo to Laguna Los Guanacos

3½–5 hours, 10.5km, 420m ascent

Head around the right (northeastern) side of Laguna Martillo. Pass sporadic **campsites**, climbing over a small peninsula to reach a tiny clearing on the lake's northern 'hammerhead' section, after 30 to 40 minutes. Proceed for five minutes to the outlet (the Río Guérrico) and head downvalley through soggy meadows on the stream's northern side under an impressive row of rock spires in the Montes Lindenmayer to reach **Laguna Zeta** (424m), 30 to 40 minutes on.

Follow a small inlet stream of this Z-shaped lake southeast for five minutes to rejoin the marked route (which takes a more difficult short cut over scrubby ridges without passing Laguna Zeta). Continue northwest past a beaver pond to **Laguna Rocallosa** (GPS 54° 58.999 S, 67° 47.425 W). The route skirts the north shore of this small, elongated lake before rising over a crest into a waterlogged basin and climbing to a marker cairn on a small rock outcrop above **Laguna Islote** (Islet Lake; GPS 54° 58.575 S, 67° 47.802 W).

Cut up diagonally rightward into low *lenga* forest, then make a very steep and muddy ascent directly against the slope to finally reach a grassy ledge beside a streamlet. (Due to heavy erosion this rather unsatisfactory section of the circuit may be rerouted at some future time.) Climb on, still quite steeply, through a grassy chute out of the trees, then traverse up northward to meet a stream coming from a broad barren plateau (GPS 54° 58.037 S, 67° 47.440 W). There are more marvellous views back south to the rugged Montes Lindenmayer and Laguna Alta (High Lake), a hanging lake with an outlet cascading into the Valle Guérrico, and northwest (along the Beagle Channel) to Ushuaia and the Cordillera Darwin. Peaks on the neighboring Isla Hoste also stand out.

Head up about 50m to the right of the stream past icy tarns, continuing northeast across the barren sloping plateau to reach **Paso Virginia** (829m), 1½ to 2¼ hours from Laguna Zeta. This point, the highest on the circuit, gives new vistas northeast across the Beagle Channel. Directly ahead the land falls away abruptly into Laguna Los Guanacos, a classic glacial lake in a deep, spectacular trough.

Take extra care in this section, which most trekkers approach tired from the ascent. Keeping well away from the often dangerously corniced precipice rim, walk 100m rightward to where red markings lead down through bluffs. The route then makes a rapid sliding descent that zigzags through coarse, loose scree slopes toward the lake. Cross the talus fields on the northwest side of Laguna Los Guanacos to reach the lake outlet, 50 minutes to 1¼ hours from the pass. On the opposite bank are scenic **campsites** sheltered by low scrub (and by the enclosed lake basin itself).

Day 5: Laguna Los Guanacos to Puerto Williams

4–5½ hours, 14km, 530m descent

From the campsites at the outlet to Laguna Los Guanacos, drop steeply along the true left (west) side of the **Estero Virginia** into the trees. Cross the tumbling stream immediately before you come out onto the boggy terrace surrounding Laguna Las Guanacas, after 15 to 20 minutes. There are excellent **campsites** here at the edge of the *lengas*.

Head around the right (eastern) shore, then continue down across another terrace with several more beaver ponds. Many trail markings have been lost in this section. Follow a vague and somewhat rough trail, bushwhacking through coigüe forest along the right (east) bank of the stream. The trail eventually comes out into a tiny wet clearing covered with big, fleshy-leafed daisies (GPS 54° 56.686 S, 67° 44.002 W), just as the valley begins to open up. You are approximately one to 1½ hours from Laguna Las Guanacas.

Cut over rightward into fire-cleared slopes overlooking the picturesque Bahía Virginia and Caleta MacLean. Move down northeast through regenerating slopes of red *chauras*, *calafate* bushes and clover. In many places stock trails confuse the route, which follows a ridge above an abandoned seafood-processing plant (the former MacLean Centolla factory). It finally meets Isla Navarino's north coast road at the **Estero MacLean**, after a final 45 minutes to one hour. Just across the road bridge is **Los Bronces**, a picnic area (where trekkers have been known to camp).

From here, it's a pleasant 7.5km (two- to 2½-hour) walk east along the road past the Parque Etnobotánico Omora back to **Puerto Williams**. Occasional vehicles usually stop (even for trekkers who are not actually hitchhiking).

MORE TREKS

ISLA NAVARINO

Lago Windhond

In the uninhabited southern sector of Isla Navarino, Lago Windhond is a remote and utterly tranquil destination for camping and fishing. This three- to four-day, 41km trek passes through Fuegian forest, steppe and peat bogs, providing a suitable lowland alternative to Dientes de Navarino if the weather is poor.

The route goes north to south, either from the Cascada sector to Lago Windhond, returning via Rio Ukika on a dirt access road near Puerto Williams, or in reverse. Start at Cascada (ideal if the weather is good), following the directions for the first day and a half of the Dientes de Navarino trek (p217), then continue following markers to Lago Windhond. Directions are available online (www.bienes.cl/rutas). The

GPS coordinates of route markers (called *snupies*) are also online.

ARGENTINE FUEGIAN ANDES

Glaciar Martial

A hearty day trek from downtown Ushuaia leads up to Glaciar Martial (see Argentine Fuegian Andes map, p208), with fantastic panoramas of Ushuaia and the Beagle Channel. In fact, the views are possibly more impressive than the actual glacier. The trek can be lengthened by continuing over the saddle and dropping down to intersect with the route through the Valle Andorra described in the Paso de la Oveja trek (p212). Use Zagier & Urruty's 1:50,000 *Ushuaia Trekking Map*.

Minibuses that travel to Glaciar Martial leave from the corner of Maipú and Juana Fadul (round-trip AR$25) every half-hour.

You can also walk to the start of the trek (7km from town) by taking San Martín west and continuing to ascend as it zigzags (there are many trekker short cuts) to the ski run. At this point, either take the Aerosilla (AR$20; 10am-7pm) or walk another two hours to the snout of the Glaciar Martial.

Estancia Túnel & Estancia La Segunda

This easy–moderate four-day coastal trek leads to isolated ranches on the Beagle Channel east of Ushuaia. Following heavy rain, the trail can be considerably muddier and less pleasant.

From Ushuaia, take Ruta Nacional 3 (via taxi or walking) southeast to the trout hatchery (*estación de piscicultura*), 6km from the center of town. The trail begins from the bridge on the lower Río Olivia. Cross the Río Olivia and continue past Estancia Río Olivia. The route leads on for 9km round the steep-sided coastline to Estancia Túnel. On the way (3km before Estancia Túnel), the coastal Camino del Atlántico reaches the lighthouse at Punta Escarpados. From Estancia Túnel, it is possible to continue for a further 10km to Estancia La Segunda. Trekkers can choose to turn around at their fancy but the whole trek from the bridge is 38kms round-trip.

Use Zagier & Urruty's 1:50,000 *Ushuaia Trekking Map*.

TOWNS & FACILITIES

OUTSIDE USHUAIA (ARGENTINA)

Valle de Lobos (☎ 15-616383; www.gatocuruchet.com.ar) is a small cross-country skiing and dog-sledding center just off Ruta Nacional 3, about 19km from Ushuaia.

A little further along Ruta Nacional 3, **Solar del Bosque** (☎ 02901-43527; km 3020) and **Nunatak** (☎ 02901-437454; www.nunatakadventure.com; Ruta Nacional 3, km 3018) both offer lodging and outdoor activities.

Also on Ruta Nacional 3, 12.5km from the center of Ushuaia, the upmarket **Hostería Kauyeken** (☎ 02901-433041; d from US$131) is a convenient 500m south from the end of the Sierra Valdivieso Circuit (p205), at the western foot of Monte Olivia.

For transport to these places from Ushuaia, see p224.

PUERTO WILLIAMS (CHILE)

☎ 061 / pop 2500

Forget Ushuaia's claims, this burg where colts roam Main St and round-the-world sailors take refuge is the end of the world. Naval settlement Puerto Williams is the only town on Isla Navarino, the official port of entry for vessels en route to Cape Horn and Antarctica, and home to the last living Yaghan speaker.

Luis at **Turismo Shila** (☎ 061-621745; www.truismoshila.cl; Plaza de Ancla s/n; 9am-1pm & 3-7pm) can recommend local trekking guides. The store stocks maps, butane gas, and rents tents, stoves and GPS units.

Denis Chevallay at **Fuegia & Co** (☎ 061-621251; fuegia@usa.net; Patrullero Ortiz 049) offers a professional guide service (four-day trekking trip per person CH$325,000) in French, German and English, with a wealth of botanical and historical knowledge at his fingertips.

Sleeping & Eating

Argentine-run **Sur-Sur Hostal** (☎ 061-621849; www.sur-sur.com; dm/d CH$8000/40,000) has its own restaurant.

Bright hostel **Refugio El Padrino** (☎061-621136; ceciliamancillao@yahoo.com.ar; Costanera 267; dm CH$10,000) sits right on the channel with an outdoor deck. The recommended **Residencial Pusaki** (☎061-621116; pattypusaki@yahoo.es; Piloto Pardo 260; s/d CH$10,500/21,000) welcomes travelers with comfortable rooms and memorable meals (reserve with advance notice).

Essential trekking provisions can be bought at various minimarkets in Puerto Williams, although prices are high.

Bonhomie abounds at **Angelus** (☎061-621080; Centro Comercial 151; closed Sun), is a popular pub, ideal for a beer, homemade pie or crab pasta. The bar at the **Club de Yates Micalvi** (☎061-621042; beer CH$2000; open late, closed Jun-Aug), Puerto Williams' legendary yacht club at the docks, comes alive after 9pm. As watering holes go, this may be like no other. A grounded German cargo boat, the Milcalvi was declared aregional naval museum in 1976 but found infinitely better use as a floating bar, frequented by navy men and yachties.

Getting There & Around

As the island taxi service is inconsistent, ask your lodging or the airport transfer driver about trekker shuttles around the island.

The following forms of transport have fewer winter departures.

AIR

From November to March, **Aerovías DAP** (☎061-621051; www.dap.cl; Plaza de Ancla s/n) flies to Punta Arenas (one-way CH$52,000) Wednesday through Saturday and Monday. Often passengers are wait-listed until the company has enough bookings to run a flight. Note the checked baggage limit is 10kg (CH$1000 per extra kilogram). A shuttle (CH$3000) takes passengers to town, otherwise it's a half-hour walk. To get to the airport, make transportation arrangements with your hostel.

Aeroclub Ushuaia (in Ushuaia ☎02901-421717; www.aeroclubushuaia.org.ar) flies to Puerto Williams from Ushuaia (one-way US$120) in the morning three times per week.

BOAT

The Patagonia ferry of **Transbordadora Austral Broom** (www.tabsa.cl) sails from Puerto Williams to Punta Arenas two or three times a month on Friday (reclining seat/bunk CH$72,500/87,500, 38 hours). Meals are included.

Ushuaia Boating (☎061-621227, 098-2695812; www.ushuaiaboating.com, in Spanish; Maragano 168; one-way CH$60,000) runs zodiac boats to Ushuaia at 9.30am and 4pm daily from September to March. The boat trip takes 40 minutes, but a bus (included) first transfers passengers from Puerto Williams to Puerto Navarino (1½ hours). Reservations can be made at Angelus (see Sleeping & Eating).

THE YAGHAN WORLD

Precious little remains of the resilient Yaghanes, a canoe people who once traveled the waterways skin-diving for mussels. A 15-minute walk east of town along the waterfront leads to the mestizo Yaghan settlement of Villa Ukika, with a crafts store selling books and whale bone knives. You can also visit the gorgeous new **Museo Martín Gusinde** (☎061-621043; cnr Araguay & Gusinde; donations requested; 9am-1pm & 2.30-7pm Mon-Fri, 2.30-6.30pm Sat & Sun), focused on Yaghan history.

USHUAIA (ARGENTINA)

☎02901 / pop 58,000

Annually drawing hundreds of thousands of visitors, Ushuaia occupies a narrow escarpment between the Beagle Channel and the snowcapped Martial Range. Though remote, it is plugged into modern commerce with a critical mass of stores, cafes and restaurants.

Information

The **oficina de turismo** (☎02901-432000, outside of Tierra del Fuego 0800-3331476; www.e-ushuaia.com, in Spanish; San Martín 674; 8am-10pm Mon-Fri, 9am-8pm Sat, Sun & holidays) is very helpful, while **Club Andino Ushuaia** (CAU; ☎02901-422335; www.clubandinoushuaia.com.ar; Fadul 50; 10am-12.30pm & 2-9pm Mon-Fri, 10am-2pm Sat in summer) sells maps and organizes some treks and climbs.

The **APN office** (☎02901-421315; pntf@tierradelfuego.org.ar; San Martín 1395;

9am-4pm Mon-Fri) give advice on trekking Parque Nacional Tierra del Fuego.

Supplies & Equipment

Compañía de Guías de Patagonia (☎ 02901-437753; www.companiadeguias.com.ar; San Martín 654) guides multiday treks and provides logistical support for remote expeditions.

For tailored trips or winter excursions with a backcountry ski element, try **Gotama Expediciones** (☎ 02901-436991, 1560 5301; www.gotama-expediciones.com); it also rents avalanche transceivers.

Deportes Todo Terreno (☎ 02901-434939; www.dttushuaia.com.ar; San Martín 903) sells outdoor gear, including tents and ice-climbing tools.

Casa Fuegia (☎ 02901-430767; San Martín 1240) sells white gasoline (known as diluyente industrial).

Sleeping & Eating

Camping Municipal (Ruta Nacional 3; camping free) is 10km west of town, en route to Parque Nacional Tierra del Fuego.

Several kilometers northwest of Ushuaia's center near the lower chairlift station, CAU's **Camping Pista del Andino** (☎ 02901-435890; www.lapistadelandino.com.ar, in Spanish; Av Alem 2873; camping per person AR$15) has campsites with good facilities and rental bikes. Phone for a free pick-up.

Catering to backpackers are the ample **Antarctica Hostel** (☎ 02901-435774; www.antarcticahostel.com; Antártida Argentina 270; dm/d AR$50/170), with a cool balcony kitchen and beer on tap; and the artsy **Yakush** (☎ 02901-435807; www.hostelyakush.com.ar; Piedrabuena 118; dm AR$55), with a breakfast of *medialunas (croissants)*, coffee and maté (traditional tea).

Family-run **Galeazzi-Basily B&B** (☎ 02901-423213; www.avesdelsur.com.ar; Valdéz 323; tw AR$120, five-person cabins AR$180) rolls out the welcome mat with good rooms and excellent cabins just uphill from the center of town.

El Turco (☎ 02901-424711; San Martín 1040; mains AR$21; closed Sun lunch) is popular for cheap eats, pizza and pasta.

A worthy splurge, **María Lola Restó** (☎ 02901-421185; Deloquí 1048; mains AR$35; noon-midnight Mon-Sat) deeply satisfies with seafood pasta, smothered steaks and heaping desserts.

Getting There & Away

In January and early February, airline and bus tickets to/from Ushuaia must be booked well in advance.

AIR

The airport departure tax is AR$13. Taxis to/from the modern airport (USH), 4km southwest of downtown on the peninsula across from the waterfront, cost AR$25, and there's local bus service along Maipú.

Aerolíneas Argentinas (☎ 02901-421218; Roca 116) flies several times daily to Buenos Aires (AR$540, 3½ hours), sometimes stopping in Río Gallegos (AR$360, one hour) or El Calafate (AR$384, 70 minutes).

Lade (☎ 02901-421123; San Martín 542) flies to Buenos Aires (AR$363) and El Calafate (AR$280).

Lan Argentina (in Argentina 0810 9999 526; www.lan.com) goes to Punta Arenas, Chile (AR$480), and Argentine destinations.

Aeroclub Ushuaia (☎ 02901-421717, 421892; www.aeroclubushuaia.org.ar) flies to Puerto Williams, Chile (AR$360), at 9am on Monday, Wednesday and Friday.

BOAT

Zodiac boats run daily, weather permitting, to Puerto Williams (AR$360; 40mins). Visit **Ushuaia Boating** (☎ 02901-436153; www.ushuaiaboating.com; Godoy 190; closed Sun) for schedules.

BUS

Ushuaia has no bus terminal. **Tecni-Austral** (☎ 02901-431408/12; Roca 157) has 5am buses for Punta Arenas (AR$175, 12 hours) via Río Grande (AR$60, four hours) on Monday, Wednesday and Friday, stopping in Tolhuin.

Transportes Pasarela (☎ 02901-424582) shuttles trekkers to Laguna Esmeralda (per person AR$40) and Lago Fagnano (per person AR$120), with hostel pick-ups and a two- to three-passenger minimum.

Trekkers Directory

CONTENTS

ACCOMMODATION

Finding lodgings is only difficult during the seasonal vacation rush between Christmas and mid-February. Book Parque Nacional Torres del Paine and El Chaltén accommodations well in advance. While larger towns and tourist centers offer a wide range of accommodations, connecting villages on Ruta 40 or the Carretera Austral have mostly basic family-run accommodations and an expensive lodge or two. Most local tourist offices have an up-to-date list of lodgings and can check availability.

Never hesitate to ask to see a room before making a decision.

Some high-end establishments quote rates on US dollars, we have maintained these rates here.

Camping

Organized campsites are widespread and generally offer good services, with flush toilets, hot showers and a grill or *quincho* – a common cooking shelter for rainy weather.

Campsites fill up quickly in the busy summer holiday season, and can get noisy. Argentina usually has a per-person rate (of around US$5) while Chilean campsites usually charge per site (up to US$20 for five people); ask for a discount if you're alone.

For camping in Chile, your best resource is Turistel's *Rutero Camping* guide, with maps and distances. Santiago's **Sernatur** (www.sernatur.cl) has a free pamphlet listing campsites throughout Chile.

WILD CAMPING

The term 'wild camping' means pitching your tent outside established campsites or campsites. All Argentine and some Chilean national parks have now banned wild

PRACTICALITIES

- For news in English, check out *Santiago Times* (www.santiagotimes.cl) or Buenos Aires Herald (www.buenosairesherald.com)
- Argentina's *Clarín* (www.clarin.com in Spanish) or Chile's *El Mercurio* (www.elmercurio.cl, in Spanish) give comprehensive national news
- The electricity current operates on 220V, 50 cycles
- Gadgets plug into outlets that accept two rounded prongs (Chile) or three angled flat prongs (Argentina)
- Use the metric system except for tire pressure (measured in pounds per square inch)

camping, and only allow camping at park-designated sites along the trails. During the busy summer holiday period, when cheap accommodation is scarce, wild camping close to roads and towns is common among local backpackers, though it calls for some discretion – see Responsible Trekking (p36).

Casas de Familia & Rural Homestays

There is no better way to steep yourself in local culture than staying at a *casa de familia*. Especially in the south, it's common for families to rent rooms to visitors. This is a great way to get off the gringo trail and enjoy rural hospitality. Guests do not always have kitchen privileges but usually can pay modest prices for abundant meals or laundry service. Tourist offices maintain lists of such accommodations, which are particularly common in Chile.

There are many organized networks in Chile's south, most notably in Chiloé, Lago Ranco, around Pucón and Patagonia. For options in Patagonia, check out Coyhaique's **Casa de Turismo Rural** (www.casaturismorural.cl). For countrywide options inquire at tourist offices.

Hospedajes, Pensiones & Residenciales

Aside from hostels, these are Patagonia's cheapest accommodations, offering sometimes homey, simple accommodations, usually with foam-mattress beds, hard pillows, clean sheets and blankets.

Especially in high season, room rates may be the same for single or double occupancy, but singles can try to negotiate a price if there are many vacancies. Bathrooms and shower facilities are usually shared and a basic breakfast is usually included in the price.

Hostels

A new generation of hostels in traveler hot spots offers budget travelers far more stylish and service-oriented lodgings. They usually set aside a few well-heeled doubles for couples that want a social atmosphere but greater creature comforts.

Independent backpacker hostels advertise in regional travel publications and pamphlets, like **Backpackers Chile** (www.backpackerschile.com), with many European-run listings. Most places don't insist on a Hostelling International (HI) card, but charge a bit more for non-members. The local affiliates of HI are **Asociación Chilena de Albergues Turísticos Juveniles** (www.hostelling.cl; Hernando de Aguirre 201, Oficina 602, Providencia, Santiago) and **Hosteling International Argentina** (☎ 11-45118723; www.hitravel.com.ar; Florida 835, Piso 3, Oficina 319b, Buenos Aires). There are also many non-HI hostels.

Hotels

In Chile and Argentina, the term *hostal* indicates a higher-end accommodation and not a youth hostel. However, there can also be very cheap hotels with few amenities, it's hard to judge by name alone. Patagonia's increasing popularity means that the range of hotels available has improved. Though midrange hotels can be overpriced, the luxury category is quite decadent (and expensive).

Refugios

Within some Chilean national parks, **Conaf** (Corporación Nacional Forestal; ☎ 02-6630000; Av Bulnes 285, Centro; 9.30am-5.30pm Mon-Thu, 9.30am-4.30pm Fri) maintains rustic shelters *(refugios)* for trekkers, which unfortunately lack upkeep due to Conaf's limited budget. In some of the more popular parks, most notably Torres del Paine, private concessions (franchises) manage comfortable and well-appointed *refugios* with bunks, mattresses, showers and even restaurants. Private reserves sometimes have *refugios* set up along their trails.

In Argentina's national parks, *refuigos* are usually run by concessionaires and can be quite clean and efficient. Those around

BOOK ACCOMMODATION ONLINE

For more accommodation reviews and recommendations by Lonely Planet authors, check out www.lonelyplanet.com/hotels. You'll find the true, insider lowdown on the best places to stay. Reviews are thorough and independent. Best of all, you can book online.

Bariloche are comparable in standard to mountain huts in New Zealand or Europe, with a fee payable to the resident hutkeeper. (Note that some hostels call themselves *refugio* although they are not really 'huts' at all.) *Refugios* can quickly become overcrowded in wet weather and during the holiday season; it is recommended that you carry a tent even in areas where there are good *refugios*.

BUSINESS HOURS

In general, bank hours are from 10am to 4pm, weekdays, and offices are normally open from 9am until noon, then from 2pm to 6pm. In Argentina, shops generally stay open until 8pm or 9pm. In the bigger cities, supermarkets and larger shops often stay open throughout the day, but in more remote areas the siesta break can be as long as four hours. Government offices and many businesses have adopted a more conventional 8am to 5pm schedule.

In summer, tourist offices in larger centers are generally open daily, at least from 9am to 6pm; in smaller towns tourist offices are usually closed on Sunday (sometimes also Saturday).

Ranger stations and information centers in national parks and reserves are usually open daily, but regional Conaf and APN offices are generally open Monday to Friday from 9am to 5pm or 6pm.

Restaurant hours in Argentina are typically 12pm–11pm. In both countries, resaurants close during the lull, from approximately 3.30am–7.30pm.

CHILDREN

The Patagonian Andes' rugged terrain and weather generally makes these mountains unsuitable for trekking with children under nine years of age. Overnight treks require packing a full range of camping gear. It is impractical, and at times unsafe, for parents to carry the additional weight of a tired, bored child on their backs, or to expect a child to carry the provisions necessary for a multi day trip.

The most family-friendly areas are Parque Nacional Torres del Paine and the Fitz Roy area of Parque Nacional Los Glaciares, due to their marked trails, extensive infrastructure and doses of creature comforts. The Lakes District and Araucania also provide good bases for families who want to get some trekking in.

Overnight trekking with younger children should be limited to shorter-distance routes and day treks. Treks rated easy or easy–moderate include Termas Lahuen Co to La Unión, Pampa Frutilla, Laguna Torre and routes in the Lapataia area of Parque Nacional Tierra del Fuego (see Table of Treks, p16) and are suitable for children.

Children walk slower and need more frequent rest stops than adults. The distance and duration of the trek you choose should be based on the children's capabilities, rather than your own with a bit taken off. Remember that children are very sensitive to environmental extremes. This makes them more prone to hypothermia, heatstroke, heat exhaustion and sunburn. It's important to bring a good range of clothing for varying conditions in addition to plenty of food and water.

Lonely Planet's *Travel With Children* by Cathy Lanigan offers lots of practical advice on this subject.

CLIMATE

The vast, unbroken stretch of ocean to the west and south of the South American continent leaves the Patagonian Andes exposed to the saturated winds that circle the Antarctic land mass. The north–south line of the range forms a formidable barrier to these violent westerlies (known to English speakers as the Roaring Forties and the Furious Fifties), which dump staggering quantities of rain or snow on the ranges of the Patagonian Cordillera.

By Andean standards, the average height of the Patagonian mountains is relatively low, but they capture virtually all the airborne moisture and leave the vast Patagonian plains on the leeward side in a severe rain shadow. Nowhere else on earth do precipitation levels drop off so dramatically over such a short distance. Having left their moisture behind in the Andes, the now dry and cold westerly winds sweep down across eastern Patagonia towards the Atlantic, drying out the already arid steppes even more.

The strong maritime influence makes for highly unpredictable weather in the Patagonian Andes. Particularly in spring or early summer, fine weather may deteriorate

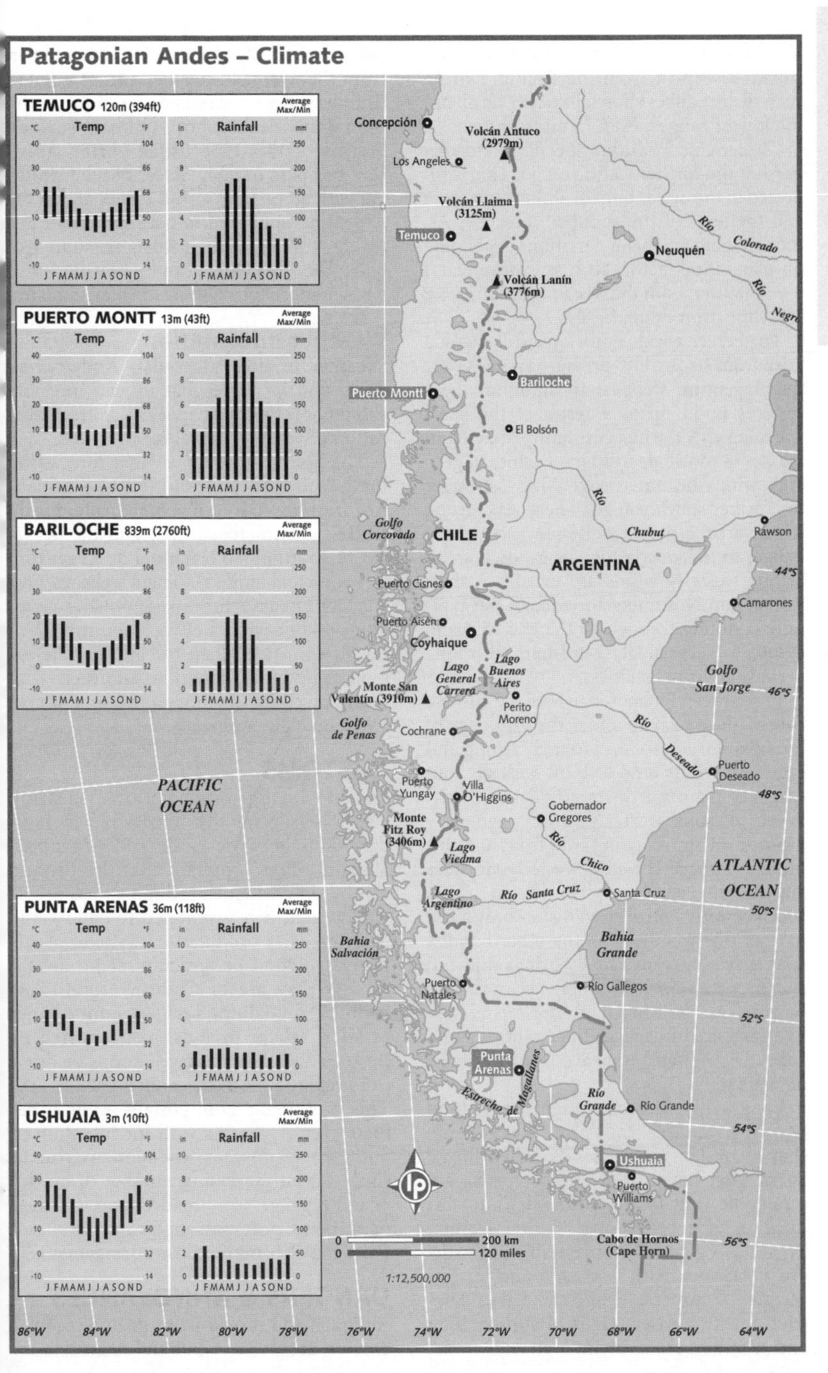
Patagonian Andes – Climate
TEMUCO 120m (394ft)
PUERTO MONTT 13m (43ft)
BARILOCHE 839m (2760ft)
PUNTA ARENAS 36m (118ft)
USHUAIA 3m (10ft)
Average Max/Min
Temp
Rainfall
PACIFIC OCEAN
ATLANTIC OCEAN
CHILE
ARGENTINA
Concepción
Los Angeles
Volcán Antuco (2979m)
Volcán Llaima (3125m)
Temuco
Neuquén
Volcán Lanín (3776m)
Bariloche
Puerto Montt
El Bolsón
Golfo Corcovado
Chubut
Rawson
Puerto Cisnes
Camarones
Puerto Aisén
Coyhaique
Lago General Carrera
Lago Buenos Aires
Monte San Valentín (3910m)
Perito Moreno
Golfo San Jorge
Golfo de Penas
Cochrane
Puerto Deseado
Puerto Yungay
Villa O'Higgins
Gobernador Gregores
Monte Fitz Roy (3406m)
Lago Viedma
Lago Argentino
Santa Cruz
Bahia Salvación
Bahia Grande
Puerto Natales
Río Gallegos
Punta Arenas
Estrecho de Magallanes
Río Grande
Ushuaia
Puerto Williams
Cabo de Hornos (Cape Horn)
1:12,500,000
200 km
120 miles

almost without warning, as violent westerly storms sweep in from the Pacific. During such disturbances snowfalls occur on all but the lowest ranges, even in midsummer.

Climatic conditions become steadily harsher the further south you go. This is reflected in the upper limit of alpine vegetation and the level of the summer snowline. Although there are major variations depending on many local factors such as exposure and precipitation, both the tree line and summer snowline drop dramatically.

The severe winds notorious to Patagonia arise from strong low-pressure systems over the Argentine steppes. In summer, these systems build up as a result of the sun's warming effect, while constantly drawing in masses of moist air from the Pacific. In general, winds become progressively stronger the further south you go, where very strong winds area a major nuisance and even a danger to trekkers in high or exposed areas. Strong westerly winds are usually at their worst from November to January, but typically continue through to the end of April. Winter is surprisingly wind-free, with long periods of virtual stillness.

In southern Patagonia, where the climate comes more heavily under the influence of the subantarctic zone, extremely strong and incessant winds tend to blow westerly, but can vary from northwesterly to southerly. West to southwesterly winds generally indicate an approaching cold front and imminent storms. If a new westerly storm is approaching, winds may again begin to turn southwesterly and very cold after only a few days of fine weather. On the other hand, a southerly airstream usually brings fine and stable conditions, although accompanied by very cold weather. Thunderstorms with lightning are unusual in the Araucanía and Lakes District and unheard of in southern Patagonia.

Long wispy streams of high cirrus cloud known as 'mares' tails', and heavy lens-shaped or lenticular clouds called 'hogs' backs' that hover above higher peaks are a possible (but by no means definite) indication of a breakdown in the weather. Weather is generally more stable in northern Patagonia, with less wind and longer, warmer summers. From the Lakes District down to Aisén, signs of approaching bad weather often include strong, moist and suspiciously warm winds blowing in from the north. In northern areas isolated thunderstorms sometimes build up in the mountains during hot summer weather. Storms of this type usually bring heavy rain but pass quickly. Areas of the Cordillera with an easterly aspect (generally on the Argentine side) tend to have somewhat less severe weather, though frosts are more frequent because of higher valley elevations and a much more typically continental climate.

Weather Information

Weather in the Patagonian Andes is so fickle and localized that official forecasts should only be considered as a general indication of what to expect on your trek.

The best up-to-date weather forecasting for the southern Andes is available (in Spanish) from the **Dirección Meteorológica de Chile** (www.meteochile.cl) and the **Servicio Meteorológico Nacional de Argentina** (www.meteofa.mil.ar). Their websites give weather forecasts for the administrative regions and provinces of each country (click on 'Prognóstico', then the appropriate region or province) as well as an overview of recent precipitation levels and temperatures (click on 'Climatología').

CUSTOMS

Except during busy periods, clearing customs is generally hassle-free in both directions between Chile and Argentina. Visitors often complain that the process can be slow when traveling by bus.

Note that it is prohibited to enter Chile carrying dairy products or any kind of unprocessed food or agricultural product – even if they are of Chilean origin. This includes foodstuffs such as honey, milk powder, salami or mushrooms (dried or fresh). Foods like packaged soups or dried pre-prepared meals or canned fish are OK. This is particularly important if you bring food from Argentina with the intention of doing a trek immediately upon arriving in Chile. At an increasing number of border posts, luggage is unloaded and scanned or sniffed before passengers may proceed. Fines may be imposed for infringements.

DANGERS & ANNOYANCES

Although you should never get too complacent about security, Chile and Argentina are unquestionably safer places for foreigners than certain countries immediately to their north. Serious incidents such as assaults are rare outside large cities, and almost unheard of in the countryside.

The risk of robbery can be minimized by wearing an inconspicuous money belt under your clothes when traveling (off the trail). In busy places such as bus and train stations, keep cameras and other valuable items out of sight and avoid putting your bag down. Don't pack valuables in the top of your pack and use small padlocks to deter petty theft (such as when staying at hostels). On the whole, trekkers are an honest and upright bunch, so you're less likely to be a victim of theft or other crime up in the mountains.

DISCOUNT CARDS

An ISIC international student card or youth card or ID will grant varying discounts at some museums and tourist sites, though most national parks do not offer reductions. Some bus companies offer 25% discounts to students. Senior discount cards are not generally used.

EMBASSIES & CONSULATES

Argentina and Chile have diplomatic representation throughout the world. A quick internet search will turn up the *embajada Argentina* (Argentine embassy) or *embajada Chilena* (Chilean embassy) in your home country and the nearest consulates to you.

Embassies & Consulates in Argentina

Australia (☎ 011-4779 3500, www.argentina.embassy.gov.au/; Villanueva 1400, 1426 Buenos Aires)
Canada (☎ 011-4808 1000, www.dfait-maeci.gc.ca/argentina; Tagle 2828, C1425EEH Buenos Aires)
France (☎ 011-4312 2409, www.embafrancia-argentina.org; Santa Fe 846, 4th fl, Retiro Buenos Aires)
Germany (☎ 011-4778 2500, www.embajada-alemana.org.ar; Villanueva 1055, C1426BMC Buenos Aires)
Ireland (☎ 011-5787 0801, www.embassyofireland.org.ar; Av del Libertador 1068, 6th Floor, Edificio Bluesky, C1112ABN Buenos Aires)
Netherlands (☎ 011-4338 0050; www.embajadaholanda.int.ar in Dutch; Olga Cossenttini 831, 3rd fl, Edificio Porteño II, Puerto Madero Buenos Aires)
New Zealand (☎ 011-4328 0747, www.nzembassy.com/argentina; Carlos Pellegrini 1427, 5th Floor, CP1011 Buenos Aires)
United Kingdom (☎ 011-4808 2200, http://ukinargentina.fco.gov.uk.en; Dr Luis Agote 2412, C1425EOF Buenos Aires)
USA (☎ 011-5777 4533, http://agrgentina.usembassy.gov; Av Colombia 4300, C1425GMN Buenos Aires)

Embassies & Consulates in Chile

Australia (☎ 02-5503500, www.chile.embassy.gov.au; Isidora Goyenechea 3621, 12 & 13 Floors, Las Condes, Santiago)
Canada (☎ 02-3629660, www.dfait-maeci.gc.ca/chile) Nueva Tajamar 481, 12th fl World Trade Center, Torre Norte, Santiago)
Germany (☎ 02-4632500, www.santiago.diplo.de, Las Hualtatas 5677, Vitacura, Santiago)
France (☎ 02-4708000, www.france.cl) Av Condell 65, Providencia, Santiago
Ireland (☎ 02-6960278, aylwin@netline.cl) Isidora Goyenechea 3162, 8th Floor, Oficina 801, Las Condes, Santiago)
New Zealand (☎ 02-2909802, www.nzembassy.com/chile; Huérfanos 1294, 3rd fl, Santiago)
United Kingdom (☎ 061-244727; www.britemb.cl; Cataratas del Niagara 01325, Punta Arenas)
USA (☎ 02-2322600, www.usembassy.cl; Av Andrés Bello 2800, Las Condes, Santiago)

FOOD

Local Food & Drink

Fish and seafood are the great specialty of Chilean cuisine. Salmon is not native to Chile, yet salmon farming has had a controversial boom along Chile's southern coast, and it is served widely in restaurants. In the Fuegian islands, king crab, known as *centolla*, is harvested. In Chile, it is typical to order a *menu del dia* for lunch, a set plate that usually includes a soup or salad, meat and a side dish and sometimes dessert.

Argentine food is typified by meat dishes, especially beef and Patagonian lamb, accompanied by salads, though pasta, pizza and gelato-style ice cream are also notable. *Asados* (open-fire whole lamb or beef roasts) are a cultural experience; a mixed-grill uses almost every part of the cow.

In both countries, *empanadas* (meat or cheese pastries) are a cheap takeaway snack; they're much larger in Chile. Wine, grown in both countries, is generally very good. If your choice is the cheap box variety, bet on the Chileans. Bottled beer is sold widely and microbrews are enjoying a boom in Argentine Patagonia, where even some *refugios* serve homebrews. Draft beer is known as *chopp*.

In restaurant listings, we have listed options in the order of cheapest (including self-catering) to most expensive.

On the Trek

With the exception of Parque Nacional Torres del Paine, trekkers need to pack in all their food. The longer the trek, the more carefully you should plan your meals. When selecting food, try to balance bulk and weight against nutritional value. A person needs at least 700gm daily. Always carry two days' extra rations for unplanned side trips, emergencies or slower-than-expected progress.

Dehydrated foods such as rice and noodles are compact and keep well, but make sure to check the cooking times on the package. Packet soups are lightweight, tasty and need only a few minutes' cooking time. With potato flakes or couscous, you just need to add boiling water. See the boxed text Provision Picks below for more recommendations.

Some trekkers make their own gorp (high-energy mix of dried fruit and nuts) for snacks. It's a good idea to carry some additional fruit and vegetables, at least in dried form. Note, however, that it is prohibited to take unprocessed dairy and agricultural products across the border from Argentina into Chile – an important consideration if you intend doing a trek immediately after crossing into Chile.

Packets of sweet, flavoured drink powders (such as Tang) are available in local supermarkets and make a refreshing source of glucose on the trek. Herbal teas, including the native *boldo* and *manzano*, are available in tea bag form and are ideal for an after-dinner brew. Trekkers are likely to be offered *yerba mate*, a high-caffeine beverage native to Argentina but popular in all of Patagonia.

At *refugios* and popular campsites, rats and mice will often nibble at unattended food (or anything else vaguely edible). As rodents may carry hantavirus (see Health & Safety, p256) – and can easily chew through

PROVISION PICKS

Cheese (*queso*) Excellent in Argentina

Condensed milk (*Dulce de leche* or *manjar*) Caramelised condensed milk eaten as a spread for bread and cakes

Dried fruits (*frutas secas*)

Dulce de batata & dulce de membrillo A semisolid dessert made from sweet potato and quince, respectively

Fruitcake (*pastel de pascua*) Full of calories and if packed carefully won't crumble too much; just the thing for a sunny southern Christmas day

Home-made chocolates Especially good in San Carlos de Bariloche, San Martín de los Andes, Calafate and other towns in southern Argentina

Instant oatmeal Try pre-mixing with raisins, cinnamon, sugar and powdered milk

Muesli A nourishing mixture of grains that requires no cooking

Mushrooms (*callampas*) Dehydrated mushrooms available in small packets

Mussels (*cholgas*) Available dried at markets in Chile

Packet soups

Pasta and spaghetti (*fideos*) A wide range is available in Argentina

Porridge (*harina tostada*) Toasted wheat flour mixed with milk to form a kind of instant porridge

Walnuts (*nueces*) Especially good in Chile

Wholemeal bread (*pan integral*) Available in larger supermarkets and health-food stores your expensive pack or tent – it is best to store food suspended in a sturdy bag from a ceiling beam or tree branch.

BUYING FOOD

Try to buy all necessary food (and other supplies) in a larger regional center, where prices will generally be lower, quality better and range wider. With the exception of certain specialized freeze-dried products, a similar range of food suitable for backpacking is available as in Australasia, Europe or North America.

Although farms near the start of (and sometimes along) many trekking routes sell home-baked bread, cheese or eggs, it is unwise to depend on local food supplies. Trekkers should carry enough food to last the whole trek.

WHEN TO EAT

Few restaurants open for breakfast, and most open between 11.30am and 3pm for lunch and 7pm and 11pm for dinner, although Argentines dine even until midnight. In small towns many restaurants stay closed on Sunday. Since many Patagonian markets or food stores keep sporadic hours, only set hours are listed.

WILD FOOD

Along many trails native and introduced plants provide occasional treats. Permits are required for fishing. Streams have trout and, increasingly, large salmon that have escaped ocean hatcheries. These wild foods can only supplement your diet, and should not be depended on.

Berries

The most common treats are the abundant native berry species. February and March are the best berry producing months. None of the edible-looking fruits that grow in Patagonia are poisonous (although many are unpalatable).

Blackberries Introduced European blackberries (*moras* in Spanish) grow along trails in the Araucanía and Lakes District.

Calafates These seedy, purple-blue berries grow on thorny bushes in southern Patagonia and Tierra del Fuego. A traditional folk song claims 'whoever eats the *calafate* comes back to Patagonia for more'.

Frutilla de Magallanes An intensely sweet miniature 'strawberry' found half-buried in moist soil in southern Patagonia and Tierra del Fuego.

Murtas These lightly tart red berries grow in bushes trailside in the Araucanía and Lakes District and are sold at local markets.

Wild strawberries Related to cultivated strawberries, but the berries are smaller and less abundant.

OTHER WILD FOODS

Several other Patagonian wild foods are interesting from a culinary and botanical viewpoint:

Nalca The thick, succulent stems taste vaguely similar to celery, though sourer, and can be stewed with sugar like rhubarb. The harder skin of soft thorns must be stripped off.

Pan del Indio These round, rubbery growths attach to the trunks and branches of southern beech. They look like champignons and have a musty fungal taste.

Piñones Starchy nuts of the *araucaria* tree found in the Araucanía and northern Lakes District. They fall in late summer. Roasted

WATER

The Patagonian Andes is one of the purest sources of fresh water anywhere, but if you're staying in cities and towns, ask first before drinking. It's likely to be fine. For information, see Health & Safety (p261)

HOW TO: MOUNTAIN MOCACHINOS

Real coffee on the trail is an affordable (and for some, indispensible) luxury. Here's how to do it. Don't buy any of those expensive contraptions in camping stores back home. At a larger Chilean or Argentine grocery store, pick up a US$1 'coffee sock' (*media*), a white cloth filter pouch topped with a circular wire to drape over a cup. Argentina has decent coffee at good prices, but watch for low-quality grounds with sugar already added. Powdered milk, hot chocolate packets and restaurant sugar samples complete your caffeine kit.

or boiled *piñones* taste like a chestnut with a slightly resinous aftertaste.

GUIDES & PORTERS

Patagonian guides range from those with international or national certifications to the neighbor's teenage son with a few idle hours. Either may be fine, if you know what you are looking for. It is useful to find out what a guide's qualifications are – ask if a guide has first aid knowledge or a kit, or speaks another language. In Argentina, national parks only allow Argentine guides certified to work in that park to guide.

Apart from organized trips run by operators, trekkers do not normally use or need guides in the Patagonian Andes (although climbers often engage a mountain guide). The use of porters to carry gear and supplies is rare, although some routes (such as multiday horse-riding trips outside national parks) can be done with pack animals.

However, using a local guide, particularly in parts of Chilean Patagonia where trail signage is sparse or nonexistent, can be useful as well as culturally educational and a good investment in the local economy. For ideas, check out the boxes on Sustainable Patagonia, p22 and p148. If you do use a guide, it is customary to tip.

HOLIDAYS

Many religious and national holidays are celebrated in Chile and Argentina (including Easter and Christmas), when government offices and businesses are closed. (If the holiday falls on a midweek day or weekend day, it's often moved to the nearest Monday.) In addition, the general summer holiday (vacation) period begins around Christmas and continues until mid-February. Some provincial or regional public holidays are also celebrated locally.

The following national public holidays fall within the extended summer season:

Todo Los Santos (All Saints' Day) November 1
Inmaculada Concepción (Immaculate Conception) December 8
Navidad (Christmas Day) December 25
Año Nuevo (New Year's Day) January 1
Semana Santa (Easter Week)
Día de las Malvinas (Malvinas Day; Argentina only) April 2
Día del Trabajador (Labor Day) May 1
Glorias Navales (commemorating the naval Battle of Iquique; Chile only) May 21
Revolución de Mayo (May Revolution of 1810; Argentina only) May 25

TRAVEL INSURANCE

Buy a policy that generously covers you for medical expenses, theft or loss of luggage and tickets, and for cancellation of and delays in your travel arrangements. It may be worth taking out cover for mountaineering activities and the cost of rescue. Check your policy doesn't exclude walking/hiking/trekking as a dangerous activity.

Buy travel insurance as early as possible to ensure you'll be compensated for any unforseen accidents or delays. If items are lost or stolen get a police report immediately – otherwise your insurer might not pay up.

INSURANCE

Most trekkers assume that Patagonia's major national parks have a doctor, EMT or organized rescue group but this is quite simply not the case. Since rural areas and parks have little to no local budget for emergency evacuations, it is important for trekkers to take this responsibility upon themselves by having good coverage. Buy travel insurance as early as possible to ensure you'll be compensated for any unforeseen accidents or delays. For health insurance information, see p254.

INTERNET ACCESS

Finding access to the internet is usually not a problem except in the most out-of-the-way places. Internet cafes are common and many public telephone offices also offer internet access with broadband connections. Rates are typically from around US$1 per hour (but can be as much as US$8 per hour in touristy or remote places). For internet resources, see Planning (p22).

LEGAL MATTERS

Always carry your documents and always be courteous and cooperative. Penalties for common offences are similar to those given in much of Europe and North America. However, the possession, use or trafficking of drugs – including soft drugs such as cannabis – is treated very seriously and results in severe fines and imprisonment.

Never attempt to bribe a police officer.

MAPS

Mapping in Chile and Argentina is mainly carried out by the military. The central mapping authority in both countries is called the Instituto Geográfico Militar (IGM). Most other locally produced maps are (to a greater or lesser extent) based on IGM maps of either country.

It is almost impossible to buy IGM topographical maps outside the national capitals, so if you are passing through Buenos Aires or Santiago be sure to buy all maps there. It is, however, possible to order IGM maps either by mail or online, but delivery time within the respective country may take up to two weeks.

Unfortunately maps of large sectors of the southern Cordillera at any useful scale are still not available. Maps of a scale less than 1:100,000 – the next size downward is usually 1:250,000 – are generally unsuitable for accurate ground navigation. In Argentina topographical maps are sometimes only updated every few generations, so some key maps are now woefully out of date.

Buying Maps

CHILEAN MAPS

The **Chilean IGM** (☎ 02-4606863, fax 4608294; www.igm.cl; Dieciocho 369, Santiago), near Toesca metro station, is open Monday to Friday from 9am to 5.30pm.

The Chilean IGM has divided the country into 12 sections (*secciones*), or mapping zones, given a letter from A to L. All Chilean treks in this book are within the (southern) mapping zones G to L. The standard IGM series covering southern Chile is scaled at 1:50,000. Generally these are topographically quite accurate, though trekking routes are often not properly indicated. Maps in the 1:50,000 series cost around CH$8600. Photocopies of out-of-print maps are available the next working day for the same price.

At the IGM sales office (*salón de ventas*) folders of maps can be viewed freely. To order, quote the map's name, number and mapping zone (eg *Volcán Puyehue*, No 27, Sección H). All maps can be ordered online from the Chilean IGM website.

In some areas, most notably the Chilean Araucanía, **Conaf** (☎ 02-6966677, fax 6715881; 5th Floor, Oficina 501, Av Bulnes 285, Santiago) has produced excellent color maps of many popular national parks and reserves, including Reserva Nacional Malalcahuello-Nalcas and Parque Nacional Nahuel Buta, at scales between 1:35,000 and 1:110,000. These are available free (after you have paid the park or reserve entry fee), and are accurate enough for navigation.

ARGENTINE MAPS

The **Argentine IGM** (☎ 011-4576 5576; Av Cabildo 381; (1426) Buenos Aires) is open Monday to Friday from 8am to 1pm.

The 1:100,000 map series covers the Patagonian Andes of Argentina. Unfortunately, many maps are hopelessly out of date and

MAPS IN THIS BOOK

The maps in this book are based on the best available references, sometimes combined with GPS data collected in the field. They are intended to show the general routes of the hikes we describe. They are primarily to help locate the route within the surrounding area. They are not detailed enough in themselves for route finding or navigation. You will still need a properly surveyed map at an adequate scale – specific maps are recommended in the Planning section for each hike. Most chapters also have a regional map showing the gateway towns or cities, principal transport routes and other major features. Map symbols are interpreted in the legend on the inside front cover of this book.

On the maps in this book, natural features such as river confluences and mountain peaks are in their true position, but sometimes the location of villages and routes is not always so. This may be because a village is spread over a hillside, or the size of the map does not allow for detail of the path's twists and turns. However, by using several basic route-finding techniques (see p253), you will have few problems following our descriptions.

show topographical information poorly, especially in the important provinces of Río Negro and Neuquén. The 1:100,000 maps cost around AR$5–10 per map. Color photocopies of out-of-print maps are available while you wait for AR$35 (AR$10 in black and white)

To buy Argentine IGM maps, first view and order them at the adjacent map library (*mapoteca*), then pay when you pick them up at the sales counter. In theory, maps may also be purchased online but the site has problems.

TREKKING MAPS

For some of the most popular trekking areas (including the parks of Nahuel Huapi, Los Glaciares and Torres del Paine as well as the Argentine Fuegian Andes), contoured topographic maps produced specifically for trekkers by independent cartographic publishers are available. **Zagier & Urruty** (☎ 011-4572 1050; www.patagoniashop.net) in Buenos Aires or **Sendas & Bosques** (☎ 02972-427836; www.sendasybosques.com.ar) in San Martín de los Andes produce Argentine maps. JLM Mapas (see Small-Scale Maps, p236) offers Chilean maps with large-scale insets that may also be of use to trekkers. Bariloche-based **Aoneker** (☎ 02944-433945; Moreno 69, oficina 3, Bariloche) has a new series of trekking maps, mostly at scales of 1:125,000 and 1:150,000, for Chile and Argentina. You can contact the company or purchase maps via CAB Bariloche (p124).

Large-scale Maps

Essential for serious backcountry navigation, large-scale maps cover smaller areas in greater detail.

Small-scale Maps

Small-scale maps that give an overview of a wide area are very useful for planning your trip. A problem with many such locally produced maps, however, is that they tend to feature only one side of the Andes – a Chilean map will often give poor coverage even to adjacent areas in Argentina, and vice versa.

Both the Chilean IGM and the Argentine IGM (see Buying Maps, p235) produce their own separate 1:250,000 series of maps that cover the entire Patagonian Andes.

PLACE NAMES

Patagonia is bigger than the human imagination, at least when it comes to map making. Many mountains remain unnamed, or, on the flip side, there's an endless number of lakes named 'Laguna Verde' or 'Lago Escondido', and rivers called 'Río Blanco'. Many land features honor battles or heroes from the wars of independence, with names such as Cordón Chacabuco, Lago O'Higgins and Cerro San Martín.

Nomenclature often shows indigenous origins, particularly in the Araucanía and Lakes District, where place names are largely based on local Mapuche dialects. Spanish and Mapuche words found in place names are listed in the Language section (p266). See also the Glossary (p272) for common terms used in the route descriptions.

The Chilean **JLM Mapas** (☎/fax 02-364808; General de Canto 105, Oficina 1506, Providencia, Santiago) publishes a range of regional maps that cover all of the Patagonian Andes, including the 1:450,000 Lagos Andinos – Temuco a Bariloche (the Araucanía), the 1:250,000 Ruta de los Jesuitas – Puerto Montt a Bariloche (Lakes District), the 1:1,100,000 Camino Austral (central Patagonia) and the 1:1,250,000 Patagonia Sur – Tierra del Fuego. The excellent Turistel Sur guidebooks to southern Chile and southern Argentina are worth buying just for their detailed color maps.

MONEY

It is important that you carry at least one alternative form of payment, including a credit card, travelers cheques or cash. Although the euro has gained some acceptance as an alternative, the US dollar (US$) remains the Latin American 'shadow currency' of choice. All prices in this guidebook are quoted in national currency, unless the provider lists with US$.

ATMs

ATM machines are prevalent throughout both countries, known as *redbanc* in Chile and *cajeros automáticos* (ATMs) in Argentina. They are the easiest and most convenient way to access funds. Your bank will likely charge a small fee for each transaction. Instructions are usually in Spanish and English; choose the option 'foreign card' *(tarjeta extranjera)* before starting the transaction. You cannot rely on ATMs in small Patagonian towns.

Cash

Although their relative values are vastly different, both Chile and Argentina use a currency called the peso. A simple dollar sign ($) is often used to show prices in local pesos.

The Chilean peso (CLP) comes in notes of the denominations 500, 1000, 5000, 10,000 and 20,000 pesos. Coins are in one, five, 10 and 100 peso denominations.

The Argentine peso (ARS) is made up of 100 centavos. Coins come in denominations of one (rare), five, 10, 25 and 50 centavos, and one peso. Notes come in denominations of two, five, 10, 20, 50 and 100 pesos. Formerly pegged 1:1 to the US dollar, the Argentine peso was floated in early 2002 and its value against the dollar may fluctuate greatly.

Credit Cards

In both Chile and Argentina, MasterCard, Visa, American Express and Diners Club are accepted in higher-end hotels and restaurants, as well as by some transport services and tour operators. A surcharge (*recargo*) – typically around 5% – is sometimes charged; some stores give a discount for cash payments instead.

Credit cards can acquire cash advances at ATMs, but expect to pay a high commission (up to 6%) after currency conversions and service fees are factored in.

Money Changers

Banks exchange foreign currencies at reasonable rates. Exchange bureaus (*casas de cambio*) can be found in tourist towns and larger regional centers. They tend to give somewhat better rates than banks. Most larger hotels will exchange US dollars in cash (though rarely in travelers cheques).

On the Trek

Except for more popular routes that have *refugios* (huts) or other trekking infrastructure (such as the Nahuel Huapi Traverse or the Paine Circuit), there isn't usually much need for – or even opportunity to spend – money on the trek itself. At times trekkers may need cash to pay for camping or perhaps even to buy produce like cheese, bread or eggs from farms along the way. It's nevertheless advisable to carry plenty of cash if you will be away from towns for a lengthy period of time.

Taxes & Refunds

In Chile, it is sometimes possible to legally avoid the 18% *Impuesto de Valor Agregado* (IVA, or value-added tax) by paying for (usually more upmarket) accommodation in US-dollars cash. In Argentina, foreign visitors may obtain refunds of the IVA on purchases of Argentine products of US$70 or more at certain participating stores upon their departure from the country.

See also Departure Tax & Arrival Fees (p242).

Tipping

Patrons tip about 10% of the bill in restaurants. Taxi drivers don't expect tips, but it's customary to round up to the nearest peso. For professional guiding services, tips follow the international standard.

Travelers Cheques

In remote areas of southern Chile and Argentina exchanging travelers cheques for a reasonable rate is not always easy. Heavy commissions are often charged.

PERMITS & FEES

Some Argentine national parks charge an entry fee of AR$15 (valid for one week). In others, such as Parque Nacional Los Glaciares, there is no fee. Entry fees are not normally charged to Argentine provincial parks.

In Chilean national parks and reserves, the fee also ranges from nothing to as much

> **PUBLIC & PRIVATE PROPERTY**
>
> Many of the treks in this book pass through private property (although this may not always be obvious) where public access is freely permitted. If you are in any doubt, however, ask a local person before entering private property.

as CH$15,000 in Parque Nacional Torres del Paine, which charges foreigners more than locals, a growing trend. Officially, trekkers are required to obtain permission – though usually not a permit as such – to hike in all Argentine national parks and in many of those in Chile. In general, the more heavily visited national parks take trekking permits most seriously. Refer to the Permits & Regulations headings in each trek description for more information.

A small (but possibly increasing) number of farm owners within or at the edge of national parks charge a 'toll' to cross through their property. Such is the case of Fundo El Caulle (p90), which at least compenses with excellent infrastructure for trekkers.

PHOTOGRAPHY & VIDEO

Few trekkers will want to go without a camera. Make sure you have extra batteries, a USB stick to download photos on to, and an adapter for your charger. If you are camping for weeks on end, it may be a challenge to find a place to charge rechargeable batteries.

Photographing People

Especially in the countryside of Chile, it is considered very bad manners to photograph or video a person without first asking permission. If you are unable to ask, at least be discreet. Usually a person will consent, but may ask you to send them a copy of the photo – so make sure it's a good shot!

Restrictions

The photographing of military and some telecommunications installations is prohibited in Chile and Argentina for security reasons. Of course, the ban only applies from close range.

TELEPHONE

The telephone systems in both Chile and Argentina are now very modern and relatively inexpensive. Public telephone offices (*centros de llamados* in Chile and *locutorios* in Argentina) can be found around the centers of all cities and – even very small – towns. Street telephones are increasingly rare. Reverse-charge or collect (*cobro revertido*) calls overseas are simple to make, as are credit card calls. Calls are charged on a timed basis. Per-minute rates from public telephone offices to the United States and Europe are generally from around US$0.60 per minute, but higher to Australia and many other places.

Mobile Phones

Chileans and Argentines widely use mobile (cell) phones. The larger telephone companies – **Entel** (www.entelphone.cl) and **Telefónica** (www.telefonica.cl) in Chile; **Telefónica de Argentina** (www.telefonica.com.ar) and Telecom Argentina (www.telecom.com.ar) in Argentina – rent out mobile phones from around US$30 per month.

Coverage is almost complete in cities and larger towns, but although mobile phones sometimes work in parts of national parks or reserves close to highways or settled areas, the network is generally too limited to be a reliable form of communication on the treks.

Phone Codes

Area codes are used throughout the Patagonian Andes and you'll need to dial them first before dialing the number, except when you are within the area code. Area codes begin with ☎0. If dialing from abroad, dial the country code, then the area code without the ☎0, then the local number.

Chile's national telephone code is ☎56. Argentina's national telephone code is ☎54.

Phonecards

Called *tarjetas telefónicas*, phone cards are widely available and are made by many companies in many price ranges.

Lonely Planet's ekno Communication Card, specifically aimed at travelers, provides competitive international calls (avoid using it for local calls), messaging services and free email. Visit www.lonelyplanet.ekit.com for information on joining and accessing the service.

Satellite (World) Phones

Although heavy and extremely expensive, satellite (world) phones allow trekkers to make calls from anywhere. Satellite phones cost from around US$1500 to buy or US$250 per month to rent, plus from US$2 per minute to use – you also pay for incoming calls.

Companies like **Nextel** (www.nextel.com), **RentCell** (www.rentcell.com) and

DEPARTURE TAX & ARRIVAL FEES

Chilean departure tax for international flights of under/over 500km is US$8/26 or its equivalent in local currency.

Note that arriving US air passengers pay a one-time fee of US$132, valid for the life of the passport. Reciprocity fees are also applied to Australians (US$56) and Canadians (US$132). This must be paid in cash and in US dollars. Officials collecting the fee most often won't have change; bring exact cash if possible.

The fee is not charged to those entering overland.

Worldcell (www.worldcell.com) rent out international and satellite phones.

TIME

Normally, Argentina is three hours behind Greenwich Mean Time (GMT) and Chile is four hours behind GMT. However, in Chile Daylight Saving Time runs from the first Sunday on or after 9 October until the first Sunday on or after 9 March. In Argentina, Daylight Saving Time is not observed at all. This means that for most of the trekking season the two countries share the same time (ie, three hours behind GMT). In recent years, Chile has extended the period of Daylight Saving Time by up to one month due to power shortages.

Note that 24-hour times are normally used in bus timetables etc.

TOILETS

Throughout Chile and Argentina, toilet paper and personal hygiene items should go in the wastebasket next to the toilet. The plumbing simply can't handle more, so please do your part; clogged toilets can be a major frustration.

TOURIST INFORMATION

In both Chile and Argentina, there are well-organized tourist offices (*oficinas de turismo*) in all regional centers and many larger towns, often located on the main plaza or at the bus terminal. During the summer months (December to February) temporary tourist offices often operate in quite small towns. Staff is generally helpful and often knows some English. Local tourist offices can supply lists covering accommodation in all price ranges; tourist maps and pamphlets are generally available free of charge.

The Chilean national tourist service, **Sernatur** (www.sernatur.cl), has offices in many larger centers. For information on trekking in local parks and reserves contact the local office of Corporación Nacional Forestal (Conaf). For online tourist information on Chile go to www.visit-chile.org. Specific email enquiries can be directed to infochile@chiletourdesk.com.

The Argentine national tourist agency, **Sectur** can provide general online information about Argentina. For information on trekking in national parks contact the local office of the Administración de Parques Nacional (APN; www.parquesnacionales.gov.ar). Details of local tourist offices are given under the Gateway and Access Town headings in the regional chapters.

VISAS

For entry to both Chile and Argentina, citizens of most western European (including European Union) countries as well as citizens of Australia, Canada, New Zealand and the United States do not require a visa for stays of up to 90 days. (Note that this may not immediately apply to all of the 10 countries due to join the European Union in 2004.) Entry requirements may change over time and you should check on the current situation before departing.

As obtaining a visa for stays of longer than 90 days can be time-consuming and expensive, most trekker-travelers arrange their trip so that they cross into the neighboring country before their 90 days is due to expire then simply return to be granted another stay of up to 90 days.

Transport

CONTENTS

GETTING THERE & AWAY

ENTERING THE COUNTRY

Most short-term travelers touch down in Buenos Aires or Santiago, while those on a South American odyssey are more likely to sidle in at their leisure – via bus from Peru, boat or bus from Uruguay, or 4WD trip from Bolivia. Entry is generally straightforward so long as your passport is valid for at least six months beyond your arrival date. For general information on visas and tourist tickets, see p239.

When entering by air, you officially must have a return ticket, though this is rarely asked for once you're in country. However, it is commonly asked for by the airline in the country of origin. For those planning to travel indefinitely, the only way out of this predicament is to buy a cheap, fully refundable onward flight (say, Mendoza to Santiago, Chile) or buy a cheap international bus ticket online.

Those traveling by bus usually avoid the costly arrival fee (see p242) required for some nationalities at Chilean airports.

AIR

Airports & Airlines in Argentina

International flights usually arrive at Buenos Aires' **Aeropuerto Internacional Ministro Pistarini** (code EZE; ☎ 011-5480-6111, tourist information 011-4480 0224), a 40-minute bus or cab ride out of town. Aerolíneas Argentinas, the national carrier, enjoys a good reputation for its international flights although national flights are notoriously prone to delay. Basic information on most Argentine airports can be found online at **Aeropuertos Argentina 2000** (www.aa2000.com.ar in Spanish). Airports include the following:

Bariloche (code BRC; ☎ 02944-422 767)
El Calafate (code ECA; ☎ 02902-491 220/30)
Río Gallegos (code RGL; ☎ 02966-442 340/4)
Ushuaia (code USH; ☎ 0291-424 422)

The following airlines fly to and from Argentina and are listed here with their telephone numbers in Argentina; numbers that aren't toll-free are Buenos Aires numbers.

Aerolíneas Argentinas (code ARG; ☎ 0810-222 86527; www.aerolineas.com)
AeroSur (code ASU; ☎ 011-4516 0999; www.aerosur.com)
Air Canada (code ACA; ☎ 011-4327 3640/44; www.aircanada.ca)
Air France (code AFR; ☎ 011-4317 4700/11/22; www.airfrance.com)
Alitalia (code AZA; ☎ 0810-777 2548, 011-4310 9970; www.alitalia.com)
American Airlines (code AAL; ☎ 011-4318 1111; www.aa.com)

THINGS CHANGE...

The information in this chapter is particularly vulnerable to change. Check directly with the airline or a travel agent to make sure you understand how a fare (and ticket you may buy) works and be aware of the security requirements for international travel. Shop carefully. The details given in this chapter should be regarded as pointers and are not a substitute for your own careful, up-to-date research.

Avianca (code AVA; ☎ 011-4322 2731; www.avianca.com)
British Airways (code BA; ☎ 0800-666 1459; www.britishairways.com)
Continental (code COA; ☎ 0800-333 0425; www.continental.com)
Copa (code CMP; ☎ 0810-222 2672; www.copaair.com)
Delta (code DAL; ☎ 0800-666 0133; www.delta.com)
Gol (code GLO; ☎ 0810-266 3232; www.voegol.com.br)
KLM (code KLM; ☎ 0800-222 2600, 011-4326 8422; www.klm.com)
LAN Airlines (code LAN; ☎ 011-4378 2222; www.lan.com)
Líneas Aéreas del Estado (LADE) (code LDE; ☎ 0810-810-5233, 011-5129 9000; www.lade.com.ar)
Lloyd Aéreo Boliviano (code LAB; ☎ 011-4323-1900/05; www.labairlines.com)
Lufthansa (code DLH; ☎ 011- 4319 0600; www.lufthansa.com)
Pluna (code PUA; ☎ 011-4120 0530; www.pluna.com.uy)
Qantas (code QFA; ☎ 011-4144 5800; www.qantas.com)
TACA (code TAI; ☎ 0810 -333 8222; www.taca.com)
Transportes Aéreos de Mercosur (code TAM; ☎ 0810-333-3333; www.tam.com.py)
United Airlines (code UAL; ☎ 0810-777 8648; www.united.com.ar)
Varig (code VRG; ☎ 0810-266 6874; www.varig.com.br)

Airports & Airlines in Chile

Most long-distance flights to Chile arrive at Santiago, landing at **Aeropuerto Internacional Arturo Merino Benítez** (code SCL; ☎ 02-690 1752; www.aeropuertosantiago.cl) in the suburb of Pudahuel. Chile's international airline LAN has an excellent reputation. In Patagonia, airstrips serviced by air taxis or small airlines include Futaleufú, Chile Chico, Cochrane, Villa O'Higgins and Puerto Williams. Major airports include the following:

Balmaceda (code BBA; ☎ 067-272 126) near Coyhaique
Osorno (code ZOS; ☎ 064-247 555)
Puerto Montt (code PMC; ☎ 065-486 202)
Punta Arenas (code PUQ; ☎ 061-745 400)
Temuco (code ZCO; ☎ 045-554 801)

Many major national and international airlines have offices or representatives in Santiago.

Aerolíneas Argentinas (airline code AR; ☎ 800-610 200; www.aerolineas.com.ar)
Air Canada (airline code AC; ☎ 02-337 0022; www.aircanada.com)
Air France (airline code AF; ☎ 02-290 9300; www.airfrance.com)
Alitalia (airline code AZ; ☎ 02-378 8230; www.alitalia.com)
American Airlines (airline code AA; ☎ 02-679 0000; www.aa.com)
Avianca (airline code AV; ☎ 02-270 6600; www.avianca.com)
British Airways (airline code BA; ☎ 02-330 8600; www.britishairways.com)
Copa (airline code CM; ☎ 02-200 2100; www.copaair.com)
Delta (airline code DL; ☎ 800-202 020; www.delta.com)
Iberia (airline code IB; ☎ 02-870 1070; www.iberia.com)
KLM (airline code KL; ☎ 02-233 0991; www.klm.com)
Lan (airline code LA; ☎ 600-526 2000; www.lan.com)
Lloyd Aéreo Boliviano (LAB; airline code LB; ☎ 02-688-8680; www.labairlines.com)
Lufthansa (airline code LH; ☎ 02-630 1655; www.lufthansa.com)
Qantas (airline code QF; ☎ 02-232 9562; www.qantas.com)
Swiss International Airlines (airline code LX; ☎ 02-940 2900; www.swiss.com)
Taca (airline code TA; ☎ 800-461 133; www.taca.com)

BAGGAGE RESTRICTIONS

Airlines impose tight restrictions on carry-on baggage. No sharp implements of any kind are allowed onto the plane, so pack items such as pocket knives, camping cutlery and first-aid kits into your checked luggage. Camping gas or fuel is not allowed. Empty all fuel bottles and buy what you need at your destination.

Flights to Puerto Williams, Chile are particularly strict on luggage; travelers are only allowed 10kgs, which can be a challenge for those backpacking.

United Airlines (airline code UA; ☎ 02-337 0000; www.united.com)
Varig (airline code RG; ☎ 02-707 8001; www.varig.com)

Tickets

From almost everywhere, South America is a relatively costly destination, but discount fares can reduce the bite considerably. Contacting a travel agency that specializes in Latin American destinations often turns up the cheapest fares. Or try these online bookers:

Ebookers (www.ebookers.com)
Expedia (www.expedia.com)
Flight Center (www.flightcenter.com)
Flights.com (www.eltexpress.com)
Kayak (www.kayak.com)
STA (www.statravel.com)
Travelocity (www.travelocity.com)

Australia & New Zealand

Lan and Qantas share a flight from Sydney to Santiago, stopping in Auckland. Aerolíneas Argentinas flies direct to Buenos Aires from Sydney and Auckland. Another way to get to Buenos Aires is to travel via the USA (Los Angeles, Dallas or Miami) with either American Airlines or United Airlines, but it's a much longer flight.

Canada

Air Canada operates the only nonstop flight from Canada to Buenos Aires, which leaves from Toronto. Air Canada, American Airlines and Delta offer connections to Santiago from Toronto.

Continental Europe

To Buenos Aires, there are direct flights from Paris (with Air France or Aerolíneas Argentinas), Madrid (with Aerolíneas Argentinas) and Frankfurt (with Lufthansa). There are regular direct flights from Madrid to Santiago with Lan and Iberia. STA Travel (www.statravel.com) has offices in Austria, Denmark, Finland, Sweden, Switzerland and Germany.

South America

Buenos Aires and Santiago are well connected to most other capital cities in Latin America. Many airlines fly daily between the capitals.

In Patagonia from November through mid-March, **Aerovías DAP** (☎ 061-213 776; www.dap.cl) flies from Punta Arenas to Ushuaia in Tierra del Fuego, and offers charter service from Puerto Natales to El Calafate.

Recommended agencies:

ASATEJ (☎ 011-4114 7544; www.asatej.com) In Argentina.
Student Travel Bureau (☎ 011-3038 1555; www.stb.com.br) In Brazil.

DEPARTURE TAX & ARRIVAL FEES

Chilean departure tax for international flights of under/over 500km is US$8/26 or its equivalent in local currency. Arriving US and Canada air passengers pay a one-time fee of US$132, valid for the life of the passport; it also applies to Australians (US$56). The fee must be paid in cash, bring exact change if possible.

Departure taxes on international flights out of Argentina are generally not included in the price of your ticket. Make sure you ask. If the departure tax is not included, you must pay it in Argentine pesos ($54) or US dollars (US$18) after check-in and have the tax sticker placed on your ticket.

UK & Ireland

Direct services to Buenos Aires are available with Aerolíneas Argentinas and many other airlines. Varig connects to Buenos Aires via Rio de Janeiro and São Paulo. At the time of writing there were no direct flights between London and Santiago. Connections from the UK go through Madrid, Buenos Aires and the US.

Journey Latin America (☎ in UK 020-8747 3108, in Ireland 1800 818 126; www.journeylatinamerica.co.uk) specializes in travel to Latin America and is a good place to start your inquiries.

USA

From the USA, the principal gateways to South America are Miami, New York, Los Angeles, Atlanta, Chicago and Dallas. Delta, American Airlines and United fly to Buenos Aires and Santiago. Aerolíneas Argentinas or Lan Chile may do a leg of the journey or all of it.

Exito (www.exitotravel.com) is recommended as one of the best specializt sites for online bookings.

LAND

There are numerous border crossings between Argentina and Chile. Generally, border formalities are straightforward as long as all your documents are in order. Except in far southern Patagonia, every land crossing involves crossing the Andes. Always check road conditions, especially if you have a flight scheduled on the other side of the mountains.

The following are listed from Chile to Argentina:

Temuco to Zapala This good road crosses the Andes over the 1884m Paso de Pino Hachado, directly east of Temuco along the upper Río Biobío near Reserva Nacional Malalcahuello-Nalcas and Parque Nacional Conguillío. Buses run at least daily.

Pucón to Junín de los Andes This attractive but largely unsurfaced road route across Paso Mamuil Malal gives access to Parque Nacional Villarica and for the ascent of Volcán Lanín. It is served by buses running between Temuco and San Martín de los Andes.

Puerto Fuy to San Martín de los Andes A scenic route first by ferry across Lago Pirehueico (accessible by daily bus from

THESE ROADS TO NOWHERE

Ranking among the world's ultimate road trips, Argentina's **Ruta 40** and Chile's **Carretera Austral** parallel the backbone of the Andes, running thousands of unpaved bone-crunching kilometers alongside ancient forests, glaciers, estancias and sprawling steppe. Highway is a glorified name for these gravel tracks rutted with potholes and washboard surface. Yet travelers can savor a landscape without Starbucks and strip malls.

Don't skimp on careful planning and a good dose of prudence. Particularly on Ruta 40, where distances between towns are long and stock fences make impromptu camping impossible, each night's stop should be predetermined.

To the north of the Carretera Austral, ferry services are inadequate for the amount of traffic and only runs regularly during summer – so don't even bother outside summer. The harsh climate can make maintenance a nightmare, with rock slides common and landslides closing sections of the road for days.

On the now partially paved Ruta 40 conditions from December to March are generally fine, but heavy precipitation can render some parts inaccessible. In other months snow may cover the route and chains are recommended. At all times winds can be severe – we've seen toppled Volkswagons to prove it.

In preparation, we suggest:

- Get your vehicle checked out prior to departure
- When possible, reserve ferry crossings in advance
- Drive only during the day, as curves are not marked with reflectors
- Carry extra food, water and even gas, as a breakdown or empty tank can leave you marooned. It is smart to top off your tank whenever you see a gas station as it may be a long, long time before you find another one
- Always carry a spare tire (*neumático*) and make sure the vehicle has a car jack (*una gata*)
- High-speed turns on loose gravel roads are a recipe for disaster, so take your time and enjoy the scenery
- Stop if someone looks like they might need help
- Avoid a pocked windshield by giving other vehicles a wide berth

If planning to cross the border, start your trip with all papers in order, permission to take the vehicle out of the country (if it isn't yours) and the required insurance. Extra fuel, produce and dairy products can't cross borders. All of the larger towns listed in this book have some sort of gas station.

Panguipulli) then by bus via Paso Huahum to San Martín de los Andes.

Osorno to Bariloche The most important international route in the Lakes District, and usually the quickest way across the border. A good surfaced road goes via Entrelagos across the Paso Puyehue and around Lago Nahuel Huapi. Numerous international buses run this route.

Petrohué to Bariloche The famous, scenic 12-hour bus–boat combination runs over the Andes between Argentina and Chile.

Futaleufú to Esquel Since Volcán Chaitén's eruption, this has been the main transit route to access the region. It leads from a popular white-water destination to the gateway for Argentina's Parque Nacional Los Alerces. Minibuses run most days in summer.

Coyhaique to Río Mayo An unsurfaced route via Paso Coyhaique to a village on Argentina's Ruta 40. There are several international buses per week in either direction between Coyhaique and Comodoro Rivadavia on the Atlantic coast.

Chile Chico to Los Antiguos A good access to Ruta 40 and Argentine town of Perito Moreno, El Calafate and El Chaltén. It goes east along the southern shore of Lago General Carrera (whose name changes to Lago Buenos Aires at the Argentine border).

Cochrane to Bajo Caracoles The most isolated of the international pass routes, the unpaved route leads through the Valle Chacabuco across Paso Rodolfo Roballos. There is no public transport and traffic is extremely thin.

Puerto Natales to El Calafate Probably the most beaten route down here, linking the gateway towns of Torres del Paine and Los Glaciares national parks. Buses run daily throughout the summer.

Puerto Natales to Río Turbio An uninteresting route but may be your fastest way of getting to Río Gallegos. Frequent buses run across the border.

Punta Arenas to Río Gallegos Daily buses in summer, a five- to eight-hour trip because of slow customs checks and a rough segment of Argentine Ruta Nacional (RN) 3.

Puerto Williams to Ushuaia This route across the Beagle Channel is the most southerly border crossing possible. Various boat and plane options exist, and a ferry service (which has operated at times in the past) may resume in the future.

For Visa information, see p239.

Bus

Crossing between Chile and Argentina does not involve too many hassles. Just make sure that you have your passport and any proper visas beforehand. Those leaving Chile must present the *Tarjeta Internacional entrada-salida* (a stamped paper) that they received upon entering the country, or pay a fine.

Car & Motorcycle

Motorists traveling through the Lakes District in both countries and the Chilean Araucanía shouldn't have too many problems. These well-traveled routes offer sufficient services. However, travelers on Argentina's Ruta 40 and Chile's Carretera Austral will find few repair shops or gas stations (see p243).

Always travel prepared with a repair kit, plenty of food and water, a spare tire or two and extra fuel. If using a remote border crossing in Patagonia, it can get tricky, since you are not technically allowed to take extra fuel across borders.

It can be costly and bothersome to take a car from Chile to Argentina since special insurance is required; rentals also require a notarized permission. For more information, see p247.

Hitching

The Spanish term for hitching is *viajar a dedo*, literally 'to travel by finger'. Hitching

LOCAL TRANSPORT TO & FROM THE WALKS

Treks in this book indicate the various possibilities for access. Most are accessible by bus or simply walking from the nearest town. For groups or those with time constraints, chartered taxis (called *fletes* in Chile and *remises* in Argentina) may be the best way of getting to the start of the trek. Out of season, hiring a taxi may be essential if tourist buses are no longer running. Especially in Argentina (such as in Ushuaia and El Bolsón), fixed prices apply to certain trailheads. You can ask your hotel or hostel for the going rate.

in Chile and Argentina is reasonably reliable along the main routes during the busy summer holiday period, but remember that for many local backpackers hitching is the only affordable way to see their country, so try not to compete with them for rides unless there is no other viable means of transport. On lonelier stretches of road you may have to wait a long time – even days – for a ride, but drivers in remoter regions are more inclined to stop.

GETTING AROUND

AIR

With fresh competition, flights have become more affordable in Chile and Argentina and are sometimes cheaper than a comfortable long-distance bus. Other than taking leisurely ferries, flights are often the only option to guarantee you reach isolated regions of the south in a timely manner. Always ask the difference between round-trip fares and one-way trips, because the former is often cheaper.

Airlines in Argentina

The national carrier, **Aerolíneas Argentinas** (☎ 0810-222 86527; www.aerolineas.com), offers the most domestic flights, but it's not necessarily better than its competitors. In fact, the airline's reputation for delays has become so bad that you should never rely on an Aerolíneas Argentinas flight to make a connection. Aerolíneas also maintains a two-tier pricing system: only residents qualify for the cheapest tickets. Other airlines with domestic flights are **Lan** (☎ 011-4378 2222; www.lan.com) and **Líneas Aéreas del Estado** (LADE; ☎ 011-5129 9001; www.lade.com.ar), the air force's passenger service. The latter specializes in Patagonia.

Nearly all domestic flights (except for LADE's hops around Patagonia) have connections only through **Aeroparque Jorge Newbery** (☎ 011-5480 6111; www.aa2000.com.ar), a short distance from downtown Buenos Aires. Flying with certain airlines on certain flights can be financially comparable or even cheaper than covering the same distance by bus, but demand is heavy and flights, especially to Patagonian destinations in summer, are often booked well in advance.

In Argentina, these taxes must be paid upon departure.

Airlines in Chile

Lan (☎ 600-526 2000; www.lan.com) is the biggest and longest-established Chilean carrier, with up-to-date planes and the most extensive system of connecting cities and international service. Check for weekly specials on the website for in-country flights. Competitor **Sky Airline** (☎ 600-600 2828; www.skyairline.cl, in Spanish) is sometimes cheaper, also with many destinations.

In Chilean Patagonia, a handful of regional air-taxi services take passengers to small airports. Prices are quite reasonable and service is usually efficient. Since air taxis are not required to insure passengers (as airlines are), you are taking on an extra risk. Dealing with older planes and harsher climatic conditions, in some cases, their collective track record is poor.

In Chile, there is a departure tax of about CH$11,000 to CH$14,000 for domestic flights, usually included in the ticket price.

BOAT & FERRY

While most of Argentine Patagonia offers little in the way of boat travel, the Chilean side overflows with opportunities.

From Puerto Montt south, Chilean Patagonia and Tierra del Fuego is accessed by a web of ferry lines through an intricate maze of islands and fjords. So, while bus services south between Puerto Montt and Coyhaique must pass through Argentina, the ferries sidle down past spectacular coastal scenery. It's important to note, however, that the end of the high season also marks limited ferry service.

Navimag's ferry service from Puerto Montt to Puerto Natales (see p198) is one of the continent's great travel experiences. The following information lists the principal passenger ferry services:

Catamaranes del Sur (☎ 02-231 1902; www.catamaranesdelsur.cl)
Mar del Sur (☎ 067-231 255)
Naviera Austral (☎ 065-270 430)
Navimag (☎ 02-442 3120; www.navimag.com)

Transbordador Austral Broom (☎ 061-218 100; www.tabsa.cl)
Transmarchilay (☎ 065-270 000; www.transmarchilay.cl, in Spanish)

Common routes include:

Chiloé to Chaitén Transmarchilay, Naviera Austral and Navimag run between Quellón, on Chiloé, and Chaitén in summer. There are also summer services from Castro to Chaitén. At the time of writing, this service was temporarily suspended due to volcanic activity in Chaitén; check first.
Hornopirén to Caleta Gonzalo In the summer, Naviera Austral ferries loop around from one side of Parque Pumalín to the other at Caleta Gonzalo, about 60km north of Chaitén. Due to volcanic activity in Chaitén, this service may be temporarily suspended; check first.
La Arena to Puelche Ferries shuttle back and forth across the gap, about 45km southeast of Puerto Montt, to connect two northerly segments of the Carretera Austral.
Mainland to Chiloé Regular ferries plug the gap between Pargua and Chacao, at the northern tip of Chiloé.
Puerto Ibáñez to Chile Chico Mar del Sur operates automobile/passenger ferries across Lago General Carrera, south of Coyhaique. There are shuttles from Chile Chico to the Argentine town of Los Antiguos.
Puerto Montt to Chaitén Naviera Austral runs car-passenger ferries from Puerto Montt to Chaitén.
Puerto Montt to Puerto Chacabuco Navimag goes from Puerto Montt to Puºerto Chacabuco, with bus service continuing on to Coyhaique and Parque Nacional Laguna San Rafael.
Puerto Montt to Puerto Natales Navimag departs Puerto Montt weekly, taking about four days to puddle-jump to Puerto Natales. Erratic Patagonian weather can play havoc with schedules.
Puerto Williams to Ushuaia This most necessary connection still has no regular ferry but does have regular motorboat service.
Punta Arenas to Tierra del Fuego Transbordador Austral Broom runs ferries from Punta Arenas' ferry terminal Tres Puentes to Porvenir; from Punta Delgada, east of Punta Arenas, to Bahía Azul; and from Tres Puentes to Puerto Williams, on Isla Navarino.

BUS

In Argentina

Most Argentines get around by bus and the comforts are similar to those in Chilean counterparts. Larger luggage is stowed in the hold below, security is generally good (especially on the first-class buses) and attendants always tag your bags (and should be tipped).

Hundreds of bus companies serve different regions but a few bigger lines (listed here) really dominate the long-haul business.

Andesmar (☎ 0261-412 2710, 011-6385 3031; www.andesmar.com in Spanish) Serves the entire country.

Chevallier (☎ 011-4016 7000; www.nuevachevallier.com in Spanish) Serves the entire country.

Via Bariloche (☎ 0800-333 7575; www.viabariloche.com.ar) Serves most destinations in the Lake District and Patagonia.

Shuttle service **Chalten Travel** (www.chaltentravel.com) provides transportation between El Calafate and Torres del Paine and travels Argentina's Ruta 40 to Bariloche.

In Chile

Long-distance buses in Chile have an enviable reputation for punctuality, efficiency and comfort, although prices and classes vary significantly between companies. By European or North American standards, fares are a bargain. Long-distance buses generally have toilet facilities and sometimes serve meals on board; if not, they make regular stops. On Chile's back roads and throughout Patagonia transportation is slower and buses (*micros*) are less frequent, older and more basic.

The nerve center of the country, Santiago has four main bus terminals, from which buses leave to northern, central and southern destinations. Chile's biggest bus company is **Tur Bus** (☎ 600-660 6600; www.turbus.cl, in Spanish), with an all-embracing network of services around the country. It is known for being extremely punctual. Online purchases (retrieve tickets at the counter) are discounted or holders of the Tur Bus club card (obtained in their offices) receive 10% off one-way fares and frequent-rider points toward free trips. Destinations covered in this book include Temuco, Pucón, Osorno, Puerto Varas, Puerto Montt, Coyhaique and Punta Arenas.

Its main competitor **Pullman** (☎ 600-320 3200; www.pullman.cl, in Spanish) also has extensive routes throughout the country, including the island of Chiloe and Puerto Natales. The Pullman Pass loyalty card offers much the same benefits as that of Tur Bus.

Classes

The cheapest class, *clásico*, *pullman* or *común* (common), features around 46 seats that barely recline, two on each side of the aisle. Don't expect great bathrooms. The next step up is *executivo* and then comes *semi-cama*, both usually mean around 38 seats, providing extra legroom and calf rests. *Semi-cama* has plusher seats that recline more fully and buses are sometimes double-decker. The pinnacle of luxury, *salón cama* sleepers seat only 24 passengers, with only three seats per row that almost fully recline. Super-exclusive infrequent *premium* services enjoy seats that flatten with fold-down leg rests to resemble a flat bed. Note that movie quality does not improve with comfort level.

On overnighters breakfast is usually included. You can sometimes save a few bucks by not ordering dinner and bringing a deli picnic. If you have any doubt about the type of service offered, ask for a seating diagram.

Normally departing at night, the *salón cama* and premium bus services cost upwards of 50% more than ordinary buses, but you'll be thankful on long-haul trips. Smoking is prohibited on all buses.

Reservations

Advance booking is a good idea on very long trips or on rural routes with limited services (such as along the Carretera Austral). Except during the holiday season (Christmas, January, February, Easter and mid-September's patriotic holidays), it is rarely necessary to book more than a few hours in advance.

CAR & MOTORCYCLE

Particularly for trekkers who intend to visit out-of-the-way areas (such as Parque Nacional Perito Moreno), the advantages of having your own means of transport are considerable. Road tolls are charged on some sections of the Panamerican Hwy in southern Chile. Apart from the main highways, roads in the south are usually unsurfaced.

Gas is heavily subsidised in Argentina's Patagonian provinces (Neuquén, Río Negro, Chubut, Santa Cruz and Tierra del Fuego), where it only costs around half as much as in Chile. Carry extra fuel when travelling in remote areas.

Note that it can be costly and bothersome to take a car from Chile to Argentina since special insurance is required as well as a notarized permission if the car is not yours.

Automobile Associations

In Argentina, the **Automóvil Club Argentino** (☎ 011-4802 6061; www.aca.org.ar in Spanish; Av del Libertador 1850, Palermo, Buenos Aires), has offices, service stations and garages throughout the country, offering **free road service** (☎ 0800-888 84253) and towing in and around major destinations. ACA membership costs AR$55 per month.

The **Automóvil Club de Chile** (☎ 600-464 4040, 02-431-1000; www.automovilclub.cl, in Spanish; Andres Bello 1863, Santiago) has offices in most major Chilean cities, provides useful information, sells highway maps and rents cars. Membership costs CH$9000 per month.

Both clubs grant discounts to members of its foreign counterparts, so don't forget to bring your card.

Bring Your Own Vehicle

Chile is probably the best country on the continent for shipping a vehicle from overseas, though Argentina is feasible. Getting the vehicle out of customs typically involves a degree of routine but time-consuming paperwork. For shipping a car from Chile back to your home country, try the consolidator **Ultramar** (☎ 02-630 1000; www.ultramar.cl).

Driving License

In Chile and Argentina, technically you're supposed to have an international driving permit to supplement your national or state driver's license, although we have found that this is rarely enforced. It's still useful, since some rental agencies require an International Driving Permit as well as the license from your home country.

Fuel & Spare Parts

Have your vehicle thoroughly checked before travelling. Even tiny Patagonian hamlets usually have at least one competent and resourceful mechanic but repairs could set you back a good while.

In Chile gas is known as *bencina*, in Argentina it's *nafta*. Argentine Patagonia, home to much of the country's oil fields, boasts reduced gas prices. Each town has *estaciones de servicio* (gas stations) but keep an eye on your gas gauge on the long stretches in-between. Throughout Patagonia it's smart to carry extra fuel.

Hire

To rent a car in Argentina you must be at least 21 years of age and have a valid driver's license and a credit card. Chile requires renters to be 25 years old or older. In most cases you must have an international driving permit, but renters rarely ask for this.

Weekly rates are the best deal. Although unlimited-kilometer deals do exist, they are much more expensive. A 4WD vehicle is significantly more expensive. One of the cheapest places to rent a car is Bariloche; if you're heading down to Patagonia or plan to drive for a while, this is a good place to rent. Reserving a car with one of the major international agencies in your home country sometimes gets you lower rates. Agencies in Chile include **Hertz** (☎ 02-601 0477; www.hertz.com), **Avis** (☎ 600-368 2000; www.avischile.cl) and **Budget** (☎ 02-598 3200; www.budget.cl). Argentina has many agencies; a few are **Avis** (☎ 0810-4480 9387; www.avis.com.ar) and **Hertz** (☎ 0810-222 hertz; www.milletrentacar.com.ar).

Insurance

All vehicles must carry *seguro obligatorio* (minimum insurance) and additional liability insurance is highly desirable. Car-hire companies offer the necessary insurance. Check if there are any limitations to your policy. Traveling on a dirt road is usually fine (indeed necessary in many parts of the country), but off-roading is strictly off limits. Check before renting to see if your credit card includes some sort of car rental insurance.

Road Hazards

Farm animals and stray dogs wander around on the roads – even highways – with alarming regularity, and visitors from European and North American countries are frequently disconcerted by how pedestrians use the motorway as a sidewalk.

Road Rules

Anyone considering driving in Argentina should know that Argentine drivers are aggressive and commonly ignore speed limits, road signs and even traffic signals. Chilean drivers are restrained and even sluggish by comparison.

Driving after dark is not recommended, especially in rural areas, where pedestrians, domestic animals and wooden carts are difficult to see on or near the highways. Motorcycle helmets are obligatory, although this law is rarely enforced.

You won't often see police patrolling the highways, but you will meet them at roadside checkpoints where they conduct meticulous document and equipment checks. Equipment violations can carry heavy fines. Chile's police enforce speed limits with fines; bribing them is not an option.

TRAIN

There are no direct rail services from Buenos Aires to cities in the Patagonian Andes, although it is possible to first travel by bus to the city of Viedma (950km south of Buenos Aires on the Atlantic coast), then take the **Tren Patagónico** (☎ 02920-422 130, 427 413; www.trenpatagonico.com.ar in Spanish) to Bariloche. Train buffs will want to take the narrow-gauge **La Trochita** (☎ 02945-451403 in Esquel; www.latrochita.org.ar), Argentina's famous narrow-gauge steam train which runs from Esquel to El Maitén.

In Chile, train travel has fewer departures and is slower and more expensive than bus travel. **Empresa de Ferrocarriles del Estado** (EFE; ☎ 600-585 5000; www.efe.cl, in Spanish offers a 12-hour, once-daily rail service in either direction between Santiago and Temuco. For details and prices, check the website.

Clothing & Equipment

CONTENTS

Your clothing and equipment will be – at times, quite literally – your life support system. For the Spanish names of items, see the Language chapter (p266).

CLOTHING

A secret of comfortable walking is to wear several layers of light clothing, which you can easily take off or put on as you warm up or cool down. Use three main layers: a base layer next to the skin; an insulating layer; and an outer, shell layer for protection from wind, rain and snow.

For the upper body, the base layer is typically a shirt of synthetic material such as polypropylene, with its ability to wick moisture away from the body and reduce chilling. The insulating layer retains heat next to your body, and is often a windproof synthetic fleece or down jacket. The outer shell consists of a waterproof jacket that also protects against cold wind.Lower body layers generally consist of shorts or loose-fitting trousers, polypropylene underwear and waterproof overtrousers.

NAVIGATION EQUIPMENT

Maps & Compass

You should always carry a good map of the area you are trekking in (see, p235), and know how to read it. Before setting off on your trek, ensure that you understand the contours and the map symbols, plus the main ridge and river systems in the area. Also familiarize yourself with the true north–south directions and the general direction in which you are heading. On the trail, try to identify major landforms such as mountain ranges and gorges, and locate them on your map. This will give you a better understanding of the region's geography.

Buy a compass and learn how to use it. The attraction of magnetic north varies in different parts of the world, so compasses need to be balanced accordingly. The entire area of Patagonia is within the so-called South Magnetic Equator (SME) zone, and only compasses balanced for South American countries or southern Africa are suitable. Compasses set for magnetic conditions in Australasia, Europe or North America tend to give inaccurate readings. If buying a compass in South America, check whether the needle dips down at one end when held horizontally, as this indicates improper balancing. Magnetic deviation in the Southern Andes is minimal, and ranges from close to 8°E in parts of the northern Araucanía to about 14°E in the islands around Cape Horn. 'Universal' compasses are available that function correctly anywhere in the world.

Global Positioning System (GPS)

Originally developed by the US Department of Defense, the GPS is a network of more than 20 earth-orbiting satellites that continually beam encoded signals back to earth. Small, computer-driven devices (GPS receivers) can decode these signals to give users an extremely accurate reading of their location – to within 30m, anywhere on the planet, at any time of day, in almost any weather. GPS receivers will only work properly in the open. The signals from a crucial satellite may be blocked (or bounce off rock or water) directly below high cliffs, near large bodies of water or in dense tree cover and give inaccurate readings.

Remember that a GPS receiver is of little use without an accurate topographical map. The receiver simply gives your position, which you must then locate on the local map. To assist GPS users with navigation, latitude and longitude are given for points on some treks. Note that some maps in Chile and Argentina show only the metric Universal Transverse Mercator (UTM) grid, in which case you will have to calibrate your GPS receiver – a simple process – so that it gives readings in UTM coordinates.

BUYING TIPS

BACKPACK

For day hikes, a day-pack (30L to 40L) will usually suffice, but for multiday treks you will need a backpack with 65L to 90L capacity. Choose a lightweight internal frame pack with strong fabric and sturdy zippers. It should have cushioned straps and rest comfortably on your hips. Try on packs loaded with full weight and line your bag with a heavy-duty trash bag for extra waterproofing.

BINOCULARS

Compact lightweight binoculars (8 x 25 or 10 x 25) are a must for bird- and animal-watchers, and are also useful for surveying the route ahead. Inexpensive brands are available locally.

FOOTWEAR

Light to medium hiking boots are recommended for day hikes, while sturdy boots are necessary for extended trips with a heavy pack. Most importantly, they should be well broken-in and have a good sole. Waterproof boots with non-slip soles (such as Vibram) are recommended. Buy boots in warm conditions or go for a walk before trying them on, so that your feet can expand slightly, as they would on a walk. Don't fail to break in your boots before your trip – even if it means wearing them to the grocery store.

Most walkers/hikers/trekkers carry a pair of sandals or thongs (flip flops) to wear at night or rest stops. Sandals are also useful when fording waterways.

GAITERS

In snow, deep mud, shallow stream crossings or scratchy vegetation, gaiters will protect your legs and help keep your socks dry. The best are made of strong fabric, with a robust zip protected by a Velcro flap, and secure easily around the foot.

ICE AXE & CRAMPONS

An ice axe and crampons may be necessary if you intend climbing the higher summits (such as Volcán Lanín or Monte Tronador) early in the season, but for general summer and fall (autumn) trekking the considerable weight of ice-climbing equipment is hard to justify.

OVERTROUSERS

Choose a model with long leg zips so that you can pull them on and off over your boots.

SLEEPING BAG & MAT

Sleeping bags should have a rating of at least –10°C. Down fillings are warmer than synthetic for the same weight. Mummy bags are the best shape for weight and warmth.

An inner sheet helps keep your sleeping bag clean, as well as adding an insulating layer. Silk 'inners' are lightest, but they also come in cotton or polypropylene.

When buying a GPS receiver, consider its weight, bulk and battery life. Cheaper hand-held GPS receivers cost as little as US$100, while new compact models costing around US$400 are integrated within a (bulky) wrist watch that allows you to take readings more conveniently.

GPS receivers are more vulnerable to breakdowns (including dead batteries) than the humble magnetic compass – a low-tech device that has served navigators faithfully for centuries – so don't rely on them entirely.

Altimeter

Altimeters determine altitude by measuring air pressure. Because pressure is affected by temperature, altimeters are calibrated to take lower temperatures at higher altitudes into account. However, discrepancies can still occur, especially in unsettled weather, so it's wise to take a few precautions when using your altimeter.

- Reset your altimeter regularly at known elevations such as spot heights and passes. Do not take spot heights from

Self-inflating sleeping mats work like a thin air cushion between you and the ground; they also insulate from the cold. Foam mats are a cheaper but less comfortable alternative.

SOCKS

Synthetic and wool-blend hiking socks are the most practical option. They should be free of ridged seams in the toes and heels.

STOVES

Fuel stoves fall roughly into three categories: multifuel, methylated spirits (ethyl alcohol) and butane gas. Stoves using butane gas are the easiest to operate. True, butane doesn't win many environmental points but it is much easier to come by than liquid fuels. Multi-fuel stoves are versatile but need pumping, priming, and lots of cleaning. However, they tend to be sooty and require frequent maintenance.

Petrol (gasoline) is known as *bencina* in Chile and *nafta* in Argentina, while kerosene is called *parafina* or *kerosén*. Locally sold petrol is often full of impurities, so it's best to filter it before use. *Bencina blanca* and *nafta blanca* are the local terms for white gasoline. In Argentina, white gas is usually sold as industrial solvent (*solvente industrial*).

Liquid fuel such as white gas can be found at hardware stores, and butane cartridges are readily available in camping supply shops. Airlines prohibit the carriage of any flammable materials and may well reject empty liquid-fuel bottles or even the stoves themselves.

SUNGLASSES

Sunglasses should be carried on all higher treks, particularly early in the season when snowfields may have to be crossed. Use dark UV-Polaroid lenses that block out all UV, and most infrared, rays and reduce glare off snow or water surfaces. Mountaineering (glacier) sunglasses are robust but tend to be poorly ventilated and uncomfortable in hot conditions.

TENT

A three-season tent will suffice in most conditions. The floor and the outer shell, or fly, should have taped or sealed seams and covered zips to stop leaks. The weight can be as low as 1kg for a stripped-down, low-profile tent, and up to 3kg for a roomy, luxury, four-season model. Dome- and tunnel-shaped tents handle windy conditions better than flat-sided tents.

TREKKING POLES

Trekking poles give stability and absorb jolting on steep descents. They can help prevent knee pain (see Knee Strain, p257) and keep you stable on river crossings and in windy conditions.

WATERPROOF JACKET

The ideal specifications are a breathable, waterproof fabric, a contoured hood allowing peripheral vision, capacious map pocket, and a heavy-gauge zip protected by a storm flap.

villages where there may be a large difference in elevation from one end of the settlement to another.

- Use your altimeter in conjunction with other navigation techniques to fix your position. For instance, taking a back bearing to a known peak or river confluence, determining the general direction of the track and obtaining your elevation will give you a pretty good fix on your position.

Altimeters are also barometers and are useful for indicating changing weather conditions. If the altimeter shows increasing elevation while you are not climbing, it means the air pressure is dropping and a low-pressure weather system may be approaching.

Route Finding

While accurate, our maps are not perfect. Inaccuracies in altitudes are commonly caused by air-temperature anomalies. Natural features such as river confluences and mountain peaks are in their true position, but sometimes the location of villages and trails is not always so. This may be because

HOW TO USE A COMPASS

This is a very basic introduction to using a compass and will only be of assistance if you are proficient in map reading. For simplicity, it doesn't take magnetic variation into account. Before using a compass we recommend you obtain further instruction.

Reading a Compass

Hold the compass flat in the palm of your hand. Rotate the bezel so the red end of the needle points to the N on the bezel. The bearing is read from the dash under the bezel.

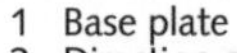

1 Base plate
2 Direction of travel arrow
3 Dash
4 Bezel
5 Meridian lines
6 Needle
7 Red end
8 N (north point)

Orienting the Map

To orientate the map so that it aligns with the ground, place the compass flat on the map. Rotate the map until the needle is parallel with the map's north-south grid lines and the red end is pointing to north on the map. You can now identify features around you by aligning them with labeled features on the map.

Taking a Bearing from the Map

Draw a line on the map between your starting point and your destination. Place the edge of the compass on this line with the direction of travel arrow pointing towards your destination. Rotate the bezel until the meridian lines are parallel with the north-south grid lines on the map and the N points to north on the map. Read the bearing from the dash.

Following a Bearing

Rotate the bezel so that the intended bearing is in line with the dash. Place the compass flat in the palm of your hand and rotate the base plate until the red end points to N on the bezel. The direction of travel arrow will now point in the direction you need to hike.

Determining Your Bearing

Rotate the bezel so the red end points to the N. Place the compass flat in the palm of your hand and rotate the base plate until the direction of travel arrow points in the direction in which you have been hiking. Read your bearing from the dash.

a village is spread over a hillside, or the size of the map does not allow for detail of the trail's twists and turns. However, by using several basic route-finding techniques, you will have few problems following our descriptions:

1 Be aware of whether the trail should be climbing or descending.
2 Check the north-point arrow on the map and determine the general direction of the trail.
3 Time your progress over a known distance and calculate the speed at which you travel in the given terrain. From then on, you can determine with reasonable accuracy how far you have traveled.
4 Watch the path – look for boot prints and other signs of previous passage.

BUYING & HIRING LOCALLY

High-quality trekking equipment is available in both Chile and Argentina yet prices are steep for these import items. This applies particularly to tents. Rainwear and thermal garments are more widely available. It's still advisable to bring all necessary gear with you. In addition to outdoor stores, fishing/hunting suppliers normally have a small range of general outdoor gear.

When renting equipment, try it out before getting on the trail. Ask to set up your rental tent at the shop, checking for tears and that all the stakes are present. It's also useful to try out a rental stove.

Gear available for hire includes tents (US$15), backpack (US$14), stoves (US$10), ice axe (US$10), crampons (US$10). These are daily rates and are approximate.

CHECK LIST

This list is a general guide. Read ahead for considerations for selecting appropriate clothing and equipment.

CLOTHING

- boots and spare laces
- gaiters (waterproof)
- hat (warm), scarf and gloves
- jacket (waterproof)
- overtrousers (waterproof)
- runners (training shoes), sandals or thongs (flip flops)
- shorts or skirt and trousers
- socks and underwear
- sunhat
- sweater or fleece jacket
- thermal underwear
- T-shirt and shirt (long-sleeved with collar)

EQUIPMENT

- backpack with liner (waterproof)
- first-aid kit*
- food and snacks (high-energy), and one day's emergency supplies
- insect repellent
- map, compass and guidebook
- map case or clip-seal plastic bags
- pocket knife
- sunglasses
- sunscreen and lip balm
- survival bag or blanket
- toilet paper and trowel
- torch (flashlight) or headlamp, spare batteries and bulb
- water container
- whistle (for emergencies)

OVERNIGHT TREKS

- cooking, eating and drinking utensils
- dishwashing items
- matches and lighter
- portable stove and fuel
- sewing/repair kit
- sleeping bag
- sleeping mat
- spare cord
- tent, pegs, poles and guy ropes
- toiletries
- towel (small)
- water purification tablets, iodine, Steripen or filter

OPTIONAL ITEMS

- altimeter
- backpack cover (waterproof, slip-on) or trash bag (as pack liner)
- binoculars
- camera, spare film and batteries
- candles
- emergency distress beacon
- Global Positioning System (GPS) receiver
- groundsheet (lightweight)
- mobile phone**
- notebook and pen/pencil
- swimsuit
- trekking poles
- travel alarm clock

*see the First-Aid Check List, p254
**see Mobile Phones, p238

In Santiago try: **Andes Gear** (☎ 02-2457076, www.andesgear.cl in Spanish); Las Condes 13451); **Lippi** (☎ 02-2256803, fax 02-2231472, www.lippioutdoor.com; Av Italia 1586, Ñuñoa). The most-established 'outdoor' company or **Patagonia Sport** (☎/fax 02-2229140, www.patagoniasport.cl in Spanish; Almirante Simpson 77, Providencia).

In Buenos Aires try: **Camping Center** (☎ 011-4794 5534, www.camping-center.com.ar in Spanish); **Rupal Mountaingear** (☎ 011-4702 9017, www.rupalnet.com in Spanish; 11 de Septiembre 4555 or you could also try **Vagabundo** (☎ 011-4780 3469; Blanco Encalada 2679).

Health & Safety

CONTENTS

Trekking in southern Chile and Argentina poses few real health hazards. Regional hygiene standards are high and only a handful of diseases and organisms can harm travelers, though these are mostly confined to areas outside the mountains themselves.

BEFORE YOU GO

For travel in Patagonia only common sense health precautions need to be taken. It's wise to have thorough medical and dental checkups before you begin your journey. Treks in this book can be physically demanding and most require a reasonable level of fitness. Even if you're tackling the easy or easy–moderate walks, it pays to be relatively fit, rather than launch straight into them after months of fairly sedentary living. If you're aiming for the demanding walks, fitness and mountain experience are essential.

Unless you're a regular walker, start your get-fit campaign at least a month before your visit. Take a vigorous walk of about an hour, two or three times per week and gradually extend the duration of your outings as the departure date nears. If you plan to carry a full backpack on any walk, carry a loaded pack on some of your training jaunts.

INSURANCE

If your health insurance doesn't cover you for medical expenses abroad, consider getting extra insurance; check www.lonelyplanet.com for more information. Make sure it covers you for walking and remote-area rescue. Find out in advance if your insurance plan will make payments directly to providers or if it will reimburse you later for overseas health expenditures.

REQUIRED & RECOMMENDED VACCINATIONS

Chile and Argentina require no vaccinations for entry from any country, but if you are visiting neighboring tropical countries consider prophylaxis against typhoid, malaria and other diseases.

FIRST AID

Trekkers should know what to do in the event of a serious accident or illness. Consider taking a basic first-aid course (preferably tailored to outdoor recreation) before you go.

For basic first aid points, see Traumatic Injuries (p262). Accident and illness prevention is key to wilderness travel; read Safety on the Trek (p263) for more advice. You should also know how to summon help in case of a major accident or illness; see Rescue & Evacuation (p264).

MEDICAL CHECK LIST

- Acetaminophen (paracetamol) or aspirin
- Adhesive or paper tape
- Antibacterial ointment for cuts and abrasions
- Antibiotics
- Antidiarrheal drugs (eg loperamide)
- Anti-inflammatory drugs (eg ibuprofen)

- Antihistamines (for hayfever and allergic reactions)
- Bandages, gauze swabs, gauze rolls
- Elasticised support bandage
- Iodine tablets or water filter (for water purification)
- Insect spray (optional)
- Nonadhesive dressing
- Oral rehydration salts
- Paper stitches
- Pocket knife
- Scissors, safety pins, tweezers
- Sterile alcohol wipes
- Steroid cream or cortisone (for allergic rashes)
- Sticking plasters (Band-Aids, blister plasters)
- Sun block
- Sutures
- Syringes & needles – ask your doctor for a note explaining why you have them
- Thermometer

INTERNET RESOURCES

There is a wealth of travel health advice to be found on the internet. For further information, Lonely Planet (www.lonelyplanet.com) is a good place to start. The WHO (World Health Organization; www.who.int/ith) publishes a superb book called *International Travel and Health*, which is revised annually and is available online at no cost. Website MD Travel Health (www.mdtravelhealth.com) provides complete and very detailed travel health recommendations for every country and is updated daily.

It's a good idea to consult your government's travel health website before departure, if one is available:

- Australia (www.dfat.gov.au/travel)
- Canada (www.travelhealth.gc.ca)
- UK (www.dh.gov.uk/en/healthcare/healthadvicefortravelers)
- USA (wwwn.cdc.gov/travel)

FURTHER READING

Lonely Planet's *Healthy Travel Central & South America* is a handy, pocket-sized guide packed with useful information including pre-trip planning, emergency first aid, immunization and disease information and what to do if you get sick on the road.

Other useful health guides for walkers include:

- *Medicine for Mountaineering & Other Wilderness Activities*, by James A Wilkerson, is an outstanding reference book for the layperson. It describes many of the medical problems typically encountered while trekking.
- *The Mountain Traveler's Handbook*, by Paul Deegan, includes chapters giving medical and safety advice as well as valuable information on all aspects of travelling in mountainous regions.

IN ARGENTINA & CHILE

AVAILABILITY & COST OF HEALTH CARE

In Argentina and Chile the medical care in major urban centers is generally good, but it may be difficult to find assistance in remote areas. Remote areas in Chile usually have a posta – a medical clinic, usually staffed by a paramedic with extremely limited medication and little diagnostic equipment. Since Argentine Patagonia has better access to urban centers, injured trekkers have better options closer at hand.

Most doctors and hospitals expect payment in cash, regardless of whether you have travel health insurance. For a list of additional physicians, dentists and laboratories, go to The US Embassy website at http://usembassy.state.gov.

If you develop a life-threatening medical problem you'll probably want to be evacuated to a country with state-of-the-art medical care. Since this may cost tens of thousands of dollars, be sure you have insurance to cover this before you depart. You can find a list of medical evacuation and travel insurance companies on the US State Department website at http://travel.state.gov.

Most pharmacies in Chile and Argentina are well stocked and the pharmacists are fully trained. As many drugs that require a prescription elsewhere are available over the counter, it's always advisable to know the generic (scientific) name of the medication you need.

INFECTIOUS DISEASES

Hantavirus

The potentially deadly hantavirus (known locally simply as *la hanta*) is spread through the saliva and feces of the native long-tailed rat, whose populations are known to rise dramatically after unusually wet winters. Since its recorded appearance in the mid-1990s near El Bolsón, hantavirus seems to have spread through parts of southern Chile and adjacent areas of Argentina. Most affected are Chile's Región VII (or Biobío), Región VIII (or Maule) and Región X (Los Lagos) and around El Bolsón.

Hantavirus causes the disease known as Hantavirus Pulmonary Syndrome (HPS). Early symptoms of HPS are fever and muscle aches, which occur one to five weeks after infection, followed by shortness of breath and dry coughing. The disease then progresses rapidly and treatment is urgent. The antiviral drug Ribaviron (Virazole) is effective in treating HPS, but only when given early. Of the currently 100 or so annual human cases of HPS in Chile (and perhaps a dozen more in Argentina), around 25% are fatal.

It's wise to avoid entering *refugios* (huts) that have been closed for any period of time. Always bring a tent.

Hydatid Cysts

The hydatid tapeworm is a 6mm-long tapeworm that forms cysts in the entrails of sheep (though it may also infect cattle or pigs). The eggs of the hydatid are generally passed on to humans through contact with dogs that have fed on the entrails of infected animals. Hydatid cysts occur when the parasite establishes itself in organs of the body – especially the liver or lungs – and develops gradually over a number of years. This condition (known in Spanish as *hidatidosis*) is extremely serious, and requires surgery to remove the cysts.

To control hydatids, an extensive government program is now underway to educate farmers not to allow their dogs into areas used for slaughtering animals, to dispose of entrails properly and to treat dogs regularly with antiparasitic drugs. Hydatids were once found all over the world, but these simple precautions have largely eradicated this parasite from countries as far apart as Iceland and New Zealand.

It is advisable not to pet suspect dogs – such as those on more remote farms – or other canines that may be infected with hydatids, and to properly boil, filter or sterilize all water when passing through grazing country. Washing hands thoroughly before handling food will also greatly reduce the likelihood of infection. In wilder (especially forested) mountain areas, the risk of contracting hydatids is virtually nil.

Tetanus

This disease is caused by a organism that lives in soil and in the feces of horses and other animals. It enters the body via breaks in the skin. The first symptom may be discomfort in swallowing, or stiffening of the jaw and neck; this is followed by painful convulsions of the jaw and whole body. The disease can be fatal. It can be prevented by vaccination, so make sure your shots are up to date before you leave.

Travelers Diarrhea

Simple things like a change of water, food or climate can all cause a mild bout of diarrhea, but a few rushed toilet trips with no other symptoms is not indicative of a major problem. More serious diarrhea is caused by infectious agents transmitted by fecal contamination of food or water, using contaminated utensils, or directly from one person's hand to another. Paying particular attention to personal hygiene, drinking purified water and taking care of what you eat, as outlined earlier in this section, are important measures to take to avoid getting diarrhea on your trek or travels.

Dehydration is the main danger with any diarrhea, particularly in children or the elderly as it can occur quite quickly. Under all circumstances fluid replacement (at least equal to the volume being lost) is the most important thing to remember. Weak black tea with a little sugar, soda water, or soft drinks allowed to go flat and diluted 50% with clean water are all good.

With severe diarrhea a rehydrating solution is preferable to replace lost minerals and salts. Commercially available oral rehydration salts (ORS) are very useful; add them to boiled or bottled water. In an emergency you can make up a solution of six teaspoons of sugar and a half-teaspoon of salt to 1L of boiled or bottled water.

You need to drink at least the same volume of fluid that you are losing in bowel movements and vomiting. Urine is the best guide to the adequacy of replacement – if you have small amounts of concentrated urine, you need to drink more. Keep drinking small amounts often and stick to a bland diet as you recover.

Gut-paralysing drugs such as diphenoxylate or loperamide can be used to bring relief from the symptoms, although they do not actually cure the problem. Only use these drugs if you do not have access to toilets, eg if you must travel. These drugs are not recommended for children under 12 years, or if you have a high fever or are severely dehydrated.

In the following situations antibiotics may be required: diarrhea with blood or mucus (dysentery), any diarrhea with fever, profuse watery diarrhea, persistent diarrhea not improving after 48 hours and severe diarrhea. These suggest a more serious cause of diarrhea, and gut-paralysing drugs should be avoided. In these situations, a stool test may be necessary to diagnose what organism is causing your diarrhea, so you should seek medical help urgently. Where this is not possible, the recommended drugs for bacterial diarrhea (the most likely cause of severe diarrhea in travelers) are norfloxacin 400mg twice daily for three days or ciprofloxacin 500mg twice daily for five days. These are not recommended for children or pregnant women. The drug of choice for children would be co-trimoxazole with dosage dependent on weight; a five-day course is given. Ampicillin or amoxycillin may be given in pregnancy, but medical care is necessary.

Two other causes of persistent diarrhea in travelers are giardiasis and amebic dysentery.

Amebic Dysentery

This is characterized by a gradual onset of low-grade diarrhea, often with blood and mucus. Cramping abdominal pain and vomiting are less likely than in other types of diarrhea, and fever may not be present. It

COMMON AILMENTS

BLISTERS

To avoid blisters make sure your hiking boots are well worn in before you hit the trail. Your boots should fit comfortably with enough room to move your toes; boots that are too big or too small will cause blisters. Similarly for socks – be sure they fit properly and are specifically made for walkers; even then, check to make sure that there are no seams across the widest part of your foot. Wet and muddy socks can also cause blisters, so even on a day walk, pack a spare pair of socks. Keep your toenails clipped but not too short. If you do feel a blister coming on, treat it sooner rather then later. Apply a simple sticking plaster, or preferably one of the special blister plasters that act as a second skin.

FATIGUE

A simple statistic: more injuries happen towards the end of the day than earlier, when you're fresher. Although tiredness can simply be a nuisance on an easy walk, it can be life-threatening on narrow exposed ridges or in bad weather. You should never set out on a walk that is beyond your capabilities on the day. If you feel below par, have a day off or take a bus. To reduce the risk, don't push yourself too hard – take rests every hour or two and build in a good half-hour lunch break. Towards the end of the day, take down the pace and increase your concentration. You should also eat properly throughout the day; nuts, dried fruit and chocolate are all good energy-giving snack foods.

KNEE STRAIN

Many walkers feel the judder on long steep descents. Although you can't eliminate strain on the knee joints when dropping steeply, you can reduce it by taking shorter steps, which leave your legs slightly bent and ensure that your heel hits the ground before the rest of your foot. Some walkers find that tubular bandages help, while others use hi-tech, strap-on supports. Walking poles are very effective in taking some of the weight off the knees.

will persist until treated and can recur and cause other health problems.

If you think you have amebic dysentry, you should seek medical advice; treatment is the same as for giardiasis.

Giardiasis

Symptoms include stomach cramps, nausea, a bloated stomach, watery, foul-smelling diarrhea and frequent gas. Giardiasis can appear several weeks after you have been exposed to the parasite. The symptoms may disappear for a few days and then return; this can go on for several weeks.

Seek medical advice if you think you have giardiasis, but where this is not possible, tinidazole or metronidazole are the recommended drugs. Treatment is a 2g single dose of tinidazole or 250mg of metronidazole three times daily for five to 10 days.

Rabies

This potentially fatal viral infection is not currently found in Patagonia, although there have been outbreaks in northern regions of both Chile and Argentina in recent years (where it is carried mainly by the free-tailed bat).

ENVIRONMENTAL HAZARDS

Altitude

Lack of oxygen at high altitudes (over 2500m) affects most people to some extent. The effect may be mild or severe and occurs because the air pressure is reduced, and the heart and lungs must work harder to oxygenate the body.

Symptoms of Acute Mountain Sickness (AMS) usually develop during the first 24 hours at altitude but may be delayed up to three weeks. Mild symptoms include headache, lethargy, dizziness, difficulty sleeping and loss of appetite. AMS may become more severe without warning and can be fatal. Severe symptoms include breathlessness, a dry, irritative cough (which may progress to the production of pink, frothy sputum), severe headache, lack of coordination and balance, confusion, irrational behavior, vomiting, drowsiness and unconsciousness. There is no hard-and-fast rule as to what is too high: AMS has been fatal at 3000m, although 3500 to 4500m is the usual range.

For trekkers, the generally lower elevation of the Andes in Patagonia virtually eliminates the danger of altitude sickness (known as *soroche* or *puna*). The threat of AMS is significantly greater for mountaineers in Patagonia, however, as they tend to get to higher altitudes, ascend more quickly and stay there for longer periods. In the treks featured in this book, altitude sickness is extremely unlikely except perhaps for the ascent of Volcán Lanín (altitude 3776m).

Treat mild symptoms by resting at the same altitude until recovery, usually a day or two. Paracetamol or aspirin can be taken for headaches. If symptoms persist or become worse, however, *immediate descent is necessary*; even 500m can help. Drug treatments should never be used to avoid descent or to enable further ascent.

The drugs acetazolamide and dexamethasone are recommended by some doctors for the prevention of AMS; however, their use is controversial. They can reduce the symptoms, but they may also mask warning signs; severe and fatal AMS has occurred in people taking these drugs. In general we do not recommend them for travelers.

To prevent acute mountain sickness:

- Ascend slowly – have frequent rest days, spending two to three nights at each rise of 1000m. If you reach a high altitude by trekking, acclimatization takes place gradually and you are less likely to be affected than if you fly directly to high altitude.
- It is always wise to sleep at a lower altitude than the greatest height reached during the day if possible. Also, once above 3000m, care should be taken not to increase the sleeping altitude by more than 300m per day.
- Drink extra fluids. The mountain air is dry and cold and moisture is lost as you breathe.
- Evaporation of sweat may occur unnoticed and result in dehydration.
- Eat light, high-carbohydrate meals for more energy.
- Avoid alcohol as it may increase the risk of dehydration.
- Avoid sedatives.

Bites & Stings

LEECHES

Common in the wet rainforests of archipelagic Chile, leeches are not dangerous to your health. Often present in damp rainforest conditions, leeches attach themselves to your skin to suck your blood. Trekkers often get them on their legs or in their boots. Salt or a lighted cigarette end will make them fall off. Do not pull them off, as the bite is then more likely to become infected. Clean and apply pressure if the point of attachment is bleeding. An insect repellent may keep them away.

SPIDERS

Two species of spider are found in lowland areas of northern Patagonia.

Chilean Recluse Spider

The venomous Chilean (or brown) recluse spider, or *araña del rincón* in Spanish, is a pale-yellow to reddish-brown 4cm-long spider, often identifiable by a violin-shaped marking on its head. It is found in Chile and Argentina to as far south as 43°S (about the latitude of Chaitén and Esquel) in dark, sheltered sites both in buildings and outside. As its name suggests, the Chilean recluse spider is shy and unaggressive and will only bite when threatened.

The spider's extremely toxic, necrotizing venom causes intense pain, and the skin around the bite becomes red, swollen and blistered – sometimes eventually gangrenous. Chills, fever, nausea, muscle aches or other flu-like symptoms are common. In around 2% of cases, hematuria (blood in the urine) heralds acute renal failure and death. The Chilean recluse spider is responsible for several fatalities each year, so even suspected spider bites should be treated urgently – within a maximum time of 72 hours. Treatment is normally with cortisone and antihistamines. An antivenin exists, but it is not fully tested and its use remains controversial.

Black Widow

Known as *araña de trigo* in Spanish, the black widow spider – the same species found in parts of the USA – is also found in the Araucanía, Lakes District and, most recently, Última Esperanza's Parque Nacional Torres del Paine. The black widow female is up to 1cm in length with long legs and a round abdomen with red markings on its underside and back, while the male is smaller with red and white stripes on its abdomen.

A black widow's bite is distinguished by a double puncture wound. Its venom is neurotoxic, blocking the transmission of nerve impulses, but is rarely fatal. Symptoms are similar to an attack of angina pectoris, with heart pain reaching into the left arm, rapid pulse rate and cold skin, but can be satisfactorily treated with calcium injections. If treated properly and promptly, the victim will completely recover.

TÁBANOS

A collective term for several species of horsefly, most often referring to large red-black ones that are more a nuisance than a threat. The scourge of the Patagonian Andes, *tábanos* appear roughly between Christmas until late January, first in the forests of the Araucanía and the Lakes District, and later in central Patagonia. They are far less common in windy southern Patagonia. Spells of hot, dry weather typically bring out swarms. Regular insect repellents don't work for long, if at all.

Some say black or blue clothing attracts the insects, while others claim that eating fresh cloves of garlic – until your sweat and blood taste noxious – acts as a natural repellent. Hikers with flexible schedules might be best suited to schedule southern Patagonia for this period, although the season is not entirely predictable.

TICKS

The Patagonian Andes are completely free of ticks.

Cold

HYPOTHERMIA

This occurs when the body loses heat faster than it can produce it and the core temperature of the body falls.

It is frighteningly easy to progress from very cold to dangerously cold due to a combination of wind, wet clothing, fatigue and hunger, even if the air temperature is above freezing. If the weather deteriorates, put on extra layers of warm clothing: a wind and/or waterproof jacket, plus wool or fleece hat and gloves are all essential. Have something energy-giving to eat and ensure that everyone in your group is fit, feeling well and alert.

Symptoms of hypothermia are exhaustion, numb skin (particularly toes and fingers), shivering, slurred speech, irrational

or violent behavior, lethargy, stumbling, dizzy spells, muscle cramps and violent bursts of energy. Irrationality may take the form of sufferers claiming they are warm and trying to take off their clothes.

To treat mild hypothermia, first get the person out of the wind and/or rain, remove their clothing if it's wet and replace it with dry, warm clothing. Give them hot liquids – not alcohol – and some high-energy, easily digestible food. Do not rub victims: instead, allow them to slowly warm themselves. This should be enough to treat the early stages of hypothermia. The early recognition and treatment of mild hypothermia is the only way to prevent severe hypothermia, which is a critical condition.

FROSTBITE

If you trek in very cold conditions, such as early or late in the season and/or at high elevations, there may be a (minor) risk of frostbite. The term refers to the freezing of extremities, including fingers, toes and nose. Signs and symptoms of frostbite include a whitish or waxy cast to the skin, or even crystals on the surface, plus itching, numbness and pain. Warm the affected areas by immersion in warm (not hot) water or with blankets or clothes, only until the skin becomes flushed. Frostbitten parts should not be rubbed. Pain and swelling are inevitable. Blisters should not be broken. Seek medical attention immediately.

Heat

Although Patagonia has a cool climate, heat exhaustion may occasionally become a real concern, especially in exposed volcanic country above the tree line. One way to avoid the heat is by getting an early start, then taking it easy during the hottest part of the day.

DEHYDRATION & HEAT EXHAUSTION

Dehydration is a potentially dangerous and generally preventable condition caused by excessive fluid loss. Sweating combined with inadequate fluid intake is one of the commonest causes in trekkers, but other important causes are diarrhea, vomiting, and high fever – see Diarrhea (p256) for more details about appropriate treatment in these circumstances.

The first symptoms are weakness, thirst and passing small amounts of very

INDECENT EXPOSURE

In the mid-1980s British scientists at Halley Station in Antarctica noticed that their ozone measuring instrument seemed to have gone wrong – ozone levels were vastly lower than had ever been recorded before. Unfortunately, it was not their instrument that had gone wrong, but the ozone itself – ozone levels over Antarctica in springtime were dropping to a fraction of the regular amount.

Soon after, they were able to isolate the culprit: chlorofluorocarbons (CFCs), which are man-made gases used in aerosols, refrigeration, air-conditioning, industrial solvents, asthma inhalers and fire control. Most of the time these gases are innocuous, but in the Antarctic springtime the combination of very cold temperatures and the return of sunshine to the polar region allow the CFCs to rapidly gobble up the stratospheric ozone, resulting in the famed ozone hole. Once the Antarctic temperatures start to warm as spring progresses, the ozone begins to recover, only to be depleted again when the next spring arrives.

Ozone protects the Earth's surface from UV radiation, the stuff that causes sunburn, among other things. Without it, sunburn and skin cancer become very serious concerns. The ozone hole has impacted Southern Patagonia more than any other inhabited area on earth. It is particularly bad during the spring, when its UV rays are most powerful. Visitors should wear brimmed hats and sunglasses, slather on the sunscreen and be particularly mindful of children.

The adoption and strengthening of the 1987 Montreal Protocol has cut the quantity of CFCs in the atmosphere and Antarctic ozone levels are beginning to recover, but it's a slow process and it will take another 50 years or so to get back to normal ozone levels. In the meanwhile, consult NASA's Total Ozone Mapping Spectrometer website at u http://jwocky.gsfc.nasa.gov for UV readings around the planet and information on ozone depletion in general.

Jocelyn Turnbull, PHD

concentrated urine. This may progress to drowsiness, dizziness or fainting on standing up, and finally, coma.

It's easy to forget how much fluid you are losing via perspiration while you are trekking, particularly if a strong breeze is drying your skin quickly. You should always maintain a good fluid intake – a minimum of 3L a day is recommended.

Dehydration and salt deficiency can cause heat exhaustion. Salt deficiency is characterized by fatigue, lethargy, headaches, giddiness and muscle cramps; salt tablets are overkill, just adding extra salt to your food is probably sufficient.

HEATSTROKE

This is a serious, occasionally fatal, condition that occurs if the body's heat-regulating mechanism breaks down and the body temperature rises to dangerous levels. Long, continuous periods of exposure to high temperatures and insufficient fluids can leave you vulnerable to heatstroke.

The symptoms are feeling unwell, not sweating very much (or at all) and a high body temperature (39° to 41°C or 102° to 106°F). Where sweating has ceased, the skin becomes flushed and red. Severe, throbbing headaches and lack of coordination will also occur, and the sufferer may be confused or aggressive. Eventually the victim will become delirious or convulse. Hospitalization is essential, but in the interim get victims out of the sun, remove their clothing, cover them with a wet sheet or towel and then fan continually. Give fluids if they are conscious.

SNOW BLINDNESS

This painful temporary condition results from sunburn on the eye's surface (cornea). To prevent it, avoid walking on snow or in bright conditions without sunglasses. Treatment only relieves the pain, the condition usually resolves itself within a few days and there are no long-term consequences. To treat, try putting cold cloths on closed eyelids. Antibiotic and anesthetic eye drops are not necessary.

Sun

Protection against the sun should always be taken seriously. Particularly in the rarified air and deceptive coolness of the mountains, sunburn occurs rapidly. Slap on the sunscreen and a barrier cream for your nose and lips, wear a broad brimmed hat and protect your eyes with good quality sunglasses with UV lenses, particularly when walking near water, sand or snow. If you burn in spite of precautions, apply calamine lotion, aloe vera or other commercial sunburn relief preparations.

Water

Patagonia boasts some of the purest water sources in the world. Even in urban Chile and Argentina, water is rarely a health problem. In remote, lightly visited mountain areas, water taken from springs or small streams close to a spring source is almost certain to be fit for drinking untreated provided there is no source of contamination upstream – such as a farm or campsite.

The high concentration of trekkers in popular national parks such as Torres del Paine and Nahuel Huapi, however, is beginning to seriously affect the quality of water, even in lakes and streams well away from trails. As water from such sources may contain harmful pathogens (especially those causing giardiasis, amebic dysentery and hydatid cysts), it is wise to sterilize it. Don't collect water downstream from abandoned mines or other human infrastructure such as ski resorts as it may contain toxic impurities that cannot be removed by standard methods of purification.

WATER PURIFICATION

Normally, boiling water is the simplest way of treating it for human consumption. Due to the generally low elevations of treks in the Patagonian Andes, boiling water for five minutes should be long enough to kill all pathogens. If boiling is your main method of purification, carry plenty of stove fuel.

An excellent option is a Steripen, a compact wand that purifies water through a quick laser treatment.

Chemical sterilisation using chlorine drops or tablets (Drinkwell, Puritabs, Steritabs or other brand names) will kill many, but not all, pathogens. Iodine is very effective in purifying water and is available in tablet form (such as Potable Aqua), but follow the directions carefully and remember that too much iodine can be harmful. Adding vitamin C (which is an additive

in drink powders such as Tang) to iodized water eliminates the unpleasant taste and color of iodine, but wait until the iodine has had time to work.

Many trekkers carry a pump-filter (such as those made by Katadyn, MSR or PUR) to remove water contaminants; ensure that your unit filters out pathogens like giardia.

TRAUMATIC INJURIES

Detailed first-aid instruction is outside the scope of this book, but here are some tips and advice. Walkers should consider taking a first-aid course before hitting the trail to ensure they know what to do in the event of an injury.

Fractures

Indications of a fracture (broken bone) are pain (tenderness of the affected area), swelling and discoloration, loss of function or deformity of a limb. Unless you know what you are doing, you shouldn't try to straighten an obviously displaced broken bone. To protect from further injury, immobilize a nondisplaced fracture by splinting it, usually in the position found, which will probably be the most comfortable position.

Fractures of the thighbone require urgent treatment as they involve massive blood loss and pain. Seek help and treat the patient for shock. Fractures associated with open wounds (compound fractures) also require more urgent treatment than simple fractures, as there is a risk of infection. Dislocations, where the bone has come out of the joint, are very painful, and should be set as soon as possible.

Broken ribs are painful but usually heal by themselves and do not need splinting. If breathing difficulties occur, or the person coughs up blood, medical attention should be sought urgently, as it may indicate a punctured lung.

Internal Injuries

These are more difficult to detect, and cannot usually be treated in the field. Watch for shock, which is a specific medical condition associated with a failure to maintain circulating blood volume. Signs include a rapid pulse and cold, clammy extremities. A person in shock requires urgent medical attention.

Major Accidents

Falling or having something fall on you, resulting in head injuries or fractures, is always possible when walking, especially if you are crossing steep slopes or unstable terrain. Following is some basic advice on what to do in the event of a major accident. If a person suffers a major fall:

- make sure you and other people with you are not in danger
- assess the injured persons condition
- stabilize any injuries, such as bleeding wounds or broken bones
- seek medical attention (see p255)

For emergency numbers see p264.

If the person is unconscious, immediately check whether they are breathing – clear their airway if it is blocked – and check whether they have a pulse – feel the side of the neck rather than the wrist. If they are not breathing but have a pulse, you should start mouth-to-mouth resuscitation immediately. In these circumstances it is best to move the person as little as possible in case their neck or back is broken.

Check for wounds and broken bones – ask the person where they have pain if they are conscious, otherwise gently inspect them all over (including their back and the back of the head), moving them as little as possible. Control any bleeding by applying firm pressure to the wound. Bleeding from the nose or ear may indicate a fractured skull. Don't give the person anything by mouth, especially if they are unconscious.

You'll have to manage the person for shock. Raise their legs above heart level (unless their legs are fractured); dress any wounds and immobilize any fractures; loosen tight clothing; keep the person warm by covering them with a blanket or other dry clothing; insulate them from the ground if possible, but don't heat them.

Some general points to bear in mind are:

- Simple fractures take several weeks to heal, so they don't need fixing straight away, but they should be immobilized to protect them from further injury. Compound fractures need urgent treatment.
- If you do have to splint a broken bone, remember to check regularly that the

splint is not cutting off the circulation to the hand or foot.
- Most cases of brief unconsciousness are not associated with any serious internal injury to the brain, but as a general rule in these circumstances, any person who has been knocked unconscious should be watched for deterioration. If they do deteriorate, seek medical attention straight away.

Sprains

Ankle and knee sprains are common injuries among hikers, particularly when crossing rugged terrain. To help prevent ankle sprains, wear boots that have adequate ankle support. If you do suffer a sprain, immobilize the joint with a firm bandage, and, if feasible, immerse the foot in cold water. Distribute the contents of your pack among your companions. Once you reach shelter, relieve pain and swelling by keeping the joint elevated for the first 24 hours and, where possible, by putting ice on the swollen joint.

Take simple painkillers to ease the discomfort. If the sprain is mild, you may be able to continue your walk after a couple of days. For more severe sprains, seek medical attention as an X-ray may be needed to find out whether a bone has been broken.

WOMENS HEALTH

Thrush (Vaginal Candidiasis)

Antibiotic use, synthetic underwear, tight trousers, sweating, contraceptive pills and unprotected sex can each lead to fungal vaginal infections, especially when traveling in hot, humid or tropical climates. The most common is thrush (vaginal candidiasis). Symptoms include itching and discomfort in the genital area, often in association with a thick white discharge. The best prevention is to keep the vaginal area cool and dry, and to wear cotton rather than synthetic underwear and loose clothes. Thrush can be treated by clotrimazole pessaries or vaginal cream.

Urinary Tract Infection

Dehydration and 'holding in' can result in urinary tract infection and the symptoms of cystitis, which can be particularly distressing and an inconvenient problem when out on the trail. Symptoms include burning when urinating, and having to urinate frequently and urgently. Blood can sometimes be passed in the urine. Drink plenty of fluids and empty your bladder at regular intervals. If symptoms persist, seek medical attention because a simple infection can spread to the kidneys, causing a more severe illness.

SAFETY ON THE TREK

Although trekking is generally one of the safest mountain activities, trekker injuries and deaths do occur – despite most serious accidents being preventable. Above all, trekkers should avoid getting themselves into dangerous situations, especially when trekking off-trail. Falls due to slipping on wet grass, loose scree, mossy rock or icy paths are among the most common hazards. High winds in southern Patagonia also cause bad tumbles.

TREK SAFETY – BASIC RULES

- Allow plenty of time to accomplish a walk before dark, particularly when daylight hours are shorter.
- Study the route carefully before setting out, noting the possible escape routes and the point of no return (where it's quicker to continue than to turn back). Monitor your progress during the day against the time estimated for the walk, and keep an eye on the weather.
- It's wise not to walk alone. Always leave details of your intended route, number of people in your group, and expected return time with someone responsible before you set off; let that person know when you return.
- Before setting off, make sure you have a relevant map, compass or GPS device (see p253), whistle, and check the weather forecast for the area.

Watch for signs of impending bad weather and descend or seek shelter if conditions start to look threatening. Trekkers should always carry a completely waterproof rain jacket (and preferably overpants) regardless of how good the weather seems. Avoid crossing exposed areas in poor weather and don't camp in any spot without natural shelter. Even in areas with *refugios*, carrying a tent will ensure you always have shelter in an emergency. Also carry basic supplies, including food containing simple sugars (such as chocolate) to generate heat quickly, and lots of fluid to drink.

BAMBOO CANE

A bamboo-like cane (known as *quila* or *colihue*) grows in the understorey of all but the most southerly temperate rainforests. On bushwhacked tracks sharp cut-off canes may stick out of the ground, making potentially dangerous obstacles. Walk very carefully where any track leads through bamboo, especially on steep muddy descents.

CROSSING RIVERS

Only a few of the treks described in this guidebook involve a serious river crossing, as most larger streams have bridges. However, a serious wade may be necessary in late spring and early summer (mid-November to late December) when thawing snow swells streams, or after heavy summer rain. Remember that while heavy rain quickly makes rivers impassable, mountain stream levels fall almost as fast as they rise. Fast-flowing glacial streams call for the greatest caution as fine sediment often clouds the water, making it difficult to gauge the depth. Streams of glacial origin usually reach their highest level in late afternoon (after the sun's intensity has begun to wane), so a morning crossing will always be easier.

Trekking parties should nevertheless be well practised in river-crossing techniques. The safest place to cross a river is usually just downstream from a long pool. Undo the waist buckle and loosen the shoulder straps of your pack. This makes it easier to slip out of your backpack and swim to safety if you lose your balance and are swept downstream. Use a walking pole, grasped in both hands, on the upstream side as a third leg, or go arm in arm with a companion, clasping at the wrist, and cross side-on to the flow, taking short steps.

USEFUL PHONE NUMBERS

	Chile	Argentina
Emergency	☎ 133	☎ 107
Police	☎ 133	☎ 101
Directory assistance	☎ 103	☎ 110

DOGS

On the whole, Patagonian pups are placid. However, do not pet working sheepdogs – not pets, they don't like being touched by strangers. At times trekkers have to pass by farmhouses guarded by decidedly unfriendly dogs. Remember that it's you who is encroaching on its territory. Avoid eye contact – a sign of territorial challenge – and retreat discreetly or make a wide circle around the farmyard. Picking up hard projectiles should earn you instant respect, as would throwing rocks with loose aim.

Bites from farm dogs should be treated seriously, as the animals may carry parasites that cause hydatid cysts (p256) or, in rare cases, rabies (p258).

LIGHTNING

If a storm brews, avoid exposed areas. Lightning has a penchant for crests, lone trees, small depressions, gullies, caves and cabin entrances, as well as wet ground. If you are caught out in the open, try to curl up as tightly as possible with your feet together and keep a layer of insulation between you and the ground. Place metal objects such as metal-frame backpacks and walking poles away from you.

ROCKFALL

Even a small falling rock could shatter your hand or crack your skull, so always be alert to the danger of rockfall. Trail sections most obviously exposed to rockfall lead below cliffs fringed by large fields of raw scree – don't hang around in such areas. If you accidentally loosen a rock, loudly warn any other trekkers who may be below you.

RESCUE & EVACUATION

As help might be many days away, trekkers should aim to be as self-reliant as possible. Keep in mind that, aside from the popular national parks of Torres del Paine and Los Glaciares, you may not see other hikers. Often parks are underfunded, with few rangers to cover vast territories and no medical staff. Particularly in remote and sparsely populated areas (such as central Patagonia), your best first option may be to seek assistance at a nearby farm or ranch (*estancia*).

In most circumstances, evacuation by helicopter will not be an option. If a helicopter is available you may be required to give some kind of assurance of payment – ensure that your travel insurance covers this.

Emergency Communications

Although mobile (cell) phones occasionally work in parts of a few national parks or reserves close to regional towns, the mobile network is far too limited to be a reliable form of emergency communication.

Satellite (world) phones can be used from virtually anywhere, but are extremely expensive to own and operate (see Telephone, p238). Larger *estancias*, ranger stations (*guarderías*) and staffed *refugios* – such as those in the national parks of Nahuel Huapi and Torres del Paine – usually have a two-way radio that can be used in an emergency situation.

Distress Signals

If you need to call for help, use these internationally recognized emergency signals. Give six short signals, such as a whistle, a yell or the flash of a light, at 10-second intervals, followed by a minute of rest. Repeat the sequence until you get a response. If the responder knows the signals, the response will be three signals at 20-second intervals, followed by a minute pause and a repetition of the sequence.

Search & Rescue Organizations

In case of an emergency, rescues may be carried out by national park, (border) police or military personnel. The *Cuerpo de Socorro Andino de Chile* (www.socorroandino.cl; jefatura@socorroandino.cl) is a special volunteer organisation that carries out mountain rescues in the Chilean Andes. Its website features an online registration form (*avisos de salida*) where you can register details of your party members and intended route.

Language

CONTENTS

Both Argentinians and Chileans speak Spanish, called *castellano* in Spanish, a term generally preferred in the Americas to *español.* In the cities quite a number of people know some English, but in the countryside this is rare. In certain parts of the south, small but influential communities of German, Italian, English, Croatian and even Welsh settlers continue to speak their languages. In some areas indigenous tongues still survive, the most notable being the Mapuche dialects of the Lakes District. Most Mapuche Indians are now able to speak Spanish as well as or better than their traditional languages.

SPANISH

On the whole, Spanish is not difficult, and you should try to gain some knowledge of simple conversational Spanish before you travel. Being able to communicate even at a very basic level with locals will be helpful and satisfying. Because of the common Latin roots in many English and Spanish words, it can be surprisingly easy to understand written Spanish. Spelling follows simple phonetic rules, and pronunciation is not difficult. Despite the common Hispanic colonial past of Chile and Argentina, there are some differences between the forms of Spanish spoken in each country. Lonely Planet's *Latin American Spanish* phrasebook has more on those differences.

PRONUNCIATION

c as the 's' in 'see' before **e** and **i**; elsewhere, as English 'k'
h invariably silent
j a guttural version of English 'h'
ll/y as the French 'j' in Jean-Jacques or, more strongly, as the English 'j' in Jessie Jackson
ñ as the 'ny' in 'canyon'

ARGENTINE SPANISH

Argentine Spanish has some interesting features. Pronunciation and accent have been heavily influenced by Italian immigration, which has given this dialect a pleasant, melodic sound. Vowels are often lengthened and pronunciation is more decisive. Many Italian words have also been absorbed into the national vocabulary. Another strong characteristic of Argentine Spanish is the continued universal usage of the archaic word *vos,* meaning 'you'. *Vos* (pronounced 'boss') completely replaces *tú* as the familiar singular form, and in the present tense requires special verb conjugations such as *vos pagás, vos tenéis, vos sos* ('you pay', 'you have', 'you are'). The sounds represented by the letters 'll' and 'y' are either pronounced like a French 'j', as in Jean-Jacques, or more strongly like an English 'j', as in Jessie Jackson.

CHILEAN SPANISH

Chilean Spanish is invariably spoken rapidly, and often has a high-pitched, lilting intonation that makes it immediately recognisable. Many Chileans appear to speak without moving their mouths very much, and often seem to swallow their words. The habit of dropping the letter 's' is almost universal in Chile, making it hard to tell whether nouns are in the singular or plural form. Some Chileans, particularly in the south of the country, are inclined to pronounce the consonants 'll' and 'y' in a similar way to the Argentinians, though with less force. Chileans have developed lots of local idioms and slang. Don't be too surprised or worried if you have difficulty understanding the Chileans at first – persist and you'll soon enough get the hang of it.

GREETINGS

Good morning!
¡Buenos días!

Good afternoon!
¡Buenas tardes!
Hello!
¡Hola!
See you later!
¡Hasta luego!
Goodbye!
¡Adios/Chau!
Farewell!
¡Que le vaya bien!

BASIC CONVERSATION

My name is…
Me llamo…
What's the time?
¿Qué hora es?
Where are you from?
¿De dónde es Usted?
Do you live here?
¿Vive acá?
Wait for me here.
Espéreme aquí.
I'm sightseeing.
Estoy paseando.
It's a very beautiful spot.
Es un lugar muy lindo.
We're touring the area.
Estamos conociendo.

TIME, DAYS & NUMBERS

Eight o'clock is *las ocho*, while 8.30 is *las ocho y treinta* (eight and thirty) or *las ocho y media* (eight and a half). However, 7.45 is *las ocho menos quince* (eight minus fifteen) or *las ocho menos cuarto* (eight minus one quarter).

Times are modified by morning *(de la mañana)* or afternoon *(de la tarde)* instead of am or pm. Use of the 24-hour clock (military time) is also common, especially with transportation schedules.

What time is it?	*¿Qué hora es?*
It's one o'clock.	*Es la una.*
It's two/three o'clock.	*Son las dos/tres.*
At three o'clock…	*A las tres…*

today	*hoy*
tomorrow	*mañana*
yesterday	*ayer*

Monday	*lunes*
Tuesday	*martes*
Wednesday	*miércoles*
Thursday	*jueves*
Friday	*viernes*
Saturday	*sábado*
Sunday	*domingo*

1	*uno*
2	*dos*
3	*tres*
4	*cuatro*
5	*cinco*
6	*seis*
7	*siete*
8	*ocho*
9	*nueve*
10	*diez*
11	*once*
12	*doce*
13	*trece*
14	*catorce*
15	*quince*
16	*dieciséis*
17	*diecisiete*
18	*dieciocho*
19	*diecinueve*
20	*veinte*
21	*veintiuno*
22	*veintidós*
30	*treinta*
31	*treinta y uno*
40	*cuarenta*
50	*cincuenta*
60	*sesenta*
70	*setenta*
80	*ochenta*
90	*noventa*
100	*cien*
101	*ciento uno*
102	*ciento dos*
200	*doscientos*
1000	*mil*
1100	*mil cien*
2000	*dos mil*
100,000	*cien mil*

TREK PREPARATIONS

Where can we buy supplies?
¿Dónde podemos comprar víveres?
Can I leave some things here a while?
¿Puedo dejar algunas cosas acá por un rato?
Where can we hire a mountain guide?
¿Dónde podemos alquilar un guía de montaña?
I'd like to talk to someone who knows this area.
Quisiera hablar con álguien que conozca este sector.
How much do you charge?
¿Cuánto cobra Usted?

We are thinking of taking this route.
Pensamos tomar esta ruta.
Is the trek very difficult?
¿Es muy difícil la caminata?
Is the track (well) marked?
¿Está (bien) marcado el sendero?
Which is the shortest/easiest route?
¿Cuál es la ruta más corta/más fácil?
Is there much snow on the pass?
¿Hay mucha nieve en el paso?
We will return in one week.
Volverémos en una semana.

TRANSPORT

When does the next bus leave for...?
¿Cuándo sale el próximo bus a...?
I'd like to charter a boat/taxi.
Quisiera contratar un bote/remise.
Come to pick us up in five days.
Venga a buscarnos en cinco días.
Can you take me to...?
¿Puede llevarme a...?
I'd like to get off at the turn-off.
Quisiera bajar en la bifurcación.
I'll hitchhike.
Viajo a dedo.
We're leaving tomorrow.
Partiremos mañana.

CLOTHING & EQUIPMENT

altimeter	*altímetro*
anorak/rain jacket	*campera/chaqueta impermeable*
backpack/rucksack	*mochila*
batteries	*pilas/baterías*
billy/cooking pot	*olla*
bootlace	*cordón de bota*
boots	*botas*
camping stove	*cocinilla/calentador (Arg)/ anafe (Ch)*
candles	*velas*
canteen/water bottle	*cantimplora*
cap/beanie	*gorro*
carabiner	*mosquetón*
compass	*brújula*
crampons	*grampones/trepadores*
gaiters	*polainas*
gas cartridge	*cartucha de gas*
gloves	*guantes*
ice axe	*piolet/piqueta (Arg)*
pocketknife	*cortaplumas*
provisions/ food supplies	*víveres/abastecimientos*
runners/tennis shoes	*zapatillas*
rope	*cuerda*
sleeping bag	*saco de dormir*
sleeping mat	*colchoneta aislante*
sunglasses	*gafas de sol*
tent	*carpa*
torch/flashlight	*linterna*
trekking poles	*bastónes*
white gasoline	*nafta blanca (Arg)/ bencina blanca (Ch)*

ON THE TREK

How many kilometers to...?
¿Cuántos kilómetros son hasta...?
How many hours' walking?
¿Cuántas horas son caminando?
Does this track go to...?
¿Va este sendero a...?
How do you reach the summit?
¿Cómo se llega a la cumbre?
Where are you going to?
¿A dónde va Usted?
May I cross your property?
¿Puedo cruzar su propiedad?
What's this place called?
¿Cómo se llama este lugar?
We're doing a trek from... to...
Estamos haciendo una caminata desde... a...

DIRECTIONS

adjacent	*al frente/contiguo*
ahead/behind	*más adelante/atrás*
ascent/descent	*subida/bajada*
before/after	*antes/después (de)*
below/above	*debajo/encima de*
beside	*al lado de*
between	*entre*
early/late	*temprano/tarde*
east/west	*este/oeste*
flat/steep	*llano/empinado*
height/depth	*altura/profundidad*
here/there	*aquí/acá, allá*
high/low	*alto/bajo*
near/distant	*cerca/lejos*
north/south	*norte/sur*
on the other side of	*al otro lado de*
southern	*austral/meridional*
(to the) left/right	*(a la) derecha/izquierda*
towards/away from	*hacia/desde*
up/down	*arriba/abajo*

MAP READING

Do you have a better map?
¿Tiene un mejor mapa?
Can you show me on the map where we are?
¿Puede señalarme en el mapa dónde estamos?

MAP FEATURES

altitude difference	*desnivel*
contour lines	*curvas de nivel*
frontier mark	*hito*
map	*mapa/carta*
metres above sea level	*metros sobre el nivel del mar/ msnm*
spot height	*cota*
tree line (timber line)	*nivel del bosque*

WEATHER

What will the weather be like?
¿Qué tiempo hará?
Tomorrow it will be cold.
Mañana hará frío.
It's going to rain.
Va a llover.
It's windy/sunny.
Hace viento/sol.
It's raining/snowing.
Está lloviendo/nevando.
It has clouded over.
Se ha nublado.
The rain slowed us down.
Nos atrasó la lluvia.
At what time does it get dark?
¿A qué hora caye la noche?

WEATHER CONDITIONS

clear/fine	*despejado*
cloud	*nube*
fog/mist	*neblina/niebla*
frost	*helada*
good/bad weather	*buen/mal tiempo*
ice	*hielo*
overcast/cloudy	*nublado*
rain/to rain	*lluvia/llover*
snow/to snow	*nieve/nevar*
spring melt/thaw	*deshielo*
storm	*tormenta/tempestad*
summer	*verano*
whiteout/clag	*borrina/encainada*
wind	*viento*
winter	*invierno*

CAMPING

Where is the best place to camp?
¿Dónde está el mejor lugar para acampar?
Can we put up the tent here?
¿Podemos armar la carpa acá?
Is it permitted to make fire?
¿Está permitido hacer fuego?
There is no firewood.
No hay leña.
I have a gas/petrol stove.
Tengo una calentador (Arg)/anafe (Ch) a gas/bencina.
I'm going to stay here two days.
Voy a quedarme dos días aquí.

DIFFICULTIES

Help!
¡Soccoro!
Fire!
¡Fuego!
Careful!
¡Cuidado!
We've lost the way.
Hemos perdido el camino.
I'm looking for…
Estoy buscando…
Is it dangerous?
¿Es peligroso?
Can you help me?
¿Puede ayudarme?
I'm sick.
Estoy enferm(o/a).
I'm thirsty/hungry.
Tengo sed/hambre.
I've been robbed.
Me han robado.
I don't understand.
No entiendo.
Please speak more slowly.
Por favor, hable más despacio.
Can you repair this for me?
¿Puede arreglarme ésto?

PEOPLE

backpacker	*mochiler(o/a)*
cowboy	*gaucho (Arg)/huaso (Ch)*
foreigner	*extranjer(o/a)/gring(o/a)*
hut warden	*refugiero*
indigenous person/ Indian	*indigena/indi(o/a)*
mountain guide	*guía de montaña/baqueano*
mountaineer	*andinista/montañese (Arg)*
park ranger	*guardaparque*
police	*gendarmería (Arg)/ carabineros (Ch)*
rancher	*estancionero*
traveler	*viajero*

NATIONALITIES

What country do you come from?
¿De qué país viene?
I'm (a/an)…
Soy…

The following alternative forms ending in 'a' are for women; those ending in 'o', for men.

American	*Estadounidense/ Norte American(o/a)*
Argentinian	*Argentin(o/a)*
Australian	*Australian(o/a)*
Belgian	*Belg(o/a)*
British	*Britan(o/a)*
Canadian	*Canadiense*
Chilean	*Chilen(o/a)*
Dutch	*Holandés(a)*
English	*Inglés(a)*
French	*Francés(a)*
German	*Alemán(a)*
Irish	*Irlandés(a)*
Israeli	*Israelita*
New Zealander	*Neozelandés(a)*
Scot	*Escocés(a)*
Swede	*Suec(o/a)*
Swiss	*Suiz(o/a)*
Welsh	*Galés(a)*

WAYS OF TRANSIT

circuit	*circuito*
highway	*carretera*
path/trail	*sendero/picada/senda*
road/vehicle track	*camino*
route (unmarked)	*huella/ruta*
shortcut	*atajo*
sidewalk/footpath	*vereda*

ARTIFICIAL FEATURES

border post	*aduana*
bridge/footbridge	*puente/pasarela*
campground	*camping*
caravan park	*autocamping*
ditch	*zanja*
farm	*finca/chacra (Arg)/fundo (Ch)*
fence	*cerco/alambrado*
homestead	*caserío*
house/building	*casa*
hut/mountain shelter	*refugio*
jetty/landing pier	*muelle*
lighthouse	*faro*
park entrance	*portada (Arg)/portería (Ch)*
pit toilet	*letrina*
ranch	*estancia*
ranger station	*guardería*
ski field	*cancha de esquí*
ski lift/ski tow	*aerosilla/andarrivel*
stockyard/corral	*galpón*
town/village	*pueblo/aldea*

EMERGENCIES

Help!	*¡Socorro!/¡Auxilio!*
Help me!	*¡Ayudenme!*
Thief!	*¡Ladrón!*
Fire!	*¡Fuego!*
police	*gendarmería (Arg)/ carabineros (Ch)*
doctor	*doctor*
hospital	*hospital*
Leave me alone!	*¡Déjeme!*
Go away!	*¡Váyase!*
I've been robbed.	*Me han robado.*
They took my...	*Se me llevaron...*
money	*el dinero*
passport	*el pasaporte*
bag	*la bolsa*

TRAIL TERMS

accommodation/ lodgings	*alojamiento*
to arrive	*llegar*
bivouac	*vivac*
to camp	*acampar*
campfire/fireplace	*fogata/fogón*
camping area	*campamento/campismo*
campsite	*sitio/area (de acampar)*
to carry	*llevar*
climb/to climb	*escalada/escalar*
firewood	*leña*
to fish	*pescar*
to follow	*seguir*
ford/wade	*vado*
hike	*caminata/andanza*
horse ride/by horse	*cabalgata/a caballo*
mountaineering	*andinismo/alpinismo*
rubbish	*basura*
signpost	*cartel indicador*
traverse	*traversía*
to walk/go on foot	*caminar/ir a pie*

VEGETATION

branch	*rama*
bush/shrub	*arbusto*
flower	*flor*
grass	*pasto*
leaf	*hoja*
lichen	*liquen*
moss	*musgo*
root	*raíz*
tree	*árbol*

WILDLIFE

beaver	*castor*
cat	*gato*

cow/cattle	*vaca/ganado bovino*
deer	*ciervo*
dog	*perro*
duck	*pato*
eagle	*águila*
fish	*pez*
flea	*pulga*
fly	*mosca*
fox	*zorro*
frog	*sapo/rana*
hare/rabbit	*liebre/conejo*
hawk	*halcón*
horse	*caballo*
horsefly	*tábano*
seagull	*gaviota*
sheep	*oveja*
swan	*cisne*
trout	*trucha*
vulture	*buitre*
wild pig	*jabalí*
woodpecker	*carpintero*

LANDFORMS

Andean meadow	*alpage/coironal*
avalanche	*alud/avalancha*
bay/cove	*bahía/caleta*
beach	*playa*
bog/swamp	*pantano/mallín*
branch of a lake/river	*brazo*
brook	*riachuelo*
cairn	*mojón/pirca*
cave	*cueva/caverna*
chasm	*abismo*
cliff	*acantilado/barranco/farellón*
coast, shoreline	*costa*
crag	*peña/peñón*
crater (of a volcano)	*caldera*
creek/small river	*estero/arroyo*
crevasse	*grieta*
drainage basin	*hoya/cuenca*
face of a mountain	*muralla/vertiente*
fjord/sound	*fiordo/seno*
forest	*bosque*
frontier/border	*frontera/límite*
gap/narrow pass	*portillo/pasada*
glacier	*ventisquero/glaciar*
gorge/canyon	*cajón, barranco/garganta*
hill	*morro/colina/loma*
hillside/mountainside	*faldeo/ladera*
iceberg	*témpano*
island	*isla*
lake	*lago/laguna*
landslide	*derrumbe*
location/spot	*lugar/paraje*
lookout	*mirador*
moor	*turbal/mallín*
moraine	*morrena*
mountain	*cerro/montaña/monte*
mountain chain	*cordillera/cordón*
national park	*parque nacional*
névé/permanent snowfield	*neviza/campo de nieve*
outlet stream	*desagüe*
pass	*paso/portezuelo/abra*
pinnacle	*pináculo/aguja/diente*
plain/flat terrain	*llanura/planicie*
plateau/tableland	*meseta*
range/massif	*sierra/mazico*
rapid	*catarata*
reserve	*reserva*
ridge/spur	*filo/espolón/cresta*
river	*río/quebrada*
riverbank/shoreline	*ribera/orilla*
riverbed	*cauce/lecho*
scoria	*escoria*
scrub/underbrush	*matorral/sotobosque*
slope/rise	*cuesta/pendiente*
(snow) cornice	*cornisa (de nieve)*
source of a stream	*nacimiento*
spring	*fuente/manantial*
steppe/plain	*estepa/pampa*
stone/rock	*piedra*
strait	*estrecho*
stream junction	*horqueta/confluencia*
summit/peak	*cumbre/cima/pico*
thermal springs	*termas/aguas calientes*
torrent/gushing stream	*chorro*
valley	*valle*
volcano	*volcán*
waterfall	*salto (de agua)/cascada*

MAPUCHE & TEHUELCHE

Although there's no need to learn any Mapuche or Tehuelche, the significance of certain place names (particularly in the Araucanía and the Lakes District) will be clearer if you can decipher a few words of indigenous origin. Most spellings given below are as used in local place names (which reflect Spanish phonetics) and some of the words differ both in spelling and pronunciation from the original Mapuche.

antu	**sun/day**
buta	**large/great**

calfu	**blue**
cautín	**a native duck**
che	**people**
co	**water**
coli/colu	**brown**
copa	**green**
cuel	**hill**
cura	**rock/stone**
cuy cuy	**log bridge**
filu	**snake**
futa	**big**
gol	**stake/stick/pole**
huapi	**island**
hue	**place/location**
hueico	**tiny lake/puddle**
huille	**south**
huiqui	**thrush**
iñim	**bird**
lafquén	**sea/lake/plain**
lemu	**forest**
leufú	**river**
llanca	**a semi-precious blue stone**
lonco	**head**
lonko	**clan chief**
mahuida/mavida	**mountain**
mallín	**moor**
mañque	**condor**
mapu	**land/earth**
milla	**gold**
nahuel	**jaguar**
ñamcu	**eagle**
ñiri	**fox**
pangui	**puma**
pile/pilén	**frost/ice**
pillán	**volcano**
pire	**snow**
poco	**frog**
puelche	**warm northerly wind in Patagonia**
púlli	**mountainside**
quilla	**moon**
repú	**path/track**
traful	**confluence/river junction**
tromén	**cloud**
tue	**ground/soil**

Glossary

The following words or terms have been used throughout the text as defined below.

A

aduana – border or customs post (Spanish)
aerosilla – chairlift
Aisén – also spelt Aysén; Chile's wild and thinly-settled XI Región in central Patagonia
albergue – hostel (Spanish)
alerce – large conifer mainly found in wet areas of the Lakes District
alerzal – a stand of *alerces* (Spanish)
almacén – small store that sells provisions (Spanish)
amphitheatre – rounded glacial cirque enclosed by high rock walls
Andean – pertaining to the Andes, the world's longest and second-highest mountain range
andinist – Andean mountaineer
APN – Administración de Parques Nacionales; the national-park authority of Argentina
araucaria – Monkey-puzzle tree with a unique umbrellalike form, found throughout the Araucanía; known in Argentina by the Mapuche word *pehuén*
Araucarian – see Mapuche
arrayán – native myrtle with orange-red bark, usually found growing on waterlogged sites
arroyo – stream or creek (especially in Argentine Spanish)
asado – whole sheep or calf grilled on a spit around a large open charcoal fire; popular in Argentina

B

bahía – bay (Spanish)
bandurria – black-necked ibis; often seen on pastures or wetlands throughout Patagonia
biota – flora and fauna of a national park or other area
bushwhacking – trekking on off-tracks through (dense) forest

C

CAB – Club Andino Bariloche; the largest mountain club in South America
calafate – thorny bush of the *Berberis* genus, particularly common in southern Patagonia
caminata – trek or hiking trip (Spanish)
camino – road, but locally sometimes also used to mean 'foot track' (Spanish)
campsite – place offering organized camping; campsites generally have basic facilities such as toilets and showers, and may charge a fee
camping libre – free campsite without facilities (used mainly in Argentine national parks)
campsite – used in each trekking stage of this guidebook for any suitable place where camping is allowed; a campsite may be 'wild' (if local regulations permit this), at a campsite designated by the park authority, or at a campsite
CAP – Club Andino Piltriquitrón; the local mountain club in El Bolsón
Carabineros de Chile – Chilean police force (also responsible for patrolling the frontier and for immigration control)
Carretera Austral – 1137km unsurfaced 'Southern Highway' that runs south from Puerto Montt to Villa O'Higgins in southern Aisén
casa de cambio – currency exchange bureau
casa de familia – private household that takes in paying guests
centro de inform – information center (Spanish)
cerro – mountain summit (Spanish)
chaura – species of low ericalike shrub that produces edible berries
chilco – native Patagonian fuchsia species
Chilote – inhabitant of the island of Chiloé
Chubut – Argentina's central Patagonian province, centerd around the Río Chubut
chucao – small ground-dwelling bird often heard (sometimes seen), mainly in the forests of the Lakes District and central Patagonia
cirque – high rounded precipice, formed by the weathering action of ice and snow, typically found at the head of a small alpine valley
club andino – mountain club (literally 'Andean club'; Spanish)

club de montaña – mountain club (Spanish)
Codeff – Comité Nacional Pro Defensa de Fauna y Flora; conservation organisation based in Santiago de Chile
coigüe – group of three evergreen species of southern beech; known as *coihue* in Argentina
colectivo – in Argentina, a public bus; in Chile, a shuttle taxi that stops to pick up passengers (Spanish)
colihue – native bamboo species
Comarca Andina del Paralelo 42 – Andean region centerd around the Argentine town of El Bolsón
Conaf – Corporación Nacional Forestal; Chilean forestry and national-park authority
confitería – small cafe-restaurant (Spanish)
contour – to move along a slope without climbing or descending appreciably Cordillera – the long chain of the Andes
Cordillera de la Costa – range of lower mountains running between the Andean Cordillera and the Pacific coast
crevasse – deep fissure in a glacier

D

downclimb – descent that is steep enough to require trekkers to use their hands for support and/or safety

E

entrada – entrance gate (Spanish)
estancia – large cattle or sheep property (Spanish)
estero – stream or creek (especially Chilean Spanish)

F

filo – ridge or spur (Spanish)
4WD track – rough road suitable only for four-wheel drive vehicles
fumarole – vent near or on a volcano from which gases and steam are emitted
fundo – farm, normally smaller than an *estancia* (especially Chilean Spanish)

G

gaucho – Argentine cowboy
Gendarmería Nacional – Argentine equivalent of the Chilean Carabineros
geyser – vent emitting hot water and steam, can sometimes erupt violently
glaciar – glacier (Spanish)
glissade – snow-sliding technique used to descend snow slopes
GPS – Global Positioning System; device that calculates position and elevation by reading and decoding signals from satellites
gringo – term (not necessarily disrespectful) for a foreigner of northern European descent (Spanish)
guanaco – Patagonian cameloid species (related to the llama)
guardaparque – national-park ranger (Spanish)
guardería – national-park ranger station (Spanish)

H

Hielo Norte – the northern continental icecap, which lies entirely within the Aisén region of Chile
Hielo Sur – the larger southern continental icecap
hito – (natural or artificial) surveying point that marks the international border (Spanish)
hospedaje – small, usually family-run, hotel (Spanish)
hostal – hotel (Spanish)
hostería – similar to a *hospedaje* (Spanish)
huaso – Chilean cowboy; in its wider sense, *huaso* simply means a country person
huemul – rare species of native Andean deer

I

icecap – vast dome-shaped glacier covering a mountain range in high-precipitation regions (see Hielo Norte, Hielo Sur)
icefall – very steep broken-up section of a glacier
IGM – Instituto Geográfico Militar; military cartographic institutes in both Chile and Argentina
intendencia – Argentine term for the administration center of a national park

L

lago/laguna – lake (Spanish)
lenga – most common deciduous species of southern beech
librería – bookstore (Spanish)

M

Magallanes – Chile's southernmost XII Región, which includes Chilean Tierra del Fuego
Magellanic forest – southern Patagonian forest (composed mainly of *lenga* and *ñirre*)

mahuén – plants of the genus *Mahuenia*, a rather atypical member of the cactus family, which grow in spiny, lawnlike mounds in dryland areas
mallín – area periodically inundated and typically covered by open swamp vegetation
Mapuche – group of ethnically related tribes that inhabit(ed) both sides of the Andes of northern Patagonia
mara – Patagonian hare
maté – a bitter brew served in gourds and sipped through metal straws **meseta** – tableland
menú – fixed-price meal (Spanish)
mirador – lookout or viewing point (Spanish)
mochilero – backpacker (Spanish; as in English, the word doesn't tell you whether the person concerned is trekking or simply using a backpack as convenient travel luggage)
mogote – species of tumbleweed found in dry areas of eastern Patagonia; also known as *mata spinosum*
monito del monte – mouse oopossum; small marsupial that inhabits the forests of the Araucanía and Lakes District
monte – term used in Argentina to describe the scrub-covered hill country fringing the eastern Patagonian precordillera; also used more generally to mean 'mountain summit', when it is synonymous with the Spanish *cerro*
moraine – rock debris carried by glaciers and dumped as the ice melts
msnm – *metros sobre el nivel del mar*, or 'meters above sea level' (Spanish)

N

ñandú – native ostrich of the Patagonian steppes; also called rhea
névé – permanent snowfield in the high alpine zone (French)
ñirre – small deciduous southern beech species; spelt *ñire* in Argentina
Nothofagus – botanical name of the southern beech genus, the most dominant trees of the Patagonian Andes
notro – also called *ciruelillo*, a common shrub that produces flamboyant red flowers

O

off-tracks – (trekking routes) not following any real walking track
out-and-back – trek whose route involves backtracking
outlet – place where a stream flows out of a lake

P

pampa – field or meadow; also used in Chile and Argentina to describe the vast steppes of eastern Patagonia (Spanish)
parque nacional – national park (Spanish)
party – used in this guidebook to mean a group of two or more trekkers
Patagonia – see exended definition (p26)
pehuén – see *araucaria*
pensión – boarding house or guesthouse (Spanish)
peter out – to gradually disappear (of a path or route)
petro – small biting gnat; usually found in lowland areas grazed by livestock
picada – foot track, usually less well-defined (mainly Argentine Spanish)
pilme – see *petro*
playa – beach (Spanish)
pobladores – the settlers of a remote region
portada – national-park entrance gate (Argentine Spanish)
portería – national-park entrance gate (Chilean Spanish)
precordillera – Andean foothills that fringe both sides of the main range, the Cordillera (Spanish)
proveeduría – canteen or small store (such as at a campsite or *refugio*) that sells basic provisions
puente – bridge (Spanish)
puesto – small hut or primitive shelter, usually on a more remote part of an *estancia*, where ranch workers can sleep a night or two (Spanish)
puma – South American mountain lion (related to the cougar of North America), sometimes referred to locally as *el león*

Q

quila – collective term (of Mapuche origin) for about half a dozen species of vigorous native bamboo
quincho – communal shelter used for cooking or campfires (Spanish)

R

reducción – Indian reservation (Argentine Spanish)

refugio – mountain hut or 'refuge' (Spanish; pronounced ref-oo-he-o)
remís – taxi (Argentine Spanish)
reserva nacional – national reserve (Spanish)
reserva natural estricta – restricted area of national park where public access is strictly controlled, and generally allowed only under the supervision of national-park personnel (Spanish)
residencial – boarding house or guesthouse (Spanish)
rhea – English word for *ñandú*
río – river (Spanish)
ruca – traditional thatched house of the Mapuche people

S

scree slide – slope of loose rock (known as scree or talus), below steep rocky mountainsides prone to weathering
scrub line – low, weather-beaten brush (usually *lenga*) on a high mountainside
seccional – *guardería* subordinate to the main APN *intendencia* (Argentine Spanish)
senda/sendero – path or foot track (Spanish)
serac – large, prominent block of ice typically seen on steep glaciers or icefalls (French)
Sernap – Servicio Nacional de Pesca; the Chilean authority responsible for regulating commercial and recreational fishing
Sernatur – Servicio Nacional de Turismo; the organisation which runs tourist offices in Chile
sierra – mountain range (literally 'saw'; Spanish)
southern beech – see *Nothofagus*
stage – individual section of a longer trek
switchbacks – sharp bends in a path that takes a winding route directly up or down a steep slope

T

tábano – collective term for two or more kinds of horseflies that infest forested areas in the Araucanía and Lakes District from early summer to midsummer
tarn – small highland lake
taxi colectivo – see *colectivo*
Tehuelche – an indigenous people who inhabited the steppes of southeastern Patagonia
termas – thermal springs (Spanish)
trailhead – point from which a trekking route begins (eg a car park, roadside, or national park ranger station)
trans-Andean – leading across the main range of the Andes
tree line – the altitude (which drops steadily from north to south) above which trees can no longer survive due to the severity of the climate
true left/true right – 'true' indicates the side of a river (or valley) from the perspective of a trekker facing downstream (or downvalley)

V

Valdivian forest – derived from the local Spanish term *bosque valdiviano*, this is the species-rich temperate rainforest that grows in the wettest areas of Andean foothills of the Lakes District and the north of central Patagonia
ventisquero – alternative word for glacier (Spanish)

W

wild camping – pitching a tent outside a campsite or a national park–authorised campsite

X

XI Región – see Aisén
XII Región – see Magallanes

Behind the Scenes

THIS BOOK

This guidebook was commissioned in Lonely Planet's Melbourne office, and produced by the following:

Publisher Chris Rennie
Associate Publisher Ben Handicott
Commissioning Editor Bridget Blair, Janine Eberle
Coordinating Cartographer Tony Fankhauser
Assisting Cartographers Alison Lyall, Ross Butler
Managing Cartographer Shahara Ahmed
Cover Designer Brendan Dempsey
Cover Layout Designer James Hardy
Project Manager Jane Atkin
Thanks to Simon Tillema, Wayne Murphy & Julie Sheridan
Production [recapture]

OUR READERS

Myra & Ron, Tom Aguirre, Carmen Auer, Michael Ausema, Marcos Baltuska, Guy Barker, William Burton, Humberto Cordero, Paul Corwin, Erin Crampton, Ryan Daly, Zuzana Druckmullerova, Janet & Paul Edstein, Joshua Feyen, Marisa Field, Mirjam Hedstrom, Ute Hilbig, Cooper Holoweski, Evan Hunter, Thomas Lothian, Brenda Lukas, Linda Mackenzie, Jonathan Nicholls, Tegwen Northam, Ludvik Pardubicky, Michael Rehm, Marcelo Rocha, Peter Salenieks, Herve Schnitzler, Richard Sheets, Morgan Simon, Jiri Smitak, Horst Stauder, Mirthe Van Der Kam, Arne Van Hofwegen, Carlos Zanoni, Don Zobel,

ACKNOWLEDGMENTS

All photographs by Lonely Planet Images, and by Michael Coyne p9 (#4), p11 (#4); Grant Dixon p6 (#3), p10 (#3 bottom); Jason Edwards p2 (#3); Roberto Gerometta p4 (#5); Ralph Hopkins p11 (#2); Holger Leue p6 (#4); Carolyn McCarthy p4 (#4), p5 (#1) p7 (#1); p10 (#3 top), Gareth McCormack p 8 (#3, #1), p12; Aaron McCoy p3 (#3); Mark Newman p8 (#5); Craig Pershouse p5 (#2); Woods Wheatcroft p2 (#5); Eric Wheater p3 (#4); Brent Winebrenner p7 (#2)

THANKS FROM THE AUTHOR

My sincere gratitude goes out to the dedicated people who call Patagonia home and work tirelessly toward its preservation. Their expertise was instrumental. I have been fortunate to continue the outstanding work of the late Clem Lindenmayer.

Freelance hiker Ben Witte made key contributions toward the Araucanía chapter – I thank you. I am also indebted to my fellow hikers, Francisco Vio and his team, Sendero de Chile in Coyhaique, Daniela Castro, Dagoberto Guzmán, Luis Tiznado,

THE LONELY PLANET STORY

Fresh from an epic journey across Europe, Asia and Australia in 1972, Tony and Maureen Wheeler sat at their kitchen table stapling together notes. The first Lonely Planet guidebook, *Across Asia on the Cheap*, was born.

Travelers snapped up the guides. Inspired by their success, the Wheelers began publishing books to Southeast Asia, India and beyond. Demand was prodigious, and the Wheelers expanded the business rapidly to keep up. Over the years, Lonely Planet extended its coverage to every country and into the virtual world via lonelyplanet.com and the Thorn Tree message board.

As Lonely Planet became a globally loved brand, Tony and Maureen received several offers for the company. But it wasn't until 2007 that they found a partner whom they trusted to remain true to the company's principles of travelling widely, treading lightly and giving sustainably. In October of that year, BBC Worldwide acquired a 75% share in the company, pledging to uphold Lonely Planet's commitment to independent travel, trustworthy advice and editorial independence.

Today, Lonely Planet has offices in Melbourne, London and Oakland, with over 500 staff members and 300 authors. Tony and Maureen are still actively involved with Lonely Planet. They're travelling more often than ever, and they're devoting their spare time to charitable projects. And the company is still driven by the philosophy of *Across Asia on the Cheap*: 'All you've got to do is decide to go and the hardest part is over. So go!'

Denis Chevallay, Rodrigo Traub, Christian Morales, Hernan Jofre, Luis Turi, the Galeazi-Basilys, Patti Pusaki, Nicolas Rodriguez, Jorge in Villa O'Higgins and Peter in Pucón. Thanks also to park rangers Jose Linnebrink, Gonzalo Cisternas Lopez, Luis Montecinos, Alejandro Caparros and Servando Rovere. Dr Jorge Muñoz at Sernageomin and Manuel Cerda at Centro GPS offered technical help. After many solo hikes, sharing the Paine Circuit with super duo Meg and Dave was an incredible treat. Thank you Janine Eberle, my commissioning editor, and the talented team at Lonely Planet.

A funny thing happened after I completed the book's last trek: I forgot my boots in El Chaltén! Thank you Gerardo and Eva, dear Claire, Sandra and Gus for ferrying them thousands of kilometers back to me. Because I think I'll need them again.

SEND US YOUR FEEDBACK

We love to hear from travelers – your comments keep us on our toes and help make our books better. Our well-travelled team reads every word on what you loved or loathed about this book. Although we cannot reply individually to postal submissions, we always guarantee that your feedback goes straight to the appropriate authors, in time for the next edition. Each person who sends us information is thanked in the next edition – and the most useful submissions are rewarded with a free book.

To send us your updates – and find out about Lonely Planet events, newsletters and travel news – visit our award-winning website: **lonelyplanet.com/contact.**

Note: we may edit, reproduce and incorporate your comments in Lonely Planet products such as guidebooks, websites and digital products, so let us know if you don't want your comments reproduced or your name acknowledged. For a copy of our privacy policy visit www.lonelyplanet.com/privacy.

Index

000 Map pages
000 Photograph pages

LONELY PLANET OFFICES

Australia
Head Office
Locked Bag 1, Footscray, Victoria 3011
☎ 03 8379 8000, fax 03 8379 8111
talk2us@lonelyplanet.com.au

USA
150 Linden St, Oakland, CA 94607
☎ 510 893 8556, toll free 800 275 8555
fax 510 893 8572
info@lonelyplanet.com

UK
2nd fl, 186 City Rd,
London EC1V 2NT
☎ 020 7106 2100, fax 020 7106 2101
go@lonelyplanet.co.uk

PUBLISHED BY LONELY PLANET PUBLICATIONS PTY LTD

ABN 36 005 607 983

Cover photograph: Cuernos del Paine and Lake Pehoe, Torres de Paine National Park, Chile, Francesc Muntada/Corbis. Many of the images in this guide are available for licensing from Lonely Planet Images: www.lonelyplanetimages.com.

Printed by SNP Security Printing Pte Ltd.
Printed in Singapore.